Resisting Reagan

Resisting Reagan

The U.S. Central America Peace Movement

CHRISTIAN SMITH

The University of Chicago Press
Chicago and London

CHRISTIAN SMITH is assistant professor of sociology at the University of North Carolina, Chapel Hill, and the author of *The Emergence of Liberation Theology*, also published by the University of Chicago Press.

The University of Chicago Press, Chicago 60637
The University of Chicago Press, Ltd., London
©1996 by The University of Chicago
All rights reserved. Published 1996
Printed in the United States of America

05 04 03 02 00 99 97 96   1 2 3 4 5

ISBN: 0-226-76335-8 (cloth)
ISBN: 0-226-76336-6 (paper)

LIBRARY OF CONGRESS CATALOGING-IN-PUBLICATION DATA

Smith, Christian (Christian Stephen), 1960-
    Resisting Reagan: the U.S. Central America peace movement /
Christian Smith.
        p.   cm.
    Includes bibliographical references (p.) and index
    1. Central America—Relations—United States. 2. United States—
Relations—Central America. 3. Central America—Politics and
government—1979- 4. Peace movements—United States—History.
5. Peace movements—Central America—History. 6. Religion and
politics—United States—History. I. Title.
F1436.8.U6S65   1996
303.48′2730728—dc20   96-3141
                                                    CIP

Map by John Sanderson, Horizon Design, Wakefield, Mass.

For Zachary,

whom I love with my whole heart.

Contents

Illustrations follow page 208.

Tables and Figures

tables

Figures

Acknowledgments

One of the gratifying rewards of completing a book is having the chance to recognize those who contributed to its realization. Topping the list, Steve Rytina has been for me an invaluable source of advice, support, and encouragement, to whom I am indebted in multiple ways. Another sociologist simultaneously as nice, hilarious, and analytically incisive as he I have not met. He deserves much more honor, for contributing both to this book and to my career, than the recognition I can offer here. Thanks, Steve.

I am also deeply indebted to the many movement activists and government officials who took me and my tape recorder into their busy lives to share their experiences, thoughts, and feelings regarding U.S. Central American politics. These include Sam Hope, Ken Butigan, Cindy Buhl, Dennis Marker, Gail Phares, Fran Truitt, Bob Bonthius, Mike Clark, Anne Shumway, Betsy Crites, Jane Guise, Phyllis Taylor, Bob Van Denend, Pat Van Denend, Tom Quigley, Joe Nangle, Jim Rice, Angela Berryman, Clark Taylor, Kevin Kresse, Dick Junkin, Ross Gelbspan, Lonna Harkrader, an anonymous Sanctuary worker from Ithaca, New York, an anonymous congressional aide involved in anti-movement investigations, and the former head of both the CIA and FBI, Judge William Webster.

Many thanks to Nathan Hatch and Michael Hamilton of the Evangelical Scholarship Initiative, Notre Dame, Indiana, and to Joel Carpenter of the Pew Charitable Trusts, Philadelphia, Pennsylvania, for funding a year's reprieve from teaching to write the bulk of this manuscript. And thanks to Jonathan Raymond, and especially to Stan Gaede, both of Gordon College, for managing the logistics of that reprieve. Were it not for these supporters, this book would today be nothing more than unfinished files on my hard drive.

I am grateful to Sam Hope and Mike Clark for the chance they took in allowing me to send my survey questionnaires to a sample of their

Witness for Peace mailing list. And thanks to the hundreds of Witness for Peace and Sanctuary activists who completed and returned their surveys. Thanks, too, to Laura Hoseley, for transcribing written survey text.

Stan Gaede, Nina Liou, and Eldon Kenworthy read my entire manuscript, and offered me tremendously helpful encouragement and feedback for revisions. David Meyer, good soul that he is, read it twice and also offered extremely helpful suggestions both times. In addition, Judith Blau, Ross Gelbspan, Dennis Marker, and my Spring 1995 Social Movements seminar students read portions of the manuscript and provided me with insightful feedback.

I am indebted to Kristi Batstone for efficient and indispensable research assistance early on, and to Kris Wood, Jill Pernigotti, and Inez Diaz for helping to code questionnaires. Thanks, too, to Cristy Wilson, Gary Becker, Stephen Smith, and the cataloguing staff at Harvard's Widener Library for help in tracking down statistical data; and to an old friend, John Sanderson, of Horizon Design, who designed and produced the map in chapter 1.

I cannot forget to thank Doug Mitchell, my editor at University of Chicago Press, for his interest, advice, and class. It was a pleasure to work with him.

Finally, many months of complete immersion in the detailed literature on low-intensity warfare, torture, state repression, and foreign policy driven by stupendous ignorance, arrogance, and malice produced in me recurrent bouts of smoldering and hardly expressible rage, heartache, and depression. Not all knowledge is sweet to acquire. There were times—computer humming, books strewn everywhere—when I just sat at my desk and wept. To the extent that this book is a balanced sociological analysis, and not an emotional diatribe, it is so because my wife, Emily, and my good friend Mitch MacDonald spent a lot of time listening to me fume, vent, and grumble. In his own way, Stan Gaede, too, helped me bracket my feelings so as to strengthen the integrity of this work. For this, I am sincerely grateful to each of them.

Acronyms

AFSC   American Friends Service Committee
AID   Aid for International Development
AP   Associated Press
ARA   U.S. Department of State Bureau of Interamerican Affairs
CALC   Clergy and Laity Concerned
CARP   Collegiate Association for the Research of Principles
CAWG   Central America Working Group
CBI   Caribbean Basin Initiative
CDS   Sandinista Defense Committee
CIA   Central Intelligence Agency
CISPES   Committee in Solidarity with the People of El Salvador
CITCA   Carolina Interfaith Task Force on Central America
CRTF   Chicago Religious Task Force on Central America
DIS   Defense Investigative Service
ESF   Economic Support Fund
FEMA   Federal Emergency Management Agency
FF   Freedom Fighters
FMLN   Farabundo Martí Front for National Liberation
FSLN   Sandinista Front of National Liberation
FSO   Foreign Service Office
IBC   International Business Communications
ITFCA   InterReligious Task Force on Central America
INS   Immigration and Naturalization Service
JPF   Jewish Peace Fellowship
MLN   National Liberation Movement
NCC   National Council of Churches
NEPL   National Endowment for the Preservation of Liberty
NICA   Nicaragua Interfaith Committee for Action
NJA   New Jewish Agenda
NSC   National Security Council
NSDD   National Security Decision Directive
OPEC   Organization of Petroleum Exporting Countries
PAC   Civil Defense Patrols

PRG   Political Reference Group
PSYOP   Psychological Operations
RIG   Restricted Interagency Group
SMO   Social Movement Organization
TEC   Tucson Ecumenical Council Task Force on Central America
UCLA   Unilaterally Controlled Latino Assets
USAID   U.S. Aid for International Development
USCC   United States Catholic Conference
WFP   Witness for Peace

Introduction

"I grew up in a very middle-class neighborhood. So it was incredible to hear Salvadorans talk about their horrible experiences. I had always heard about people far away, but they had never been 'real.' This hit me like a bomb. When I realized that I could make a difference, I jumped all over it, and my life changed."

"The tales of horror wrought by our tax dollars were infuriating and very contradictory to our alleged national ideals. They shattered my whole worldview. And they made me care again about social and political issues after a ten-year period of apathy."

"After World War II and the Nuremberg Trials, I could not stand to be an accomplice to crimes against humanity. I had to get involved. And it changed my life. I learned to speak with a conviction, a passion, and an articulateness that I had never experienced before. I found myself doing things, like being the spokesperson at demonstrations, that I had never done before."

"I had no other choice but to get involved if I was to remain faithful to the Christian Gospel and its option for the poor, the persecuted, for those hungering and thirsting for justice."

"While visiting Nicaragua, I was asked to conduct a funeral for a man found shot in the back and decapitated by the U.S.-backed Contras. I never will forget the look of sadness in his pregnant wife's eyes and the smell of his dead body. It drove home to me the obscene arrogance and thoughtlessness of U.S. policy. And what do you do with that?"

"I have been profoundly and eternally changed by this struggle. I have more faith, passion, and self-confidence. In spite of the dark hours of fear, the tears, and occasional exhaustion, I received a far greater gift than I could ever give."

"As a Jew, I know what it means to be persecuted. If it hadn't been for a few kind people, no Jews would have escaped the Holocaust. Now it was my turn to take risks on behalf of others."

"It was probably one of the most memorable things that ever happened to me. I felt as though in my own little way, I helped defeat the Contras and bring to the U.S. some truth about what was really going on in Central America."

For most of human history, political and military elites have directed the foreign affairs of their tribes, kingdoms, and nations as they have seen fit, largely unencumbered by the concerns of the common people over whom they rule. Generations of ordinary women and men—those who pay the taxes, forge the swords, and watch their sons marched off to battle—have had little say about exactly which wars ought to be fought, which treaties ought to be signed, and which territories ought to be colonized. Common people have paid the costs, and sometimes enjoyed the benefits, of their leaders' ventures in foreign relations. But, with few exceptions, they have been excluded from participating in the decisions about the nature and direction of those ventures.

Recent history, however, has witnessed a difficult, faltering, yet clearly perceptible, upheaval from below. The ideals of human equality and participation that Hebrew prophets and Greek philosophers once proclaimed and subsequent centuries dimmed reemerged from the rubble of medieval Europe. In recent decades, those ideals have been amplified into a "participation revolution" around the world. From Algiers to Prague to Beijing, from Soweto to Santiago to San Francisco, ordinary people are increasingly acting on the idea that all people, and not just elites, ought to participate significantly in shaping the decisions and structures that affect their lives. This "participation revolution" has not left untouched the domain of international relations and foreign policy making—long restricted to the control of elites. In the United States, this recent drive toward greater citizens' participation in matters of foreign policy has expressed itself dramatically in a number of contentious grassroots social movements. These include the anti–Vietnam War, the Free South Africa, and the Nuclear Freeze movements. The importance of many of these social movements has been matched by a plethora of popular and academic literature describing, analyzing, and explaining them.

One of the most interesting and significant of these foreign policy–oriented grassroots movements in the U.S. was the Central America peace movement of the 1980s. In this movement, more than one hundred thousand U.S. citizens mobilized to contest the chief foreign policy initiative of the most popular U.S. president in decades. Ordinary Americans marched in the streets, illegally housed refugees fleeing persecution, traveled to Central American war zones, committed civil disobedience at demonstrations, and hounded their political representatives to stop the U.S.-sponsored war in Central America—all on the assumption, as the above quotations indicate, that common people can and should shape national foreign policy.

AN UNEXAMINED MOVEMENT

Amazingly, however, the U.S. Central America peace movement of the 1980s has received scant attention in both the popular and academic literature. No more than a few scholars—whether sociologists, political scientists, or historians—have studied this movement in depth. Indeed, many scholars appear unaware that it ever existed.[1]

This lack of attention to the U.S. Central America peace movement is baffling, for many reasons. First, the broader political battle over U.S. Central American policy in the 1980s, within which the peace movement was a major contender, was the most conspicuously protracted and volatile political struggle of the decade. Indeed, the Central America issue has been described by analysts as "the most bitter and divisive since the Vietnam War" (Arnson 1988: 35) and "the most divisive foreign policy issue in the United States since the Vietnam War" (Falcoff 1984: 361). Should not all the major actors in such a struggle be examined and understood?

Second, the Central America peace movement itself was a crusade of major proportions. It mobilized more committed activists, generated more political conflict, sustained itself over a longer period of time, and made a greater political impact than did, for example, the much studied anti-nuclear movement of the same decade. As we will see, the Central America peace movement actually ended up absorbing much of the faltering anti-nuclear movement. Does not such a major social movement deserve to be accounted for and analyzed?

A third reason why scholarly inattention to the Central America peace movement is so baffling is that this movement was characterized by a unique and fascinating feature, "what one seasoned Latin Americanist called '*a foreign policy first*'" (Falcoff 1984: 362). That is, it was largely initiated, organized, and led by people of faith, mostly Christians. The role of the churches in this protest movement was at least as vital as it was in the civil rights movement of the 1950s and '60s. According to Reuther (1986: viii), "For the first time since the Vietnam war, the United States government is faced with a major challenge to its policies of global control, a challenge spearheaded by the American religious community." Such widespread faith-based opposition to a major U.S. foreign policy initiative suggests important theoretical and practical questions about the relationship between religious faith and politics. Perhaps social scientists studying the relationship of faith and politics in the 1980s were too preoccupied with the fanfare surrounding the New Religious Right to notice the faith-based protests at the other end of the political spectrum. But, does not such faith-generated disruption merit our study and understanding?

For whatever reasons, the Central America peace movement has, in fact, received relatively little scholarly attention. The entire academic literature on the movement to date consists of a few journal articles (Wiltfang and McAdam 1991; Fields 1986), a handful of highly focused Ph.D. dissertations (Ovryn Rivera 1987; Clark 1988; Hildreth 1989; Stout 1989; Coutin 1990; Hannon 1991), and one book (Lorentzen 1991). Many of these works are very good empirical and interpretive studies. But, as it stands, this small body of literature on the U.S. Central America peace movement is inadequate, not only because of its size, but also because the works themselves are quite limited, in at least three ways. First, with the exception of Hildreth, all of the studies are based on relatively small samples of the movement's population. Lorentzen's insightful exploration of women in the Sanctuary movement, for example, is based on interviews with only twenty-nine women participants. Second, with the same single exception, all of these works reflect a narrow geographical focus. Hannon's interesting analysis of Pledge of Resistance activists, for example, limits itself to participants in the Boston, Massachusetts, area. Although these works offer many important insights, attempts to generalize their findings to the movement as a whole are quite problematic. The third limitation is that all of these analyses—without exception—focus on only one of the numerous social movement organizations represented in the entire movement. Hence, no work has been published to date that attempts to analyze the movement broadly by examining together a variety of primary movement organizations at a national, movement-wide level.

THE BIG PICTURE

In this study I have tried to answer a number of key questions concerning the *who, what, why,* and *how*s of the Central America peace movement: What historical events, social forces, and cultural influences shaped the broad sociopolitical environment that generated the movement? What effect did subsequent changes in these forces and events have on it? Who actually initiated it? And why and how did they do so? What kinds of people then joined the Central America peace movement? And how and why were they mobilized into activism? What strategies and tactics did the movement employ to achieve its goals?

How and why did these strategies and tactics change over time, and to what effect? How did media coverage affect the movement's struggle with the state? In what ways and to what effect was the movement repressed by its antagonists? What significant changes, intended and unintended, did it accomplish? In what ways did it succeed and fail, and why? How did Central America activism change the lives of movement participants? What caused the movement's eventual demise? What can we learn from this movement about the force of faith in politics? And how can understanding this movement provide theoretical insight into the nature and dynamics of social movements generally?

The scope of this study is broad. But care has been taken not to sacrifice depth. This book investigates the macro-level social forces that generated the Central America peace movement, but also the people at the grass roots who actually made the movement happen on a daily basis. It explores the emergence of a movement, but also the ongoing maintenance, transformation, and decline of that movement over time. This study draws on quantified data from two national surveys of movement activists, but also on more than thirty in-depth interviews with movement activists around the country. As a result, it offers an unusually comprehensive analysis of the Central America peace movement.

OVERVIEW OF THE STUDY

I attempt in this book to weave together narrative, analysis, and theory. Like a novelist or historian, I wish to tell the story of an important and fascinating human and political struggle. At the same time, like a criminal investigator or research scientist, I also attempt systematically to isolate and analyze the components of that struggle— the properties, motives, beliefs, actions, strategies, and consequences of the people and groups involved—to understand better exactly what happened and why. Finally, like a philosopher or social theorist, I seek to draw from this story general observations about the nature of human social life and action. If my weavings succeed, this book should be as relevant to the interests of any thinking person concerned with the U.S. and Central America as it will to those of political activists working for social change and of sociologists, political scientists, and historians who read and write for academic journals.

This book is divided into four parts. Part 1 seeks to explain the social and political context of the Central America peace movement. In chapter 1, I examine the historical sources of Central America's revolutions and wars of the 1970s and '80s. Chapter 2 then explores the reasons why the United States became so deeply entangled in those hostilities. Chapter 3 describes the specific kind of warfare—"low-intensity warfare"—the United States promoted in Central America, along with its consequences.

Part 2 focuses on the emergence of the Central America peace movement in the early 1980s. Chapter 4 provides a brief, descriptive overview of the origins and development of the major activist organizations of the movement. In chapters 5 and 6, I use a political process model of social movements to explain the macro-social forces and events that created the environment which brought the Central America peace movement to birth. Chapter 7 then focuses at the micro-level on the characteristics of the individual activists who led and participated in the movement, and seeks to understand who joins social movements and why.

Part 3 then concentrates on the ongoing maintenance and transformation of the Central America peace movement throughout the decade. Chapter 8 studies the strategic and tactical choices the movement was forced to make in its struggle to alter the nation's Central American policy. Chapter 9 then analyzes the all important political battle to control the framing of the Central American reality in public discourse, particularly in the mass media. Chapter 10 examines the efforts on the part of the U.S. government and other groups to harass, discredit, and repress the Central America peace movement, and the various effects of these efforts. Chapter 11 goes on to explore many of the internal problems that plagued the movement from within and hampered its political effectiveness. And chapter 12 employs the political process model again, to explain the movement's eventual decline at decade's end.

Finally, part 4 steps back and assesses the Central America peace movement from a number of vantage points. Chapter 13 considers the movement's political, social, and cultural impact, identifying ways the movement succeeded and failed. And chapter 14 explores various ways the case of the Central America peace movement both confirms and challenges important assumptions and theories in the academic literature on social movements.

part one
Setting the Context

THE SOURCES OF CENTRAL AMERICAN UNREST

Men who can graft the trees and make the seed fertile and big can find no way to let the hungry people eat their produce. Men who have created new fruits in the world cannot create a system whereby their fruits may be eaten. And the failure hangs over the State like a great sorrow. . . . In the souls of the people the grapes of wrath are filling and growing heavy, growing heavy for the vintage.

John Steinbeck, *The Grapes of Wrath*

In early January 1982 an exhausted Salvadoran teenager named José Valdes, assisted by a small group of Tucson churchgoers, crossed the Mexican border into Arizona. Two months earlier, Valdes' village, located in El Salvador's Morazán province, had been assaulted by one of his government's U.S.-trained army battalions. In that attack, and others like it throughout the province, nearly a thousand peasants had been massacred in one month. Valdes' father, mother, and uncle were interrogated and murdered by army soldiers in the alley beside his house. His sister was also dead, first raped, then shot in the back of the head. And Valdes' two older brothers were forced by soldiers into a military vehicle and driven to an unknown destination—he knew he would never hear from either of them again. Now sitting in the cool sanctuary of a local Presbyterian church, the confused and depressed José Valdes falteringly told his helpers about the army attack and his narrow escape. After a pained minute of silence, one of the group explained to Valdes that they were helping refugees like him to safety. Another explained that they were also organizing politically to do everything possible to stop their country's financial and military support for his country's genocidal army. Valdes nodded, then asked for a place to lie down and rest. That night, the group made plans to transport Valdes to a church in Wisconsin that would help him start on a new life in the U.S. Afterwards, half of them stayed behind to discuss details of an upcoming national protest against U.S. aid to El Salvador.

Throughout the 1980s, in scenes like this, tens of thousands of North Americans were driven to humanitarian and political action on behalf of José Valdes and millions of others like him suffering the horrors of U.S.-sponsored war in Central America. Together, these North Americans became the U.S. Central America peace movement. In order adequately to understand this movement, we must begin by comprehending the situational context of its birth and life. In particular, we must understand the war that brought together the lives of José Valdes and the group of Tucson churchgoers. This chapter, therefore, answers the following question: Why did Central America erupt into such disruptive political and military violence in the 1970s and '80s.

A HISTORICAL LEGACY

Civil strife, political struggle, and military clashes have been part of life in Central America for all of its known history. Well before the Spaniards came to Central America, the indigenous peoples were familiar with the tensions and violence attendant to periodic struggles between cities over land, political control, natural resources, and trade routes (Willey and Shimkin 1973; Bricker 1981). Scholars agree that, in the sixteenth century, violence between the natives' rival cities partly contributed to their own conquest by the Spanish. For example, in 1536, the treacherous massacre at Otzmal, of more than forty leaders of the Xiu nation by Nachi Cocom, ruler of the Sotuta, sparked a civil war: "Coming so shortly before the final phase of the Spanish Conquest, [that violence] sealed the fate of the northern Maya by reviving old hatreds and effectively preventing a united stand against the Spaniards. . . . Exhausted by civil war, betrayed by some of their own leading native houses, and decimated by disease, the Maya were unable to resist the better-armed Spaniards and finally succumbed to the invaders' superior might" (Morley and Brainard 1983: 175–76).

However, although "the 'peaceful' and 'pious' Maya engaged in their share of violence" (Willey and Shimkin 1973: 479), the Spanish Conquest set in motion a long tradition of violence and exploitation more intense and calamitous than anything previously known in Central America. Pedro de Alvarado, a man "infamous for his cruelty and inhuman treatment of his foes" (Morley and Brainard 1983: 576)—along with Christóbal de Olid and Francisco Hernández de Córdoba—began the military conquest of Central America in 1524 (Parker 1964: 44–45). The military technology of the Spanish was more

EL SALVADOR
Central America's smallest and most densely populated nation. In 1980, rebels of the Farabundo Martí Front for National Liberation (FMLN) led an insurrection against the military regime. Over the 1980s, the U.S. sent more than a billion dollars in military and economic aid to help the Salvadoran government defeat the FMLN. The ensuing civil war lasted the entire decade, with more than 115,000 dead, a million refugees displaced, and no clear victor, until a peace accord was signed in 1991. 70 percent rural poverty rate.

GUATEMALA
Ruled by a repressive military-controlled government since 1945, when the constitutionally-elected, reformist government of Jacobo Arbenz was overthrown by a U.S.-planned military coup. Since 1965, with U.S. military aid, the state has fought insurgent guerrillas in a thirty year-long civil war, killing 200,000 and displacing one million Guatemalans. 60 percent rural poverty rate.

NICARAGUA
Ruled by the Somoza family dictatorship since 1936, civil war erupted in 1978, and the Sandinista Front of National Liberation (FSLN) seized power in 1979. In response, the Reagan administration created the Contras, who waged a war from Honduras and Costa Rica against Nicaragua, in which more than 30,000 died. The Contras failed to overthrow the FSLN. 57 percent rural poverty rate.

HONDURAS
The hemisphere's second poorest nation and closest U.S. ally in Central America, Honduras became in the 1980s the staging base for extensive U.S. and Contra military activity in the region. 77 percent rural poverty rate.

COSTA RICA
Central America's most democratic, literate, and equitable nation. After a revolution in 1948, the government outlawed the army and developed a relatively progressive social welfare system. Costa Rica initially cooperated with the U.S.-sponsored war against Nicaragua, but in 1987 its President Oscar Arias broke with the Reagan administration by mediating a successful regional peace agreement. 40 percent rural poverty rate.

Fig. 1.1

lethal, their authorities more repressive, their diseases more deadly, and their economic structures more exploitative than anything the Maya had ever known. The Conquest was for the natives "an unmitigated calamity . . . of genocidal proportions"—by 1650, between 65–85 percent of the native population in Central America and Mexico had died (Jonas 1991: 14).

In the centuries that have followed, Central America has been riddled with chronic violent social conflict. From the early near genocidal enslavement of natives to the crushed Quisteil rebellion of 1761 to Guatemala's bloody counterinsurgency campaign of the 1960s, Central America has seen almost a half-millennium of endemic military, political, and economic repression and violence.

THE ROOTS OF THE 1980S CRISIS

Nevertheless—even in view of this legacy of violent conflict—the Central American crisis of the 1970s and '80s was extraordinary. The number of Central Americans who lost their lives, the resources spent to fuel the conflict, the intensity of international tensions generated, the amount of physical destruction wreaked, and the numbers of refugees displaced far exceeded any other Central American conflict since the Conquest. What, then, were the root causes of this recent conflict, more intense and destructive than anything seen in centuries? The complete answer, of course, is complex, and scholars differ on points of emphasis. But a broad agreement has emerged in a considerable body of literature on the subject.[1] Simplified, the essential points of that agreement are that: 1) inequitable land distribution has generated poverty and misery for the majority of Central Americans, which has given rise to acute discontent; 2) Central American elites have typically employed repressive violence against expressions of discontent, successfully crushing individual protests, yet breeding added grievances; 3) the recent modernization of Central American societies has generated both new miseries and opportunities for protest, upon which the aggrieved poor have increasingly capitalized; and 4) the ensuing confrontations eventually escalated in the 1970s and '80s—through vicious cycles of protest and repression—into a devastating regional conflict of crisis proportions. This explanation maintains that the conflict of the 1980s is the outcome of a long history of inequity and subjugation extending back to the Spanish Conquest. It is necessary, therefore, to explore further that history.

According to Brockett (1990: 14), "Before the Conquest, northern Central America had a substantial population living in well-developed, complex societies." Although those societies were struggling to manage their own social tensions and transformations, three particular features are noteworthy. First, the natives the Spanish found were not "primitives" or "savages." They were descendants of a prosperous, sophisticated civilization that between 300 and 900 A.D. had made great achievements in agriculture, astronomy, mathematics, sculpture, architecture, hieroglyphics, and metallurgy (Skidmore and Smith 1984: 15; Morley and Brainard 1983). And, while the classic Maya civilization "had been in a long decline before the Conquest, its influence continued throughout the area" (Brockett 1990: 14). Second, while the Maya had their share of sickness and suffering, their agricultural system generally produced enough food to feed the entire population. Thus—while avoiding romantic depictions of native life—we can say that hunger and malnutrition appear not to have been widespread (Barry 1987: 5). "At no time before the conquest did the Indians suffer the systematic material deprivation that has characterized Guatemala since 1524. Malnutrition was not a chronic condition of the Indian population, as it is today" (Jonas 1991: 13–14). Third, in contrast to the European notion of land as individually deeded private property, the Maya typically owned land communally (Anderson

1984). Land was not surveyed and deeded, bought and sold. "To the Indian, private and individual ownership of land was as meaningless as private ownership of the sky, the weather, or the sea" (Browning 1971: 16). Communal land was cultivated by individuals and groups largely to produce locally consumed basic necessities. Thus, the majority of pre-Columbian Central Americans had sufficient access to the fruit of the earth.

The Spanish changed all that. They had come to the new world to acquire riches and status, for Spain and for themselves. But they quickly exhausted the easily appropriated wealth in Central America, looting gold and selling slaves (Brockett 1990: 17). Thus, the colonists had to find new sources of riches. They did not have an abundance of capital, but they did have plenty of land about them, which in their minds nobody properly "owned." They also had an adequate supply of cheap labor: the remaining natives who hadn't been sold off as slaves, and later—as those natives died from disease and famine—imported slaves from Africa (Stein and Stein 1970). Exploiting this opportunity, the colonizers forcibly seized the best tracts of land, forming them into large estates, called haciendas or *latifundios*. The natives were left to cultivate communal plots of land, as yet unseized, and later small plots called *minifundios*. Since a domestic market for agricultural products was minuscule, the colonists experimented with growing tropical crops for export to Europe. Thus began the long history of agro-export development, and its dual structure of land tenure, that still dominates Central American economies today (DeWalt and Bidegaray 1991).

The first major crop to succeed was cacao, due to a robust demand for chocolate in Europe. By 1600, however, the conditions that made cacao profitable had changed, and cacao was replaced by indigo and cochineal, and to a lesser extent, tobacco, as the dominant tropical export crops (Skidmore and Smith 1984: 289). With the periodic need to develop new export crops, and the sometimes deteriorating conditions of production, colonists increasingly pushed further into the countryside, seizing more and more of the best land from the natives. Naturally, as the export-crop *latifundios* expanded, the communal lands and lands remaining for food-crop *minifundios* shrunk (Brockett 1990: 19–20). Increasingly, the natives suffered famine and hunger, as a small elite possessed the majority of productive land while the greater part of the population possessed smaller plots of more marginal land. By the end of the eighteenth century, the preponderance of the natives' communally owned land had been appropriated (Barry 1987: 7).

Then, nineteenth-century land grabbing stimulated by a coffee boom prompted "a massive assault upon village lands" (McCreery 1976: 457). In El Salvador, for example, the state actually outlawed remaining communal lands, granting land titles to anyone who cultivated export crops on a previously communal piece of property (Brockett 1990: 25). Land seizures were also motivated by the demand for cheap labor: hacienda owners "needed and wanted more land, not to raise more crops, but to take the land from the Indians in order to force them to leave their holdings and to become dependent on the hacienda for land and work" (quoted in Spykman et al. 1988: 52). Besides the injustice of having their land stolen, the natives suffered the abuse of forced labor—an essential component of the system's success—through slavery, work quotas, compulsory labor drafts, and debt peonage (Spykman et al. 1988: 47–50). A contemporary observer (quoted in Sherman 1979: 207) described the natives' experience:

> They go to the farms and other places of work, where they are made to toil from dawn to dusk in the raw cold morning and afternoon, in wind and storm, without other food than the rotten or dried-out tortillas, and even of this they have not enough. They sleep on the ground in the open air, naked, without shelter. Even if they wish to buy food with their pitiful wages they could not, for they are not paid until they are laid off. . . . So the Indian returns home worn out from his toil, minus his pay and his mantle, not to speak of the food that he brought with him. He returns home famished, unhappy, distraught, and shattered in health. For these reasons, pestilence always rages among the Indians.

According to Jonas (1991: 15), "These methods of organizing the work force were maintained by coercion and terror. Violent abuse of the indigenous population became routine, essential to making the system work."

Indians and peasants did resist and rebel frequently (Bricker 1981). But this resistance merely offered the landowners a rationale for continuing their repression of the native population. Protests were crushed and punished by political-military forces that backed the landowners. Eventually, this created what Huizer (1972: 52–61) calls a "culture of repression": a pervasive attitude of passive resignation among natives, and later mestizo peasants, who were aware of their exploitation, but equally aware of their inability to escape it.

With time, hacienda owners developed new export crops. After cacao and indigo came coffee in the nineteenth century, and bananas, cotton, sugar, and beef in the twentieth century. But, Jonas rightly argues (1991: 15), while "the particular export changed over time . . . the basic structure of the mono-export economy remained constant." A minority of Central American elites profited handsomely—even if erratically—by selling cheaply produced commodities in overseas markets, causing misery for the mass of natives and peasants dispossessed of their food-producing land and forced to labor (Durham 1979).

AN EXPLOSIVE CONTRADICTION

By the second half of the twentieth century, an explosive social contradiction had developed in Central America. On the one hand, agro-export economies had produced staggering amounts of landlessness, hunger, and unemployment for the majority of the population. The living standards of the poor actually deteriorated, even as elites profited from rapidly growing national economies linked to an expanding world economy.[2] On the other hand, new organizational and political opportunities for grassroots protest and rebellion developed. Peasants and laborers thus found themselves possessing, perhaps as never before, the means to challenge the system under which they had suffered for so long. By the 1970s, Central America had become a powder keg ready to ignite.

First, the misery of the majority had intensified. Between 1950 and 1979, land devoted to sugar and cotton crops increased nearly tenfold. Meanwhile, the per capita amount of land used to grow basic food crops decreased dramatically (Table 1.1). By 1978, ninety times more of Central America's land was growing export crops than basic food crops. Between 1975 and 1981 alone, the per capita production of corn and beans declined by 11 percent. The number of landless peasants tripled between 1960 and 1980, such that the average rural poverty rate in the early 1980s grew to 60 percent. Rural unemployment figures stood at 42 percent in Guatemala, 47 percent in El Salvador, and 24 percent in Nicaragua. Malnutrition was rampant, and child malnutrition was increasing in most countries (Table 1.2). Income, despite overall national growth, grew more unevenly distributed (Brockett 1990; Barry 1987; Wiarda 1984; also see Weeks 1985; Bulmer-Thomas 1987). Thus, the objective grounds for widespread discontent—injustice, increasing misery, and early death—were epidemic.

Table 1.1. Per Capita Basic Food Cropland (Hectares)

Country	1950	1979	Change(%)
Costa Rica	.325	.160	-51
El Salvador	.220	.080	-64
Guatamala	.450	.190	-58
Honduras	.520	.420	-19
Nicaragua	.630	.440	-30

Source: FAO, Food Security in Latin American and the Caribbean, June, 1984

Table 1.2. Malnutrition in Central America

Country	Calorie deficit, poorest half of population[a]	Child Malnutrition (%)	Change in Child Malnutrition 1965-75 (%)
Costa Rica	8	57	-10
El Salvador	35	75	+46
Guatemala	39	81	+18
Honduras	32	73	+29
Nicaragua	16	57	+51

Source: Brockett 1990; Barry 1987.
Note: [a] Percent of minimum caloric need lacking.

But discontent alone was not enough to ignite the Central American powder keg. For discontent was nothing new for the majority of Central Americans. Potential rebels need more than grievances to sustain protest and insurgency. They also need political opportunities and facilitating organizations (Smith 1991; McAdam 1982). In fact, Central America's poor in the 1960s and '70s did experience both an expansion of political opportunities for rebellion and an increase in the strength of organizations that would facilitate protest.

Modernization and development in Central America were accompanied by the loosening of some traditional mechanisms of social control. Local patronage relationships, which had maintained peasants' subordination to landowners in the hacienda system, began to erode in the mid-twentieth century as agro-export agriculture became increasingly commercialized (Brockett 1990: 6). For many, personal patronage ties were supplanted by more impersonal market-oriented, wage-labor relationships, a situation which created a political open space, a degree of independence from scrutiny by elites. Furthermore, according to Wiarda (1984: 14–15):

A number of the reforms [the United States] helped to finance in the name of development—U.S. style political parties, trade unions, farmers' cooperatives, and the like—had the practical effect of destroying many traditional institutions (patronage, clan, family networks), without really institutionalizing viable modern ones, thus leaving an institutional vacuum and eventually precipitating the fragmentation and social unraveling [the United States] had sought to prevent.

Political opportunity also befell would-be rebels in Central America in the 1970s as a by-product of shifting international political relations. The United States, long a hegemonic presence in Central America, had been declining in influence in the region since the mid-1960s (Wiarda 1984: 17). The situation took a major turn in the mid-1970s, however, when newly inaugurated U.S. President Jimmy Carter made concern for human rights the guiding principle of his foreign policy toward Central America. In a memo sent to embassies in the region, the Carter administration argued that since change was both natural and inevitable, the United States should define itself as the ally of progressive, democratic forces. Carter threatened to cut off aid to regimes that violated human rights. This partially restrained the repressiveness of some Central American regimes—such as Anastasio Somoza's in Nicaragua—thus partially shielding mobilizing forces of opposition (Booth 1985: 130). This abatement of repression is often found to aid the emergence of insurgencies (Benford 1992: 1881).

Organizational strength for potential rebellion increased through a widespread penetration of peasant and worker communities in the 1960s and '70s by outside organizers who brought with them new ideologies and organizational skills. Prominent among these were religious missionaries and pastoral agents, influenced by the reforms of Vatican II, Medellín, and liberation theology (Smith 1991; Berryman 1984). Also important were union organizers, development workers, and political party activists (Brockett 1990: 6). Finally, revolutionary guerrillas, sometimes with Cuban support, worked to re-educate and organize the poor (Valenta and Valenta 1984; Blasier 1983; Leiken 1984b). Increasingly, indigenous organizations—such as labor unions, political parties, student groups, peasant federations, base Christian communities, worker cooperatives, and guerrilla groups—were being founded that helped to mobilize widespread rebellion (Eckstein 1989; Booth 1985; McManus and Schlabach 1991; Montgomery 1983). Typically, such agents were important, for, in addition to building organizations that facilitated protest, they "help[ed] to break down the domination of traditional patrons by offering alternative sources of economic assistance and protection. They [were] able to promote peasant mobilization not only because of their organizational expertise but also because they facilitate[d] the transformation of attitudes from those of powerlessness . . . to those of solidarity and strength" (Brockett 1990: 6–7). Thus, by the 1970s, reformist and revolutionary movements in Central America experienced a concurrent growth in organizational strength, political opportunity, and deep grievances potentially sufficient to mobilize widespread activism. The Central American powder keg was set to explode.

THE IGNITING SPARK

The spark that actually ignited that powder keg was a succession of social and economic shocks in the 1970s that rocked Central America, especially traumatizing the poor and frustrating the middle classes. Central American economies had boomed in the 1950s and '60s, reaping the benefits of participation in an expanding global economy. But trouble hit when oil prices rose sharply in 1973 and again in 1979. Since Central American countries had no domestic energy substitutes, they had to import all of their oil. As oil prices climbed, Central American economies struggled to cope (Wiarda 1984: 15). Then, in the later years of the 1970s, international market prices paid for sugar, coffee, bananas, and other export products began fluctuating wildly, in an overall downward direction, creating further havoc for these economies (Booth 1985). Rational economic planning became difficult, and imported goods, including petroleum, became that much more expensive. Consequently, the foreign debt burdens of Central American countries swelled, prompting pressures to implement austerity programs and to export even more agricultural commodities (Brockett 1990: 63). Real wages in every country but Costa Rica declined (Bulmer-Thomas 1987).[3]

To make matters worse, two devastating earthquakes struck Central America, in Nicaragua in 1972 and Guatemala in 1976. The epicenter of the 1972 quake was Managua's downtown shopping and commercial area. As many as twenty thousand people died in it, while four hundred thousand people—three-quarters of Managua's population—were left homeless (Bermann 1986: 253). Guatemala's earthquake killed twenty-five thousand people, injured seventy thousand, and left more than a million homeless. Ninety percent of the destroyed homes in the capital were in poor neighborhoods. In subsequent months, fifty thousand people migrated to Guatemala City, increasing the ranks of the hundreds of thousands of homeless already there (Jonas 1991: 95).

These shocks together culminated in the late 1970s into a crisis. Unemployment, corruption, homelessness, landlessness, hunger, and frustration were escalating rapidly (Graham 1984). No regime in power seemed to be responding to the problems adequately. Some— such as Anastasio Somoza's, in exploiting earthquake relief funds— simply took advantage of the dismal times for personal gain. Finally, by the end of the 1970s, a deepening world economic recession further crippled the internationally dependent Central American economies (Weeks 1985). The damaging effect of this global recession was "the final straw" (Wiarda 1984: 16).

All of this was particularly egregious because it followed so closely on the heels of rapidly rising expectations among the majority of Central Americans. The great economic growth of the 1950s and '60s "had created a growing middle sector and a limited working class. These groups wanted an improvement in their standard of living, and they hoped it would be dramatic and soon" (Brockett 1990: 41). The 1960s U.S.-initiated Alliance for Progress also dramatically raised the hopes of the poor for a better life (Smith 1991: 111–15). And such projects as the "Agency for International Development, Peace Corps, literacy, road-building, and other programs . . . [had raised] popular expectations to potentially revolutionary proportions" (Wiarda 1984: 14). When these high hopes were dashed by the economic shocks of the 1970s, unrest of revolutionary proportions, in fact, did erupt. Popularly supported revolutionary guerrilla armies in Nicaragua, El Salvador, and Guatemala began to challenge regimes in power.[4] And as these rebel armies increasingly drew grassroots support, those countries were thrown into bloody civil wars. The Central American powder keg was ignited.

POLITICAL INTRANSIGENCE AND REPRESSION

Economic misery and frustration alone, however, did not generate Central America's explosive crisis in the 1970s and '80s. Equally responsible for turning difficulty into disaster was the "political cloture" besetting the Central American regimes in Nicaragua, El Salvador, Guatemala, and, to a lesser extent, Honduras (Wiarda 1984; Lafeber 1984). These governments exhibited an astounding reactive intransigence in the face of moderate efforts toward economic, political, and military reform. In so doing, they only threw gasoline on the blaze of rebellion that was spreading in Central America.

This defiance of change was not new. Since the Conquest, challenges to the status quo almost always met tenacious resistance and violence, if necessary, from elites. This pattern continued into the twentieth century. For example, in El Salvador in 1932, hungry peasants in the country's western highlands, led by the socialist Agustin Farabundo Marti, rose in a poorly organized rebellion and, with machetes in hand, marauded, looted, and occasionally killed local landowners and officials. The well-equipped Salvadoran army, summoned by the area landowners, quickly suppressed the uprising. Retribution followed, as the army massacred ten to twenty thousand peasants and Indians in the next two weeks, most of whom had not even participated in the rebellion (Anderson 1971; Skidmore and Smith 1984: 311).

> Jorge Sol Castellanos, an economist born into the Salvadoran oligarchy, was a high school student at the time. He recalls how the young members of the oligarchy were thrilled by the army's violent suppression of the uprising and formed their own para-military group called the "Civic Guard" to help out. Together they slaughtered thousands. (Hoeffel 1984: 100)

That incident—*La Matanza,* "The Massacre"—has ever since defined the mentality of Salvadoran elites toward even moderate efforts to transform their social system. "Today the same policy of extermination is in effect," says Sol. "They use the same expression: '*Muerto el perro, se acabo la rabia*' (Kill the dog and the rabies is gone)" (Hoeffel 1984: 100). In a 1980 speech to the annual Salvadoran Coffee Growers Association meeting, one landowner quipped to a thunderous applause (quoted in Frontline 1986): "I'm not bothered by what's happening these days. We faced a similar situation in 1932, and in 1932 the situation was handled appropriately. Shouldn't we be able to handle the current situation just as well?" Similarly, in 1980, National Guard Commander Colonel Vides Casanova asserted, "Today, the armed forces are prepared to kill 200,000–300,000, if that's what it takes to stop a Communist takeover" (Sklar 1988: 50).

Such was the response of many Central American political regimes to the growing unrest in the years leading up to the crisis of the 1980s. Unable or unwilling to quell the rising clamor for change through economic development and moderate political reforms that benefitted the majority of people, defensive Central American economic and political elites resorted to brute force (Coleman 1991). Military counterinsurgency campaigns, political imprisonment, rural destabilization, paramilitary death-squad assassinations, "disappearances," and widespread torture became commonplace in many countries.

In Guatemala, for example, nine years of progressive reform were reversed in 1954 when a U.S.-backed military coup repealed a major land reform program and outlawed political parties, labor unions, peasant leagues, and workers cooperatives (Schlesinger and Kinzer 1983). This radicalized progressive forces, eventually generating a guerrilla insurgency. Consequently, the military government has had to fight against a fierce counterinsurgency campaign since 1965, in which fifty thousand to one hundred thousand individuals, mostly civilians, have died (Weaver 1984: 545; Carmack 1988). In 1976, when U.S. President Jimmy Carter pressed the Guatemalan government to improve its human rights record, the worst in the hemisphere, or face an end to U.S. aid, the Guatemalans told Carter—who they referred to as "Jimmy Castro"—to keep the aid and stay out of their business. By 1991, the number of casualties from the Guatemalan civil war had grown to two hundred thousand (Jonas 1991: 2, 195).

In Nicaragua, Anastasio Somoza García and his two sons, Luis and Anastasio, who ruled as dictators from 1936 to 1979, controlled a powerful National Guard whose repression "rose in proportion to the strength, visibility, and success of . . . opposition movements" (Booth 1985: 93–94). During their rule, beatings, political detentions, torture, and executions all were utilized to maintain control. The ruthless repression of forces of change by the Guard was especially brutal from 1974 until the fall of the Somoza regime in 1979. During this period,

atrocities by National Guard troops—random murders, rapes, destruction of property, looting, and brutality toward any oppositional suspect—reached epidemic proportions. . . . The Guard executed many scores of preteenagers and repeatedly attacked Red Cross ambulances and their crews. . . . Barbarity against ordinary citizens became . . . commonplace (Booth 1985: 166, 173).

In the last weeks of the insurrection, the Guard murdered ABC television correspondent Bill Stewart in front of his own camera crew. His execution was shown on U.S. television that night. Despite sweeping opposition from every sector of Nicaraguan society and calls from international organizations to step down, Somoza displayed a remarkable political intransigence. His position was intractable. Eventually, even his friends and allies entreated him to resign. But the more widespread and insistent the challenge was to his regime, the more hardened his position became. U.S. negotiators urged Somoza to turn over power to a moderate, transition regime, in order to preempt a total leftist military victory. But Somoza remained stubborn until it was too late. As his position became more desperate in the summer of 1979, a recalcitrant and spiteful Somoza ordered his air force to bomb indiscriminately his own cities, including Managua. Residential neighborhoods were demolished. In the final months of the insurrection, three to four hundred Nicaraguans were being killed each day. Between 1977 and 1979, the war and related epidemics killed between forty to fifty thousand Nicaraguans (Booth 1985: 183).

In El Salvador, the 1972 election of a center-left, reformist Christian Democrat, José Napoleón Duarte, was fraudulently obstructed by the right-wing candidate Arturo Molina. When election returns began projecting a Duarte victory, the radio broadcast was cut off. When broadcasts resumed, a Molina victory was declared. Ensuing protests and a military mutiny, launched by young officers, were crushed. Duarte was arrested, tortured, then exiled. Through this experience, "the notion that structural reforms could be attained through the ballot box [was] widely discredited. . . . Dissidents increasingly opted out of the formal political structure and engaged in antisystemic participation, aimed at its destruction" (Schulz 1984: 201). The Molina regime, successive regimes, and sympathetic paramilitary death squads, responded with massive repression, assassinations, and massacres. Oppositional military forces often struck back with equal ferocity. Often, violent repression occurred in broad daylight. Protesters demonstrating against another fraudulent election in 1977, for example, were fired on by government security forces. More than one hundred died. In 1979, the National Police and Guard fired on a crowd protesting on the Metropolitan Cathedral steps against the arrests of opposition party leaders. Two dozen demonstrators died (Schulz 1984; Brockett 1990: 148–53). In January 1980, government troops opened fire on two hundred thousand peaceful demonstrators marching in San Salvador, killing 67 and injuring 250 (Schulz 1984: 212). Overall, the scope and scale of the repression in El Salvador was staggering. The progressive Catholic church was terrorized. Priests, nuns, lay leaders, and even the Archbishop, Oscar Romero, were assassinated. Entire towns and villages were attacked, often leaving casualties numbered in the hundreds. In 1979, government attacks were killing a thousand people a month (Skidmore and Smith 1984: 313). In the 1980–81 period alone, death-squad forces abducted and killed more than twenty-one thousand civilians (Fagan 1987: 78). Overall, many tens of thousands of Salvadorans lost their lives in the repression (Brockett 1990: 155). In response, "armed resistance . . . spread into rural areas as small guerrilla organizations formed with a broad range of political and ideological orientations. Gradually, what had seemed only isolated acts of terrorism became recognized as a full-scale revolution" (McDonald 1985: 538).

Thus, in most parts of Central America the pattern was similar: pressure for moderate reforms intended to rectify injustice and poverty met intransigent repression, which resulted in increasing radicalization, rebellion, and often revolution. By the late 1970s, U.S. President John F. Kennedy's famous words of 1962—"Those who make peaceful revolution impossible make violent revolution inevitable"— proved to be more prophetic than his speechwriters could ever have imagined.

SUMMARY

In the 1970s, centuries of exploitation, deprivation, and violent repression culminated in the outbreak of revolutionary insurgencies across Central America. Long-standing grievances were intensified by the economic and social shocks of the decade. And the emergence of new political opportunities and new indigenous organizations transformed Central America's historical "culture of repression" into a disruptive "culture of insurrection." Armed revolutionaries across Central America began to exult, as history's tide finally seemed to be turning in their favor. What the protesters and guerrillas did not adequately anticipate, however, was how deeply disturbing their revolutions would be to their immense neighbor to the north.

Two

United States Intervention

In no part of the Constitution is more wisdom to be found, than in the clause which confides the question of war or peace to the legislature, and not to the executive department. . . . The strongest passions and most dangerous weaknesses of the human breast—ambition, avarice, vanity, the honorable or venial love of fame—are all in conspiracy against the desire and duty of peace. . . . The trust and temptation would be too great for any one man.

James Madison, *Helvidius*

"Central America is the most important place in the world for the United States today." Thus spoke Jeanne Kirkpatrick—President Reagan's ambassador to the United Nations—in 1981 (*Newsweek* 1981). That was a curious assertion. No previous U.S. policy maker had ever voiced such a claim. Indeed, in 1981, the majority of Americans knew or cared little about Central America.[1] But Kirkpatrick's pronouncement was no rhetorical misstep, no case of political hyperbole. However curious a statement, it accurately reflected what would be the consistent policy analysis and commitment of the new administration she served. Two years later, President Reagan himself declared (1983): "The national security of all of the Americas is at stake in Central America. If we cannot defend ourselves there . . . the safety of our homeland would be put in jeopardy. . . . If Central America were to fall . . . our credibility would collapse, our alliances would crumble." Thus, Reagan argued (1983) that, on the necessity of achieving his policy goals in Central America, "no issue is more important . . . for the protection of [U.S.] vital interests." Clearly, Central America was at the top of President Reagan's foreign policy agenda. The question is, how did it get there?

MAINTAINING U.S. HEGEMONY OVER CENTRAL AMERICA

Historically, the United States' dealings with Central America have reflected a contradiction. On the one hand, the U.S. has always con-

sidered Central America a region of geopolitical importance. Many
believe its close proximity to the U.S. makes it "America's soft under-
belly," and its security vital for the protection of the U.S. mainland. Its
strategic location—bridging both the Atlantic and Pacific Oceans and
North and South America—makes it an important region for international transportation and communication, and the projection of U.S.
military might (Wiarda 1984; Best 1987: 5).

On the other hand, Central America has historically been a very
low priority in U.S. foreign policy, almost always subordinate to concerns in Europe, Asia, and the Middle East (Karnes 1984: 65; Falcoff
1984). Since these countries lack major military installations, strategic
resources, or massive U.S. investment, the U.S. has typically understood Central America as having only "latent" or "potential" strategic importance. With more weighty international problems on its
hands, the U.S. has tended to ignore Central America (Wiarda 1984:
25; Best 1987: 6).

This contradiction—regarding Central America as important while
simultaneously neglecting it—has been reconciled through the U.S.
domination of Central America. That is, while the U.S. has considered
Central America to be strategically important, it nonetheless has been
able to afford generally to neglect the region because it had established
a dominance there that was never seriously contested by other major
powers. Thus, the "confident neglect [was] born of unchallenged
hegemony" (Best 1987: 6). This U.S. domination was based on (Best
1987: 5–6) "a 'hegemonic presumption' that Central America was
part of the U.S. 'historical,' even 'natural,' sphere of influence, often
strengthened by a belief in the U.S.' historic duty, be it to 'manifest
destiny' or 'continental democracy,' to exert that influence." Such a
presumption is evident, for example, in this 1927 statement by U.S.
Under Secretary of State Robert Olds (quoted in Kornbluh 1987: 2):
"The Central American area . . . constitutes a legitimate sphere of
influence for the United States. . . . We do control the destinies of Central America, and we do so for the single reason that [our] national
interest absolutely dictates such a course. There is no room for any
outside influence other than ours in this region."

This U.S. domination of Central America has been sustained over
many decades through friends and force. When U.S. interests seemed
safe, the security of Central America was entrusted to friendly local
governments and private U.S. interests, such as U.S.-based multinational corporations. When, however, the U.S. saw problems emerging

that it did not trust its regional allies to manage, the U.S. would resort to various forms of more direct intervention (Best 1987: 6). The resulting history of U.S.-backed regimes and U.S. interventions in Central America is too long and intricate to review adequately here. Suffice it to recall a few better-known examples: multiple military interventions in Honduras between 1911–25 and in Nicaragua between 1909–33; U.S. involvement in the overthrow of Guatemala's Arbenz regime in 1956; U.S. support of the Somoza dictators from 1933–79 and of Cuba's Fulgencio Batista for decades before 1959; the Bay of Pigs fiasco of 1961; and the military invasions of the Dominican Republic in 1965, of Grenada in 1983, and of Panama in 1990. In effect, the U.S. has dominated Central America politically, economically, and militarily since at least the mid-nineteenth century.

President Reagan's keen interest in Central America can only be comprehended against the backdrop of the real and perceived erosion of that U.S. hegemony not only in Central America, but around the world. The 1970s were a troublesome time for the U.S. In that single decade, the U.S. anxiously watched its ability to manage world events—for decades something largely taken for granted—deteriorate steadily. The Vietnam debacle set for the 1970s a tone of introspection and insecurity. Watergate reinforced that tone, creating in American citizens a profound distrust of their own government. Meanwhile, in 1973 frustrated Americans, waiting in long lines for expensive gasoline, felt "held hostage" at home by Arab OPEC ministers. Later, fifty-two Americans were held hostage for 444 days by seemingly crazed revolutionaries in Iran who had easily toppled a long-standing U.S.-backed ally. The Ayatollah's disciples chanted denunciations of the "Great Satan," while the President seemed completely impotent to win the hostages' freedom. The "Vietnam syndrome" thorn was driven further into the American flesh when a U.S. military hostage-rescue mission broke down in the Iranian desert and was aborted for want of spare parts. Economically, after 1973 growth in real U.S. wages ended, just as U.S. economic rivals in Western Europe and Japan were gaining competitive ground. Politically, between 1974 and 1981 new governments not aligned with the U.S. took power in thirteen countries.[2] Most importantly, the Soviet Union invaded Afghanistan—and all the United States seemed able to do about it was boycott the 1980 Olympics and cut U.S. wheat sales to the Soviets, which hurt American farmers. After all of this, in the U.S.'s own "backyard," a longtime American ally in Nicaragua was overthrown by the "Yankees-are-the-

Enemy-of-Mankind" Sandinistas—some said with help from President Carter. Next, the regime in El Salvador seemed poised to fall into the hands of the FMLN socialists. Once again, in many eyes Carter seemed to be assisting the rebels by restricting aid to the embattled Salvadoran regime. By the end of the 1970s America's self-confidence was shaken. The economy was sputtering. The government seemed bloated and crippled. Traditional faith in U.S. national moral virtue and can-do determination was unraveling. And the military seemed incapable of containing the Soviets and prevailing against insurgents in the third world. President Carter both summarized and reinforced the dismal '70s spirit by pronouncing that he had discovered a deep malaise in the American people.

Ronald Reagan promised to change all that. He promised to expand the economy, clean out the government, revitalize the military, stand up to communists, and restore American pride. He pledged to stand tall, draw the line, and roll back the enemy. Americans liked what they heard. They elected him President.[3]

President-elect Reagan wanted, upon inauguration, to "hit the ground running," to quickly demonstrate America's newfound courage and resolve. Three factors—necessity, priority, and opportunity—made Central America appear an expedient "proving ground" for Reagan's new approach. First, events in Central America were at a critical point: the Sandinista regime was consolidating power in Nicaragua and the FMLN guerrillas had recently launched a major offensive in El Salvador. There was thus an urgent necessity to address the situation in Central America one way or another. Second, Reagan and most of his advisers regarded Central America as a "vital interest" to U.S. national security.[4] If the U.S. could not prevail in Central America, they believed, it would lose credibility in the eyes of its friends and adversaries, Marxist-Leninism would quickly spread throughout the region through a "domino effect," and the U.S.'s "strategic rear" would be threatened (Vaky 1984: 237–40). Thus, Central America appeared a strategic priority.[5] Third, Reagan's advisers believed that success could be won fairly quickly in Central America. Alexander Haig, Reagan's first Secretary of State, according to Destler (1984: 321), "sniffed an opportunity for a dramatic, low-cost policy success—a lot of visible pressure, followed by an evident improvement in the region, and the administration could claim that its toughness was bearing immediate fruit." Thus, Central America appeared to present the best "test case" to demonstrate America's renewed strength and determination. Secretary Haig advised his chief: "Mr. President, this is one you can win" (Kenworthy 1991: 202).[6]

THE LOGIC OF REAGAN'S STRATEGY

The idea of "winning" in Central America in this way assumed a distinct interpretive analysis of Central America that Reagan and most of his advisers confidently took as the self-evident truth. This interpretive analysis was framed by three major beliefs.[7] The first was that the real cause of unrest in Central America—and the third world generally— was Soviet and Cuban adventurism. This Cold War assumption had guided U.S. foreign policy for decades, although it had fallen on hard times during the Carter years (Schoultz 1987). Reagan brought it back to the White House with fervor. "Let's not delude ourselves," Reagan warned in 1980 (quoted in LaFeber 1984: 302), "the Soviet Union underlies all the unrest that is going on [in Central America]." A year later, Alexander Haig asserted (quoted in Falcoff 1984: 361): "We consider what is happening [in El Salvador] is part of the global Communist campaign coordinated by Havana and Moscow. . . . What is clearly evident to us is that the leftist movement, the rebel activity, its command, control, and direction, now is essentially in the hands of external forces." And, three years later, Reagan reaffirmed: "Central America has become the stage for a bold attempt by the Soviet Union, Cuba, and Nicaragua to install communism, by force, throughout this hemisphere" (Reagan 1983; also see Haig 1984: 88–89, 122–24).

The second belief framing Reagan's approach to Central America was that the real reason the U.S. had ever failed to prevail against communist expansionism—particularly in Cuba and Vietnam—was because of U.S. timidity and indecisiveness. With regard to Cuba, according to Pastor (1987: 231): "Reagan blamed President Kennedy for not saving Cuba when he had the chance: 'We have seen an American President walk all the way to the barricade in the Cuban Missile Crisis and lack the will to take the final step to make it successful.' Presumably, the 'final step' would have been an invasion to remove Fidel Castro."

Similarly, Reagan did not think of Vietnam as an immoral or foolish war. Vietnam itself was not a mistake. To the contrary, Vietnam was, in Reagan's words, "a noble cause" (LaFeber 1984: 274). What *was* a mistake was the irresolute manner in which the U.S. prosecuted the war in Vietnam. For Reagan, avoiding "another Vietnam" meant not timidly evading all military engagements in the third world, but decisively winning third world conflicts through the courageous and resolute application of necessary force. "The Caribbean," lamented Reagan (quoted in Pastor 1987: 231), "is rapidly becoming a Communist lake in what should be an American pond, and the United States resembles a giant, afraid to move." For Reagan, the giant simply needed to rouse the courage for decisive action.

The third belief framing Reagan's interpretive analysis of Central America was that both the Sandinistas and the FMLN rebels were totalitarian, Marxist-Leninist communists—inherently expansionistic, undemocratic, irreformable, and untrustworthy (Schoultz 1987: 128–39). The Sandinistas, Reagan warned (quoted in Kenworthy 1987: 163), were "a cruel clique of deeply committed Communists at war with God and man." "I haven't believed anything they've been saying since they got in charge," Reagan told a group of news reporters (quoted in Vaky 1984: 249), "and you shouldn't either." Under Secretary of Defense Fred Iklé (1983: 555), referring to Nicaragua, underlined the threat: "Leninist regimes are particularly dangerous: once entrenched, they tend to become irreversible, and they usually seek to export their totalitarianism to other nations." Thus, the White House tagged the Sandinistas "terrorists," "genocidal," "Murder, Inc.," a "cancer," "hardline communists," people who "hijacked" their own country and brought to the region a "Central American gulag," a "communist reign of terror," and a "totalitarian dungeon." Elections in Sandinista Nicaragua were labeled "Soviet-style shams" that had dragged Nicaragua "behind the iron curtain." In a radio broadcast, Reagan accused the Sandinistas of "exporting drugs to poison our youth and linking up with terrorists of Iran, Libya, the Red Brigades, and the PLO" (Kenworthy 1987: 166; Lamperti 1988: 29; Kornbluh 1987: 173, 193–94).

Together, these three beliefs clearly determined Reagan's options in Central America. To begin, simply waiting and watching for positive developments was unthinkable, for, as Jeanne Kirkpatrick (quoted in Rubin 1984: 301–2) put it in 1981, "the deterioration of the U.S. position in the hemisphere has already created serious vulnerabilities where none previously existed, and threatens now to confront this country with the unprecedented need to defend itself against a ring of Soviet bases on and around our southern and eastern borders." Similarly, attempting diplomatically to negotiate terms with the Sandinistas or the FMLN rebels that would satisfy U.S. national security interests was equally senseless. For, the very *existence* of the Sandinistas and the FMLN was thought to threaten U.S. national security. The Sandinistas and the FMLN would never assent to U.S. demands, it was believed, and shouldn't be trusted even if they promised to. As Elliott Abrams, Assistant Secretary of State (quoted in Kenworthy 1987: 169), argued, "It is preposterous to think we could sign a deal with the Sandinistas and expect it to be kept." Similarly, Under Secretary Iklé (quoted in Vaky 1984: 244) claimed of the FMLN: "We can no more negotiate an acceptable political solution with these people than the social democrats in revolutionary Russia could have talked Lenin into giving up totalitarian Bolshevism." Hence, diplomatic negotiations were seen to represent at best a distraction and at worst a deceitful and fatal trap guaranteeing U.S. defeat. "This Administration believes," a senior official acknowledged (quoted in LeoGrande 1986: 116), "that a negotiated settlement with these guys [the Sandinistas] . . . would be a life-time insurance policy for the revolution." Thus, *a priori*, real negotiations were considered unacceptable (Roberts 1990).

With the procrastination and negotiation options removed from the table, the only logical option that remained was force. The FMLN had to be extinguished and the Sandinistas ousted. But neither were going to surrender or resign voluntarily. They had to be pushed. Force was thought to be the only means of achieving U.S. goals in Central America (Haig 1984: 123–29).[8] Thus, although some of Reagan's key advisers had their doubts,[9] the decision was made to confront Central American communists with a strong show of force.

DRAWING THE LINE

The Reagan administration began its first term with a flurry of dramatic public threats and private plans for military intervention in Central America. Secretary Haig was the point man (Smith 1984). In interviews and press conferences, Haig announced that with the new U.S. policy—in contrast to Carter's approach—concern for human rights and social reforms would be subordinate to the issues of security and the fight against "terrorism" (Pastor 1987: 232). He warned that the U.S. was going to "draw the line" against Soviet and Cuban adventurism in Central America by "going to the source of the problem." This meant blockading or invading Cuba—a plan which Haig had formally proposed to the National Security Council in June 1981. The possibility of eventual direct U.S. military action in Central America was publicly entertained (Best 1987: 33). Presidential Counselor Edwin Meese stated that the U.S. "could not rule out any means" in opposing the FMLN in El Salvador—including, presumably, sending U.S. combat soldiers (Pastor 1987: 236). Public and congressional concerns about blundering into "another Vietnam" were summarily dismissed (Vaky 1984: 235). The correct historical analogy, administration officials argued, was not Vietnam but Greece of 1945–48 (Vaky 1984: 235). The Reagan administration minimized human rights abuses by friendly right-wing regimes. The State Department rewrote internal papers to downplay rightist threats to democracy. "Haig even speculated that three American nuns killed and raped at a Salvadoran army checkpoint might have been victims of 'an exchange of fire' while running a roadblock. Ambassador Kirkpatrick said that the nuns were political activists on behalf of the opposition" (Rubin 1984: 302). The State Department then produced a "White Paper" which claimed to document with indisputable proof Soviet, Cuban, Vietnamese, and Ethiopian shipments of hundreds of tons of arms to El Salvador through Nicaragua (Falcoff 1984: 361). Diplomatic teams were sent to Europe and Latin America with the White Paper in hand to line up support for U.S. action in Central America (Rubin 1984: 302).

Furthermore, Carter-era diplomats in Central America—most notably the Ambassador to El Salvador, Robert White—were promptly and visibly removed from office and replaced with more loyal Reagan associates (Destler 1984: 321; Rubin 1984: 303–4). Reagan suspended wheat and chemical feedstock sales, economic aid, and Export-Import bank guarantees to Nicaragua and opposed its loan requests to the World Bank and the Inter-American Development Bank (Rubin 1984: 302; Kornbluh 1987: 99). Reagan began promoting a $113.7 million aid package to the Salvadoran military government and looking for ways to restore aid to the Guatemalan army cut off by President Carter (Falcoff 1984: 361–62; Jonas 1991: 148). And plans were made to train sixteen hundred Salvadoran soldiers at U.S. military bases (Schulz 1984: 232). With U.S. support, anti-Sandinista paramilitary brigades began training in Florida and California (Walker 1987: 6). The CIA drew up secret plans to assemble, train, arm, and direct a commando force of five hundred Cuban exiles to conduct paramilitary operations against Nicaragua and "special Cuban targets." And Argentina's right-wing military regime was also engaged to draw up plans to train one thousand Nicaraguan exiles—mostly ex-members of Somoza's National Guard—to overthrow the Sandinistas. In December 1981, Reagan approved both plans for implementation (LeoGrande 1987: 203).[10]

The administration proceeded confidently with these initial plans to confront and roll back what it saw as Marxist communism in Central America. But to its great surprise, the public and Congress reacted negatively. "Almost immediately the president and his secretary of state faced a roar of domestic opposition which caught them utterly off balance. Congress was flooded with letters, visits, and phone calls protesting the administration's proposals" (Falcoff 1984: 362). According to Destler (1984: 321), "Haig's dramatic acts and declarations brought headlines and television cameras. At first the administration encouraged this coverage, only to find public communications to the White House running 10–1 *against* the new approach." Reagan and Haig were stunned. They thought that a landslide election victory had provided the public mandate to confront communism aggressively in Central America. But now the public and Congress were resisting.

Soon, certain Reagan advisers became alarmed about jeopardizing their domestic economic agenda by pushing the Central America plan too hard and fast (Kenworthy 1991: 204). The White House reacted by de-escalating media attention on Central America. According to Falcoff (1984: 362):

> Within weeks the administration was furiously backpedaling from its original rhetoric. For example, in a television interview with Walter Cronkite on March 3, 1981, President Reagan redefined Haig's comment about "going to the source" as using "diplomacy, trade, a number of things" to persuade the Soviets to alter their role in the area. "I don't think in any way," the president assured his listeners, "that he was suggesting an assault on Cuba." A few days earlier, somewhat shellshocked from sustained barrages of hostile questions, Secretary Haig exclaimed to journalists, "I wouldn't want anyone here to think that we are not very concerned about, if you will, the [human rights] improvements that are necessary in the Salvadoran regime."

The State Department also chastened journalists for sensationalizing the Central America story and inflating its importance to a proportion "five times as big as it [really] is" (Rubin 1984: 307).

But aside from temporarily reducing media attention on Central America, this early domestic opposition did not actually alter any of Reagan's fundamental intentions toward or strategies for Central

America (Smith 1984). Given the administration's premises about the Central American situation, it would have been manifestly irresponsible to do so. Reagan remained fully committed ideologically and politically to confronting and rolling back communism in Central America.[11] Abandoning Central America, reverting to stalling tactics, and pursuing real negotiations to their conclusion all remained, in the minds of most White House officials, out of the question.

POLITICAL PUBLIC RELATIONS

The White House did learn, however, from this initial public outcry that achieving its objectives in Central America would require greater political shrewdness. If sectors of the public and Congress had unwarranted fears of confronting communism, they could be persuaded, placated, or kept in the dark. But ultimately, the administration felt, those fears—which themselves were largely responsible for the Central American danger in the first place—must not be allowed to keep the President from doing whatever would be necessary to protect vital U.S. national security interests.[12] Thus, the White House pressed on with its original intent to use force in Central America. But it now began to work more carefully to cultivate support for and counter opposition to its policy, both with Congress and the American public. It did so primarily through public diplomacy campaigns, participation in peace negotiations, and congressional accommodation.

First, the White House took more proactive steps to try to win public opinion on Central America. Public resistance to the administration's Central American policy was strong and widespread. In 1982 an National Security Council paper on Central America noted, "We continue to have serious difficulties with U.S. public and congressional opinion, which jeopardizes our ability to stay the course." And, in 1983 an interagency strategy paper conceded, "Efforts have failed to produce domestic or international understanding and support. The present U.S. policy faces substantial opposition, at home and abroad" (both quoted in Kornbluh 1987: 159). Reagan himself complained to his advisers in 1983, "I have not succeeded in explaining to the public why they should care about Central and South America." He responded by signing directive NSDD 77, "Management of Public Diplomacy Relative to National Security." The directive sought "to strengthen the organization, planning and coordination of various aspects of public diplomacy . . . those actions of the U.S. Government

designated to generate support for our national security objectives."
The purpose of NSDD 77 was later expressed candidly by John Kelly,
Deputy Assistant Secretary of the Air Force and specialist in low-
intensity warfare (quoted in Kornbluh 1987: 159): "The most critical
special operations mission we have today is to persuade the American
public that the communists are out to get us. If we can win this war of
ideas, we can win anywhere else."

NSDD 77 authorized a Special Planning Group under the National Security Council to "be responsible for the overall planning, direction, coordination and monitoring of implementation of public diplomacy activities." Two major suborganizations were created to carry
out these "perception management operations," the Office of Public
Diplomacy for Latin America and the Caribbean and the White House
Outreach Group on Central America (Kenworthy 1987). In addition,
the National Security Council contracted with I.D.E.A. Inc.—a public
relations firm directed by National Security Council courier-to-the-
contras Robert Owen—to carry out public relations campaigns in the
U.S. on behalf of the contras and to establish private contra-support
groups (Nelson-Pallmeyer 1989: 66). Finally, White House officials
successfully worked the mass media to get their messages across to the
prime-time public. Common publicity techniques, which the Reagan
presidential campaign had utilized skillfully to win the White House—
such as strategic press leaks, not-for-attribution "backgrounder"
interviews, "strategic polling," and well-timed, one-liner photo
opportunities—were employed to promote the administration's Central American policy. One administration official explained the public
diplomacy campaign in this way: "The idea is to slowly demonize the
Sandinista government, in order to turn it into a real enemy and threat
in the minds of the American people, thereby eroding their resistance
to U.S. support for the contras and, perhaps, to a future U.S. military
intervention in the region" (quoted in Kornbluh 1987: 166).

Second, the White House began to express greater public interest in
negotiating peace in Central America. In 1982, for example, when
Mexican President López Portillo proposed a new peace plan, the
administration agreed to participate in talks, as it did in most subsequent third-party efforts to negotiate peace. In fact, however, we now
know, the administration had no true interest in peace negotiations.
Although a few officials, such as Assistant Secretary of State Thomas
Enders, appear to have viewed negotiations as a genuine potential
solution to the region's conflicts, most top administration officials

considered the Sandinistas and the FMLN untrustworthy negotiators and were entirely unwilling to see negotiations to a conclusion (Goodfellow 1987). According to one administration official (quoted in Riding 1982): "We were cool to the [López Portillo] initiative from the beginning, but we were effectively ambushed by Congress and public opinion. We had to agree to negotiate or appear unreasonable."[13] U.S. participation in ongoing peace talks, in other words, was mere "showcase negotiation," maintained primarily for domestic political reasons (Roberts 1990; Vanden and Walker 1991: 170–72). By publicly expressing a willingness to pursue a diplomatic resolution, the White House both undermined opponents' charge that the President was simply a warmonger spoiling for a fight and justified its use of force as a necessary "stick" to pressure enemies into making concessions in negotiations to win the "carrot" of peace.[14]

The third means the White House used to garner support for and counter opposition to its Central American policy—until 1983 at least—was limited accommodation with Congress. As it worked in Congress for military aid for friendly Central American regimes, the White House assumed a more compromising approach, "settling for three quarters of a loaf when necessary, accepting, in form at least, Congressional preconditions" (Destler 1984: 324). The administration official in charge was Assistant Secretary of State Thomas Enders, a relatively pragmatic career diplomat. His main purpose was to win the necessary aid support from moderate Democrats. To begin, the administration bowed to congressional oversight and agreed to certify human rights improvements in El Salvador every six months as a condition for new aid. The administration consistently claimed to Congress that progress was indeed being made (Schulz 1984: 233; see de Onis 1981b, 1981c).

> It publicly described the country as run by a reformist government battling extremists from both the insurgent left and the death-squad right. It claimed that its own strategy was primarily a political one, with military aid serving only as a shield to protect successful reforms against insurgent sabotage. Given a chance, it argued, Duarte would undercut the appeal of the left and restrain the abuses of the armed forces (Blachman and Sharpe 1988: 4).

Many in Congress challenged the administration's claims.[15] But by simply agreeing to certify human rights reforms, the White House was at least offering a formal gesture of flexibility toward Capitol Hill moderates.[16] An additional effort to accommodate congressional concerns was the introduction, in 1982, of the Caribbean Basin Initiative (CBI), a "Marshall Plan for Central America." The CBI provided $400 million in economic assistance to the region.[17] More importantly, the CBI encouraged regional trade and investment, with a focus on developing nontraditional exports for market in the U.S. (Ross 1985; Torres Rivas 1988; Stein 1988). The White House advanced the CBI partly to demonstrate to Congress that it was genuinely concerned with Central American economic development. In doing so, the administration implicitly backed away from its previous claim that poverty and injustice were unrelated to revolutions in Central America, and positioned themselves closer to congressional moderates (Smith 1984: 490).

RETAKING THE POLITICAL OFFENSIVE

The White House's accommodating approach, however, did not last long. By early 1983, administration hard-liners—such as U.N. Ambassador Jeanne Kirkpatrick and National Security Adviser William Clark—were growing impatient with Thomas Enders. The war in El Salvador against the FMLN was going very badly for the Salvadoran army.[18] In Nicaragua, the Sandinistas were engaged in a rapid military buildup. Regional allies were reported to have lost confidence in the administration's efforts. And at home, congressional opponents were preparing a campaign to cut off Contra aid (Rubin 1984: 308–9; Dickey 1983: 663). Kirkpatrick and Clark pressed the President for a change of course. They argued that success demanded significantly more military aid for the Salvadoran army and the Contras. Appeasing Congress, they contended, only encouraged obstructionism. "As long as a group in Congress keeps crippling the President's military assistance program," complained Fred Iklé (quoted in Destler 1984: 330), "we will have a policy always shy of success." On the other hand, CIA Director William Casey argued that a fully funded Contra force might overthrow the Sandinistas by the end of the year (Rubin 1984: 309; see Kenworthy 1985).

The President was persuaded. He decided to retake the political offensive to win public and congressional approval for an all-out military defeat of the FMLN and the Sandinistas. Thomas Enders soon was reassigned as ambassador to Spain and William Clark placed in charge of Central American policy. A string of dramatic actions followed. In February, U.S. and Honduran troops conducted a $5 million military exercise, labeled "Big Pine," near the Nicaraguan border. The troops practiced repelling an imaginary invasion of a "red army" from the country "Corinto"—clearly Nicaragua, which possessed a nearby seaport by that name (Kornbluh 1987: 140). In April, the President, in an unusual move, addressed a joint session of Congress with a forceful and pointed appeal to Congress and the American people to support his Central American policy. "I do not believe," he asserted, "there is a majority in the Congress or the country that councils passivity, resignation, defeatism, in the face of this challenge to freedom and security in our hemisphere."[19]

In May, Reagan cut Nicaragua's sugar import quota almost 90 percent, in a way reminiscent of the confrontational slashing of Cuba's quota twenty-five years earlier (Pastor 1987: 242). The White House also unilaterally lifted the arms embargo against Guatemala and publicly resumed arms sales to the military (Jonas 1991: 199). In June, the President ordered the closing of all Nicaraguan consulates in the U.S. Meanwhile, the number of Central American military personnel training at the Pentagon's "SouthCom" base in Panama was increased ninefold to twenty-nine thousand a year (Kornbluh 1987: 99, 128). In July, the administration announced more large-scale joint military maneuvers with Honduras. Dubbed "Big Pine II," this six-month operation involved four thousand troops and nineteen ships, and included practice amphibious landings on Central American soil by U.S. Marines (Dickey 1983: 664–65). Also in July, the White House appointed a national bipartisan commission, headed by former Secretary of State Henry Kissinger, to devise new policy recommendations for Central America. Its final report largely affirmed the administration's view of Central America, recommending massive economic and military assistance to allies and increased pressure against the Sandinistas and the FMLN (Lowenthal 1985). Finally, in October, the U.S. invaded and overthrew the government of the Caribbean island of Grenada, clearly demonstrating its willingness to employ U.S. combat troops to intervene in the region when considered necessary. If the Sandinistas ever doubted the U.S.'s readiness to invade Nicaragua and overthrow their regime, they doubted no more.

President Reagan's renewed high-profile approach to Central America again drew domestic protest. Unlike Alexander Haig's political offensive of 1981, however, domestic criticism and opposition in 1983 and thereafter did not surprise nor daunt the White House. For the remainder of the decade, President Reagan remained steadfast in his public fight to achieve his policy objectives in Central America. As he later declared in a 1985 battle over Contra aid, even if Congress did reject aid for the Contras, "we are not going to walk away from them, no matter what happens"—a promise the President, the Iran-Contra scandal later proved, was deadly serious about keeping.

Three

LOW-INTENSITY WARFARE

I love killing. I have been killing for the past seven years. There's nothing I like better. If I could, I'd kill several people a day.

Contra Chief of Military Operations for Misura, 1984[1]

The White House's resurgent efforts on Central America, under the new leadership of National Security Council adviser William Clark, adopted a different war strategy than Alexander Haig's. In 1981, Haig had advocated forceful and direct U.S. military engagements with the enemy, such as a U.S. naval blockade of Cuba. But the early 1980s saw the emergence in Washington military and intelligence circles of a new, unconventional approach to war making—called "low-intensity warfare"—that was to significantly shape the White House's Central American policy.

Low-intensity warfare as a school of thought extended the "flexible response" strategy employed by the U.S. military in the Vietnam War, but the use of proxy soldiers in Central America was a direct response to the U.S. loss in Vietnam.[2] The U.S. military learned the hard way in Vietnam that vastly superior military technology and hardware do not guarantee victory in small-scale, third-world conflicts. That is because these conflicts are not fundamentally military, argue low-intensity warfare authors, but political and ideological in nature. In Vietnam, the Vietcong employed a combination of political, economic, psychological, and military measures to win the war. Low-intensity warfare advocates contend that future U.S. success in similar conflicts demands adopting and employing the enemy's own measures against it.

Victory, thus conceived, does not so much consist in destroying the enemy physically, but rather in isolating, demoralizing, and delegitimating the enemy politically. The ultimate goal is to undermine the enemy's credibility as a viable political alternative. This is achieved through long-term political, economic, psychological, and military forms of aggression—always short of full-scale, direct battle—which, over time, discourage civilian support for the enemy (Sarkesian 1986).[3]

> Tactics range from psychological warfare (aimed at winning "the six inches between the peasant's ears," instead of territory) to massive saturation bombing of populated areas in "liberated zones." . . . The underlying goal is to remove the masses as a support for revolutionary forces and recruit them into the rearguard of "national security" (Barry, Vergara, and Rodolfo Castro 1988: 83).

In low-intensity warfare, the traditional distinction between combatants and noncombatants disappears. The civilian population of the country in question is a major target. In the words of Colonel John Waghlestein (1985: 42), commander of the Army's 7th Special Forces, low-intensity warfare is "total war at the grassroots level."

William Clark, who was by 1983 in control of Central American policy, and others in the administration believed that low-intensity warfare would be a strategy much more effective than Haig's for defeating communism in Central America. For one thing, it did not require the employment of U.S. troops in Central American combat, since proxy armies could be utilized to fight instead. Also, low-intensity warfare was less understood by and less visible to the American public, making it less likely to generate domestic political opposition. Furthermore, this kind of warfare was relatively inexpensive to wage. As CIA Director William Casey (quoted in Kornbluh 1987: 7) remarked, "It takes relatively few people and little support to disrupt the internal peace and economic stability of a small country." Additionally, intelligence reports claimed that the Sandinistas and the FMLN would be quite vulnerable to low-intensity warfare tactics. Finally, many of the administration's actions already taken in Central America dovetailed well into the new strategy. Thus, previous commitments, domestic political constraints, and the Central American reality all converged to make low-intensity warfare the administration's war strategy of choice (Walker 1987: 14).

Through a variety of tactics, this strategy aims to make civilian support for the enemy unbearably costly, while making compliance with allies appear beneficial. In Central America, waging this kind of "total war at the grassroots level" involved the following methods.

MILITARY AND ECONOMIC AID

The U.S. first needed to furnish massive military aid to regional allies—the Salvadoran, Honduran, and Guatemalan regimes and the Contras—since the costs of waging war far exceeded these U.S. friends' economic capacity to pay themselves (see figure 3.1). U.S. economic aid was also needed to "stabilize" fragile political allies (see figure 3.2).[4] El Salvador was the largest Central American recipient of U.S. aid. Between 1981 and 1983, El Salvador received $744 million in U.S. "security" aid alone. In 1985, the U.S. granted $744 million in total aid to El Salvador. That amount equaled 20 percent of that country's GNP and the total expenditure of the entire Salvadoran government (Gorostiaga and Marchetti 1988: 129). The U.S. also sent Special Forces trainer-advisers to El Salvador and Salvadoran officers to train at Fort Benning, Georgia. By late 1983, the U.S. had trained nine hundred Salvadoran officers, half of the entire officer corp (Hudson 1990: 224).

Honduras was the second largest regional recipient of U.S. assistance. Military aid to Honduras skyrocketed 2,344 percent in six years, from $3.4 million in 1980 to $79.7 million in 1986. In the four years after 1981, Honduras had received a total of $285.5 million in military aid from the U.S. (Vanden and Walker 1991: 162). According

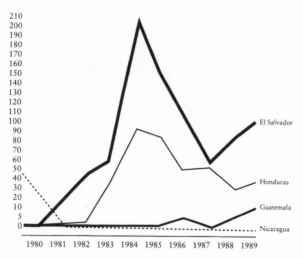

Fig. 3.1. U.S. Foreign Military Aid to Central America ($ U.S. million). Source: *International Finance* 1986, 1992; *Statistical Abstract of Latin America* 1990.

to Kornbluh (1987: 136–37): "By 1985, Honduras was the eighth leading recipient of U.S. military and economic aid in the world. U.S. military training programs in Honduras also escalated. Between 1980 and 1984, the number of U.S. military advisors rose from seven to 349." Honduran military and security forces grew from eleven thousand in 1979 to twenty-three thousand in 1985. Between 1980 and 1984, the number of Honduran military personnel training at the U.S. Army School more than doubled to well over five hundred a year (Gold 1987: 45).

In Guatemala, the situation was different. The most important phase of Guatemala's counterinsurgent low-intensity warfare was fought between 1980 and 1983. U.S. ability to support directly the army's counterinsurgency campaign was technically constrained by President Carter's aid embargo imposed to penalize Guatemala's grisly human rights record. "In fact," according to Jonas (1991: 195), "what was billed as a military aid 'ban' or 'cutoff' was only partial, as military contacts and arms transfers continued." In June of 1981, for example, the Commerce Department approved a $3.1 million sale of military vehicles (Schoultz 1983: 197–98). Altogether, Guatemala received $17.61 million in military and economic aid from the U.S. between 1978 and 1983. Furthermore, the U.S. had collaborated with the Guatemalan military in devising its original low-intensity warfare

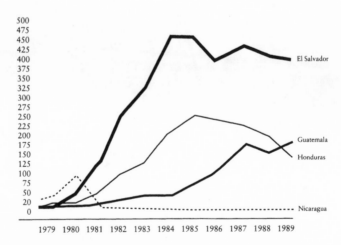

Fig. 3.2. U.S. Foreign Aid to Central America ($U.S.million). Source: *International Finance* 1986, 1992.

plan, called "Program of Pacification and Eradication of Communism" (Jonas 1991: 198, 205).

The Nicaraguan Contras received U.S. aid through many channels. In 1980, President Carter had expended $1 million to begin organizing a counterrevolutionary force. In 1981, Reagan authorized another $19.5 million to expand the covert operation. In two separate 1983 bills, Congress approved $19 and $24 million in aid to the Contras. In June 1985, Congress approved another $27 million. By the spring of 1986, the Contras had received a total of $130 million in U.S. aid. Then, in June, 1986, Congress authorized another $100 million to continue the Contra war (Kornbluh 1987b). Even more of the Contras' aid, however, was furnished secretly through the CIA (Chamorro 1987; Woodward 1987). For example, in 1984 the CIA was feeding Edén Pastora's Democratic Revolutionary Alliance $400,000 a month. In one instance, the CIA also provided $500 million worth of weapons, logistical support, and communications technology to the Contras in secret by retaining legal title to purchased equipment while turning it over to the Contras. Besides congressional appropriations and CIA funding, the White House provided an additional $50 million in Contra aid through third-party solicitations and $3.8 million through a diversion of profits from covert arms sales to Iran (Kornbluh and Byrne 1993; Kornbluh 1987a: 211). By 1988, the Contras had received more than $1 billion in U.S. aid (*New York Times* 1988b).

In addition to standard forms of military aid to Central America, the U.S. Agency for International Development in El Salvador, as in other countries, used U.S. food aid for political purposes: to undermine the FMLN, draw support for the army, and create gratitude, trust, and dependence on the U.S. (Garst and Barry 1990: 147–83). One U.S. congressional report stated, "Despite their innocuous labels, these [food] programs are used to prosecute the war and repair its damages, rather than to change the conditions that sparked and continue to fuel rebellion" (Hatfield, Leach, and Miller 1987: 4).[5]

Finally, low-intensity warfare called not only for overt military and economic aid to allies, but also covert funding for friendly political organizations and movements. In Nicaragua, for example, the CIA funded opposition newspapers and labor unions associated with traditional political parties to criticize the Sandinistas (Robinson 1992; Walker 1985: 178). In El Salvador in 1984, the CIA gave financial support to the Unión Popular Democrática, a confederation of unions which represented the main electoral base of the White House's favored candidate, José Napoleón Duarte. In the end, the U.S. spent more than $10 million on the 1984 election to ensure Duarte's victory (Karl 1988: 180).

Overall, in 1985 the U.S. was spending *twenty times* more on foreign aid to Central America than it had in 1978. Taking all the costs together—economic and military aid, military exercises and construction, and regional Army and Marine force maintenance—by mid-decade the U.S. was spending about $9.5 billion annually for its security policy in Central America (Cohen and Rogers 1986: 42).[6]

ECONOMIC AGGRESSION

Fighting the low-intensity war in Central America also involved the material and economic strangulation of enemies, particularly the Sandinistas. Damaging the Nicaraguan economy served the Reagan administration in two ways. First, economic breakdown could destabilize Nicaragua politically and possibly lead to the collapse of the Sandinista regime. Second, economic decline, even if externally facilitated, could be construed to demonstrate that all alternatives to free-market capitalism would inevitably fail (Vanden and Walker 1991: 166–67). By 1983, the Reagan administration had already suspended Nicaragua's foreign aid, slashed its sugar quota, suspended wheat and feedstock sales, and obstructed multinational loans to Nicaragua. By 1984, the NSC was drawing plans for a naval blockade of Nicaragua (Woodward 1987: 335). In the following years, the economic strangulation continued.

On May 1, 1985, the President declared a state of national emergency and imposed a full economic embargo against Nicaragua. While the embargo was ignored by every other nation, it did block $58 million worth of Nicaraguan exports to the U.S. and $110 million worth of imports to Nicaragua. The net cost of the embargo to Nicaragua in 1985 alone totaled $50–$90 million (Barry and Preusch 1988: 213).[7] In addition, the State Department took steps to prevent the reestablishment of private transaction credit links for firms trading with Nicaragua. With private corporate credits eliminated, imports and exports had to be transacted on a cash basis, which dramatically constricted trading (Conroy 1987: 69–70). Also, the U.S. attempted, sometimes successfully, to block shipments of humanitarian aid to Nicaragua. In September 1986, for example, the relief agency Oxfam

America tried to ship $41,000 worth of seeds, rakes, shovels, wrenches, chain saws, hammers, and water pipes to Nicaragua to alleviate food shortages. The shipment was terminated by the U.S. government, however, as "inconsistent with current U.S. foreign policy" (*New York Times* 1986c). Similarly, in 1988, the U.S. government blocked a fourteen-vehicle shipment of food and medical supplies, donated by the Veterans Peace Convoy, at a Mexican border town in Texas (*New York Times* 1988a, 1988b). After a twenty-five-day standoff, nine members of the convoy were maced and arrested by Federal agents when they tried to cross the border bridge (*New York Times* 1988e, 1988f, 1988h).

Another major element of economic aggression involved the military sabotage of economic infrastructure and means of production. The CIA itself carried out bombing attacks on various Nicaraguan facilities, considered too sophisticated for the Contras to execute—at least twenty-two in one eight-month period. The CIA also created a special Latin American commando force called "Unilaterally Controlled Latino Assets" (UCLAs). "Our mission was to sabotage ports, refineries, boats, bridges, and to make it appear that the Contras had done it," explained one Honduran UCLA (quoted in Kornbluh 1987b: 29). In January 1984, CIA-supported commando teams mined all of Nicaragua's major harbors in an attempt to disable international trade. Ten ships from six nations were damaged, seventeen seamen were injured or killed in explosions, incoming shipments of goods were delayed for weeks, several shipping lines suspended imports altogether, and shipping insurance costs increased. The U.S. mines continued to explode for six months (Conroy 1987: 69; Kornbluh 1987b: 30–31).

Most of the CIA's work of economic sabotage, however, was executed indirectly through the Contras. Early on, some in the White House hoped that the Contras might achieve a military overthrow of the Sandinistas. It soon became apparent, however, that the Contras were incapable of such a victory. For, while they could raid villages or destroy bridges and retreat to Honduras, the Contras remained unable to capture and hold Nicaraguan territory. Hence, the Contras' primary role in the low-intensity war shifted to economic vandalism and military harassment. From the beginning, the Contras proved better able to destroy civilian than military targets. Indeed, their first attacks, in March 1982, consisted in destroying two bridges in northern Nicaragua (Pastor 1987: 238). In the years that followed, the Contras concentrated on destroying highways, bridges, oil refineries, customs warehouses, fuel tanks, grain storage facilities, government buildings, schools, health clinics, and fields of crops. In September 1983, the Contras even attempted to bomb Managua's Augusto Sandino Airport with a propeller-driven twin-engine Cessna which had five-hundred-pound bombs strapped under each wing (Woodward 1987: 271). The millions of dollars of damage inflicted by the Contras helped undermine Nicaragua's economic recovery and reforms following the revolution.

In addition to destroying infrastructure, the Contras also developed a policy of "terrorizing the civilian population so they would be afraid . . . to help produce badly needed export crops. . . . Crops could not be harvested in northern areas of the country because of the danger to the farmworkers" (Vanden and Walker 1991: 164–65). This contributed to food shortages and a decline in export goods. Another consequence was the exacerbation of Nicaragua's already severe labor shortage. Nicaragua was building up its army, in part, to repel Contra attacks. But this shifted labor out of the agricultural and industrial sectors into the nonproductive defense sector. In 1980, the Sandinista Army was quite small—about 16,500 soldiers. But by late 1983, Nicaraguan armed forces had expanded to 25,000 and the popular militia force to 60,000. As the Contra war intensified, by 1988, the armed forces expanded to 75,000 (Lamperti 1988: 37; also see Vanden and Walker 1991: 158; Walker 1987: 5). In 1984 alone, "the Sandinistas organized 10,000 [new] recruits, mostly young men, into Irregular Warfare Battalions, removing them from productive work" (Barry, Vergara, and Rodolfo Castro 1988: 89).

Similarly, the Contra war increasingly diverted government expenditures into defense costs. In 1980, defense expenditures comprised only 11 percent of the Nicaraguan government's budget (International Finance 1982). The rest of the funds were primarily spent on economic investment and social programs. But by 1985, defense spending had grown to more than 50 percent of the budget, leaving much less money for more productive uses. Hence, "many of the most successful social programs, implemented in 1979 and 1980, had been slowed or halted by the economic demands of the war. Fewer new schools and clinics were constructed and agricultural and industrial production suffered because available currency was being used to support the war effort" (Conroy and Pastor 1988: 220). According to Miles (1986: 30), the goal was "to squeeze the economy by forcing a massive diversion of resources into defense. The strategy aimed to exacerbate social problems and tensions, eroding popular support for the revolution by making it ineffective in people's lives."

While U.S. economic aggression was most conspicuous toward Nicaragua, other forms of economic aggression were waged in El Salvador and Guatemala to undermine the guerrilla movements. Government counterinsurgency forces, for example, often burned crops and destroyed villages in guerrilla-controlled areas to disrupt the guerrillas' social and material support networks. In Guatemala, as a result of crop burnings, the 1983 food harvest was 60 percent lower than normal (Jonas 1991: 95).

POLITICAL ISOLATION

The U.S. worked in a variety of ways politically to isolate its enemies from other nations. In the case of Nicaragua, in an effort to generate negative international public opinion, the Reagan administration continually decried real and invented civil and human rights abuses by the Sandinistas, whom they repeatedly branded as "Communists."[8] As the human rights–monitor group Americas Watch observed (1984: 46–47): "The Reagan Administration [used] human rights criticism of Nicaragua as an instrument of warfare . . . of military policy." The Sandinistas, for their part, gave the Reagan administration plenty of material to work with. Less experienced in governing than in seizing power over their country, the Sandinistas made a number of costly political blunders. Early in their rule, the Sandinistas badly mishandled the integration of the Miskito Indians of the Atlantic Coast into their program of revolutionary social reconstruction, seriously violating their civil and human rights. Seeing an obvious sign of totalitarian rule, the Reagan administration relentlessly condemned these violations. They were, charged Jeanne Kirkpatrick with more than a little exaggeration, "more massive than any other human-rights violation that I'm aware of in Central America today" (Diskin 1987: 86).

Similarly, the White House repeatedly called attention to religious repression of the Catholic hierarchy in Nicaragua, accusing the Sandinistas of gross religious persecution. Many of the administration's charges—that the Sandinistas capriciously closed down the Catholic radio station and expelled priests—had some basis in fact. Such acts lent themselves to substantiating the charge that the Nicaraguan rulers were totalitarian communists. Other White House accusations, however, were sheer fabrications. For example, in 1985 President Reagan

charged that "the Sandinistas seem always to have been anti-Semitic.
. . . After the Sandinista takeover, the remaining Jews were terrorized
into leaving" (Cohn and Hynds 1987: 107). Such undocumented allegations continued, despite cables from the U.S. embassy in Managua
stating that no such antisemitism existed. "We've pointed out the distortions time and time again and been totally ignored or told to shut
up," one embassy official reported. "It seems they must be using our
reports as toilet paper" (quoted in Kornbluh 1987: 174, 259).[9] The
U.S. also actively worked to discredit Nicaragua's elections. In 1984,
for example, the CIA offered bribes to opposition leaders to withdraw
their candidacies. The treasurer of Nicaragua's Conservative Party, for
example, reported that the CIA had offered his party $300,000 and
four of its leaders $50,000 each to withdraw from the election. When
some, such as Arturo Cruz, did withdraw, the State Department
denounced the elections as Soviet-style, "rubber-stamp" shams (Kornbluh 1987: 177; Nelson-Pallmeyer 1989: 47).

In addition to efforts to generate negative international public opinion toward Nicaragua, the U.S. also employed diplomatic means to
isolate the Sandinistas. The State Department exerted intense diplomatic pressure on the Mexican government to reduce its economic and
political support for Nicaragua. These efforts partially succeeded, as
Mexico began curtailing its oil shipments to Nicaragua in 1984. Similarly—though less successfully—the U.S. pressured France, West Germany, Spain, Austria, Italy, and the Scandinavian countries to cut aid
to Nicaragua, which from 1980 to 1983 had increased 38 percent
(Kornbluh 1987: 115–18). Finally, the U.S. also successfully pressured
the post–cold war Soviet Union to curtail its 1989 assistance to
Nicaragua (Vanden and Walker 1991: 168). Often, U.S. diplomatic
efforts to isolate the Sandinistas were quite coercive. For example,
when Costa Rican President Oscar Arias proposed a peace plan for
regional reconciliation, the Reagan administration

> used a number of political and economic tactics to express its displeasure. . . . These tactics included the nondisbursement of . . . six months
> of U.S. economic assistance to Costa Rica, the failure to appoint a new
> U.S. ambassador, a campaign to force the resignation of a liberal Arias
> advisor, maneuvers to block international bank loans to Costa Rica, and
> restrictions on Costa Rican exports to the U.S. (Honey and Avirgan
> 1987).

In El Salvador, the major domestic program used to politically isolate the FMLN was the agrarian reform of 1980–84. The centerpiece of the reform was a land-redistribution program that, if fully implemented, would have redistributed 40–45 percent of the nation's land to more than three hundred thousand peasant families. The reform was designed, financed, and carried out by U.S. advisers, led by Roy Prosterman, who had designed an almost identical program for Vietnam during the 1960s. In fact, both programs were given the exact same name, "Land to the Tiller" (Brockett 1990: 153–61; Barry and Preusch 1988: 147–53). This particular land reform program had the rare blessing of El Salvador's military command, because while, for some, its objective was genuine rural development, for others it was merely a public relations campaign for counterinsurgent pacification. Many of its planners, in other words, viewed the program as a "tactical land reform." In the words of the U.S. AID mission in San Salvador, it was "a political imperative to help prevent political collapse, strike a blow to the left, and help prevent radicalization of the rural population" (Barry and Preusch 1988: 150). The idea was to undercut the basis of the FMLN's domestic and international support, namely, moral outrage over economic inequity. In fact, because they were poorly planned, underfunded, weakly managed, subverted by El Salvador's right wing, and ultimately aimed more to change perceptions about land inequality than inequality itself, the reforms eventually failed.

The flip side of politically isolating enemies was politically embracing and promoting allies. Guatemala was considered by the Reagan administration a very important country strategically. Hence, the White House did everything possible politically to support the right wing and its war from 1981 on. This included establishing public ties with military and civilian forces, despite their links to death squads; accepting campaign donations from the extreme right-wing MLN party; defending Guatemala's human rights record to Congress and in State Department reports; denouncing human rights organizations, such as Amnesty International, when they condemned Guatemala's human rights record; attempting to fund Guatemala's security force's Telecommunications Center, which facilitated "disappearances"; and pressing Congress for an end to the aid embargo (Jonas 1991: 197–99). Similarly, in El Salvador, the Reagan administration took extraordinary measures to champion Duarte's "democratic center" regime against its critics in El Salvador and the U.S. who claimed it was merely "window dressing" for the military, which exercised real power (Barry, Vergara, and Rodolfo Castro 1988: 88).

PSYCHOLOGICAL WARFARE

Successful low-intensity warfare also called for psychological aggression and ideological propagandizing. A CIA manual on psychological warfare (quoted in Frederick 1987: 124), written for Contra officers, explained: "Conceived as the military target of a guerrilla war, the human being has his most critical point in his mind. Once his mind has been reached, the political animal has been defeated, without necessarily receiving bullets." For this reason, as early as 1983, the CIA was spending $80 million annually developing psychological warfare strategies to use against the Sandinistas (Walker 1985: 182).

One of the main forms of psychological warfare conducted against Nicaragua was the ever present threat of a U.S. invasion. The goal was to wear down the Sandinistas and the Nicaraguan people mentally and emotionally through the constant anxiety and intimidation generated by a succession of invasion scares. As one Pentagon official stated: "We're playing a little cat-and-mouse game with them, putting a little squeeze on, making them wonder what's going to happen next" (Rubin 1984: 313). The continual threat of a U.S. invasion was maintained primarily through a series of U.S. military maneuvers: "In 1981, the U.S. held two military exercises in the region. In 1982, there were five exercises, in 1983 there were 10. By 1984, the number of U.S. military exercises had grown to 20" (Cohen and Rogers 1986: 45).

In the spring of 1984, "Ocean Venture 84" and "Grenadero I" transported thirty-three thousand U.S. troops to the region. And in the spring of 1985, "Big Pine III" and "Universal Trek" brought nine thousand U.S. troops to Honduras (Gold 1987: 41). A White House official (quoted in Kornbluh 1987: 147) explained: "One of the central purposes [of the maneuvers] is to create fear of an invasion . . . to push very close to the border, deliberately, to set off all the alarms." Other threatening signs complemented the psychological impact of the maneuvers. The 1983 U.S. invasion of Grenada was intended as much to intimidate the Sandinistas as to oust Grenada's leftist regime. Nicaraguan airspace was conspicuously violated, too, by strategically timed flights of U.S. high-altitude reconnaissance planes that emitted thunderous sonic booms (Vanden and Walker 1991: 162). Finally, administration officials often leaked to the press information about contingency plans for a U.S. invasion of Nicaragua (Gorman and Walker 1985: 110).

The U.S. also waged an electronic media war against the Sandinistas. In 1985, seventy-four foreign commercial, U.S. government (e.g. Voice of America), clandestine Contra, and religious radio stations transmitted programs into Nicaragua. These far outnumbered Sandinista media in power and number (Frederick 1987). Foreign stations often broadcast anti-Sandinista, pro-Contra messages and news reports. Many of the stations were paid by the CIA to do so (Chamorro 1987: 25–26; Nelson-Pallmeyer 1989: 45).[10] Mainstream stations, for example, often warned listeners of the "communist threat" of Nicaragua, sometimes reporting fictitious attacks by the Nicaraguan army on foreign territory (Frederick 1987). More militant programs regularly accused the Sandinistas of atrocities, such as "burning churches, kidnapping Nicaraguan children and sending them to Cuba, stealing land from campesinos, creating food shortages by sending Nicaragua's food to the Soviet Union, and killing old people in order to make soap" (Nelson-Pallmeyer 1989: 45).

The psychological facet of Guatemala's low-intensity warfare, by contrast, focused on the social and emotional control of its rural population. In zones where guerrillas were strongly supported, up to twenty thousand peasants were forced to relocate to "model villages" established by the military. There, all aspects of life were subject to elaborate psychological and social controls by the army. Since the scorched-earth land sweeps (see below) had destroyed local supplies of essential provisions, these internal refugees became entirely dependent on the army for all basic necessities. Provisions were rationed, movement was limited, and all of life was subject to surveillance. Residents were told that the army was protecting them from the guerrillas and were required to participate in heavy schedules of ceremonies, talks, discussions, and group-dynamics exercises aimed at "winning the people over" to the cause of the army (Aguilera Peralta 1988: 160–61; Manz 1988; Jonas 1991: 150–51). In addition, the Guatemalan army organized masses of male adult peasants into "Civil Defense Patrols" (PACs). By 1985, almost a million civilians—12 percent of the total population—had been mobilized into PACs. Patrol members were obliged to perform twenty-four-hour patrols every ten to fifteen days, monitoring roads, bridges, and buildings for guerrilla activities. Often, in an attempt to create guilt, shame, and internal division among the peasants, PAC members were forced to go on "guerrilla hunts" and sometimes stone or machete to death fellow villagers accused of being subversives. PAC members who defected and civilians who refused to participate were blacklisted and punished severely, often with death. Politically, PACs were designed to drive a wedge between civilians and guerrillas and to verify loyalty to the government on the basis of participation in the militias. Psychologically, PACs undermined independence of thought and action in communities and generated civilian dependence on the army (Aguilera Peralta 1988: 162–63; Davis 1988: 28; Jonas 1991: 150–51, 164–65).

Psychological warfare in El Salvador—introduced to the Salvadoran army by U.S. advisers in 1983—primarily focused on persuading guerrillas to defect and join the government forces.[11] Colonel James Steele, Commander of the U.S. Military Group in El Salvador from 1984 to 1986, observed (1988: 321): "There is an interest in PSYOP [psychological operations] and civic action within the Salvadoran armed forces that's far greater than anything that we saw in Vietnam. It's an integral part of what they're doing. The idea of getting people to defect is central to the plans of every brigade. They are training Psychological Operations experts for every unit."

Guerrilla defections undermined the confidence of the revolutionary movement. And they often provided valuable intelligence information, as a Salvadoran army spokesperson noted (C-5 Spokesperson 1988: 324, 326):

> The origin of psychological operations in El Salvador was part of a general change in the Salvadoran Army behavior. During the 1980–1982 period they had a policy . . . that they generally did not take prisoners. . . . The [U.S.] advisors convinced the Salvadorans that you can get intelligence out of prisoners. That when treated properly the value of a prisoner who decides to give information is much greater than the prisoner who is dead. It may be more satisfying to see them dead, but in terms of utility, it is better to have the guy alive. . . . It is now quite commonplace in the brigades to have informants who were former guerrillas.

El Salvador's psychological warfare strategy also established a "model village" program called "Project One Thousand," referring to the thousand new villages it aimed to create. It was designed, in part, by the same U.S. AID workers who had designed the model village program for Guatemala. In it, five hundred thousand displaced Salvadorans were to be settled in specially built communities under government control (Fish and Sganga 1988: 94).

SELECTIVE REPRESSION

Total war at the grassroots level also required the exercise of "selective repression." Selective repression strategies—designed by Central American military commanders and U.S. military advisers—targeted community leaders considered sympathetic to the enemy to be harassed, tortured, or killed, to create examples for the rest of the community. The goal was to discourage, through intimidation, widespread support for or participation in enemy activities. Guatemala's counterinsurgency campaign, for example, utilized a carefully designed strategy of selective repression:

> First, government security forces chose selected community leaders for kidnapping, torture, and assassination. . . . Second, the government threatened and killed religious leaders, because it believed that they served as a major link between the peasants and the guerrillas. . . . Third, the army bombed and harassed key villages, on the pretext that these villages served as strategic support populations for the guerrillas (Davis 1983: 166–67).

The pattern was similar in El Salvador, where, although selective repression was used by both the government forces and the FMLN, right-wing death squads were particularly notorious for tens of thousands of targeted executions. "They take an entire family from their home, and the next day the bodies are found strung up in the outskirts of town with their faces tied together, as if kissing each other. . . . In December, disfigured bodies began to appear with signs that read, 'Merry Christmas, people. We are ridding you of terrorists'" (Cayetano Carpio 1988: 39).

Two Salvadoran students (quoted in Fish and Sganga 1988: 30) described the army-sponsored death-squad activity at their university which, between 1980 and 1984, killed more than a thousand students:

> A list of eleven names was issued, giving the named university teachers and students eight days to leave the country or be executed. Our names were both on this list. Three days later they came and dumped four corpses on the steps of the campus to frighten us more. They left the bodies for two hours and then came back to pick them up again. This shows that it was a well-coordinated action. They wanted to scare us off so that we wouldn't continue to demand respect for human rights.

A former Salvadoran Treasury policeman (quoted in Fish and Sganga 1988: 108), interviewed on British television, described the grisly methods used to torment those targeted for selective repression:

Putting people's heads in buckets of excrement, electrical torture? Oh, this is nothing. Electric shocks—nobody will die unless it is too severe. But if you cut somebody, their skin, or you take somebody's eyes, this is actually what they did at the torture. With a pencil, you take one eye out and you say, "If you don't talk I will take another one." And you say, "I will pull your teeth out," and they do—one by one. Or . . . you take the . . . genital organ. . . . This is torture. And this person bleeds to death, and then you laugh around him, drink, smoking marijuana, using LSD, all kinds of drugs. And you feel bad after the torture takes place. After the person disappears, you throw the person away. You say, "This guy was hard to kill. . . ." This is how they fight terrorists, Communists—to eliminate a person—this is it. They are trained to eliminate.[12]

In Nicaragua, many Contra units also engaged in brutal, though less well coordinated, forms of selective repression. The human rights group Americas Watch reported that politically targeted gang rapes, emasculation, premortem skinning, and eye-gouging were common practices of the Contras. Edgar Chamorro (quoted in Vanden and Walker 1991: 164–65), a civilian Contra chief who resigned in disgust over Contra violation of human rights, later reported that "the atrocities . . . were not isolated instances, but reflected a consistent pattern of behavior by our troops. There were unit commanders who openly bragged about murders, mutilations, etc. . . . They told me it was the only way to win the war, that the best way to win the loyalty of the civilian population was to intimidate it and make it fearful of us."[13]

Such an approach was apparently encouraged by U.S. advisers. A CIA manual, *Psychological Operations in Guerrilla Warfare,* designed to help train Contra officers, stated in sections on "Implicit and Explicit Terror" and "Selective Use of Violence for Propagandistic Effects" that "a guerrilla force always involves implicit terror because the population, without saying it aloud, feels terror that the weapons may be turned against them," and "it is possible to neutralize [i.e. execute] selected targets, court judges . . . police and state security officials, CDS chiefs" (quoted in Vanden and Walker 1991: 165). The Contras' selective repression especially targeted civilians working for the Sandinistas' social revolution. Cooperative farms, food-storage buildings, schools, health clinics, and day-care centers became prime targets for Contra attacks (Collins 1986: 143–49). Community organizers, teachers, and health-care workers were regularly abducted or murdered. By 1985, 88 rural Sandinista health facilities had been destroyed (Kornbluh 1987: 41). In all, 130 teachers, 40 doctors and nurses, 152 technicians, and 41 other professionals were killed by Contras (Vanden and Walker 1991: 165–66).

SCORCHED-EARTH LAND SWEEPS

Finally, counterinsurgent low-intensity warfare involved army "scorched-earth land sweeps." These were designed, according to Garst and Barry (1990: 150), "to separate the guerrillas from their civilian supporters. If the local communities are the 'sea in which the fish swim,' as China's Mao Tse-tung put it, then the strategy is obvious: drive the fish out of the sea and/or dry up the water."

In El Salvador, military effectiveness in land-sweep tactics demanded a highly mobile, decentralized, offensively deployed army, permanently stationed in the field as "troops without quarters." To achieve this, after 1983, with the help of U.S. advisers, the Salvadoran army doubled the number of infantry brigades, organized and deployed new search-and-destroy units, reinforced its helicopter units, and mobilized long-range reconnaissance patrols, anti-terrorist battalions, navy attack battalions, and "Immediate Response Battalions." The objective of these units was to wear down the guerrillas and estrange them from the civilian population by forcing the guerrillas to stay constantly on the move (Barry, Vergara, and Rodolfo Castro 1988: 87). Between 1983 and 1990,

> the Salvadoran army . . . employed a variety of means to break the link between the guerrillas and their popular base. At the urging of U.S. advisors, the Salvadoran armed forces . . . adopted such tactics as aerial bombing and military sweeps of contested and guerrilla-controlled areas. In addition, crops [were] burned and supplies to these zones cut off, all in an effort to force the relocation of suspected guerrilla supporters to military-controlled areas (Garst and Barry 1990: 150).

Such destruction was justified on the grounds that living in a guerrilla-controlled area makes one an enemy combatant. In the words of Colonel Carlos Aviles, a Salvadoran army spokesman (quoted in Fish and Sganga 1988: 60), "In the conflict zones, there simply aren't any civilians. The people who move in zones of rebel persistence are identified as guerrillas. Good people—those who are not with the guerrillas—are not there." Given this assumption, it was sometimes thought necessary to depopulate entire areas. As another Salvadoran army colonel said (quoted in Fish and Sganga 1988: 63): "Take the population away from the guerrillas, that's the way to win. [Guerrilla influence is] like malaria in this area. You can do two things: you can treat people for malaria for as long as you stay in the area, for the next 3,000 years maybe, or you can drain the swamp and not have to worry about malaria any more." Thus, in a single December incident, "some 900 civilians, including women and children, were taken from their homes in and around the village of El Mozote and killed by government troops during a sweep" (Schulz 1984: 230).

In Guatemala, similarly, according to Jonas (1991: 149): "the goal was literally to 'drain the sea' in which the guerrilla movement operated and to eradicate its civilian support base. The principal techniques included depopulation of the area through 'scorched-earth' burnings, massacres of whole village populations, and massive forced relocations. Entire sectors of the population (overwhelmingly Indians) became military targets."

The villages targeted by the Guatemalan army for attack, even when armed by the guerrillas for self-defense, according to Aguilera Peralta (1988: 158; also see Davis 1983: 167), "were not prepared to fight against helicopter-transported troops. The military actions, seemingly directed indiscriminately against all inhabitants, affected noncombatants such as children and the elderly. . . . The army adopted a scorched-earth tactic, which included the destruction of buildings and of fields ready for sowing and the killing or dispersal of livestock and domestic animals."

Finally, in the case of Nicaragua, the constant, widespread hit-and-run tactics of the Contras closely resembled the scorched-earth land sweeps of El Salvador and Guatemala's counterinsurgency forces. And the Contras' economic aggression, selective repression, and indiscriminate terrorism, described above, all aimed to destroy popular support for the Sandinista revolution.

THE HUMAN COSTS

For the people of Central America, the U.S.-sponsored low-intensity war was anything but low in intensity. It was devastating. Tens of millions of dollars worth of property and infrastructure were destroyed. The region's economic development was ruined, reversing decades of growth. Hundreds of thousands of Central Americans were killed and maimed. Millions were displaced. In Nicaragua, by the end of 1985, two-and-a-half years of the Contra war had killed 3,652 civilians, wounded 4,039, and seen 5,232 civilians kidnapped, mostly by the Contras (Kornbluh 1987: 27). More than 250,000 Nicaraguans had been displaced from their homes, and more than seven thousand children orphaned by the fighting (Williams 1987: 258). By the same year, the total cost of the low-intensity war for the Nicaraguan economy surpassed $1 billion (Kornbluh 1987: 121). By the end of the decade, that cost had risen to more than $4.5 billion (Vanden and Walker 1991: 169). By 1987, a total of fifteen thousand combatants and fifteen thousand civilians had died in the Contra war (Sivard 1991: 22).[14] The war produced more than twenty thousand wounded Nicaraguans, "many of whom were so maimed that they would be wards of the state for the rest of their lives" (Vanden and Walker 1991: 166).

In El Salvador, even more died in the struggle between the military regime and the guerrillas. The army, security forces, allied death squads, and the FMLN all killed large numbers of Salvadorans.[15] The death toll mounted early. Civilian deaths in 1981 had risen to 13,353 from 8,062 the previous year, mostly the victims of the counterinsurgency forces (Schulz 1984: 230).[16] That carnage continued throughout the decade. By 1985, right-wing death squads alone had murdered more than forty thousand Salvadorans (Hudson 1990: 233). By that same year, El Salvador's economic output per capita had declined to a level 50 percent below that of 1979 and real wages for agricultural workers fell 60 percent below wage levels of 1979 (Stein 1988: 196). By 1990, El Salvador's war had claimed a total of fifty thousand civilian and twenty-five thousand combatant lives (Sivard 1991: 22). In addition, more than a million Salvadorans—25 percent of the nation's total population—fled their homes as refugees (Fagan 1988: 59).

Guatemala's counterinsurgency war, however, was the most brutal of all. Jonas notes (1991: 146): "There is no more painful chapter in the history of modern Guatemala than the events of 1980–1983. At the human level, it is a tale of wholesale slaughter and genocide by the new death squads [and] counterinsurgent security forces." She continues (1991: 149):

> The statistics are staggering: over 440 villages were entirely destroyed; well over 100,000 civilians were killed or 'disappeared' (some estimates, including top church officials, range up to 150,000); there were over 1 million displaced persons (1 million internal refugees, up to 200,000 refugees in Mexico). . . . Accompanying these massive popula-

tion displacements was the deliberate destruction of huge areas of the highlands (burning forests, etc.) to deny cover to the guerrillas.[17]

The three-year counterinsurgency war left well over a hundred thousand Guatemalan children as orphans and almost 12 percent of the total population displaced (Jonas 1991: 95, 185).

Finally, Honduras—which for serving as the main military and intelligence base for the Contras and U.S. forces was nicknamed "U.S.S. Honduras"—suffered as well. Some two hundred students, peasants, and union leaders "disappeared" between 1981 and 1985 (Gold 1987: 46). Hundreds of Hondurans were evicted from their land for the U.S. military to build airfields and military bases. Drug and alcohol abuse and sexually transmitted diseases, including AIDS, spread rapidly near military installations (Gold 1987: 44–45). And Contra activities in Honduras displaced twelve thousand Honduran farmers near the Nicaraguan border (Kornbluh 1987: 216).

Altogether, the 1980s low-intensity wars in Nicaragua, El Salvador, and Guatemala killed more than two hundred thousand Central Americans and created between 1.8 to 2.8 million refugees (Fagan 1988: 76; Sivard 1991: 22). In addition, the region's economy was ruined—by 1985, real income per capita had declined 33 percent in seven years (Gorostiaga and Marchetti 1988: 119).

PERSONAL STORIES

Behind these staggering statistics lay countless, untold personal stories of terror and anguish. In the end, we will see, it was not abstract statistics but these personal stories that generated the U.S. Central American peace movement. Before going on to investigate that movement, therefore, we end this chapter by recounting three such stories of war in Central America. The first story is that of Brenda Sánchez-Galan, a Salvadoran refugee arrested in 1984 in Texas by the U.S. Immigration and Naturalization Service, along with two sanctuary workers who were transporting her to safety. Her story is told by Renny Golden and Michael McConnell (1986: 64–65), two other sanctuary organizers.

> In 1980, when Brenda was a high-school student in San Salvador, a demonstration erupted near her school. Salvadoran military tanks pulled into the crowd and soldiers shot down fleeing demonstrators. The sisters in charge of Brenda's school instructed the students to go home immediately.

Making her way through the streets, the terrified 15-year-old saw Salvadoran military personnel execute persons in the street. She ran to escape their reach. In her flight she saw an old man motioning her to come into a ground-level parking garage. She ran into the garage. There, huddled in the rear part of the building, a hundred persons were crammed. The old man lowered and bolted the door against an approaching government tank. . . .

Then there was silence. The tank had stopped in front of the garage door. A Salvadoran soldier ordered the door to be opened. The old man . . . refused. In the suspended silence that followed, the adults in the front . . . moved the children hand over hand, overhead, to the rear of the garage. . . .

The tank pumped round after round of 50-calibre machine gun fire into the garage. Bodies crumpled upon one another. Brenda remembered lying among the children and whimpering babies, soaked in blood. In the room was the sound of the dying. Then the soldiers broke into the garage and began to cart the bodies, like refuse, into trucks. Those still alive were ordered by an officer to be silent about what they had seen or they would be killed.

Brenda . . . soon left school to begin training to be a medical assistant in order to work with the Lutheran Church and Green Cross at a refugee center near San Salvador. She worked with the center's physician, Dr. Ibarra. [Later] Dr. Ibarra was interrogated by the military because of his refusal to submit lists of patients for military approval. . . . The military insisted that he was helping "subversives." He was arrested, brought to national police headquarters, and tortured for six months. They wired his thumbs behind his back, tied ropes on his wrists, then hoisted him on pulleys until his arms were pulled from their sockets. Finally . . . he was released and eventually left the country.

Soldiers returned to the apartment building where Brenda and other medical assistance workers lived. They intended to "interview" church medical workers whom they felt were aiding communists. One night Brenda's co-worker was dragged from her apartment and brought to national guard headquarters where she was gang raped and tortured. In the morning the soldiers led her into the town square and forced her to bend over. Then a soldier inserted a machine gun in her rectum and pulled the trigger. She was three months pregnant. The fetus was torn from her womb and sliced in half.

When Brenda learned of her co-worker's abduction, she sought refuge with the Lutheran church. She took nothing with her but her one-year-old daughter, Bessie.

The second story, from Nicaragua, is based on the victim's sworn affidavit. It is told by Reed Brody (1985: 119–20), former Assistant

Attorney General of New York State, who traveled to Nicaragua to investigate allegations of Contra atrocities.

Digna Barreda de Ubeda of Esteli, a mother of two, is the niece of two well-known religious leaders, Felipe and Mary Barreda, who were tortured and killed by the contras [in December, 1982]. On May 3, 1983, Digna and her husband, Juan Augustin, were visiting the land they had received under the agrarian reform program in the village of Zapote. . . . The couple was staying there with her uncle, who, it turned out, was collaborating with the contras and who had denounced the couple as Sandinista spies.

That evening after dinner, five contras came to the house, beat up Juan Augustin, stole a gold chain and watch Digna was wearing, and tied their hands and took the two of them away. . . . Three of the men went back to talk to the uncle. Upon returning: "They beat my husband brutally. . . . And then, the three who talked with my uncle raped me so brutally that I still have scars on my knees. They put me face down. They raped me through the rectum too. And all this in front of my husband."

The captives were then taken further on where they met a group of 55 contras. There they were interrogated and beaten and Digna was again raped in front of her husband. . . . After eating, they continued on until at 4:00 A.M. they reached a camp of tents marked "made in U.S.A." There, while some of the contras slept, others interrogated Digna, "torturing me, pressing my eyes, separating my toes and raping me brutally again." Juan Augustin, who still was tied up, asked the contras to kill him, but he was told that they were going to take him to Honduras, beating him on the way, where "Benito Bravo," a contra leader, was waiting to kill him. And they "kicked him and beat him again and again". . . .

On the fourth day . . . the contras called one of the hostages, Juan Valladares, and asked him if he loved Thomas Borge (Nicaragua's Minister of the Interior) and the revolution. When Valladares replied that he did, "they laid him down on the ground and they gouged out his eyes with a spoon, then they machine-gunned him and threw him over a cliff". . . . On the fifth day: "Five of them raped me at about five in the evening. . . . They gang raped me every day. When my vagina couldn't take it anymore, they raped me through my rectum. I calculate that in five days they raped me 60 times." That day, they let Digna go . . . but not before the contra who was assigned to lead her back to the road raped her. . . . Her husband escaped during a battle 15 days later.

Her difficulties were not over, however. Her house in Esteli was set on fire and she was forced to move. Her father and two brothers were robbed and kidnapped. One of the brothers returned after having been taken to Honduras while the other is still missing. Another campesino was also kidnapped with her brothers, and reportedly had his penis cut off.

The final story, from Guatemala, is told by sociologist Susanne Jonas (1991: 145). It is based on the testimonies of survivors of a massacre at the village of San Francisco, Guatemala, where on July 17, 1982, the army killed 352 people.

The soldiers separated the men off to one side, telling them that there was going to be a meeting, and locked them up in the courthouse of the village-farm. The soldiers then rounded up the women from their various homes and locked them up at another location along with their children. . . .

At about 1:00 P.M., the soldiers began to fire at the women inside the small church. The majority did not die there, but were separated from their children, taken to their homes in groups, and killed, the majority apparently with machetes. It seems that the purpose of this last parting of women from their children was to prevent even the children from witnessing any confession that might reveal the location of the guerrillas.

Then they returned to kill the children, whom they had left crying and screaming by themselves, without their mothers. Our informants, who were locked up in the courthouse, could see this through a hole in the window and through the doors carelessly left open by the guard. The soldiers cut open the children's stomachs with knives or they grabbed the children's little legs and smashed their heads with heavy sticks.

Some soldiers took a break to rest, eating a bull—the property of the peasants—that had been put on to roast. Then they continued with the men. They took them out, tied their hands, threw them on the ground, and shot them. . . . It was then that the survivors were able to escape, protected by the smoke of the fire which had been set to the building. Seven men . . . managed to escape. It was 5:30 P.M. The massacre continued, and when about six people were left, the soldiers threw grenades at them, killing all but two. Since it was already night, these two escaped by the window, covered with blood but uninjured. One of them was shot, the other lived. . . . He arrived in Chiapas, Mexico at 11 a.m. the following day.

Were all Central America's victims able to testify, hundreds of thousands of similar stories could be told.

Yet, in the early 1980s, few U.S. citizens knew anything about the human costs of the U.S.-sponsored war in Central America. Those who did often protested vociferously. The war, however, continued. But as the Central American reality increasingly came home to more and more Americans, those voices of protest eventually grew into an organized, national resistance. The Central America peace movement—determined to confront the Reagan administration and end the war in Central America—was born.

Part Two
The Movement Emerges

Four

Launching the Peace
Movement

> Their conclusion was always the same . . . that a fight must be put up, in this
> way or that, and there must be no bowing down. The essential thing was to save
> the greatest possible number of persons from dying. . . . And to do this there
> was only one resource: to fight the plague. There was nothing admirable about
> this attitude; it was merely logical.
>
> Albert Camus, *The Plague*

The U.S. Central America peace movement was not a unified, mono-
lithic entity. Few social movements are. It was, instead, a broad assembly of individual and collective actions and organizations, all of which
challenged U.S. Central American policy in some way.

Many of the movement's actions were isolated, relatively uncoor-
dinated deeds of protest and solidarity. Handfuls of demonstrators in
small towns held candlelight vigils publicly to mourn El Salvador's
war dead. U.S. cities "adopted" and supported individual Nicaraguan
cities. Community groups shipped truckloads of clothing and tools to
Guatemala's poor. Angry dissidents threw blood on the walls of government buildings. Community leaders wrote searing op-ed articles
for local newspapers opposing aid to El Salvador. Ideologically directed consumers bought Nicaraguan-grown coffee in support of the Sandinistas. Activist groups aggressively campaigned and voted against
politicians who supported aid to the Guatemalan military. Middle-
class citizens undertook hunger strikes and war-tax resistance. Outraged dissenters floated beach balls, painted to resemble explosive
mines, in U.S. harbors to protest the mining of Nicaraguan harbors.
Suburban homeowners planted in their front yards memorial crosses
bearing names of individual peasants killed in Contra attacks. These
kinds of grassroots expressions of activism reflected the movement's
broad-based diversity and energy.[1]

But what gave the U.S. Central America peace movement its greatest potency and endurance in contesting U.S. policy were its national movement organizations. These organizations mobilized hundreds of thousands of activists across the country, coordinating their energies into targeted strategies of collective action. The most important ones were Sanctuary, Witness for Peace, and the Pledge of Resistance.[2] After only three years of existence, Sanctuary had mobilized more than seventy thousand U.S. citizens to participate in breaking federal immigration laws in order to confront the Reagan administration with the consequences of its low-intensity war in Central America (Golden and McConnell 1986: 3). Witness for Peace activated more than four thousand U.S. citizens to risk their lives by traveling to Nicaraguan war zones to see first-hand the effects of U.S. policy and to return home to struggle to stop it (Taylor n.d.). And in two years, the Pledge of Resistance mobilized eighty thousand U.S. citizens collectively to threaten mass civil disobedience if the U.S. invaded or escalated its war in Central America (Butigan 1991).

This chapter briefly tells the stories of *how* these organizations formed and what collective actions they produced. It is primarily descriptive. Future chapters will explore why they emerged and what can be learned about social-movement dynamics from their experiences. Those chapters will be more analytical in nature. But first, the descriptive histories.

SANCTUARY[3]

Jim Corbett woke up on the morning of May 5, 1981, knowing that he had to do something about the arrested hitchhiker. He did not know, however, that what he was about to do would launch a social movement.

Corbett was a forty-six-year-old semi-disabled Quaker who, with his wife, Pat, raised goats on a ranch outside Tucson, Arizona. The night before, a fellow-Quaker friend of Corbett's, Jim Dudley, had been stopped by the U.S. Border Patrol on his way back from a trip to Mexico, shortly after picking up a Salvadoran hitchhiker. Dudley was on his way to Corbett's house to return a van he had borrowed and to discuss the planned construction of a chapel in a Mexican village. The hitchhiker was arrested. Dudley was interrogated for half an hour and accused of smuggling an illegal alien before being released.

When Dudley finally arrived at Corbett's, he was visibly disturbed. The frightened hitchhiker, he told Jim and Pat, had begged Dudley in the final moments before the abduction to lie about his Salvadoran identity. "Tell them I work for you and we are traveling together," he had pleaded. Dudley now wondered aloud whether he had made a mistake telling the truth. Couldn't he have tricked or eluded the Border Patrol somehow? Jim and Pat thought not. "Once you're stopped, there's not too much you can do."

But as they discussed the incident, their concern for the arrested hitchhiker grew. They remembered news stories reporting El Salvador's civil war and the assassination of El Salvador's Archbishop Oscar Romero and four North American churchwomen. They recalled that only ten months earlier twenty-seven middle-class Salvadorans had been discovered trying to cross the scorching desert seventy miles west of Tucson. The Salvadorans' paid smugglers—"coyotes"—had gotten lost and abandoned them, and they were forced to drink urine and cologne before the Border Patrol recovered them. Half of the twenty-seven had died of thirst and exposure. The remaining survivors were taken in by several Tucson churches. Frank Shutts, another Quaker also visiting Corbett that night, said that he had heard rumors of entire planeloads of deported Salvadorans being murdered at the San Salvador airport by death squads, as examples to others who might consider fleeing the country.

"There must be some way to intervene for these people," Corbett said. But none of them knew how. Helplessly, they shrugged their shoulders, noting that the night was getting late and Dudley had to catch a bus to Albuquerque. Frank Shutts drove him to the station. And the Corbetts went to bed. But Jim Corbett did not sleep well. He could not escape the thought of Dudley's arrested hitchhiker being sent home to a death-squad assassination.

In the morning Corbett resolved to follow up on the matter. He called the offices of the U.S. Immigration and Naturalization Service (INS) and the Border Patrol, who told him that they could not give out information on detainees. Corbett then remembered that his name was the same as that of a well-known former Tucson mayor. He called back the Border Patrol office and said in a commanding voice, "This is Jim Corbett here in Tucson, and I need the name of the Salvadoran you picked up late yesterday at the Peck Canyon roadblock. His name, and where he's being held." It worked. The officer looked up and gave him the information.

After a few more phone calls to a local immigration-rights organization, the Manzo Area Council, Corbett learned that the arrested hitchhiker could not be deported without a hearing if an INS G-28 form designating legal council was signed and filed. So, Corbett drove to the Santa Cruz jail, near Nogales, where Nelson, the hitchhiker, was being held. There Corbett met Nelson, who signed the G-28. Corbett also met two other arrested refugees who told him chilling personal stories of abduction and torture in El Salvador. He concluded that their lives would be in danger if they were deported, so he decided to file G-28s for them as well. The jailer said he had no more of the forms, so Corbett drove to the nearby Border Patrol office, where officers delayed him a half hour before giving him G-28s.

Back at the jail, Corbett was told he had to wait before he could see the two other prisoners again. Thirty minutes passed. Corbett grew impatient. He had to leave Nogales soon to get the G-28s filed at the Tucson INS office by five o'clock. He asked again to see the Salvadorans. "Who was it you were waiting for?" the jailer asked. "Oh, you wanted to see those guys? The Border Patrol took them twenty or thirty minutes ago. They're all gone. And there's no way to know where they went."

Corbett was stunned—he had been hoodwinked by agents of his own government. This was not a bureaucratic confusion, he fumed, but a deliberate effort to deprive refugees of their legal rights and deport them as swiftly as possible to what he considered a likely death.

Jim Corbett, it turns out, was the wrong person for the Border Patrol to cross. He was no dolt. With full scholarships, he had completed a philosophy degree at Colgate University in three years and a master's degree in philosophy at Harvard in one year. Corbett was a nonconformist who believed in the Quaker values of honesty and plain speech and who despised abuses of power. A free-thinking and outspoken man, he had lost three separate jobs in one-man-stand protests over the mistreatment of other employees. The Border Patrol stunt was not about to deter him.

The Corbetts borrowed $4,500 against the value of a trailer they owned and bailed four Salvadoran women and a baby out of jail. These refugees, who lived in a small apartment on the Corbett's property, spent hours talking with Jim and Pat about the violence in El Salvador and the terrors of refugee life. Through them, the connection between "the refugee problem" and the U.S.-sponsored war in Central America became increasingly clear. Jim Corbett began to press the system harder to protect Salvadoran refugees from deportation. But the harder he pressed, the more disillusioned and frustrated he became with the INS and the Border Patrol.

On May 30, Corbett and a companion drove to Los Angeles to search in El Centro, a major INS detention center, for the refugees who twenty-five days earlier had been hastily transferred out of the Santa Cruz jail while he waited to see them. When a refugee-rights paralegal had recently traveled to El Centro to process G-28 forms, an INS official took the G-28s out of her hand, tore them up, and threw them in a trash can. Corbett was determined this time to find the refugees he was looking for, especially Nelson, Jim Dudley's arrested hitchhiker.

What he found instead—when a prisoner in the room who knew Nelson interrupted Corbett's conversation with the jail superintendent—was that Nelson had already been deported to El Salvador. Corbett couldn't believe his ears. Nelson's deportation was illegal, since Corbett had filed his G-28 on May 5! The superintendent, Mr. Aguirre, had told Corbett upon arrival that he had no record of Nelson. But when the outspoken prisoner insisted otherwise, Aguirre quickly ordered all the prisoners back to their cells and Corbett to leave immediately. Corbett, now angry, refused. Then Aguirre noticed that Corbett's companion had been recording the entire conversation with a tape recorder. Aguirre demanded he hand it over. Corbett replied the guards would have to take it by force, and that they wanted to leave now. Aguirre locked the room's doors and demanded the recorder. Corbett began to lecture Aguirre about refugees' rights. Aguirre stormed out of the room in a rage. After a few minutes, he returned and released them.

The experience was enraging. The U.S. government, Corbett saw, was violating its own law and risking the lives of thousands of Central American refugees. It had to be fought. Corbett began writing a series of "Dear Friend" letters to five hundred Quaker meetings and individual Quakers around the country explaining the plight of the refugees. In them, he criticized INS practices and solicited donations to help pay bond to free jailed Salvadoran refugees while their asylum applications were under review. This was the only legal recourse available for helping illegal aliens. In his first letter, however, Corbett alluded to the possibility of the need to violate immigration laws. "I can see," he wrote, "that if Central American refugees' rights to political asylum are decisively rejected by the U.S. government or if the U.S. legal system insists on ransom that exceeds our ability to pay, *active resistance* will be the only alternative to abandoning the refugees to their fate."

In the nineteenth century, Quakers had helped to organize an underground railroad to help slaves escape the antebellum South. Corbett was now beginning to envision a similar contemporary movement to assist Central American refugees. "The creation of a network of actively concerned, mutually supportive people in the U.S. and Mexico," he wrote, "may be the best preparation for an adequate response [to unjust INS policy]. A network? Quakers will know what I mean."

By June, Corbett and the Manzo Area Council had raised $150,000 to bond refugees out of jail. The Corbetts had twenty Salvadorans living on their property and many refugees living with families from various Tucson churches. But the more money they raised, the more the INS increased the cost of bail for Central Americans—though not for Mexicans. Bail jumped from $250 to $1,000 to $3,000 per alien and more. It was a losing battle.

Another problem was that Central Americans applying for political asylum were being systematically discriminated against by the INS. Granting asylum implicitly acknowledged the existence of gross violations of human and political rights by regimes and forces supported by the U.S. Since this embarrassed the Reagan administration, political asylum for Central Americans was almost always denied. From 1983 to 1986, for example, only 2.6 percent of Salvadorans and 0.9 percent of Guatemalans requesting asylum were approved. This compared to 60.4 percent of Iranians, 51 percent of Romanians, and 37.7 percent of Afghans approved. Thus, bonding Central American refugees out of jail was really only postponing their deportation. Corbett began to despair of the bail-bond strategy. Rather than bonding refugees out of jail for exorbitant sums of money, he reasoned, why not help smuggle the refugees to safety, keeping them out of jail in the first place? Still, for the time, he continued to raise bond money.

June 26 was a turning point. On that day, Corbett took three Salvadorans, who had fled El Salvador under threat of death, to the Tucson INS office to apply for political asylum. He knew their applications would eventually be denied. But the INS had always allowed asylum applicants to go free, under custody of local ministers, while their applications were on appeal—long enough, Corbett still hoped, for the Salvadoran civil war to end. On this day, however, the Tucson INS director, William Johnson, ordered the three applicants arrested and placed bail at $3,000 each. Corbett desperately protested. This

LAUNCHING THE PEACE MOVEMENT

was his only means for working within the system, he argued. If the INS started arresting asylum applicants, Corbett insisted, the churches would have no choice—they would be forced to take their refugee operation underground. According to Corbett, Johnson replied that he was acting under orders from the State Department, that granting asylum to Salvadorans embarrassed the U.S. administration, and that hitherto all applicants would be arrested and sent to El Centro. Corbett and Johnson argued for an hour. At five o'clock Corbett was asked to leave. "We're not just going to abandon these people to their fate," the Quaker warned.

Shortly thereafter, Corbett began putting his intimate knowledge of the desert terrain to use guiding refugees across the border himself and escorting them around INS roadblocks to friends and relatives in Tucson. That such an act broke the law mattered little to Corbett by then. To him, protecting aliens whose lives were in danger was a moral imperative. The Nuremberg trials—which Corbett's lawyer father, Jim recalled, discussed at the family dinner table—had proven that. Corbett next organized a collection of sympathetic students, housewives, professionals, and retirees into a "tucson refugee support group," which began coordinating a group smuggling operation.[4] The number of refugees aided by their *pro bono* "evasion services" steadily increased. By mid-August, Corbett himself was making one to two trips a day transporting undocumented aliens to Tucson in his pickup truck.

Members of the Manzo Area Council and the newly formed Tucson Ecumenical Council Task Force on Central America (TEC), to which Corbett belonged, however, were more reluctant to break the law. They understood and supported Corbett's work, but chose themselves to continue working to bail Salvadorans out of El Centro. By mid-July they had raised another $175,000 in collateral and freed 115 refugees—every Salvadoran in the detention center.

By late summer, Corbett was beginning to run out of places to leave the refugees. His house was overflowing with Salvadorans, many of whom had serious emotional and drinking problems, and his wife, Pat, had come to the end of her rope. Corbett approached a number of area churches about housing illegal aliens, but each one declined his request. Then, in early autumn, after a TEC meeting, Corbett took aside John Fife, the forty-one-year-old pastor of Tucson's Southside Presbyterian Church, which hosted TEC's meetings. "John," he said, "we're running out of places to stash people. What about letting the refugees stay in your church?" Fife, it turns out, had already been weighing the possibility of sheltering illegals for weeks. He believed in principle that it was the right thing to do. But he hesitated, concerned for his family's welfare should he be arrested. He told Corbett he would raise the idea at the church's next elders' meeting.

John Fife had a long history of justice activism. Many of his seminary professors were German-emigré scholars who condemned the passivity of the German Protestant churches in the 1930s and '40s. Fife had marched from Selma to Montgomery in 1965, and had been arrested at sit-ins protesting whites-only public facilities and for picketing the suburban lawns of slum landlords. Fife had also done ministry on Indian reservations and in the slums of Canton, Ohio. Still, Fife struggled with Corbett's proposal for several days. No one knew how the government would react to a church willfully committing a felony.

By Southside's next elders' meeting, however, Fife had made up his mind. His faith and ethics gave him no choice but to take in the refugees. To do otherwise, he judged, would be immoral. He explained this to the elders at the meeting, and, after five hours of discussion, they agreed. By a seven-to-zero vote, with two abstentions, the elders decided to shelter illegal aliens in their church building. The next Sunday, Fife announced the decision to the entire church. Within a few weeks, Fife and others from TEC were joining Corbett in transporting the undocumented refugees. Although members of Southside agreed to act as discreetly as possible, it only took a month for the Tucson INS to hear the rumors that city ministers were openly defying immigration laws. Shortly before Thanksgiving, an INS lawyer approached TEC activist Margo Cowan in the city courthouse and told her, "We're not sure what Fife and Corbett are up to. But tell them to quit or we're going to have your asses."

Cowan and Fife called an emergency TEC meeting in Fife's living room. "We can do two things," Fife surmised. "We can continue on and wait for them to indict us. Or we can quit." After a brief discussion, everyone agreed the legal route was grossly inadequate, that they couldn't quit. Fife then observed that there was an alternative to waiting passively for the inevitable arrests. They could go public. "Beat 'em to the punch," Fife said. That way, they could claim the high moral ground and openly explain themselves to the media and their denominations before the INS could brand them just another bunch of "coyotes" and lock them away.

The group, excited now, then had the idea of declaring Southside

Presbyterian a sanctuary for refugees. The ancient Hebrews, Fife remembered, declared entire cities sanctuaries of refuge for accused criminals. Christian churches during the Roman Empire and in medieval England had offered themselves as sanctuaries for fugitives of blood revenge. And during the Vietnam War, many churches sheltered conscientious objectors. This idea of sanctuary fit nicely with Corbett's notion of a new underground railroad. The group also realized that public sanctuary could give the refugees a platform to tell their stories about atrocities experienced in Central America—the very stories that had mobilized those in the TEC group to get involved in the first place. Fife agreed to put the idea to his church for approval.

After much soul-searching and self-education, in January 1982 the members of Southside Presbyterian voted 59 to 2, by secret ballot, to endorse the sanctuary idea. The day of the public declaration was set for March 24—the second anniversary of Archbishop Romero's assassination. Tim Nonn, of TEC, sent letters to congregations around the country that worked with refugees, asking them to join the sanctuary declaration. Five churches in the San Francisco Bay area and churches in Los Angeles, Washington, D.C., and Lawrence, Long Island, agreed also to declare sanctuary. The Episcopal Diocese of Ohio, the Unitarian Universalist Service Committee, the Arlington Street Church in Boston, and the Social Justice Commission of the Catholic Archdiocese of San Francisco sent endorsements. Nonn worked full-time for weeks before the big day, trying to generate media interest and church support.

On the morning of March 24, Fife and others set up a table on the church steps and hung two banners, which read in Spanish, "This is a Sanctuary of God for the Oppressed of Central America" and "Immigration, Don't Profane the Sanctuary of God." By 10:00 A.M., forty news reporters and television crews, including several Europeans and one from Canadian broadcasting, had arrived to cover Southside's public declaration of the movement that was henceforth known as Sanctuary. A church openly breaking federal law was big news.

Corbett began the news conference by telling the reporters that he had been smuggling refugees across the border for months. Manzo Area Council lawyers then explained the injustice of immigration laws. Next, Fife read a letter he had sent the previous day to Attorney General William French Smith and other state and INS officials, which announced the church's violation of the law and declaration of sanctuary. "We believe the current policy and practice of the U.S. Government with regard to Central American refugees is illegal and immoral," it read. "We will not cease to extend the sanctuary of the church to undocumented people from Central America. Obedience to God requires this of us." Finally, a Salvadoran, Alfredo, masked to hide his identity, spoke of the violence in El Salvador which drove him to seek political asylum in the U.S.

That night, three hundred supporters marched in candlelight procession from the Tucson Federal Building to Southside for an ecumenical service observing the welcome of undocumented Salvadoran refugees into the church. Many pastors and rabbis from around the country spoke of the need to endure hardship to defend the poor. The crowd sang stirring renditions of "Through It All" and "We Shall Overcome." Fife closed with a benediction. An undercover Border Patrol agent in attendance later filed this report with his superiors:

> Aside from the old people, most of them looked like the anti-Vietnam war protesters of the early 70s. In other words, political misfits. . . . It seems that this movement is more political than religious, but that the ploy is going to be Border-Patrol "baiting" by that group in order to demonstrate to the public that the U.S. Government, via its jack-booted gestapo Border-Patrol agents, thinks nothing of breaking down the doors of their churches to drag Jesus Christ out to be tortured and murdered. I believe that all political implications should be considered before any further action is taken toward this group.

The INS decided to treat Sanctuary publicly as a trivial novelty that would soon fade into insignificance. No arrests were made. In fact, however, it was later revealed that the INS was deeply worried about Sanctuary and initiated a covert investigation of the movement by paid infiltrators.

In its first year as a sanctuary, Southside Presbyterian harbored sixteen hundred Salvadorans on their way to more permanent homes around the country. And, with national and religious media giving front-page coverage on the movement, word about Sanctuary spread quickly. Steadily, churches scattered across the country began declaring public sanctuary. The movement became truly nationalized, however, when in August 1982 Jim Corbett—feeling overwhelmed by the day to day demands of refugee work in Tucson—asked the Chicago Religious Task Force on Central America (CRTF) to take over the job of coordinating Sanctuaries across the country. The CRTF had been founded, in response to the 1981 murders of four North American churchwomen in El Salvador, to lobby against military aid to that country. Their first year of efforts, however, produced so little fruit that they began to consider shifting their focus to grassroots political education. Corbett's request was enticing. But members of CRTF felt inadequate for the task. But after searching in vain for weeks for a more experienced group, the CRTF—green though they were—finally agreed to become the national headquarters of Sanctuary.

The CRTF aggressively promoted Sanctuary, recruiting churches by phone and publishing and distributing thirty thousand copies of Sanctuary how-to manuals. By early 1983, more than forty-five churches and synagogues had declared public sanctuary and more than six hundred "secondary Sanctuary groups" had offered their endorsements and support. The movement was spreading from New England to southern California. An entire clandestine communication and transportation network—a new underground railroad—was now up and running. Refugee families were being smuggled across the border by the likes of Corbett and driven to Tucson, Los Angeles, and San Antonio. From there a pony express of cars and vans shuttled them across the continent to anxious families waiting to receive them. At first, railroad "conductors"—teachers, truck drivers, businesspeople, farmers—relayed messages through the network with passwords and codes and disguised refugees with wigs and moustaches. But eventually—as the system became routine, no arrests were made, and the coded messages proved more confusing than helpful—the secrecy was abandoned.

The movement's identity soon began to evolve. Sanctuary began as a movement of hospitality that aimed to provide for the humanitarian needs of vulnerable refugees. But Sanctuary quickly become more than that. It grew into a *political* movement that sought to end the human oppression generated by the U.S.-sponsored war in Central America. As more and more churches and synagogues considered declaring sanctuary, they were forced to learn the reasons why so many traumatized and anguished Central Americans were flooding northward. And, by choosing to shelter undocumented refugees, Sanctuaries publicly declared their belief that violence and human rights abuses were epidemic in Central America, that the U.S. was guilty of promoting and financing the violence and atrocities, and that open mass civil disobedience was necessary to confront Washington and demand an end to its bloody war. Thus, heightened grassroots political awareness and the spread of Sanctuary fueled each other.[5]

In 1983, other churches and synagogues made public declarations of sanctuary. Religious groups were by then declaring sanctuary at a rate of more than two a week. In the first six months of 1984, the total number of sanctuaries had more than doubled to 150. And eighteen national religious denominations and commissions had publicly endorsed Sanctuary. Clearly, the Sanctuary movement was not fading into trivial insignificance, as the INS had hoped. Publicly downplaying Sanctuary's importance was not working. So the INS shifted to a more aggressive strategy. In February, 1984, Texas Sanctuary workers Stacey Lynn Merkt and Sister Diane Muhlenkamp were arrested for transporting undocumented refugees. *Dallas Times-Herald* reporter Jack Fischer, who was covering their work, was arrested as well. One month later, TEC Director Phil Conger and Southside volunteer Katherine Flaherty were arrested. In April, Texas Sanctuary worker Jack Elder was arrested. Six months later Merkt and Elder were indicted again on additional charges. Then, in January 1985, the Justice Department announced the indictment of sixteen Arizona Sanctuary workers, including Corbett and Fife, three nuns, two priests, a nurse, a housewife, and a graduate student. The long-awaited, direct confrontation with the government had arrived.

The arrests, however, only served to increase the movement's visibility and produce an outpouring of support from around the country. The National Council of Churches condemned the arrests. Groups of Roman Catholic bishops and religious orders issued statements affirming Sanctuary as biblical and moral. In one week after the Arizona indictments, registration for a TEC-organized national symposium on Sanctuary jumped from three hundred to fifteen hundred participants. The city of Los Angeles and the state of New Mexico declared themselves Sanctuaries. By mid-1985, the number of declared Sanctuaries had climbed to 250. Two years later, the number had grown to four hundred. Despite opposition, the Sanctuary movement was continuing to attract an expanding number of people willing to break federal law to protect aliens and protest U.S. Central America policy.

WITNESS FOR PEACE[6]

On Saturday afternoon, April 9, 1983, thirty dazed North Carolinians stepped off an old yellow school bus in El Porvenir, Nicaragua, and began to wander aimlessly through the smoldering wreckage of the previous night's attack. The sight was devastating. This thriving village and tobacco farm situated on the Honduran border, named "The Future" in Spanish, had been assaulted by U.S.-backed Contra forces. Hours later, the thirty *gringos* stood before the scorched remains—the smoking piles of ashes, mangled tin roofs, burnt crops, scattered mortar shells, and wounded and shellshocked survivors—overwhelmed by the ruin and anguish.

The thirty North Carolinians were traveling on a one-week fact-finding tour, organized by Gail Phares, an ex-Maryknoll nun who had worked with the poor in Nicaragua in the 1960s. In the 1970s, at the urging of the Central Americans she worked with, Phares had returned to the States to work for change in U.S. Central American policy. In 1982 Phares moved to North Carolina, created the Carolina Interfaith Task Force on Central America (CITCA), and began searching for ways to raise awareness about Central America in her new state. When the Contra war surfaced in the media, she decided to lead a group of church people to Nicaragua to see the situation for themselves. Only a few hours after they had arrived in Managua late Friday night, reports of a Contra attack reached Phares and her collection of middle-aged, middle-class religious leaders, pastors, college teachers, and assorted housewives and retirees. At 4:00 A.M. Saturday morning, with little sleep, Phares's group boarded their bus and headed for the village. Ten hours and two stops at other attacked villages later, the exhausted group trudged through the remains of El Porvenir, trying to absorb the horror that lay before them.

"Look over there on that hill," implored a young local militia soldier guarding the village's remains, pointing to a hut a few hundred yards away, across the Honduran border on the horizon. "Those are the Contras that attacked us. That is the headquarters of Suicide, their commander. They can see us now."

Jeff Boyer, one of the delegates who years earlier had worked for the Peace Corps in a nearby Honduran village, just on the other side of the mountains, peered through his binoculars and saw Contra soldiers wandering about. "Why aren't they shooting now?," he asked.

"Because you are here with us," the youth replied. The wheels began to turn in Boyer's mind. He and others began thinking they should stay the night.

"It's past three o'clock and time to leave," the anxious bus driver insisted. "We need to get out of here and back on the paved road before dark." Phares agreed. But the Nicaraguans did not want the group to leave. They asked them to come see one more house. Inside stood a young mother, shaking. She was in shock. The floors and walls were splattered with blood. A pair of children's shoes lay on the floor in the middle of the room, also stained with blood. The group was told that the woman's mother and three children—an infant and two toddlers—had been wounded in the Contra assault and had been taken away by ambulance that morning. No one knew if they were alive or dead. The trembling mother began to sob. Many in the delegation began to cry. Boyer reached out and held the woman, crying, "What the hell are we doing? We can't just leave these people."

The bus driver was shouting. The bus was getting ready to leave. The hesitant delegation slowly headed back to the bus, saying farewells, embracing the villagers, promising never to forget them. Boyer mumbled in Spanish, "Take care, ma'am," withdrew to the bus, and broke down, weeping bitterly. "Holding that woman was the most empty gesture I have ever made in my life," Boyer later recalled. "To this day, I think we failed those people. We should have stayed." Later, the group learned that the mother's wounded infant died in the hospital.

The bus ride back to Managua was bleak and painful. The delegates burned with rage, helplessness, and guilt. They knew whose tax dollars funded the Contras. They knew it was their own country responsible for devastating El Porvenir, that their own government had shattered that young mother's life. And they knew that the Contras would probably return after dark with more destruction and death. Phares tried to console the group by talking about the need to return home and tell the truth about the Contras. "Somehow," she repeated, "we have to do something to stop our government's war on these people."

Boyer brooded over the young soldier's words: "*Because you are here with us.*" Finally, he blurted out, "Look, if the United States is funding this, then let's put fifteen hundred volunteers here to stop this fighting! If all it takes to prevent the killing is a bunch of U.S. citizens in town, then let's do it, let's hold a big vigil in the war zone!" At first, the group laughed off the idea. But the more they thought and talked about the proposal, the more they liked it. The mood in the bus began to shift from guilt and powerlessness to indignation and resolve. Back in Managua, the group spent the rest of the week meeting with Nicaraguan religious, educational, and political leaders, including four Sandinista Commandantes, to learn more about the Nicaraguan situation. In each meeting they posed their idea of a massive U.S. citizen's peace vigil in the war zone and solicited support and advice. Reactions were mixed. But by the end of the week, they had won the approval of evangelical church leaders and the president of Nicaragua, Daniel Ortega.

On the April 15 plane ride home, Phares, Boyer, and Gil Joseph, a University of North Carolina professor, sat together and drafted an outline of their plan. They wanted to organize one thousand people from all fifty states—including celebrities such as Bob Dylan and Bianca Jagger—who were willing to risk their lives by traveling to the war zone and, "standing with the Nicaraguan people," hold a high-visibility peace vigil in clear view of the Contras. The assembly would then return home and spread the word to the media, their religious communities, families, and friends about the government's dirty proxy-war against Nicaragua. They decided to call the event "Action for Peace in Nicaragua." D-Day was set for July 4—two-and-a-half months away. All that remained was to find a national religious organization to sponsor and organize the event.

That, however, proved impossible. Phares, Boyer, and Joseph spent two weeks on the phone and on the road trying to get any number of organizations to sign on to organize the trip. Although many liked the idea, no one would actually take it on. Two months, they said, was not enough time for such an immense and risky project. Boyer and Joseph, in despair, were ready to give up. Phares suggested they sleep on it. A day later they agreed together, "Okay, we'll do it ourselves."

The next six weeks were spent working the telephones in Phares's CITCA office. A small crowd of volunteers, including many members of the first trip, worked around the clock to recruit and train delegates for the July 4 trip. They tapped into the networks of Clergy and Laity Concerned (CALC), the American Friends Service Committee (AFSC), the New York–based InterReligious Task Force on Central America, and local Central America task forces across the country. Gail Phares contacted every religious and political connection she had from her previous work, asking them to join the trip, organize their state, donate money. By July, the volunteers had gathered 153 people from forty states for their "Action for Peace in Nicaragua."[7]

This second delegation arrived in Managua on July 3. They spent the first two days getting acquainted with the Nicaraguan situation, meeting with church, Sandinista, and opposition leaders, visiting social projects and churches, reading local newspapers. Many of them were quite impressed with the social achievements of and popular support for the Sandinista revolution. This, they thought, was not the totalitarian Nicaragua portrayed by the White House and the U.S. news media.

On July 5, the group woke at 4:00 A.M., ate a rice-and-beans breakfast, and began the thirteen-hour bus trip to the refugee town of Jalapa, near the Honduran border. Because of torrential rains and worry about mined roads, the buses arrived three hours later than scheduled. But when they finally did appear, the whole town seemed to come out to greet them. After a merry reception held at the local movie theater, a prayer service concluded the evening's events and the group settled down for a night's sleep in the local high school.

The next morning, the delegates met with a group of Nicaraguans, mostly women, for an emotional, three-and-a-half hour prayer vigil, held on the basketball court behind the high school. The North Americans read passages from the prophet Isaiah and from Thomas Jefferson on the imperative of social justice. The group then presented gifts, including a copy of the U.S. Declaration of Independence, to the Nicaraguans and asked forgiveness for the United States' betrayal of its own revolutionary ideals. Then they prayed. Between each prayer, the North Americans spoke in ritual unison, "For killings and kidnappings funded by us, forgive us and pray for us." Soon, the somber Nicaraguans spontaneously began to answer with quaking voices, "You are forgiven." Back and forth passed the liturgical confessions and pardons until the whole group, overcome by tears, fell silent. Then, the Nicaraguans began to tell, one by one, stories of sons and daughters recently killed, kidnapped, and dismembered by the Contras. At the mention of the name of each killed loved one, the Nicaraguans reverently repeated "Presente," meaning that the person's spirit lived on. With each story of death, the grieved North Americans asked the mothers for their forgiveness. And each suffering mother answered, "You are forgiven."

That afternoon, the North Americans and Jalapans held a peace march, complete with banners, around the city courtyard. They then moved to a field, situated between the Contra positions and the town, held hands in a long line, and sang songs of peace. Delegates planted U.S., Nicaraguan, and United Nations flags in the field. After, some delegates helped plant corn with Nicaraguans. Others met with Nicaraguans throughout the town, ate together, prayed together, exchanged photographs, and pledged to work for peace.

The emotional and spiritual impact of the days' events on the

North Americans proved to be extraordinary. The morning prayer vigil was particularly moving. Phyllis Taylor, a Jewish nurse who became deeply involved in Central America activism, later remembered,

> A profound thing happened to me. When the first mother started telling her story, she began very strong, but started to cry when she got to the day of her son's death. The next mother was the same. By the third mother, they were in tears, I was in tears, we were all in tears, holding each other. The profound thing was that, in comforting each other, the mothers were able to distinguish me from my government. That was a phenomenal breakthrough for me. A strongly self-conscious Jew, I had grown up never having allowed anything German in our house, with a tremendous dislike for Palestinians, without ever even knowing one! Now here I was, this mother not condemning me, but forgiving me, even though her child had died brutally at the hands of my government. It was incredibly moving.

Henri Nouwen, a Dutch theologian and author, said, "I had never been so deeply touched as when those women looked at us and said, 'You are forgiven.' The experience shook up my understanding of faith and left me unable to write anything for months." Similarly, Fran Truitt, a retiring United Church of Christ minister, who went on to become a prime mover in Witness for Peace, later recalled, tearfully,

> After the morning vigil, the oldest of the mothers of those killed came up to me, of all the people. I called for a translator. It was an eternal moment for me. She said, "I have been blessed by God, for I have given the blood of my son for the salvation of our people. I want to share that blessing with you, to share with your people." I fell on my knees, and she kissed me on the forehead. I looked up to the translator and he had tears streaming out of his eyes. The woman's name was Maria Garcia Lopez. But she became the incarnation of Mary for me. I didn't know what all that meant, I just knew it was a very religious moment. It was very sobering, both a blessing and a burden. I was supposed to be retiring. But now I felt chosen. And what do you do with that?

"It was a powerful experience that affected us all very seriously. It made a tremendous impact," recalled Mike Clark, another delegate who later became director of Witness for Peace. "We had seen and experienced something that demanded a response. All of us came back with a solemn mission to carry out."

Before returning to the States, the group met in Managua with the U.S. ambassador to Nicaragua, Anthony Quainton, and told him their story. They showed him pieces of shrapnel from U.S.-manufactured mortar shells they found in bombed villages. Theology professor Jorge Lara Braud charged the U.S. with "legalized murder" and pastor William Sloan Coffin challenged Quainton to resign in protest. Quainton responded with the official administration's views of the dangers of communism in Central America. This man, the stunned delegates realized, was not talking about the Nicaragua they had come to know in the last few days. Perhaps none of their government's statements on Nicaragua could be trusted. That night, the group held a candlelight vigil outside the U.S. embassy gate, singing "Ain't Gonna Study War No More."

The next morning, forty of the delegates met to begin making plans to establish a permanent North American presence in the war zone. They believed that nothing short of a permanent vigil would have any impact on U.S. policy. Eventually, they chose a task force of nine, which worked all day and through the night. By dawn, they had written a plan they called "Project Witness." Three permanent vigilers would be stationed near border areas where Contras attacked. They and their Nicaraguan co-workers would receive short-term delegations of ten to twenty people. As had been done on the first two trips, the delegates would see the Nicaraguan situation for themselves, go to any village under Contra assault, and report the truth back to the U.S. media and churches. Delegates would be expected to live with Nicaraguans, share the risks of Contra violence, "face death if need be," and become first-hand sources of information on Nicaragua alternative to the U.S. government.

The 153 delegates returned home and began to tell their story in many hundreds of newspaper articles, radio and television interviews, and church pulpits. They received local, regional, and national press coverage, including an article in *Newsweek* and an essay by William Sloan Coffin, "Nicaragua is Not Our Enemy," in the *New York Times*. A three-page draft of the "Project Witness" proposal was circulated widely among church and peace groups. David Sweet, a Santa Cruz Latin American history professor; Jim Wallis, of *Sojourners* magazine; and Henri Nouwen began touring the country calling for peacemaking in Central America and recruiting new delegates. Many from the July trip, who had now become full-time volunteers, worked their own religious denominations and organizations for support. In short order, Clergy and Laity Concerned, the American Friends Service Committee, the Fellowship of Reconciliation, the InterReligious Task

Force, the Quakers, the Presbyterian Church U.S.A., the United Methodist Church, the *Catholic Worker* and *Sojourners* magazines, Washington D.C.'s Religious Task Force on Central America, and many other denominations and organizations were lending organizational and financial support for a permanent vigil in Nicaragua.

By August, a National Steering Committee was formed that met on regular telephone conference calls. In October, twenty key leaders met at the Convent of the Good Shepherd in Philadelphia to hammer out a statement of purpose and principles and to hire a coordinator. After struggling through many disagreements (to be discussed in chapter 11), they defined Witness for Peace as "prayerful, biblically-based, non-violent, and politically independent." By mid-November, Witness for Peace had raised more than $38,200 in cash and pledges and had been awarded an additional $13,000 in grants. Around the country, twenty-seven local support groups and seven regional offices worked on publicity, recruitment, and fund-raising. Applications to be long- and short-term delegates began pouring in. According to Phyllis Taylor (1990): "It was wonderful and prophetic and crazy in the beginning. You know, people used their own money and their own travel. We set up trainings in our house. People were asking what our policy was, we didn't have any so we just made them up on the spot. It was that kind of wonderful chaos in the beginning."

The first long-term delegates flew to Nicaragua on October 18. Then, the first official short-term delegation was launched with much fanfare on December 2, the third anniversary of the murder of the four U.S. churchwomen in El Salvador. *Sojourners* had hired a top-notch media relations specialist, Dennis Marker, who packaged Witness for Peace for the media as a "shield of love" for the Nicaraguan people, "ordinary people doing a radical thing." The media ate it up. Witness for Peace gained coverage in every major national newspaper. NBC's *Today* show even provided live coverage of the delegation's peace procession in the town of Ocotal.

Short-term delegations began to flow to Nicaragua—from Missouri, South Dakota, New York, Illinois, Maine, all over the country—one after another, at a steady rate of four a month.[8] Delegation after delegation usually encountered the same kind of deeply disturbing experience as had the first two groups—establishing friendships with Nicaraguans, seeing for themselves both the Sandinista revolution and the anguish of the war, weeping with parents whose children and spouses were killed by the Contras, and vowing to return home and struggle to end the killing. Witness for Peace had hit upon a tactic, it seemed, that transformed people, that disturbed and electrified U.S. citizens into fervent political action against their own government. Soon, wave after wave of delegates began returning home on fire with a mission to tell their troubling stories to anyone who would listen and organize to end the U.S.-backed Contra war.

The number of long-term delegates in Nicaragua quickly jumped from three to twenty, increasing capacity to receive a growing number of short-term delegates. Over the course of the decade, a total of four thousand short-term and two hundred long-term delegates traveled to Nicaragua with Witness for Peace, generating the basis of a massive, grassroots domestic opposition to the administration's Central America policy. In time, Witness for Peace was mailing its newsletter to forty thousand readers and its recruitment and fund-raising letters to more than one million contacts a year. Witness for Peace organized more than 1,000 local media and congressional contacts in 380 cities and 49 states. The organization became a regular source of information on Nicaragua for newspapers across the country. And the national office repeatedly helped coordinate major political campaigns to end the Contra war. Anticipating the May 1988 congressional vote on aid to the Contras, for example, Witness for Peace organized an "End Contra Aid!" call-in that generated eleven thousand protest calls to Capitol Hill offices. Thus, the guilt and rage of thirty tired North Carolinians wandering through the smoking wreckage of El Porvenir had been transformed into a well-coordinated challenge to the President's low-intensity war.

THE PLEDGE OF RESISTANCE[9]

On a cold week in early November of 1983, fifty-three Christian peace and justice activists gathered for a retreat at the Kirkridge Retreat Center in northeastern Pennsylvania. These activists, mostly movement leaders and representatives of peace organizations, who called themselves the New Abolitionist Covenant, had been convening each year at Kirkridge for fellowship, Bible study, prayer, and political reflection. But this year, the shadow of an impending crisis loomed large over the assembly. Eight days earlier, almost seven thousand U.S. troops had invaded the Caribbean island of Grenada and deposed its leftist government. Many at the retreat—who were in close communication with alarmed Nicaraguan church leaders—feared that the

Grenada invasion was merely a dress rehearsal for the Pentagon's main event: an imminent, full-scale U.S. invasion of Nicaragua.

A sense of urgency and danger weighed heavily on the group as they talked and prayed. Before the retreat's end, a consensus emerged on the need for an organized resistance to such an invasion. Jim Wallis and Jim Rice of *Sojourners* magazine drafted a brief statement called "A Promise of Resistance," which was revised through group discussion and signed by thirty-three of the gathered activists. The statement vowed that, if the U.S. invaded Nicaragua, its signers would gather as many North American Christians as possible to "go immediately to Nicaragua to stand unarmed as a loving barrier in the path of any attempted invasion." It also called upon Christians to "encircle, enter, or occupy congressional offices in a nonviolent prayerful presence with the intention of remaining at those offices until the invasion is ended." *Sojourners* sent copies of the statement to every member of Congress, to the Departments of State and Defense, to the CIA, and to President Reagan. Every retreat participant presented the plan to their own organizations and denominations. And *Sojourners* printed the statement in the December issue, publicizing it to religious activists across the country.

In the first months of 1984 an array of religious organizations endorsed the Kirkridge statement and lent organizational support.[10] With input from these groups, the contingency plan was refined, rewritten, and republished in the August issue of *Sojourners*. Now titled "A Pledge of Resistance," the new plan downplayed the original idea of traveling to Nicaragua to intercept U.S. forces and focused primarily on the occupation of congressional offices. The article described a newly formed implementation plan and communications network—Witness for Peace's seven new regional offices had volunteered to serve as regional communication centers—and published the names, addresses, and phone numbers of regional coordinators.

Meanwhile, in Berkeley, California, a doctoral student in theology and peace activist by the name of Ken Butigan was, by happenstance, given a copy of the *Sojourners* issue that carried the Kirkridge statement. Nine months earlier, Ken had received a letter from someone in Nicaragua he didn't know. The letter said, in short:

> Listen, we're telling you this: your government is killing our children. We're telling you now so later you cannot say that you didn't know. We're asking you to take steps to stop this killing at a time when we have such hope for our country.

Butigan was deeply affected by the letter. He knew down deep that the letter was right. He and others in his anti-nuclear activist group formed an East Bay chapter of Witness for Peace. Increasingly, however, Butigan felt the need for a U.S.-oriented strategy to complement Witness for Peace's work in Central America. When he read the Kirkridge statement in *Sojourners*, it clicked. "Thirty-three people signed this," he said to himself, "why not three hundred people or three thousand or three million people making this pledge?" Not knowing there were organizers on the East Coast already working on it, Butigan sat down and wrote a pledge document called "A Commitment to Stop the Killing in Central America." He circulated it in the Bay area, explaining his idea to a number of activist groups. But it fell flat. Nobody responded.

A puzzled and discouraged Butigan, however, soon received a call from David Hartsough of the AFSC's San Francisco office, who had heard of the document. They met and debated Butigan's idea for an hour and a half. In the end, Hartsough said, "This is a great idea. We should make it happen across the country!" Hartsough gave Butigan a desk, a phone, AFSC's name, and fifty dollars a week pay. Butigan went to work organizing his version of the Pledge. About this time he discovered *Sojourners'* August revision of the Pledge and rewrote it to say, simply, "If the United States . . . significantly escalates its intervention on Central America, I pledge to join with others . . . in acts of legal protest and civil disobedience as conscience leads me." He then convinced a few people from local Sanctuary, the Committee in Solidarity with the People of El Salvador (CISPES), anti-nuclear, feminist, and environmental groups to help collect signatures.

On Tuesday, October 9, 1984, Butigan and his colleagues held the first mass public signing of the Pledge of Resistance. They set up a table and a public address system in front of the San Francisco Federal Building at 11:00 A.M. In the first hour, seven hundred people signed the Pledge. Two hundred of them explained over the microphone to the gathered crowd exactly why they felt compelled to sign on and possibly go to jail. More than half of those explained they did so because of their religious faith. Butigan was thrilled by the response. In the following days the Pledge campaign took off.

Butigan then learned through David Hartsough that *Sojourners* was convening a meeting on October 16 at their Washington, D.C., office. It was to be attended by representatives of eighteen major peace, justice, and anti-interventionist groups to hammer out the organizational details of the emerging Pledge. Butigan got himself invited. At the meeting, different parties advanced disparate visions of how the Pledge should operate. Some argued for an unwritten Pledge with spontaneous protests emerging as conscience led. Others called for a more structured campaign involving coordinated leadership, training seminars, and mass-mail fund-raising. At an opportune time, Butigan passed around a copy of his version of the Pledge, told of his October 9 public signing in San Francisco, and argued for a highly organized but nationally decentralized Pledge. In the end, Butigan's suggestion won out. An "analyst group" was established to monitor and interpret U.S. activities in Central America.[11] An eight-member "signal group" was organized to consult with the analyst group and decide if and when to activate the national network of Pledge protesters.[12] The existing regional Pledge offices were continued and the number expanded from seven to ten. A National Pledge Clearinghouse was set up in the National Council of Churches' Interfaith Task Force on Central America (ITFCA) office in New York. Finally, following Butigan's rewritten version, the decision was made to expand the Pledge to protest not only a U.S. invasion but any major military escalation in Central America, and to offer an optional legal protest to complement the civil-disobedience pledge. With a national organization now in place, Butigan returned home and quickly wrote a hundred-page Pledge of Resistance handbook, called *Basta! No Mandate for War.* Containing detailed information on Central America, the Pledge, nonviolence, and the logistics of protest, it was published by New Society Publishers and distributed nationally.

Meanwhile, Pledge groups were rapidly forming all over the country, collecting signatures, sponsoring nonviolence training seminars, and organizing mailing lists, phone-trees, and affinity groups. Pledge organizers were amazed by the public's positive response. By December, activists had collected 42,352 signatures, half pledging civil disobedience. "In fifteen years of activism," remembered Boston-area Pledge organizer Anne Shumway, "I never saw anything explode the way the Pledge did. It just took off. At public signings, people were just lining up to sign on." Likewise, Janice Hines, the regional coordinator for Texas, Arkansas, and Oklahoma, remarked, "The response was just amazing. The idea caught on so fast and generated so much excitement, we were just trying to keep up with it." Florida, Virginia, North Carolina, and Texas collected 1,000 signatures each. Colorado collected 1,650, Wisconsin 2,000, Massachusetts 2,100, and New Jersey 3,000. Pledge groups at Tufts University and University of California campuses began to organize a national boycott of college classes in the event of a U.S. invasion of Nicaragua. And national organizations—such as the National Lawyers Guild, the League of United Latin America Citizens, the Jewish Peace Fellowship, and Church Women United—continued to endorse the Pledge. To make the message clear, *Sojourners* sent the Department of State copies of the 42,352 signed Pledge forms.

By December, Pledge groups in northern California had collected five thousand signatures. In a few months, that number would grow to nine thousand. Having outgrown the AFSC office, Butigan opened a Pledge office in downtown San Francisco, staffed by two paid organizers and an army of volunteers. They began conducting five nonviolence training sessions a week, which trained fifteen hundred new activists in six months. Pledge activists began holding "peace maneuvers" at the San Francisco Federal Building, role-playing the major demonstration they believed was imminent. And the thousands of Pledge signers were given cards to deliver to their local congressional offices threatening to return to take over and occupy the offices if the U.S. invaded Nicaragua.

By early 1985, the Pledge of Resistance had mobilized the potential to create major social disruption in the event of a U.S. invasion of Nicaragua. The number of local Pledge groups had grown to more than two hundred and the number of Pledge signers had grown to fifty thousand. Activists were trained and communication networks were in place. The Pledge was ready and waiting for the White House to make the wrong move.

In May, the Congress refused to approve $14 million of Contra aid requested by the Reagan administration. In response, one week later, the White House imposed a full trade embargo on Nicaragua. But Pledge leaders were now divided. Should the Pledge react with full force? Or should it "save its ammunition" for a more important political showdown? The national signal group chose to wait. But many local Pledge leaders—including those in Boston and San Francisco—decided to act, despite worries that most of their people might not participate, since the embargo was not really an invasion. Their fears proved groundless, however, as thousands of activists held demonstrations in eighty cities and sixteen states over the next days. In Boston, twenty-six hundred protesters demonstrated and 559 were arrested for occupying the Federal Building. And in San Francisco, three thousand activists engaged in legal protest while six hundred were arrested for committing civil disobedience. In its first major show of force, despite the absence of an official national signal, more than ten thousand Pledge activists demonstrated across the country and more than two thousand were arrested for nonviolent civil disobedience.

As Pledge leaders began to realize that the U.S. might never invade Nicaragua directly with U.S. forces but already was attacking Nicaragua through the Contra armies, Pledge protests began to focus primarily on Contra aid votes in the Congress, arms shipments to Central America, and U.S. military maneuvers in the region. In June, only one month after the first embargo demonstrations, the Congress hastily passed $27 million in aid for the Contras. In response, Pledge activists, this time activated by the national signal group, staged demonstrations again in more than two hundred cities and forty-two states in which more than twelve hundred protesters were arrested for acts of civil disobedience.[13] The Pledge organization, now deeply engaged in political battle, was feeling a surge of confidence and energy. By September, Pledge groups had been organized in more than three hundred U.S. cities and the number of Pledge signers had grown by 40 percent to seventy thousand. In nine months, that number would grow again to its peak of eighty thousand.

Originally, many Pledge organizers, focused on the immediate post-Grenada crisis, expected the Pledge campaign against a U.S. invasion of Nicaragua to last only a few months. Ken Butigan recalls, "When the Pledge first began, I remember bringing a three-month budget to our first meeting. Someone said, 'Hell, we're not really going to be doing this for three months, are we! This will all be over in three months, won't it?' We all hoped so. But we just didn't know." In fact, the Pledge of Resistance spent the next five years mobilizing one campaign of demonstrations after another. All told, the Pledge marshaled forces to fight eight separate congressional Contra aid votes, as well as numerous Salvadoran aid votes, and carried off five major thematic public-awareness campaigns.

In 1986 alone, in response to four successive Contra aid votes in Congress, the Pledge sustained seven months of protest that involved one thousand separate demonstrations and vigils in which some two thousand Pledge protesters were arrested. Tens of thousands of Pledge activists protested in myriad ways. They occupied congressional offices for days; blocked gates of Contra-training military bases; staged funeral processions and mock "die-ins" in city streets and congressional offices; ran "Stop the Lies" advertisements in newspapers and radio stations and distributed sixty thousand "Stop the Lies" tabloids across the country; blocked morning rush-hour traffic with street marches and sit-ins; fasted in protest for weeks on the Capitol steps; rented planes and flew huge "U.S. Out of Nicaragua Now!" signs over big college football games; trespassed on National Guard bases and blocked airplane runways to obstruct military shipments; staged cross-state marches concluding with rallies at government offices; erected plywood walls in shopping centers painted with the names of hundreds of Nicaraguan civilians killed by Contras; held "Lie of the Week" vigils outside local pro-Contra congressional offices; held a four-day "People's Filibuster" in the Capitol Rotunda; rallied at shopping malls during the Christmas season, unfurling banners and singing politicized versions of Christmas carols; and, with banners and chants, birddogged 160 campaign appearances of forty pro-Contra congressional candidates seeking re-election.

Pledge activism continued strongly into 1987. In response to a major deployment of National Guard troops to Honduras in February, protesters held demonstrations and vigils outside one hundred congressional offices and sent many thousands of letters and postcards to congressional representatives. North Carolina Pledge members, for example, sent more than a thousand letters of protest to their newly elected senator, Terry Sanford. The Pledge then took the lead in organizing "April Mobilization" in Washington, D.C., in which one hundred thousand people marched for peace and justice in Central America and South Africa. Afterward, 567 protesters were arrested at a major civil disobedience action at CIA headquarters. Next, the Pledge launched a "Summer of Resistance" that focused on blocking the shipment of arms from the U.S. to Central America. Five hundred protested at the psychological warfare base in Arlington Heights, Illinois, where sixty-seven were arrested for climbing the base's fences. More than two hundred protested at the Van Nuys Air National Guard base, where thirty-four were arrested for leafletting. In Northern California, three thousand protested at the Concord Naval Weapons Station, where four hundred were arrested for blocking train tracks leading to the docks. In addition, members of the Baltimore Pledge twice disrupted the Iran-Contra hearings in Washington, unfurling banners and demanding a deeper investigation of the scandal. And a group of Vietnam veterans held a "Nuremberg Action," where they vigiled and leafletted against Contra aid twelve hours a day for three months.

At summer's end the Nuremberg Action group began a forty-day fast and nonviolent blockade of trains and trucks carrying munitions to the Concord Naval Weapons Station. On September 1, Brian Willson, one of the veterans, was run over by an oncoming train while kneeling on the tracks. The train cut off both legs and inflicted severe head injuries. Among the numerous reactions around the country, ten thousand outraged protesters—including Jesse Jackson, Joan Baez, and Daniel Ellsberg—marched on Concord, demanding an end to the war. Afterward several hundred demonstrators tore up one section of train tracks, while others halted all Concord arms shipments by mounting an ongoing, twenty-four-hour human blockade of trains that would last, with the involvement of one thousand protesters, more than two years. They were joined on September 30 by Willson himself, then recently released from the hospital. Altogether, in 1987, twelve hundred Pledge activists were arrested in hundreds of demonstrations.

But by the end of 1987, many Pledge protesters were growing weary of the struggle. Nevertheless, the Pledge continued in its work for two more years. During the fall and winter of 1987–88, 120 Pledge groups and fifty other Central America organizations coordinated a five-month protest campaign, called "Days of Decision," which helped successfully to defeat two new administration requests for Contra aid in February and March of 1988. After the second defeat, the White House deployed thirty-two hundred U.S. troops to Honduras. Fearing an invasion of Nicaragua, the Pledge helped to mobilize tens of thousands to protest in two hundred demonstrations in 150 cities in which nine hundred protesters were arrested. In April, the Pledge orchestrated nonviolent direct action campaigns at thirty military installations supporting the war in Central America, where hundreds were arrested. In October, the Pledge led a coalition of Central America groups in its "Steps to Freedom" campaign, where activists protested in seventy demonstrations across the country. The campaign culminated in a major demonstration at the Pentagon building, where fifteen hundred activists blocked entrances, occupied the heliport, and planted on the lawn five hundred crosses with names of Salvadoran civilians killed in the war. Five hundred protesters committed civil disobedience and 240 were arrested.

In 1989, the Pledge organized nationally coordinated demonstrations and vigils around President Bush's inauguration, the Salvadoran elections, President Cristiani's inauguration in El Salvador, and the

Panama invasion. In May, Pledge activists staged a series of surprise, high-visibility actions, where rappellers hung huge "Stop U.S. Aid to the Death Squad Gov't in El Salvador" signs at local and national landmarks, such as Washington, D.C.'s National Press Building, San Francisco's Coit Tower, Philadelphia's Independence Hall, St. Louis's Union Station, Chicago's Daley Plaza, Minneapolis' Franklin Avenue Bridge, and Boston's Transportation Building. In November and December, Pledge groups responded to renewed U.S.-funded military actions in El Salvador with more than seven hundred protests across the nation in which 2,440 people committed civil disobedience and 1,452 were arrested. And on March 24, 1990, the Pledge helped organize a rally in Washington, D.C., to mark the tenth anniversary of Archbishop Oscar Romero's assassination. Weathering a chilly snowstorm, fifteen thousand people marched and 580—the most of any single Pledge action—were arrested for demonstrating in front of the White House.

CONCLUSION

The Central America peace movement generated in the United States a political mobilization of major significance. Well more than a hundred thousand U.S. citizens had been activated into a fierce, extended struggle against a tremendously popular U.S. President. Year after year they had organized thousands upon thousands of demonstrations, vigils, rallies, and blockades. More than a hundred thousand had engaged in legal protests, many tens of thousands had broken state and federal laws to resist U.S. policy, and more than ten thousand had gone to jail for nonviolent civil disobedience. It was the most protracted, acrimonious political battle and the most enduring and contentious social movement of the decade. The question to which we now turn is: Exactly how and why did such a major movement emerge?

Five

Grasping the Big Picture

Neither the life of an individual nor the history of a society can be understood without understanding both. Yet people do not usually define the troubles they endure in terms of historical change and institutional contradiction. . . . What they need . . . is . . . the sociological imagination. . . . The sociological imagination enables us to grasp history and biography and the relations between the two within a society. That is its task and its promise.

C. Wright Mills, *The Sociological Imagination*

History is made by people. Not by mysterious collective forces or abstract social causes. Specific flesh-and-blood human beings, all of us, continually act—individually and collectively, intentionally and unintentionally—to construct and reconstruct our societies and cultures. In so doing, we become the creators of the social worlds we inhabit and co-authors of the social story we call history. But, as ordinary experience often painfully demonstrates, no one is free to make history exactly as they would like. For everyone acts in historical, sociocultural contexts that not only guide action but also constrain the potential range and results of human action. This is what Karl Marx meant when he wrote (1978: 595): "Humans make their own history, but they do not make it just as they please. They do not make it under the circumstances of their own choosing, but under circumstances directly found, given, and transmitted from the past. The tradition of all dead generations weighs like a bad dream on the mind of the living."

The same social dialectic—that human agents alone make history and society, but always and only under conditions made by history and society—also affects the life of social movements. Organized efforts to shape history through disruptive collective activism are subject to the same influences and constraints that condition all human action. Social movements' experiences of emergence, struggle, and decline, of success, stalemate, and failure are profoundly influenced by their particular historical and social contexts. This means that any good social-movement analysis must account for both the complex motives and actions of the actual people who produce the social movement *and* the multifaceted social-structural environment within which those people collectively act. In other words, unidimensional theories—whether focused on mobilized material resources, relative deprivation, collective identity, or any other single variable—are inadequate.

Recognizing the need for a multi-variable theory of social movements, scholars in the last fifteen years have been working to identify an array of key social factors and forces that shape social-movement dynamics (see, for instance, McAdam, McCarthy, and Zald 1988). One of the most illuminating multidimensional explanatory models to emanate from this work has been the political process theory. This approach argues that movements emerge and prosper only when challengers enjoy concurrently expanding political opportunities, strong facilitating organizations, and rising insurgent consciousness (McAdam 1982; Smith 1991).

This chapter and the next seek to explain the specific events and forces that produced the social context out of which the Central America peace movement was mobilized. I address the question of why and how did that movement emerge and sustain itself as successfully as it did. To answer this, I utilize a political process model, with the intent of accounting for both sides of the social dialectic, both the history-making human action and the action-shaping social environment. When we examine the big picture, we see that the cards of history were dealt in such a way that virtually guaranteed the Central America peace movement's eruption and continuance.

EXPANDING POLITICAL OPPORTUNITIES

According to the commonsense view, social movements emerge when people become angry about some social condition and organize to demand a political change. This view is correct, insofar as it goes. We know from years of research, however, that grievances, no matter how deeply felt, cannot by themselves produce a social movement. Two other essential factors are needed. The first is sufficient political opportunities to act upon those grievances with some hope of success. The second is the availability of strong organizational networks to facilitate a movement. To fully understand the emergence of the Central America peace movement, then, we need to recognize the combination of forces and events that together produced a social-structural context characterized not only by irrupting grievances, but also by expanding political opportunity and growing organizational strength.

In this chapter, we explore the relatively open structure of political opportunities enjoyed by those who opposed the Reagan Central America policy. Such opportunities arose from the combination of tremendous political attention focused on Central America in the 1980s and the profound lack of national consensus about the appropriate U.S. role in Central America. Central America persistently held the political spotlight for years, while the American public, academic and policy elites, and the legislative branch all remained deeply divided over the issue. Thus, the Reagan administration lacked both the public inattention and the political "united front" that would have been necessary to steamroll, marginalize, or demoralize the incipient grassroots Central America peace movement.[1]

The Presidential Preoccupation

Marriage, it is wryly said, is the chief cause of divorce. Analogously, Ronald Reagan was the primary cause of the Central America peace movement. This is true in a trivial sense, but also in a somewhat more significant way. "Ronald Reagan was the father of the Central America peace movement," in the words of Witness for Peace activist Fran Truitt, because he made Central America a national political preoccupation. Rather than implementing his plans as inconspicuously as possible—as Nixon had done with Chile in 1973—the President's concerns with Central America were prominent, persistent, and alarming.

The mass media took up and perpetuated this preoccupation. Following the President's cue, it held Central America in the media spotlight for most of the decade. Writing in the early 1980s, Pastor (1982: 28; also see Falcoff 1984: 372–76) observed: "Last March [1981], 792 foreign journalists, more than were in Vietnam during the height of the war, were in El Salvador to observe an election for a constituent assembly. The political, economic, and military turmoil in Central America . . . has been on the front pages of American newspapers and on the television news shows for months."

Indeed, the conflict in Central America would remain prominent in the news for most of the decade. The *New York Times*, for example, went from providing sparse coverage of Central America in the 1970s to publishing an average of 3.4 new articles and editorials on Central America *a day* during the eight years of the Reagan presidency (see figure 5.1). Television news coverage of Central America also exploded during the Reagan presidency, growing from a total of only *eleven* news stories on Nicaragua and El Salvador for the entire three years of 1975–77 to an average of 550 network television news stories on Nicaragua and El Salvador per year for each year of President Reagan's term of office (see figure 5.2). The publishing industry published an enormous quantity of books on Central America, increasing its yearly output on the subject during the height of the political struggle on average to nearly five times that of the preceding years (see figure 5.3). By 1989, an accumulated total of 549 books, monographs, and booklets on Central America had been published during Reagan's presidency (Books in Print 1989).[2]

This presidential and media preoccupation roused public attention to the issues, as the White House intended. But, in many ways, this focused attention often served to strengthen the position of the President's opponents. To begin, the President's high-profile approach to Central America, which was perpetuated by the mass media, eliminated the possibility of public indifference to the region. Witness for Peace organizer Mike Clark explains (1992): "The single most important factor was that the President made it impossible for people to ignore Central America. If he would have made it possible for us to

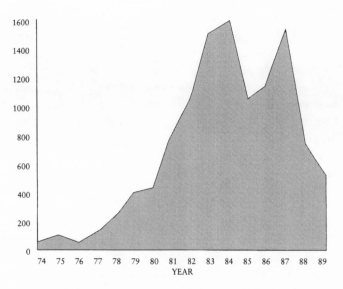

Fig. 5.1. *New York Times* Articles on Central America: 1974—1989. Source: *New York Times* Index.

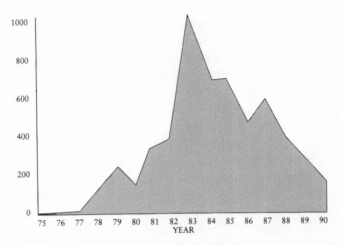

Fig. 5.2. Television Network News Stories on El Salvador and Nicaragua: 1975-1990. Source: *Television News Index and Abstracts 1975-1990*

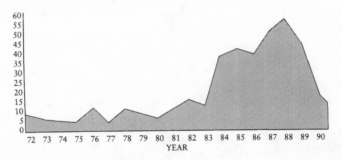

Fig. 5.3. Books about Central America Published: 1972-1990. Source: Cumulative Book Index 1972-1990. Note: Excluding books on Central American archeology, travel, crafts, juvenile literature, and poetry.

ignore it, I think we would have. But it was his obsession for eight years. So we were helped enormously by the fact that Reagan focused on Central America as the most dangerous and sinister threat."

Witness for Peace organizer Bob Van Denend agrees (1992): "Witness for Peace owes a lot of its success to Reagan. I don't know that we could have been successful without a President like that. He was so bent on Central America, and it was so much in the news, that it was easy for people to be aware of it. And it was easy for us to raise money, too."

Opponents of the President's Central American policy did not have to struggle against public apathy to raise general awareness about the region, as do champions of a great many causes. The President accomplished that work for them himself, giving people concerned with Central America's fate a great deal of free publicity.

Furthermore, the President created political opportunity for the Central America peace movement by making their concern the lightning-rod issue of the decade. Like most presidents, Ronald Reagan was opposed by a set of natural political adversaries, especially liberals and leftists of various sorts, who disliked his beliefs and politics on a host of issues not necessarily related to Central America. The President's preoccupation with Central America, however, channeled their broad hostility toward him into specific political resistance to his Central America policy. Falcoff observes (1986: 8): "Nicaragua has become controversial in the United States because President Reagan has made it that way. By openly declaring himself an enemy of the Sandinista regime, he has automatically strengthened its appeal for people who vehemently oppose his policies at home and abroad."

The President's sustained focus on Central America, in other words, strengthened the Central America peace movement's ability to mobilize the energy of those predisposed in general to resist the President.

Reagan's high-profile approach to Central America also served the interests of his opponents by evoking a deep-seated fear in the American public. Although the newly elected president enjoyed great public popularity, many Americans remained uneasy about his reputation as a "warmonger" spoiling for a fight (Destler 1984: 322). His tone on Central America policy only heightened this concern. Many Americans interpreted the President's words and actions as Ken Butigan (1991) did:

> You start with the Reagan administration's project, very confrontational, an acute military buildup, threatening the people of Central America. With all of that, and the "Evil Empire" rhetoric, there was a sense that anything is possible with this administration. That was underscored—not created—by Grenada. There was a growing sense that Nicaragua really was under attack. And Al Haig wanted to "go to the source." The White House really seemed to be salivating to go in and use force.

All of this touched a sensitive nerve for the American public, evoking a sense of deep anxiety. To understand why, we need to consider the effects of the Vietnam War on the American psyche.

The Vietnam Syndrome

Today, the Vietnam War and the turmoil it produced seem a distant memory of another era. Between then and now lay OPEC oil embargoes, the political reemergence of Islam, a decade of Republican conservativism, the collapse of communism, the structural weakening of the U.S. economy, a host of ethnic conflicts, and the Gulf War. But when Ronald Reagan took office in 1981, the U.S. withdrawal from the Vietnam War was only eight years old. And despite the strong tendency in American culture then to try to forget the war had ever happened, the incubus of Vietnam still haunted the nation. The American people and many of their leaders suffered under what former NSC Advisor Zbigniew Brzezinski called "a very deep philosophical-cultural crisis" that came to be known as "the Vietnam syndrome"—the strong and widespread aversion to U.S. intervention in third world conflicts (Klare 1992: 42–43). This aversion afforded tremendous political leverage to those committed to contesting President Reagan's Central America policy.

In the early 1980s, Vietnam-syndrome worries over Central America were ubiquitous. Peace activists were not the only ones troubled by the possibility that, in the words of one bumper sticker, "El Salvador is Spanish for Vietnam" (Bonner 1981). Many journalists, such as Tad Szulc (quoted in Herring 1991: 183), warned that the President's policy was a "scenario for absolute disaster," destined to entangle the country "in an endless, Vietnam-style guerrilla war in the Salvadorean mountains and jungles." In Congress, liberals and moderates debating military aid to Central America also dreaded the risk of sliding into another Vietnam. According to McCartney (1986), "Again and again, as the debate reached a climax on the House floor, the specter of American troops bogged down in an indecisive war haunted many members of the House." "Here we go again! Gulf of Tonkin Day," warned Representative Andrew Jacobs (D-Ind.), for example, reading 1964 newspaper headlines stating that no U.S. troops would be sent to Vietnam. "We ought to know by now that when they send the guns it does not take long before they send the sons." Vietnam, one legislator remarked (quoted in Herring 1991: 183, 185), was "a ghostly presence; it's there in every committee room, at every meeting."[3]

A number of Vietnam-era political figures also openly worried about replaying Vietnam. George Ball, a Lyndon Johnson Under Secretary of State, for example, warned of the refrains he was hearing in the political battle over El Salvador (quoted in Kaiser 1982): "The music and words sound like plagiarization. I have the feeling that we've heard it all before, but in another setting." The U.S. military also approached the Central America question with Vietnam on its mind (Herring 1991: 183–84):

> "All I want to do is win one war, that's all, just one," an advisor [in El Salvador] told a reporter. . . . "It'll be like winning the World Series for me." Another advisor expressed fear of a repetition of the final days of April 1975. "If the sense spreads that the U.S. will desert them," he said of the Salvadorans he is working with, "I don't know what they'll do. It's Vietnam all over again." Among senior U.S. military officers . . . Vietnam was a "silent obsession. It lurks in nuances and ellipses, even when the discussion is about something else. . . ." The presence of Vietnam in the military mind was clearly manifest in September 1983 in the famous Freudian slip of Marine Corp Commandant General P. X. Kelley who, before a committee of Congress, inadvertently used the word Vietnam when he meant to say Lebanon.

Fear of another Vietnam even reached into the White House, where some advisers worried that the administration's course, if not carefully plotted, might lead to disaster (Woodward 1987: 117; Gwertzman 1984; Sklar 1988: 72; Rubin 1984: 307; see Fields 1986).

The President did his best to counter the Vietnam syndrome, which he considered only "a temporary aberration" (Klare 1992: 45). He repeatedly asserted that Central America offered "no comparison with Vietnam. And there's not going to be anything of the kind" (Herring 1991: 182). "In no sense are we speaking of participation in combat by American forces," Reagan (quoted in Lewis 1983) assured the public. "There is no parallel whatsoever with Vietnam." But such statements proved ineffective in dispelling widespread fears about U.S. involvement in Central America.

At other times, the administration tried to use the specter of Vietnam to leverage support for its policy. For example, Secretary of State George Shultz wrote (1985): "Broken promises. Communist dictatorships. Refugees. Widened Soviet influence, this time very near our borders. Here is your parallel with Vietnam and Central America." Shultz also claimed that if the Congress failed to approve Contra aid, "we will be faced with the agonizing choice about the use of American combat troops" (quoted in Sklar 1988: 265–66; also see Gwertzman 1985). Representative Newt Gingrich (R-Ga.; quoted in Herring 1991: 185) warned that the same people opposing Contra aid "were wrong about South Vietnam and watched it become a dictatorship and watched the boat people flee . . . [and] were wrong about Cambodia and watched 'The Killing Fields.'" But, again, the White House was unable through these kinds of arguments to scare up consistent support for its policy. No matter how it was framed, Vietnam seemed invariably to work against the President. This translated into political opportunity for the emerging Central America peace movement in at least three distinct ways.

First, the Vietnam syndrome helped to predispose U.S. public opinion against the administration's approach to Central America. According to Sobel (1989: 116), "Gallup polls from 1981 to 1983 showed that roughly two-thirds (62% to 74%) of those aware of the situation in El Salvador thought it was likely that it 'could turn into a situation like Vietnam.'" The majority of Americans simply believed that the U.S. should steer clear of Central American military conflicts (see, for instances, Clymer 1985; Gailey 1985; Shipler 1986; Sobel 1989; Blachman and Sharpe 1988: 25–26; Bowen 1989). At no time in the entire decade did a majority of Americans support Contra aid, military aid to El Salvador, sending U.S. troops to Central America, or the President's handling of Central America in general (see figures 5.4 and 5.5). Few Americans wanted to see American soldiers fighting and dying in the jungles of Honduras and El Salvador. Most Americans would rather have seen funds spent on U.S. domestic problems (Miller 1981; Roberts 1982b; *New York Times* 1983d, Gailey 1985; Gruson

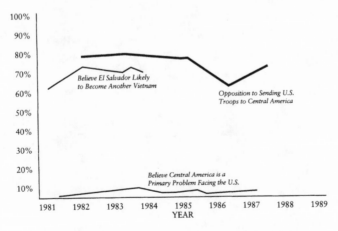

Fig. 5.4. Public Opinion on Central America. Source: Sobel 1989.

1983; Moberg 1987; Sklar 1988: 192). Ignorance of the region and racism toward its people also contributed to a public aversion to involvement in Central America (Moberg 1987).[4] All of this provided the emerging Central America peace movement a reservoir of sympathetic public opinion into which it could tap to help resist White House policy. The burden thus fell on the administration, and not the movement, to spend its energy trying to secure public backing.

In addition to the weight of general public opinion, the legacy of Vietnam propelled widespread anxieties among national leaders about the possibility of inflaming the painful wounds of social division and turmoil of the late 1960s and early 1970s. The prospect of replaying draft-card burnings, the 1968 Chicago Convention, the Weathermen, and Kent State was unbearable. Many in power understood that, in the words of former NSC analyst Robert Pastor (1982: 38–39), "the unilateral use of U.S. troops [in Central America] . . . would be so internally divisive as to make the Vietnam demonstrations of the 1960s appear only a minor historical prelude to the anti-war riots of the 1980s." Given this perception—and the fact that the emerging Central America movement actually appeared to be mobilizing the capacity for exactly that kind of disruption—for many congressional leaders, the prudent course of action seemed to be the avoidance of any significant military involvement in Central America.

The final dimension of political opportunity enjoyed by the incipi-

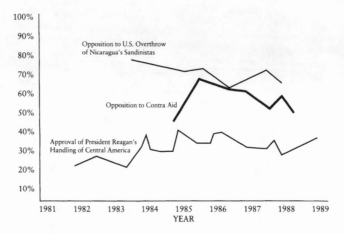

Fig. 5.5 Public Opinion against President Reagan's Central American Policy. Source: Sobel 1989.

ent Central America peace movement involved apprehensions on the part of the U.S. military. One consequence of the loss in Vietnam was an antipathy on the part of the Pentagon to engage in unpopular or restricted military actions. The military, in fact, *was* prepared to fight a war—indeed, more than a few military leaders may have been eager to do so.[5] But they would fight only on two conditions. First, the American people had to genuinely support the war. "One of the lessons of Vietnam," reported a high Pentagon official (quoted in Roberts 1982a), "is that we can't engage in a war that is not supported by American public opinion." Second, they would fight only if they were given the freedom to prosecute the war with full force—Vietnam-style limited incrementalism was unacceptable. Both of these conditions, however, constrained the Reagan administration's military options. For both public opinion and Congress were clearly opposed to sending American combat troops to Central America, not to mention an all-out U.S. war in the region.[6] Thus, the White House's lack of unambiguous backing from the Pentagon translated into an opportunity for grassroots opponents of administration policy to exercise the political power of protest (Rubin 1984: 305).

In sum, the Vietnam debacle strongly predisposed the American public and the majority of Congress against President Reagan's policy in Central America and curtailed the military's willingness to exercise its force in Central America. This restricted the White House's freedom to act, and furnished political leverage to the growing movement committed to defeating the President's Central America policy.

Divided Government and Elite Defection

Modern political systems tend, by nature, to be dominated by relatively small groups of elites who control great concentrations of national wealth and power. Despite the appearance and limited reality of pluralistic democracy, these "power elites" remain the primary shapers of national foreign, military, and economic policies. Through easy access to and control over the positions and people of government, business, and the media, they exercise a decisive influence not only on the character of major policies, but also on the agendas and terms of national policy debates. As such, ruling elites typically enjoy the capacity to preempt, suppress, or coopt challenges to their interests, including those of protest movements. In a dynamic social world, however, openings of political opportunity present themselves to challenger movements when power elites become internally divided.

Regime crises and elite defections of various sorts generate political instability that enhances the relative power of opposition forces (see, among other works, Skocpol 1979; Shorter and Tilly 1974; Brinton 1965; Schwartz 1976; Piven and Cloward 1979; Meyer 1990). When the U.S. Central America peace movement began to mobilize in the early 1980s, it encountered a situation of divided government and elite defection—precisely the kind of conditions that fosters the successful emergence of movements contesting state policies.

At the broadest level, in the late 1970s and early 1980s, the entire U.S. federal government was moving rapidly into what Ginsberg and Shefter (1990; also see Burnham 1982) call a "postelectoral era" characterized by low voter turnout, weakened political parties, and electoral deadlock. This new era brought an increasingly heavy reliance by political adversaries on institutional weapons of combat, such as congressional investigations, judicial battles, media revelations, and political prosecutions. Also, a system of "dual sovereignty" emerged, where both Congress and the White House attempted to assemble the capability to govern independently, without reference to each other. The ultimate consequence of this shift away from election-based allocations of real power to govern was "governmental disarray" (Ginsberg and Shefter 1990: 32–36): Ginsberg and Shefter observed (1990: 2):

> Because contemporary elections fail to establish conclusively who will—or will not—exercise power, conflict over this question continues to rage throughout the political system. This exacerbates the historic fragmentation of government in the United States, further weakening the American state and making it difficult to achieve collective national purposes. Contending groups are increasingly able to seize portions of the state apparatus and pursue divergent and often contradictory goals.

This governmental disarray and weakened ability by the state to govern decisively were never as visible as in the political struggle over Central America policy. Ginsberg and Shefter (1990: 166–67) wrote further that "the example that has most frequently been commented on involves policy toward Central America. At the same time that the administration was seeking to mobilize support in the Central American region for the contra forces in Nicaragua, House Speaker Jim Wright and other members of Congress were conducting their own negotiations with Central American heads of state premised on the American abandonment of the contras."

This disarray presented an opening of political opportunity for

Central America peace activists to challenge administration policy. It did so precisely because the structure of the situation simultaneously eroded the decisiveness of electoral outcomes, including that of the presidential election of 1980, divided U.S. political elites, and decreased the state's overall governing effectiveness on this high-profile issue.

In addition to these general political consequences of the emerging "postelectoral era," White House Central America policy stood vulnerable to challenges from grassroots Central America activists because of the rancorous partisan split that developed in the 1980s between the legislative and executive branches of government. Congressional Democrats viewed the new Republican administration and its "Reagan Revolution" as a dangerous political threat that needed to be countered. But the President's strong popularity with the American people meant they needed to proceed carefully in their political opposition. Central America offered congressional Democrats an ideal issue with which to sustain a political attack on the White House, because public opinion on it so strongly opposed the President and U.S. involvement. Central America, in other words, was one weak spot in the Reagan agenda where Democrats discovered they had political leverage to counter the President. According to Destler (1984: 322), "they suddenly had a foreign policy issue on which they could take the offensive." According to Falcoff (1984: 377), "the Democratic approach was purely negative: to make the Central American issue a permanent embarrassment for the administration." Led by a group of vocal legislators—such as Michael Barnes, Edward Boland, Gerry Studds, David Bonior, Christopher Dodd, and Joseph Moakley—congressional Democrats capitalized on the Central America issue by engaging the President, with "unrelenting attacks," in an ongoing, politically costly battle (Felton 1983: 668). To what extent this was motivated by genuine concern for the Central American people or by political expediency is uncertain. What is certain is that this partisan conflict generated a key political opportunity for grassroots activists seeking to defeat the administration's policy. It provided a partially effective institutional channel through which to direct their grassroots opposition.

Understanding the partial effectiveness of working through Congress to restrain White House foreign policy brings us back to the legacy of Vietnam. The Vietnam War represented the apex—until the 1980s, at least—of a two-hundred-year-long process of the enlargement of the foreign policy powers of the executive branch (Sundquist

1981; Falcoff 1984: 370–72). President Johnson's 1964 sending of a half million U.S. troops without a declaration of war and President Nixon's 1969 secret bombing of and 1970 invasion of Cambodia revealed the degree to which Congress's constitutional right to declare foreign wars had been abrogated by the "imperial presidency" (Lake 1976). At the war's end and after the Watergate scandal, Congress responded by instituting a set of new laws, procedures, and organizational provisions designed to safeguard against presidential abuses of power that threatened constitutional democracy in the U.S. (Arnson 1988: 37). These safeguards sought to access information about executive activities, to restore congressional legislative authority in foreign policy, and to establish limits on executive-ordered covert operations (Sharpe 1988: 18). The 1972 Case-Zablocki Act, for example, required the president to report to Congress the making of any secret executive agreements. The 1973 War Powers Resolution required any president committing U.S. troops to hostile actions to inform Congress within forty-eight hours with a written explanation of the justification and nature of the commitment; if the Congress rejected the deployment, the president was obliged to withdraw the troops within sixty days. And the Hughes-Ryan amendment of 1974 compelled the president to report promptly all CIA covert operations to appropriate congressional committees, which could then monitor or even obstruct those operations (Sharpe 1988: 18–20; also see Destler 1981).

In addition to this congressional reassertion of control over foreign policy, administration opponents were aided by a decisive shift in the composition of key congressional committees. Although Congress as a whole had shifted in a conservative direction in 1981, three committees that handled administration requests for aid had become more liberal. According to Destler (1984: 322–23; also see Best 1987: 35):

> The Senate may have swung sharply to the right, but the new members of the Foreign Relations Committee were foreign policy liberals . . . or moderates. . . . This atypically liberal committee, with its moderate chairman, Charles Percy (R-Ill.), not one to dominate his colleagues, would be passing on administration policies. Helms was isolated as a hard-line conservative, and among the other Republicans only Majority leader Howard Baker (R-TN) and Richard Lugar (R-IN) were reliable administration supporters. The shift at House Foreign Affairs was more visible and dramatic. . . . In 1981, committee Democrats, seeking activist leadership to challenge the new administration, replaced veteran [chairman Gus] Yatron with a liberal sophomore, Michael Barnes

(D-MD). . . . His activism gave critics a focal point, an alternative power center to schedule hearings and publicize dissenting views. Finally, the Foreign Operations Subcommittee of House Appropriations continued to offer an impediment to administration proposals. It had the power of first review for actual aid appropriations, and a de facto veto power over "reprogramming," shifting of funds from one aid account to another. Its moderate, idiosyncratic chairman, Clarence Long (D-MD), was reinforced in his skepticism about military aid by six very liberal Democrats. Thus, administration majorities on the thirteen-man subcommittee were hard to find. So when the administration showed (intentionally) its toughness and (inadvertently) its political vulnerability, there were strategically placed critics ready to resist.

This post-Vietnam legislative legacy and the liberal domination of key committees afforded Central America activists working through Congress the institutional potential to challenge White House policy. The activists successfully exploited this political opportunity of divided government. At the same time, however, they soon discovered that this political leverage carried its own significant limitations and drawbacks, which we will explore in chapter 8.

Another manifestation of elite division in the U.S. political system in the 1980s that served to strengthen the political hand of the Central America peace movement was the vocal opposition to President Reagan's Central America policy articulated by a host of respected foreign policy analysts and strategists—including former diplomats, former State Department, CIA, and NSC officials, academic political scientists, and Washington think-tank scholars. Few of these policy elites disputed administration strategy with the conscious intention of strengthening or endorsing the grassroots Central America peace movement. Their positions were motivated more by simple intellectual conviction and political self-interest. But these foreign policy specialists' critical analyses of the President's policy—calling it, for example, "arrant nonsense" (Rogers and Meyers 1982: 15)—lent valuable credibility and affirmation to those championing an anti-administration cause.

Broad and vocal opposition to the White House from within the foreign policy establishment is explicable on two grounds. First, a multitude of foreign policy analysts—especially academic political scientists—genuinely believed White House policy was ill conceived, unwarranted, and calamitous in its consequences. They felt morally and intellectually obliged to criticize the President's policy and to advocate an alternative U.S. strategy in Central America. There were also political dynamics and personal vendettas generating this opposition as well. Many of these foreign policy makers were "exiled" in 1981 from positions of power, removed by the Reagan administration, often indelicately. According to Schoultz (1987: 9–10):

> President Reagan's team sought to minimize conflict within the executive branch by permitting only one point of view to be represented among the individuals making U.S. policy toward Latin America. According to one observer, the administration conducted "one of the most thorough purges in State Department history." . . . An attempt was clearly made to simplify policy making by eliminating divergent policy perspectives. . . . Diplomats were not simply removed from their posts; they were in effect fired from the Foreign Service. . . . According to George Gedda, "virtually all of the career diplomats who guided Central America policy during the Carter years either saw their careers set back or found themselves . . . out of the Foreign Service altogether."

Rubin (1984: 303–4) wrote, for example,

> Ambassador to El Salvador Robert White . . . was ousted within 10 days and offered no new assignment. Other ARA [Department of State's Bureau of Inter-American Affairs] personnel, like Deputy Assistant Secretary James Cheek . . . were sent to posts outside the hemisphere. Ambassador Lawrence Pezzullo, who remained in Nicaragua well into 1981, later became diplomat-in-residence at a U.S. university. . . . [President] Carter's last assistant secretary of ARA, William Bowdler, was dismissed within 24 hours of Reagan's inaugural, although, as a Foreign Service officer (FSO), he could normally have expected an ambassadorial post.

"By tradition," writes Schoultz (1987: 9), "high-ranking FSOs enter retirement at a department ceremony, during which they are presented with the flag that had stood in their last office. Mr. Bowdler, who had risen through the ranks during a thirty year career to become Ambassador to South Africa, Guatemala, El Salvador, and finally Assistant Secretary of State, received his flag in the mail in a manila envelope." This abrupt and sometimes discourteous changing of the guard helped to generate a tremendous amount of resentment among many establishment foreign policy makers. Many of them, in turn, spent much of the decade publicly and disparagingly analyzing the policy of the administration that had turned them out of office. Battles over political turf helped generate significant division within the foreign policy elite. This represented, in part, in the words of David Meyer (1990: 96), nothing more than a rear-guard action against a new ascendent group, designed not to empower new groups but to prevent the entrenchment of a new elite. . . . Many of the architects of U.S. defense policy for the 20 years before Reagan's presidency attacked the new administration's policies. That was at least partly a reaction to the presence of a new contingent . . . in an unaccustomed position of power. The old guard . . . was . . . concerned with restoring previous foreign and military policies.

This division among policy elites, and the scathing criticism of administration policy it engendered, may not have been intended to "empower new groups," such as the Central America peace movement. But empowerment was assuredly one of its unintended consequences. When many experienced policy makers and foreign diplomats, such as Ambassador Robert White, for example, wrote in journals and testified before Congress that (quoted in Schoultz 1987: 63, 137) "the Salvadorans on whom the success of the Reagan formula depends are rotten to the core," that "it is a grave, and if we continue it, fatal, error to believe that we are confronting primarily a case of Communist aggression in Central America," that "the United States is not producing evidence" of Nicaraguan arms shipments to El Salvador "because they do not have it," and that the President's policy assumptions reflect "towering ignorance," the position of grassroots opponents of the President's policy automatically acquired increased plausibility and regard.

White House Policy Blunders

President Reagan's preoccupation with Central America, the Vietnam syndrome, and division among U.S. political elites created a favorable structure of political opportunities within which the Central America peace movement could act. In addition, as the movement mobilized and struggled over the years, a series of political mistakes and scandals associated with the administration's Central America policy damaged the White House's political power and indirectly enhanced the relative power of the Central America peace movement.

The White House's first significant political mistake was the extremely assertive and sometimes imperious and shrill tone of its initial campaign to confront what it believed was communist aggression in Central America. Many in Congress and the American public felt the administration was being too pushy and alarmist and reacted with skepticism and resistance. According to Best (1987: 40), "The exaggerations, distortions, and even misrepresentations by administration figures created a clear 'credibility gap' with many in Congress and the public, and helped to provoke a wave of counter-rhetoric." Falcoff (1984: 372) writes that congressional resistance to White House policy was

> nourished by the Reagan administration's own maladroit actions. In the early months of 1981, for example, an exasperated Secretary Haig threatened at one point to recur to already appropriated "emergency funds" if Congress failed to authorize the requested amount of military aid for El Salvador or, worse still, to go over the heads of Congress and appeal directly to the American people. This sort of thing was bound to alienate even administration supporters in the Senate and House.

In the face of immense public and congressional reaction, the administration quickly backed off and toned down its rhetoric. However, although for two years it attempted cooperation with Congress, the White House still continued to pursue overt and covert military solutions to its problems in Central America. This eventually led to the administration's next significant political fumble.

In March 1983, the administration's covert support for the Nicaraguan rebel army, the Contras, was, through a flurry of press reports, becoming an increasingly "open secret." In April, four congressional committees insisted on being briefed by White House officials on the exact nature and scope of the covert support. What was divulged rankled many in Congress, who felt crossed because administration actions appeared to violate "the Boland Amendment," a law passed in December 1982 prohibiting U.S. aid targeted to overthrow Nicaragua's Sandinista regime. Chairman of the Western Hemisphere Affairs Subcommittee of House Foreign Affairs, Michael Barnes (D-Md.), for example, complained (quoted in Felton 1983: 703), "Congress intended to prohibit the administration from trying to take paramilitary action against Nicaragua, but they [the administration] have ignored it. I think they're in pretty obvious violation of the law." Piqued Democrats on Barnes's subcommittee reacted by passing a more exacting version of the Boland Amendment that strictly limited Contra aid funds (Destler 1984: 329). In addition, for the time being, they "gutted" the President's annual budgetary request for Central American aid, giving the administration "the most severe beating it has yet met in Congress" (Felton 1983b: 736).

One year later, the White House again angered congressional leaders of both parties with another political misstep. Desperate for emergency funds for El Salvador and the Contras, the administration decided to bypass two key congressional committees and attach a $21 million aid package to a Senate low-income energy assistance bill. But because this "violated jurisdiction, which is sacrosanct in Congress," the Republican-controlled Senate Appropriations Committee rejected the President's request (Felton 1984a: 542). Committee Chairman Pete Domenici (R–N. Mex.) bristled about the "extemporaneous, under-the-gun" administration lobbying. "If the State Department," he fumed, "is going to manage the remaining activities in the way they have managed this so far, I guarantee them and I guarantee the President, they are going to fail." Chairman of the bypassed Senate Intelligence Committee, Barry Goldwater (R-Ariz.), also was furious at the White House's actions (Felton 1984a: 542).

That altercation was suddenly eclipsed, however, by the political tidal wave that broke over Capitol Hill on the week of April 9, 1984. It was revealed that the CIA had, with the President's approval, orchestrated the mining of Nicaraguan harbors. This incident provoked a firestorm of criticism from political leaders around the world. In Washington, congressional Democrats and Republicans seethed because not only was the mining flagrantly illegal, but appropriate congressional committees had not been properly informed by the White House of such activities (Felton 1985: 711). Senator Patrick Moynihan (D-N.Y.), for example, resigned in disgust as Vice-Chairman of the Intelligence Committee, protesting the lack of appropriate notification. Committee Chairman Goldwater sent a blistering open letter to William Casey, the head of the CIA, in which he wrote (quoted in Felton 1984: 833):

> It gets down to one, little, simple phrase: I am pissed off! . . . Bill, this is no way to run a railroad and I find myself in a hell of a quandary. I am forced to apologize to the members of the Intelligence Committee because I did not know the facts on this. . . . The President has asked us to back his foreign policy. Bill, how can we back his foreign policy when we don't know what the hell he is doing? . . . Mine the harbors of Nicaragua? This is an act violating international law. It is an act of war. . . . I don't like this. I don't like it one bit from the President or from you. . . . In the future, if anything like this happens, I'm going to raise one hell of a lot of fuss about it in public.

The White House attempted to defend the legality of the mining as an act of "collective self-defense," which only further infuriated members of Congress. The whole incident provoked weeks of "intensive battling" in Washington that left the Central America issue an "open wound" on Capitol Hill (Felton 1984b: 835). Eventually, CIA Director Casey issued apologies to select members of the Senate for his failure to inform them about CIA involvement in the harbor minings (Felton 1984c: 957). The next month, however, angry congressional leaders discovered that the CIA again had failed to apprise them of covert CIA involvement in El Salvador's 1984 presidential election on behalf of the White House's favored candidate, José Napoleón Duarte (Felton 1984: 1091).

Six months later, another major scandal damaged the President's political position on Central America. In October 1984, the national press reported the discovery in Honduras of two secret training manuals written and published by the CIA and distributed to Nicaraguan Contra officers (Sklar 1988: 177–87). The first, entitled *Freedom Fighters Manual,* used comic-book graphics to illustrate thirty-eight forms of sabotage of government-owned property and economic infrastructure. The manual taught "how to damage office equipment, clog toilets, slash tires, puncture gas tanks, destroy engines of government vehicles, tear down electrical and telephone wires, set warehouses on fire, and manufacture molotov cocktail bombs" (Kornbluh 1987: 43). The second and more politically damaging manual, *Psychological Operations in Guerrilla Warfare,* gave lessons on, among other things, how to "create martyrs" for the Contra cause and terrorize a population by kidnaping and assassinating civilians and government officials. One passage (quoted in Kornbluh 1987: 45) instructed: "It is possible to neutralize [i.e. murder] carefully selected and planned targets, such as court judges, magistrates, police and state security officials, etc. For psychological purposes, it is necessary . . . to gather together the population affected, so that they will be present, take part in the act, and formulate accusations against the oppressor."

The later manual, which the Washington Post called the "CIA's Murder Manual," violated a 1976 Presidential Executive Order, issued by Gerald Ford, that prohibited U.S. government involvement in assassinations. It also violated the moral sensibilities of many Americans and congressional leaders who believed that, in the words of Edward Boland (quoted in Felton 1984: 2875), the manual "should never have been produced by any element of the U.S. government. It espouses the doctrine of Lenin, not Jefferson." The 1984 manual scandal killed any consideration of Congress passing a Contra aid bill until March of 1985. Instead, Congress, led by the House Intelligence Committee, quickly approved an even more strictly worded Boland Amendment, which prohibited any government agency from expending any funds toward "supporting, directly or indirectly, military or paramilitary operations in Nicaragua by any nation, group, organization, movement, or individual" (Sharpe 1988: 26).

The administration's support for the Contras, it seemed, had finally been curtailed. But the White House was determined to keep the Contras fighting and set about to circumvent the law, thus setting itself up for the next and biggest politically damaging exposé of the decade: the Iran-Contra scandal. On October 5, 1986, an American mercenary named Eugene Hasenfus was captured by Nicaraguan troops when his plane, carrying ten thousand pounds of U.S. NSC-supplied ammunition, rifles, and grenade launchers to the Contras, was shot down over Nicaragua. Hasenfus's capture and a paper trail of evidence led to revelations of a major illegal White House enterprise to aid the Contras.[7] In the following months, the country learned that the NSC—under the leadership of Lt. Col. Oliver North, working out of the White House—had organized a network of private support for the Contras, had secretly raised millions of dollars for the Contras from foreign governments, including $30 million from Saudi Arabia, and had diverted to the Contras millions of dollars of profits from secret and illegal arms sales to Iran. According to the report of the Tower Commission that investigated the Iran-Contra affair (quoted in Barry, Vergara and Castro 1988: 80), "The National Security Council [was] led by reckless cowboys, off on their own wild ride, taking direct operational control of matters that are the customary province of more sober agencies. . . . A kind of parallel government came into being, operating in secret, paying scant heed to laws, deceiving Congress and avoiding oversight of any kind."

The country also learned that, since 1984, the CIA had been secretly aiding the Contras, providing communications support, and seeking political backing in Europe and South America. All of this transpired with the knowledge, approval, or involvement of National Security Adviser Robert McFarlane, CIA Director William Casey, National Security Adviser John Poindexter, Secretary of State George Shultz, Secretary of Defense Caspar Weinberger, and, the record now shows, President Reagan and Vice President Bush (Draper 1987; Sklar 1988: 326).

The Iran-Contra affair hit Washington and the nation like a bombshell. The NSC and CIA operations blatantly violated the congressional ban on aid to the Contras. White House lies and an NSC coverup constituted an obstruction of justice and violated public trust in the executive. Furthermore, arms sales to Iran in exchange for the release of U.S. hostages held in Lebanon brazenly contradicted President Reagan's public condemnation of negotiating with terrorists. In the words of one White House official involved in the operations (quoted in Ignatius 1986): "Legality was viewed as an obstacle that had to be gotten around. That was the spirit of the program." All of this seriously sapped the President's political strength on Central America and further eroded already weak congressional support for the Contras. Although the administration did its best at damage control, one senior White House official remarked that the scandal was "probably an unrecoverable disaster for the contras," and for the administration's Central America policy (Brinkley 1986b). Most of the White House's ardent advocates for the Contras left or were removed from office in the wake of the revelations (Millett 1988: 401). Although Congress would subsequently approve moderate amounts of "nonlethal" and "humanitarian" aid in 1987 and 1988, especially after a Contra-Sandinista cease-fire agreement, Congress would henceforth refuse to approve military aid to the Contras.

These political fumbles and scandals—the administration's alienating rhetoric, the CIA's lack of communication with Congress, the mining of Nicaraguan harbors, the discovered CIA manuals, and the Iran-Contra affair—had the indirect effect of bolstering the position of the Central America peace movement. They did so by generating public and congressional hostility and resistance to the administration, by discrediting the logic undergirding the White House's Central America policy, and by weakening the moral persuasiveness and political power of the President to win military aid for the Contras and El Salvador. Altogether, these political blunders, the high-profile nature of the Central America issue, the Vietnam syndrome, and the deep division among government and policy elites afforded Central America peace activists a relatively open structure of political opportunities upon which to capitalize in their struggle to defeat the President's Central America policy.

STRONG ORGANIZATIONAL NETWORKS

Would-be peace activists cannot exploit political opportunities, however favorable they may be, without mechanisms that enable them to form groups, communicate, make decisions, and execute coordinated actions. The successful emergence of a social movement, in other words, requires bridging the gap between aggrieved individuals at the micro-level and favorable political conditions at the macro-level. These disparate levels are best linked through meso-level organizational structures—institutionalized networks of communication, decision making, and action—that facilitate the mobilization and deployment of protest. Organizations perform this function by coordinating members, leaders, information networks, recruitment mechanisms, group identities, communication channels, solidary incentives, and enterprise tools in ways that channel the energy of insurgent consciousness into effective collective action for political change. The remainder of this chapter examines the formation of an organizational structure strong enough to sustain the Central America peace movement's emergence and ongoing struggle. We begin by examining a type of organization that was absolutely critical in generating the life of the Central America peace movement.

Movement Midwives

The emergence of a social movement usually consists, in part, in the formation of new movement organizations dedicated to directly carrying on the movement's struggle. We may call these "movement carriers." But, typically, movement-carrier organizations themselves are born into existence only with the help of supportive, preexistent organizations. These antecedent organizations intentionally foster the initial emergence of a movement by helping to organize movement carriers, without ever actually themselves becoming movement-carrier organizations. This kind of organizations we may call "movement midwives," in recognition of their deliberate efforts to help in the "birthing" of movements while retaining identities distinct from those of the resultant organizations.[8]

The Central America peace movement was neither self-begotten nor created *ex nihilo*. Rather, it was constructed with assistance from and out of materials found in preexisting organizations. Many of these organizations themselves were not primarily interested in Central America issues. But, just as nurse midwives do not actually conceive nor bear the children they help to deliver yet play a vital role in their delivery, these organizations neither actually "caused" nor "became" the Central America peace movement yet played an absolutely indispensable role in facilitating that movement's emergence. Specifically, they lent their financial resources, leadership abilities, building facilities, legal advice, organizational sponsorships, membership lists, and communications networks to help construct new movement-carrier organizations.[9]

The story we have narrated thus far clearly highlights the importance of movement midwives in the emerging life of the Central America peace movement. Sanctuary was launched from an underlying organizational platform provided by the Manzo Area Council, the national organization of the Society of Friends (Quakers), the Tucson Ecumenical Council, the Southside Presbyterian Church, the Unitarian Universalist Service Committee, the Chicago Religious Task Force on Central America, and other organizations. Without the prior existence and support of this complex of organizations, Sanctuary simply would not have appeared. Similarly, Witness for Peace in various ways was indebted for its life to the Carolina Interfaith Task Force on Central America, Clergy and Laity Concerned, the American Friends Service Committee, the New York InterReligious Task Force on Central America, the Fellowship of Reconciliation, the Presbyterian Church U.S.A., Sojourners Peace Ministry, the Convent of the Good Shepherd, and a host of other denominations and peace organizations that assisted its formation. The Pledge of Resistance was born and sustained only through the collective contribution of the New Abolitionist Covenant retreat group, *Sojourners* magazine, the San Francisco office of the American Friends Service Committee, Witness for Peace, and the more than thirty other organizations that early on endorsed, sponsored, and promoted the Pledge.[10]

Jim Wallis, of *Sojourners* magazine and community, noting the particular importance of support from institutional church structures in facilitating religious activism (1991: 11–12), observes a "crucial partnership between the church as a movement and the church as an institution. Grassroots groups, national organizations, churches, councils of churches, and whole denominations are working closely together on a variety of [social] concerns. . . . That creative cooperation now makes many things possible that were not possible before, and undergirds the church's witness on many critical issues."

Especially vital for newly forming Central America peace movement carrier groups were the financial resources that many religious denominations furnished activist groups. In the three years between 1984 to 1987, for example, the United Methodist Church alone gave $10,000 to the Sanctuary movement, $20,000 to Witness for Peace,

$2,500 to a Witness for Peace Women's Delegation, $25,290 to the InterReligious Task Force on Central America, $2,250 to the National Sanctuary Defense Fund, $2,500 to the Christic Institute—which was prosecuting a lawsuit against twenty-nine individuals involved in the Iran-Contra affair—and a total of $75,332 to five other organizations engaged in Nicaragua activism (Wilson 1988: 88–89). With this kind of giving, Witness for Peace was able to raise, in its first five *weeks* of existence, $25,000 in cash, $13,000 in grants pledged, and four pledges for regional offices totaling to $1,100 per month (Griffin-Nolan 1991: 68).[11] According to Witness for Peace organizer Betsy Crites (1992),

> The churches were important because our board of advisors were religious leaders, representative heads of churches, and they would sign our direct-mail fund-raising letters. Some were also judicatories that would grant church funds to our programs. That lent legitimacy and funding. The Church of the Brethren and the United Church of Christ supported long-term delegates, paying the bill for long-termers who were from their denominations. The Mennonites provided us a number of months of free housing in Managua for our long-termers. We also got big grants from the Presbyterians and the Unitarian Universalists. All of that was very important help.

Equally important was the extensive and immediate publicity that religious organizations provided newly emerging movement carriers by promoting them throughout their communication networks. Such infusions of money and diffusion of publicity at critical moments in organizations' development can make the difference between political insignificance and the rapid expansion to positions of influence.

Interestingly, for all of their importance in assisting the formation of new movement carriers, preexistent movement-midwife organizations appeared to have been fairly ineffective in actually directly mobilizing insurgent protest. Their established stability and bureaucratic formality seem to produce a certain sluggishness that inhibits the kind of high-intensity organizing needed to mobilize insurgency. Recall, for example, that after returning from their April 1983 trip to Nicaragua, Gail Phares, Jeff Boyer, and Gil Joseph spent two weeks trying to get only one out of many national religious organizations to agree to organize their proposed July "Action for Peace" trip. The entire project was almost aborted when, fearing its risks and immensity, no national organization would take it on. According to Phares (1992), "The people I called thought it was a great idea, that it had to be done.

But a week later they would call me back and say, 'My board of directors think I'm too busy to take this on.'" Clergy and Laity Concerned,
the American Friends Service Committee, the InterReligious Task
Force on Central America, and many other national groups eventually proved very helpful providing contacts, publicity, and sponsorship
to the Witness for Peace mobilization. But it took a small team of
impassioned entrepreneurs working the phones around the clock for
six weeks to actually carry the embryonic dream of Witness for Peace
to its next critical stage.

Similarly, at the October 16 Washington, D.C., meeting to organize
the Pledge of Resistance, it was agreed that the National Council of
Churches' New York InterReligious Task Force on Central America
would take primary responsibility to coordinate the Pledge nationally. But, despite the commonly agreed-upon urgency to mobilize quickly, the Pledge languished for weeks afterwards. As reported by Jim
Rice (1992), a Sojourners community activist who eventually took up
the coordination of the Pledge, "The Pledge took a while to get organized nationally. The InterReligious Task Force was supposed to take
it on. But it just didn't get it going and nothing really happened. Finally they said they just couldn't do it, so we said, 'Fine, we'll do it.' We
took over and pulled the national infrastructure together over the next
two weeks working full-time. Two of us just started calling contacts
until we had state coordinators set up across the country."

Once again, the more established preexistent organization—which
did play a very important *supportive* role for many Central America
peace movement carrier groups—proved ineffective in its attempt to
directly mobilize insurgency. Such work was better accomplished by
movement entrepreneurs working in more informal, flexible, and fervent contexts. Appropriate functional specialization, in other words,
by different types of organizations related to a budding movement
appears critical for the successful emergence of protest.

Feeder Organizations

Movement-midwife organizations help to build a social movement's organizational strength by facilitating the initial formation of
new movement-carrier organizations. But another type of preexistent
organization, not actually belonging to a social movement, can also
fortify the organizational strength of a movement by serving as a con-
duit that channels an ongoing supply of new members to the movement. These organizations function for social movements as do tribu-

tary streams for rivers, collecting and routing elements from a wide social or geographical area into one single, strong current flowing in a common direction. We may call these "feeder organizations." Virtually any existing group can function as a feeder organization. In the history of social movements, all sorts of organizations have done so, including political parties, ethnic clubs, student associations, consciousness-raising discussion groups, churches, drinking associations, black colleges, labor unions, kinship groups, hunting and athletic clubs, religious orders, and service organizations. Two types of feeder organizations particularly important in supplying new activists for the Central America peace movement were established religious organizations and preexistent political activist groups. Innumerable individual churches, synagogues, and denominational organizations, combined with already activated grassroots political groups, provided structural conduits that over the decade channeled tens of thousands of their members into Central America activism.

The important role of churches and synagogues as feeder organizations is most obvious in the Sanctuary movement, where entire congregations would vote to become involved in refugee work. Simply by being members of religious congregations that eventually declared Sanctuary, tens of thousands of Americans were drawn into the Central America peace movement, entirely apart from any original interest in Central America activism. Usually, it only took the initiative of an individual member or leader of the congregation or of someone in another local church already involved in the movement to introduce a church or synagogue to Sanctuary and energetically press the congregation to declare Sanctuary (Hildreth 1989: 80–83; Lorentzen 1991: 34–45). Typically, the decision-making process was politically educational for the congregation's members (Golden and McConnell 1986: 131–37; Little 1989). The testimonies of refugees given to the congregations were particularly enlightening.

Preexistent feeder organizations, both religious and political, were also essential to the Pledge of Resistance's rapid growth. According to James Hannon (1991: 262), "Most recruitment to the Pledge took the form of bloc recruitment from pre-existing groups." In his study of the Boston-area Pledge, Hannon observed (1991: 261–62), "The importance of pre-existing, cooptable groups and networks is quite clear in the case of the Pledge. Of my twenty-one informants, all but two were members of pre-existing groups which joined the Pledge together and went on to constitute their own affinity group or formed the core of an affinity group which collected additional members from among Pledge recruits."

Pledge leaders used the credibility and communication channels of sponsoring organizations to promoted the Pledge. According to Hannon (1991: 265):

> By October 1984, the national steering committee of the Pledge had incorporated secular and more partisan organizations who represented the national leadership of the anti-intervention movement. . . . Each of these national organizations had their own supporters who could now view the Pledge as a representative and politically-astute coalition. All of the member organizations were able to publicize the Pledge through their own membership networks and publications. The availability of the mailing lists of these organizations facilitated the direct mail efforts of the national Pledge office which reached supporters throughout the country.

Furthermore, at the level of individual relationships, through a "strength of weak ties" dynamic (Granovetter 1973), information about the Pledge quickly spread like a virus across and within a broad range of existing religious and political groups, attracting a multitude of already organized members to Pledge activism. Hannon wrote (1991: 262), "Individual members of groups such as church congregations, political organizations, and residential cooperatives learned about the Pledge from colleagues in other groups. . . . In turn, they would educate other group members about the Pledge and begin the process of recruitment and the formation of affinity groups."

This was the conscious intention of national Pledge organizers who, in an article titled "Organizing a Local Pledge Campaign" published in the *Pledge Handbook* (Emergency Response Network 1986: 25), encouraged local Pledge organizers to foster "networking between the Pledge Campaign and already established solidarity, peace, justice, and religious groups. The Pledge Campaign should not, except in rare cases, start from scratch. The campaign depends in large measure on groups networking together and inviting those organizations to circulate and promote the pledge, participate in specific tasks of the campaign, etc."

Finally, churches were also important recruiting grounds for Witness for Peace. According to Gail Phares (1992), "Most of the people who do Witness for Peace are sent to us from their churches." In many cases, information about Witness for Peace would travel through church networks by informal word of mouth, especially through the stories told by delegates returning home from Nicaragua. Most of the entire first year's delegations were recruited by the 156 delegates on the original July 1983 trip. Phares recalls (1992): "We put out a call to the first 156 people and asked them to recruit and lead delegations. Within six weeks, we had booked a year's schedule of delegations from states all over the country, going one after another, being led by those first 156 people."

This kind of word-of-mouth recruiting in churches was fairly effortless, according to Mike Clark (1992): "In the early years, 1984–1986, you could literally say, 'We're sending a trip in two months,' and twenty people immediately signed up. There were thousands of church people in the U.S. who wanted to have such an experience and recruiting delegations was fairly easy." Often many religious denominations approached Witness for Peace with already fully organized delegations (Crites 1992).

Witness for Peace activists, however, did not rely solely on spontaneous, word-of-mouth recruitment. Sometimes, contacts in feeder organizations were used to "prime the pump." Gail Phares has said, "I'd call Father Jim Lewis in the Episcopal diocese and say, 'Hey Jim, I need a doctor from Charolette and someone else from Greensborough.' And he goes and gets them. And I'd call sister Joan Jersky at the Catholic diocese and say, 'Hey, can you recruit someone from here and here?' Then the word passes around and one person who's been gotten will then go and recruit somebody else themself."

The highly organized network of religious organizations made this kind of recruitment possible. According to Fran Truitt (1990): "Even if you don't know people, you know how to get in touch with people, because you are part of the universal church. That's how we have been able to do all sorts of projects." Jane Guise, of the Boston-area AFSC, recalls her intermediary role feeding people, at Witness for Peace's request, into the movement (1990): "I put together the first Witness for Peace delegation from New England. My role in a lot of these things has been as a catalyst. I got something in the mail from Witness for Peace informing me of the work and inviting me to put together a local delegation. I thought it was a wonderful thing to support. My delegation was formed through already-existing networks and contacts. We had staff in every state at that time that recommended people they knew."

In addition, hoping to exploit fully these rich sources of new activists, Witness for Peace deliberately marketed its cause to the members of religious feeder organizations, employing the communication networks of these religious groups. Witness for Peace President Sam Hope (1992) offers an example:

> When a Presbyterian church leader would protest and get arrested, for instance, we would have a photographer there and would take his story with pictures and send it to the Presbyterian church headquarters with the headline, you know, "Church Moderator Arrested at the Capitol." This had a very powerful effect. It would get on the church wires and go out like an alternate news network. The religious news network was very important to us. We would have long-term delegates come back to the U.S. and tell their story to religious reporters, of what they'd seen and heard in Central America, who would then write it up in the *National Catholic Reporter* or *The Methodist* or the *Episcopal Witness* magazines. This had enormous impact drawing people in, because their readerships were in the millions. That was a tool that was very effective.

Additionally, some Witness for Peace organizers strategically recruited delegates in preexistent organizations. Gail Phares, for example, explains her style (1992):

> I sit down and decide who I want on delegations—which towns still need interfaith task forces, which churches still need to be influenced—and go after them. It's very intentional. I do personal letters and phone calls. If you want to impact the church, you've got to get the right church people going, not just Joe Schmoe. You need him too, but you also need plenty of people who can have an impact. Recruiting takes real effort. Some people think they send out a brochure and a bunch of letters and wha-la, they're going to have a delegation. What really helps is person-to-person contact, telephone calls where you say, "You've got to go on this delegation." If I really want someone to go, I'll get all kinds of people working on it, their pastors, colleagues, friends, saying "Hey, you've really got to do this." You have got to pat them on the back, be affirming, really work on them.[12]

Whether self-recruited or deliberately recruited by Central America peace movement activists, the bulk of Central America activists were channeled into the Central America peace movement through preexistent religious and political feeder organizations. In addition to the above evidence, this study's survey data clearly confirms the special significance of religious feeder organizations in building the Central America peace movement's membership. Of the Sanctuary activists surveyed, 35 percent first heard about the Sanctuary movement through their church or synagogue, 13 percent through a religious publication to which they subscribed, and 9 percent through their religious denomination's promotion of Sanctuary. Of Witness for Peace activists surveyed, 19 percent first heard about Witness for Peace through a religious publication they read and 9 percent through contacts at their church or synagogue. Thus, well over one-half of Sanctuary and more than one-quarter of Witness for Peace activists were acquired by the movement through preexistent religious feeder organizations.[13] We will further examine reasons for this dynamic among religious groups in the next chapter.

Demise of the Nuclear Freeze

In addition to gaining new members through a multitude of feeder organizations, the Central America peace movement also acquired many thousands of new activist members when a competing wave of the American peace movement began rapidly to recede. In the early 1980s, shortly after Ronald Reagan was first elected president, the nuclear freeze movement broke into the American political arena with astonishing swiftness and energy. In a handful of years, it mobilized millions of activists in opposition to the Reagan administration's nuclear arms policy. The movement appeared to be riding a wave to success when on June 12, 1982, one million demonstrators marched in New York City in support of the freeze. But the freeze campaign was plagued by underlying strategic and political defects, including the lack of public education about nuclear issues, the cooptation of the proposal by opportunistic politicians, and the Reagan administration's tenacity in promoting its nuclear arms policy. By mid-1983 the freeze began to show signs of breakdown. A year later, the freeze movement had all but collapsed.

As the nuclear freeze campaign was beginning to disintegrate in 1983, the Reagan administration launched a renewed political offensive on its Central America policy, generating an explosion of media stories about the Central America crisis (see figures 5.1, 5.2, and 5.3) and a surge of political momentum for the Central America peace movement. This attracted the attention of many freeze activists, who began increasingly to get involved in Central America peace work. According to Molander and Molander (1990: 49–50), "As the freeze and other antinuclear war movement groups struggled to keep people focused on nuclear weapons–related issues, across the country local chapters of ESR, PSR, Ground Zero, and other peace and social justice groups turned their attention to [the Central America crisis]." And Meyer says (1990: 64, 67): "The institutionalized [freeze] movement was . . . unable to respond effectively to new political issues; it could not . . . incorporate growing public concern with escalating conflict in Central America. . . . The freeze movement ceded the political space for social movements to other issues and groups. . . . Heightened conflict in Central America . . . came to occupy much activist concern, drawing antinuclear movement resources and support."

Besides not suffering from the same organizational and political problems that were damaging the freeze campaign, the Central America peace movement enjoyed the distinct advantage of possessing what to many activists seemed a more concrete, manageable protest issue. Pledge of Resistance organizer Ken Butigan, who was originally involved in the anti-nuclear movement, explains (1991):

> The Central America movement absorbed many people from other movements, especially from the anti-nuclear movement. They just flowed into Central America work. You see, as terrible as a nuclear holocaust would be, it is also somewhat abstract. It's the ultimate "big one," further down the road. Anti-nuclear activists in the early 1980s came to see that reversing the arms race would mean reversing the trajectory of human culture. It's a long-term haul. So some of the edge came off. Then you start to hear about real human beings next door being killed right now because the U.S. has a gun to their heads. And you have the Sanctuary movement with refugees in living rooms talking about that horror. So, many people just moved on from the anti-nuclear movement to Central America activism.

Witness for Peace Director Mike Clark, who was a leader in the New York freeze campaign, concurs (1992):

> The blunting of the anti-nuclear movement was important. There was an energy on the part of activists and progressive people in the religious community who took their energy and jumped into Central America activism. They were not just looking for another cause, they weren't action-junkies, just people who, when presented with a moral crisis that looked somewhat more manageable, got involved. The Central America movement still would have happened without the freeze's demise. But it wouldn't have been as momentous without the preceding anti-nuclear movement that people, particularly from the progressive religious community, had participated in. When the anti-nuclear movement failed to produce results, people went around, like a river around rocks, and found some other place to channel their basic commitment to creating a better world.

The importance of the nuclear freeze campaign's demise in bolstering the Central America peace movement's organizational strength is also evident in this study's survey data. Central America peace activists had a great deal of prior experience in a variety of other social movements, as we will see in chapter 7. But the movement in which Central America activists had the greatest prior involvement was the anti-nuclear arms movement. Sixty-six percent of Sanctuary and 78 percent of Witness for Peace activists reported involvement in the anti–nuclear weapons freeze campaign before joining Sanctuary and Witness for Peace. For both groups, the period of greatest influx into the Central America movement by anti-nuclear activists was exactly the time of the nuclear freeze campaign's disintegration: 1983–84 for Sanctuary activists and 1984 for Witness for Peace delegates. Undoubtedly, the freeze campaign's failure was the Central America peace movement's fortune.

Movement-Carrier Groups

Thousands of preexistent movement midwives and feeder organizations played supportive roles in facilitating the Central America peace movement's emergence and growth. But it took the mobilization of more than fifteen hundred movement-carrier groups in all fifty states to execute the essential political work of the movement. Some of these Central America organizations were started from scratch. Others had been intact political-activist groups that in the early 1980s were converted from other issues to Central America activism. These Central America peace movement carriers were local, regional, and national organizations that engaged in a variety of activities, including educational work on Central America, direct-assistance operations, Central American refugee work, political organizing, and disruptive-protest campaigns. Together they provided a sufficiently strong organizational infrastructure to sustain the movement's challenge to the administration's Central America policy throughout the decade.

How were authority, identity, decision making, membership, and communication typically structured in Central America organizations? A comprehensive analysis of the organizational structures of fifteen hundred local, regional, and national Central America groups involved in combinations of political, educational, refugee, and direct-assistance work is beyond the scope of this study. We can, nevertheless, make some valuable observations about the organizational structuring of the movement's three main national carrier groups: Sanctuary, Witness for

Peace, and the Pledge of Resistance. These groups were organized as loosely knit, decentralized activist networks coordinated by regional and national organizations of limited authority. Rather than reflecting the hierarchical, centralized command structure, bureaucracy, and organizational standardization of many more traditional political associations and social movement organizations, these Central America groups typically exhibited numerous features of the so-called "new social movements" and direct-action campaigns. These included tendencies toward egalitarianism, decentralization, community building, nonviolence, and consensus decision making (Epstein 1991).

Sanctuary, for example, was composed of 423 largely autonomous congregations that were minimally coordinated by regional organizations and, nationally, by the Chicago Religious Task Force on Central America. In the words of Ignatius Bau (1985: 174), "Sanctuary is . . . not a movement focused on a few visible, charismatic leaders. There is clearly a network of churchpeople, lawyers, and social workers coordinating the movement. However, there are no hierarchies, no formal organizations, no regulations regarding membership. There is no requirement of either uniformity or conformity."

James Hannon (1991: 271) described regional groupings of the Pledge of Resistance similarly:

> The Pledge was designed to be a network of affinity groups. The significance of the network identity was that no attempt would be made to fuse individuals and groups from varying backgrounds and political positions into an organization that would agree on a wide range of policies and procedures. Beyond a commitment to oppose an escalation of U.S. militarism in Central America and a commitment to non-violence and consensus decision-making, there were no demands for any party line.

Each regional grouping of the Pledge was coordinated nationally by a signal committee which would follow events in Central America and, when necessary, call for unified national protests. Nevertheless, regional and local Pledge groups ultimately retained their own autonomy and were allowed to act or not act at their own discretion.

Witness for Peace was in some ways the most centrally controlled organization. Nevertheless, for most of its life, it was decentralized through ten regional offices which took primary responsibility for recruitment and political organizing (Clark 1992). The national office, which changed locations several times, was primarily responsible for coordinating long- and short-term delegations. Once delegates returned from Nicaragua, the regional and national offices of Witness for Peace did attempt to support and coordinate their political activism. A few official local chapters of Witness for Peace were formed, but most Witness for Peace activists continued their political work within their original churches, affinity groups, and activist organizations.

This decentralized organizational structure that characterized the Central America peace movement's national organizations derived partly from an attraction by leaders and members to a "prefigurative politics" movement culture, partly from the functional imperatives of sustaining, with limited resources, national political campaigns involving diverse constituencies, and partly from the fact that the movements' most important leaders lived all over the U.S. The structures, in other words, were both ideologically fitting and functionally necessary.

What actually held together this loosely knit, widely scattered activist network? The answer is, three things: AT&T, the personal computer, and the U.S. Postal Service. First, more than anything else, the Central America peace movement was built on the national network of telephone lines, through conference calls, faxes, phone-trees, and innumerable person-to-person calls. The original formation of Witness for Peace in 1983 by delegates of the July Action for Peace trip, for example, required, in the words of Mike Clark (1992), "endless telephone conference calls about forming an organization, some vessel to embody this charisma we had experienced." Fran Truitt recalls what transpired (1990):

> Soon after the Jalapa trip, I got a phone call from Buddy Summers, one of the delegates. He was calling to set up a conference call on a future date. He had called down the list and I just had happened to answer the phone—things like that, by the way, make you believe in God when you have moments of doubt. Anyway, about a week later there were five of us on the telephone: David Sweet, Buddy Summers, Paddy Lane, Jim McLeod, and myself. We decided then that we needed to get organized to continue sending people down to Nicaragua. Over time, a fascinating community developed over the telephone through conference calls. I became chair of the personnel committee. I learned how to type, use a computer, and a fax machine.

Multi-party conference calls were, according to Ken Butigan, also essential in organizing the Pledge of Resistance.

Telephones were also useful for rapidly deploying thousands of activists in protest actions. Particularly effective were phone-tree sys-

tems and phone banks staffed by volunteers. According to Ken Butigan (1991):

> In the early years, we had fourteen phone-bank centers set up around
> the Bay Area. We had arranged people who were committed to come in
> at a moment's notice to call everyone on our list. That meant calling six
> to nine thousand people, which would take a few days. Later we moved
> to the phone-tree model, where, in the event of a national signal, mem-
> bers of the communications committee would call all the representa-
> tives of the hundreds of affinity groups and say, "Look, tomorrow
> morning at seven do such-and-such." The committee called each group
> which then spread the word among themselves.

The Philadelphia-area Pledge created a similar system (Taylor 1990):
"We had a mailing list, a newsletter, and a hugely complicated phone-
tree: ten people would call ten people who would call ten people. Different groups cooperated to promote events. The religious people had
agreed that if there were an invasion, we would all meet at St. Joseph's
Church at 10 A.M. for civil-disobedience training, at 11 A.M. for a worship service, and then to action. The system worked amazingly well."

Personal computers, which became widely available in the early-to
mid-1980s, were also critical organizing tools, because they enabled
organizers to efficiently generate mailing lists, newsletters, and fund-
raising campaigns. Utilized together with the third factor linking
together this decentralized movement—the relatively inexpensive
bulk-mail system of the U.S. Post Office—organizers were able to
mobilize tens of thousands of activists for political lobbying and
protest. James Hannon (1991: 268–69) described how the Boston-
area Pledge office coordinated thousands of Pledge signers using the
personal computer and the U.S. mail system:

> The early organizing efforts of the Pledge were a spectacular success. A
> computerized mailing list of all local signatories of the Pledge was
> established early. Informational mailings to affinity group spokes went
> out on a monthly basis and other mailings, including notifications of
> special events and fundraising appeals, were sent occasionally to all sig-
> natories, who eventually totaled 3,400. The Pledge office, located after
> the first few months at the Congregational Church in Harvard Square,
> became a clearinghouse for information concerning Central America as
> well as the locus for Pledge organizing.

Anne Shumway, a key leader in the Boston-area Pledge, recalls
(1990): "At first I tried to keep a list by hand myself. But it was too

much. So one of our women who was a computer expert volunteered her time. We assembled thousands of names. And we had a phone network, a phone tree. Our organizing was almost all done by phone. I would call 30 designated leaders, who would all call their people, and so on. It worked well."

According to Ken Butigan (1991), the national Pledge office simply replicated the decentralized "hub-and-spoke" system established by regional coordinators for communicating with their local groups: "We sent out, for example, bundles of Pledge newspapers—of which at the peak we were printing 40,000 copies—from the national office to regional and local organizers who, in turn, sent them out to their people. So we did not have to compile a national mailing list of all individual U.S. activists. We only sent material to representatives who did the rest of the work."

Witness for Peace also combined computerized member lists and the mail system to generate a great deal of focused political pressure. Sam Hope (1992) describes their systems:

> We had several ways of putting out alerts which really worked well. Every few weeks we would use our computer list to do a mailing to people who had committed to certain tasks in their area. We would get political information from the Central American Working Group and then feed that out across the nation. That was terribly effective. We would absolutely flood the State Department with calls. We could hog the switchboard for hours, if we wanted to. I mean, they declared several times that they had never gotten so many calls in all their history. We also coded our computer mailing list by congressional district so we could target all of our people in certain congressional areas if we wanted, not just the media-contacts there. Our political pressure was very well targeted. Sometimes, I remember, when it was a last-minute vote, we would even send out overnight telegrams to our people in key districts, saying, "Vote for this House bill by number on this day. Here are the swing votes and this is how it is stacking up." Then everybody in that district would absolutely flood their congressional representative with calls.

If the telephone, computer, and postal service were key in organizing the Central America peace movement nationally, the formation of multi-organization coalitions was fundamental in organizing the movement regionally. AFSC staff member and Sanctuary organizer Jane Guise (1990) reported:

> In Boston there was a mushrooming number of Central America groups. The human rights and peace movements have fads, you know,

and there is a body of people, more politically than religiously motivated, who will pick up on issues that seem to have promise. All of a sudden there developed many grassroots groups. So we formed a coalition of about eighty organizations. This included solidarity groups that had been formed for each Central American country, labor unions, and other special-interest groups. Building networks and coalitions like this requires solid, full-time organizers doing behind-the-scenes work to keep them together and moving. That's what I did.

And according to Fran Truitt (1990), "All around Maine, a number of local peace-action groups formed, all around the state. And we developed a Maine Coalition for Central America. If there needed to be action, between us all we know who will be there and how to get others there. Our coalition generates constant letters to the editor and all kinds of activism."

Forming multi-group coalitions was particularly important for the Pledge of Resistance, given the nature of its purpose and strategy. Pledge organizer Anne Shumway (1990) recollects, "We were in coalition with every other regional group working on Central America. Boston is very good on coalition politics." Likewise, Phyllis Taylor (1990) recalls, "Many Central America groups sprung up in the Philadelphia area. We cooperated by trading mailing lists and trying to coordinate calendars to minimize the duplication of protest events and meetings." The formation of regional coalitions was also an important element of Sanctuary work.

> In addition to our general Central America coalition, we developed a regional network of about 180 Sanctuary groups that continued for years. We also had a key-contact list in New England of about 40 people who communicated to their own groups. The Sanctuary coalition meetings we held were very well attended for years, spontaneously almost. We didn't have to work to get people out. They themselves felt that they needed to come, to receive each other's support. (Guise 1990)

But while national networking and regional coalition building was essential, the Central America peace movement's greatest energy for protest and ultimate source of political leverage was the activism of hundreds of thousands of protest organizers at the grassroots level. In other words, to paraphrase U.S. House Speaker Tip O'Neill, ultimately, all activism is local. Organizationally, the basic building blocks of local activism were church and synagogue Central America committees and—typically for the less religiously inclined—"affinity groups." As to the church groups,

In most dioceses there developed Justice & Peace offices and commit-tees which were articulate and active. Many dealt with a variety of domestic issues, but on the international side, Central America ruled the waves. That was just the issue that people were passionate about. Few other issues at that time galvanized as much concern in these groups. These Justice & Peace groups were there in Des Moines and every other diocese mobilizing and pressing their bishop on the Central America issue. (Quigley 1990)

Religious Central America committees were also common in Protes-tant and Anabaptist churches and denominations.

For the formation of local Jewish activist groups, two progressive Jewish organizations were particularly important: the three-thousand-member Jewish Peace Fellowship (JPF), founded in 1941, and the forty-five-hundred-member New Jewish Agenda (NJA), founded in 1980. In addition, the Union of American Hebrew Congregations, a Reformed umbrella organization, opposed President Reagan's Central America policy (Falcoff 1984: 368). Both JPF and NJA were respon-sible for mobilizing many of their members to become involved in Central America activism, whether through a committee in their syn-agogue or a local JPF or NJA chapter.

The second major building block of local Central America activism was the affinity group, first developed in 1977 by the Clamshell Alliance in their Seabrook anti-nuclear campaign (Epstein 1991: 65). Affinity groups are small clusters of ten to fifteen activists which func-tion as coordinated units of protest. Affinity group members typically train for civil disobedience together, restrain each others' inappropri-ate emotions and behaviors during protests, and, when arrested, sup-port each other in jail. The groups are also responsible for sending rep-resentatives to regional council meetings to shape policy through consensus and receive the council's directives. Pledge organizer Anne Shumway (1990) reported, "We tried to organize everyone into affin-ity groups if they didn't already come in that way. All of our organiz-ing was done on the affinity-group model, which came out of Seabrook." And Ken Butigan (1991) noted: "Our organizational structure was imported wholesale from the anti-nuclear movement." These groups proved superior to masses of unsystematically connect-ed individuals as means of preparing for and executing Central Amer-ica protest actions.

Affinity groups enhance commitment to a larger organization by func-tioning as an intermediate organization that enhances the experience of solidarity through greater homogeneity and agreement. Interpersonal solidarity bonds promote faithful attendance at movement activities, particularly at events which involve some personal risk. Also, the pleasure associated with affinity group participation and the group's identity as an activist collective are likely to prolong individual and group participation in the activities of the larger organization, even when participants begin to feel some disenchantment with the strategies or culture of that organization. The affinity group structure also resonates with some of the central values of the Pledge, including decentralization, consensus-decision making, and the importance of community. (Hannon 1991: 300)

Local Central America organizers in religious Justice and Peace committees and movement affinity groups across the country together mobilized a tightly organized movement. According to Anne Shumway (1990), "One of the phenomenal things about Pledge was the great grassroots organizing. Yes, there was a national signal group that would tell the grassroots to do an action. But the grassroots people were themselves tremendously organized. Each region had its own list of many thousands of names. We had a weekly coordinating committee meeting. All kinds of stuff."

This high degree of organization is also reflected in Ken Butigan's account (1991) of the Bay-Area's effervescent Pledge organizing:

> In the first years, we had about 200 very good affinity groups that were affiliated with the Pledge. We had two poorly paid staff people. It was genuinely a dynamic, grassroots thing, consensual-based. The staff was seen as complementing and reinforcing the work of the committees. We had all kinds of committees—Media, Finance, Logistics, Materials, and Transportation committees. We also had a "Pledge Working Group" that met weekly, consisting of representatives from each committee and the staff together. We made decisions. Finally, we had monthly "Spokescouncil" meetings, involving representatives of different affinity groups, at which anyone from any group could come and speak.

Thus, primarily through the coordinated action of a host of local, regional, and national movement-carrier groups, the Central America peace movement was able to present a well-organized, sustained challenge to President Reagan's Central America policy.

Religious Human Rights Lobbies

Movement midwifes facilitated the organization of new movement carriers. Feeder organizations and the demise of the nuclear freeze helped channel new members into the Central America peace movement. All of this strengthened the more than fifteen hundred local, regional, and national Central America peace movement-carrier groups that emerged across the country. Much of the movement's political activism was mobilized and expressed directly by and through these carrier groups. Yet, there existed one other preexistent organizational structure that complemented and amplified the work of the new movement-carrier groups: the national religious human rights lobbies that operated in Washington, D.C. These established religious lobbying organizations fed up-to-date political information from Washington back to grassroots activists and provided established channels through which those activists could direct focused political pressure.

Washington, D.C., is replete with interest groups and lobbying organizations of all kinds. Among them, a cluster championing international human rights and humanitarian foreign policies on Capitol Hill and in the White House—largely an outgrowth of the anti–Vietnam War movement—had become particularly influential since the late 1960s (Powell 1986; Winsor 1987). Fueled by growing interest in peace-and-justice concerns among many religious communities and encouraged by a President sympathetic to both human rights concerns and religious involvement in politics, the religious sector of the human rights lobbies grew increasingly important throughout the 1970s.[14] According to Falcoff (1984: 366–68),

> The Vietnam War marks not only a division within America's foreign policy elites but also the widening and diversification of the foreign policy public. . . . The most significant addition to this wider public have been the secretariats and social justice commissions of the Roman Catholic and mainstream Protestant churches. The case of the Roman church is particularly interesting in the light of the conservative tradition of the American hierarchy, as well as its historic reluctance to become involved . . . in controversies outside the area of personal morality. . . . The Protestant churches have pursued similar foreign policy goals through both the National Council of Churches and their individual denominations. . . . [This has resulted in] the emergence of what for lack of a better term must be called a clerico-leftist foreign policy lobby in Washington.

Livezey concurs (1989: 14–15):

> In the expansion of the nongovernmental human rights movement in the United States since the Vietnam War, nothing has been more important than the increasing role of the U.S. religious community. . . . In the

late 1960s these organizations emerged as major actors in a growing
[human rights] movement, and adopted distinctive roles within the
movement that helped shape its ideology and strategy. . . . A very broad
cross section of the U.S. religious community counts itself as part of the
international human rights movement. Indeed, the human rights work
of religious organizations . . . is so great that the organizations formed
specifically to promote human rights [e.g. Amnesty International] constitute merely 'the tip of the iceberg.'

For reasons we will see more clearly in the next chapter, the conflict
in Central America became *the* issue which in the 1980s dominated the
agendas of these religious human rights lobbies—particularly those of
the United Church of Christ, United Methodist, Presbyterian, American Baptist, Mennonite, and Quaker denominations (Keller 1982).
Consequently, among Washington lobbying organizations, the political
battle over Central America was itself dominated by these religious lobbies.[15] According to U.S. Catholic Conference staff member Thomas
Quigley (1990), "The U.S. Catholic Conference and the National
Council of Churches took the lead in generating awareness and concern
and taking public positions on Central America. The major church
structures were off the mark early and set a pattern. Over time, there
developed an increasing religious hostility to the Reagan policy. This
was gradually picked up more and more by peace movement activists."

Religious lobbies were the first to react against the President's Central America policy. Falcoff (1984: 361–62; also see Destler, 1984:
333) indicated that in 1981, when the White House first proposed
sending more than $113 million in aid to El Salvador, "Congress was
flooded with letters, visits, and phone calls protesting the administration's proposals . . . spearheaded . . . by the Washington lobbies of the
Catholic and mainline Protestant churches." Religious groups sustained this oppositional leadership throughout the decade. For example, Falcoff observed (1984: 367), "The Methodist Church has
become, according to one report, 'the busiest center of El Salvador
lobbying' in the nation's capital."

About the 1987 battles over Contra aid, Hertzke wrote (1988:
234–35): "Cokie Roberts of National Public Radio, interviewed on
the 'MacNeil-Lehrer News Hour,' said that on the day of the House
vote against the president's aid package to the Contras, the church
groups were 'the strongest lobby against this package.'" Religious lobbies simply barraged the political system with oppositional pressure.

The Protestant churches have . . . sent representatives to testify on Central American issues before appropriate congressional committees; they . . . have lobbied intensively on Capitol Hill for a cutoff of U.S. military aid to El Salvador and in many cases have arranged contacts for lawmakers and aides visiting El Salvador, Guatemala, and elsewhere in the region. They have kept up a steady stream of anti-administration arguments in church publications and sermons. On Central America policy, perhaps the most important activity of the churches has been sponsorship of a letter-writing campaign to members of Congress. . . . A weary recipient of this sort of correspondence, Representative Peter Kostmayer (D-PA), noted, perhaps not remarkably, that his mail was running "100 percent against aid." (Falcoff 1984: 367–68)

This kind of religious opposition to the administration's Central America policy attracted a great deal of media attention. Quigley recalled (1990):

We got a lot of attention for our resistance, because the media loved to contrast the typical conservativism of bishops on other issues with the progressive, counter-administration position on Central America. I read that contrast a thousand times. There was a lot of focus on the bishops saying "No!" to Ronald Reagan, especially given all of the Catholics supposedly in his administration. Here are these Catholic bishops going against their President. The media goes for that kind of thing.

All of this gave the religious lobbies a considerable amount of political influence on the Central America issue. Schoultz observed (1987: 22), "It is impossible to make sense out of U.S. policy toward Latin America without acknowledging [the human rights lobbies'] impact—their growing impact—upon policy. Without an understanding of these participants, for example, the close congressional vote on aid to the Nicaraguan Contras in 1985 and 1986 are simply inexplicable. The beliefs of these Washingtonians now count heavily in the construction of U.S. foreign policy toward Latin America." According to Falcoff (1984: 372), the "clerico-leftist foreign policy lobby" was able to "restrict [administration policy] greatly and force the White House to expend far more 'energy and political capital' than it had originally anticipated."

These influential religious human rights lobbies represented another preexisting organizational resource—in addition to movement midwives and feeder organizations—that enhanced the Central America peace movement's organizational capacity. These established political lobbies did not displace the movement carriers' work of mobilizing and deploying disruptive grassroots protest. Rather, like the movement midwives, they played a distinct role that complemented the work of the movement carriers. Their functional specialization was twofold. First, they informed grassroots Central America activists—through telephone hot lines, newsletters, and action alerts—about the political challenges and opportunities in Washington. Second, they represented the will of tens of thousands of Central America activists, in a more standard interest-group style of persuasion, to political decision makers in Washington.

Social movement analysts of the past—in efforts to define social movements as not pathological and psychological but rational and political, yet qualitatively different from standard institutionalized forms of politics—have emphasized the distinction between "members" and "challengers" (for example, Tilly 1978; Gamson 1975). According to this distinction, members are those who enjoy access to routine decision-making processes because they possess sufficient political and economic resources required to gain entry. Challengers, on the other hand, are those who lack bargaining leverage and whose interests are consequently excluded from institutional political participation. Members can pursue their interests through standard, institutionalized means of political influence, while challengers must resort to the "negative inducements" of confrontation, force, and disruption. This conventional distinction has served social movement analysts well as a conceptual tool, providing the rationale for the making of important analytical distinctions between such phenomena as the civil rights movement's Student Nonviolent Coordinating Committee (a challenger), the American Medical Association (a member), and soccer-game riots (nonpolitical collective behavior). But this distinction does not come without liabilities. When applied as an ontological reality in empirical analysis, for example, the member-challenger distinction can mislead and obfuscate.

While real-world "members" are fairly ubiquitous, few concrete social movements actually involve protagonists who are unambiguously "challengers." In fact, the majority of modern social movements possess *moderate* amounts of political and economic resources, enjoy *limited* access to political decision making, employ both disruptive *and* institutionalized means of political influence, mobilize new movement-carrier groups *while simultaneously* collaborating with established political organizations, and vocalize a mix of conciliatory, persuasive, *and* confrontational rhetoric.[16] The member-challenger distinction poses the danger of allowing the analytical concept to mischaracterize the empirical reality as either-or, rather than recognizing the existence of and exploring the interaction between these coinciding member- and challenger-like qualities in movements.

We have already seen this ambiguous nature in the Central America peace movement. Its entrepreneurs both mobilized their own new insurgent movement-carrier organizations and worked with established groups, such as the Roman Catholic Church. Activists illegally took over and occupied congressional offices, but also wrote their representatives the usual constituents' letters of appeal. The movement's leaders correctly perceived political opportunity in a divided government, but concurrently, we will find in the next chapter, seethed with frustration at an intransigent and impenetrable political system. The movement's protagonists were not society's disinherited and deprived, forced by a dearth of resources to take to the streets. Rather, they were the educated middle class, committed to the political goal of transforming U.S. Central America policy. In their effort to exploit the full range of organizational and political means of achieving that goal, these movement actors utilized all of the available resources possible. They freely drew on resources of preexistent movement midwives. They tapped religious and political feeder organizations for all the new members that could be recruited. They also collaborated fully with established religious lobbies which—by employing a more conventional political vocabulary and syntax than the insurgent movement-carrier groups—complemented and amplified the work of the movement's emerging protest organizations. We can conclude that the principle that shaped the overall organizational structure of the Central America peace movement was decentralized multi-organizational functional specialization, not consolidated negative inducement by excluded challengers.

CONCLUSION

We began this chapter by observing that any good social-movement analysis must account for both the complex motives and actions of the people who produced the social movement *and* the multifaceted social-structural environment within which those people collectively acted. In this chapter, we have investigated ways the broader political and organizational environment facilitated the emergence of the Central America peace movement. We now turn to the second half of the social dialectic and explore the element of human motives, investigating the sources of the insurgent consciousness that ignited and fueled the Central America peace movement. But just as this chapter's examination of the macro-structural environment maintained a reference to the human agency that ultimately generates all social structure, so the next chapter's approach will recognize the decisive influence of social structure on individual consciousness.

Six

The Social Structure of Moral Outrage

> Anger at the failure of authority to live up to its obligations, to keep its word and faith with its subjects, can be among the most potent of human emotions and topple thrones.
>
> Barrington Moore, *Injustice*

Early opponents of President Reagan's Central American policy found themselves facing a relatively favorable structure of political opportunities that facilitated mobilization for activism. They also enjoyed a variety of organizational networks that helped to expedite the generation of the movement. In the absence of these two supportive macrosocial conditions, the Central America peace movement never could have sustained its widespread, decade-long struggle against the President's Central American policy.

At the same time, we know that expanding political opportunity and strong organizational capacity alone could not have generated the Central America peace movement, for together they only provided the structural potential for collective political action. What prompted would-be Central America peace activists actually to exploit that potential was the irruption among them of an insurgent consciousness, of the kind of moral outrage that incites disruptive political activism.[1] Explaining the causes of that rise of insurgent consciousness is the task to which we now turn.

INSURGENT CONSCIOUSNESS

What exactly motivated Central America peace movement activists to mobilize themselves into a social movement? More generally, what compels any person to engage in disruptive political activism?

Human beings are, at their core, normative and moral creatures. This means that people's actions are formed not only by their understanding of what is, but also by their sense of what *should* be. People draw on the resources of their cultural traditions and, through a process of lived experience, develop within and among themselves standards of what is right and wrong, appropriate and inappropriate, obliged and prohibited, just and unjust. These standards may be more or less conscious and formal. But they usually operate as potent guides and measures of thought, feeling, and action. People conduct their lives, in part, to fulfill the imperatives of their normative standards. And people judge themselves and those around them according to how well they have done so.

When someone violates their own normative and moral standards, they often experience some sense of regret, disappointment, frustration, self-criticism, guilt, or shame. When other people violate those standards, people often react with some mixture of astonishment, annoyance, disapproval, indignation, or hostility. Sometimes people keep their disapproval to themselves. At other times, they openly express it. Sometimes, people go even further and take action to try to stop what transgresses their beliefs and feelings of what should and should not be.

Many social movements represent exactly this kind of action, where people's sense of what is right and just is so seriously violated that they feel compelled not only to express disapproval, but to organize to set things right. Factory workers strike because their sense of fair wages and work conditions are violated. Environmentalists protest because their convictions about the responsible use of the earth are disregarded. Racial minorities revolt because their sense of equity and dignity is abused. Social movements and political protests, in other words, are deeply rooted in the normative and moral nature of human persons.

The Central America peace movement is no exception. That movement erupted, in part, because President Reagan's Central American policy deeply violated the moral beliefs and normative standards of tens of thousands of U.S. citizens. For them, the prospect of using U.S. tax dollars to invade Nicaragua, to sponsor the Contra war against Nicaragua, to prop up El Salvador's military machine and political system, to militarize Honduras, and to deport vulnerable Central American refugees to life-threatening situations was so noxious, so morally reprehensible, so contrary to their convictions that they felt compelled to mobilized a political movement to stop these things from happening. Exactly why and how those people came to feel that strongly about the President's policy is the subject we explore in this chapter.

We will be particularly concerned to explain a unique feature of the Central America peace movement—its religious character. This movement was largely initiated, organized, led, and joined by people of faith, mostly Christians and Jews. The question is, why? Why exactly did religion play such a dominant role in the Central America peace movement? Most important contemporary Western social movements—the anti-Vietnam, anti-nuclear, environmental, student, and women's movements—have been largely secular in character. In the West, religiosity generally tends to be negatively associated with both conventional and unconventional forms of political participation (Barnes and Kaase 1979: 118; Conway 1985; Millbrath and Goel 1977). So, why were people of faith more likely to become activists in *this* movement? Part of the answer, we will see, is that many religious people in the U.S. were socially located in a way that made them very aware, concerned, and educated about the problems of Central America long before Ronald Reagan even took office.

Religious Teachings on Peace and Justice

If human action is profoundly shaped by normative and moral considerations, then a reasonable place to begin exploring the many forces that helped ignite an insurgent consciousness among Central America activists, especially religious activists, is with recent religious social ethics. Both the Christian and Jewish traditions include ethical orientations that lend themselves, under some conditions, to this-worldly political activism. In the twentieth century, many schools of social ethics in the Catholic, Protestant, and Jewish traditions were developing especially strong emphases on social justice, peace, and political engagement. For religious activists, these social teachings served as a general backdrop to the political events of the 1980s, providing a supportive orientation toward and legitimation for involvement in the Central America peace movement.

Modern Roman Catholic social ethics, for example, commenced with the 1891 publications of Pope Leo XIII's encyclical *Rerum Novarum* ("Of Things New," also known as "The Condition of the Working Classes"). In the decades that followed, popes and bishops' councils built upon the foundation of *Rerum Novarum,* taking, over a ninety-year period, progressively broader and stronger stands on social and political issues. Popes Leo XIII, Pius XI, and Pius XII in their letters and addresses developed Catholic social doctrine by sounding the themes of the immorality of economic exploitation, the right to fair compensation for labor, the need for structural social analysis, the reality of collectivized sin, affinities between socialist and Christian values, the demand for an equitable distribution of wealth, and the priority of the common welfare over the right to private property (Dorr 1983).

In the early 1960s, Pope John XXIII expanded Catholic social teachings with his encyclicals *Mater et Magistra* ("Christianity and Social Progress," 1961) and *Pacem in Terris* ("Peace on Earth," 1963). In them he stressed the social obligations of private property, the state's right to own the means of production, the dangers of third world neocolonialism, and the legitimacy of political cooperation with non-Christians toward socially honorable goals. Then, in 1967, Pope Paul VI issued *Populorum Progressio* ("On the Progress of Peoples"), which expressed a stronger stand on sociopolitical issues than any previous encyclical. Paul VI called for bold social transformations to lift the poor out of hunger and misery. He condemned past colonialism, recent forms of neocolonialism, and vast inequities of power between nations as the causes of world poverty. The ideology and principles of liberal capitalism, he argued, could never sustain a just economic order. Furthermore, the encyclical stated, people are entitled to be the shapers of their own futures (Dorr 1983).

The 1970s and 1980s saw a host of papal and episcopal documents that emphasized peace, justice, and the protection of human dignity. Particularly important was the Synod of Bishops Second General Assembly document *Justice in the World,* which declared, "Action on behalf of justice and participation in the transformation of the world fully appear to us as a constitutive dimension of the preaching of the Gospel . . . of the Church's mission for the redemption of the human race and its liberation from every oppressive situation" (Gremillion 1976: 514). Also important were Pope Paul VI's *A Call to Action* (1971), Paul VI's *Reconciliation—the Way to Peace* (1975), the U.S. Bishops' *The Challenge of Peace* (1983) and *Economic Justice for All* (1986), and Pope John Paul II's *The Social Concerns of the Church* (1988) (Henriot, DeBerri, and Schultheis 1988).

This developing body of social doctrine had profound effects on many Catholics. It defined this-worldly social matters as integral concerns of committed Christians, thus encouraging the faithful to engage themselves in economic, political, and cultural issues. It promoted a critical attitude toward violence, social injustice, political oppression, the violation of human dignity, the basic principles of liberal capitalism, and the domination of the poor by the rich. Catholic social doctrine also created an opening for dialogue with the left and prudent collaboration with socialists and other non-Christian activists. It urged Catholic laity to seize the initiative in struggling for bold social transformations to achieve peace and justice (Gremillion 1976: 3–124; Dorr 1983; Smith 1991: 110–11, 124–26). Hence, when in the 1980s, many Catholics mobilized in the Central America peace movement, many of them were, in their minds, acting consistently with the directives of ninety years worth of papal and episcopal teachings.

Mainline Protestant social ethics of the twentieth century also developed a strong emphasis on Christian engagement in political action for peace and justice. This tradition's roots extend back to nineteenth-century Christian activism to abolish slavery and the antebellum involvement of Christians—such as Washington Gladden, Richard Newton, Lyman Atwater, and Joseph Cook—in political reform for greater economic equity and political participation (Craig 1992; Stackhouse 1987). This legacy was continued by turn-of-the-century and early twentieth-century progressive social gospel writers and activists— among others, Walter Rauschenbusch, Josiah Strong, Charles Sheldon, and Shailer Matthews—who called for the reformation of urban, industrial America according to Christian principles of love and equality, toward building the kingdom of God on earth (Fishburn 1993; White and Hopkins 1976). In the twentieth century, mainline Protestant social ethics continued in its strong emphasis on social and political activism as many leaders of individual denominations, the U.S. National Council of Churches, and the World Council of Churches championed a host of peace and justice causes. The denominational leadership of the United Methodist Church, for example, issued many official statements and resolutions, established numerous agencies and programs, and devoted a great deal of money to progressive and sometimes radical political causes in the name of Christian faith (Iosso 1993).

Echoing and reinforcing the politically activist social ethics of most mainline Protestant denominations in the two decades before the Central America peace movement, the U.S. National Council of Churches (NCC)—whose membership represented about one-half of all U.S. Protestants—also advanced politically progressive pronouncements and policies advocating and sponsoring political activism by Christians for peace and justice. Billingsley writes (1990: 176):

From its founding in 1950 until approximately the mid-1960s, the NCC took a mainline moderate-to-liberal American position on domestic and foreign policy questions. . . . But from the early 1960s, NCC pronouncements and expenditures abroad started to reflect a new and different political agenda, an agenda that embraced many assumptions and prescriptions of the emerging secular liberal-left. On virtually every major foreign policy issue, for example, the council was strongly critical of the United States while at the same time it was apologetic for or only mildly critical of the Soviet Union and other Marxist regimes.

Over the years, the NCC issued pronouncements, advocated policies, and promoted Christian activism—taking mostly progressive positions—on the social and political issues of educational reform, black civil rights, nuclear energy, environmentalism, domestic poverty, criminal-justice reform, unemployment and welfare policy, farm subsidies, budget and tax policy, consumer and corporate affairs, labor-union issues, military conscription, the nuclear arms race, SALT II, the Nuclear Freeze, the Strategic Defense Initiative, the Reykjavik Summit, chemical and bacteriological weapons production, and U.S. foreign relations with the Soviet Union, Eastern Europe, South Africa, Angola, Mozambique, Zimbabwe, Namibia, Libya, Ethiopia, China, Japan, Korea, the Philippines, Afghanistan, Pakistan, India, Vietnam, Cambodia, Cuba, Grenada, Central America, Israel, Iran, and Lebanon (Billingsley 1990; also see Singer 1975; Evans 1973). Further reinforcing the influence of the NCC, for decades before the 1980s, the NCC's international counterpart, the World Council of Churches, exhorted American mainline Protestants to engage themselves in social and political activism for justice and peace by advancing many progressive statements and programs in support of international peace, human rights, just political systems, racial equality, humanizing technology, sustainable economic systems, and third world social development (Bock 1974; Duff 1956; Howell 1982: 27–57).

In the 1970s, even some sectors of conservative Protestantism—whose historical roots also extend back to the nineteenth-century Protestant tradition of social and political activism—joined the growing religious insistence on the necessity of political engagement for peace and justice. In that decade, evangelicalism's relative political homogeneity gave way to an increasingly diverse pluralism when, influenced by the social ferment of the 1960s, a movement of progressive and radical evangelicals emerged in the early 1970s (Quebedeaux 1974). That movement—represented in the 1973 "Chicago

Declaration of Evangelical Social Concern," in the organizations Evangelicals for Social Action, JustLife, and the Sojourners community, in the publication of *Sojourners* and *The Other Side* magazines, and in the leadership of Jim Wallis, Ronald Sider, and John Alexander, among others—blended conservative Protestant and Anabaptist theology with progressive-to-radical politics (Fowler 1982: 115–39; Skillen 1990: 141–61; Sider 1974). Not only did many radical evangelicals participate in the Central America peace movement, but *Sojourners* magazine also played a key role in organizing and promoting both the Pledge of Resistance and Witness for Peace.

The tradition of the historic peace churches—the Mennonites, Quakers, and Brethren in Christ—also contributed to the growing religious focus on peace and justice. Organizations such as the American Friends Service Committee and the Mennonite Central Committee carried forward the four-hundred-year-old Anabaptist commitment to pacifism, social service, and simple living with an increasingly sharp focus on third world development, refugee and disaster relief, advocacy for the poor, and disarmament (Dyck 1980a, 1980b; AFSC n.d.). Although the historic peace church tradition typically discourages direct political participation—since governments are agents of violence—some of its social values helped draw many Anabaptists into forms of Central America activism that involved nonviolent direct action and witness to the State. The conception of Witness for Peace as a nonviolent "shield of love," for example, was especially attractive to many Anabaptists (Bonthius 1990). And the AFSC played a critical role in sponsoring and facilitating many Central America peace movement organizations and activities, including the San Francisco Pledge of Resistance.

The Jewish ethical tradition—informed by notions about humans made in God's dignifying image, love of neighbor, defense of the weak and poor, *tikkun olam* ("healing the world"), and the need to oppose social evil and establish *salom* ("peace and social well-being")—readily lent itself to promoting political action for justice and peace (Shapiro 1978; Greenberg 1977: 69–77). A number of developments in twentieth-century Jewish social ethics further reinforced that tendency (Blanchard 1975; Fackenheim 1968; Hirsch 1970, 1971; Israel 1970; Lipman 1970; Twersky 1982). Most importantly, the Holocaust and the Nuremberg trials that followed drove home the need for both the proactive, forceful confrontation of sociopolitical evils and the ethical obligation to disobey military and governmental orders and actions that violate human rights (Breslauer 1983: 1–2; Braude 1970). The Holocaust helped to clarify for many Jews the universalistic, humanizing meaning of being a chosen people—in contrast to the Nazi ideology of the superior Aryan race. John Roth (quoted in Breslauer 1983: 51), for example, writes: "After Auschwitz, the only way in which it can make good sense to say that a group or an individual is chosen is if that conviction leads men to empty themselves in service that meets human need" (also see Agus 1981, 1983; Wiesel 1972; Cohen 1973, 1979; Freidman 1974; Shatz 1978). Furthermore, the valiant but inadequate actions of a minority of European Christians to protect Jews against the Nazis, in contrast to the majority of German Christians who cooperated with the Nazi regime, underscored for many Jews their moral tradition's call to risk life and limb on behalf of others in danger (Greenberg 1977: 75–76). Developments in twentieth-century American Jewish social ethics that were significant for the Central America peace movement were also provoked by the Vietnam War, as many Jewish leaders grappled to formulate a Jewish response to the challenges of Vietnam for the country and for Jewish youth (see, for instance, Winston 1978; Wein 1969). Out of this engagement emerged a body of literature which contained, among other positions, a distinctively Jewish justification for a pacifist position on war (see, for instance, Kimmelman 1968; Schwarzschild 1966; Siegman 1966; Simonson 1968; Gendler 1978) and for civil disobedience against an unjust state (see, for instance, Konvitz 1978; Broude 1970; Landman 1969; Roth 1971; Zimmerman 1971; Kimmelman 1970; Greenberg 1970; Kirschenbaum 1974).

It would be simplistic and misleading to argue that these schools of religious social ethics themselves actually generated the insurgent consciousness of the Central America peace movement. But by providing theological pointers to political action for peace and justice, they did afford many religious activists a legitimating theoretical background and ideological impetus for involvement in that movement. Had these traditions of religious social ethics been absent from the social worlds of Christians and Jews, the Central America peace movement would have emerged with much greater difficulty, if at all. These religious traditions were vital preconditions for the irruption of insurgent consciousness. But to understand the more proximate causes of moral outrage and political commitment, we must attend to other, more experiential and organizational factors. Prominent among them is the

North American relational connection to Central America through church missionary work.

The Missionary Connection

"Go and make disciples of all nations, baptizing them . . . and teaching them to obey everything I have commanded you." These were the last instructions, according to the New Testament, that Jesus of Nazareth gave his disciples before ascending to heaven. Since then, this command, which Christians call the "Great Commission," has propelled innumerable evangelists to spread the Christian faith to the corners of the earth. In the later part of the twentieth century, one major field of North American missionary efforts, both Catholic and Protestant, was Central America.

In the 1920s, there were less than three hundred North American Protestant and almost no Catholic missionaries working in Central America (Connors 1973; Beach and Fahs 1925). By the early 1960s, however, more than eight hundred Protestant missionaries from fifty-eight missionary agencies and more than five hundred Catholic missionaries from scores of religious orders were sent to live and work in Central America (U.S. Catholic Mission Association 1993; Directory 1960). This missionary presence grew steadily for almost two decades until its peak in 1979, when the total number of North American missionaries in Central America had expanded to 2,234 (see figure 6.1).[2] This means that, given what appears to have been an average annual missionary turnover rate of about 6 percent, we can estimate that approximately 3,900 North American religious workers served in Central America over the twenty-two-year period from 1959 until the commencement of the Reagan administration. The period of time when the greatest number of North American missionaries were serving in Central America was precisely the years before and after the Nicaraguan revolution, the Salvadoran insurrection and civil war, and the bloody Guatemalan counterinsurgency campaign.

This decades-long involvement of almost four thousand North American pastoral workers in Central America had important consequences for the political struggle over Central America in the U.S. in the 1980s. First, it supplied a large group of religious workers very knowledgeable and concerned about the region who became vocal advocates for Central America back home. AFSC organizer Angela Berryman explains (1990), "A lot of the church involvement, especially for Catholics, goes back to the 1960s and Pope John XXIII's call for religious people to go to Latin America. Very many priests and nuns went. The majority lived in poor communities and didn't hobnob with the elite. Of course, they couldn't help but be affected by what they saw and heard. So there was an experiential, personal bond created over those many years."[3]

These personal bonds with the poor motivated the missionaries to work back in their North American churches to raise awareness about Central America.

> There was a group of North Americans who had served in Central America mostly as missionaries, and had grown to love it and understand it as much as any North American can. They functioned as a constituency that was constantly trying to draw people's attention to the concerns of Central America. Their work helped prepare the ground over several decades. When things began to happen there in the 1970s and 80s, they became an important resource, particularly for the religious community. I doubt you could find a missionary today who knows very much

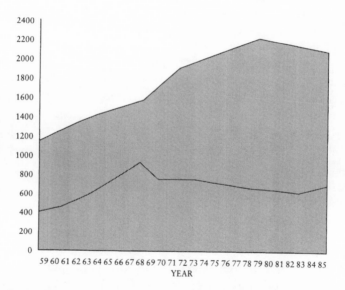

59 60 61 62 63 64 65 66 67 68 69 70 71 72 73 74 75 76 77 78 79 80 81 82 83 84 85
YEAR

Fig. 6.1. North American Protestant and Catholic Missionaries to Central America: 1959-1985. Source: *Annual Report on U.S. Catholic Overseas Mission 1992-1993; Mission Handbook 1973, 1986; Directory of North American Protestant Foreign Mission Agencies 1962; Directory of North American Protestant Missionaries Overseas 1968.*

about Bosnia-Herzegovina. But right now I could call one hundred people I know who had once served in Guatemala. (Clark 1992)

These thousands of missionaries had a bridging effect between Central and North America, generating a multitude of strong relational bonds between North American religious leaders, pastors, and congregations and their counterparts in Central America:[4] These ties helped create in many North American religious communities a feeling of personal identification with the people of Central America. Witness for Peace leader Betsy Crites tells us (1992), "With Central America, there were strong religious ties that created a great awareness. My husband was a priest in Honduras, for example. So, you have missionaries in Central America deeply in love with Central Americans and torn apart by the suffering of those people. Their pain meant that we North American Christians could not help but get involved and respond."

Religious commonalities provided a natural basis for this personal identification. Mike Clark, director of Witness for Peace, recalled (1992), "The Central American people shared the sort of religious assumptions that, for example, the core people of Witness for Peace shared. You didn't have to learn about a very different religious tradition to relate to them. These were Catholics and Protestants who sang the same hymns we did."

As a result, for many North American church people, potentially alien foreigners came to feel like spiritual family. Through this relationship, these North Americans became increasingly interested in the concerns of their Central American brothers and sisters and better educated about the social and political problems of Central America.

> One factor that made the Christian church, especially Catholics, so ready to respond to the situation in Central America was the prior involvement of many people in the Church who worked in Latin America in the 1960s and 70s. Many had gone down to "save" Latin America or to do good things, a la Peace Corps, with religious motivations. Many of them came back to the U.S. having been radicalized by Latin America, or at least profoundly affected by Latin America. They were changed. So when the U.S. media began focusing on Central America in the early 80s, the ground was prepared for a response by the parts of the religious community that had been affected by Latin America and had become aware of poverty and human-rights concerns. There had been an engagement in Central American political issues. (Quigley 1990)

For all of these reasons, when Central America became a political concern in the U.S. in the 1980s, many in the U.S. religious community were primed to attend closely to the issue.

Finally, this missionary connection provided church people in the U.S. their own firsthand source of information on Central America that in the 1980s served as an alternative to the information and analysis advanced by the Reagan administration. According to Crites (1992): "Catholic priests and nuns and Protestant missionaries were all sending the word back to their counterparts in the U.S.: 'This is what's really going on here, not what Reagan is saying.' That was very disturbing for the religious community in the U.S." These reports tended to carry great authority for North American religious people because they came from priests, nuns, and pastors, and because they were based on direct, personal experience.

> These were people living in Central America for long periods of time, who had become very knowledgeable and conscious of the reality there. So, in the 1980s when Reagan began hyping Central America, these people said, "Well, that's not my experience. I don't think that's true at all." That was the beginning. The Central America movement capitalized on that person-to-person experience. When a missionary has a real feel for Central America and someone in the U.S. turns around and declares that the problem is communism, they say, "You know, that's not so. My experience is very different than that." That experiential base is much more powerful than an intellectual one.[5] (Berryman 1990)

The missionary connection gave many U.S. Christians a reason to question White House pronouncements on Central America. In time, that doubt would grow into political resistance. Marker observes (1992):

> There were large numbers of missionaries and church people already in Central America. How many missionaries were in Vietnam? Almost none. And the church basically went along with Vietnam. But in the case of Central America, the church resisted. Because you actually had people from every church—Baptists, Methodists, every denomination, every Catholic order—saying, "What Ronald Reagan is telling you about Central America is simply not true." That message was coming back from trusted people on the ground in Central America.

Eventually, the sharp contrast between White House statements and the reports of the missionaries they trusted led many U.S. Christians to conclude that the President was not simply ill-informed, but was intentionally deceiving the U.S. public about Central America. This conclusion, combined with a growing awareness of the human suffering in Central America, helped to generate in the U.S. church community a passionate opposition to President Reagan's policy.

Liberation Theology

The North American missionary connection was not the only factor attracting the attention of U.S. church people to Central America in the 1970s and '80s. Years before Ronald Reagan declared a crisis in Central America, a major religious movement in Central and South America—liberation theology—had already engrossed the interest of and exerted a powerful influence on many Christians in the U.S.

Liberation theology emerged in the Latin American church in the late 1960s, heavily influenced by the revolutionary mood of the time and by neo-Marxist social analysis. It taught that God is working in history to liberate humanity from every injustice and oppression—whether spiritual, cultural, economic, or political.[6] Liberation theology taught that the church must make a "preferential option for the poor" and join in the political struggle, God's struggle, for justice for the oppressed. By becoming an agent of social transformation, the church participates in the realization of history's true end: the new society of God's kingdom (Smith 1991: 25–50). Liberation theology was a radical departure from the conservative theological and social orientation that characterized the Latin American church for most of its history. In 1968, in Medellín, Colombia, the Latin American Catholic bishops endorsed a set of official church documents that reflected a liberation theology orientation. By 1972, the influence of liberation theology had spread—through radicalized bishops, theologians, priests, nuns, and lay pastoral workers—to millions of people in Latin America (Smith 1991: 150–88).

This radical movement did not go unnoticed in the United States where, we have seen, so many church people were aware of the concerns of their Latin American counterparts. Liberation theology also made a considerable impact in the North American churches. Pledge of Resistance leader Ken Butigan has said (1991), "There was an experiment of truth going on all over Latin America in the 1960s and 70s with liberation theology, to the point where even the bishops began to proclaim the preferential option for the poor. Many North Americans were hearing the proclamation from Christians in Nicaragua, El Salvador, Chile, and Brazil that God loves the poor and opposes oppression. We in the U.S. were very much evangelized by them."

Liberation theology made its way to the U.S. through a variety of channels. It was transmitted through innumerable North American bishops, foreign-missions boards, religious orders, denominational bureaucrats, seminary professors, and missionaries that had regular, direct contact with church people in Central America. It was diffused through the Maryknoll Order's publishing house, Orbis Books, which translated and published many important works of Latin American liberation theology—including Gustavo Gutierrez's groundbreaking *A Theology of Liberation* (1973), which has sold more than one hundred thousand copies in the U.S. Furthermore, in the 1970s a number of important North American Protestant and Catholic theologians— such as Harvey Cox, John Coleman, and Robert McAfee Brown— wrote and taught extensively about liberation theology. Books that especially helped to diffuse liberation theology in the U.S. included Argentine liberation theologian José Miguez Bonino's *Doing Theology in a Revolutionary Situation* (1975), written specifically to explicate liberation theology for a North American audience, and Robert McAfee Brown's *Theology in a New Key: Responding to Liberation Themes* (1978). In addition, in 1975, exiled Chilean liberation theologian Sergio Torres organized a conference in Detroit titled "Theology in the Americas," which brought together for extended dialogue many North American theologians and Latin American liberation theologians (Torres and Eagleson 1976). In these ways, liberation theology was disseminated throughout North American church circles, especially in more progressive religious communities. By the end of the 1970s, virtually every Christian seminary and divinity school in the U.S. was offering course work in the theology of liberation, most Christian bookstores were selling books on liberation theology, and many Catholic and mainline Protestant believers had heard about liberation theology.

Thousands of North American Christians, especially politically progressive Christians, came to value this radical theology and absorbed many of its key themes and assumptions. Ideas about Christian-Marxist dialogue, the God of the oppressed, the Exodus as liberation, the option for the poor, the gospel of justice, the politically engaged church, the historic significance of the poor, and liberation spiritualities gained considerable currency among many U.S. theologians, priests, nuns, ministers, teachers, and lay people. Between 1973 and 1987, seventy-six U.S. religion and history students wrote doctoral dissertations about Latin American liberation theology or black, feminist, or other types of liberation theology, many of which were published (UMI 1973–87). By the end of the 1970s, many U.S. Christians looked with admiration and anticipation to liberationist believers in Latin America—especially in Central America—for spiritual inspiration and insight. Thus, events in Central America again commanded the attention of many U.S. church people. The more U.S. Christians adopted the views of liberation theology, the more they came to identify with poor Central American Christians struggling for justice. This identification was a major impetus behind U.S. Christians' involvement in the Central America peace movement (Epstein 1991: 13, 203; Davidson 1988: 24; Crittenden 1988: 25, 108, 178). The liberationist struggle of Christians in Central America, observes Witness for Peace organizer Ed Griffin-Nolan (1991: 39), "inspired and called people in the U.S. to action."

Of particular interest to North American students of liberation theology was the Nicaragua revolution of 1979, which exhibited many religiously fascinating and unprecedented features that reflected the liberationist struggle for justice. In Nicaragua, there had been widespread religious opposition to the Somoza regime in the years before the revolution. In 1979, Managua's Catholic archbishop Obando y Bravo had publicly sanctioned the use of violence against the collapsing regime. Many liberationist Christians had actually participated in the armed insurrection, to such an extent that the FSLN formally acknowledged the important role Christians played in defeating Somoza. After the revolution, four Catholic priests became high-ranking officials in the Sandinista government and the Nicaraguan church became acrimoniously divided over political matters. All of this generated a great deal of tension within the national hierarchy and with the Vatican (Berryman 1984; Dodson and O'Shaughnessy 1985).

Many in the U.S. church community became fascinated not only by these religious aspects of the revolution, but also by what appeared to be the Nicaraguan people's struggle to build a new and different kind of society in the third world. Seeing Nicaragua's distinctive mixed economic system and non-aligned foreign policy, they felt very hopeful about the revolution's potential for improving the living standards of Nicaragua's people while promoting economic equity. According to Griffin-Nolan (1991: 39): "Revolutionary Christians throughout Latin America saw Nicaragua both as an example and as a beacon of hope. U.S. Christians seeking to change their own society saw Nicaragua as an experiment and a sign of hope." According to Witness for Peace organizer Mike Clark (1992):

People had a strong sense that something new might be entering history in Nicaragua. And you know you might have one chance in a generation to be part of that. People said, "If this is it, then, by God, I need to see what it's about and be part of it." This had an incredible draw bringing people to Nicaragua. We saw Nicaraguans struggling to make a different life for themselves, and a government, although not without its problems, that was actually concerned about the poor. We also saw the first major 20th century revolution where religion had played an absolutely central role, supporting the revolution and not opposing it. It really seemed something new in history was coming to birth. I can't tell you how important that was in impressing North Americans.[7]

For these Christians, President Reagan's Central American policy—so determined to counter the Nicaraguan revolution and oust the Sandinistas from power—was not just a matter of faulty political analysis and judgment. It represented the reversal of liberation theology's historical project, the frustration of the poor's aspirations for justice, and the destruction of one of the third world's greatest hopes. For these U.S. church people, such a policy was absolutely intolerable. To them, what was at stake was not self-interest or geopolitical politics, but spiritual truth and historic destiny.

Religious Murders

Nicaragua was not the only focus of attention for U.S. church people with missionary connections and Christians influenced by liberation theology. In the late 1970s, the struggle for human rights and social justice in El Salvador captured the interest of many politically aware Americans. But again, the U.S. religious community, especially the Roman Catholic church, was socially situated to have special reason to be informed about, involved in, and outraged by events there. For its counterpart, the church in El Salvador, played a major role in challenging El Salvador's military-political regime and, for so doing, paid dearly.

On March 24, 1980, the Roman Catholic Archbishop of San Salvador, Oscar Romero, was gunned down by a right-wing assassin while celebrating mass with his congregation. He died within minutes. Romero had been a popular and outspoken champion of peace and human rights in El Salvador. His bold, public confrontations with the government and military made him a renowned symbol of the church's opposition to violence, oppression, and injustice. One day after Romero, in a church homily, ordered Salvadoran soldiers to disobey their commanders by refusing to kill civilians, a right-wing death-squad group linked to the military had him murdered. The gunman was never brought to justice (Brockman 1982). This assassination sent shock waves through the Catholic church in Central and North America and Europe. Nine months later, four American churchwomen—three nuns and a lay missionary—performing religious and social work in El Salvador were driving together from the San Salvador airport at night when they were abducted by government security forces, raped, and murdered. Their bodies were found the next morning, buried in shallow roadside graves. The Salvadoran government conducted no serious investigation. Again, Roman Catholics in Central and North America were horrified and outraged (Brett and Brett 1988).

The assassination of Romero and the murder of the four churchwomen had an immense political effect in the U.S. religious community. To begin, it heightened awareness about violence and injustice in Central America for many previously uninformed church people. According to Epstein (1991: 204), this led "many American Catholics to feel a personal connection to El Salvador and a personal responsibility for U.S. policy in Central America." "They may not know where El Salvador is," explained Rev. J. Bryan Hehir, U.S. Catholic Conference's (USCC) international director, about American Catholic laity (quoted in Keller 1982: 898), "but they know killing a bishop while he's saying mass is not something they ought to be passive about." The murders also mobilized thousands of U.S. Catholics and sympathetic Protestants actively to oppose U.S. Central American policy. According to Arnson (1988: 54), "Religious groups, particularly the Catholic church and Protestant denominations, led public opinion in opposition to U.S. support for authoritarian regimes. Persecution of the church and of the poor was the taproot of this activism, which swelled dramatically after the 1980 murders of Archbishop Romero and four U.S. churchwomen in El Salvador." For many Central America peace movement activists, the religious murders were their introduction to the movement. One Witness for Peace delegate, a Presbyterian minister, reported on her 1991 questionnaire: "The assassination of Oscar Romero began my awareness of Central America specifically. After that event I became involved in worship, organizing, and protests." Romero's assassination, in particular, unified the U.S. bishops in political opposition to U.S. aid to El Salvador. According to USCC staff member Thomas Quigley (1990), "By 1980 and through the 1980s, there was a readiness on the part of our bishops to be more deeply involved in U.S. policy on El Salvador at a very specific level. There was almost no hesitancy across the whole ideological spectrum of bishops about taking a stand. The bishops felt that one of theirs, Oscar Romero, had been slain."

Perhaps more importantly, the murders of the four churchwomen especially compelled members of Catholic women's religious orders to mobilize for Central America activism.

> The murder of the four women in El Salvador was particularly signifi-cant in turning on religious women here in the U.S., who are already well organized within the church community. They are very significant. It's usually not priests, but religious women, who do much of this work. Tens of thousands of people have been murdered in Central America. But the rapes and murders of the four in El Salvador gave religious women in the U.S. much more of a bond to identify with, a real burden to carry. There is a big difference between simply opposing aid to El Sal-vador, which the bishops did after Romero's murder, and being ignited by moral outrage to activism. It was religious women, not the bishops, who pulled the people together, who organized and carried out the movement. (Berryman 1990)

As a result of the shocking murders in El Salvador, hundreds of new religious activist groups were formed across the country. Boston-area Sanctuary organizer Jane Guise tells of her experience (1990): "The killings of Romero and the religious women certainly had a big impact on me. It was shocking. I actually knew one of the women, Nora Carr. After their murders, I started a weekly vigil at Park Street, in Boston, which still continues. A local group of religious orders also formed an organization called the Catholic Connection. And we organized a coalition for an education and petition drive on Central America and Salvadoran refugees."

Additionally, the murders further radicalized and incited to deeper commitment many religious activists already involved in the newly emerging Central America movement. One Catholic immersed in Sanctuary work recalled in her 1991 questionnaire: "I had already been involved in some activism. But Oscar Romero's death was the beginning of my *serious* commitment to a life of prayerful activism."

Finally, Romero and the four women came to serve as "sacred icons" in the Central America peace movement—often present in its speech, ritual, and narrative—ever inspiring in activists a renewed resolve, hope, and readiness to sacrifice. As one female Methodist pastor and Sanctuary activist explained on her 1991 questionnaire, "Archbishop Romero, whose presence lives so strongly in the people of El Salvador, has taught me about crucifixion and resurrection. As I experienced Romero, this gave me tremendous hope. I realized that you can't kill the light, no matter how much darkness surrounds it, the light will and does break through. This gives some hope to press on."

Similarly, in many U.S. church communities, Romero and the four women became emblems of the immorality of U.S. Central American policy, martyrs for the gospel cause of justice and liberation, moral symbols around which vigils, demonstrations, and rallies were called, and inspiring heroes in whose memory ensuing battles to end U.S. involvement in Central America were waged (see, for instance, Collins 1990; Davidson 1988: 68). Recall that the 1989 White House demonstration commemorating the ninth anniversary of Romero's assassination, although many years into a wearying struggle, produced the largest number of arrests, 580, of any Pledge of Resistance protest.

Stories of Refugees

The Central American missionary connection, liberation theology, and the religious murders in El Salvador all worked to generate an unusual level of interest in and concern for Central America among church people in the U.S. These factors also provided the occasion for the beginnings of hostility toward U.S. Central American policy. But absolutely nothing ignited in U.S. citizens the fierce insurgent consciousness for activism more than personal encounters with the traumatized victims of the U.S.-sponsored war in Central America. Nothing so deeply disturbed and enraged so many Americans, sending them headlong into the struggle to defeat White House policy, as hearing flesh-and-blood men, women, and children tell heartrending stories of hunger, terror, disappearances, torture, executions, rape, and mass murder.

Such personal encounters between Central and North Americans were well facilitated by the fact that vast numbers of Central American refugees poured into the U.S. in the early 1980s. In 1960, less than 4 percent of all U.S. immigrants had come from Central America, the Caribbean, and Mexico combined. By the early 1980s, Central American refugees, fleeing political repression and military brutality, were flooding into the U.S. (Pastor 1982: 35–36; see LeMoyne 1987). Between 1979 and 1982, a half-million Salvadorans fled the political violence in their country and came to the United States. By 1982, an estimated 250,000 Nicaraguans, 10 percent of that nation's entire population, had been driven by the violent insurrection and revolution to emigrate to the U.S. (Pastor 1982: 36). By 1983, Guatemala's counterinsurgency war had displaced one million people—14 percent of the entire population—and up to two hundred thousand of them had fled to Mexico (Jonas 1991: 164). Many Guatemalan refugees continued on into the U.S. As the story of Jim Corbett and Sanctuary demonstrates, refugee contact with Americans, particularly with U.S. church people, was inevitable. That contact, it turned out, had politically momentous consequences. "The Sanctuary refugees actually brought the war in Central America *here* to the U.S. The refugees told their dreadful stories, while the U.S. government told a very different story. This human contact helped move anyone with a conscience, even people not previously politicized, to become active. This helped escalate the movement. This human contact was very much at the heart of the movement" (Berryman 1990).

Bob and Pat Van Denend were Central America activists who, as part of the Overground Railroad, helped transport undocumented Central American refugees from Georgia, through Kentucky, and on to contacts in Ohio. Their experience, told in a 1992 interview, illustrates this process:

> We got local church people involved in our work by having refugees stay in their homes. When refugees came through, we put together pot luck dinners, invited lots of area church people, and asked refugees to tell us their stories. The effect was amazing. I mean, there was never a dry eye in the place after they were done. Horrible, horrible stories. Incredible stories. People were very deeply touched. We would even bring in translators who weren't activist types, but after translating those stories, they *became* activists. There was direct human contact. People could see these were real, hurting people, not a bunch of radical, scary Marxists, but people with families and kids that had endured absolutely horrible experiences. It really touched people personally.

And the political effect?

> This was a tremendous organizing tool, one of the best I have ever seen. Real powerful stuff. After hearing refugees tell their stories, these mainstream church people were more than willing to transport and house refugees, donate money, whatever. They also became very skeptical, at the very least, of the White House line about what was going on in Central America.

The power of Central American refugees' personal stories of repression and war to move North Americans emotionally and politically is demonstrated in these statements of Sanctuary and Witness for Peace activists, written on their 1991 questionnaires (two of which were already quoted in the Introduction):

> Listening to Guatemalan indians profoundly changed our view of things. Spending this time with people who are the victims of U.S. policy intensified my commitment to resist it. Through them, I saw the grotesque genocidal behavior of our government and our complicity with it through our tax dollars.

> I became involved in Central America work by hearing the stories of refugees. Their accounts engaged me on a deep emotional level. So, I set about educating myself, and became very committed.

> Initially, I disbelieved our refugee's stories of personal peril, bestial treatment by the army, rampant murder of villagers, and persecution of family. It was too incredible to me. Eventually, I realized he was telling the truth. And I saw the terrible toll this experience had had on this man and his family. It was very disturbing.

> The refugees introduced me first-hand to gross injustice and violence. Through their stories, I learned an awful lot about the dark side of my government.

> After seeing those beautiful brown faces, hearing their personal tragedies, stories of torture, brutality, tragedy so horrendous it offends love, you realize it can kill the human spirit. But the crucifixion has taken on new meaning for me: it is through suffering, I have learned from the refugees, that we learn compassion.

> Hearing the testimonies of Salvadoran refugees in Sanctuary, whose stories greatly differed from the tale my government was spreading, was for me the beginning of a decade of ongoing political activism.

The refugees' personal stories were greatly effective in generating this kind of insurgent consciousness for two reasons. First, they effectively transformed the Central American crisis for Americans from a broad and abstract issue in the news into a specific, concrete reality sitting in one's church or living room. Distant matters of foreign policy, national security, and aid appropriations suddenly became embodied in flesh-and-blood human beings with comprehensible autobiographies that elicited strong responses of emotional identification. Hearing refugees' personal stories, in other words, was an experience of relevance-magnification.

Phenomenological sociologists, such as Alfred Schutz, Thomas Luckmann, and Peter Berger have persuasively argued that people's consciousness is primarily formed by the practical concerns of *everyday life*. Berger writes: "All consciousness, religious or other, [is rooted] in the world of everyday *praxis*" (1967: 128). And Schutz states (1971: 222, 227; also see Berger and Luckmann 1966: 19–46):

> The wide-awake man within the natural attitude is primarily interested in that sector of the world of his everyday life which is within his scope and which is centered in space and time around himself. The place which my body occupies within the world, my actual Here, is the starting point from which I take my bearing. . . . We have an immanently practical interest in it, caused by the necessity of complying with the basic requirements of our life. . . . The selective function of our interest organizes the world . . . in strata of major and minor relevance.

From this perspective, human beings, driven by the need to impose meaning and order on an otherwise chaotic sensory experience, socially construct and inhabit "life-worlds" that sustain a meaningful sense of reality. The inherent fragility and precariousness of those socially constructed life-worlds are counteracted by the intersubjective reality reinforcement and functional reliability of each world's shared "stock of knowledge." That is, the artificial "reality" appears ontologically real and epistemologically believable only to the extent that its assumptions are collectively embraced by those who inhabit that life-world and its prescriptions prove pragmatically functional in the course of empirically lived experience. To be believable and, therefore, meaningful, the implications and dictates of people's constructed realities must "work," they must "perform" when it comes to the problems and challenges of everyday life. What primarily determines the substance of any life-world's "stock of knowledge" for the people who inhabit that life-world, therefore, is their everyday pragmatic concerns. This is why Alfred Schutz (1971: 262) claimed that people's "paramount reality" is the reality of everyday life.

Practically speaking, this means that facts which are known, but only from a distance or in the abstract, can engage an individual at a cognitive level, but will not likely make a deep impression on the individual's consciousness or significantly alter their behavior. On the other hand, events that break into individuals' everyday experience and impose themselves as problems or challenges on empirically lived, commonplace existence stand a much greater chance of modifying or transforming consciousness and behavior. Schutz wrote (1971: 228): "It is characteristic of the natural attitude that it takes the world and its objects for granted until counterproof imposes itself. . . . We have no reason to cast any doubt upon our warranted experiences which, so we believe, give us things as they really are. It needs a special motivation, such as the irruption of a 'strange' experience not subsumable under the stock of knowledge at hand or inconsistent with it, to make us revise our beliefs."

Theoretical problems elicit, at most, theoretical responses and hypothetical solutions. But a concrete problem that impinges on people's everyday life is likely to evoke the concrete response of the pragmatic search for an effective solution. Abstract issues are interesting, perhaps, but ultimately inconsequential. Personally experienced, everyday issues, however—especially emotionally gripping ones—become unavoidably relevant. They impose themselves on human consciousness. This is exactly how the refugees and their stories functioned for their North American audiences: they irrupted as "a strange experience not subsumable under the stock of knowledge at hand," making Central America concrete, problematic, and unavoidably and painfully relevant.

The precise reason why this relevance was so unavoidable and painful suggests the second reason why the refugees' stories were quite effective in sparking insurgent consciousness: what the North Americans learned from the refugees' accounts deeply violated their moral standards. Human beings, we have argued, are, at the core, normative creatures. They are propelled, guided, and constrained by more or less conscious standards of the way things ought to be. When people's standards are violated, they often react in disapproval and anger. When dearly held standards are egregiously violated, people sometimes take action to try to oppose and prevent further violations. The refugees' gruesome experiences of deprivation, kidnapping, rape, torture, and execution—now thrust into the everyday lives of North Americans—flagrantly and heinously violated many of the North Americans' cherished, fundamental moral standards of human decency, civil rights, and political legitimacy. This evoked compassion and outrage. When the North Americans realized that many of those violations were not only being tolerated, but actually facilitated and sponsored by their own government, operating in their name, with their own tax money, the North Americans burned with culpability and guilt. This emotional combination of compassion, outrage, personal culpability, and guilt proved to be a potent formula for political resistance.

This disposition to act against that which deeply violates one's cherished moral norms is reflected clearly in Pledge of Resistance organizer Ken Butigan's summary (1991) of the cumulative effect of the factors we have thus far reviewed:

> You have the missionary connections, with missionaries coming back and missionizing their own people about what is really going on in Central America. Then you have the role church people played in the Nicaraguan and Salvadoran revolution. Then you have the witness and martyrdom of people like Oscar Romero and the four church women. People became aware of this cognitive dissonance: we are sending millions of dollars of military aid to a place the size of the San Francisco Bay area where, at the same time, tens of thousands of people were being slaughtered. Then here are these refugees in your own living room telling you about their brother executed or mother raped in front of their own eyes. When all of this came together, the embers struck, the flames started, and the organizing began. We had to do something to take the next step. What can you do? You simply cannot name the intolerable and not do something about it. Actions have to follow a confrontation with the intolerable.

Interestingly, this particular experience of politically educational mass mobilization—thousands of citizens being moved to political action by the personal stories of refugees—appears to be historically unprecedented. Scores of political movements through the years have mobilized in the name of political freedom, higher wages, cultural autonomy, civil rights, national independence, environmental protection, religious sovereignty, and gender equality. But never before in the history of disruptive politics has a movement been triggered, as this movement was, by people's personal encounters with the victims of their own nation's aggression sitting in their own living rooms and sharing stories of tragedy and anguish. Never before had so many thousands of "the enemy" broken into the everyday lives of ordinary people and, through simple human contact, provoked such an emotionally and morally driven commitment to political resistance. This unique and powerful experience of encounter was the strategic linchpin of the Sanctuary movement's political efforts. It was the primary energy that fueled much of the Central America peace movement.

With regard to the Pledge of Resistance, for example, Ken Butigan explains (1991), "There is no question but that the work of Sanctuary and the refugees' dreadful stories helped generate the Pledge of Resistance. The Pledge would not have been one-tenth of what it was without that groundwork having been done. It had an incalculable effect, a multiplier effect. Many, many of our organizers, in fact, came directly out of Sanctuary work."

Thus, Central America peace movement activists—particularly Sanctuary organizers—stumbled upon, were mobilized by, then further capitalized on the power of abhorrent violations of moral convictions confronting people in their everyday-life existence to provoke the insurgent consciousness that generated and sustained political disruption.

Geographical Proximity

Listening to the heartrending stories of refugees in one's church or living room was only one way to be exposed to the tragedy of Central America. Another was to hear the stories of Central Americans in *their* churches and living rooms, to actually see for oneself the Central American story unfold. If the refugees brought the war to the U.S., asked many U.S. citizens interested in learning more about the region, why not reciprocate and bring the U.S. to the war? This is precisely what many Americans did. During the 1980s, tens of thousands of U.S. citizens traveled to Central America for a firsthand encounter with revolution, injustice, repression, and war. The results often matched those produced by the refugees' stories told in the U.S.: Americans came home deeply affected by what they had seen and heard, committing themselves to resist and defeat President Reagan's Central America policy. According to Lars Schoultz (1987: 5), "Most of the church groups that opposed the Reagan policy did so because of their members' first-hand experiences in Latin America, experiences that were often so strongly offensive that they created a passionately committed opposition."

Gail Phares has commented (1992), "You have to find ways to make Central America real. Central America is like talking about the moon. People don't know where it is or why they should be concerned about it. Bringing Central Americans to the U.S. has an impact on people. But the best thing is to get them down there. Once they've been down, they will always be changed."

All of this was made possible by one simple fact: Central America is very close to the U.S.—a few hours flight from Miami—and airfare to Central American destinations were relatively inexpensive. AFSC organizer Angela Berryman explains (1990):

> Nicaragua is just two days drive from the U.S. border, as Ronald Reagan often repeated to emphasize the threat of communism. But this proximity was a two-edged sword, for it gave many North Americans the opportunity to see Central America for themselves. That hasn't happened in any other world region in a way that actually affected U.S. foreign policy. People opposed Vietnam because U.S. soldiers were there. But with Central America there was much more of a sense of identification because there were so many Americans traveling there.

And see it they did. By 1986, more than one hundred thousand U.S. citizens had toured Nicaragua to observe its revolution firsthand (Falcoff 1986: 6; see Courtney 1987a). In 1985 alone, forty thousand Americans traveled to the land of Sandino. The volume of foreigners, especially Americans, traveling to Nicaragua was so large that tourism provided the fifth largest source of foreign-exchange earnings, employing twenty-five thousand Nicaraguans directly and indirectly (Burns 1987: 102). Tens of thousands of Americans also traveled to El Salvador, Guatemala, and Honduras in the 1980s, to see for themselves the area that had become the focus of so much political controversy. By 1987, more than 230 different North American organizations were sponsoring and organizing educational trips to Central America (Central America Resource Center 1986).

Many, if not most, of the Americans who traveled to Central America were church people—especially mainstream Protestants and progressive Catholics. Most traveled with tour groups sponsored by denominations, church committees on social justice or hunger, religious orders, and social-change organizations. In a short time, an entire organizational network developed to coordinate these tours (Falcoff 1986: 7). Dick Junkin, a Presbyterian sent by his denomination in 1983 to be a Central American "peace associate," who in four-and-one-half years coordinated forty-five tours himself, recalled in a 1991 interview: "I quickly became aware that I was only one small part of a much larger phenomenon. I made contacts with colleagues in every country doing the same thing. There were groups running these tours all over Central America. The Presbyterians probably did more than any other denomination. But there were others, plenty of others. There was an entire network of people down there—mostly people of faith—running these travel groups."

According to Junkin (1991), some of the visitors were actively recruited by their religious organizations, but many others were recruited through informal relational networks: "We would have one delegation down and they would return home and talk about their trip. Word would spread and we would get these telephone calls asking us to take such-and-such a group. Traveling to Central America was just as much a grass-roots groundswell as an institutionally organized thing."

Witness for Peace was only one of a multitude of groups bringing delegations to Central America. But Witness for Peace maintained a unique niche in the system: it was the only group that intentionally transported delegations to battle areas to witness the destruction, document cases of human rights abuses, and—they hoped—discourage Contra attacks through their presence. Hence, Witness for Peace's strategy, compared to that of other tour groups, involved the greatest personal risk for delegates. This element of risk was purposeful. Bob Bonthius, Witness for Peace organizer and participant in the original July 1983 delegation to Jalapa, said in a 1990 interview, "We realized pedagogically that the way you change people's thinking is by engaging them in risk-oriented action. Direct, personal, risk-taking exposure is really the best pedagogy for social action, a life-changer in a way that no amount of didactics ever is. We knew that was key because it had happened to us in Jalapa."

Whatever the degree of risk, however, Central America travel generally affected the North American pilgrims in a way similar to the effects produced by the stories of refugees. "These tours," wrote Mark Falcoff (1986: 7–8),

> are intended to have a concrete impact upon American foreign policy. In very large measure, they do. Returning visitors deluge their local newspapers and congressional representatives with letters. To what degree has Nicaraguan revolutionary tourism affected U.S. policy? . . . It has helped to create a domestic political constituency where none existed before—an impressive network of lobbying and letter-writing activities that constitute a serious obstacle to the Reagan administration's Central American policies.

Dick Junkin (1991) recounted the kind of shock he observed Central America travel had on visiting Americans:

> Most people from the U.S. were utterly unprepared to deal with the kind of poverty and suffering they saw in Central America. Nor were they pre-

pared for the depth of Christian commitment and hope and faith they encountered. We just don't experience that in this country. People go down and are just smashed in the face by both suffering and hope. There were even conversion experiences, like career military people totally overwhelmed. Years later, I still run into people who tell me, "I still think about our trip. It won't let me go." No question but that people come back from that experience motivated to defeat Reagan's policy.

Central America travel could be quite disorienting and confusing for many Americans, calling into question their basic assumptions, world-views, and commitments. Many confronted disturbing perspectives of their own government. As Witness for Peace activist Betsy Crites (1992) related:

> These poor Nicaraguans would say, "Please go back and tell your President Reagan we want peace. We don't want to hurt your country." They would say, "We understand your situation. We know what it's like not to have a democratic country. We once lived under a brutal dicta-tor." Nicaraguan *campesinos* saw the contradiction of so many thousands of good-willed American citizens coming to visit them, while the U.S. government waged war on them, and concluded, "Obviously the United States cannot really be a democratic country." That was a new and troubling thought for most Americans.

One sixty-nine-year-old Witness for Peace delegate wrote in a 1991 letter to the author: "It is not easy to feel patriotic when one goes to a cemetery to view with survivors the mass graves of 34 victims of a U.S. mine explosion and of 80 children strafed on a airstrip runway as they were about to be evacuated." Bob Bonthius (1990) described the emotional consequences he experienced and observed in typical delegates traveling Nicaragua:

> You go to Nicaragua with a nice concern for the poor and anxiety over a U.S. invasion. But then you get there and are hit with three very strong emotions. One is guilt, when you see what your country is doing. The second is outrage. You get absolutely galvanized by anger. The third emotion is hope—not your hope, but theirs. The hope of the Nicaraguans was just a marvelous thing, as they struggled to build a new society. And the idea that we could help them by getting the U.S. off their backs was inspiring. Together, these three deeply internalized emotions provided a powerful impetus for activism.

Firsthand encounters with Central America often produced shocking confrontations with poverty and suffering, troubling challenges to people's political worldviews, and intense feelings of guilt, outrage, and hope that deeply impressed the consciousness of many North American visitors. Many returned home, like Jeff Boyer and Gail Phares, committed to confronting and reversing U.S. Central America policy. Witness for Peace President, Sam Hope, recalled in a 1992 interview:

> I remember, at a demonstration in Washington, the moderator of the Presbyterian Church—a denominational leader, 65 years old, Seminary president, author, everything else—saying to the crowd, "I stayed in the home of a Nicaraguan last January named Manuel Rivera. I promised him then that I would tell his story here in the U.S. I have since learned that he has been killed by the Contras. So I feel even more strongly that I must tell his story. I would rather not get arrested for the first time in my life. But I'm afraid I must. Manuel Rivera is the reason." Then he goes up, kneels down to pray, gets arrested, and is led off to jail.

This kind of thing happened because the firsthand experience of Central America—like the stories of refugees—thrust into people's everyday-life consciousness a reality that deeply violated their moral sensibilities. Traveling to the region suddenly made the people of Central America very real and their afflictions very relevant. In the words of one Witness for Peace delegate, Aynn Setright (quoted in Griffin-Nolan 1991: 198), "The cause I came here crusading has been replaced by the people, the individuals I've met." People had witnessed the intolerable, in Ken Butigan's words, and were compelled to respond with action.

Frustration with Conventional Politics

Most Americans believe that their political system, though imperfect, ultimately responds to the will of the people. Thus, when so many Americans took action to end the intolerable suffering they heard in refugees' stories and saw firsthand in Central America, they expected their political system to listen and respond. Rather quickly, however, they learned otherwise. That was radicalizing. Part of the anger that fired the Central America peace movement resulted from people's early experiences of frustration with the standard mechanisms of political influence. Almost every normal channel of power in the institutionalized political process proved inadequately responsive to, if not impervious to, the concerns of opponents of White House policy.

To begin, as we will see below, President Reagan steadfastly disregarded the majority of Americans' consistent opposition to his Central

American policy. Rather than acknowledging or honoring the will of the American people, the President pressed on year after year with covert military campaigns, requests for massive aid packages, trade embargoes, repeated military maneuvers, secret CIA operations, and thinly veiled threats of invasion. Even the constraints of the U.S. Constitution and congressional statutes did not restrain the President's determination to intervene aggressively in Central America. This presidential disregard for public opinion incensed many U.S. citizens concerned about Central America.

Many refugee advocates also found the INS largely indifferent to and sometimes contemptuous of their concerns in the year before the formal declaration of Sanctuary. This had a radicalizing effect. Originally, the first Sanctuary activists had wanted to employ legal means to help the refugees. But their efforts to do so were frustrated by unhelpful, antagonistic, and sometimes devious immigration officers. For example, had the Santa Cruz Border Patrol, El Centro's director, Mr. Aguirre, or Tucson INS Director William Johnson been more forthright and cooperative with Jim Corbett, the Sanctuary movement might never have emerged at all. But refugees were illegally deported, bail charges were inordinately inflated, and refugee advocates were lied to and stonewalled. Consequently, some, like Corbett and John Fife, felt forced to resort to defiant and illegal tactics, which escalated the entire conflict.

Likewise, early opponents of military aid to El Salvador found working with Congress a fruitless means of political action. At the beginning, many opponents of the administration's policy hoped that Congress would reject requests for military aid if the facts were known. They wrote, called, and met with their representatives, collected petition signatures, and testified repeatedly in congressional hearings. The Catholic bishops and Protestant leaders especially urged an end to Salvadoran aid (de Onis 1980a, 1980b, 1981a, 1981e; *New York Times* 1981g, 1981i, 1981j, 1981k, 1982c, 1982d; Briggs 1981, 1982). Even the Pope denounced foreign interference in El Salvador (Kamm 1982). Two-thirds of Americans polled reported wanting the U.S. to "stay out" of El Salvador (Roberts 1982). But in the end, those voices were disregarded. In early 1981, the Reagan administration requested a military aid package for El Salvador. Activists and church leaders around the country worked very hard to defeat the aid, lobbying, testifying, and writing thousands of letters opposing the President's request (see, among other works, Coston 1981; de Onis 1981a;

Alvarez 1981; *New York Times* 1981f). Congressional leaders were deluged with mail, between 75 and 100 percent of which opposed the aid. "I've never gotten so much reaction on any other issue," remarked Representative Clarence Long (D-Md.; quoted in Miller 1981), "People literally stop me in the street and tell me . . . to stop this involvement." Despite these lobbying efforts, Congress approved sending $25 million in military aid and fifty-four U.S. military advisers to El Salvador (Bonner 1981).

Aid opponents repeatedly encountered similar frustrations in the following years. Despite massive lobbying campaigns, widespread public opposition, and the support of liberal democrats, for eight years Congress would never terminate military aid to El Salvador. "There was always a fresh atrocity for Washington to be outraged about," writes Leogrande (1991: 127), "yet U.S. military aid kept flowing." Eventually, many activists concluded that, as long as they restricted themselves to the conventional mechanisms of political influence, they would never achieve their goals. As Americans who opposed the administration's Central American policy grew increasingly frustrated by the unresponsiveness of standard, institutionalized political means of influence—elections, opinion polls, petitions, lobbying campaigns—they increasingly shifted to unconventional means of influence: marches, blockades, demonstrations, occupations, and organized mass civil disobedience. Concerned involvement developed into insurgent consciousness. And public opinion unfolded into public disruption.

International Protests

We have examined a complex of forces and events that together generated the moral outrage and political commitment we call insurgent consciousness: the legacy of Christian and Jewish social ethics, the missionary connection to Central America, the influence of liberation theology, the outrage of religious murders, radicalizing stories of refugees, easy travel to Central America, and frustration with the results of conventional political action. Together, these forces and events were more than enough to generate the energy that activated and sustained the Central America peace movement. But one other relatively minor factor deserves mention: protests against President Reagan's Central America policy in Canada and Europe that affirmed the U.S. protesters' activism.

On January 31, 1981, fifteen thousand Germans demonstrated

against U.S. military aid to El Salvador, storming through downtown Frankfurt shouting "Yankee go home!" and throwing paint on and slashing the tires of American cars (*New York Times* 1981b). Five weeks later, one thousand Swedes gathered in Stockholm's main square to protest American involvement in El Salvador, projecting pictures of Salvador's war casualties on a huge screen (*New York Times* 1981e). Five days later, hundreds of Canadian demonstrators heckled a visiting President Reagan outside Ottawa's Parliament building for his El Salvador policy (Giniger 1981). Then on July 19, 1981, as President Reagan and other Western leaders gathered in Ottawa for an economic summit, five thousand Canadians, protesting U.S. support for the Salvadoran government, demonstrated at the U.S. Embassy, shouting "Yankee go home!" (*New York Times* 1981o). On October 7, a dozen Belgians occupied the Salvadoran Embassy in Brussels to protest that country's junta and U.S. influence in Central America (*New York Times* 1981p). One month later, fifteen thousand Parisians marched through central Paris to protest U.S. involvement in Central America (*New York Times* 1981q). On March 19, 1982, hundreds of Dutch protesters marched to the U.S. Consulate in Amsterdam, placed crosses bearing names of four Dutch journalists killed by the U.S.-funded Salvadoran army, smashed windows with stones, and threw paint on the walls. Damages, which forced the Consulate's closing, were estimated at $30,000 (*New York Times* 1982f, 1982j). The next day, several hundred Dutch demonstrators marched to the U.S. Embassy in the Hague and burned an American flag to protest President Reagan's support of the Salvadoran regime (*New York Times* 1982g). Four days later, demonstrators in Bonn, Germany, lay down in the road to block the entrance to the U.S. Embassy to protest American policy in El Salvador—twenty-six people had to be forcibly removed by the police (*New York Times* 1982i). Three days later, West Berlin riot police had to use tear gas to disperse ten thousand protesters demonstrating at a U.S. air base against U.S. policy in El Salvador (*New York Times* 1982k). On that same day, four thousand German protesters threw stones and paint at the American Consulate in Bremen to protest U.S. aid to El Salvador (*New York Times* 1982l). On April 3, twenty-five hundred Swiss demonstrators marched in Bern to demand that their government condemn the Reagan administration's El Salvadoran policies (*New York Times* 1982m). On May 3, 1983, hundred of demonstrators protested the death of a West German doctor killed in an ambush the previous week by U.S.-funded Contras, while, in West Berlin, five hundred marched through the streets in silent tribute to the slain doctor. Placards read: "The murders are the work of imperialist lackeys in Central America. . . . Without the support of the U.S., the gangs from Honduran territory could not threaten the revolution in Nicaragua" (*New York Times* 1983e). On March 6, 1985, hundreds of thousands of Spaniards marched in protest in cities across Spain against an impending scheduled visit by President Reagan; while at a Madrid rally of seventy-five thousand people, speakers condemned the President's trade embargo against Nicaragua (*New York Times* 1985c). In July 1985, West Berlin police used clubs and tear gas to disperse one hundred German demonstrators throwing stones and lighting fires in the street to protest U.S. policy toward Nicaragua (*New York Times* 1985h; also see Apple 1982). If U.S. Central America peace movement activists ever wondered in the back of their minds whether they were crazy, overreacting, or the only ones who saw things this way, these kind of protest actions by citizens of allied nations certainly reassured them otherwise.

SUMMARY

Social movements, I have argued, are deeply rooted in the normative and moral nature of human persons. They emerge when people's sense of what is right and just are so seriously violated that they feel compelled not only to express criticism, but to mobilize for collective action to force an end to the violation. Flagrant and egregious breaches of moral principles and normative sensibilities, in other words, often engender an insurgent consciousness that animates political activism.

But clearly not everyone in a society experiences the same sense of violation. Usually, the drive to mobilize activism is limited to a small minority of people. The generation of insurgent consciousness is always socially located, it is heavily conditioned by people's social-structural positioning. How do we explain this? Here we benefit from the sociology of knowledge's insights into the socially grounded nature of people's awareness, beliefs, and understandings. Specifically, we see that an insurgent consciousness forms primarily among people who enjoy two structural characteristics that affect the social distribution of knowledge. People must be "cognitively accessible" to information about events that violate their moral sensibilities. And people must be "subjectively engageable," that is, culturally and socially situated so that these violations are likely to become high priorities in their personal relevance-structures.[8]

First, our case indicates that the people who are more likely to acquire an insurgent consciousness are those who enjoy "cognitive accessibility," that is, organizational and relational positioning that affords exposure to norm-violating information. Most Americans oppose—in theory—gross violations of human rights, foreign aid for violently repressive military regimes, and the systematic deportation of endangered political refugees. But most Americans were not in the position to know in detail the full extent to which the Reagan administration's policy tolerated and promoted these practices. The majority of Americans' major source of information on Central America was the U.S. news media. But the mass media, we will see in chapter 9, generally portrayed a superficial and incomplete picture of the Central American conflicts and gave considerable airplay to the White House interpretation of the Central American reality. Hence, while most Americans opposed the President's policy generally, most Americans were not actually mobilized to disruptive political action by an insurgent consciousness.

However, one particular subset of the American population, the religious community, *was* in a position to have access to alternative, credible, detailed information about what was going on in Central America. It was among church people exactly that insurgent consciousness was first ignited. Church groups in the U.S. did not have to rely primarily on news media accounts or White House press briefings, because they had their own trusted sources of information on the ground in Central America: missionaries, social service workers, pastors, members of religious orders, denominational leaders, and bishops. They were relationally and organizationally well positioned to be exposed to information that deeply violated their moral sensibilities. In short, they were cognitively accessible.

But cognitive accessibility alone does not generate insurgent consciousness. Mere access to credible, detailed information about events one finds to be objectionable or repugnant does not guarantee an energized commitment to activism. Also required for the formation of insurgent consciousness is the element of "subjective engageability."

Again, most informed Americans must have had some idea that civilians were being killed in El Salvador, that Central American refugees were fleeing grave dangers, that the Contras violated human rights. Most Americans probably were, in fact, concerned about these problems. But for most U.S. citizens, these injustices and atrocities remained essentially abstract and remote, detached from the immediate affairs that shaped their lives. It is not that most Americans were necessarily callous. They simply lacked the cultural and social positioning that would have infused these violations with a sense of personal immediacy and urgency.

Many Christians and Jews, however, were, in fact, "subjectively engageable." They were culturally and socially located in a way that ranked the Central American crisis in their personal and collective relevance-structures as a matter of personal, immediate concern. Christians and Jews both possessed fermenting traditions of social ethics that emphasized justice, peace, and political commitment. Church people enjoyed relational ties to Central America, through missionaries and organizational counterparts, that heightened their interest in and awareness of the region and its problems. Liberation theology further engaged the interest of many progressive people of faith, particularly evoking personal investment in the Nicaraguan revolution. The 1981 murders of Archbishop Romero and the four churchwomen made the Salvadoran civil war a matter of personal identification for millions of Catholics and attentive Protestants. More importantly, personal confrontations with the tragic consequences of Central America—through refugees' stories and firsthand travel to the region—thrust the previously abstract issue into the paramount reality of people's everyday consciousness. These stories and travels put a human face on the crisis, moving many people of faith at deep emotional levels, generating for thousands an intense, personal involvement in the issue. Together, for many in the religious community, these factors helped turn public concern into personal crusades. This account of variability in insurgent consciousness among the American people reflects a "micro-structural" approach. That is, it points beyond differences in people's personal attributes to socially patterned, situational factors that condition people's likelihood of feeling the moral outrage and political commitment we call insurgent consciousness. Central America peace movement activists may not have necessarily been more compassionate than nonactivists. But they appear to have been more cognitively accessible and subjectively engageable than nonactivists. And both cognitive accessibility and subjective engageability are matters of social location, of organizational and relational positioning, not individual inclination.

It is no accident that the U.S. Central America peace movement emerged primarily out of the religious community. It is no accident that the otherwise often conservative Catholic bishops were some of the most vehement and persistent critics of U.S. aid to El Salvador. It is no accident that the Pledge of Resistance was dreamed up by a collection of Christian activists gathered to study the Bible and pray. It is no fluke that the Sanctuary movement originated among church people in Tucson, Arizona, and not, say, leftists in Boston. It is no coincidence that Sanctuary was sparked by a North American's disturbing encounter with a frightened Salvadoran hitchhiker and Witness for Peace by a few North Americans' disturbing encounter with a battle-traumatized Nicaraguan mother. All of these seemingly idiosyncratic and, in some ways, counterintuitive occurrences are comprehensible in terms of socially patterned micro-structural factors of explanation.

CONCLUSION

Moral outrage, religious obligation, emotional passion, personal commitment. These were the forces that drove the Central America peace movement for a decade. President Reagan's Central American policy so deeply violated the sense of right, of justice, of decency of so many U.S. citizens, especially people of faith, that they believed they had no choice but to do whatever they could to defeat it. To do otherwise would have been an abdication of moral responsibility, a failure to live up to one's own identity-commitments, an unacceptable compromise with the intolerable. This insurgent consciousness, irrupting in the context of open political opportunities and strong organizational capacity, generated and propelled this social movement of major proportions.

Before proceeding to analyze important facets of the ongoing maintenance and struggle of the Central America peace movement in part 3, we first examine one more key issue concerning the movement's emergence. Thus far, we have spoken of the Central America peace movement as mobilized by North Americans, particularly religious people. Next we explore in much greater depth the question of exactly what kind of people participated in the Central America peace movement and how and why they became involved.

Seven

THE INDIVIDUAL ACTIVISTS

To know who you are is to be oriented in moral space, a space in which questions arise about what is good and bad, what is worth doing and what not, what has meaning and importance for you and what is trivial and secondary. . . . We come here to one of the most basic aspirations of human beings, the need to be connected to, or in contact with, what they see as good, or of crucial importance, or of fundamental value. And how could it be otherwise, once we see that this orientation in relation to the good is essential to being a functioning human agent?

Charles Taylor, *Sources of the Self*

The previous two chapters have suggested that the emergence of the Central America peace movement can be understood as resulting from a favorable combination of forces and events that expanded political opportunity for, supplied strong organizations to sustain, and provoked an insurgent consciousness among potential participants in that movement. The synchronistic existence or occurrence of these key macro-social events, organizational structures, and micro-structural contexts were essential in bringing the Central America peace movement to birth. In their absence, the movement certainly never would have materialized.

Yet social movements do not consist simply of abstract structures and contexts, of impersonal forces and events. Social movements are, at bottom, real, flesh-and-blood human beings acting together to confront and disrupt. They are the collective expressions of specific people, of concrete men and women struggling together for a cause. Bringing our focus down from macro-social events and structural contexts to real, concrete human beings in this way raises a set of questions that in this study have so far gone largely unaddressed. Namely, exactly what kinds of people participated in the Central America peace movement? Why did *they* tend to join or become recruited into the movement? What personal characteristics or circumstances may have predisposed them to become activists? And by what processes or mechanisms were those particular people mobilized for activism? Answering these questions—which address the issue social movement scholars call "differential recruitment to activism"—is the task which this chapter takes up.

The evidence I use to answer these questions was gathered through two national surveys of and twenty-eight in-depth interviews with Witness for Peace and Sanctuary activists. In 1991, I mailed a six-page, twenty-eight-item questionnaire (closed- and open-ended questions) to a sample of 1,190 former Witness for Peace short-term delegates, randomly drawn from that organization's total list of four thousand former delegates. An almost identical questionnaire was mailed to representatives of all four hundred declared Sanctuary organizations listed in the Chicago Religious Task Force on Central America's 1987 Sanctuary directory.[1] Four hundred and fifty-two Witness for Peace and 129 Sanctuary questionnaires were completed and returned. More than one hundred open-ended follow-up questionnaires, asking for written explanations and interpretations of findings from the first questionnaires, were sent to respondents who had voluntarily waived their anonymity by writing their names and addresses on their original questionnaires. In addition to these surveys, I interviewed twenty-eight movement activists—from seven states representing the northeast, south, southwest, and west coast regions of the country—about their motivations and experiences as participants in the Central America peace movement.[2] By employing these multiple methodologies to examine two very different organizational segments of the Central America peace movement, I hope to capture a fairly accurate picture of those involved in the national movement as a whole.

A GROUP PORTRAIT OF THE ACTIVISTS

What kind of people actually got involved in the Central America peace movement? Table 7.1 represents a comparison of the characteristics of Central America peace movement activists with those of all adult Americans. Examining this and other tables, we see emerging a distinctive group profile of the movement activists, one which also sheds light on the issues raised in the literature on differential recruitment to activism.[3]

Attitudes and Values

To begin, we see that both Witness for Peace and Sanctuary activists strongly reflect social and political attitudes and values con-

Table 7.1. Comparison of Central America Peace Activists and All Adult
Americans, 1985

Trait	Sanctuary Activists	Witness for Peace Delegates	All Adult Americans[a]
Average age (years)	44***	45***	37
Married (%)	70*	51***	63
Married, without children (%)	65***	77***	50
Caucasian (%)	98***	96***	86[b]
Female (%)	63**	52	52[c]
Median annual household income ($)	31,155***	31,174***	24,986[d]
Completed 4 years of college or more (%)	91***	90***	19[e]
Mean number of prior social movements participated in	7.3***[f]	8***[f]	?<1[f]
Member of one or more political organization (%)	77[g]***	85[g]***	<10[h]
Regularly attend religious services (%)	63***	58***	42
Traveled to Central America before sanctuary (%)	16***	—	<4[i]
Politically leftist in 1979 (%)	23***	25***	7[j]
Postmaterialists (%)	59[k]***	68[k]***	16[d]
Materialists (%)	0[k]***	0[k]***	23[d]
N	(129)	(452)	(239,279,000)

*** = p<.001 ** = p<.01 * = p<.05

Source: Statistical Abstract of the United States 1987, 1990; Inglehart 1990; U.S. Department of
Transportation 1975-1990; General Social Survey 1990; Knoke 1990; Walker and Baumgartner
1990; Wood 1990.
Notes: [a]18 years of age and older. [b]16 years of age or older. [c]14 years of age and older. [d]For 1987.
[e]25 years of age and older. [f]Difference in means based on likely estimate—not known data—for all
adult Americans. [g]Other than Sanctuary or Witness for Peace. [h]For 1986. [i]Conservatively estimated
from U.S. Department of Transportation, 1975-1990. [j]For 1990. [k]For 1991.

gruent with and supportive of those of the Central America peace
movement. A comparison of the bottom three traits in table 7.1
reveals major differences in political ideology and in Inglehart's (1990)
scale of "Postmaterialist" values between the activists and all adult
Americans. Sanctuary activists were five times more likely and Witness
for Peace activists were almost six and one-half times more likely to
have been politically leftist in 1979 than the average American. In the
context of American politics in the 1980s, such an ideological orientation would clearly predispose one to be very critical of the Reagan
administration's military policies and sympathetic to the cause of
Nicaragua's Sandinista government and, possibly, El Salvador's

FMLN guerrilla insurgency. Table 7.1 also indicates that more than three and one-half times as many Sanctuary activists and more than four times as many Witness for Peace activists were pure Postmaterialists than were all adult Americans. The activists, in other words, were much less concerned with the values of economic and physical security that informed most of the White House's policies than with the values of social participation and relational fulfillment that are strongly associated with joining in social movement activism (Inglehart 1990). Conversely, while almost one-quarter of adult Americans are pure Materialists, not one of the hundreds of Sanctuary or Witness for Peace activists was. This distribution is even more striking when we consider that Central America activists tended to be older, while Postmaterialist values are strongly associated with youth.

Evidence on the activists' occupational backgrounds seems to corroborate their value-sympathy with the movement. Table 7.2, which compares the proportion of activists' occupations with that of adult Americans, demonstrates that Central America peace movement activists were recruited heavily from *human service* occupations. They are religious workers, social workers, clergy, health care administrators, teachers, legislative activists, and nurses. They are not, generally, manual laborers, secretaries, accountants, business managers, technicians, or sales clerks. This data accords with other studies which socially locate political activists as drawn from "new class" backgrounds (McAdam, McCarthy, and Zald 1988: 712). But what might this say about values? When asked to explain this contrast in the follow-up survey, respondents unanimously maintained that the occupational differences reflect value differences. On the whole, they maintained, people gravitate to human service occupations who are more relationally empathetic, who wish to minimize human suffering, and who want to make a positive impact on their social world. By contrast, they asserted, people generally gravitate to business and technical occupations who are less people-oriented, more concerned with making money, and more interested in shaping the material than the social world. This interpretation, which reflects the perspectives and prejudices of human service workers, seems overstated, at least. But it is not entirely implausible. In fact, studies have shown that new-class, human-service occupations do attract or produce people with more liberal or progressive attitudes and values than business people and unskilled operators (among others Brint 1984; Bruce-Briggs 1979; Gouldner 1978).

Interviews with Central America peace movement activists confirm

Table 7.2. Occupational Ratio of Central America Peace Movement Activist to All Americans, 1985 (Relative frequency of activists employed in occupation vs. Americans employed)

	Sanctuary	Witness for Peace
Non-clergy religious worker	107[a]	114[a]
Clergy	56[a]	39[a]
Health administrator	24	6.8
Social worker	9.5	17.23
Academic administrator	5.2	2.2
Government/legislative worker	1.8	4.7
Teacher	3.9	4.4
Nurse	2.9	2.8
Attorney	2.2	2.9
Doctor/dentist	1.3	2.3
Science professional[b]	1.4	.23
Medical technician	.61	.65
Business manager	.48	.29
Accountant	.25	.36
Secretary	.16	.24
Sales person	.13	.13
Skilled operator	.12	.09
N	(129)	(452)

Source: Statistical Abstract of the United States 1990, 1987.
Notes: [a]Compared to Americans employed in these fields in 1988. [b]Includes engineers, architects, computer analysts and programmers, chemists, and research scientists.

these findings on attitudes. Among Sanctuary activists, for example, according to Jane Guise (1990), "Protestants tended to come from the more liberal end of the spectrum and Catholics were not parish priests but mostly women from religious orders, who tended to be more independently-minded. In the Jewish sector, it was also the more liberal congregations that developed the Jewish sanctuary network."

Witness for Peace delegates also tended to hold sympathetic values and attitudes. Fran Truitt (1990) describes Witness for Peace delegates as mostly "deeply committed, radical leftist humanists and Christians." And Mike Clark (1992) affirms, "When I think about the delegations that I led, there were very few people who were in favor of U.S. policy. They were going to be staying with people who had family members killed because of it! The people who went were mostly from the Judeo-Christian community, generally had been involved in social activism, and tended to be politically progressive."

These shared values tended to help to expedite the intended political effects of the Witness for Peace experience. Joe Nangle (1992), for example, observed that "as things moved along people became 'converted' in a very short time. You know? I mean, it took me 8 years working in Latin America before I realized what I was really seeing. Eight years! But it took merely a few weeks for the Witness for Peace folks to get on track. Now, what would that mean? Were they already there? Liberal, if you will? Or even radical? Perhaps." And, according to Dick Junkin (1991): "Many Christians who came to Central America were already ideologically committed. Sure, we would get some politically uncertain people and a few dyed-in-the-wool Reaganites. But the predominance were people in sympathy with Central American revolutionary movements, or at least open enough to go see for themselves."

Altogether, these survey and interview findings suggest an important, though not surprising, relationship between adherence to values and attitudes that resonated with the Central America peace movement and the likelihood of someone actually joining or being recruited into that movement. But the exact difference these values made is not entirely clear. For the total number of Central American peace activists almost certainly did not exceed one-half of 1 percent of the entire adult American population. If so, this leaves more than 6.5 percent of American leftists and 15.5 percent of American Postmaterialists who did *not* participate in the Central America peace movement—respectively, thirteen and thirty-one times the number who did. This suggests that while compatible attitudes and values may be a necessary condition of recruitment to high-risk activism, they remain an insufficient condition. Sympathetic attitudes and values may have predisposed our activists to participate, but it appears that they alone did not induce participation. Other influences must have also been at work.

Prior Activist Experience

The Central America peace activists studied here exhibit a long history of actual experience in social movements. According to the findings presented in table 7.1, the average Sanctuary and Witness for Peace activist had participated in more than seven other distinct social movements before becoming involved in the Central America peace movement.[4] This is a number at least seven times larger than that for all adult Americans. More specifically, table 7.3 shows the percent of Central America peace activists who had previously participated in

Table 7.3. Prior Social Movement Involvement by Central American Peace
Activists (%)

Prior Movement	Sanctuary	Witness for Peace
Anti-nuclear weapons	66	78
Civil rights	58	56
Anti-vietnam	54	59
Environmental	53	60
Anti-poverty	51	57
Women's movement	36	46
Anti-apartheid	33	47
Pro-choice	31	30
Anti-nuclear power	28	33
1960s student movement	18	20
Corporate responsibility	17	16
Gay/lesbian rights	13	18
N	(129)	(452)

Table 7.4. Central America Peace Activists' Prior Protest Experience (%)

	Sanctuary	Witness for Peace
Previously participated in political protests, demonstrations, marches, sit-ins or vigils	65	77
Previously committed non-violent civil disobedience or tax resistance	29	37
Previously were arrested for protesting or committing civil disobedience	14	24
N	(129)	(452)

each of twelve different U.S. social movements. One-third of all Central America activists had prior experience in the women's, anti-apartheid, pro-choice, and anti-nuclear power movements. More than half had participated in civil rights, anti–Vietnam War, environmental, and anti-poverty campaigns. And, two-thirds or more had participated in anti–nuclear weapons work. How deeply were they involved in these movements? Table 7.4 shows the kinds of protest activities Central America peace movement activists had engaged in before joining in Central America work. Two-thirds or more had participated in lawful forms of disruptive protest, about one-third had joined in illegal forms of political confrontation, and one-fifth to one-quarter had actually been arrested for their prior participation in civil disobedience. In short, the majority of Central America peace movement activists were not political novices, but were quite experienced in prior social movement activism.

The observations of leaders in the Central America peace movement again confirm these findings. According to Ken Butigan (1991), "There were a lot of older, more experienced people involved in the Pledge. Here in the Bay area, there were definitely people from the Vietnam and Civil Rights era helping to organize. Some of them were doing sit-ins at lunch counters in the late 1950s."

Clark Taylor (1990) agrees: "People involved in the Pledge were church groups, academics, neighborhood organizations—anyone with a long history of leftist activism gravitated to it. There was something about the Pledge that called for resistance that caught these people's imaginations."

Bob Bonthius (1990) observes similarities in Witness for Peace activists: "Many of the people who got involved in Witness for Peace were people who had actually had Central America experience and seen a long history of U.S. repression. They had prior experience in church peace and justice work or third-world travel. Many also had come up through the civil rights movement and were pacifists."

According to Betsy Crites (1992), early Witness for Peace recruiting strategies ensured contact with politically experienced people: "We started recruiting and advertising in places that we thought the right kind of people would see it. They were peace and justice people, early on, they had to have been."

This prior experience is significant because it appears to have both radicalized participants and familiarized them with the "script" used to play the "social activist" role. From this perspective, these activists seem to have been engaged in a long-term role-transformation process which had gradually deepened their commitment to and participation in political activism. With each successive social movement involvement, these activists appear both to have become more comfortable with their participation in activism and to have engaged in a broader range of more challenging and disruptive activist tactics. We have already seen in chapter 6 that mobilization into the Central America peace movement—through the stories of refugees, the murders of Romero and the four religious women, and Central America travel— typically involved a process of increased political radicalization. Three additional pieces of evidence from the surveys substantiate this interpretation. First, as noted above, many participants came to the Central America peace movement already somewhat radicalized (see table 7.1). Second, the Central America peace movement clearly helped to advance that process of radicalization. A comparison of the reported political stance of survey respondents in 1979 to their stance at the time of their Central America activism shows that 43 percent of Sanctuary and 44 percent of Witness for Peace activists grew more radical in the intervening time period. And of them, 19 percent of Sanctuary and 23 percent of Witness for Peace activists reported undergoing a major radicalization experience, involving a leftward shift at least one-third of the way across the entire ideological spectrum. On the other hand, only 4 percent of all Sanctuary and 7 percent of all Witness for Peace activists grew more politically conservative in the same time span.[5] Betsy Crites (1992) informs us that many of those Witness for Peace delegates with little prior activist experience actually joined with the conscious intent of becoming radicalized: "I would hear people in the training say, 'I want to be transformed. I know I have some changing to do.' And you know, this wasn't supposed to be a group therapy thing, but some people almost seemed to approach it as, 'I need to face something like this, to shape me up and get me active.' And it did."

The third piece of telling evidence is that larger proportions of both Sanctuary and Witness for Peace activists engaged in legal and illegal forms of political protest and were arrested for civil disobedience *during* their Central America activism than beforehand. In other words, the extent of their collective involvement in all types of disruptive protest tactics increased with their participation in this new movement.[6]

Central America peace activists, then, not only held sympathetic values and attitudes, but were also familiar with the processes and techniques of political protest through their considerable prior experience in two decades of social movement activism. And these prior experiences not only helped to shape their political values and attitudes. They also helped to form their personal identities in such a way that these people had come increasingly to think of themselves as "political activists." This meant that when the Central America crisis arose in the early 1980s, these men and women not only felt opposed to the Reagan policy and thought it to be wrong, as did most Americans, who nevertheless did not become mobilized into Central America peace activism. They also had developed personal activist-identities which made participation in the movement a natural expression and affirmation of who they thought themselves to be as people. Hence, their familiarity with the role requirements of activism and very sense of "self" helped induce their mobilization into the movement.

Biographical Availability

Reviewing survey and interview evidence, we see that Central America peace activists reflect in their social class and life-cycle statuses a tremendous amount of biographical availability for social movement activism (see table 7.1). To begin, as a whole they were significantly older than the population of adult Americans. Being on average middle-aged, rather than in their twenties or thirties, they were largely beyond the exacting tasks of earning educational degrees, establishing new careers, and raising young children, which can compete with the demands of activism.[7] Fran Truitt (1990) describes Witness for Peace delegates as "older people, a lot of older middle class people. Very few were students."[8] And Angela Berryman (1990) recollected:

> What type of people were active in the Central American movement? I'll tell you my small but telling experience from when a number of us did a protest sit-in at the CIA office in the Federal Building. We were sitting there and someone said, "During the Vietnam war we would have wished that someone with a grey hair was sitting with us. Now we wish that someone without a grey hair were here sitting with us." Although young people did participate in the Central American movement, the middle-aged have been the really significant actors. It was an older crowd, for example, that signed the Pledge. And they were the likely ones to have visited Central America, which was key. In the early 1980s, university campuses were more conservative and career-oriented. Central America very much engaged people who had lived through the Vietnam war.

According to Pastor (1982: 34), the middle-age presence in the Central America peace movement reflects a kind of political nostalgia:

> The formative political experience of an entire generation—the baby boom generation [born in] the late 1940s and early 1950s—was marching against the [Vietnam] war and turning the U.S. government around. In some ways, this was as heady an experience for this generation as winning World War II was for their parents. And just as the older generation enjoys recapturing the memory of its experience in movies or by marching in veterans' parades, the younger generation is ready to recapture its lost youth by marching against another war alongside a new generation ready to develop its own anti-war experience.

Anne Shumway (1990), however, interprets the issue in a somewhat more purposeful and altruistic light: "The age range in the Pledge was different from Vietnam, where there was a predominance of young people. I would say there were more middle-age and older people involved with Central America. Why? We had been through it once with Vietnam and we really knew what war meant. We knew what war could do."

In addition to being older, the Central America peace activists were relatively well-to-do financially, enjoying household incomes about 25 percent higher than that of the average adult American.[9] Fran Truitt (1990) observes, for example, that Witness for Peace delegates were "middle class, and a few wealthy people have gone too." And according to Sam Hope (1992), "Because of the cost of going on Witness for Peace, delegates would tend to have been more middle class than poor, more white, pretty equally male and female was my observation. They also seemed to be generally college educated." Anne Shumway (1990) remarked: "These weren't people on the margins." Central America peace activists were also very well educated, almost five times more likely than the average adult American to have earned a bachelor's degree or more. Indeed, among Witness for Peace and Sanctuary activists respectively, 44 percent and 46 percent had earned Master's degrees and 13 percent and 14 percent had earned doctorates.

Furthermore, Witness for Peace activists, at least, whose involvement took them into dangerous war zones, were much less likely than the average adult American to be married and thus responsible for and accountable to a spouse and possibly children. According to Betsy Crites (1992), "They generally would have had to have been single and free, single was the norm. We obviously couldn't take children, but we did take married couples. There were married couples that did it. There were even some that got married while they were there. And then there were some retired people that had joined, who were really inspiring."

Sanctuary activists, on the other hand, were actually *more* likely to be married than the average adult American.[10] However, most importantly, among both groups, the married activists were significantly more free of daily child care responsibilities than the typical married American. Thus, their activism did not place an extra burden of family nurturance on their spouse or hinder or endanger their relationship with their dependent children.[11]

Finally, these peace movement participants were drawn from occupations that facilitated availability for activism. Examining table 7.2, we see that, compared to the occupational distribution of all adult Americans, these Central America activists tended to be drawn disproportionately from time-flexible occupations. According to Anne Shumway (1990), "People who signed the Pledge, especially for civil disobedience, had to have a certain amount of flexibility in their lives, so they wouldn't lose their jobs." The typical work schedules of clergy, religious workers, social workers, teachers, legislative workers, and academic and health administrators are much less structurally rigid than the typical nine-to-five-with-coffee-break routines of business people, office workers, and manual operators. Thus, when the refugees in sanctuary need to go clothes shopping, the college professor is able to take them any afternoon after classes. But the secretary can't go until after dinner or on the weekend. Likewise, for a Presbyterian minister, a twenty-day trip to Nicaragua means finding guest preachers for two weeks and postponing the elders meeting. But for a business accountant, it means spending an entire year's worth of vacation time. Thus, Bob Bonthius (1990) recalls:

> Some short-termer delegates were retired. But mostly they were professionals who could call their own shots. If clergy really want to get away for a week or two they can work it out, justifying it as part of the mission of their churches. Sisters of religious orders have freedom too. These are people who are a little more independent than the nine-to-five people. The nine-to-five people would have had to take it out of vacation or sick leave. Whereas some religious workers, such as denominational officials, were actually commissioned to go as part of their jobs.

Thus, people involved in the Central America peace movement were those who not only enjoyed relatively high degrees of emotional, relational, and financial freedom to participate, but also those who could expect to generate less friction trying to mesh the demands of activism with those of work.

Relational Links to Activism

Central America peace movement participants also possessed an unusually large number of relational ties to activism. These served both as channels through which the activists were initially recruited into the movement and as social attachments that sustained their involvement over the years of struggle. Table 7.5 summarizes the

Table 7.5. Personal and Organizational vs. Impersonal Sources of Activists'
Introduction to Sanctuary and WFP (%)

Sanctuary		Witness for Peace	
Church or synagogue	35	34	Other WFP activists
Prior SMO membership	20	19	Religious publication
Other sanctuary activists	15	16	Family or friends
Religious publications	13	12	Prior SMO membership
Denominational promotion	9	9	Church or synagogue
Secular mass media	8	5	Secular mass media
		5	WFP mailing
Relational/organizational	79	71	Relational/organizational
Impersonal	21	29	Impersonal
Total	(100)	(100)	
N	(129)	(452)	

sources by which activists were first introduced to Sanctuary and Witness for Peace. It shows that in 70 to 80 percent of cases, knowledge
about the Central America peace movement was diffused through personal relationships and organizational memberships (since many personal relationships are formed within the context of formal organizations, such as churches, it is impossible to disaggregate the numbers
for the two).[12] Quite clearly, the vast majority of Central America
activists were exposed to the movement by friends, family members,
fellow political activists, and fellow church and synagogue members.

The activists, however, were not only first introduced to the movement through their relational and organizational ties, most of them—
84 percent of Sanctuary and 56 percent of Witness for Peace
activists—were also *drawn into* the movement through face-to-face
discussions with like-minded people (see table 7.6). Hence, making a
commitment to activism appears to have been a more relational than
private process. Bob Van Denend (1992), for example, recalls the
group affirmation he received for his initial desire to do a Witness for
Peace trip: "We were involved in a peace group that met in our backyard and also a regular pot-luck dinner with a group of Quakers. We
passed the Witness for Peace brochure around at these meetings and
everybody said, 'Yes, this is absolutely right.' People communicated
that they believed that it was the right thing for me to do."

The importance of relational ties in diffusing knowledge of and
evoking commitment to the movement is also clear in the answers sur-

Table 7.6. Relational Links to Central American Activism (%)

	Sanctuary	Witness for Peace
Respondents whose decision to join movement emerged from small group discussions among like-minded people	84	56
Friends on a Witness for Peace trip or in Sanctuary	16	59
Friends involved in Central America peace movement	18	32
N	(129)	(452)

vey respondents wrote to open-ended questions about how they became involved in activism, of which the following are representative:

> My son-in-law belonged to another church that was one of the first in our city to declare Sanctuary. That prompted some of us in my church to press to declare Sanctuary. (Fifty-three-year-old, female, Catholic college administrator.)

> We knew a priest who was transporting two Salvadoran refugees north and I heard them speak. They asked for our help. On that cold February night, I was dumbstruck, compelled to respond. I thought, "If it were my children, pray God, would someone help them?" (Thirty-eight-year-old, female, Methodist child care worker.)

> Central American first came into my consciousness mainly through people I knew. I talked with all kinds of people involved in it. I got to know Bill Weber, one of the great spirits of the Protestant world, through working together on a local missions project in Boston. He was an early leader in Witness for Peace, on the National Steering Committee, and I found out he was leading a short-term delegation to Nicaragua so I went with him in 1987 and two times more since then. He is one person who definitely helped me get involved in Witness for Peace. (Fifty-four-year-old, male, Protestant university professor.)

> I was taking a theology course taught by a former Witness for Peace delegate, who shared his experience with the class. I decided I wanted to go too. (Thirty-four-year-old, female, Unitarian Universalist minister.)

> I was good friends with some strong anti-nuke folk. Their attitude of resistance got me fired up to do Central America work. (Thirty-seven-year-old, male, Catholic teacher.)

> Our rabbi gave a sermon about Central American refugees, which sparked my interest. I then joined our social action committee and vol-

unteered with one other person to take on the Sanctuary project. (Forty-five-year-old, female, Jewish interior designer.)

We were visiting an old, old friend of ours in Indonesia, a Dutch Jesuit that we worked with years ago organizing labor unions. He talked to us late into the night about liberation theology and Witness for Peace. (Sixty-two-year-old, female, retired Episcopal.)

I have friends who have been missionaries in Peru for 25 years and introduced me to Gustavo Gutiérrez's liberation theology in 1973. Then in the 1980s, members of my church helped get me involved in Central America. (Thirty-two-year-old, female, Catholic social worker.)

I was learning Spanish because my husband worked for the U.S. Agency for International Development. To practice Spanish, we attended Spanish Mass, where we met and became friends with a couple of radical priests and a nun. We began a Central America reading-and-discussion group and progressively became more radical. Eventually, my Spanish teacher asked me to go with her on a delegation. (Fifty-year-old, female, Catholic social worker.)

My husband was interested in Central America and decided to go on a delegation. I resisted, but finally I decided to go rather than stay home and worry about him. That trip changed my life! (Thirty-seven-year-old, female, Quaker grade school teacher.)

A friend of mine told me that a Salvadoran refugee was going to speak in our community. I went to hear him speak and my consciousness was raised and I became involved. (Thirty-seven-year-old, female, Jewish, at-home parent.)

A close friend of mine and I were fed up with Reagan's foreign policy. We discussed it a lot and decided to join a peace and justice group, which helped us get more deeply involved. (Twenty-one-year-old, female, Catholic counselor.)

Furthermore, beyond the initial introduction and commitment, the activists' ongoing participation itself appears to have been accompanied and reinforced by relational ties to the movement (see table 7.6). Among Sanctuary activists, about one out of six friends was also involved in Sanctuary or in the Central America peace movement. Well more than one-half of Witness for Peace delegates traveled to Central America with a friend. And fully one-third of friends of Witness for Peace activists were themselves activists in the Central America peace movement. We see, then, that Central America peace activists were people who possessed extensive relational ties that exposed and recruited them to the movement and offered participation-sustaining companionship during the activism.

Organizational Ties to Activism

We have already seen in chapter 5 the important role movement midwives and movement-feeder organizations played in generating the Central America peace movement. Evidence from our surveys also highlights the indispensability of organizational ties in determining who did and didn't join the Central America peace movement. In table 7.1, for example, we see that 77 percent of Sanctuary and 85 percent of Witness for Peace activists were members of one or more political organizations during the two years prior to their Central America activism—compared to less than 10 percent of all adult Americans. Most Central America activists also had strong ties to religious organizations. Table 7.1 shows the activists regularly attending religious services at rates 40 and 50 percent higher than the national average. Interviews make plain that these prior organizational involvements were the contexts in which many activists became mobilized. Fran Truitt (1990), for example, notes that "in Maine, the people I recruited were people who would respond to speaking engagements, especially at churches, and who would hear the story and want to go. They were all Christians, Catholics and Protestants. I think that's where most delegates came from." Likewise, Phyllis Taylor (1990) observes:

> In the beginning, the Pledge here was very specifically based in religious organizations. It involved a lot of nuns from religious orders, for example. This was very exciting because it was the first time they had ever done anything political. We worked with sisters helping them to think through the issue of civil disobedience. One women's order, the Sisters of St. Joseph, even worked out a formal procedure to help assist their members in doing civil disobedience.

In almost all cases, by the nature of the project, Sanctuary activists were mobilized specifically as members of churches and synagogues (see table 7.7). Written survey responses also accent the importance of organizational ties in mobilizing Witness for Peace activists as well:

> It was through my activism in the anti-nuclear movement that I became aware of the Central America reality. Our Clergy and Laity Concerned group met monthly for a potluck, to hear a speaker, and discuss a sub-

Table 7.7. Types of Sanctuary Groups, 1987

Groups	Number	Percent
Protestant Churches	93	22
Anabaptist Churches	80	19
Unitarian Universalist Churches	67	16
Roman Catholic Churches	65	15
Jewish Synagogues	41	10
Ecumenical Religious Groups	25	6
Cities	24	6
Universities	15	4
Other Secular Groups	13	3
Religious Groups	371	88
Secular Groups	52	12

Source: Chicago Religious Task Force Sanctuary Directory 1987.

ject. Through this education and activism I learned of Witness for Peace. (Thirty-one-year-old, male, Quaker film projectionist.)

I volunteered with Pax Christi in my spare time, where friends invited me to join an Interfaith Committee on Central America. From there I learned of Sanctuary and Witness for Peace and became involved in marches, vigils, and demonstrations for peace in Central America. (Fifty-nine-year-old, female, Catholic refugee worker.)

In the early 1980s, I worked with Mennonite Central Committee doing literacy work with two Catholic sisters in Louisiana. They had fellow members of their religious order working in El Salvador who sent letters to my co-workers. That's how I got interested in Central America. (Twenty-nine-year-old, male, Mennonite mental health caseworker.)

Being around this university has helped to develop leftist ideology and involvement in activism. This school is a hothouse for social movements. You couldn't be here and not be involved with what was going on in the rest of the world. (Fifty-four-year-old, male, Protestant university professor.)

I was involved in the Kalamazoo Friends Meeting and the St. Thomas More Student Church. Many of us there got interested in CISPES and Sanctuary, which, in turn, got me involved with Witness for Peace. (Sixty-three-year-old, female, Quaker social worker.)

I became involved through a Hispanic youth group I attended that was very liberal and socially conscious. We met weekly and Central America issues were often part of our discussions. (Twenty-five-year-old, male, Catholic production inspector.)

I was involved in Elders for Survival, which protested Livermore Labs nuclear weapons work. Two of our members went to Nicaragua, came back, and turned us on to Witness for Peace. (Sixty-six-year-old, female, Unitarian retired educator.)

I have always been part of a small peace and justice group from our church. We together began discussing the possibilities, risks, and goals of traveling with Witness for Peace and eventually decided to go. (Forty-two-year-old, male, Mennonite college professor.)

Altogether, the evidence suggests that our Central America peace activists enjoyed not only biographical availability for and relational ties to activism, but also high levels of organizational ties to social movement participation.

Relational Support for Activism

Biographical availability and organizational and relational ties to activism are clearly important. But a micro-structural explanation that accounts for only these three factors still leaves a number of questions unanswered (McAdam and Paulsen 1993). Exactly how do social ties to activism function to mobilize activists? Is the mere *existence* of a tie sufficient? Or does the type or quality of the relationship matter? How do relationships with people *not* tied to activism affect potential activists' decisions about participation? Further, how do social movement recruits negotiate between relationships that support and those that oppose their activism? And what factors might affect the significance of that support and opposition? The identity-salience of the supporters and opposers? Geographical distance? Frequency of contact? In what follows, we attempt to begin to answer some of these questions.

In their surveys, Witness for Peace activists were asked to identify the two people who most strongly supported and the two who most strongly opposed their Central America activism. They were asked to specify both the *type* of relationship and the *frequency* of communication they had with each of these people. The results of these questions are striking. To begin, we observe in table 7.8 that fully one-half of all Witness for Peace activists had absolutely nobody oppose their Central America activism. They encountered nothing but support for or indifference to their decision to join Witness for Peace, travel to Nicaragua, and fight against U.S. policy in Central America. Comparatively, only 2 percent of Witness for Peace activists had absolutely

Table 7.8. Relationship Offering Witness for Peace Delegates First or Second
Strongest Supporter and Opposer (%)[a]

Relationship	Supporter	Opposer
Friend, Acquaintance, Work Colleague	51	15
Spouse	37	5
Fellow Church/Synagogue Member	24	4
Fellow Member of Political/Social Organization	20	.2
Witness for Peace Spokesperson	17	.2
Clergy	13	1
Children	8	5
Parents	7	26
Family Relatives	4	19
Nobody	2	50
N	(452)	(452)

Note: [a]Percentages do not add to 100 because categories combine percentages of first and second
strongest supporter/opposer.

nobody support their activism. These differences in the absolute
amount of support and opposition of any kind are substantial.

Furthermore, we can observe a pattern in the *type* of relationships
that tended to support and oppose the activists. Specifically, other than
"nobody," the most frequent opponents of activism tended to have
been parents and family relatives. Considering that the average Witness
for Peace activist was 45 years old in 1985, we can safely suppose that
these are mostly relationships of secondary authority and relevance.
Indeed, one would almost *expect* elderly parents and family relatives
to worry about such involvements. But one would likely not make one's
final decision based on their opinions. On the other hand, the most likely supporters of activism were friends, work colleagues, spouses, fellow church and synagogue members, and fellow social activists—all
relationships of far greater immediacy and importance. Furthermore,
we see in table 7.9 that the Witness for Peace activists received support
from people with whom they communicated very frequently and
encountered opposition from people with whom they interacted very
infrequently. Thus, on the whole, the Witness for Peace activists appear
to have been supported by people whose opinions were more important, whose presence was more consistent and direct, and whose communications were more frequent than those who opposed them. Thus
the identity salience, social proximity, and frequency of communication

Table 7.9. Frequency of Communication of Witness for Peace Delegates with Strongest Supporter and Opposer (%)

Frequency of Communication	Supporter	Opposer
Constantly	13	1
Daily	27	7
Few Times a Week	19	7
Once a Week	18	11
Few Times a Month	13	10
Monthly or Less	10	63
Total	(100)	(99)
N	(452)	(452)

Table 7.10. Support and Opposition for Witness for Peace Activism from the Two Most Important People in Respondents' Political Reference Group (%)

Two Most Important People	Support	Opposition
Both of two	47	1
One of two	40	11
None	14	88
Total	(101)	(100)
N	(452)	(452)

of supporters and opponents of activism all appear to be important influences in differential recruitment.

To explore more precisely the matter of relational support for activism, I also asked Witness for Peace activists to identify their core "political reference group" (PRG)—that is, the two people whose opinions on social and political issues they most sought out and respected. In this way we moved beyond suppositions about the nature of people's relationships to rely on the respondents' own specific evaluations. Table 7.10, which shows the PRG members' opinion about the activists' involvement in Witness for Peace, reveals considerable differences in support and opposition. The vast majority of activists had at least one, if not both, members of their PRG supporting their participation in Witness for Peace. Conversely, an equally vast majority had neither of their core PRG opposing their activism. People who actually became mobilized into Central America peace activism, in other words, tended to be those who enjoyed support and encouragement from the people whose social and political opinions and judgments they most sought out and respected.

Our evidence confirms the critical influence of all four micro-structural factors in sorting out who became Central America peace activists and who did not. Compared to the population from which they were drawn, our Central America peace activists enjoyed considerably more biographical availability for, relational and organizational ties to, and relational support for social movement activism. These key situational factors, along with people's greater prior activist experience, may account for the fact that, although millions of Americans shared values and attitudes supportive of the Central America peace movement, only a minority of them actually became mobilized into movement activism.

Summary

Forming a composite picture based on our findings thus far, the typical Central America peace activist appears to be a white, forty-five-year-old human service worker—probably a church, health, social-work, or academic professional. He or she—more likely a she—is a person of deep religious faith who actively participates in church or synagogue. Our typical activist possesses a Master's degree in their field, possibly even a doctorate, and enjoys a comfortable household income. The structure of their profession affords them the time flexibility to become involved in political activism, an opportunity they take advantage of. Our typical activist is also either unmarried and without children or, if married, childless or with children who are grown and almost out of the house.

Ideologically, our typical Central America activist tends to lean toward the political and cultural left, although they probably dislike thinking in traditional left-right political categories and don't belong to any traditional leftist political parties or organizations. In any case, they are generally suspicious of, if not antagonistic toward, most Reagan administration policies. Indeed, more concerned with issues of human rights, social equality, political participation, and the aesthetic and environmental quality of life than with securing a strong economy and national defense, they almost certainly voted in 1980 for either Jimmy Carter or John Anderson.

Central America activism is not our typical activist's first experience in extra-electoral politics. Indeed, they have been involved in four or five different political movements during the twenty-five years since their college days—most likely the civil rights movement in the late 1950s and 1960s, the anti-war movement in the late 1960s and early

1970s, environmental and poverty work in the 1970s, and the Freeze campaign in the early 1980s. Before ever particularly knowing much about Central America, they had participated in a few protest marches and demonstrations and perhaps had even committed and been arrested for civil disobedience. For this reason, they don't feel particularly uncomfortable thinking of themselves as political activists.

Finally, most of the social and professional circles in which our typical Central America activist circulates are supportive of their political commitments. Indeed, their Central America activism has been strongly encouraged by an identifiable network of friends, family members, and work colleagues, many of whom are also Central America peace activists. These relationships provide an ongoing reinforcement of our activist's political values and attitudes as well as companionship and support that helps to mitigate the risks and sacrifices inherent in political activism.

MORAL COMMITMENTS AS MOTIVATIONS

Sympathetic values and attitudes, prior activist experience, biographical availability, and relational and organizational ties to and relational support for activism go a long way toward explaining who became Central America peace activists and who did not. But another dimension of the actual process of deciding to become an activist deserves closer attention. In examining how activists actually went about deciding to join the movement and what considerations they took into account in their decision making, we discover a number of curious findings.

For example, the surveys asked Sanctuary and Witness for Peace activists how much they had calculated the costs and benefits of their potential participation before joining the movement. Table 7.11 shows that these Central America activists reported more likely than not having calculated the costs and benefits only a little or not calculating them at all. Why would people willfully breaking federal immigration laws and traveling to third world war zones have done so little reckoning?[13]

Furthermore, the surveys also asked the activists to recall how costly—in time, money, relationships, and lost opportunities—they expected, before becoming involved, their Sanctuary and Witness for Peace activism would be. Table 7.12 shows that almost one-third of respondents who went on to become activists anticipated beforehand

Table 7.11. Respondents Calculating the Costs and Benefits of Activism (%)

	Sanctuary	Witness for Peace
Calculated a lot	20	21
Calculated somewhat	23	25
Calculated a little	29	26
Did not calculate	28	28
Total	(100)	(100)
N	(129)	(452)

Table 7.12. Expected Costs of Central American Activism (%)

	Sanctuary	Witness for Peace
Very or extremely costly	14	11
Rather costly	17	19
Somewhat costly	28	27
Hardly costly	32	28
Not at all costly	9	15
Total	(100)	(100)
N	(129)	(452)

that doing so would be "rather," "very," or "extremely" costly. These numbers are corroborated by many of the comments about the anticipated costliness of activism that respondents wrote on their surveys, including the following:

> When I left for Nicaragua, I thought my marriage was over because my husband said that if I actually went he would divorce me.

> This was 1983 and I expected the worst. I knew full well that any one of us could be badly injured or killed traveling out in the war zones.

> My boss told me that if I went to Central America, there would not be a job waiting for me when I came back.

Did activists like these, who knew that participation could or would be exceedingly costly, merely calculate that the expected rewards of participation would outweigh the high anticipated costs? Or was another dynamic at work?

Two important facts are worth bearing in mind here. First, unlike the case in many social movements, the primary potential beneficiaries of Central America peace movement success would have been the people of Central America, not U.S. movement activists or even U.S. citizens generally. In other words, this is a case of a doubly altruistic motive involving, first, a "*public* good" enjoyed, second, by a public *different* from the one to which the activists themselves belonged. Not only would the good have been consumed by people who did not contribute to providing it, but the good would *not* have been consumed by those who *did* contribute to providing it. The second relevant fact is that Central America peace activists were attempting to reverse the highest-priority foreign policy initiative of one of the most popular, persistent, and ideologically committed U.S. presidents in history. The objective probability of the movement achieving ultimate success was low. Why then would thousands of reasonable decision makers, with an immense variety of potential activities to choose from, commit to engage in one exacting very high personal costs yet holding out little promise of success that, even if achieved, would not primarily be of tangible benefit to themselves or their own society?

A series of additional findings compound the enigma. First, curiously, many of the Sanctuary and Witness for Peace activists claimed that they did not really experience the "costs" of their activism as costs. On many surveys, respondents qualified their answers to questions about the costs of activism by writing in the margins statements like these:

> That's a difficult question to answer because it makes "costs" sound too negative.

> I cannot *not* act on my beliefs, so I didn't think about it in terms of costs and benefits.

> I don't look at the high costs of my work in a negative sense, I just had to spend a lot of time and money.

> I can't describe my experience as costly. It was a gift!

These are intriguing comments. One wonders how to make sense of the notion of "rewarding costs" or "positive costs."

Next, Sanctuary activists who seriously underestimated the costs of activism were no more likely to spend fewer years involved in the movement than were those who correctly estimated or overestimated the costs of activism. One would think that activists who got more trouble than they originally bargained for—that is, who discovered activism to be much more costly than expected—would likely reconsider the cost-benefit ratio and perhaps drop out of the movement earlier than those who didn't. But statistical analyses of the data reveal no relationship whatsoever between people's over- or underestimations of the costs of activism and the number of years of their involvement as activists.

Furthermore, all of the survey respondents who reported having *not* calculated the costs and benefits of activism beforehand (see table 7.11) proceeded to answer the question about how costly, before becoming active, they expected their activism to be. If they never calculated, how could they have anticipated degrees of costliness? Furthermore, their answers conform to a broader, statistically significant pattern in the data, in which amount of calculation and degrees of expected costliness are positively associated ($r = .251^{**}$). In other words, the more the respondents had calculated the costs and benefits of activism beforehand, the more costly they tended to have estimated those costs would be. How exactly ought we to interpret these "uncalculated" expectations of cost and this pattern of association?

Finally, besides gathering data on activists' calculations and expected costs, the surveys also measured the depth and breadth of each participant's involvement in Central America activism. Respondents reported both the average number of hours they spent on Central America activism per week and the variety of political protest activities in which they participated as a part of their Central America activism.[14] Table 7.13 shows the correlations between the respondents' expected costs and ability to "free-ride" and their depth and breadth of involvement in activism. Apparently, the more costly Sanctuary and Witness for Peace activists expected beforehand that their participation would be, the *more* deeply and broadly those activists actually became involved in activism. And the more Sanctuary workers were afforded greater opportunities to free-ride by virtue of working on larger Sanctuary task force committees, the *more* hours they actually spent doing Sanctuary work. Higher expected personal costs and greater opportunities to free-ride did not discourage, but actually promoted greater personal participation in activism.

How are we to make sense of these findings? The most plausible interpretation is that the majority of these activists were motivated primarily by moral commitments that overrode not only the ordinary limits of acceptable action alternatives, but also perhaps the normal process of decision making itself.[15]

Such an interpretation assumes that all human actions are prompted and guided by two irreducible motives: pleasure and morality. On

Table 7.13. Correlation Coefficients for Factors Affecting Differential Levels of Central America Activism

	Hours Spent in Activism	Breadth of Activist's Political Activities
Greater expected costs of WFP activism	.115*	.121*
Greater expected costs of sanctuary activism	.040	.257**
Larger sanctuary core group	.305**	.103
N (Witness for Peace)	(452)	(452)
N (Sanctuary)	(129)	(129)

** = p<.01   * = p<.05

the one hand, people act to satisfy the ubiquitous desire for self-interested pleasure.[16] On the other hand and concurrently, people act to affirm the inescapable imperatives of their moral commitments.[17] These two fundamental motives are irreducible: as sources of valuation they cannot be reconciled or integrated into one all-encompassing utility. Pleasure motives are oriented toward *consequences* of action and the achievement of ends subjectively defined as desirable. Morality motives, on the other hand, are concerned with the *intentions* of actors and the discharging of what are believed to be objectively existing normative obligations. The former revolve around options and interests and seek self-satisfaction, while the latter revolve around imperatives and commitments and strive for identity affirmation. Charles Taylor writes (1989: 4) that moral acts, "involve discriminations of right and wrong, better or worse, higher or lower, which are not rendered valid by our own desires, inclinations, or choices, but rather stand independent of these and offer standards by which they can be judged."

In philosophical language, pleasure is a *teleological* motive—impelling action because of certain desired ends it will achieve—while morality is a *deontological* motive—prompting action because the action is right in and of itself, entirely apart from whatever ends it may produce. In addition to being irreducible, the two motives, are also recurrently in conflict: satisfying one's own pleasure often requires compromising moral commitments, and abiding by moral commitments often requires sacrifices of pleasure.[18]

Human selves, then, are best understood as internally divided, engaged in perpetual, creative inner conflict. People seek to balance their moral commitments and their pleasures, to negotiate a judicious mix of the two, rather than to maximize either. Exactly how they adjudicate between these irreducible and often conflicting motives in choosing courses of action depends largely upon the nature of the actions themselves and the social contexts in which they take place. In some situations—such as choosing vacation destinations—the pleasure motive predominates. In others—such as rescuing one's children from a burning building—moral imperatives largely govern behavior. Most actions and contexts, however, are not that clear-cut and thus involve the significant interplay of both motives. The majority of human activities, in other words, are indeed performed with "mixed motives."

Participation in Central America peace activism, we presume, was prompted by a mix of pleasure-seeking and morality-affirming motives, the exact balance of which probably differed from activist to activist. But given the nature and context of this Central America activism, the motive of abiding by moral commitments appears to have been primary for most of the participants. In other words, the majority of activists became involved more because they believed it was the right and necessary thing for them to do, *whatever the outcome*, and not primarily because they calculated that the probable consequences of their individual participation warranted their involvement and justified the costs it would entail. Thus, engaging in activism represented a response to moral obligations and the dictates of conscience more than the calculated pursuit of either selective incentives or an end-state collective good.

Most of the activists' accounts, gathered in interviews and surveys, confirm this interpretation. The following quotes, some of which have appeared in previous chapters, are representative:

> With regard to motivation, I must say that the moving spirit for Sanctuary was faith in the gospel of Jesus. I had no other choice but to get involved if I was to remain faithful to the Christian Gospel and its option for the poor, the persecuted, and those hungering and thirsting for justice.

> I stayed in the home of a Nicaraguan last January named Manuel Rivera. I promised him then that I would tell his story here in the U.S. I have since learned that he has been killed by the Contras. So I feel even more strongly that I must tell his story. I would rather not get arrested for the first time in my life. But I'm afraid I must. Manuel Rivera is the reason.

> Jim Corbett spoke to our group about the plight of the refugees and I felt I couldn't, in good conscience, *not* help in any way possible.

After the morning vigil, the oldest of the mothers of those killed came up to me, of all the people. I called for a translator. It was an eternal moment for me. She said, "I have been blessed by God, for I have given the blood of my son for the salvation of our people. I want to share that blessing with you, to share with your people." I fell on my knees, and she kissed me on the forehead. I looked up to the translator and he had tears streaming out of his eyes. The woman's name was Maria Garcia Lopez. But she became the incarnation of Mary for me. I didn't know what all that meant, I just knew it was a very religious moment. It was very sobering, both a blessing and a burden. I was supposed to be retiring. But now I felt chosen.

As a Jew, I know what it means to be persecuted. If it hadn't been for a few kind people, no Jews would have escaped the Holocaust. Now it was my turn to take risks on behalf of others.

These testimonies are spoken in the language of identity-affirming moral obligation, not ends-oriented rational instrumentalism. Indeed, for these people and the tens of thousands like them, there were, in a sense, ultimately no choices to be made here, no probabilities to weigh or results to consider. They had "no other choice." They "could not have *not* helped in any way possible." In the end, it didn't matter whether they would win or lose. They were simply "chosen." All that remained was to perform faithfully the tasks morality demanded. As John Fife of Southside Presbyterian Church, Tucson, Arizona, explained after his trial about a fifteen-year-old Salvadoran boy who had come to his church for help after his family had been killed (quoted in Tomsho 1987: 206): "The haunting thought that came to me was, if that was my boy, what would I want the church to do? We had no choice. None of us ever had a choice. Our only choice was whether we wanted to sell our souls."

Understanding the participation of activists in the Central America peace movement in these terms makes the curious evidence on calculation and expected costs intelligible. To the extent that the activists' involvements were motivated by moral commitments, many participated *in spite of* the very high expected costs (table 7.12), not because some other probable consequences were figured to outweigh those costs. This helps to explain the lack of the participants' calculation of the costs of activism (table 7.11). Their primary recognition of the moral obligation to participate tended to render option-evaluating, cost-benefit analyses irrelevant. As the activist cited above stated: "I cannot *not* act on my beliefs, so I didn't think about it in terms of costs and benefits."

This perspective also helps to explain why many activists did not experience "costs" as costs. Spending or losing time, money, energy, and opportunities in order to voluntarily discharge the moral obligations one has internalized can often, in fact, be experienced as affirming and even rewarding. "Costs" as necessary means to ends actually become transubstantiated into integral elements of positively regarded experiences.[19] Thus, survey respondents could claim: "I can't describe my [objectively "costly"] experience as costly. It was a gift!" And Fran Truitt could simultaneously name her calling out of retirement to fight Contra aid a blessing and a burden.

Furthermore, this approach transforms the very meaning of the calculation process itself by reversing the order of the evaluation and the conclusion: "calculating" the costs of activism appears to represent not so much a mechanism for making decisions, but a process of reckoning or coming to terms with the practical implications of what one has *already* decided to do because of other values and commitments. People first realized that they must and would become politically involved, *then* they sorted through the practical implications of what that involvement would entail. This interpretation explains the positive association found between expected costs and the amount of prior calculation. The more costs the already-committed-to participation promised to exact, the more attention the activists had to give to sorting out the implications of those costs. More importantly, this interpretation explains the positive associations found between expected costs and opportunities to "free-ride" and the depth and breadth of the activists' involvements (table 7.13). The "expected costs" were, in fact, not factors plugged into a decision-making formula. Rather, they were reflections of an awareness on the part of the incipient activists of just how deeply they were already committed to becoming involved and of the probable costs of that involvement. Moreover, larger Sanctuary task force committees were not viewed as opportunities for free-riding—why would a profoundly morally motivated person wish to free-ride?—but as encouraging and reinforcing resources for accomplishing the tasks people felt responsible to discharge. In other words, for people internally motivated by moral commitments, the effect was one of strength-in-numbers, not shirking-behind-numbers.

So, why would thousands of people, with an immense variety of potential activities to choose from, commit to engage in one exacting very high personal costs yet holding out little promise of success that, even if achieved, would not primarily be of tangible benefit to themselves or their own society? The most plausible answer appears to be: only if they were primarily motivated by moral commitments. But to clarify the implications of this answer and connect it to the conclusions of the first half of this chapter and the previous two chapters, we must state that Central America peace movement activists were not necessarily extraordinary saints or ethical virtuosos. Indeed, this view does not require that people become angels before discharging moral obligations in their actions. According to our model, theoretically, most people, given the right experiences and circumstances, should be capable of equivalent expressions of morally driven behavior. What determined that *these* particular people became Central America peace activists, and not some others, was not that they were moral superhumans, but primarily that they possessed the right backgrounds and were found in the right place at the right time. It was this population's unique combination of religious commitments, structural links to Central America, available organizational capacities, supportive political values and attitudes, prior social movement experiences, biographical availability, relational and organizational ties to activism, and relational support for participation coalescing in the context of opening macro-political opportunities that significantly advantaged their chances of recruitment into this particular movement. The activists' differential recruitment, in other words, was just as socially structured as was their moral outrage.

A PROFILE OF MOVEMENT LEADERS

Before concluding this exploration of who joined the Central America peace movement and why, we narrow the focus here to briefly examine the specific men and women who emerged as the movement's national leadership. What might we learn from them about differential recruitment to movement leadership?

Perhaps the best way to characterize the Central America peace movement national leaders is to say that they closely resemble the movement's rank-and-file activists, only more so. This is not surprising, of course, since leaders, whether intentionally or not, tend to create and shape movements in their own image. Thus, by all accounts—including personal observations of, the available literature on, and interviews with the movement's leadership—these leaders were, first, and predictably, leftist-progressive in political ideology. As the movement's main ideologues, tacticians, and spokespeople, they not only shared the movement's values and attitudes, they, so to speak, *were* the movement's values and attitudes.

Second, virtually all of these national leaders possessed a tremendous amount of experience in previous social movements and community-organizing campaigns. As such, the social role of "political activist" was central to all of their personal identities. As far back as the 1930s, for example, Bob Bonthius, who was then a college student and absolute pacifist, had worked with A. J. Muste and the Fellowship of Reconciliation organizing opposition to President Roosevelt's attempts to "get the U.S. into war with the Allies" (Bonthius 1990). More recently, Central America peace movement leaders were especially likely to have been deeply involved in the civil rights movement. Sanctuary's John Fife, for example, had participated in the 1965 march from Selma to Montgomery, Alabama (Golden and McConnell 1986: 47). Dick and Phyllis Taylor had taken part in the 1961 Freedom Rides through the deep south. In the 1950s, Fran Truitt organized civil rights campaigns to challenge racism in the Columbus, Ohio, public education system, as did Jane Guise in the Detroit, Michigan, schools in the 1960s. Anne Shumway did voter registration work in California. David Hartsough joined the lunch counter sit-ins in Washington, D.C., in 1959. And Witness for Peace leader Bob Bonthius had worked in Hattiesburg, Mississippi, as a voter registration volunteer in the 1964 Freedom Summer campaign (Truitt 1990; see also McAdam 1988: 199–240). Indeed, in most cases, if the Central America peace movement leaders had not been involved in the civil rights movement—as was the case for Gail Phares and Joe Nangle, for example—it was because they were out of the country at the time, working as missionaries in Central or South America.[20] According to Truitt (1990): "99 percent of the original group that formed Witness for Peace had either worked in the civil rights movement and/or were former missionaries to Central America. Only one person out of the whole lot of us, Paddy Lane, was too young to have done civil rights work."

The anti–Vietnam War movement figured almost as importantly in these leader's autobiographies. Betsy Crites (1992), for example, recalls, "I was very heavy into anti-Vietnam. My father and mother took me to the marches, we marched together when I was in high school. Then I went to college in 1968 and the anti-war movement was really getting strong then, so I was deeply involved. The only thing I regretted about going to Peru in 1970 was that I missed much of the last part of the anti-Vietnam struggle."

The following story told by Phyllis Taylor (1990) conveys the kind of depth of involvement in the anti-war movement typical of those who later became Central America peace movement national leaders:

> In New Jersey, we used to blockade ammunition train and boat shipments to Vietnam. For a wedding present, Dick and I requested a canoe to do this blockade work. Later it was impounded by the government as evidence on an espionage charge. One day 19 of us were sitting on the train tracks. They were using water cannons to knock us off. But Dick didn't get knocked off. He was run over by a slow moving train and rolled underneath. Amazingly, none of his limbs lay across the tracks and he wasn't seriously hurt. He said he felt the presence of Jesus protecting him. Anyway, that was my first arrest. We spent the night in jail, where, incidently, the youngest member of our group was gang-raped. Next day we were all given $50 fines, which we refused to pay. So we got 10 days more for contempt of court.

Anne Shumway, who lived in the socially conservative city of York, Pennsylvania, actually received death threats when she brought Jane Fonda to town for an anti-Vietnam campaign in the 1960s. And Sam Hope, as a North Carolinian pastor in the mid-1960s, after preaching sermons about Vietnam and being branded a communist, was so intent on seeing the country firsthand that he took his wife and three children and moved there, working for the Vietnam Christian Service from 1966 to 1968.

In addition to this extensive prior political and social movement experience, the national movement leaders were quite seasoned—mostly because of their reformist work in church denominations—in the tactics and processes of "bureaucratic insurgency."

> One factor that made Witness for Peace operational was that the original founders thought organizationally and structurally. Each of us had five to thirty years of experience at community leadership. Also, virtually all of us had a "lover's quarrel" with the church, recognizing its instrumental capacity to sanction the powers that be. None of the original group were anarchists. We thought structurally and organizationally, and really wanted to work the system. Each of us had previously struggled with the system in one way or another, organizing to reform our churches. There was an anger and hope that made us feel that we

couldn't just abandon these church structures, but that we had a voca-
tion to work through them, to do what we called a "righteous jujitsu"
on them. (Bonthius 1990)

Central America peace movement leaders also resembled a more
ideal-type version of the rank-and-file activists in their biographical
availability. Most were middle-aged. According to Bonthius (1990),
"The founders of Witness for Peace were all very mature. There were
very, very few young people." All were very well educated, typically
possessing graduate degrees, especially seminary degrees. Most were
financially secure enough, primarily because of their ages or because
of simplified standards of living, to be able to focus their attention on
political matters. Clark Taylor, for example, explains: "I have been to
Central America more than twenty times now. It helps that I am financially stable and comfortable, that we own our house outright." And
according to Fran Truitt (1990): "Sam Hope left a $50,000 a year job
to come work for Witness for Peace for $13,000. This is a movement
that really calls people. It is important to understand the kind of depth
of commitment, the passion that motivates people."

Passion certainly appears to have motivated Sam Hope's activism,
but, equally important, his acquired relative financial security enabled
that activism. Furthermore, most of the national movement leaders
had minimal family responsibilities to obstruct their time- and energy-
intensive organizing. Many—including Ken Butigan, Jim Wallis,
Cindy Buhl, Joe Nangle, Joyce Hollyday, and Yvonne Dilling—were
single.[21] Others—including Anne Shumway, Bob Bonthius, and Fran
Truitt—had many years earlier divorced spouses who opposed their
political activism.[22] Still others, who were married—such as Dick and
Phyllis Taylor, Bob Bonthius and Fran Truitt, Angela and Phillip
Berryman, Betsy and Joe Crites, and Bob and Pat Van Denend—were,
as couples, partners in political activism. The remainder—including
John Fife, Gail Phares, Jim Corbett, and Sam Hope—were married to
spouses flexible and gracious enough to at least tolerate their spouses'
devotion to activism. Very few of these movement leaders were parents of young children, and those who were worked as full-time
salaried organizers. Finally, most movement leaders enjoyed occupations that facilitated their activism. Indeed, almost all were full-time,
paid political activists.

The Central America peace movement's national leadership also mirror with greater clarity the rank-and-file activists in their relational and organizational ties to activism so clearly revealed in chapters 4 and 5. This was true of these leaders by definition. Simply by virtue of who they were, all of the national leaders were plugged into extensive networks of politically active friends and associates and religious and political organizations. Indeed, those relational and organizational ties were both the causes and results of these people's rise to positions of national leadership.

Finally, as in the histories of the rank-and-file activists, only more so, little in the stories of these national leaders indicates significant ends-oriented instrumentalism at work in their political activism. They do not appear to have been motivated to participate primarily by the promise of accomplishing some future goal. Obviously, they very much longed to overturn White House Central America policy. But, most fundamentally, these leaders were motivated not by that longing, but by a resolution to fulfill what they understood to be their inescapable moral commitments. As Ken Butigan (1991) insisted in a previous chapter: "We had to do something to take the next step. What can you do? You simply cannot name the intolerable and not so something about it. Actions have to follow a confrontation with the intolerable."

For this reason, the typical first, though not only, response of these national leaders to questions about their movement's success and failure was to say simply, "If nothing else, we were faithful." Sam Hope's (1992) candid reply to this question of success probably expresses this morally motivated orientation best:

> Success should be measured in terms of faithfulness. There are certain fights worth fighting even though you may lose. You've got to fight the good fight even if you know you won't win. At first, I thought, David and Goliath and goddamn, we were going to knock them in the head. But after a while I began to see we weren't. Still, I kept struggling, even to this day, knowing that we were just going to get beat up. I knew that if we didn't fight, we would be letting down sisters and brothers in Central America who I cared about deeply. I felt that not fighting would be a dishonorable thing to do and I simply was not going to be that kind of person.

Again, this is the language and logic of moral obligation, a language and logic that permeated the activist worlds of these national leaders.

"EPIPHANAL TURNING POINTS"

Besides the accentuated demographic and situational resemblance of the Central America peace movement's national leaders to the movement's grassroots activists, one other common characteristic of these leaders deserves mentioning. Time and again, as they told their stories, it became clear that critical in the development of most of their identities as political activists were what perhaps may best be called "epiphanal turning points" or "crises of dedication." As these leaders constructed and reconstructed, for themselves and for others, their own identities as committed political change agents, prominent in their personal narratives were pivotal episodes, sometimes momentously wrenching or awakening experiences, the repercussions of which seem to have driven and defined the meaning of their lives as activist ever since. Fran Truitt's "religious" encounter with Maria Garcia Lopez transfigured into the Virgin Mary in Jalapa, Nicaragua, recounted above, was one such moment. Often these crises of dedication involved family tragedies somehow associated with activism. In other cases, they consisted of revelatory or unforgettable events that served as points of "political conversion." Here we retell six very different examples at some length, the initial recountings of which by the activists were often difficult and tearful.

Sanctuary organizer Jane Guise disclosed her "crisis of dedication" more than halfway through her interview (1990). After discussing her involvements in the anti–Vietnam War movement, she paused for a moment, then continued:

> My oldest daughter was in the church youth group at that time and became quite involved in the Vietnam issue. Then, in 1971, she was killed in an automobile accident, at the age of seventeen. [Pause.] It was one of those inexplicable tragedies in life. My oldest daughter, had she lived, would have been a significant bridge person, at the very least, between the races so much in conflict. She already was that in our church. Certainly, my motivation for my human rights work has some relationship to my daughter. At the time I remember feeling very frustrated, thinking: what can I do for her? The anti-war and human rights committee I happened to be working on at the time was a very fitting opportunity to deepen that kind of commitment. That's a piece of how it came about for me. But I also know of others for whom the death of a loved one played a role in motivating their activism.

This kind of tragic collision of the intensely personal and the obdurately political also emerged in Anne Shumway's story (1990):

> My oldest daughter is, or was, married to a Guatemalan. He was killed some years ago. In the early 1980s there was a massacre in his village and many people were killed. His family had to leave and go to Guatemala City. But I have two Guatemalan grandchildren through him. They are for me a personal connection to the atrocities in Guatemala. When I traveled to Guatemala, it was a tremendously powerful experience. I could not even visit my son-in-law's family because it would have endangered their lives. And having two Guatemalan grandchildren who look very Guatemalan, it was overwhelming to hear stories about children being tortured, torn apart, killed, the horror, just overwhelming. That reality reenforces everything I have been doing in this movement.

Epiphanal turning points did not always involve tragedies like these. Bob Van Denend, for example, became profoundly burdened, almost obsessed, with Central America during a trip to Guatemala he made in 1976 to work with earthquake victims. There was nothing overtly traumatic about his trip, yet something about it haunted Van Denend for years, and drew him like one possessed into Central America activism in the 1980s. He recalls (1992):

> In 1976, I lived in Guatemala for three and a half months building houses after the earthquake. The trip was very haunting to me, a real life-changing event. I never really could put it all together. But there were all these churches coming down, delivering stuff. I especially remember a guy from a Christian college, he had flowered Bermuda shorts and a plaid shirt on and a camera. I remember him walking into a lean-to shack where this destitute family was living and literally pulling this girl outside to take pictures of her so he could put it on his brochure and do whatever else he wanted with it. That image really haunted me for a long time. Like, you know, "This is really wrong." The whole thing became a haunting spiritual call like I had never experienced before in my whole life. It's hard to explain, but when I say haunting, I mean it was life-changing. Because of it, I didn't pursue a career and still don't have one. We went right into working with the poor in Appalachia. But over the next years it became clear that I really needed to resolve the whole unforgettable Central America thing, that I needed to work it out. By the time Witness for Peace came around, I was ready to go to the border and catch Contra bullets, basically, to protest U.S. policy. Our Quaker peacemaking group was saying, "Look, if something happens to you, we'll take care of your family." I mean it was dramatic, heavy stuff and we were scared to death. But I had come to the point

where I was compelled to go. It was calling me, just a haunting, personal thing.

Phyllis Taylor's crisis of dedication also happened during a trip to Central America (1990):

My husband had done his conscientious-objection alternative service for the Korean War in El Salvador from 1954–56. After we were married in 1967, Dick and I traveled to Salvador, Guatemala, and Mexico for three weeks to see that part of Dick's life. It had a tremendous impact on me. I was so horrified, we went to a village where two hundred children had just died of a measles epidemic, while our children were at home immunized and fine. Then in El Salvador we saw a barrio with one water spigot for two thousand people. That was my first experience with rural poverty. I decided then that I would become a nurse in order to work in Central America. It was profound for me. I came back, became badly ill, and was hospitalized. But I started calling nursing schools from the hospital bed and soon enrolled at a Catholic school. After seeing Central America, I was so passionate and outspoken, my teachers had to ask me to stop talking in class.

Fran Truitt's original epiphanal turning point—the narrative of which, interestingly, was structurally similar to her religious encounter in Jalapa, Nicaragua—was neither tragic nor haunting. It was, rather, a liberating and validating revelation. Like Van Denend's, its significance would not have been apparent to surrounding observers. But for Truitt, the experience was life-transforming. She remembers (1990):

There was a small but, for me, critical incident in my life. Rochester civil rights worker Mrs. Harper Sibley, who was confronting Xerox about racism, came to Columbus and many leading local women met in a home to hear her speak. This was the late 1950s and I was just confronting our school board about racism in the schools. As a result, my neighbors had stopped talking to me and I began getting hate mail. It was a baptism by fire in the world! Anyway, all the chairs in this house were full, and I was the youngest woman, so I sat on the floor. Mrs. Sibley told her entire story and finished. Then, of all the women there, she looked directly at me and said: "You understand what I'm saying, don't you?" And I said: "Yes, I do. But people tell me I'm ahead of my time." And she looked right at me and said: "You're not ahead of your time. You just know what time it is." Now, that may not seem like a big deal, but it was a key moment in my life. Somehow, I absolutely knew then that Christ was out in the world, going before us, and that we had to follow. It told me that I was not really crazy for fighting racism. So, from then on, I really pressed on, doing more civil rights work, inner-city organizing, anti-war activism, anti-hunger work. I just became very involved, known in central Ohio and my denomination as a leader for justice. Because of all of this I ended up getting a divorce.

Finally, Ken Butigan's epiphanal turning point or crisis of dedication was also an unexpected revelation of sorts, not about himself, but about the true nature of the political-military system he had begun to challenge. Again, to Butigan's comrades the episode may not have seemed extraordinary. But for Butigan himself, it represented the decisive crossing of a threshold which allowed no turning back. He recalls (1991):

> My baptism into the peace movement came in 1981 when I was involved in trying to stop the first *U.S.S. Trident* submarine in the Puget Sound from getting loaded with their weapons. We were thirty-five scruffy people coming together, praying, thinking, and getting out there on the water to oppose the single most destructive weapon in human history. The *Trident* itinerary was secret, but we had people watching up and down the coast. When it did come, we deployed people in rowboats to get out in front of the submarine, to get them to stop for one moment to reflect on what they were doing. All of a sudden, out of nowhere ninety-nine Coast Guard and Navy craft appeared: cutters, Zodiaks, helicopters, airplanes, out of nowhere. Here were frightened nineteen-year-old kids pointing M-16s at us and blowing us out of our boats with water cannons. It was like war. The water was very choppy that day and we were very far out. It was frightening. The experience had a tremendous impact on me. I realized then that my government was willing to use extraordinary force to try to stop a handful of nonviolent people trying to make a simple statement about mega-violence. The image that spontaneously appeared in my mind was an iron fist in a velvet glove: consumerism and human rights for the white, middle class cloaking a ruthless readiness to use brute force to hold on to power. That was a real education for me that, for some reason, totally solidified my commitment. I resolved then to learning how to use the tactics and strategies of nonviolent direct action. I was even ready to sacrifice my career, so I pushed my Ph.D. off to the side and plunged into political activism.

Clearly, the particulars of these epiphanal turning points were unique in each person's experience. Yet the common features and functions of these pivotal episodes are too interesting and significant to disregard. Whether traumatic, exhilarating, or sobering, these critical moments all appear to have unexpectantly broken into these people's lives. They all jolted their subjects' basic perceptions of reality, elucidating for them a new awareness of what is truly valuable in life. As an event, each in its own way accumulated and conveyed greater significance to those who experienced it than the standard cultural "recipe knowledge" interpretations would have prescribed. Each was personally costly in its consequences, terminating marriages, higher degrees, and careers. And each had the practical effect of inspiring and energizing an intense commitment to long-term political activism.

Recognizing the frequency of these "epiphanal turning points" and "crises of dedication" in the autobiographies of Central America peace movement leaders raises intriguing questions. Does something common in the experiences of social movement leaders *require* or *call forth* the social construction and reconstruction of such autobiographical events? And if so, exactly why and how? Do these crisis-of-dedication narratives function to justify the personal costs of activism? Do they operate as "frame alignment" mechanisms sustaining and deepening political commitment? Does the telling and retelling of epiphanal turning-point stories serve as a solidarity-building ritual among activists, as do stories of, for example, "the first arrest?" Or should we simply accept their face-value significance as unpredictable historical ordeals that at one time inspired dedication to activism? Furthermore, we might ask: Are epiphanal turning points unique to the experience of those who become movement leaders, or are they common fixtures in the lives of "ordinary" grassroots activists as well, as Hannon's (1991) work might suggest? If there is a difference, why? Finally, how might these retrospective autobiographical interpretations alter over the years with the leaders' changing experiences of activism? How, in other words, might political success, stalemate, burnout, failure, or withdrawal metamorphize the telling or meaning of these stories? It remains beyond the capacity of this study to answer these questions. But they certainly deserve further investigation.

CONCLUSION

Examining the issue of what kind of people became involved in the Central America peace movement, we have discovered that the activists were distinguished both by their long-term histories of acquiring "political activist" identities and by their circumstantial and relational environments, which facilitated and supported political activism. We have also discovered the central importance of moral commitments as deontological motives that overrode the logic of teleological instrumentalism in the decision-making process by which activists came to join the movement. Finally, we noted with interest the importance of "epiphanal turning points" in the lives of Central America peace movement leaders, which suggested a number of intriguing questions about the formation and transformation of social-activist identities.

Having explored in this and the previous three chapters the initial *emergence* of the U.S. Central America peace movement, we turn now to investigate various aspects of the ongoing struggle to *maintain and advance* the movement over the entire decade of the 1980s. We begin in chapter 8 by examining key dilemmas about strategy and identity that Central America peace activists were forced to confront.

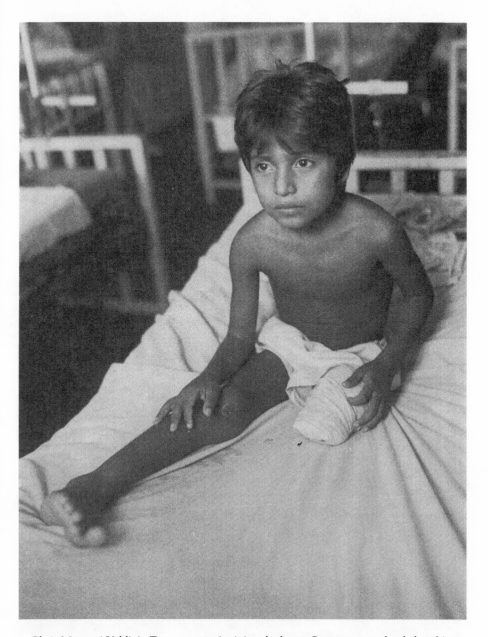

Pl. 1. Marconi Valdivia Zamora, age six, injured when a Contra mortar landed on his home in Siuna, Nicaragua, on December 20, 1987. The attack was part of a widespread offensive in which dozens of civilians were killed and hundreds wounded. A Contra spokesman in Washington, D.C., subsequently admitted that the offensive was launched prior to the January 1988 congressional vote for $36 million in Contra aid, to impress the U.S. Congress that the Contras remained a viable fighting force. By 1987, the Contra war had wounded 20,000 and killed 30,000 Nicaraguans. The death toll of El Salvador's civil war was 75,000. Guatemala's civil war produced 100,000 civilian deaths and more than 100,000 children orphaned. © 1987, Paul Dix.

Pl. 2. Jim Corbett assists Guatemalan refugee Juana Beatriz Alvarez over the border fence between Mexico and the U.S. © *Arizona Daily Star,* by Ron Medvescek.

Pl. 3. Southside United Presbyterian Church declares itself the first public sanctuary for Central American refugees on March 24, 1982. The signs read, "INS: Don't profane the sanctuary" and "This is the sanctuary of God for the oppressed of Central America." Speaking is the Reverend John Fife. Sitting to his right are Gary MacEoin and Jim Corbett. To his left is a Salvadoran refugee whose protective alias is "Alfredo." © 1982, *Tucson Citizen,* by Peter Weinberger.

Pl. 4. March 24, 1983. Four Guatemalan refugees prepare to tell their stories at Luther Place Memorial Church, the first publicly declared sanctuary church in Washington, D.C. On the far right is the church's pastor, John Steinbruck. © 1983, Rick Reinhard/Impact Visuals.

Pl. 5. July 1983. On Witness for Peace's first delegation, 153 U.S. Christians join with residents of the town of Jalapa, Nicaragua, for a peace vigil at the edge of town. The man in the hat is Bob Bonthius. © 1983, Richard Taylor.

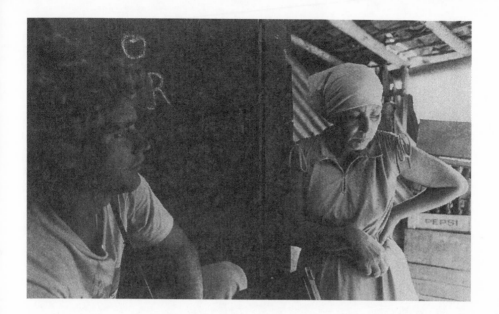

Pl. 6. Witness for Peace long-term delegate Larry Lehman interviews a survivor of a 1985 Contra attack on Jinotega, Nicaragua, to document war casualties and atrocities. © 1985, Paul Dix.

Pl. 7. On January 17, 1985, Jim Wallis holds a news conference in front of the U.S. State Department to deliver to authorities 42,352 pledges, gathered from around the country, to protest with massive civil disobedience a U.S. invasion of Nicaragua. By 1986, eighty thousand Americans had signed the Pledge of Resistance. © 1985, Rick Reinhard/Impact Visuals.

Pl. 8. April 20, 1985. Crowds of demonstrators protest Contra aid on the west side of the U.S. Capitol Building in a coalition-sponsored, multi-issue "April Action for Peace, Jobs, and Justice" campaign. © 1985, Rick Reinhard/Impact Visuals.

Pl. 9. December 11, 1986. Pledge of Resistance demonstrators protest administration deceptions in front of the White House. © 1987, Rick Reinhard/Impact Visuals.

Pl. 10. September 15, 1987. A Witness for Peace "Days of Decision" campaign rally against Contra aid, near the U.S. Capitol Building. The five-month campaign helped to defeat two administration requests for Contra aid in February and March of 1988. Crosses and coffins commemorate and protest Contra war victims; piled on the table are some of the campaign-generated letters to U.S. Senators. © 1987, Rick Reinhard/Impact Visuals.

Pl. 11. May 15, 1989. Baltimore Pledge of Resistance member Dick Ochs, in one of a series of Pledge-coordinated "surprise actions" across the country, dangles from the atrium of the National Press Building, two blocks away from the White House, calling for an end to U.S. aid to El Salvador. © 1989, Ken Butigan.

Pl. 12. December 2, 1989. Protesting the murder of four Salvadoran Jesuits and their housekeepers by the U.S.-backed Salvadoran military, religious activists pray for peace in Central America on the White House sidewalk; forty-seven were arrested for praying without a permit. © 1989, Rick Reinhard/Impact Visuals.

Pl. 13. March 24, 1990. Protesters against U.S. aid to El Salvador demonstrate at a "Romero Peace Plaza" in front of the White House, in a coalition-organized tenth-anniversary commemoration of the assassination of Salvadoran Archbishop Oscar Romero. Fifteen thousand participated in the day's protests, in which 580 were arrested for demonstating in front of the White House. © 1990, Rick Reinhard/Impact Visuals.

Part Three
Maintaining the Struggle

Eight

NEGOTIATING STRATEGIES AND COLLECTIVE IDENTITY

Action is built up in coping with the world. . . . By making indications to himself and by interpreting what he indicates, the human being has to forge to piece together a line of action. In order to act, the individual has to idenitfy what he wants, establish an objective or goal, map out a prospective line of behavior, note and interpret the actions of others, size up his situation, check himself at this or that point, figure out what to do at other points, and frequently spur himself on in the face of dragging dispositions or disouraging settings.

Herbert Blumer, *Symbolic Interactionism*

The emerging U.S. Central America peace movement did not receive a predetermined, self-evident political program to guide its actions. All of the key strategic and tactical questions had to be answered all along the way. Whom should the movement be portrayed as representing? How broadly or narrowly should the movement define its goals? Against whom should the movement exert political pressure? Through what specific actions should that pressure be exerted? When should the movement expend its political resources and when should it conserve them? How centralized or decentralized should the movement be? With whom should the movement form alliances? What should be the purposes and limits of those alliances? How would the movement know when it had succeeded or failed? How should the movement respond to apparent successes and failures? These were the kinds of issues that had to be decided and re-decided by Central America peace movement activists over the course of the entire decade, as both the subjective experiences of the activists and the objective political and military circumstances in the U.S. and Central America changed over the years.

In recent years, social-movement studies have been preoccupied with a supposed opposition or contrast between resource mobilization theory and new social movements theory (see, for instance, Klandermans and Tarrow 1988; Dalton, Kuechler, and Bürklin 1990). Often, the theoretical debate has been cast as one of "strategy" versus "identity" (see, for instance, Cohen 1985). Such a theoretical opposition, however, is unnecessary and misleading. Political strategy and collective identity are both essential and complementary facets of the life of any social movement. By choosing and implementing strategies and tactics, movements automatically construct and solidify their own collective identities, and by doing so help to specify the kinds of strategies and tactics they can appropriately employ. In this chapter we illuminate this reciprocal process by investigating some of the fundamental strategic and tactical dilemmas with which the Central America peace movement grappled throughout the 1980s. By struggling with and resolving these dilemmas, Central America peace activists both committed the movement to specific strategies and tactics *and* helped construct their movement's collective identity.

NARROW THE ISSUE OR CONFRONT THE BIG PROBLEM?

For many Central America peace movement activists, military aid to the Nicaraguan Contras and El Salvador was merely the tip of the iceberg. The real problem with the U.S. and Central America, in their estimation, was much deeper and more profound than that. A growing historical awareness in the movement helped form a belief that Reagan military aid was actually more a symptom than it was the actual problem. The problem itself, in the minds of many activists, was a long history of U.S. imperialism intent on the geopolitical domination and economic exploitation of Central America. As Joyce Hollyday wrote in the opening lines of a *Sojourners*-published Central America study guide, *Crucible of Hope* (1984: 5), the nations of Central America "all hold in common . . . the fact that since at least 1898 their histories have been dominated by the interests of the United States rather than their own. That reality has been at the root of the region's brutal repression and civil strife."

What ultimately needed to be challenged and changed was not simply the aid and immigration policy of the Reagan years, but the entire one-hundred-year-old political, military, diplomatic, economic, and cultural posture of the U.S. toward Central America. The paramount goal of many Central America peace activists involved a fundamental transformation of inter-American relations and, therefore, necessarily, of the U.S.'s understanding of its own unique role in the world. Danny

Collum made this clear in the Pledge of Resistance handbook, *Basta!* (1986: 13):

> The only long-term solution to the economic misery that fuels the rebellions in Central America is a fundamental reordering of those nations' economic and political systems. . . . What the countries of Central America and the Caribbean need most is the freedom to determine their own future. They must be able to create the systems, institutions, and international alliances that will best serve their peoples' needs. That is what the long decades of U.S. economic and military domination have most denied them. As long as that domination continues, the cycle of grinding poverty, revolt, and war can only escalate. . . . If there is ever to be peace, justice, and genuine democracy in Central America and the Caribbean, it will be when the people of the United States realize that those countries are not our backyard. They are other people's homes.

This conviction presented a significant problem. For challenging and defeating the specific, unpopular foreign aid program of one president was one thing, an imaginably attainable goal. But transforming a century-old posture of international relations deeply embedded in both U.S. political culture and state bureaucracy was another matter altogether. Thus, the Central America peace movement confronted a strategic dilemma. If it defined its central grievance as the narrow issue of annual military aid appropriations or, for Sanctuary activists, U.S. immigration policy, it might win the battle but lose the war. That is, it might succeed, for example, in ending Contra aid for the time being but fail in changing the underlying policy paradigm that had generated one hundred years of military aid, Marine interventions, CIA-sponsored coup d'états, support of exploitative Central America oligarchies, and political and economic domination by multinational corporations. Even with victory now, without ending U.S. imperialism, one or two presidents later, the U.S. might again be exporting massive amounts of military equipment and training to Central America. Defining the grievance narrowly seemed like knowingly slapping Band-Aids on cancer (see Cohen and Rogers 1986b: 45–49).

On the other hand, if the Central America peace movement was to define its main grievance broadly and, from its perspective, honestly, confronting America with what was understood to be the U.S.'s own imperialistic hegemony and interventionism, it would almost certainly relegate itself to political irrelevance and ineffectiveness. Anti-imperialist analyses, however accurate they may be, do not sell well in the

American marketplace of ideas. Nor does the rhetoric of U.S. exploitation, cultural hegemony, and systemic interventionism. Furthermore, compared to killing a specific military aid bill in Congress, transforming the entire historical posture of foreign relations of a world superpower appeared simply too vast a political goal to effect. The big problem, in other words, for many seemed politically too big to confront. In the language of "frame alignment theory" (Snow et al. 1986), frame bridging and frame amplification seemed feasible, but frame extension and frame transformation appeared impossible and self-defeating. Thus, while Central America peace activists believed that, ultimately, they were facing something like political cancer, it also appeared that, realistically, what seemed like the mere Band-Aid of attacking immediate and narrow issues might be the only feasible remedy at their disposal.

This strategic dilemma created an ongoing, frustrating tension among these activists. Narrowing the issue seemed pragmatically necessary, but also shortsighted, deficient, and intellectually dishonest. Confronting the big picture did appear truly essential. But doing so also promised to derail the movement's immediate political momentum, kill its popular appeal, and reduce its chance of winning any short-term victories. Could the movement really afford to focus on long-term education toward a foreign-policy paradigm shift while every day hundreds of innocent Nicaraguans and Salvadorans were dying at the hands of brutal militias financed with U.S. tax dollars? At the same time, could the movement really afford to ignore the ultimate, entrenched political source of the immediate problems? Central America peace activists argued these issues and questions throughout the decade. Their debate was not simply one over strategic choices, but inevitably also over the movement's very identity. Would this be an anti-war movement? An educational movement for awareness and consciousness-raising? An isolationist movement? A liberal humanitarian movement protecting refugees? A leftist solidarity movement in support of revolutionary change in Central America? A radical anti-imperialist, anti-interventionist movement? Or something else?

On the one side, many argued on moral and strategic grounds for the need to focus attention on the larger issues, to see each problem as part of a single political cloth. They believed it was essential to draw connections between the Monroe Doctrine, U.S. banana plantations in Honduras, Salvadoran death squads, U.S. CIA covert activities, the migration of refugees, Anastasio Somoza and his ilk, drug smuggling, and even the nuclear arms race and domestic poverty in the U.S. Sanctuary activist William Sloane Coffin, for example, argued for this kind of "frame extension" tactic at the 1985 Arizona Inter-American Symposium on Sanctuary (1985: 180–81):

> Foreign policy to an extraordinary degree reflects a government's attitude toward its own people. . . . Our foreign aid today to Central America is making the rich richer, the poor poorer, and the military more powerful. Isn't that exactly what is happening in our own country?. . . . If my analysis is correct . . . we in the sanctuary movement can no longer separate foreign policy from domestic policies, and we may have to recognize that the best way to change the former lies in a change of the latter. I realize that by making these connections, the sanctuary movement may lose some of its middle-class adherents, but only by making these connections will the movement gain converts among the poor in this country, especially blacks, who tend to resent so much attention being lavished on "foreigners" when they could use a little more attention themselves.

Similarly, in 1982, a group of academics and policy makers initiated a project called Domestic Roots of U.S. Foreign Policy, whose purpose was to "explore the links between current U.S. policies in [Central America] and major institutions and issues in U.S. domestic politics . . . to highlight the continuity between domestic policy initiatives and current policies in the region" (Tushnet 1988: i).

Many others, however, on pragmatic grounds, opposed tackling such a broad agenda. Break the larger problem down into little bits, they argued, and deal with them separately, one at a time. Bob Bonthius, who helped establish Witness for Peace, was a particularly strong advocate of narrowing the issue to a manageable size to increase the chances of success. He explains (1990):

> From the start of Witness for Peace, we were quite willing to define a modest focus for the whole organization. What we bit off was modest enough to chew, we were able to chew it. That jived with our experiences about how to develop an effective organization: you have to keep a very, very limited focus, hold to it, recruit around it, organize around it, and raise money around it. We have done that since the beginning, despite all the discussions about becoming involved with domestic issues to link the whole world. You have to decide your issue. You don't have time for them all. You can't be everywhere all at the same time. That limited purpose made our task doable at the grassroots.

Thus, Witness for Peace board member Clark Taylor observed (1990):

"Witness for Peace's ultimate goal was to stop imperialism, change U.S. policy, and withdraw U.S. dominance. But our immediate goal was to stop the Contras. That was our slogan and cause." Interestingly, in the late 1980s, when Witness for Peace leaders in Washington began considering moving into material-aid work to Nicaragua under the slogan "repair the damage," the long-term delegates in Nicaragua staged a virtual insurrection in opposition, arguing that this violated their core mission and smacked of paternalism (Crites 1992).

Overall, those who advocated narrowing the issue and defining limited grievances tended to win the debate, perhaps because their strategy's implementation was more organizationally feasible. The recruitment, training, and deployment of movement activists was almost always grounded in single, specific issues, whether refugees' rights, the invasion of Grenada, Contra abuses, support for the FMLN, or an immanent attack on Nicaragua. Once activists were mobilized and committed, they could learn about broader historical legacies, the interconnections of power, and the imperatives of empire. But this typically remained secondary, whenever it did occur. Central America peace movement organizations also tended to specialize in grievances. Sanctuary took on illegal refugees, Witness for Peace the Contras, the Pledge of Resistance an invasion of Nicaragua, CISPES (Committee in Solidarity with the People of El Salvador) the Salvadoran military, and so on. Only taken together as a single movement did these organizations address the broadest issues of U.S. involvement in Central America. And, in the movement's public discourse, the broad rhetoric of radical anti-Yankee anti-imperialism almost never occupied center stage for very long.

As a consequence, the movement's identity was fairly eclectic. When scratched below the common surface of general opposition to the administration's Central America policy, the movement operated as an umbrella that comprised multiple identities—humanitarian, isolationist, liberal, anarchist, leftist, pacifist, radical, and more. Through organizational specialization, the movement became many things for many people, which was both a strength and a weakness. Politically speaking, the movement was able to score some very important short-term victories. However, partly because broader historical and philosophical issues of the U.S. role in Central America largely had been neglected in public debate, when the sociopolitical conditions that originally had expanded political opportunity for the movement changed, Central America disappeared from the national agenda. Key battles had been won, but the conflict subsided without any significant changes in the U.S.'s fundamental posture toward Central America. This outcome was also closely related to another fundamental strategic dilemma that faced the Central America peace movement, which we examine next.

EDUCATE THE GRASSROOTS OR RUSH TO LEGISLATIVE BATTLE?

Central America peace activists also struggled over the balance between grassroots education work and political protest and lobbying in Congress. Underlying this conflict was the fact that both of these tasks possessed an allure or logic that beckoned greater investment in one and less investment, for the moment, in the other. Investment in grassroots education, for example, presents itself as an essential prerequisite for successful political activism. Anti-nuclear activists Molander and Molander (1990: 44–45) write: "Education must precede political participation or movement adherents will often misdirect their resources when they undertake political participation, the pressures on public policymakers will not be sufficiently forceful to overcome the prevailing policy inertia, and movement adherents will be unable to handle the inevitable defeats that will accompany any change process." The Molanders argue (1990: 37–38) that the nuclear Freeze movement of the early 1980s failed precisely because it neglected the essential work of grassroots education:

> It was the movement's failure to understand the role of education in movement development, not political naïveté or a lack of a sufficient political base, that was the overriding cause of its failure and decline. . . . In consciously choosing to leap into the political arena, rather than continuing their movement-building efforts at the grassroots, movement leaders abandoned those areas where the awareness-building and educational efforts had been most effective.

Thus, to avoid the dangers of "premature politics," major investments in grassroots educational work seemed essential for a successful Central America peace movement. Many movement leaders understood that. Fran Truitt (1990) said, "Witness for Peace did not go right into conventional lobbying because we wanted to build a real grassroots movement. So we started out educating at the regional and local level." The necessity of grassroots educational work became clear to

Sanctuary organizer Jane Guise (1990) through the failure of "premature politics":

> Originally, we hoped for a Vietnam era-like ever-escalating growth of anti-intervention in Central America through large demonstrations. We worked very hard building broad-based coalitions with all kinds of domestic and foreign issue groups. But in 1984, after a tremendous amount of work, we had a barely-acceptable crowd of 7,000 people at a demonstration in Boston. Trying to repeat another Vietnam-period movement and efforts to work through the media just weren't working. So I decided to make a programmatic shift, a change of focus. I realized the Sanctuary movement offered an opportunity to do in-depth education with a narrower but very significant base: declaring Sanctuary in a congregation requires that everybody pay attention to it, whether they want to or not. The little groups that started the process within congregations had tremendous commitment and holding power. Some of them worked on it steadily for years before bringing the congregation to a vote. This forced ordinary people to pay attention to the issue, like it or not. You would have folks saying, "but I don't know enough about it." And you say, "well, come to the next meeting," or "lets talk about it." This very solid, in-depth grassroots education was a very important opportunity on which we capitalized.

But grassroots education had its limits. To even its strongest advocates, grassroots education was merely a necessary means to an end, not the end itself. What really mattered was changing U.S. Central America policy, and that would only happen through political activism. Excessively investing in grassroots education seemed like ever preparing for a battle that would never be fought. Waiting too long to become politically engaged risked losing an open window of opportunity. Activists felt a constant pressure to rush to political battle, which they often did. According to Jim Rice (1992), "An unlimited supply of resources would have afforded us the luxury of doing the kind of long-term thinking and organizing that's extremely important. And there are always some people who really push that. On the other hand, Reagan was about to invade Nicaragua and Congress was always about to send millions of dollars to the Contras and El Salvador. So the imperative, the urgency of the moment took over. It had to."

Even most radical activists, scornful of the entire U.S. political system and primarily committed to oppositional protest alone, were eventually forced to link their extra-institutional protests to an institutionalized lobbying program in Congress: "The inclination of a lot of the organizers was not even to bother with the Congress, that lobbying was a joke. On the other hand, you have to organize civil disobedience around the idea of demanding that your representative take a stand and stop the policies. Even the most cynical people about the U.S. political process realized they needed to focus our work on members of Congress. So, lobbying was pretty intense" (Butigan 1991).

A price was paid, however, for lunging into urgently needed protest and lobbying activism. According to Rice (1992), "It was often detrimental to the longer-term educational work that needs doing." Angela Berryman (1990) explained that this was particularly galling in view of the frustratingly few results produced by lobbying Congress:

> There was always a love-hate relationship with the Congress. Many people put lots of energy into Congress because we needed to cut off the money to change policy. But there was a great resistance to being so dependent on the votes of Congress, resistance to dealing with the congressional cycles and chasing around various committees for such little results. There was a feeling of being manipulated by congressional votes, of simply putting out brushfires. People knew that the votes were important but resented Congress's slowness and lack of responsiveness. People in the movement were ultimately much more interested in education toward fundamental change in U.S. policy, which is resource-intensive. Unfortunately, what demanded all our attention and energy were the immediate issues being voted on by Congress.

Frustrations like these tended to push some people back into either long-term grassroots educational work or into plain oppositional protest. Since most of the movement's attention had been focused on the immediate political work of blocking U.S. military aid and preventing a U.S. invasion, when in the late 1980s macro-conditions changed and the Central America conflict began to wind down, the peace movement receded without having fundamentally changed the U.S.'s political and economic posture toward the region.

MAINTAIN A RELIGIOUS IDENTITY OR DIVERSIFY?

Another strategic decision that would significantly shape the Central America peace movement's collective identity concerned the character of the movement's national organizations. Namely, should those organizations, which were mostly conceived, founded, funded, and staffed by Christians, along with some Jews, retain their specifically religious identities? Or should they broaden out and officially embrace all creeds? This was an issue about which movement leaders had strong and conflicting convictions. In Witness for Peace, it came up as a dispute at every major gathering of leaders (Bonthius 1990).

On the one hand, many movement leaders, particularly those from the East Coast, fought hard throughout the decade to identify their organizations officially as "Christian" or "biblical," rather than "interfaith," "spiritual," or totally inclusive. Beside feeling a certain ownership by right of creating these organizations, these voices believed that the movement's greatest strength was precisely its religious constituency and identity. The U.S. government and the American people, they argued, could—whether right or wrong—comfortably ignore secular militants, radical anti-interventionists, leftist academics, assorted feminists, Muslims, gays, lesbians, and witches as fringe elements. But they could not disregard the protest demands of tens of thousands of mainstream church people. In an early memo to other Witness for Peace founders, Jim Wallis wrote (quoted in Griffin-Nolan 1991: 60):

> The stronger the religious identity, the stronger will be the Witness. The concern for a "prayerful, biblical approach" and . . . a strong Christian character is, I think, critical. . . . If the identity were more liberal and secular, or, even more problematic, left[ist] or Marxist in character, it would be easily written off by the U.S. government and press and would not attract the numbers and kind of people whom we need. . . . And risk factors of the vigil require a strong spiritual rootage, as well as keen political perspective.

Furthermore, this camp contended, creating a context in which mainstream church- and synagogue-goers would feel comfortable participating in protest was very much in the long-term interest of the entire peace and justice movement, and the religious community as well. In any case, they observed, religious and secular activists tended to employ very different styles of activism and protest. Why should alien and often alienating secular styles of protest be imposed on religious activists when they were the ones who had founded these organizations? Finally, they asked, why should their organizations feel obliged to be all things to all people? If nonbelievers wanted to get involved, they could either join one of the hundreds of existing local secular groups, such as CISPES, or start their own group.

On the other side, many movement leaders, especially those from California, championed creedal inclusiveness. Diversity, they argued, is strength. By deterring all but Christian or Bible-believing or faith-based participants, they would be unnecessarily shearing down the movement's breadth. Why exclude enthusiastic participants when the movement needed all the warm bodies it could get? Furthermore, many nonreligious leaders from previous movements, such as the Freeze, women's, and environmental movements, offered to bring a great deal of experience to the Central America struggle. Why not take advantage of their know-how for the current conflict? Finally, this camp asserted, any option other than total inclusiveness fundamentally violated the core values of the peace and justice movement. How could the movement "prefigure" the kind of world it wanted to create when it itself reflected parochialism, exclusivity, and religious imperialism in its policies and structures? If religious and secular activists could not collaborate within the same organization, how could they expect Ronald Reagan to get along with Daniel Ortega?

The principle that tended to resolved this issue, whenever it *was* resolved, was not the opinion of leaders, but the essential functional mission of each organization. Witness for Peace, for example, remained defined throughout the decade as a "prayerful, biblically based community" which, however, welcomed "others . . . who vary in spiritual approach but are one with us in purpose," as long as they were "comfortable" with the prayerful, biblical approach (Griffin-Nolan 1991: 61; Bonthius 1990). Witness for Peace's recruitment, political strategies, and especially the inherent risk of its war-zone travel supported the more specifically religious identity. "The last thing you want to be doing when people you love are getting killed," argued Yvonne Dilling at a key meeting defining Witness for Peace (quoted in Griffin-Nolan 1991: 61), "is worrying about whether your prayer is going to offend someone." The Pledge of Resistance, on the other hand, whose strategy relied on coordinated, massive civil disobedience across the nation, quickly shifted from being a primarily religious organization to being a creedally all inclusive one. Whereas excluding secular populations did not significantly impair the successful operation of Witness for Peace, it clearly would have for the Pledge of Resistance. "In the beginning, the Pledge was organized mostly by religious leaders. But quickly it became much broader and less Christian-oriented. The roots of the Pledge were faith-based, but it expanded out beyond to get as broad as possible a group of people to sign on. People realized there was a bigger audience out there that would oppose an invasion of Nicaragua on moral and ethical grounds but not faith grounds" (Berryman 1990).[1]

Finally, Sanctuary was, almost from the beginning, theoretically open to nonreligious groups. But it remained *de facto* almost entirely within churches and synagogues. Once established, little about its mission required an exclusively religious identity, and its developing decentralized structure allowed for diversity. Some cities and university groups in fact did declare Sanctuary (see table 7.7). But, overall, their actual contribution was more symbolic than substantive. The task of caring for the everyday needs of refugee families was simply more organizationally suited to churches and synagogues.

Alternative resolutions to the religious exclusion-inclusion issue carried obvious consequences for the movement's identity. Witness for Peace's decisions on the matter gave that group a decidedly Christian character and self-concept, which helped sustain the dominant religious tone in the movement as a whole. The Pledge of Resistance, on the other hand, took on a more secular-leftist character, taking the movement in a direction that gave it a feel more like that of the antinuclear movement. Both resolutions carried their own inherent set of difficulties as well. Witness for Peace constantly had to struggle with the ambiguity of being prayerful and biblical while accepting other views. A major dispute erupted in 1983, for instance, when Witness for Peace's media spokesman, Dennis Marker, discovered that one of the members of the first long-term delegation was a publicly declared socialist. According to Marker (1992):

> I was adamant. I was not going to tell the press that we are a Christian-based mission, then have it discovered that one of our first people is a communist. No way. Give me a break! It could have ruined our credibility. We had huge fights over that because he was a personal friend of one of our founders. The guy had every right to be a socialist. It had nothing to do with his politics. It simply had to do with the fact that we had a message to convey, that we had decided to be Christian-based. People wanted us to do press work around this first team going to Nicaragua and I said "No way. We're just not going to do it." So we had to fight that one out.

Witness for Peace also encountered major internal disagreement in 1985 over whether gays and lesbians could participate (Truitt 1990). Finally, even some Jews, not formally excluded by the organization's self-definition, sometimes felt ill at ease with Witness for Peace's organizational culture. Phyllis Taylor (1990) remarked:

> It was always a problem for me that the official Witness for Peace tee-shirt said: *Acción Cristiano Permanente por la Paz*. I led two national Jewish delegations when Reagan falsely accused the Sandinistas of anti-

Semitism, which made me so mad! One of the long-term delegates who met my Jewish group at the airport had to write on the tee-shirts "y Judea," which was very thoughtful. I have always had to raise the issue: why can't we do campaign of crosses *and markers*, with churches *and synagogues*? I have had to keep reminding us that "biblical" means Jewish and Christian, not just Christian.[2]

USE YOUR POLITICAL AMMUNITION OR WAIT FOR "THE BIG ONE"?

Another dilemma that especially plagued the Pledge of Resistance concerned exactly when to "call out the forces" for massive, civil-disobedient resistance. This problem stemmed from an incongruity that developed between the Pledge's original strategic design and the military strategy of the Reagan administration. Originally, the Pledge of Resistance had been mobilized as a response to the U.S. invasion of Grenada. The idea was to deter a similar overwhelming invasion of Nicaragua through the threat of widespread and massive legal protest and civil disobedience involving the takeover and occupation of federal buildings and congressional offices across the nation until the invasion was withdrawn. That provocative idea compelled eighty-five thousand people to sign the Pledge. But the expected and feared U.S. invasion of Nicaragua never happened. Or it did not occur in the way Pledge founders thought it would. Instead, the Reagan administration skillfully outmaneuvered its opposition with the strategy of low-intensity warfare. The Pledge of Resistance had prepared for another Normandy. But what it actually confronted in the Nicaraguan Contras and the CIA was something more like the Chinese-backed Vietcong than like Normandy. World War II–style beach-landing invasions simply had become outmoded—precisely because of the Vietcong's success. In fact, the U.S. *had* begun an invasion of Nicaragua, but it was a covert and incremental "invasion" executed through a surrogate army.

This posed a vexing dilemma for Pledge leaders, who knew they possessed a significant but limited amount of potential for protest. The question was: Should they adjust their strategic thinking, try to deploy their massive protests against the low-intensity Contra war, and run the risk of jumping the gun? Or should they adhere to their original vision, save their massive protest for the direct and overwhelming U.S. invasion of Nicaragua that many thought was still possible, and run the risk of watching the Contras slowly desolate Nicaragua without ever once calling out the protest forces they had so purposefully amassed? In other words, use the ammunition now and hope you don't need it later, or save it for later and hope you shouldn't have used it earlier? Bob Bonthius (1990) recalled:

> The original Kirkridge group thought there should be a mass-resistance in the event of an invasion. That set us off on a good and misleading track. It was good to recognize that nothing less than massive resistance would change U.S. policy. But it was misleading to suggest that an invasion hadn't already taken place. Many of us were saying: "Look they've already invaded and are still invading! It's just a different kind of invasion." So, the Pledge had tactical problems because it had this notion of waiting for some big invasion. Incremental penetration was far less dramatic, but that was the "invasion" we had to deal with. Because, from our point of view, no dramatic overseas landing was going to happen.

Ken Butigan (1991) concurred: "We quickly ran into the perception that the Pledge was something we were keeping in abeyance for some future catastrophic invasion. That was a very strange psychological situation to be in, to see the blood flowing across your desk from Contra attacks, disappearances, death squads, yet to be saying to people: 'This isn't bad enough, but yeah, but when the Big One happens we're going to be prepared.' We really struggled with that contradiction."

Dennis Marker (1992) remembered: "It was not fun at all. There were bad days. And managing media interest in the Pledge with that kind of problem was just a disaster."

As each month passed without a direct invasion, the alternative of abandoning the "Normandy standard," adjusting to the reality of low-intensity war, and calling out the forces against it grew increasingly inevitable. But this option—which amounted to transforming the Pledge's fundamental identity—raised three significant problems. First, no Pledge leader knew whether the tens of thousands who had pledged to protest a direct U.S. invasion would protest anything *but* that. According to Phyllis Taylor (1990):

> Many people pledged to oppose a U.S. invasion. But with the change to low-intensity warfare, which is very hard to make real to people, it seemed it would be much harder to get people to act. Instead of protesting a large-scale invasion, we were dealing with Contra aid votes, the embargo, non-compliance with the world court. That is much harder to get across to regular folks, who will alter their lives to protest overt military engagement, but not something else. Protesting low-intensity warfare just requires much more political sophistication.

Pat Van Denend (1992) remembered: "After an invasion didn't happen, many people felt they had to retract their pledge because there wasn't a full-scale invasion, it was just a Contra aid vote or something else. They felt what they had pledged to do was null and void because things had changed." And Ken Butigan (1991) recalled:

> I remember Dan Berrigan giving a speech at Berkeley castigating the Pledge because there's a war going on right now, so why are we sitting around waiting? I remember that so vividly. That was a struggle we had every day. It's not like we didn't know there was a war going on. But it was a question of discerning whether we could actually mount a strong resistance. It was very delicate then. We didn't know whether people actually would perceive the need for a strong, united public opposition.

The second problem was the trivializing or diffusing of Pledge's power by staging too many protests over less than vitally important issues. According to Dennis Marker (1992), "We couldn't call out the Pledge once a week. The reason was simple. We were afraid that it was like crying wolf. You can use the strategy of huge demonstrations only a few times and then the meaning begins to dissipate." Butigan (1991) added: "In the early days, there was a reluctance to call for civil disobedience, because we didn't want to water-down or de-value our power."

The third problem concerned the decision about which political and military events deserved massive resistance and which did not. If the original standard of action was to be abandoned, what would become the new standard? Anne Shumway (1990) recalled, "There was an ambiguity, a problem knowing at what point should we protest, when did the U.S. step over a line? It eventually became evident Reagan wasn't going to invade, that he would push as far as he could without having us in the streets. So, then, when should we decide he *had* pushed us too far and take to the streets?"

According to Marker (1992):

> Things got to be, every time that Reagan would spit in the wind or rattle his saber, we would get calls from all over saying, "Call the Pledge! Call the Pledge!" Sometimes, it would be really bad. There would be some wild, who-knows-where-it-came-from rumor flying around with people calling up saying things like, "This is it, you've got to do it! What good is it going to be if we don't use it? This is the most people we've ever had sign up to do anything. We've got to use it!" We actually had to start a rumor-control group to try to stop uncoordinated protests.

By mid-1985, the pressure to act had grown too strong to resist. The first mass protests broke out in San Francisco. In May, one week after Congress rejected the President's Contra aid package, the administration imposed a trade embargo on Nicaragua. Ken Butigan (1991) recalled that Bay-area Pledge leaders were attending a regularly scheduled organizing meeting:

> When we began, we had no plan to do anything different. We had such a high threshold that had to be met before asking people to act—which is funny because two years later we seemed to be calling people out about every other minute. But then, we didn't know if a lot of people would go for it. What's an embargo? But someone argued: the embargo is a test of the American people and if we don't respond to the test then they will move up to the next rung of the ladder. That argument was compelling, it won the day. By the end of the meeting, we had decided for the first time to call out the people for full mobilization here in the Bay area. We sent out the call.

Butigan remembered his anxiety:

> We were holding a film benefit that night, showing Charlie Clemens' *Witness to War*. The theater was packed. At the intermission, Steve Slaid gets up and announces the call for full mobilization and civil disobedience the next Tuesday. There was this moment of total silence. We were all just sitting in our chairs. We had been working blind for seven months. We didn't know if people just thought the Pledge was a neat idea but wouldn't really do it. Suddenly, everyone just jumped up out of their seats yelling and screaming in support. What a relief! Two days later we had a 300-person spokescouncil meeting, organizing the whole thing. The following Tuesday, we had two days of protest at the Federal Building, with 3,000 people doing legal protest and over 600 people arrested. Stuff was going on around the clock all over the place.

Soon, Pledge actions were being called all around the country: "The grassroots level insisted that we change our tactics to deal with the embargo, Contra aid votes, the mining of the harbors, etc. and we did change our focus. We had to, we simply had to" (Shumway 1990).

Two of the three problems associated with this tactical transition did indeed hurt the Pledge. Many of those who had pledged to oppose a direct invasion dropped out when no invasion occurred. And the eventual proliferation of protest actions did dilute the political power of Pledge resistance, compared to the power of eighty-five thousand activists together protesting an invasion. Still, enough activists did consistently protest to sustain a respectable political opposition over the six years. As for deciding on an alternative standard of action, the national signal group simply developed a new criterion, organizing periodic, fixed-day actions around Central American issues broadly. Overall, the Pledge negotiated this difficult strategy dilemma and identity transformation reasonably successfully, converting much of the protest potential it had mobilized during a time of apparent emergency into actual sustained protests within what seemed to many to be a noncrisis situation.

PLAY HARDBALL WITH CONGRESS OR COMPROMISE WHEN EXPEDIENT?

Finally, Central America peace movement leaders wrestled one other strategic dilemma. Movement leaders had to decide upon a general relational demeanor toward the U.S. Congress (see Cohen and Rogers 1986b: 49–51). Should movement representatives seek to work cooperatively with Congresspeople as insiders, when possible, or maintain a critical distance? Should they threaten the legislators with negative sanctions or try to finesse them with persuasion and positive rewards? And should they hold out for total legislative successes or compromise their way toward partial victories? The danger on the one hand was cooptation, of gradual seduction and neutralization by the established powers. Recently, a "smothering embrace" of political acceptance in Congress had helped to undermine the thrust of the nuclear Freeze movement (Meyer 1990: 221–37). The danger on the other hand was political marginalization and alienation. What would be the point of organizing a campaign for peace in Central America if the movement had estranged all potential congressional allies who might have championed their cause, however imperfectly?

These questions became particularly pertinent to the fifty-member coalition of Central America peace organizations coordinating lobbying on Capitol Hill that eventually became named the "Central America Working Group" (CAWG).[3] This was the primary, direct organizational interface between the movement and members of Congress. Thus, it was the focal point where many of the movement's internal differences and contradictions manifested themselves. Generally, the grassroots Central America peace organizations with more direct ties to people on the ground in Central America tended to be more antagonistic, distanced, and uncompromising with Congress. Whereas the more established, bureaucratized Central America organizations that had more direct contact with Congress tended toward compromise, diplomacy, and accommodation (Marker 1992; Buhl 1993).

The issue that generated the most controversy was whether to accept compromise bills offered by the Democratic leadership to approve "humanitarian" aid for the Contras. Butigan (1991) said: "There was a real split in CAWG as to whether to oppose all kinds of funding or to let non-lethal aid go through. Many were saying, 'Reagan will come back and ask for more military aid if we give them nothing.' But most of the grassroots groups hung together and opposed *any* aid, for strategic and philosophical reasons. There was a real split in the coalition."[4]

According to Cindy Buhl (1993), who coordinated CAWG, given congressional politics a "humanitarian" aid compromise bill was inevitable:

> You have to recognize, we never won a Contra aid vote in the Senate. This exercised a very significant influence on how the debate developed. We kept winning in the House and losing in the Senate. This kept the issue alive with the administration. Besides being ideologically committed, the White House kept winning in the Senate, and we were only winning in the House by very narrow margins. So both sides could always say, "We just have to change 7 votes and we'll win." Because we always lost in the Senate, sooner or later the House had to move to a compromise, in the hopes of either bringing the Senate along or increasing the margin of victory on the House side. House moderates were not voting "no" anymore on up or down votes without the promise of quick alternative compromises. Most movement people never figured that into their calculations. So the House leadership devised the idea, that, okay, if we're not going decisively to win cutting off Contra aid, we should compromise and at least try to de-escalate the level of violence and keep the Contras out of Nicaragua. Local activists are still so very angry at the House Democratic leadership about this. To choose compromise means you believe that you cannot end the war. And the grassroots didn't believe that. But if we had gone for a straight up or down vote, and another $100 million in lethal aid had passed—which was the likely outcome in my mind—then where would we be? It's really a dirty business.

However, the prospect of supporting aid to the Contras, even "non-lethal" aid, was deeply disturbing and caused multiple splits in the CAWG coalition. Again, Buhl explains (1993):

> For organizers, "non-lethal" aid was extraordinarily controversial. Nobody liked it, not even people who ultimately went along. It's not

what we wanted. But at the time it seemed like the road we had to take. For many activists, though, these were too bitter pills to swallow. They just couldn't go along with it. If your main work is to document human rights violations by the Contras, trying to balance those atrocities with Washington's *real politick* was impossible. Those who witnessed those abuses and interviewed the victims simply could not compromise. It was just too hard.

In the end, most of the CAWG groups unhappily decided to support the Democratic leadership's compromise bill.

Besides this issue of "strategic compromise," another related question tended to divide CAWG members. How tactful or confrontative should they be in face-to-face meetings with members of Congress? Some CAWG members, including CAWG coordinator Cindy Buhl, who was quite experienced with Capitol Hill politics, believed in friendly diplomacy as a rule. Why bite the hand that feeds you, they argued, even if it doesn't feed you everything you want? Other CAWG members saw no point in such delicate tact. Why beat around the bush with shysters, they asked, who don't deliver what you really want anyway? Dennis Marker (1992) described a time when this difference came to a head during a CAWG meeting with the Democratic leadership shortly after Congress had approved $27 million in humanitarian aid to the Contras:

> A bunch of us met with Tom Foley, David Bonier, and Dick Gephardt. The way these things are run, as a rule, is the politicians come in, say a few nice words about how they want to hear our views. Then, we fall all over ourselves, with our tongues hanging to our boots saying, "Thank you so much for meeting with us. We really appreciate this opportunity and your time. Blah, blah, blah." That's the typical opening statement. Then we act politely through the whole meeting. Anyway, this time, Cindy Buhl asked if I would make the opening statement, which turned out to be the last time she asked, because I was really mad about the aid vote. I said to Foley, "Thank you for meeting with us. I can't speak for all the groups, but several of us here want to make it clear that we reject your humanitarian aid. And we want to make it crystal clear that if you even think about doing that next year we are going to make your lives as miserable as possible." Foley answered, "That sounds like a threat." And I said, "No, not a threat, just a promise, at least from Witness for Peace." Well, Cindy and others were just furious. That was clearly not proper protocol, a very bad blunder from their perspective. But the Central America groups I was closest to loved it. It actually emboldened them to start voicing what

they were *really* thinking, instead of falling all over themselves in obse-
quious deference. For me, it was just such a . . . it was just the truth.
And I was in no compromising mood.

Strategy decisions about the movement's general relational demeanor
toward the powers of Congress inevitably shaped the movement's collective identity. Likewise, the reverse was true: groups within the
movement that had successfully constructed a clear sense of collective
self tended to determine more easily the kind of strategic approach
they wanted to take toward Congress. With the ongoing differences
between groups within the movement on this issue of relating to Congress, the movement as a whole tended to vacillate between the pos-
tures of cooperative insider and antagonistic challenger. This enabled
the movement to play multiple political roles, as needed. But it also
worked to undermine consistency in its long-term strategic lobbying
effort. In the end, Congress proved neither particularly cooperative
nor consistently inhospitable. For most members of Congress, Democrats and Republicans alike, the Central America peace movement was
too disruptive and intrusive to collaborate with easily, yet too disruptive and intrusive to ignore. Hence, the movement and Congress maintained an uneasy relationship of mutual need and mutual frustration.

CONCLUSION

In this chapter we have explored the complementary processes of
strategic decision making and collective identity formation in the life
of the Central America peace movement. In the next chapter, we will
explore another facet of movement strategy construction and identity
construction: the role of the mass media in shaping public discourse
about Central America. Paradoxically, though more concerned with
political appearances and symbols than political substance—or, more
accurately, by helping to generate political substance through the
manipulation of appearances and symbols—the mass media, as an
institution, played at least as important a role in shaping the struggle
over Central America in the 1980s as did the Central America peace
movement, the U.S. Congress, and the White House. It is to this key
role that we now turn our attention.

Nine

FiGHTiNG BATTLES OF PUBLiC DiSCOURSE

Those who rule the dominant institutions secure their power in large measure directly and indirectly, by impressing their definitions of the situation upon those they rule and . . . significantly limiting what is thought throughout the society. . . . Hegemony is done by the dominant and collaborated in by the dominated. Hegemonic ideology enters into everything people do and think is "natural" —making a living, loving, playing, believing, knowing, even rebelling. In every sphere of social activity, it meshes with the "common sense" through which people make the world seem intelligible; it tries to become that common sense.

Todd Gitlin, *The Whole World Is Watching*

In March 1986, a quiet Dennis Marker returned from Capitol Hill to his office, where he was met by a jubilant celebration. The entire Witness for Peace staff had worked long and hard to defeat a Contra aid vote in Congress, and the House of Representatives had just rejected the President's proposed aid package 220 votes to 210. "Yeah, we won the vote," Marker notified the merry group, "but today was really a huge defeat, a real loss." Surprised and baffled, his colleagues asked him to explain. "Until today, 'no' votes always focused on the faults of the Contra program," he said (1992), "but today, the language changed. Every 'no' voter began their speech with, 'The Sandinistas are a bunch of no-good, communist dictators,' and only then tacked on, 'but I'm still voting against Contra aid.' The ground has shifted. We won't sustain our position in the future." Undaunted by this bleak prophesy, the group returned to their celebration. Three months later, the House voted 221 to 209 to approve $100 million in aid to the Contras.

The battle over Central American policy in the 1980s was much more than a political battle over congressional votes. More fundamentally, it was a symbolic battle to construct and define reality. For congressional votes were governed not by disagreements about objective "facts," but by the relative potency of contending "packagings" or "framings" of the Central American reality. Furthermore, resisting Reagan required not simply struggling to win a political debate, but, more importantly, struggling to control the debate's agenda and vocabulary.

This chapter analyzes the battles of public discourse that constituted a key element of the Central America peace movement's struggle to defeat President Reagan's low-intensity war in Central America. Here we examine the relative cultural power of alternative interpretive "packagings" of Central America that the movement and the administration sought to establish as reality in the public imagination. We investigate the multiple factors that shaped how successful the packages' sponsors were in projecting their social constructions of the Central American reality to and through the mass media. And we trace historically key moments in the development of the struggle to define Central America, to explain better the outcome of the larger political conflict.

MEDIA BIASES AND FILTERS

What animated the conflict between the Central America peace movement and the Reagan administration, ultimately, was their very different, largely incompatible interpretations of Central America. Their divergent answers to the question, "How ought the U.S. best respond to the evolving Central American sociopolitical reality?" were rooted in very different understandings of the nature of that sociopolitical reality. Consequently, winning the battle over U.S. Central American policy required that either the Central America peace movement or the Reagan administration persuade the American public and Congress to adopt *its* analysis of Central America. One of the primary communications vehicles through which both sides sought to do so was the mass media. Generating sympathetic television, newspaper, newsmagazine, and radio coverage that would promulgate the desired framings of Central America was critical for both the Reagan administration and the Central America peace movement.

Any analysis of the battle to use the mass media to define the Central American "reality" for the American public and Congress must recognize that the mass media itself is not an open, impartial, and transparent vehicle of communication. Instead, mass media institutions are characterized by definite interests, biases, norms, and practices that significantly condition what and how material gets published and broadcasted to mass audiences. The mass media does not simply and disinterestedly facilitate reality definition, but actively participates as an influential and influencing actor in the reality-defining process (Halloran, Elliot, and Murdock 1970; Molotch and Lester 1974; Ryan 1991; Gitlin 1980). Here we examine three aspects of mass media structure and practice that influenced the administration and the peace movement's battle to interpret Central America: the definition of newsworthiness, the dictates of "objectivity," and the impact of journalists' daily routines.

News reporters, writers, editors, and producers all share a common set of assumptions about what is *newsworthy*. Only those events and ideas that are considered to be current, publicly recognized, important, and interesting make the papers and television news broadcasts. Events, experiences, and ideas judged by media producers as passé, unfamiliar, inconsequential, or dull rarely, if ever, make the news—no matter how meaningful, prevalent, vital, or revealing they actually may be. Furthermore, newsworthiness depends heavily on the availability of a "news peg"—such as a holiday, anniversary, predictable event, tragic incident, or piece of breaking news—which acts as a hook upon which to "hang" a story (Gans 1979: 168; Ryan 1991: 96–99). Moreover, the concern with what's interesting makes stories that focus on individual personalities involved in an event more newsworthy than those that analyze underlying systemic or structural, substantive issues behind an event. Finally, incidents and issues that are accompanied by emotion-evoking action visuals, one-liner "sound bites," and culturally resonant prepackaged interpretations stand a much greater chance of being judged newsworthy.

These criteria of newsworthiness were tremendously relevant for those struggling to project alternative definitions of Central America to and through the media. The ongoing Contra war, Salvadoran death squads, and the Iran-Contra affair eventually could become passé and, therefore, ignorable, according to U.S. media standards. News stories on anti-administration demonstrations could focus on a handful of violent protesters (the interesting) rather than on the peaceful majority's central grievance (the meaningful). Reports on Sanctuary could concentrate on the fact of clergy violating the law (the novel) and neglect the actual reasons why clergy felt compelled to do so (the significant). And coverage of the Iran-Contra scandal could fixate on Oliver North's personal magnetism (the individual-interest angle) yet overlook analyses of the unconstitutional security apparatus that he orchestrated (the important). Thus, Central America peace movement activists had to struggle both to make their media pitches fit the criteria of newsworthiness *and* to minimize distortions of their message when their issues *were* covered. Whereas anything the White House said was automatically considered important and interesting news, for the movement, largely unknown activists had to establish themselves as the publicly recognizable representatives of an important oppositional position.[1] They had to demonstrate currency without appearing faddish or opportunistic, and continually offer an interesting message without inviting the media to fixate on fascinating but extraneous aspects of their work.

A second industry convention that conditioned the media's treatment of Central America was the belief in the need for journalistic "*objectivity.*" Mainstream news reporters and editors uniformly believe that responsible journalism must be objective, balanced, value-free. Seeking to avoid any hint of "adversarial" or "advocacy" journalism, newsmen and women generally conceive of themselves as politically neutral reporters of facts who leave it up to the reading and viewing public to make value judgments (Hertsgaard 1989: 65–66; Ryan 1991: 176–79). In practice, this objectivity norm means that journalists tend to focus more on discrete events than on in-depth analytical interpretations of those events. They rely heavily on "official" sources of news, such as White House spokespeople, members of Congress, business leaders, and academic specialists. And they avoid stories that seem too politically critical, that quote "irresponsible" sources, or that give voice to "extremist" positions. In the interest of balance, journalists do customarily feel obliged to present opposing sides of an issue. But the range of those contending positions is usually limited to the officially acceptable views of Republican-versus-Democrat, conservative-versus-liberal, defense attorney-versus-prosecuting attorney, and the like. Thus, according to independent journalist I. F. Stone (quoted in Hertsgaard 1989: 66), "Most of the time objectivity is just a rationale for regurgitating the conventional wisdom of the day. If what you're saying challenges the stereotypes of the day, it's hard to get it printed."

The media norm of objectivity skewed the administration and movement's struggle in favor of the White House. Journalists' heavy reliance on official sources automatically gave an advantage to the White House. Often, in the interest of allowing their *audience* to make value judgments, news reporters simply presented Reagan administration views of Central America without comment or analysis (Spence 1987). In effect, the media became a "mouthpiece of the government, a stenographer to power" (Hertsgaard 1989: 66).[2] Reporters' common practice of presenting opposing sides of a debate did afford the Central America peace movement some opportunity for voice, when journalists sought out administration critics to balance White House statements. But on the whole, these opportunities carried significant limitations on the movement's capacity to counter the administration's framings of Central America. When movement spokespeople *were* tapped for contrary views, critiques that went beyond those typically voiced by oppositional Washington elites—policy makers, congresspeople, academics—were often considered too out of the mainstream for publication. Suggestions, for example, that El Salvador's FMLN guerrillas were motivated by legitimate grievances, that Salvadoran elections did not necessarily verify the existence of democracy, or that the Sandinistas actually may have accomplished some good for Nicaragua were often dismissed as "biased" or "soft on communism." Stories that did offer trenchant critiques of White House views tended to be published irregularly, since a steady flow of adversarial pieces in one publication was typically suspected as "politically motivated."[3] Finally, certain harsh but true realities—that, for example, the administration repeatedly knowingly lied about Central America, or that the President's Iran-Contra offenses may have been impeachable—were simply matters too delicate to express as serious possibilities in the media. However true they might have been, they were also unpopular with the public and Congress, and so were disregarded by the press (Hertsgaard 1989: 333–34).[4]

A third aspect of media practice that influenced the struggle to interpret Central America to and through the media was the daily *news routines* of journalists and editors. The news industry copes with scarce resources and the demand for consistent news coverage through a series of routinized practices that structure the efficient production of news—all of which shape the content of the news. The daily pressure of production deadlines, for example, forces journalists to rely on safe, conventional sources of information—"experts" from the "Golden Rolodex"—who have proven accessible and articulate (Ryan 1991: 142–43; also see Cutler 1984). According to *ABC News* White House correspondent Sam Donaldson (quoted in Cooper and Soley 1990: 45):

> To sit down while you're facing a deadline and say, "Gee, there must be some other expert we haven't thought of. Let's beat the bushes and launch a search of the city or of the country for them." Well, that takes a

> lot more time than flipping a card on the Rolodex. A second reason is that
> we know these [known] guys provide a succinct response. You can't come
> to me and say, "Sam, I know you're on deadline, you need a comment on
> such and such, go out and take a chance on Mr. X." No, I'm sorry folks,
> I don't have time to take a chance on Mr. X.

Furthermore, reporters are typically assigned to institutionalized "news
beats"—such as business or crime beats—that generate a constant supply of stories. Issues and events that are not visible to reporters on a
beat or do not fit this predetermined news structure are unlikely to
receive coverage. In addition, the vast majority of news covers
prescheduled events—such as conferences of experts, political
announcements, campaign debates, and visits from foreign digni-
taries—to which reporters and camera teams are assigned in advance
(Tuchman 1973). Consequently, the events that receive coverage are
those sponsored by groups that have the prominence and resources to
command the media's attention. Moreover, national and regional news
producers rely heavily on AP and UPI wire services and professionally
crafted news releases in deciding what is the day's news. This establishes additional barriers for grassroots challengers from below who
desire access into the reality-defining media process. If their stories or
news releases do not make the wires or impress the editor, however
important they actually may be, they will go unreported. Similarly,
newspaper, radio, and television news editors look to the *Washington
Post* and the *New York Times* to determine what is newsworthy. If a
movement's story is not reported in one of these standard-setting
papers, it probably won't be covered elsewhere. Finally, journalists
work within routinized space and format limitations. Radio stories typically must be less than forty seconds, television reports less than ninety seconds long, and newspaper articles must fit within a rather small
number of column inches, predetermined by the editor. Consequently,
stories that require significant background elaboration to understand
properly are either disregarded or distorted through oversimplification
(Ryan 1991: 147–49).

All of these content-shaping news routines significantly disadvan-
taged Central America peace movement activists. Few if any of them
were expert sources found in journalists' Rolodex files. At best, they
had to work hard over time in hopes of ever becoming trusted news
sources. Since few newspapers or radio or television news programs had
reporters assigned to a "political protest" beat, the burden lay with
Central America peace activists to make their message heard and rele-

vant within the bounds of the standard "International Affairs" or "Congressional" news beats. Furthermore, compared to their opponents, Central America peace organizations often lacked the prominence and resources needed to get their issues on major wire services or news editors' assignment lists. And some movement activists, especially inexperienced ones, often found it difficult explaining their views on Central America—which required sufficient historical awareness and critical political consciousness—briefly enough to fit journalists' standard format limitations. Winning the battle to interpret Central America, therefore, demanded that Central America peace activists learn to work *with,* and not against, journalists' news routines. It also required that they surmount the barriers formed by the media norm of "objectivity" and overcome the neglect and distortions generated by the industry's constricted criteria of newsworthiness.

FRAMING CENTRAL AMERICA

Central America did not present itself to interested U.S. citizens as an objective fact or self-evident reality. Nor could it have. Access to objective knowledge about "what was really happening" in Central America was simply unavailable. Theoretically, there abides a world of objective facticity "out there" that exists apart from anyone's comprehending of it. But no one enjoys a privileged, unbiased, unmediated knowledge of that world. All human beings can ever possess are constructed interpretations of it. While some interpretations are arguably more accurate, coherent, or truthful than others, they remain constructed interpretations nonetheless. The challenge that faced both the Central America peace movement and the White House was selling to the American public and Congress a believable interpretation of the Central American "reality" that supported their policy proposals, while simultaneously discrediting their opponent's interpretations.

This task was complicated by two major difficulties: unmanageable complexity and inadequate context. First, the Central American reality of the 1980s was tremendously complex, requiring a great deal of attention and education to understand fully. But few Americans had the interest and resources needed to grasp that complexity. Furthermore, it was nearly impossible for such sociopolitical complexity to be conveyed through the communication medias—primarily newspaper, radio, and television—through which the movement and the administration would contend for public acceptance of their interpretations. Second, a vast majority of Americans and congressional representatives lacked an adequate context for making appropriate decisions about Central America. Relatively few of them had ever visited, much less lived in, Central America. And very few possessed the kind of familiarity with Central American history and culture necessary for making informed judgments about Central American policy. These complicating difficulties produced two results. First, Central America's complexity became tremendously *oversimplified* in U.S. political discourse on the subject, reduced to simple categories and arguments that Americans could easily grasp. Second, contending interpretations of Central America proved persuasive or not to Americans vis-à-vis their resonance with *U.S.* history and culture, not Central American history and culture. Thus, systemic and situational imperatives propelled the Central America peace movement and the Reagan administration to pitch to Americans relatively glossed-over portraits of Central America, the believability of which were based more on their resonance with U.S. values and experiences than with the Central American reality itself.

Perhaps the best way to explore the battle between the Central America peace movement and the White House is through *frame analysis*. "Frames" are interpretive formulas that assign meanings to events and issues by selecting out and organizing certain elements into packaged story lines. Frames employ clusters of assertions, metaphors, anecdotes, catchphrases, exemplars, and visual images to highlight certain aspects of an event or issue that fit and promote an internally coherent interpretation, and disregard others that do not (Gamson 1989; Snow and Benford 1988; Gamson and Modigliani 1989). In this way, a frame puts a certain "spin" on an issue or event, eliciting one specific interpretation of it and excluding others. A frame establishes the boundaries of attention to an issue or event—as a picture frame does for a photograph—and provides an internal skeletal structure that determines the overall pattern of discourse on an issue or event, as a frame of a building does for its overall form and appearance (Gamson et al. 1992: 385).

An effective political frame includes a *diagnosis* of a problem, a *prognosis* for a solution, and a *motivation* providing a rationale for political involvement to help solve the specified problem (Snow and Benford 1988: 200–204). The relative robustness of any frame is determined by the emotional impact of its visual images and catchphrases, by the strength of its "cultural resonance," by the extent of its experiential credibility, and by the salience of the cultural values to which it appeals. Robust frames deeply engage their targets' emotions, are not blatantly

contradicted by relevant empirical evidence, and, perhaps most importantly, strongly resonate with primary themes deeply embedded in the
dominant cultural tradition.

From this perspective, we can speak of the Central America peace
movement and the Reagan administration as "framing" Central America for the American people and Congress. Both promoted portrayals of
the region that organized certain elements of the Central American reality into simplified interpretive packages to mobilize support for specific
political policies. To construe a Central American reality that supported its policy, the White House promoted two principal framings of Central America, the *Soviet-aggression* frame and the *fragile-democracy*
frame. To define a Central American reality that justified its policy proposals, the Central America peace movement advanced four interpretive
framings of the region, the *another-Vietnam* frame, the *botching-diplomacy* frame, the *wayward-America* frame, and the *imperial-America*
frame. Here we describe and analyze at an abstract, static level the logic,
strengths, and weaknesses of these six frames. Later in this chapter, we
examine historically the dynamic process by which these competing
frames engaged each other over the course of the decade and the political outcomes that resulted as different frames gained and lost ascen-
dancy in the struggle of political discourse.

The Reagan administration initiated the rhetorical battle to define
Central America in 1981 by promoting a *Soviet-aggression* framing of
the region. The "Central America crisis," according to this frame—first
advanced by Secretary of State Alexander Haig—was nothing other
than an external communist intrusion in the region that required a military response. Its core argument may be summarized as follows:

> *Soviet- and Cuban-style communism is now penetrating America's own
> backyard with frightening speed and success. The Marxist-Leninist San-
> dinistas have already established a Soviet beachhead in Nicaragua and
> the FMLN rebels threaten to do the same in El Salvador. After that,
> Guatemala, Honduras, Costa Rica, and Mexico will fall like dominos
> into communism's grip (Diagnosis). A window of opportunity exists to
> counter this communist aggression. If America acts decisively, these Sovi-
> et advances can be rolled back and Central America freed from commu-
> nist control. But if America fails to respond, Soviet-style communism will
> soon advance to the edge of the Rio Grande. Direct U.S. troop combat is
> unnecessary, if we act now, for the valiant Nicaraguan Contras and Sal-
> vadoran army can defeat communism themselves. All they need is U.S.
> moral, financial, and technical support (Prognosis). Soviet aggression in*

Central America is a major threat to U.S. vital security interests. A failure to confront it there jeopardizes our political credibility in the world and strategic control over our own hemisphere. As the world's only moral superpower, we have a responsibility to resist Soviet aggression anywhere, but particularly in our own backyard. Both our national self-interest and moral responsibility to champion freedom demand that we extend desperately needed Contra and Salvadoran aid now (Motivation).

Given the fact that these frames' relative persuasiveness was determined vis-à-vis their resonance with *U.S.*, not Central American, history and culture, this Soviet-aggression frame was potent (see table 9.1). For Americans, its visual images and catchphrases were emotionally engaging, its story line fit many important U.S. cold-war military experiences, and the cultural values and themes to which it appealed were among the strongest and deepest in the cultural tradition. The frame's only *fatal* weakness was a potential inability of its promoter to demonstrate clear Soviet interference in Central America, in which case the frame would become impertinent.

In the course of its eight years of attempting to form Central American policy, the White House sponsored and championed a second view of the Central American reality with its *fragile-democracy* frame, whose basic story line ran as follows:

In Central America, fragile democratic movements are struggling valiantly against inimical forces to establish lasting political freedom in the region. In El Salvador, a fledgling democracy is under siege by right-wing extremists, communist guerrillas, economic underdevelopment, and a legacy of human rights abuses. And in Nicaragua, a democratic opposition-coalition is fighting courageously for freedom against a totalitarian Marxist-Leninist state. Forces of freedom are also strengthening the fragile democracies of Guatemala and Honduras. The Central American people's yearning for freedom and democracy is extraordinary and inspiring. But anti-democratic forces in the region, attacking from all sides, threaten to extinguish freedom's flickering flame (Diagnosis). Democracy can survive and thrive in Central America. But it needs America's help. The U.S. must provide economic aid, security assistance, and political backing to friendly centrist regimes—such as El Salvador's Christian Democratic Party—and moral and financial support to the "freedom fighters" of the Nicaraguan democratic resistance. With America's help, democracy can vanquish tyranny in Central America and establish a bright future of peace and freedom (Prognosis). The United States of America—the world's symbol and bastion of democratic freedom—is entrusted with the sacred duty to promote and defend democracy throughout the world.

Table 9.1. Soviet-Aggression Frame

Symbolic Resources

VISUAL IMAGES: Ortega with Castro or in Moscow, Nicaraguans and FMLN with Soviet weapons, Arafat in Managua.

CATCHPHRASES: "Domino effect," "communist rebels," "Cuban-Soviet proxy," "Marxist-Leninist Sandinistas," "exporters of revolution," Contras as "freedom fighters," "democratic resistance."

HISTORICAL ANALOGIES: Cuba 1959, Angola 1975.

Strengths and Constraints:

CULTURAL RESONANCE: Very strong. Cold war anti-communist containment-theory imperative, Monroe Doctrine, peace through strength, antiterrorism.

EXPERIENTIAL CREDIBILITY: Very high. Communist expansionism in Eastern Europe 1946-49, Greece 1946-49, Korea 1950-53, Berlin 1961, Afghanistan 1979, Grenada 1983 often successfully countered by U.S. military force.

VALUE SALIENCE: Very high. Individual freedom, anti-communism, U.S. national security.

FRAME VULNERABILITY: High but limited. Fear of military quagmire involving unnecessary loss of U.S. soldiers lives. Revolutions in Central America reflect not Soviet expansionism but legitimate responses to redress poverty and injustice.

Today, freedom's patriots in our neighboring countries of Central America beckon earnestly for our help. We must not fail these voices of hope and freedom. We must answer their call resolutely with the support and action they so desperately need (Motivation).

This fragile-democracy frame was also quite robust, though somewhat less so than the Soviet-aggression frame described above (see table 9.2). Its catchphrases and visual images were quite strong, and its cultural resonance very strong. But the frame tended to suffer from experiential implausibility, as evidence accumulated that the purported democratic forces in Central America were not as free and clean as the administration had originally proclaimed.

Nevertheless, together, the Soviet-aggression frame and the fragile-democracy frame presented a powerful interpretive combination, defining Central America in a way—for those who accepted the frames' assumptions—as to make the White House's regional policy almost irresistible. This was especially true for Americans who were less knowledgeable about the actual political and economic situation in Central America. The two frames tapped some of America's most dearly cherished cultural values: individual freedom, anti-communism, democracy, and the resolute defense of national security. And politically, the two frames had the theoretical potential to assemble a majority coalition in Congress, with the Soviet-aggression frame appealing especially to con-

Table 9.2. Fragile Democracies Frame

Symbolic Resources

VISUAL IMAGES: José Napoleón Duarte campaigning for Salvadoran Presidency, lines of peasants braving threats of violence in election, FDN freedom fighters advancing on Sandinista soldiers.

CATCHPHRASES: "Free, fair and open elections," "Caribbean Basin Initiative," "democratic reform," "improvement in the human rights situation."

HISTORICAL ANALOGY: The Marshall Plan.

Strengths and Constraints:

CULTURAL RESONANCE: Very strong. Faith in democracy, procedural legitimacy of elections, aiding freedom's struggle.

EXPERIENTIAL CREDIBILITY: Moderately low. Recurrent abuses, corruption, and impotence of supposedly democratic forces in El Salvador, Guatemala, Honduras, and among the Contras.

VALUE SALIENCE: Very high. Freedom and democracy core cultural values.

FRAME VULNERABILITY: Moderately high. Frame undermined by ongoing death-squad and military atrocities, corrupt justice system, and increasing political weakness of El Salvador's Duarte regime; Somoza-National Guard ties, human rights atrocities, and military ineffectiveness of Nicaraguan Contras; 1984 Nicaraguan elections with Sandinista victory.

---

gressional conservatives and the fragile-democracy frame to congressional moderates.

The Central America peace movement entered the rhetorical battle with its own potent counterframes, all of which, when accepted, convincingly discredited President Reagan's Central American policy. The earliest and most visceral of these was the *another-Vietnam* frame, which enjoyed, from the start, an automatic, broad acceptance among the American people. Its core contention was thus vocalized:

> *The warmongering Reagan administration is rapidly and inextricably entangling the U.S. in the civil wars of small third-world countries in Central America. Today we send U.S. military aid and advisers. Tomorrow we will be forced to send American boys to fight and die in distant jungles for causes nobody really understands or cares about. And withdrawing from such quagmires will be difficult and humiliating (Diagnosis). Apathy today will bring disaster tomorrow. But we can avoid another Vietnam by quickly terminating now the President's frightening escalation of U.S. military involvement in Central America. The American people can demand that Congress, with its budgetary power, deny our hawkish President the fiscal ability to lead the U.S. into another bloody, protracted guerrilla war (Prognosis). Central America's problems do not have U.S. military solutions. So if the American people and Congress do*

*not block our trigger-happy President today, it's just a matter of time
before our sons, friends, husbands, and perhaps we ourselves will be
coming home from San Salvador and Tegucigalpa in body bags, and for
no good reason. We must act now to stop Reagan before it's too late!*
(Motivation).

So credible was this counterframe in the public imagination that, initially, it did not even require an organized movement to become formulated and articulated. Another-Vietnam erupted as the instantaneous,
almost knee-jerk rebuttal to Alexander Haig's Soviet-aggression campaign on Central America in 1981. This uncomplicated frame's visual
images, lifted as they were from fresh national experience, were wrench-
ingly powerful (see table 9.3). For the same reason, the frame's experiential credibility was, for most Americans, impeccable, its cultural resonance enormously strong, and its catchphrases gripping. Thus, in the
early 1980s, the another-Vietnam frame suffered virtually no internal
logical, cultural, emotional, or empirical weaknesses.[5] Outside of an
unlikely, imminent Soviet threat to U.S. territory, which would effectively nullify the frame, the another-Vietnam story line's only vulnerability was that of possible inapplicability. If Americans became confident that Central America posed no danger of dragging the U.S. into
direct combat involvement, the frame would simply become irrelevant.
But in the early 1980s such confidence was conspicuously lacking.

A second counterframe that also served well the purposes of the Central America peace movement was the *botching-diplomacy* frame.
Couched in less emotional and reactive, more rational and judicious
language than the another-Vietnam frame, this interpretation of Central
America maintained the following view:

*The U.S. has an important role to play in Central America. But the Rea-
gan administration is taking a totally wrong approach and badly
bungling U.S. affairs in Central America. By evading negotiations, arm-
ing murderers, mining Nicaraguan harbors, publishing "terrorism manuals," snubbing the World Court, etc., the administration is embarrassing
the U.S. before its allies, polarizing and radicalizing the Central American
situation, and aborting chances for reasonable and responsible solutions*
(Diagnosis). *The U.S. can help resolve the Central America crisis, but
only by ceasing U.S. covert military operation', promoting peace negotiations without preconditions, expanding U.S. development aid to the
region (contingent on respect for human rights), and encouraging
amnesty and reconciliation programs for rebels and exiles. By intelligent-
ly and prudently using less stick and more carrot, the U.S. can secure its*

Table 9.3. Another Vietnam Frame

Symbolic Resources
>   VISUAL IMAGES: Body bags returning to America, U.S. military boys wounded and dying in tropical jungles.
>   CATCHPHRASES: "Quagmire," "El Salvador is Spanish for Vietnam," "another Vietnam."
>   HISTORICAL ANALOGY: Vietnam 1964–'73

Strengths and Constraints:
>   CULTURAL RESONANCE: Very strong. American exceptionalism, historical legacy of U.S. isolationism, virtual consensus on Vietnam as well-meaning blunder.
>   EXPERIENTIAL CREDIBILITY: Very high. Vietnam a terrible destructive social trauma, President Reagan's public history of hawkish tendencies.
>   VALUE SALIENCE: Moderate. Political potency grounded in recent historical experience, not central cultural value, except indirectly through inalienable right of individuals to life and pursuit of happiness.
>   FRAME VULNERABILITY: High but limited. If communist enemy perceived as direct threat to U.S. national security and territory, interventionistic anticommunism imperative prevails.

own interests and those of Central Americans (Prognosis). Current U.S. Central America policy spells disaster. It prolongs the region's crisis by bolstering its terrorist right and inciting its terrorist left. It generates unnecessary, divisive political strife in the U.S. And it undermines international confidence in America's role as a responsible and effective world leader. It is long past time for more discerning and enlightened minds to alter U.S. Central American policy—before it is too late (Motivation).

This botching-diplomacy frame was only moderately strong in its ability to counter the administration's framing of Central America (see table 9.4). Its greatest strength was its experiential credibility—plenty of evidence suggested that the Reagan administration was botching U.S. relations in Central America. On the other hand, the frame's visual images seemed somewhat foreign and its catchphrases slightly academic. Most Americans could recall few historical analogies appropriate to this frame. The cultural values to which the botching-diplomacy frame appealed were largely secondary to those values to which the President's frames appealed. Because of its greater concern for the effectiveness and reputation of U.S. foreign relations than with the plight of the Central American people, this frame tended to remain subordinate to the movement's other primary frames. Despite these disadvantages, the botching-diplomacy frame did remain an essential weapon in the movement's rhetorical arsenal, since its logic appealed to political moderates in Con-

Table 9.4. Botching-Diplomacy Frame

Symbolic Resources
VISUAL IMAGES: Central American peasants chanting anti-American slogans and songs, U.N. and E.C. officials condemning U.S. trade embargo on Nicaragua.
CATCHPHRASES: "Counterproductive policies," "doomed to failure," "polarizing the political situation," "throwing gasoline on the fire," "peace through negotiations."
HISTORICAL ANALOGY: Bay of Pigs 1961.

Strengths and Constraints:
CULTURAL RESONANCE: Moderately strong. Cultural sub-themes of inept government, suspicion of authority, misgivings about the competence of U.S. military bureaucracy, coddling dictators, and President Reagan's hawkish proclivities.
EXPERIENTIAL CREDIBILITY: High. The conflict's ongoing irresolution, reports of atrocities, disapprobation of European and Latin American allies, criticisms by U.S. policy elites, CIA scandals all confirm.
VALUE SALIENCE: Moderately high. Desire for respectable and competent executive office, strong U.S. influence in foreign affairs.
FRAME VULNERABILITY: Moderately high but limited. If Soviet expansionism believed to be fomenting Central American revolutions, frame discredited as "liberal," "idealistic," "soft on communism."

gress and sectors of the American public that remained unpersuaded by the movement's more militant frames.

Perhaps the Central America peace movement's most dominant and enduring interpretation of Central America was the *wayward-America* frame, whose core argument could be summarized as follows:

The United States—whether because of unique national calling or mere human decency—should always act as a benevolent force in world affairs, promoting freedom, democracy, prosperity, and human welfare. But the Reagan administration is egregiously violating this principle in Central America by spending multi-millions of U.S. tax dollars to arm repressive dictators and death squads, train torturers, and equip armies that destroy villages and maim and kill women and children. In a horrible and tragic reversal of purpose, Ronald Reagan has made the U.S. an accomplice to gross and pointless evil and destruction (Diagnosis). If the majority of Americans understood the dreadful truth about Central America, they would demand change. Informed Americans can stop Reagan's catastrophic Central America juggernaut by educating the American people and lobbying for a congressional ban on funds for Reagan's Central America policy (Prognosis). Nobody wants America to stand for death, destruction, and misery. And awareness brings responsibility. Those who know the facts but fail to act become accessories to untold death and destruction. But those who oppose Reagan's policy can save

untold lives, end excruciating suffering, and help to turn America away
from its current dreadful policy. All decent Americans are morally oblig-
ated to oppose the President's policy (Motivation).

This frame proved quite effective in mobilizing opposition to the administration's Central American policy. Its visual images and catchphrases
were engaging, its experiential credibility very high, and its cultural resonance very strong (see table 9.5). Moreover, this wayward-America
frame was continually and powerfully reinforced by the Central American refugees' stories and activists' trips to Central America. Few Americans relished the thought of their tax dollars funding brutal armies to
massacre thousands of innocent women and children, or the idea of the
U.S. acting as a malevolent force in world affairs. Although a convinc-
ing Soviet-aggression frame tended to counter the wayward-America
frame, few arguments could neutralize this frame's ability to capitalize
on the emotions issuing from these violations of Americans' moral sensibilities. According to Cindy Buhl (1993):

> Most Central America activists aren't people who think Cuba has a far
> better system than ours. Maybe in New York or Berkeley. But that's not
> where most people are coming from. The two strongest constituencies I
> worked with were the churches and unions, and that's certainly not their
> philosophical outlook. Most activists are exactly the kind of people who
> bought everything about America that they were told in high school. And
> they're just trying to make that ideal come true.

One final interpretation that some Central America peace activists
brought to the political struggle was the *imperial-America* frame. Its
basic story line ran as follows:

> *President Reagan's deadly Central America policy is merely the latest*
> *chapter in a long, shameful history of U.S. imperial domination of the*
> *entire region. The Sandinistas and the FMLN have dared to throw off*
> *that domination in Nicaragua and El Salvador, and Reagan is punishing*
> *them as an example to the entire third world. Deceptive rhetoric aside,*
> *the U.S. is not really interested in freedom and democracy in Central*
> *America, but economic, political, and military hegemony. And the*
> *immoral and unjust cost of maintaining this U.S. imperialism is massive*
> *hunger, injustice, oppression, and violence for the majority of the Central*
> *American people* (Diagnosis). *For the first time in more than a century,*
> *Nicaragua stands the chance of resisting U.S. imperialism and building a*
> *free and just society. The Salvadoran opposition may face the same*
> *opportunity. But if they are to succeed, sympathetic Americans must*
> *champion their cause at home by obstructing a U.S. invasion of*

Table 9.5. Wayward-America Frame

Symbolic Resources
> VISUAL IMAGES: Women and children killed by U.S. -armed Contra and
> Salvadoran soldiers, refugees fleeing U.S.-supported military regimes.
> CATCHPHRASES: "Contra thugs," "U.S.-sponsored repression," "subsidizing cor-
> rupt Latin dictators," "showcase elections," "condoning death squads," "U.S.
> tax dollars kill women and children."
> HISTORICAL ANALOGY: Vietnam's My Lai massacre 1969.

Strengths and Constraints:
> CULTURAL RESONANCE: Very strong. Heritage of American exceptionalism, liber-
> al humanitarianism, protection of innocent life, fighting "good" wars.
> EXPERIENTIAL CREDIBILITY: Very high. Reports of religious assassinations,
> death squads, rights abuses, Contra atrocities, and refugees stories all confirm.
> VALUE SALIENCE: Moderately high. U.S. moral idealism and self-image, belief in
> universal freedom from abusive government.
> FRAME VULNERABILITY: Moderately high. Entire frame undermined by the per-
> suasion that U.S. policy is made tragically necessary by communist aggressors
> and is imperative to avert the even worse scenario of communist totalitarianism
> in Central American, in which light the frame takes on a "bleeding heart" tone.
> "Fair elections" of Central American U.S.-allied regimes further subvert this
> frame.

*Nicaragua and cutting off aid to the abusive Contras and Salvadoran mil-
itary. These expressions of solidarity will help to break the stranglehold
of U.S. imperialism so that independent, people-powered societies can
create true peace, freedom, and equity for all Central Americans* (Prognosis). *Today, Central America faces a decisive, historic turning point. If
Reagan prevails, U.S. domination of Central America and the unjust suffering and killing it causes will persist. But if Reagan is stopped, new possibilities of peace and justice will emerge. We, whose arrogant and dom-
ineering nation is guilty of so much death and destruction, must commit
ourselves to solidarity with the people of Central America and political
activism on their behalf* (Motivation).

This was a difficult frame to sell to the American public and Congress
(see table 9.6). Its language sounded far too radical and un-American to
resonate with most Americans. Unlike the wayward-America frame, it
defined U.S.-sponsored death and destruction in Central America not as
a well-intentioned mistake or the work of one recalcitrant president, but
the logical outworkings of a malignant, predatory national character—
not a self-image widely held in the U.S. Furthermore, the values, emotions, images, and experiences to which this frame appealed were not
those of the average American, but those of the conscientized Central
American—exactly the kind of person who did not need to be mobilized

Table 9.6. Imperial-America Frame

Symbolic Resources

VISUAL IMAGES: July 1979 Managua celebration of Sandinista victory, Augusto César Sandino 1927–'33

CATCHPHRASES: "Yankee imperialism," "gunboat diplomacy," "solidarity," "regional hegemony," "U.S. aggression," "right to self-determination," "people's revolution."

HISTORICAL ANALOGIES: U.S. support for Somoza 1934–'79, CIA-sponsored Guatemala coup 1954.

Strengths and Constraints:

CULTURAL RESONANCE: Normally weak—mainstream cultural hostility to charges of U.S. imperialism. But conditionally strong—if admitted, resonates with cultural animosity for imperious government, American revolutionary spirit, national sovereignty, championing underdog.

EXPERIENTIAL CREDIBILITY: Low. U.S. international affairs deemed benevolent, violations perceived as well-intentioned mistakes.

VALUE SALIENCE: Very low. Contradicts mainstream national self-image.

FRAME VULNERABILITY: Very high. Easily discredited as radical, unpatriotic, leftist, "blame America first," radical fringe.

---

to oppose White House Central American policy. Thus, for all its appeal among radicalized U.S. activists, the imperial-America frame—as a counter to the White House's Soviet-aggression and fragile-democracy frames—was fraught with disabling defects.

These six frames—Soviet-aggression, fragile-democracy, another-Vietnam, botching-diplomacy, wayward-America, and imperial-America—were by no means the only interpretations of Central America advanced in the rhetorical battles over Central American policy. Other motifs, such as regional development and solidarity with the Central American people, also entered the debate (see, for instance, Ryan 1991: 242–43). But these six were the primary frames whose themes, images, and contentions recurrently dominated the public discourse and political rhetoric about Central America throughout the 1980s.

Neither the White House nor the Central America peace movement had to rely solely on the internal logic and cultural appeal of their Central America frames. Both possessed many other resources by which to actively promote their framed interpretations to and through the mass media. Typically, not unlike consumer products, the interpretive frames described above did not sell themselves on account of their strong cultural resonance or high experiential credibility alone. Rather, to exert a significant impact on public discourse, the frame sponsors needed actively and deliberately to publicize and market their frames to journalists, news reporters, editors, and, occasionally, media managers and owners. Next we examine the resources that the White House possessed and employed to sell their Central America frames to and through the mass media.

WHITE HOUSE RESOURCES

The Reagan White House was indisputably the most media-savvy U.S. presidential administration ever to hold office. No White House media relations team prior to or since President Reagan's understood more clearly how the mass media worked, or possessed more interest in or skill for using the mass media as an instrument of policy promotion and implementation. "For the first time in any presidency," observed David Gergen, White House director of communications, "we molded a communications policy around our legislative strategy" (Hertsgaard 1989: 23). Under the adroit leadership of Gergen, White House deputy chief of staff Michael Deaver, and chief of staff James Baker (U.S. News 1981), the Reagan administration built a finely tuned organizational media machine that skillfully mastered and controlled the coverage of the national mass media for years. In the words of Leslie Janka, deputy White House press secretary from 1981 to 1983 (quoted in Hertsgaard 1989: 6): "The whole thing was PR. This was a PR outfit that became President and took over the country. And to the degree then to which the Constitution forced them to do things like make a budget, run foreign policy and all that, they sort of did. But their first, last, and overarching activity was public relations."[6]

Key to the White House media machine's success was detailed planning and coordination. Each Friday afternoon, the White House's top communications staff met over lunch at a "Friday Group" meeting to plan overall media strategy. Then, with their big-picture strategy in place, each morning at 7:30, Baker, Deaver, and Attorney General Edwin Meese met for breakfast to review overnight political developments, news coverage, and legislative priorities. A half hour later, the day's organizational directives were handed out by Baker at a meeting of senior White House staff. At 8:15 A.M., Baker, Gergen, assistant to the President Richard Darman, and White House press secretary Larry Speaks met for fifteen minutes to decide on the media "line of the day"—the single sound bite that the group wanted to lead the news coverage of all evening network news programs. Once determined, the line of the day was sent via computer to senior administration officials and via telephone conference calls to executive branch spokespeople throughout the federal bureaucracy. Throughout the day, every significant official in the executive bureaucracy would be expected to repeat to the press the day's line, thus reinforcing the chosen theme in unity. In addition, David Gergen often arranged Thursday morning and afternoon "substance seminars" to educate executive branch spokespeople about the foreign-policy or domestic issues on which the current media strategy was focused. At 8:30 A.M., Deaver and his staff met for a communications meeting to review the day's scheduled events and coordinate upcoming media events. At a 9:15 mini-briefing and again at the regular noon press briefing, White House reporters would be given the line of the day, which would usually make its way into the headlines and network newscasts (Hertsgaard 1989: 34–37; Walsh 1986; also see Stein 1986; Manoff 1986; Diamond 1985; Fields 1984; Griffith 1984; Morganthau and Clift 1984; Hamburger 1982).

James Baker's primary responsibility in this structure was to coordinate the policy agenda and the media strategy, making sure that the White House communications office, the Legislative Strategy Group, the Friday Group, and various other political-outreach groups worked together in unison (Isaacson 1982). According to Baker (quoted in Hertsgaard 1989: 23), "Implementing policy depends on getting your media operation and your political operation together, but so does running a successful political campaign. A, you've got to have a message, and B, you've got to be able to sell that message. The only thing added to that once you move into the White House is that you've got to be able to sell it not just to the public but also on the Hill. But the key to selling it on the Hill is to sell it publicly."

Michael Deaver's job was to conceive and plan a steady flow of media events that would enhance President Reagan's image and bolster current policy efforts. His specialty was packaging captivating visual images (Shapiro 1984; Broadcasting 1984). Deaver would visit each media event's location in advance, along with representatives of the television networks, to orchestrate even the smallest details in order to maximize visual effect. Deaver, for example, carefully pre-choreographed President Reagan's entire 1983 Korea trip to the demilitarized zone separating North and South Korea. After that trip, according to Hertsgaard (1989: 24–25), "the evening news shows, newspapers, and newsweeklies across the country were filled with inspiring photos of the Leader of the Free World, dressed in flak jacket, staring down the Communists through field glasses." NBC news correspondent Andrea Mitchell, who called the trip "one of the greatest advanced [sic] events of all time," remarked, "I saw the toe marks for [Reagan]. . . . When he didn't stand on his toe mark he was signaled by one of the advance men to move over into the sunshine" (Hertsgaard 1989: 25; also see Posner 1981).[7] As the plaque on deputy press secretary Larry Speaks's desk said, "You don't tell us how to stage the news, we won't tell you how to cover it."

David Gergen's primary responsibility was to handle the news journalists on a day-to-day basis (*Newsweek* 1981). Gergen participated in the daily White House press corps briefings and spent most of his day on the telephone doing "back-channel spin control" on news stories and coaxing network television officials to make maximum space available in their evening news broadcasts for White House events and speeches. Besides the continual contacts maintained with reporters, Gergen would make five to fifteen telephone calls a day to the three network news editors about an hour and a half before their final story deadlines to check on their content and discourage undesirable coverage (Hertsgaard 1989: 28–31). Tom Bettag, senior producer of the *CBS Evening News,* said (quoted in Hertsgaard 1989: 31), "A call . . . from a Gergen is no small thing. It's a sort of subtle reminder, usually over relatively small details. There was no 'Don't run that story!' They understand how much we brace at anything smacking of overt control. Usually it was more like, 'We wonder if you realize that . . .'"

President Reagan was also a key participant in this media-relations team. Despite his frequent embarrassing gaffes before the press, his apparent ignorance of the substance of many policy issues, and his persistently low public job-approval ratings, the President enjoyed the positive regard of the press and relatively high personal-appeal ratings among the public (Blumenthal 1983; *Time* 1982; Griffith 1983, 1984, 1986). Ronald Reagan—with his affable personality, sincere demeanor, and Hollywood acting experience—was extraordinarily effective in cultivating positive press relations (Matthews 1984). According to Susan Zirinsky, senior Washington producer at *CBS News* (quoted in Hertsgaard 1989: 47), "Jimmy Carter you felt sorry for, but he was always aloof and hard to get to know. But Reagan always made you laugh. It was hard not to like him." *Newsweek* editor Maynard Parker agrees: "Reagan has gotten the breaks in terms of press coverage, for the reason that most reporters covering him genuinely like the man and find it difficult to be as tough as they might like." This positive regard from the press helped the White House politically, according to Joanna Bistany, deputy assistant to the President, "A lot of what we've done [politically was] because of Ronald Reagan and his warm personality. You can get away with a lot [of unpopular politics], because he can then come up and defuse the antagonism" (quoted in Hertsgaard 1989: 47).[8]

Other important players in the White House media team included President Reagan's close adviser Richard Darman, who monitored the entire flow of written communications in and out of the White House and significantly shaped the Friday Group strategies; deputy press secretary Larry Speaks, the most visible member of the communications machine, who played the role of drawing fire from unhappy or aggressive reporters to divert their animosity away from his superiors; and pollster Richard Wirthlin, who regularly fed the White House media-relations apparatus vital public-opinion information on the President's political vulnerabilities and opportunities with various constituencies, as well as imaginative proposals for communications strategies to deal with those vulnerabilities and opportunities (Kenworthy 1991: 194; Hertsgaard 1989: 20–21).

This finely tuned and uncommonly proficient machine exploited the four advantages in media relations normally available to every presidential administration, namely, the powers to initiate, anticipate, regulate, and amplify. First, every White House administration, by virtue of the importance of the U.S. presidency, possesses the capacity not simply to influence the news, but actually *to initiate* news, to create advantageously timed news at will, to design and activate the news of the day. Thus Witness for Peace long-termer Kevin Kresse (1992) complained: "Every time Reagan sneezes, the press gives him the front page." Such power to initiate news is evident in the very feasibility of a "line of the day," but the Reagan media machine went much further than that in creating news.

On August 19, 1981, for example, the White House media-relations team scored a Vietnam-syndrome-purging public relations triumph when U.S. fighter planes shot down two Libyan jets over the Gulf of Sidra. The air strike had been originally planned for July. But Chief of Staff James Baker ordered the operation postponed for one month so as not to divert public attention away from the President's July tax-legislation victory in Congress. When the timing was right, and the Libyan planes downed, President Reagan was flown that morning to the USS *Constellation* for a staged photo opportunity. Thus, reporters were able to shoot news footage—which, according to plan, hit the networks just in time for the next evening's prime-time news broadcasts—of the fearless Commander in Chief at hostility's front lines, giving the subliminal impression that the President had actually overseen the air attack. The fact that President Reagan had slept in bed through the entire incident—as Edwin Meese later accidentally divulged to reporters—did nothing to diminish the visual impact of the planned media event (Hertsgaard 1989: 132–33; also see Alexandre 1987).

The White House applied that same capacity to create news events to strengthen their Central America campaign (Hallin 1987: 11–16). The shared belief in the existence of a "Central American crisis" was itself ultimately a social construction, mostly a political creation of Alexander Haig, that was later sustained by Ronald Reagan, William Clark, and Jeanne Kirkpatrick. Media coverage of the region was driven more by White House story leaks and press conferences than by actual significant events in Central America (see, for example, tables 5.1 and 5.2). Most conspicuously, Haig used the press and the release of the highly publicized White Paper "Communist Interference in El Salvador" in February 1981 to establish the theory that communist adventurism was to blame for Central America's unrest. Few reporters actually studied the White Paper or questioned its credibility. Most simply reported its allegations as fact. Thus, through mere public declaration, President Reagan's Secretary of State was able to generate a newsworthy "reality" where none had existed before.[9] Similarly, on November 4, 1984—election day in the U.S.—White House officials created a national-security sensation by leaking to CBS News an intelligence report claiming that the Soviet freighter *Bakuriani* was transporting Soviet MIG-21 fighter planes to Nicaragua. That action, claimed U.S. officials, warranted U.S. military retaliation. It was later admitted that no such MIGs were on board the *Bakuriani*. But this subsequent acknowledgment did not nullify the political impression of a potential military threat from Nicaragua advanced by the strategic leak of November 4.

Second, every presidential administration, by virtue of its access to privileged information, enjoys the ability to *anticipate* a great deal of breaking news, and thus get a head start on shaping the interpretive framing of that news. For example, in 1983, the Reagan White House learned that an impending government report on economic activity contained news of an upturn in new housing starts. In response, Michael

Deaver arranged to have the President flown to Fort Worth, Texas—where housing starts were increasing at an extraordinarily high rate and where polls showed Reagan needed to shore up his political support—for an upbeat photo opportunity with busy Houston construction workers at a new home development. According to Deaver (quoted in Hertsgaard 1989: 251):

> Now, the press can say, "They brought us all the way down here to Fort Worth, Texas, just to have a show and make the President look good." But the guy sitting there with his six-pack that night is looking at it and saying [here Deaver imitated the viewer, leaning sideways, cocking his head and squinting at an imaginary television set], "What's the President doing there with those hard hats? Oh! Housing starts have gone up. Things must be getting better."

Anticipating breaking news helped the administration shape the Central America debate as well. In December 1981, for example, El Salvador's Atlacatl Battalion—the first Salvadoran army battalion trained by U.S. advisers—swept through the rebel-controlled province of Morazán, massacring between seven hundred and one thousand Salvadoran peasants. The White House, it was later revealed through released documents, had evidence of the massacre through cables from the U.S. embassy in San Salvador. But the day before the President was to formally certify to Congress that El Salvador was "achieving substantial control over all elements of its own armed forces" and making "a concerted and significant effort to comply with internationally recognized human rights," the massacre was reported in the U.S. in front-page articles by Raymond Bonner of the *New York Times* and Alma Guillermoprieto of the *Washington Post*. In response to these potentially policy-damaging reports, Assistant Secretary of State Thomas Enders quickly appeared before Congress, contending persuasively that "no evidence" of a massacre existed. Shortly thereafter, newspapers such as the *Wall Street Journal* began depicting Bonner and Guillermoprieto as having been hoodwinked by a Salvadoran-rebel propaganda exercise (Hertsgaard 1989: 188–90; also see Chamorro 1987: 31–35). Through their advantage of being able to anticipate damaging news, administration officials were able to prepare to neutralize it.

Third, every White House administration, because of its possession of restricted information and power to establish ground rules with the media, enjoys the capacity to *regulate* the dissemination of important information through the media. Administration officials can choose, for example, to release to the press only some of the truth it knows on a subject (see, for instance, America 1986; Chamorro 1987: 26–31). Administration officials also can choose to hold the press at a distance, when more immediate media access would be risky. For instance, in order to minimize the political damage of President Reagan's chronic gaffe problem, the White House media-relations team made the President highly unavailable to the press (Alter, DeFrank, and Warner 1984). They restricted daily media access, scheduled fewer Presidential press conferences than any other modern White House administration, and, in 1982, even demanded that reporters refrain from asking questions of the President during Oval Office photo opportunity sessions (Broadcasting 1982; Radolf 1987; Stein 1987; Roper 1985a, 1985b; Hertsgaard 1989: 133–43). Furthermore, administration officials can choose to regulate the *contexts* in which they communicate through the media. Elliott Abrams, Assistant Secretary of State for Inter-American Affairs, for example, refused to debate on talk shows with, or even take questions from, a list of certain journalists and policy analysts he considered to be politically adversarial (Hertsgaard 1989: 61). Finally, administration officials can choose to withhold relevant information from the press altogether. During the 1983 U.S. invasion of Grenada, for instance, the administration, in a glaring act of press censorship, entirely barred the media from covering the invasion of Grenada (Friedrich 1983; Grunwald 1983). Cordoned off from the entire invasion, through deception and denial, the press was forced to rely solely on official government reports and sanitized Pentagon videotapes of the operation (Hertsgaard 1989: 205–37).

Finally, all presidents, because of the great attention their pronouncements attract, possess the ability to *amplify* issues and themes into major matters of concern. The key is repetition. In 1983, for example, polls showed a two-to-one public disapproval of President Reagan's cutbacks in federal spending on education. In response, Michael Deaver orchestrated a twenty-five-stop "excellence in education" public relations campaign, emphasizing merit pay for teachers and increased classroom discipline. According to Deaver (quoted in Hertsgaard 1989: 48–49): "The President would *say* the same thing, but we had different visuals for every one of those stops. . . . It used to drive the President crazy, because repetition was so important. He'd get on that airplane and look at the speech and say, 'Mike, I'm not going to give this same speech on education again, am I?' I said, 'Yeah, *trust* me, it's going to work.' And it did."

Six weeks later, without *any* change in the administration's actual education policy, the polls showed the public *supporting* Reagan on education two-to-one. Saul Friedman, Knight-Rider journalist, observed (quoted in Hertsgaard 1989: 49), "They understood that to shift the fulcrum of the debate, you have to do it with repetition, which the President is very good at."

Reagan effectively capitalized on this power of repetition to "shift the fulcrum of the debate" in championing his Central America policy as well (Millman 1984; Hallin 1987; Cockburn 1987). In particular, through his unrelenting repetition, Reagan managed successfully to shift the focus of the public debate over the Contra war away from the question of the wisdom of supporting the disreputable Contra forces to that of the diabolic nature of the Sandinista regime (see R. Cohen 1986). By incessantly asserting that the Sandinistas were "hardline communists," "terrorists," "Marxist-Leninist dictators," and "Murder, Inc.," Reagan was able to reframe the terms of the debate in a way that effectively undermined congressional opposition to his policy (Spence 1987: 183–87).

Thus, in its struggle to define the Central American reality from *its* perspective, the Central America peace movement confronted a formidable opponent in the Reagan White House. Besides possessing the obvious capacity to originate, define, and implement U.S. foreign policy, the Reagan administration also enjoyed the power, vis-à-vis the media, to initiate, anticipate, regulate, and amplify "facts," to establish a definition of the situation that justified its foreign policy. The administration's masterful media-relations machine exploited this power with great proficiency and success.

CONTESTING ADMINISTRATION FRAMES

Given the difficulties inherent in media norms and practices for grassroots challengers trying to shape public political discourse, and given the tremendous media advantages enjoyed by the Reagan administration, what strategies and resources were available to the Central America peace movement for using the media successfully to redefine Central America for the American people and Congress? The movement did not have the power, prominence, finances, and world-class media-relations machine of the White House. The movement *did*, however, enjoy certain attributes that afforded potential leverage against the White House position. Specifically, the movement was generating dramatic, often disruptive political actions. It had mobilized a grassroots base of tens of thousands of what seemed to be mostly ordinary people. Most of the reported evidence coming out of Central America seemed to corroborate its position. Also, its framings of Central America—especially the another-Vietnam and wayward-America frames—enjoyed high degrees of resonance with U.S. cultural values. Furthermore, the movement included a handful of organizers—most notably, Dennis Marker of Witness for Peace and the Pledge of Resistance, Cindy Buhl of the Coalition for a New Foreign and Military Policy and the Central America Working Group, and Amanda Spake of the Caribbean Basin Information Project—who understood how to work the news industry to the movement's advantage. These media-experienced organizers, working with thousands of other leaders and activists, managed successfully to exploit the movement's distinct attributes—its dramatic actions, grassroots base, empirical credibility, and cultural resonance—to help undermine, through the mass media, the administration's framing of Central America. The following pages recount, mostly in these organizers' own words, the key elements of their media strategy.[10]

Accentuate the Dramatic

Experienced movement organizers knew that to be newsworthy, they had to have a current, interesting story. So they worked to capitalize on the movement's dramatic actions. Dennis Marker explains (1992):

> My job was to translate Witness for Peace and Pledge philosophy into something the media could understand and be interested in and excited about. But why would journalists listen to a person they've never heard of? The only ways to get press attention are to have huge numbers, huge money, or a story that's just so dramatic that they can't resist. We didn't have money or numbers. The only thing left was drama. And Witness for Peace and the Pledge were golden with drama. Really, they were screaming. They gave us a perfect press strategy.

For its public launching, Witness for Peace organized a press conference and a striking religious commissioning service to send off its first delegation. In preparation, Marker spent days on the phone, calling and inviting every journalist at every press outlet he could, including all of the major national newspapers, television stations, and wire services.

> I would call and say, "Look, I've got something you're not going to believe. Twenty U.S. citizens who are going to Nicaragua to the war zone. We don't know if they're going to make it back. These are Christians,

church people, some of them are pastors who are willing to risk their lives. This is major. I don't think you want to miss it." I pitched the risk angle very big because, at the time, it was very risky. Husbands and wives were actually traveling on different delegations because they didn't want to orphan their kids, in case they got killed. We just didn't know. Well, the media just ate it up. (Marker 1992)

Marker put out press releases publicizing the idea that the delegates were going to Nicaragua to be a "human shield": ordinary Americans standing between the Nicaraguans and the Contras, using their bodies to shield innocent peasants from the deadly Contras. He has recalled (1992), "When you're little, like us, you have to have one concept that is so striking that the press *has* to cover you, and for us, that was the 'human shield.' You don't get many opportunities in life to have such a simple, marketable, dramatic concept that conveys so well what you're trying to say."

The drama strategy worked, as the Witness for Peace kickoff received widespread national media attention.[11] With this success, Marker chose to employ the same strategy of accentuating the dramatic when it came to launching the Pledge of Resistance (Marker 1992): "With Witness for Peace, it was the drama of people putting their lives at risk. With the Pledge, it was the drama of confrontation: 'We're not going to passively take it. We're laying down the gauntlet with massive civil disobedience and protest.' It's a little person's way of drawing a line in the sand. And that worked too."

Not only did the drama make Witness for Peace and the Pledge of Resistance media-worthy. It also helped to build important working relationships between Dennis Marker and news journalists. As he said (1992), "By the time we launched the Pledge, all the reporters were talking to me first call. They would hang up on someone else because they knew I might have something good. Once you get their attention, they're willing to talk to you. Also, the media are like 'blackbirds on a wire.' You get one to go, then the others think, 'We should be there, too,' which is why you always get the same coverage on all three networks."

Appeal to the Credibility of Ordinary Folk

A second component of the peace movement's media strategy was to turn the apparent ordinariness of most activists into a reality-defining advantage. The tactic was to highlight, not most activists' lack of expertise on inter-American relations, but their trustworthiness as ordinary, neighbor-next-door, everyman and everywoman kind of people. Appealing to latent Jacksonian-populist values in the American cultural tradition—belief in the integrity of ordinary working citizens and distrust for centralized governmental elites—the movement's media organizers counterposed the word of local activists against the word of Ronald Reagan and summoned people to choose between the two: "We worked to set up this choice for journalists and their readers: 'You have to decide: do you believe Ronald Reagan or do you believe the local Baptist pastor? Because you can't believe both.' We pitched the idea that these are ordinary people, credible people, they could be from your local church, could be your pastor, your priest, from the school. Trustworthy folk. This could be your mother, your grandmother" (Marker 1992).

The strategy was to connect these ordinary people with area journalists for interviews, in order to undermine President Reagan's version of Central America through their testimonies (Marker 1992):

> We would get the names of delegates before trips and tell journalists, "Just call this person in your city." So, Presbyterian ministers would be out there telling reporters, "Well, yes, I'm the minister of this church in whatevertown. And no, of course I've never been arrested before. But, I've been to Nicaragua, and I must act, out of conscience, to oppose what our government is doing there." Well, who are people going to believe? This guy? Or Elliott Abrams? *That's* the choice we wanted to confront people with.

Cultivate New Media Contacts

Projecting their Central America frames through the media required that activists build stronger links to the media. Thus, the movement organizers invested heavily in cultivating working relationships with reporters. The first step was getting the right attitude. According to Cindy Buhl (1993), "You have to learn to like working with the press. People are mostly taught to see the press as an adversary. We've had to learn to see the press as our friends, to build collaborative relationships with them."

The next step was establishing personal relationships with reporters and editors. Marker said (1992),

> The key is being personal, of finding ways to get in their faces, nicely. Big news reporters get 1,000 press releases a day, and they're going to cover one story, maybe two. So your chances of getting through to them are nil

if you just send them something. So, after you send a press release, you call and ask if they have it. You know they don't—they didn't even bother to read it. So you say, "Okay, I'll get you another." I would hand deliver it. That way, I could ask if they were in and go and shake their hand. I would call five times before getting a story. Then, once I had given them a good story, I called the next day and said how great it was, if there was anything good to say about it.

Central America peace movement media strategists stressed three key principles they practiced in developing working relationships with journalists. First, activists had to become sources of genuinely valuable information for reporters. "Good reporters cultivate a wide variety of sources. Most journalists really needed to know what was going on in Congress, who to talk to. So, if a reporter had a question, I would be available to them. We developed excellent relations in this way with Capitol Hill reporters who covered Central American issues. Mostly because we gave them the background they needed for writing the important stories" (Buhl 1993).[12]

To make the movement a source of valuable information for reporters, Amanda Spake organized regular educational sessions for Capitol Hill journalists, billed as "A Road Map to Congress." "Amanda would bring in inside people who would tell reporters what the year's key debates and arguments were going to be. The reporters and television people just ate it up, they loved it. It was like a little tour guide on Central America politics. It was also our way to get out names of talking-heads for our side, people they could contact later for interviews" (Buhl 1993).

Second, activists had to develop reputations for being trustworthy. According to Dennis Marker (1992), "You're always trying to get journalists to trust you, by consistently telling the truth, only what is accurate, only what you know. They need to know they have someone they can trust, who will be straight with them." Third, activists had to make themselves totally available to reporters. Marker recounted (1992):

I was available 24 hours a day. I said, "Here's my home number. Call me at three in the morning, don't worry about it. I'd love to talk to you." And they did. Reporters would call me in the middle of the night. "I'm so glad you called. Disturbing me? Heavens, no. Two in the morning is fine!" If they ask you for a copy of something, you get it to them in 15 minutes. You drop anything to talk to them. That's what they expect. That's what they get from the White House. That's what they got from us.

Saturate the Local News

Another key element of the Central America peace movement's media strategy was to concentrate on generating extensive local news coverage. This tactic had four advantages. First, local news coverage was easier to generate than national coverage. Second, local news coverage could target key political states. Third, widespread local news coverage was more difficult for the movement's opponents to counter. Fourth, extensive local news coverage hit the movement's intended targets—the American public and Congress—at least as effectively as national news coverage. Local news not only touches the public at a closer-to-home level, but local news, editorials, and letters-to-editors also exert a significant influence on the thinking and voting of area congressional representatives. Hence, the movement's strategy was first to get major national press and establish its identity, then to saturate the local and regional press.

Part of the very purpose of first generating national news was to gain a reputation and credibility that would attract local news coverage: "The key was piggybacking. We created a national story. Then we went to our local people and said, 'Look, just tell your *Small-Potatoes Daily* that this was covered in the *New York Times* and they'll cover it.' And they did" (Marker 1992).

According to Mike Clark (1992), Witness for Peace delegates enjoyed a notoriety that naturally attracted local press coverage. "At the grassroots level, press coverage was easy. We had people coming back from Nicaragua, which, in many places, was like coming back from Mars. People came home and were like stars. So, we got lots of free publicity, lots of television, radio, and newspaper coverage, at the grassroots level."

Witness for Peace also worked on generating publicity in specialty publications, by soliciting information about delegates' organizational, professional, hobby, or interest-group connections, and encouraging them to contact the publishers of any magazines or newsletters to which they were related:

> If a pipefitter was going, we'd get the pipefitter press. If a nun, we'd get their religious order to cover it. I would call whoever: "Do you know that one of your board of directors is doing a really dramatic thing that was covered in *Newsweek* and the *Washington Post*?" Any connection these people had. I remember one delegate was a sewing machine salesman and we tried to get into *Sewing Machine Trade* magazine. "Have him call me.

No problem. I'll figure out how to connect it." That's what you have to do. (Marker 1992)

Barrage with Empirical Contradictions

At the heart of the movement's media strategy stood the tactic of relentlessly challenging White House Central America frames by churning out a deluge of contradictory evidence. When the White House blamed Central America's turmoil on Soviet expansionism, the movement countered with details of the region's epidemic injustice and repression. When the administration claimed human rights progress by the Salvadoran regime, the movement publicized its continuing, documented military and death-squad atrocities. To President Reagan's assertion that the Contras were "Freedom Fighters" and "the moral equivalents of our founding fathers," the movement replied with damning evidence of their rampant terrorist activities. White House claims to possessing the morally choiceworthy Central American policy were rebutted with the unremitting testimony of myriad religious and legal authorities and policy makers condemning the administration policy's immorality, illegality, and ineffectiveness. Administration charges that the Sandinistas were creating a "Marxist-Leninist, anti-semitic, totalitarian dungeon" were met with signs of new-found political openness, fair elections, and social advancement in Nicaragua. White House disavowals of "another Vietnam" were countered with film footage of new U.S. military advisers arriving in San Salvador. State Department claims of Nicaraguan gunrunning to the FMLN rebels were refuted with statements of certain forthright State officials about the actual lack of verifying evidence. Denials of covert CIA operations were confronted with proof of U.S. harbor minings, terrorist manuals, and military supply operations. Taking advantage of the empirical evidence from Central America that supported their frames, movement organizers struggled to undermine White House credibility by contradicting every policy argument the administration advanced. Dennis Marker explained (1992):

> Our whole strategy was to win a few and cast doubts in the minds of the rest. We had to use a "guerilla strategy," designed to plant doubts in the public mind, to "confuse" the public, so to speak. People were going to hear from us once a month, maybe, and from Reagan every day. He had the power to amplify and we didn't. So, what could we do? Create uncertainty, so the public wouldn't solidify around Reagan's position, but say,

"Gee, I've been hearing contradictory things and I don't know what to think." So any time they'd throw out a line, we'd counter it. We thought if we could keep the public from totally believing Reagan, then they might not be so interested in paying for his policy. So we ran in and lobbed little somethings that would get attention, then ran back before we got creamed.

The movement employed a variety of sources and channels of information to contradict the President, including damaging news reports from Central America, critical film documentaries, published reports of human rights monitor groups, refugees' stories, Central American activists on speaking tours in the U.S., reports from U.S. activists stationed in Central America, and the statements and testimony of critical Central America scholars, religious leaders, and policy analysts. Witness for Peace, which actually documented Contra atrocities in Nicaraguan war zones, was especially well situated to challenge the White House. According to Mike Clark (1992): "When Witness for Peace delegates returned, they had the opportunity to tell the news media what they had seen with their own eyes, which was a story that contradicted Reagan. And often it was possible to get those contrary stories out through the media." Eventually, Witness for Peace became accepted by many U.S. politicians and journalists as a reliable source of information on the war in Nicaragua. This opened up opportunities for contributing to the public debate: "When we were the only source for information about Contra attacks, we were being quoted in Congress and the *New York Times*. We got access because we were the only people who were traveling out to the war zones. So reporters and congresspeople would quote us and use our information when debating Nicaragua" (Clark 1992).

Although the movement's imperial-America frame lent itself most to countering the President's characterization of Central America and his own policy, the another-Vietnam, wayward-America, and botched-diplomacy frames proved much more effective. The campaign to contradict the White House worked best when it appealed to the good in the U.S. and refrained from disparaging the bad. Doing so not only logically set up the possibility of isolating President Reagan and his policy, specifically, as the bad to be opposed—and not the U.S. as a whole. It also made movement arguments more plausible to average Americans, given their value commitments and worldviews (see Kenworthy 1988: 121). Throughout the decade, the movement especially strove to capitalize on its Vietnam-syndrome leverage. Cindy Buhl recalled (1993):

> Vietnam worked well at the grassroots. People viscerally reacted to getting embroiled in some two-bit third-world war not worth one American life. Initially that was Salvador, then Nicaragua. As late as our Countdown '87 campaign, a consultant did focus groups and found that Vietnam still resonated so strongly with Americans. We actually did a television commercial hinting at Vietnam, that ran in swing states. It starts with a Nicaraguan soldier, but when you hear the bolt clicking back on his gun, he turns around and he's not a Nicaraguan anymore, he's an American. A clearly hispanic campesino becomes the boy next door. It was a very powerful commercial.

Overall, the effort to contradict the White House was effective throughout the decade, as the movement *did* succeed in casting doubt in the public mind on the wisdom of President Reagan's Central American policy.

But, for its part, the White House also took steps to counter the movement's contradiction campaign. Sometimes, the administration was able successfully to smother the movement's challenges in the press through the media advantages that it enjoyed. Elliott Abrams, for example, was able to choose the opponent against whom he would debate Central America on television. After a particularly bad performance against Bishop Thomas Gumbleton on the March 19, 1986, *McNeil/Lehrer News Hour,* for example, Abrams refused ever to debate Gumbleton again and demanded to debate less-informed, mainline liberals, such as Ted Kennedy.

Other times, developing political events in Central America—partly shaped by the Reagan administration for just such an effect—undermined the movement's attempt to keep *their* issues in the spotlight. According to Cindy Buhl (1993), Salvadoran elections foiled movement efforts to focus attention on human rights abuses in El Salvador: "Duarte's 1984 election creamed us, put Salvador off the agenda for years. You couldn't get Congress to look at Salvador and we didn't have a winnable Salvador vote until 1989. It was barely all we could do to keep some of the human rights issues alive during the Duarte regime."

At other times, the administration received assistance from the political blunders of the Sandinistas and tactical mistakes by the movement's congressional allies: "Some in Congress tried to give a more balanced approach to the Sandinistas, but then Daniel Ortega went to Moscow. Timing was not Ortega's strong suit. Every time they tried to give a balanced assessment of the Sandinistas, they would be burned and less likely to try again. Eventually, none of Reagan's claims about the Sandinistas were opposed" (Buhl 1993).

Finally, sometimes, movement leaders declined to employ administration-contradicting tactics that promised to damage White House credibility because, at the time, they appeared too risky. Dennis Marker offers an example (1992):

> The CIA got caught producing a terrorism comic book about how to make Molotov cocktails, how to slash tires on police cars, terrorist tactics. At first, the press covered it. Then Reagan said the comic was to promote democracy. And the press bought it. So, I said, "Let's print up 10,000 translations, hold a press conference, and say we're going to distribute them in inner-city America because we want to promote democracy there." It was beautiful. It could not have failed. It would have forced the press to show Ronald Reagan to be directly, openly lying. Unfortunately, some of our people hated it. They said, "We don't want to be associated with terrorism." Oh! They just missed the point! Because we didn't do that, Reagan's argument was allowed to stand.

In most cases, movement efforts to use the media to challenge the President with evidence contradicting the administration's framings of Central America succeeded in their intended effect. In certain other cases, however, they were neutralized by White House counteractions and the restraint of sometimes overly cautious congressional and movement leaders.

Employ Multiple Authorities and Arguments Simultaneously

Besides the tactics described above, also integral to the movement's struggle to shape the public debate on Central America was the practice of "media triangulation," that is, of drawing on multiple anti-administration authorities and advancing several anti-administration arguments simultaneously. According to Cindy Buhl (1993), "On Nicaragua, for example, the mantra was, 'It's illegal, it's immoral, and it doesn't work.' People responded to that. If it's illegal, immoral, and doesn't work, what more do you need to know? And we had our moral people, our legal people, and people who could show why it wasn't working." Buhl went on to explain:

> We divided it up into different specialties. The ACLU and the Center for National Security Studies took on the legal arguments against the policy. Then the churches were very good on the moral and theological argu-

ments and on human rights. They argued persuasively that this policy was simply immoral. Then we brought in foreign-policy types, academics and analysts, who argued that, even given Reagan's objectives in Central America, this policy would simply not succeed. And that worked very well for us. All of those voices together commanded a hearing.

Regularly Promote New Story Lines

Finally, movement organizers maintained their voice in the media throughout the decade by regularly formulating and advancing fresh news story lines. Witness for Peace, for example, began with an inaugural press conference and commissioning service. One year later, they launched a "What We've Seen and Heard" media campaign. A year later, they promoted a new "Thousand Eyewitnesses" press campaign. In the following years, Witness for Peace helped devise a variety of campaigns, including the "Countdown '87," "Countdown '88," and "Days of Decision" campaigns. According to Dennis Marker (1992), "You must always try to find a new angle. Basically it's all the same story, but you're finding a new way to pitch it. That's the game. We always asked, 'How can we make this different, yet reinforce the same message?' Reporters don't have any problem with that. They understand it very well. They're willing to print it, as long as you make it exciting and dramatic. So we would formulate different events and campaigns and just kept releasing these things."

Witness for Peace also used a "Reagan Lies" campaign to promote a new story line (Marker 1992): "You up the ante. For a while we said, 'The administration is getting it wrong, it's not the truth.' You beat around the bush. Then at some point you've got to go the next step and up the ante. So you directly charge, 'They're lying. Purposefully lying.' You've got to do that, not only because it's true, but also to maintain the interest, to keep up the drama with the press."

To summarize, by accentuating their own dramatic actions, appealing to the credibility of ordinary Americans, carefully cultivating new media contacts, saturating local news outlets around the country, barraging the administration with damaging contradictory evidence, posing multiple anti-administration authorities and arguments, and regularly promoting fresh news story lines, the Central America peace movement activists managed successfully to project their counterframings of Central America to and through the mass media, despite the difficulties presented by media norms and practices and by the White

House's immense media advantages and skills. In so doing, the movement was able to advance to the American public and Congress an alternative definition of the Central American situation that countered the Reagan administration's and persuasively called for a major change in U.S. Central American policy. Consequently, as Central America increasingly proved the subject of a major political battle and not a political rollover, the early words of Secretary of State Alexander Haig—"Mr. President, this is one you can win"—seemed ever increasingly impetuous and presumptuous.

ADMINISTRATION COUNTERATTACKS

The Reagan administration, understandably, did not take the Central America peace movement's relative media success and consequent political strength amicably. Nor was it prepared to consider the possibility of suffering ultimate defeat. To strengthen the chances of prevailing in the public debate over Central America, and particularly over Nicaragua, certain members of the administration took more aggressive actions to promote and defend the White House's position and to undermine the opposition. In their covert, coercive, and sometimes illegal nature, these countermovement actions took on a qualitatively different character than the regular press-management work of the Deaver-Gergen-Baker media-relations team. The remainder of this chapter examines these more aggressive discourse-influencing administration actions.

William Casey, President Reagan's CIA director and fervent champion of the Contras, perceived very early in the decade that winning the domestic political battle for Central America would be difficult. He knew it would require concerted efforts to shape the news media and influence public opinion, efforts he was prepared to foster.[13] The CIA, however, was prohibited by the 1947 National Security Act and 1981 Presidential Executive Order 12333 from engaging in domestic operations intended to influence U.S. political processes, public opinion, or the media. To formally skirt these bans, in 1982, Casey transferred the CIA's senior overseas-propaganda specialist, Walter Raymond, Jr., to the NSC. There Raymond began coordinating, along with Oliver North, a major "public diplomacy" operation designed to influence and manipulate media, congressional, and public perceptions of Central America (Kornbluh and Byrne 1993: 4).[14] Raymond, who heralded public diplomacy as a "new art form," once characterized his work as "gluing black hats on the Sandinistas and white hats on [the Contras]." An NSC official who worked with Raymond explained that their operation's purpose was "to manipulate [U.S.] public opinion . . . using the tools of Walter Raymond's trade craft which he learned from his career in the CIA covert operation shop" (Parry 1992: 16). Another of Raymond's staff described their organization as "carrying out a huge psychological warfare operation, the kind the military conduct to influence the population in denied or enemy territory" (Hertsgaard 1989: 310; Sklar 1988: 245; Parry and Kornbluh 1988: 19–20).[15]

The Office of Public Diplomacy

Many of Raymond's Central America tasks were executed through the Office of Public Diplomacy for Latin America and the Caribbean, an agency created—on Raymond's recommendation—by NSC Adviser William Clark in July 1983 and given a presidential cachet (Kornbluh and Byrne 1993: 21). The Office of Public Diplomacy itself was headed by Otto Reich, a Cuban exile and fervid anti-communist. Reich's office was housed in the State Department and appeared to operate under State's oversight. But, in fact, it secretly reported directly to the NSC Central America Public Diplomacy Task Force chaired by Walter Raymond. That task force, in turn, took what Raymond called its "political guidance" from RIG, the Restricted Interagency Group—led by Oliver North, Assistant Secretary of State Elliott Abrams, and CIA Central America Task Force Chief Alan Fiers—that directed all of the Contra's political and logistical affairs. Thus, the administration's clandestine, domestic public-diplomacy operation was directed by the same coterie of people that developed and maintained the administration's covert, illegal Contra-supply operation (Kornbluh and Byrne 1993: 4–5; Sklar 1988: 247).[16]

On the surface, the Office of Public Diplomacy—with an annual budget of $1 million, plus eight professional staff on loan from the State and Defense Departments, USAID, and AID—served as a publisher and distributor of pro-administration reports and briefings on Central America (Kornbluh 1987: 163). In the first year of its operation alone, titles such as "Nicaragua's Military Buildup and Support for Central American Subversion," "The Sandinistas and Middle Eastern Radicals," and "Who Are the Contras?" were distributed to 1,600 college libraries, 520 political science faculties, 122 editorial writers, 107 religious organizations, and unnumbered news correspondents, conservative lobbyists, and members of Congress. Prominent journalists with their own television programs, such as "This Week with David Brinkley" and the "McLaughlin Group," not only were the first to receive the Office's material, but were extended open invitations for personal briefings on Central America. During its first year of work, the Office of Public Diplomacy also booked advocates for the administration's Central American policy for 1,570 lecture and talk-show engagements. Years later, Otto Reich testified in his Iran-Contra deposition, "Without blowing our own horn, it got to the point where the President of the United States, the Secretary of State, the National Security Advisor, Cabinet officials, and lots of other people relied on our information and used it verbatim. I mean, it was that good" (Parry and Kornbluh 1988: 17; Sklar 1988: 246; Kornbluh and Byrne 1993: 5).

However, the Office for Public Diplomacy's operations extended well beyond these visible informational activities to more covert efforts to influence and manipulate public opinion and the media. To begin, Reich borrowed six psychological warfare specialists from the Department of Defense to plan "psy-op" campaigns to persuade Congress and the American people to support Contra aid. In March 1985, for example, Colonel Daniel "Jake" Jacobowitz—before moving on to join the Psychological Operations Board in the Office of the Secretary of Defense—wrote for Reich a detailed confidential-sensitive "Public Diplomacy Action Plan" for an "educational campaign" targeting the U.S. Congress, media, and interest groups. Complete with analyses of goals, central perceptions, impediments, assets, themes, audiences, and timetables, the plan recommends forty-two specific, coordinated actions to amplify the "overall theme" that "the Nicaraguan Freedom Fighters (FF) are fighters for freedom in the American tradition; FSLN are evil" (see Kornbluh and Byrne 1993: 23). Three months later, Reich recruited an "A-Team" of five psychological warfare officers from the Fourth Psychological Operations Group at Fort Bragg. According to a Jacobowitz memo to Reich, their responsibilities included "looking for exploitable themes and trends, and inform[ing] us of possible areas for our exploitation" (Kornbluh 1988: 37; Parry and Kornbluh 1988: 19). Jacobowitz assured Reich that the five would "have enough [work] to keep them busy until the Contras march into Managua" (see Kornbluh and Byrne 1993: 31–32). Among the themes Reich's A-Team concocted for exploitation were charges of Sandinista anti-Semitism and "Sandinista chic," that is, an image that the Sandinista "commandantes [were] living a high life style . . . [of] corruption and drugs" (Parry 1992: 16).

The Office of Public Diplomacy then disseminated these themes throughout the media through self-described "white propaganda operations." These included planting articles and editorials actually ghostwritten by the Office of Public Diplomacy in major newspapers under the names of seemingly independent scholars, leaking false and misleading anti-Sandinista intelligence information to journalists to cover-up Contra atrocities, and anonymously arranging interviews for Contra leaders with major U.S. television news journalists (Kenworthy 1988: 112; Parry and Kornbluh 1988: 18–19; Jacoby and Parry 1987; Kornbluh and Byrne 1993: 37–38; Kornbluh 1987: 163; also see Chamorro 1987: 52–54). In a March 13, 1985, Confidential/Eyes-Only memo to Director of White House Communications Pat Buchanan, Jonathan Miller of the Office of Public Diplomacy delineated "five illustrative examples of the Reich 'White Propaganda' operation," concluding (see Kornbluh and Byrne 1993: 37–38):

> I will not attempt in the future to keep you posted on all activities since we have too many balls in the air at any one time and since the work of our operation is ensured by our office's keeping a low profile. I merely wanted to give you a flavor of some of the activities that hit our office on any one day and ask that, as you formulate ideas and plans of attack, you give us a heads-up since our office has been crafted to handle the concerns that you have in getting the President's program for the freedom fighters enacted.[17]

Besides shaping media content through these "white propaganda" operations, the Office of Public Diplomacy took more direct actions to prevent reporters from publishing stories that damaged the administration's position. Specifically, the Office monitored all of the major news outlets, identified those stories that challenged the President's interpretation of Central America, and directly pressured the responsible journalists and editors to alter their content. In one memo to Walter Raymond, Otto Reich reported that his office took "a very aggressive posture vis-a-vis a sometimes hostile press" and "generally did not give any quarter in the debate." Reich claimed that his team had "killed" purportedly "erroneous news stories" and created an atmosphere in which "attacking the President was no longer cost-free" (quoted in Parry 1992: 17; Sklar 1988: 245). In one case, after National Public

Radio (NPR) broadcasted an extended report about a Contra massacre of civilians at a Nicaraguan farming cooperative in November 1984, Reich demanded a meeting with the story's reporters, producers, and editors. According to one editor in attendance, Reich "went ballistic" over the story, castigating their "biased" coverage of Nicaragua, notifying them that their stories were being monitored, and threatening to have their federal funding cut if such stories continued (Sklar 1988: 245–46; Kornbluh and Byrne 1993: 6; Parry and Kornbluh 1988: 17; Parry 1992: 17). Another NPR foreign correspondent at the meeting (quoted in Kornbluh 1987: 164) recalled that "Reich bragged that he had made similar visits to other unnamed newspapers and major television networks. . . . Reich said he had gotten others to change some of their reporters in the field because of a perceived bias, and that their coverage was much better as a result."

In another instance—according to a George Shultz memo to President Reagan, sent "to illustrate what the Office of Public Diplomacy has been doing to help improve the quality of information the American people are receiving"—when CBS ran a documentary on Central America that "upset" President Reagan and Vice President George Bush, Reich spent more than three hours protesting to the correspondent and his bureau chief the story's "unbalanced" and "deceptive" treatment of the Salvadoran guerrillas (see Kornbluh and Byrne 1993: 35–36). Shultz wrote, "This is one example. . . . It has been repeated dozens of times over the past few months. . . . We are attempting to try to build the kinds of relationships with the news media that will enable us to dispel the disinformation and misinformation which has been so prevalent in coverage while at the same time aggressively expressing our policy objectives."

These aggressive tactics proved effective, as many news editors became more guarded about their coverage of Central America. One of NPR's foreign editors, Paul Allen—who was involved in the story that Reich had protested and who eventually resigned from NPR, in part, because of the negative fallout from Reich's visit—observed that, after Reich's reproach, NPR executives began to shy away from stories about Nicaraguan issues. According to NPR foreign-affairs correspondent Bill Buzenberg, one editor, in considering whether to air a certain story on Central America, asked, "What would Otto Reich think?" Similarly, ABC News correspondent Karen Burnes, after enduring sustained pressure from the administration for her stories on drug-trafficking and corruption among the Contras, asked to be reassigned to Ethiopia, stating, "I'll take a civil war any day before working in this city" (Parry 1992: 17; Kornbluh 1987: 256; also see Hertsgaard 1989: 186–91, 196–203).

When such forms of pressure failed to daunt journalists critical of the administration's policy, the Office of Public Diplomacy often employed whispering campaigns and character assassinations to intimidate and discredit them. In 1986, for example, a colleague of Associated Press reporter Brian Barger received a phone call from the Office of Public Diplomacy warning him that his partner was "bad news" and "a Sandinista agent." Similar calls were made to other news outlets, charging certain reporters with having "secret agendas" and promoting "deliberate distortions." When former New York State prosecutor Reed Brody published a documented report on Contra human rights abuses—many of which were verified by a classified CIA review of Brody's study released one year later—President Reagan publicly denounced him as "one of dictator Ortega's supporters, a sympathizer who has openly embraced Sandinismo." The administration even impugned the integrity of mainstream human rights groups, such as Americas Watch, for publishing meticulously documented reports which criticized not only the Contras, but also the Sandinistas, for human rights abuses. Finally, in one case, Reich's Office actually spread an unfounded story about American journalists in Managua receiving sexual favors from Sandinista prostitutes in exchange for sympathetic stories on Nicaragua. "It isn't only women," Reich claimed in the July 29, 1985, issue of *New York* magazine, explaining that the Sandinistas supplied men for gay journalists. Soon thereafter, the right-wing group Accuracy in Media, which was under secret contract with the Office of Public Diplomacy, began identifying journalists by name who allegedly received these sexual favors. Such tactics often effectively either frightened critical journalists into self-censorship or undermined their professional reputations by "controversializing" them (Kornbluh 1987: 164–65; Parry and Kornbluh 1988: 25–26; Parry 1992: 17–18).

In addition to its own in-house work, the Office of Public Diplomacy, in violation of anti-lobbying laws, secretly used taxpayers' money to finance private public relations consultants, fund-raisers, and lobbyists to promote the Contras and challenge administration critics. As early as January 1983, Walter Raymond wrote in a memo, "We will move out immediately in our parallel effort to generate private support" for public diplomacy operations. By May 1983, the White House had raised $400,000 to support the work of private pro-administration groups, such as Accuracy in Media (Parry and Kornbluh 1988: 13). The Office for Public Diplomacy's primary contractor was International Business Communications (IBC), a public relations firm owned by two former government officials, Richard Miller and Frank Gomez. Between 1984 and 1986, IBC received seven no-bid contracts totaling $441,084 to do pro-Contra media work, including writing briefing papers, creating computerized mailing lists, drafting opinion pieces, holding press conferences, and organizing national speaking tours for Contra leaders (see, for instance, Kornbluh and Byrne 1993: 39–42; Sklar 1988: 246). In turn, IBC coordinated its media and lobbying activities with other quasi-private organizations, such as Accuracy in Media, Freedom House, and conservative fund-raiser Carl "Spitz" Channell's America Conservative Trust, Sentinel, and the National Endowment for the Preservation of Liberty (NEPL). In late 1985 and the spring and summer of 1986, Channell and Miller together spent more than $1.5 million on political ads targeting pivotal congressional districts in key swing-vote states (Kornbluh 1988: 37; also see Kenworthy 1991: 206; Parry 1992: 16–17). Channell and Miller, we will see below, also both became principal players in Oliver North's illegal Contra resupply operation.[18]

While the Office of Public Diplomacy concentrated on shaping mass-media content and secretly financing congressional lobbying campaigns, another administration organization, the White House Outreach Group on Central America, specialized in disseminating pro-administration materials to business, labor, religious, veterans, and other special-interest groups. The Outreach Group hosted weekly, invitation-only forums in which representatives of over 150 organizations heard Contra leaders and high-level administration officials—including Oliver North and President Reagan himself—speak in support of administration policy. Between 1983 and 1985, Outreach Group speakers also conducted 96 seminars and delivered 225 speeches in 75 different cities (Barry and Preusch 1988: 206). Finally, the White House Outreach Group also sponsored conferences on topics such as "The Contra's Pursuit of Democracy in Nicaragua," placed pro-Contra advertisements in and ghostwrote sympathetic op-ed articles for major newspapers, and produced and distributed a series of papers and books, with titles such as "The PLO in Central America" and "Nicaraguan Repression of Miskito Indians" (Kornbluh 1987: 161). The United States Catholic Conference's Tom Quigley recalled (1990):

The Reagan administration worked awfully hard to manipulate religious institutions and language, to influence the church. The Outreach Group was very aggressive. They had specific people assigned to Roman Catholic affairs, Evangelical affairs, Protestant and Jewish affairs, and so on. They very assiduously cultivated the faith community by running a series of Wednesday afternoon talks, mostly focused on Nicaragua, on the atrocities of the Sandinistas, on an evangelical pastor who had his ear cut off, lots of stuff on alleged religious persecution in Nicaragua. I went to a few of them, when invited. But they were mostly a waste of time, dog-and-pony shows, with low levels of real information. They did succeed, however, in solidifying the support of more conservative clergymen.

Finally, Otto Reich's Public Diplomacy operations were also linked and coordinated with an extensive, multi-million-dollar CIA campaign to develop and manipulate an ostensibly self-governing "Contra Directorate" to garner congressional support for the Contra war (Chamorro 1987: 46). According to Edgar Chamorro (1987)—a former Nicaraguan businessman, descendant of four former Nicaraguan presidents, exiled Sandinista opponent, and member of the Contra Directorate from 1982 until his forced resignation in 1984 over his objections to use of the CIA's "Psychological Operations in Guerrilla Warfare" manual—the CIA secretly created the Contra Directorate in 1982, designed its entire political strategy, and instructed its members in press relations, charging them to disavow any connection with the U.S. government. Chamorro writes that the CIA hired Woody Kepner Associates of Miami for $300,000 to orchestrate its public relations campaign, sent the Directorate on a whirlwind tour of Western Europe to promote the Contras, arranged for the Directorate to meet with swing-vote members of Congress, staged contrived military maneuvers for U.S. journalists in Honduras and Nicaragua, helped to raise private funds to support the Contras, surreptitiously hired supposedly independent scholars and analysts to write and publish in U.S. newspapers pro-Contra articles and editorials, and bribed local Honduran television, radio, and newspaper journalists to produce favorable stories on the Contras. "The purpose of much of the work I have described," Chamorro wrote (1987: 41), "was actually aimed at [the U.S.] Congress. Each element [was] in itself a small piece; but the cumulative effect of the impressions, the innuendos, the appearances, the staged events, and the suggestions was enormous." Chamorro continued (1987: 41–42):

The goal was to put Congress in a position where denying aid to the Contras would be unpatriotic or un-American. . . . Although it is supposed to
be against the law for the CIA to lobby Congress or to attempt to sway
public opinion in the domestic sphere, the CIA used the Contra Directorate as a proxy arm to influence legislation both directly and indirectly.
. . . The CIA, with its extensive network of contacts and its access to vast
resources of information, directly influenced the congressional debate
and the legislative results of that debate.

When in June 1985, the disillusioned Chamorro—who originally joined
the Contra Directorate hoping to help organize an honest and
respectable political opposition to the Sandinistas—tried to testify
before Congress about the operation's ethical and political defects, the
U.S. INS immediately began deportation proceedings against him
(Chamorro 1987: 60).[19]

Oliver North's "Perception Management" Operations

Besides the work of the Office of Public Diplomacy, the White House
Outreach Group on Central America, and the CIA-created Contra
Directorate campaign, the NSC's Oliver North orchestrated his own
secret, "off-the-shelf" public relations campaign in support of President
Reagan's Central American policy. To dramatize the need for Contra
funding, for example, North fabricated a series of "discoveries" to
incriminate the Sandinistas. In 1984, for instance, North arranged to
entrap and frame a Sandinista official for narcotics smuggling. North
engaged a convicted U.S. drug smuggler, Barry Seal, to pilot a planeload
of cocaine into Nicaragua and, with a hidden camera, photograph a
Nicaraguan official who had been coaxed into carrying one of the
parcels to a second plane, which was then flown to Florida. North then
leaked the story and photograph to the press, thus seemingly authenti-
cating President Reagan's charge that the Sandinistas were poisoning
America's youth with drugs.[20] In another incident—according to former Panamanian presidential consul José Blandón, told in testimony
before the U.S. Congress—Oliver North conspired in 1986 with then
Panamanian President General Manuel Noriega to plant a shipment of
Warsaw-pact arms in El Salvador, which would then be seized by the
army as the long-missing evidence of Sandinista gunrunning to the Salvadoran guerrillas (Parry and Kornbluh 1988: 12).[21]

Oliver North also devised a number of other schemes to sway congressional Contra aid votes. Before one 1985 vote, for example, North

arranged with Contra leader Adolfo Calero to keep secret a recent sizable Saudi Arabian cash donation, in order not to undermine the President's claim that Contra supplies had run out. In a message to Calero, signed by his *nom de guerre*, "Steelhammer," North wrote, "The Congress must believe that there continues to be an urgent need for funding" (Parry and Kornbluh 1988: 12; also see Chamorro 1987: 44–45). To counter the testimony of religious authorities about Contra human rights abuses, in April of 1985, North hired a member of the Old Catholic Church, a religious sect unrecognized by the Vatican, to don the garb of a Roman Catholic priest and testify to Congress about Sandinista abuses. In a fourteen-page March 20, 1985, memo to National Security Adviser Robert McFarlane, North chronicled eighty planned public relations events designed to win an end-of-the-month Contra aid vote. North closed his memo (quoted in Parry and Kornbluh 1988: 12–13):

> In addition to the events depicted on the internal chronology, other activities in the region continue as planned—including military operations and political action. Like the chronology, these events are also timed to influence the vote: planned travel by [Contra leaders] Calero, Cruz, and Robelo [and] special operations attacks against highly visible targets in Nicaragua. . . . Director Casey has sent a personal note to [White House Chief of Staff] Don Regan on the timing matter.

In addition to implementing these tactics, North contracted with the same firms Otto Reich had engaged—Richard Miller's IBC and Carl Channell's NEPL—to fund-raise and execute carefully crafted domestic political lobbying campaigns targeting the key Southern swing-vote states of Florida, Texas, North Carolina, Kentucky, Missouri, and Tennessee (Parry 1992: 17; Kornbluh 1988: 37–39; Jacoby and Parry 1987; Parry and Kornbluh 1988: 21). The campaigns were largely financed by $3.9 million raised by Channell in 1985 and $7 million in 1986. Those funds were solicited primarily from conservative, elderly, multimillionaire widows, whom Channell entertained and flattered, but privately ridiculed as "the blue rinse brigade."[22] Channell used access to the White House as his inducement to contribute, offering a chance to meet with the President himself for contributors donating $300,000 or more. For eager supporters who could not afford that sum, Channell arranged meetings with Chief of Staff Donald Regan, Assistant Secretary Elliott Abrams, National Security Adviser John Poindexter, and Communications Director Patrick Buchanan (Kornbluh and Byrne

1993: 7; Sklar 1988: 248; Parry and Kornbluh 1988: 21). North participated in the fund-raising too. Showing his Contra-promotional slide show to individuals and groups of potential donors that Channell brought to the NSC or to the nearby Hay Adams Hotel, North would then talk about the Contra's desperate need for medicine, food, and weapons. To avoid technically engaging in illegal fund-raising, North would then leave the room, and Channell would press—with what Channell's assistant, Daniel Conrad, termed an "altar call"—for big money to help repel communism in Central America.[23] That scheme netted more than $10 million (Sklar 1988: 248–49; Kornbluh and Byrne 1993: 7).

About one-quarter of that money—the portion not used for Contra arms ($2.7 million) or the salaries and expenses of Channell, Miller, Gomez, and their subordinates ($5 million)—was spent on tours by Contra leaders through swing-vote districts, on anti-Sandinista and pro-Contra television commercials, on professional lobbyists on Capitol Hill, and on media campaigns to unseat prominent opposition congressional leaders[24] (Kenworthy 1988: 119; Kornbluh and Byrne 1993: 8–9). In February 1986, Channell's NEPL spent $100,000 on comprehensive polling research to determine the themes and audiences that would comprise the most effective Contra aid media campaign for a "Central America Freedom Program." Channell then hired the Baltimore-based Robert Goodman Advertising Agency to produce and place more than $1 million worth of television commercials, using military video footage provided by Oliver North, in decisive broadcasting areas. These "Freedom Fighters TV" commercials ran in crucial congressional districts for the eight weeks preceding the initial March vote on $100 million in Contra aid. Channell also spent $600,000 to fund a Contra speaking tour in swing-vote districts. Similarly, in the final eight days before the June 1986 Contra aid vote, Channell spent $200,000 on a last-minute volley of television ads targeting ten crucial congressmen in Kentucky, Tennessee, North Carolina, and Texas. "Communist planes can strike us in only two hours from this new base in Nicaragua," warned an ominous voiceover in a typical commercial, showing satellite intelligence photos of a Nicaraguan airfield. Then, switching to an unflattering picture of the local congressman and a display of his local telephone number, the voiceover marveled, "And still Congressman Ed Jones won't support the President. Call him" (Kornbluh 1988: 39; also see Chamorro 1987: 19–22).

On June 23, 1986, the House of Representatives approved by twelve votes the President's Contra aid request for $100 million. Walter Raymond wrote in an August 7, 1986, memo to William Casey, "It is clear we would not have won the House vote without the painstaking deliberative effort undertaken by many people in the government and outside." Oliver North awarded Carl Channell a "freedom fighter" commendation from President Reagan. And Elliott Abrams conferred a White House "meritorious honor" award upon Otto Reich's Office of Public Diplomacy, stating that it "played a key role in setting out the parameters and defining the terms of the public discussion on Central America policy. Despite the efforts of a formidable and well established Soviet/Cuban/Nicaraguan propaganda apparatus, the achievements of U.S. public diplomacy are clearly visible" (Kornbluh 1988: 38; Kornbluh and Byrne 1993: 8; Parry 1992: 18).

CONCLUSION

For the Central America peace movement, winning the battle over U.S. Central American policy necessitated prevailing in the struggle to construct and define the Central American "reality." Successfully projecting its framings of Central America through available vehicles of public discourse, particularly the mass media, was absolutely essential for the movement successfully to end the U.S.-sponsored war in Central America. This was a formidable task for the grassroots challengers, who faced a number of systemic disadvantages and capable adversaries. The mass media's entrenched norms of newsworthiness and "objectivity" and news-production routines almost uniformly presented themselves as obstacles to the movement. Furthermore, the White House media-relations team skillfully exploited the media advantages enjoyed by all presidential administrations, adroitly employing their power to initiate, anticipate, regulate, and amplify news content to promote and defend their definition of the Central American situation and undermine that of their opponents. Where the administration's more conventional use of media resources ended, administration officials like William Casey, Walter Raymond, Otto Reich, Elliott Abrams, and Oliver North stepped up to perform more covert, coercive, and unlawful forms of media influence and manipulation. Despite these obstacles and adversaries, however, the Central America peace movement managed to mount a relatively effective campaign to undermine the administration's arguments and validate their position before the America public and Congress. By accentuating their own dramatic actions, appealing to the credibility of ordinary Americans, carefully cultivating new media contacts, saturating local news outlets around the country, barraging the administration with damaging contradictory evidence, posing multiple anti-administration authorities and arguments, and regularly promoting fresh news story lines, the movement managed effectively to project their counterframings of Central America to and through the mass media.

As the Central America peace movement increasingly proved itself a threatening political challenger, capable of mounting significant resistance to the President's policy, the Reagan administration and its allies began to implement even broader, more hostile campaigns and operations to damage the movement's political credibility and power. We now turn to examine, in the following chapter, the sources, tactics, and effects of this pattern of anti-movement harassment and repression.

Ten

FACING HARASSMENT AND REPRESSION

Again and again there comes a time in history when the person who dares to say that two and two make four is punished with death. . . . The question [for them, however] is not one of knowing what punishment or reward attends the making of this calculation. The question is that of knowing whether two and two do make four.

Albert Camus, *The Plague*

On September 1, 1987, Central America peace activist Brian Willson was run over by a military munitions train while trying to block with his body U.S. arms shipments to Central America at the Concord Naval Weapons Station. Both of his legs were severed. Most Americans who heard the news were horrified. But for Tom Posey, a U.S. supplier of private armaments and mercenary soldiers to the Contras, the news of Willson's gruesome tragedy was gratifying. "I was rather delighted," Posey remarked to the press (Sklar 1988: 355).

Posey's delight with Willson's dismemberment represented far more than the sadistic pleasure of a violent, twisted individual. It also represented the logical—if extreme and uncharacteristically candid—response of a complex of organizations whose political interests the peace movement threatened. Social movements, by definition, challenge the entrenched interests of powerful groups. Because these groups invariably loathe to see their interests endangered, when a threat becomes too serious, they begin to counter the challenge by mobilizing an organized opposition (Marx 1988). Tom Posey's public declaration of delight with Willson's maiming simply represented one verbal expression of a threatened set of organized interests mobilizing increasingly active Central America anti-movement actions.

Not all of the resistance Central America peace movement activists encountered was generated by organized movement opponents. Some opposition was simply scattered and interpersonal. For example, activists often faced resistance to their Central America work from family members who either objected to their involvement in political activism in general or to their political positions on Central America specifically. According to Witness for Peace activist Betsy Crites (1992), "Lots and lots of people had to deal with resistance from their families. Some families divided over Central America. My brother and I, for example, could never agree on this. He still taunts me every time we get together, saying, 'I suppose you still think the Sandinistas are angels?'"

Central America activists also often faced opposition from work colleagues and employers, and many were demoted and even fired for their political activism (see, for instance, Millman 1984: 10; Subcommittee on Civil and Constitutional Rights 1987: 262; Griffin-Nolan 1991: 93). Finally, the peace activists were often heckled and harassed at demonstrations by hostile passersby and belligerent counterdemonstrators (see, for instance, New York Times 1981d; Clendinen 1986).

Nevertheless, the Central America peace movement also threatened the keenly felt interests of some very powerful groups, including agencies of the executive branch of the U.S. government and Central American and U.S. right-wing anti-communist groups. Unwilling as they were to see the movement succeed, many of these groups took deliberate actions—direct and indirect, legal and illegal—to obstruct, harass, and intimidate the movement's activists. This chapter examines the kinds of antagonism Central America activists encountered, the people and organizations who appear to have mobilized contrary activities, and their effects on the Central America peace movement.

ANTI-MOVEMENT ACTIVITIES

Anti-movement tactics to impede, harass, and frighten peace activists were designed to raise significantly the costs of activism and thereby to deter future participation. Such activities included the following:

Harassment of Central America Travelers

Much of the energy for Central America peace activism was generated by the moral outrage over war, poverty, and injustice felt by U.S. citizens traveling to Central America. One logical means of countering the movement, therefore, was to discourage U.S. citizens from going there. Several executive branch agencies did exactly this. In 1981, the State Department issued a travel advisory on Nicaragua, discouraging would-be visitors to the country. Thereafter, frequent travelers to this designated high-risk destination, who were marked as high-risk individuals themselves, began to encounter, for example, increasing difficulty qualifying for accident and mortgage insurance (Leahy 1987: 230). On June 7, 1983, the State Department, in a move "officially discouraging travel to Nicaragua," closed down all six Nicaraguan consulates in the U.S., making it difficult to obtain travel visas to Nicaragua (Taubman 1983). Then, on May 1, 1985, President Reagan declared a state of national emergency, which, among other things, revoked the U.S. landing rights for Nicaragua's national airline, Aeronica (Leahy 1987: 230).

In addition to these moves, government agencies began in 1984 to harass U.S. citizens traveling to Nicaragua. The FBI and Customs, under assignment by the CIA and the NSC, routinely began stopping U.S. citizens returning from Nicaragua, interrogating them in detail about their trips and professional lives, and searching, seizing, and photocopying their address books, diaries, research materials, and other personal written materials (Donner 1985: 13; Lewis 1986b, 1986c). FBI agents usually retained photocopied materials for FBI intelligence files. And Customs officials often entered information on the travelers into a Treasury computer database, the Treasury Enforcement Communication System, and possibly the FBI's Terrorist Research and Analytical Center, a computer database with information on terrorist groups (Subcommittee on Civil and Constitutional Rights 1987: 200–204; Webster 1984: 12).

On January 16, 1985, for example, Edward Haase, a Kansas City radio journalist returned from a trip to Nicaragua through the Miami airport. He was detained by U.S. Customs officials and questioned by an FBI agent, Joe Miranda, who seized and photocopied Haase's personal address book, diary, and documents about Central America peace organizations with which Haase was involved. When Haase's lawyer later demanded the FBI to return all copied materials, the FBI refused, saying that it was properly "disseminable" and, furthermore, that copies of his materials were being sent to the State Department and the INS (Lewis 1985; also see Leahy 1987: 231–33; Sklar 1988: 351). The FBI acknowledged in 1985 conducting one hundred such "interviews" with returnees from Nicaragua in one year (Donner 1985: 13). Many more hundreds were conducted over the following four years (MSN 1989; also see Demac 1984: 26).

FBI Visits

FBI agents not only interrogated Central America peace activists returning from Nicaragua at airports, they also began investigating them at their homes and jobs, questioning their friends, neighbors, landlords, and employers. They also began to question people who belonged to any Central America organization, had visited Central American embassies in the U.S., or happened to have attended a meeting with speakers critical of White House Central America policy (Subcommittee on Civil and Constitutional Rights 1987: 198).

For example, a New York man who had worked on a construction crew in Nicaragua in 1984 discovered that his landlord had been subsequently visited by FBI agents three times. That same year, another man living in New York City returned from a trip to Nicaragua to discover that the FBI had questioned two of his friends about him and his political affiliations. Both friends were frightened by the inquiry (Leahy 1987: 233). In April 1987, FBI agents in five cities visited the employers of twelve activists who had volunteered with the development assistance organization TecNica. The FBI agents asked the employers to call the volunteers into their offices, where the agents reproached them in front of their employers for "helping the communists," warning them not to travel to Nicaragua again (Sklar 1988: 357). In November 1985, a hispanic University of California student who had been quoted in a local newspaper about an anti-Contra student protest received repeated phone calls, a visit, and a lengthy interrogation by FBI agents, who insinuated that she was helping to smuggle arms to El Salvador. Soon thereafter, she received two anonymous phone calls threatening that she would "pay" if she continued her activism, and a bag of decapitated hamsters were left on her doorstep (Subcommittee on Civil and Constitutional Rights 1987: 200). In 1985, Daisy Cubias, a volunteer at the Ecumenical Refugee Council of Milwaukee, after traveling to Nicaragua, was visited once at her job and twice in her home by FBI agents. "They asked me if I knew some fellow activists were in the Communist party. They said, 'You're going around with a bunch of terrorists, and we want to help keep you clean'" (Gelbspan 1985). Between 1984 and 1989, more than one hundred activists were questioned in this manner (MSN 1989; also see Subcommittee on Civil and Constitutional Rights 1989).

Most activists who were visited by the FBI felt that the FBI agents were more interested in harassing them than in gathering intelligence information. Dennis Marker (1992) remembered: "When two guys in suits come up and say, 'We're from the FBI. Tell us what you did in Nicaragua' or 'I want to ask you about your activist friend,' of course the friends and neighbors got a little nervous. Which is just what the FBI wanted." CISPES activist Beth Perry characterized the experience of many members of her organization being questioned by the FBI: "It appears the FBI was trying to impart information, rather than collect it. From the questions that were posed, and sometimes from direct statements, the FBI seemed to be trying to raise doubts [in our minds] about our operation" (Burnham 1985; also see Millman 1984).

Tax Audits, Phone Taps, and Mail Tampering

Peace activists also became the subjects of other forms of government harassment. The first suspicion of state opposition to the movement arose in 1982, when two women—one of whom never earned more than $12,000 a year—returned from Nicaragua immediately to receive notices of IRS tax audits (Gelbspan 1985a; 1991: 25). In the following years, a disproportionately large number of Central America activists were subject to similar seemingly inexplicable tax audits by the IRS, half of whom were notified shortly after returning from trips to Nicaragua. In addition, many of the movement's organizations—including Sojourners, the National Network in Solidarity with the Nicaraguan People, the Quixote Center, the Center for Development Policy, Alternative Life, Inc., and Reichler and Appelbaum, the law firm representing the Nicaraguan government before the World Court—were subject to tax audits (Subcommittee on Civil and Constitutional Rights 1987: 158, 204, 248; Kornbluh 1987: 165). Witness for Peace organizer Sam Hope said (1992), "Whenever any government agency, the IRS or whoever, could make us do more paperwork, they did. There was always some bureaucrat or agent looking over our shoulder or questioning us about something or other. We ended up spending an inordinate amount of time doing government paperwork and other red tape."

Many Central America peace activists also experienced odd troubles with their telephones which suggested that they were being tapped by unknown surveillance agents. For example, when on September 13, 1986, a North Carolina activist made a telephone call, she heard a recording of a phone conversation she had had five months earlier. On July 29, 1986, when the travel agent of a New York legal-rights activist attempted to call her at home, a man answered, saying, "I'm her boyfriend and a policeman, I'll take a message." The activist had been alone at home at the time, her phone never rang, and her answering machine, which was turned on, had given two clicks but recorded no message. On November 11, 1985, a Wisconsin graduate student, who had done support work in Tucson during the Sanctuary trials, had a telephone conversation with a newspaper reporter about the trials interrupted by a male voice, which said, "Are you two girls still fooling around with those stories?" In subsequent conversations, loud clanking noises on her telephone line forced her to end similar conversations. In October 1985, a woman worker at the Pittsburgh Thomas Merton Center answered her telephone at home only to hear a recording of a conversation that had taken place earlier at the Center. And, on May 5, 1985, a telephone conversation between two journalists about an article they were writing on "Nicaragua and FBI Harassment" was interrupted by voices heard in the background commenting on their conversation (Subcommittee on Civil and Constitutional Rights 1987: 246, 247, 251, 255, 261).

According to Ken Butigan (1991), "Our phones at the Pledge were tapped from the beginning. In Washington, whenever we were organizing a big event, for three weeks before hand, my phone would have so much popping and snapping on it you could hardly talk. Plus, there would be harassing callers bothering us all day long."

Anne Shumway recalled (1990), "Our office phones were definitely tapped. On the week before any action, they would always begin acting up."

Finally, numerous Central America activists also reported hundreds of incidents of tampering and interference with their mail. For example, when Sara Murray, a staff worker with the Michigan Interfaith Committee on Central American Rights, sent three separate first-class mailings to constituents in a period of two months, only one out of one hundred letters was ever delivered (Burnham 1985). The Central America organization Nicaraguan Interfaith Committee for Action (NICA) experienced seventeen separate incidents of mail tampering. In April 1986, for example, two letters sent to NICA's travel agency with correct return addresses—one contained a check for a scholarship participant's airfare to Nicaragua, the other an airline ticket being returned for a refund—were never received nor returned. Many other activists discovered movement newsletters taking months to be delivered, letters they sent to established movement organizations returned and stamped "Return to Sender, Address Not Known," letters "accidentally" routed to IRS offices which opened them and stamped "Opened in Error, IRS" before returning them, and letters destroyed or opened by unknown parties, resealed with tape, and stamped "Damaged in Handling in the U.S. Postal Service" (Subcommittee on Civil and Constitutional Rights 1987: 204–5, 242–68; Gelbspan 1991: 28). Both the IRS and Postal Service, however, denied having tampered with mail for political reasons.

Witness for Peace organizer Mike Clark recalls one incident which seems to indicate the practice of some form of international covert surveillance, such as mail tampering, of Witness for Peace delegates (1992):

> Paul Fischer, one of our long-termers, was kidnapped by the Contras in the Fall of 1987 and held captive. Paul had just been through a difficult divorce and was quite emotionally unstable at the time. The Contras did a kind of mind rape on him, telling him things like they had just seen his wife on TV saying she wanted to reconcile with him if he were released. The Contras knew intimate things about the internal dynamics of his marriage, things he had written to his ex-wife but that no one, not even we, knew about. The Contras, in the middle of nowhere in Honduras, were using this to manipulate him as they pleased. Question: how did they know this stuff if long-termers' letters were not being opened? That freaked us out. It was mind-numbing. The Contras knew details about Paul's personal life that even members of his close community didn't know.

Information Gathering

Another common anti-movement activity employed against the Central America peace movement by a host of governmental and private organizations was information gathering. Applying techniques developed for criminal investigations, the FBI and other organizations—in addition to seizing the materials of travelers, questioning activists and their associates, and monitoring telephone calls, as noted above—hired informers, posed as journalists, and staked out leaders' homes to gather information, collected organizations' membership lists, photographed demonstrations, recorded the automobile license-plate numbers of protesters, collected movement literature, searched through activists' trash, reviewed their utility bills, and collected other personal information on activists for files. The purpose of this information gathering appears to have been to uncover potential subversion and political violence, to gather names for counterintelligence computer banks, to consolidate evidence for possible criminal charges, and to harass Central America peace activists.

In 1981, the FBI began a criminal investigation of CISPES, a major opponent of the administration's El Salvador policy. When that investigation failed to produce evidence that CISPES was an undeclared agent of the Salvadoran rebels, the investigation was reclassified as a "counterterrorism" probe, giving FBI agents greater leeway to investigate the activities of U.S. citizens (Lacayo 1988: 33; Subcommittee on Civil and Constitutional Rights 1988: 19–22). Twelve hundred pages of FBI documents obtained in 1988 through the Freedom of Information Act by the Center for Constitutional Rights revealed that between 1981 and 1985 the CISPES investigation had expanded into a major FBI domestic surveillance operation (Gelbspan 1991: 209). The original CISPES probe spawned 178 separate spinoff investigations, involving all fifty-nine of the FBI's field offices, which scrutinized 2,370 individuals and 1,330 organizations (Mills 1988b; Lacayo 1988; Shenon 1988b, 1988c). Any individual or group that had contact with CISPES was subject to investigation, including church, human rights, peace, labor union, college, and academic organizations (Mills 1988a; Gelbspan 1988c). Groups investigated included the Southern Christian Leadership Conference, the Maryknoll Sisters, the United Auto Workers, the American Federation of Teachers, the U.S. Catholic Bishops Conference, as well as many hundreds of Central America peace organizations (Gordon 1989; *New York Times* 1988c; Shenon 1988a; Cockburn 1989; Hitchens 1988). Although these FBI investigations were officially closed down in 1985, some evidence indicates that the FBI continued to gather information on Central America peace organizations in the years that followed (see, for example, Cockburn 1989).

In addition to investigations performed by their own agents, the FBI employed a variety of private groups to gather information on Central America peace activists and donors. The FBI, for example, hired members of the Collegiate Association for the Research of Principles (CARP), a university-campus organization affiliated with the Reverend Sun Myung Moon's Unification Church, to collect information on the Central America movement. The FBI also gathered information through the research arms of conservative groups such as the Young Americas Foundation and the Council for Inter-American Security and through publications such as *Review of the News,* a John

Birch Society paper, and *Information Digest*, the journal of the ultra-conservative foundation Western Goals, which maintains a computerized database of U.S. leftists and subversives. In addition, the FBI cooperated with and received information, directly and indirectly, from local police intelligence divisions in many cities. In January 1983, for example, a detective in the intelligence division of the Los Angeles Police Department was discovered transferring 180 boxes worth of data on political activists—more than five thousand files in all—to a variety of law enforcement and right-wing organizations, including Western Goals (Gelbspan 1988a, 1988b, 1991: 73–84, 204, 169–70; also see Webster 1984: 11).

When the FBI investigations became public in early 1988, FBI officials denied that they were politically motivated or engineered by the White House. "Nothing could be further from the truth," claimed Oliver Revell, the FBI's executive assistant director. According to Revell, FBI headquarters instructed its field offices on several occasions to take care not to violate U.S. citizens' constitutional rights. When pressed on the matter at a hearing of the Senate Select Committee on Intelligence, however, Revell conceded, "We may have seen some wavering over that line." In September 1988, the FBI's director, William Sessions, acknowledged "mistakes in judgment" by investigators, disciplined seven FBI agents, and offered to hear requests on a case by case basis to expunge from FBI files the names of people and organizations investigated (Mills 1988a, 1988b; Corn and Morley 1988; Shenon 1988c, 1988d; *New York Times* 1988j).

Sabotaging the Credibility of the Movement and Its Allies

Opponents of the peace movement attempted in a variety of ways to damage the credibility of individuals and organizations within or sympathetic to the movement. They did so in order to delegitimate the movement's political analysis in the public's eye, to neutralize newly exposed information that would damage the cause of administration policy, and to divert the movement's energies away from proactive political campaigns into defensive reputation maintenance.

One tactic used to undermine movement credibility was impugning the political integrity of movement supporters. This often took the form of suggesting that White House opponents were communists or communist sympathizers. For example, in one *Washington Post* editorial published shortly before a key Contra aid vote in Congress, White House Communications Director Patrick Buchanan wrote

(1986), "By cutting arms shipments to Nicaragua's freedom fighters, by tying the president's hands with the Boland amendment, the national Democratic Party has now become, with Moscow, co-guarantor of the Brezhnev doctrine in Central America. . . . With the vote on contra aid, the Democratic Party will reveal whether it stands with Ronald Reagan and the resistance—or Daniel Ortega and the communists."[1]

FBI agents questioning movement activists often implied or charged that the activists, their associates, or the organizations they supported were communist or communist-infiltrated (see, for instance, Sklar 1988: 357; Gelbspan 1985). Special Assistant U.S. Attorney Donald Reno, who prosecuted the Tucson Sanctuary activists, showed journalists, during the trials, a photograph of one defendant, Catholic nun Darlene Nicgorski, standing next to Tomás Borge, Nicaragua's Minister of the Interior, taken during a tour of nuns visiting Nicaragua, as proof of a link between Sanctuary activists and "Communist guerrillas down in Central America." Reno believed that Sanctuary was simply, at bottom, a conspiracy to smuggle "real hard-core Marxists" into the U.S. (Crittenden 1988: 200, 155). Anti-movement publications often labeled movement activists communism's "useful idiots" and the Central America peace movement "the Red Chorus," "communism's second front," and "the Revolution Lobby" (see, among other works, Tyson 1986; Winsor 1987; Powell 1986). In the editorial quoted above, for example, Patrick Buchanan (1986) derided "the 'useful idiots' of Lenin's depiction—the liberated nuns and Marxist Maryknolls . . . and tenured professors anxious to wow the coeds with how they picked coffee beans for the revolution." And many private organizations, from the Institute for Religion and Democracy to *Soldier of Fortune* magazine, constantly castigated in print Central America peace groups, such as Witness for Peace, as "socialist pawns" and "Sandinista sympathizers" (Hope 1992; Crites 1992).

Analogous efforts to discredit the Central America peace movement involved attempts to associate administration opponents and movement organizations with terrorism. FBI documents released in 1988 revealed that FBI agents investigating the movement had compiled a "terrorist photo album" containing seven hundred entries. Among them were Senators Christopher Dodd and Claiborne Pell, Representatives Michael Barnes and Patricia Schroeder, and former Ambassador to El Salvador Robert White—all administration opponents—who were described as having "terrorist tendencies" (Gelb-span 1991: 67–102). In 1987, John Ryan, an FBI agent sympathetic to the Central America movement, was fired for refusing to investigate an incident of minor vandalism that took place during a Central America protest because it was to be investigated as a case of "domestic terrorism/domestic violence," which carried long prison terms (Kurkjian 1987). A representative FBI report on a 1986 Pledge of Resistance demonstration in Chicago was titled "Nicaraguan Terrorist Matters: International Terrorism—Nicaragua" (Gelbspan 1988c: 16; also see Millman 1984: 10; Leahy 1987: 239).[2] And an INS proposal to fund an undercover investigation of Tucson Sanctuary activists stated: "Information has been received that indicates some of the persons they have moved are terrorists" (Crittenden 1988: 143).

The White House and private conservative organizations also took aim at journalists and academics who criticized the administration's Central American policy. For example, when in March 1986 noted U.C.L.A. Latin Americanist E. Bradford Burns published an article in the journal *Nicaraguan Perspectives*, critiquing U.S. policy in Central America, President Reagan, at a national press luncheon, publicly accused Burns of "dispersing disinformation." "God help" Burns' students, declared the President, if this was the kind of thing he was teaching them (Leahy 1987: 240–41; see Roark 1986). In 1985, a newly formed group, Accuracy in Academia, began monitoring university professors for teaching "incorrect information" that would harm U.S. national security (Meyer 1985). Their initial "secret target list" consisted of "a list of professors who had endorsed a rally opposing U.S. involvement in Central America" (Ledbetter 1985: 15). In 1986, Accuracy in Academia published a list of academics who they judged taught politically menacing "bad facts." The list included, for example, Cynthia McClintock of George Washington University, because she showed in a course a film that was critical of the Nicaraguan Contras (Leahy 1987: 239; also see Lewis 1986a).[3] In 1985, the Institute for Religion and Democracy published a Special Report which accused the Sanctuary movement of having a hidden political agenda, of having no biblical or historical basis for providing sanctuary to refugees, and of misleading the American public about danger to Central American lives (Golden and McConnell 1986: 93). In 1986, the administration circulated to congressional leaders a classified CIA document purportedly captured from the Sandinistas naming U.S. citizens and journalists who the Sandinistas planned to use in a campaign of "disinformation" to influence votes on Contra aid. Assistant Secretary of State for Inter-American Affairs Elliott Abrams argued: "What we're talking about is simply information about how elaborate and skillful" the Sandinistas are in "manipulating the Congress and the press." Some Americans, he said, "would be shocked to find their names appearing in such a document as people the Sandinistas plan to use" (Robinson 1986). Chairman of the Senate Intelligence Committee, Republican Senator David Durenberger, however, with many others, denounced the document, charging that the administration was "outrageous . . . to portray every senator and congressman who votes against lethal aid as a stooge of communism" (Jacoby and Parry 1987).

Other instances of sabotaging the credibility of the Central America peace movement and its allies sprang from the need to neutralize information damaging to White House policy. One case—in which the FBI discredited one of its own ex-agents who threatened to go public with detailed, inside knowledge of FBI misconduct—is particularly instructive. Frank Varelli was an FBI agent who had been a central figure in the four-year undercover investigation of the movement's organizations. In mid-1984, Varelli had met with U.S. Secret Service agents to discuss a report he had written on the possibility of a Libyan or Iranian assassination attempt on President Reagan during the Republican national convention. He had learned that CISPES members were considering blocking the President's motorcade and spraying red paint on his limousine to draw attention to the war in El Salvador. Varelli feared the theoretical possibility that Libyan or Iranian assassins might infiltrate the CISPES leadership and exploit the blockade plan to fire a rocket mortar at the President's car. In preparation for his meeting with the Secret Service, Varelli had taken a standard FBI lie-detector test, which showed no deception on Varelli's part (Gelbspan 1991: 178–81).[4] Two months later, Frank Varelli resigned his position after concluding that the FBI was more interested in obstructing the Central America peace movement than in countering communist terrorism and when his case agent, Daniel Flanagan, illegally withheld his compensation payments.

In 1987, Frank Varelli agreed to testify before a House Judicial Subcommittee on Civil and Constitutional Rights about FBI misdeeds during the CISPES investigation. Varelli's testimony of extensive FBI misconduct would have implicated numerous high-ranking FBI officials in criminal activities, harmed the FBI's reputation, and vindicated and bolstered the cause of many Central America peace movement organizations (Gordon 1987; Berman 1987). To neutralize Varelli, the FBI sabotaged his testimony. They altered the results of his 1984 polygraph test to show that Varelli had lied numerous times.[5] And they altered Varelli's 1984 report on the CISPES blockade to make it say that CISPES members themselves intended to "assassinate" the President during his arrival rather than, as he originally wrote, to "disrupt" the President's arrival. When congressional staff members questioned FBI officials about Varelli's allegations prior to the hearings, they were shown the altered polygraph results and warned not to trust Varelli because he was a habitual liar (Gelbspan 1991: 181). And when, during the hearings, Varelli testified that he never actually witnessed CISPES members commit any illegal acts, Representative James Sensenbrenner, a conservative Republican member of the subcommittee, contradicted him by producing the altered report which stated that CISPES had been planning to assassinate President Reagan in 1984 (Subcommittee on Civil and Constitutional Rights 1987: 172, 427–34, 440). Varelli protested vehemently that the report had been altered, and Varelli's lawyer charged, "This is a glaring attempt by the Bureau to rewrite history three years after the fact." But it was too late. Despite the existence of other evidence corroborating his claims, Varelli's credibility had been successfully torpedoed and his testimony shattered.[6] In the news, Varelli immediately became labeled "the discredited informer" who had "recanted many of his statements" (see, for instance, Shenon 1988c; Mills 1988b). Congressional committee members who had strongly suspected FBI impropriety, led by Subcommittee Chairman Representative Don Edwards, backed away from their investigation.

Finally, in September 1988, then FBI Director William Sessions made a full report on the CISPES investigation to both the Senate Intelligence Committee and the House Judiciary Subcommittee on Civil and Constitutional Rights, in which he laid blame for the ill-fated investigation squarely on the shoulders of Frank Varelli and on the naïveté of FBI managers in trusting Varelli's reports (Subcommittee on Civil and Constitutional Rights 1988: 116–56; also see Mills 1988b; Gordon 1989; Corn and Morley 1988b). Sessions stated (Subcomittee on Civil and Constitutional Rights 1988: 118):

> The case pivoted on the information Varelli provided. His background and reliability were never investigated adequately and during much of

the investigation the accuracy of Varelli's information was not adequately verified. . . . Absent the information provided by Frank Varelli,
there would not have been sufficient predication for an international terrorism investigation of CISPES. . . . By the time it was realized that Varelli's information was unreliable, the investigation had been under way for
approximately one year. The investigation would not have developed as
it did had Varelli's reliability been properly scrutinized at the outset.

Despite the fact that this plainly contradicted the FBI's actual estimation and handling of Varelli over a three-year period (see, for instance,
Gordon 1987: 289; Gelbspan 1991: 115–17), Chairman of the House
Judiciary Subcommittee on Civil and Constitutional Rights Don
Edwards complimented Sessions for "a very honest, forthright, hard-
hitting statement and the work you did. Your testimony today was very
comforting" (Shenon 1988d). Thus, with congressional acquiescence,
by sabotaging Frank Varelli's testimony the FBI dodged both his very
damaging allegations and responsibility for their scandalous investigation and deprived Central America peace activists of explosive revelations that would have validated and bolstered their movement.[7]

Another instance of sabotaging movement credibility springing
from the need to neutralize information damaging to the White House
involved a Contra kidnapping of a Witness for Peace delegation. On
August 8, 1985—the same day that President Reagan authorized the
first transfer of arms to Iran—a Witness for Peace delegation traveling
by boat down the San Juan River on a three-day "Peace Flotilla" was
fired upon, kidnapped, and held at gunpoint overnight by a regiment
of Eden Pastora's Contra forces (Kinzer 1985a, 1985b; *New York
Times* 1985j, 1985k, 1985l). Since two of the delegates were able to
report the emergency by ham radio to the Witness for Peace office in
Managua before being seized by the Contras, and since the delegation
was being accompanied by more than a dozen U.S. news reporters and
photographers, the kidnapping represented a potential public relations disaster for the White House. The Contras seemed to be demonstrating for the world firsthand that they were, indeed, dangerous terrorists. Worse, seconds before the boat's ham radio signal went dead,
the radio listeners in Managua heard machine-gun shots.[8] It seemed to
all the staff members and reporters who heard the recording of the
transmission that the Contras had executed the entire delegation. In
response, Nicaraguan President Daniel Ortega made an uninvited

and, for Witness for Peace, ill-conceived visit to the organization's Managua office to offer his condolences and support (Griffin-Nolan 1991: 137–56).

Upon hearing the news, the Witness for Peace offices in Washington and Managua immediately held press conferences. The kidnapping story received heavy print and television news coverage. That evening's *New York Post*'s headlines, like many, read, "29 Yanks Held in Jungle." According to Marker, "All the television networks sent portable-dish trucks for interviews and we were all over the news. The first day's stories were very accurate, basically saying, 'the Contras kidnapped these people and may be killing them.'" Marker continued (1992):

> The next day, it all hit the fan. And I discovered the full effect of the administration's power. All of a sudden, I couldn't get a phone call returned. Journalists I had worked with for three years, who had trusted me, wouldn't talk to me or return my calls. I mean, it was like running 100 miles an hour into a brick wall. Like being run over by a truck while sitting in my living room. I literally could not figure it out. I asked people what was going on, but they wouldn't say.

It turned out that someone at a State Department briefing had made an off-the-record comment that he had heard that the whole kidnapping had been planned by Dennis Marker and Daniel Ortega as a publicity stunt. And this ended the story's threat to the White House, as the news media began reporting the State Department's off-the-record allegation as fact. Journalists immediately began frantically searching for slight inconsistencies in Witness for Peace's handling of the incident, which they took as evidence discrediting the organization. ABC-TV's Peter Collins reported a groundless story from Nicaragua that the Sandinistas were preparing a reception for the delegation even before they were released. Newspapers across the country printed photos of Daniel Ortega sitting in the Witness for Peace Managua office. Political cartoonists began depicting the delegation as "Witless for Peace." And the *New York Post*'s August 9 headline, like others, read, "Yanks Duped by Reds." By the time the released delegation finally returned safely to their port of departure in mid-afternoon on August 9, not one news reporter was there to meet them at the dock. The dozen journalists accompanying the delegation were stunned to discover not only that no one was interested in their version of the ordeal, but that it was no longer even a newsworthy story, as media attention had turned to a plane crash in Japan and the major-league baseball strike (Griffin-Nolan 1991: 155). Later Marker was to say (1992), "That bit of State Department disinformation was a contingency plan. And this was the day. The kidnapping story was either going to be that you can't control the Contras because they in fact are terrorists. Or else that Witness for Peace is mighty suspicious, maybe commies. So they used that moment to deal with us. Certainly, all it took was a simple phone call from the White House requesting an off-the-record remark and we were basically wiped off the board."

According to Marker (1992), organizationally, the experience permanently damaged Witness for Peace:

> We never fully recovered. In a flash, we had gone from being the truthful opposition to being "suspected." Sandinista sympathizers at the very least. That affected us at all levels—national, regional, and state. Before, any local newspaper was going to cover Anne Smith traveling to Nicaragua with this group. Now, they have to say, "Well, gee, I wonder if she's a dupe?" We would still get covered. But the larger effect was like that of any good slander campaign, you know, "Do you still beat your wife?"

Disrupting Demonstrations

Occasionally, opponents of the Central America peace movement, especially private groups, attempted to disrupt movement campaigns by provoking extraneous conflict and violence during rallies and demonstrations. These disruptions usually were incited by antagonistic counterdemonstrators, not covert *agents provocateurs*. Tactically, such disruptions diverted the focus of protests away from substantive political issues and helped to create an unfavorable public image of the movement as fostering civil disorder. Virtually all Central America peace movement organizations were officially nonviolent in philosophy and trained their members in the tactics of nonviolent direct action, including appropriate responses to provocations (see, for instance, Emergency Response Network 1986: 40–50). Nevertheless, the intense emotions and tensions inherent in political protests lent themselves to verbal altercations and even violence. At a 1981 protest against U.S. policy in El Salvador during a Syracuse University commencement speech by Secretary of State Alexander Haig, for example, clashes between Haig supporters and 150 protesters erupted into shouting matches, multiple fist fights, and arrests for disorderly conduct (*New York Times* 1981m).

Members of the Collegiate Association for the Research of Principles (CARP), the university affiliate of the Reverend Sun Myung Moon's Unification Church, were particularly notorious for organizing counterdemonstrations and otherwise disrupting Central America peace movement demonstrations (see, for example, de Onis 1981e). According to FBI documents, CARP members—who ex-FBI agent Frank Varelli claims were paid by the FBI—regularly threw rocks and started fights at CISPES rallies and demonstrations (Gelbspan 1991: 76). Joseph Crews, attorney for the Southern Methodist University chapter of CISPES, recounted (quoted in Gelbspan 1988b: 6), "The Moonies were very confrontative. Most of it was verbal, but it got close to fighting a couple of times. On one occasion, we formed a human barrier between them and our own people."

Jim Rice, of *Sojourners* magazine and community, recalled of Pledge of Resistance protests (1992): "We would run into chanting Moonie-types who would come to demonstrations and were pretty aggravating and argumentative. I often had to play the role of peacekeeper, spending several hours keeping the two groups separate and defusing altercations."[9]

Group Infiltrations

Numerous Central America peace movement groups were penetrated by undercover operatives—typically FBI or INS agents and informers—who posed as concerned activists in order to infiltrate the Central America organizations and spy from the inside on movement activities. The primary motive for this clandestine surveillance was to gather possible evidence of criminal wrongdoing. A secondary but often more damaging effect was to erode mutual trust between activists and curtail the free flow of information within the movement organizations.

The details of most cases of undercover agents penetrating Central America organizations remain obscure. In some cases, organizations strongly suspected, but had no hard evidence of, having been infiltrated. Witness for Peace leaders, for example, believe—but cannot prove—that they had hired what turned out to be a saboteur posing as a sympathetic professional fund-raiser who intentionally bungled a major Witness for Peace fund-raising event, causing their organization considerable embarrassment and financial liability (Hope 1992). In other cases, all that is known is that some unknown individual within a Central America organization was spying for a government agency. In 1985, for example, after having been burglarized five times in one year, the Old Cambridge Baptist Church of Cambridge, Massachusetts, filed a Freedom of Information Act request with the FBI. The request was denied, however, because, as the FBI explained in writing, disclosure of the relevant files might "reveal the identity of an individual who has furnished information to the FBI under confidential circumstances" (Kohn 1986: 75). In yet other cases, no more than a few specifics about internal spying are known. The 1987 Tower Commission Report on the Iran-Contra scandal, for example, revealed that a CIA agent posing as a journalist was planted in the Witness for Peace Rio San Juan "Peace Flotilla" delegation that was captured by the Contras. Specifically, the report disclosed that when the boat was seized, the CIA Station Chief in Nicaragua, Joe Fernandez, called Contra leader Edén Pastora to warn him not to harm anyone on the boat because a CIA agent was among the delegates. Witness for Peace organizers believe they know which delegate was the CIA agent. But it remains unclear whether he infiltrated the delegation simply to observe activities or actually to provoke a politically damaging incident (Griffin-Nolan 1991: 141).

Two documented cases of covert spying on Central America peace organizations do exist which shed considerable light on such undercover surveillance campaigns. We know of their details only because, in one case, evidence gathered through the covert investigation was used to prosecute Sanctuary activists and because, in the other case, an FBI agent went public with his inside knowledge of FBI undercover surveillance activities (Subcommittee on Civil and Constitutional Rights 1987: 206–9).

"Operation Sojourner," the INS undercover surveillance program that investigated the Sanctuary movement, began in March 1984. Early that year, orders came from high-level INS officials, possibly through the Justice Department, to James Rayburn, a Phoenix INS investigator, approving a covert investigation of the Tucson Sanctuary churches. Rayburn had been following the Sanctuary movement, which had received much media attention, for two years. Now he was assigned to organize a covert surveillance program to infiltrate the movement. The purpose of Operation Sojourner, as Rayburn began to envision it, was not simply to break up an immigrant-smuggling ring, but to determine the "true purpose" of the movement (Rayburn suspected drug smuggling), to ascertain whether it constituted a threat to U.S. sovereignty, and to "neutralize" the positive media publicity Sanctuary had been receiving (Tomsho 1987: 161; Crittenden 1988: 190).

Rayburn employed five informants—Jesus Cruz, Salomon Graham, Lee Morgan, John Nixon, and "Gina Sanchez"—to masquerade as Sanctuary activists, infiltrate the movement, and spend the next ten months gathering evidence of criminal wrongdoing.[10] Jesus Cruz, who was Rayburn's primary informant, became a regular Sanctuary volunteer, helping to transport illegal refugees.[11] Cruz used telephone and body bugs to secretly tape-record more than one hundred church meetings, Bible studies, and private conversations with activists (King 1985; Taylor 1985; Tomsho 1987: 160, 165; Crittenden 1988: 132, 143, 179–87; Tolan and Bassett 1985). To obtain the full addresses of refugees aided by Sanctuary, Cruz called refugee families and told the parents that he wanted to send their children Christmas presents but that to do so he needed their mailing addresses (Davidson 1988: 117). The informants also recorded the license-plate numbers of vehicles parked in church parking lots during what they thought were "political" church services (Crittenden 1988: 186). There were no limits placed on the extent of Cruz's surveillance, and some of the informant's covert activities were unauthorized and improper (see, for instance, Crittenden 1988: 132, 139, 154, 225, 262; Tomsho 1987: 166). Violations of undercover guidelines were fostered by the fact that Cruz was being paid according to the amount of information he gathered, which gave him an incentive to exaggerate, entrap, and lie about what he had observed (Crittenden 1988: 256; Davidson 1988: 117). Many Sanctuary activists were suspicious of the informants from the start, especially of Morgan and Nixon, but decided to maintain an open posture to avoid a "witch hunt" mentality within Sanctuary (Davidson 1988: 88; Crittenden 1988: 163–64). In addition to the informants' spying, Operation Sojourner sought search warrants for churches, the office of the Chicago Religious Task Force on Central America, and the homes of Sanctuary activists. Sanctuary organizer Darlene Nicgorski's apartment was searched and videotaped by INS agents for possible incriminating evidence (Crittenden 1988: 189–91, 200). In the end, Operation Sojourner resulted in the indictment, arrests, trial, and conviction of eleven Arizona Sanctuary activists.

The second documented case of covert spying on Central America peace organizations involves the FBI operative Frank Varelli, who was that agency's key undercover informant in the CISPES investigation. Frank Varelli was born into a powerful Salvadoran family, son of a former director of the Salvadoran Military Training Academy, who had also been the head of the Salvadoran National Police, Minister of the Interior, and Ambassador to Guatemala. As a young man, Varelli became a born-again Protestant evangelist, preaching Christ as savior and communism as anti-Christ to crowds of tens of thousands. After an unsuccessful attempt in 1980 by FMLN soldiers to assassinate Varelli's father at home—Varelli himself participated in the deadly gun battle—Varelli's family, seeking a safer environment, emigrated to Los Angeles. Shortly thereafter, Varelli was approached by FBI agents and asked if he wanted to participate in a major FBI investigation of Salvadoran terrorism. Varelli was enthusiastic. Soon, Varelli and his family moved to Dallas, location of the FBI field office that was to coordinate the investigation. Within days, Varelli was contacted by FBI special counterterrorism agent Daniel Flanagan, who gave Varelli a new identity and put him to work (Subcommittee on Civil and Constitutional Rights 1987: 435; Gelbspan 1991: 35–36).

Varelli, it turned out, was a well-chosen operative. He was a devoted anti-communist, committed to fighting leftist terrorism on every front. His family background guaranteed Varelli access to the highest levels of El Salvador's political, military, and security agencies. Also, his experience as an evangelist had honed his abilities to read human motives, establish rapport with strangers, and communicate his message to skeptics. Varelli quickly put these assets to use.

To Central America peace movement activists, Varelli became "Gilberto Mendoza," a poor Salvadoran political-asylum applicant whose family had been murdered by death squads in El Salvador. Under this cover, Varelli quickly established himself as an eager volunteer in a number of Central America organizations. From that position, he began gathering and analyzing piles of movement literature and collecting and filing the names, addresses, and phone numbers of every activist possible (English 1989; Gelbspan 1991: 60–65). Varelli also used his family connections to open back channels of communication with intelligence agencies in El Salvador (Berman 1987: 6). Through contacts in the Salvadoran military and police, Varelli obtained lists of Salvadoran leftists who had fled to the U.S. He also gathered similar information from conservative Salvadoran think tanks and paramilitary groups and from fourteen well-placed intelligence sources Varelli personally recruited during a visit to El Salvador (Gelbspan 1991: 55, 58). Varelli fed all of this information to the FBI. According to Varelli, "The Bureau wanted to know who was wanted by the [Salvadoran] National Guard and whether there were organizations in the U.S. against Reagan's policy in El Salvador that had contacts with the same elements in El Salvador that the National Guard was seeking" (Bielski, Forster, and Bernstein 1987: 18; Subcommittee on Civil and Constitutional Rights 1987: 436).

In turn, Varelli passed U.S. intelligence information back to his Salvadoran contacts (Shenon 1988d). For example, Varelli regularly transmitted to a close family friend in the Salvadoran National Guard information on Americans considered to be administration opponents who were traveling to El Salvador and INS data on Salvadorans being deported from the U.S. (Berman 1987: 6; Subcommittee on Civil and Constitutional Rights 1987: 437). Varelli supplemented the later information by arranging for flight lists of all passengers traveling to El Salvador with TACA, El Salvador's national airline, to be surreptitiously passed to the Salvadoran National Guard by an undercover FBI agent he helped secure a job at TACA's main office in Houston, and by personal friends who worked at TACA's Los Angeles office (Gelbspan 1991: 132–34). According to Varelli, this information was used by military-linked Salvadoran death squads to assassinate deportees considered to be leftist subversives (Berman 1987: 6; Subcommittee on Civil and Constitutional Rights 1987: 437–38).

In the course of his three-year involvement in the undercover investigation, Varelli developed a crash-course curriculum on Central American terrorism for FBI counterterrorism agents, and collaborated with a private network of conservative Salvadoran expatriate businessmen, based in Miami, who organized and financed an association of anti-communist cell groups to monitor, spy on, and harass Central America peace activists (Gelbspan 1991: 97–99, 110, 102–4). In one instance, Varelli attempted to gain access to the publishing materials and letterhead of left-wing activist Gene Lantz, who published the *Hard Times News,* to covertly disseminate incriminating evidence, to ruin Lantz (Gelbspan 1991: 125, 130). In another instance, Varelli's colleagues designed a plan in which Varelli would rent an apartment next to Catholic Sister Linda Hajek, the head of the Dallas chapter of CISPES. Varelli would then establish a relationship with her, invite her over, and attempt to seduce her, while other FBI agents would videotape the encounter. "Once we do it," Varelli's colleagues told him, "we will have her in our hands" (Berman 1987: 9). Varelli claims to have declined participating in the plan. Varelli's investigation eventually proliferated into 178 separate spinoff investigations, involving all of the FBI's field offices, which scrutinized 2,370 individuals and 1,330 organizations (Mills 1988b; Lacayo 1988; Shenon 1988c).

Break-Ins

Central America peace movement organizations experienced an epidemic of political break-ins between 1984 and 1990. In more than 140 separate documented incidents around the U.S., unknown intruders broke into and ransacked the offices, churches, and homes of Central America activists (MSN 1989; Subcommittee on Civil and Constitutional Rights 1987: 209–15; Glick 1989: 2; Marker 1992; Hope 1992; Guise 1990). Over the course of these episodes, a distinct pattern emerged, indicating that these were not common property burglaries, but politically motivated break-ins intended to intimidate, obstruct, and gather information on anti-administration activists (Hirshson 1988; Schneider 1986; Kohn 1986; Sklar 1988: 351–52; Gelbspan 1984, 1985b, 1987e, 1991: 219–21; Leahy 1987: 234). The targets of the break-ins were always opponents of White House Central America policy, usually, it was later revealed, the same groups that had been under FBI surveillance. Break-ins were especially likely to occur when the individual or group targeted had either been recently quoted in a newspaper story on Central America or was away traveling in Central America. In almost every case, accessible office equipment, cash, and other items of monetary, but not political, value were left untouched. However, organizations' mailing lists, computer records, photographs, undeveloped film, correspondences, and documents on file were ransacked, stolen, or destroyed. Typically, the break-ins appeared to have been the work of professionals, experienced with disabling locks and evading and incapacitating burglar alarms. The burglars seemed to know both the activists' schedules and the exact nature and locations of the documents and records they were looking for. After one break-in at the International Center for Development Policy, for example, Jack Terrell, a senior analyst at the center, remarked (quoted in Schneider 1986), "It appears they knew exactly where to go. . . . Whoever it was did a professional job. I would bet $10,000 to a doughnut that we had a photographic intelligence mission run on us. It looks like they took pictures of every document in my office."[12]

In some cases, the trespassers left threatening messages behind. At the Central America Refugee Project in Phoenix, for example, intruders left behind bloody handprints smeared on the walls (Davidson 1988: 113).

The break-ins began in December 1983, starting with the offices of the Guatemala News and Information Center in Oakland, California. Bookkeeping records and mailing lists were stolen and files were rifled, but petty cash and office equipment were left untouched (MSN 1989: 59). The next years witnessed a flood of break-ins, of which the following are a few examples (MSN 1989: 37, 49, 57; Gelbspan 1991: 203, 1986a). In October 1984, an apartment on the premises of the First Methodist Church in Germantown, Pennsylvania, that housed a Guatemalan refugee family—whose father would later become an unindicted co-conspirator in the Arizona Sanctuary trials—was broken into. A list of all Sanctuary activists who assisted their travels from Arizona to Philadelphia was stolen, along with letters showing the addresses of their families in Guatemala. In November 1985, a list of fifteen hundred donors and activists involved in Central America issues was stolen from the Los Angeles office of a human rights organization. On May 10, 1986, intruders ransacked and tried to set fire to the home of one of the Sanctuary trial defendants while she was attending a pre-sentencing hearing in Phoenix. The intruders entered through a hole they cut in the bedroom wall, poisoned her dog, and rifled through her files. On May 17, 1987, staff at the New Institute of Central America in Cambridge, Massachusetts, found in their office their map of Nicaragua ripped off the wall, torn in pieces, and lying on the floor, and muriatic acid poured on forty computer disks containing information on the programs of other Central America solidarity groups. That was the Institute's eighth of nine eventual break-ins in three years. Occasionally, activists' automobiles were also targeted. On April 4, 1987, Catherine Suitor, a Los Angeles CISPES staff member, discovered her car had been forced open. Seven hundred dollars' worth of new clothes had been searched but left behind. All that was taken was an overcoat of a CISPES colleague containing in its pocket a list of solidarity organizations in Europe. And on March 23, 1987, while Glynnis Golden, coordinator of the AFSC Central America Program in Pasadena, California, spent one hour in the office of a Central America organization, burglars stole from her car sixty to seventy pounds of files on sanctuary and refugee assistance groups. An expensive stereo, jewelry, and a watch were left untouched (Gelbspan 1991: 31).

Local police—preoccupied with what they considered to be more serious crimes and skeptical about political motives—almost always declined to investigate these break-ins. The FBI consistently claimed the burglaries were not within their authority to investigate, since they did not involve felonies (Gelbspan 1986b).[13] In only one of the more than 140 cases of political burglary and vandalism were suspects identified or arrested (Subcommittee on Civil and Constitutional Rights 1987: 215).

Non-Arrests, Arrests, and Prosecutions

State authorities skillfully employed the power to arrest to thwart and intimidate Central America peace activists. Particularly effective in many cases were tactical decisions *not* to arrest protesting Central America demonstrators. Employing a tactical maneuver adroitly utilized in 1961 by the police chief of Albany, Georgia, Laurie Prichett, against civil rights demonstrators, municipal and federal police in many cities neutralized the effectiveness of the Central America peace movement's mass civil-disobedience campaigns by avoiding arresting protesters: "One of the tactics of the justice department and other agencies, which differed from the 1960s, was to trivialize our civil disobedience so it didn't have an impact on the press. We had lots of protesters not being arrested at all, or being arrested but detained only two hours or not detained at all. This was a conscious strategy to foil us, which worked fairly well" (Butigan 1991).

One example of non-arrest as an anti-movement tactic involved the Boston-area Pledge of Resistance. On May 7, 1985, more than twenty-six hundred Boston-area Central America activists converged on Boston's John F. Kennedy Federal Office Building to stage a mass protest against the Reagan-declared national emergency which imposed economic sanctions against Nicaragua. While two thousand activists outside the Federal Building staged a highly vocal legal protest, more than six hundred demonstrators inside the Federal Building committed civil disobedience by refusing to leave the building at its 5:00 P.M. closing time. Five hundred and fifty-nine demonstrators were arrested and locked up that evening. This experience of mass arrest energized the movement by demonstrating the Pledge's collective strength, increasing activists' identity with and investment in the movement, strengthening activists' relational networks, and building organizational *esprit de corps* (Hannon 1991: 309–15).

Events turned out differently, however, one month later, when Congress voted for $27 million of Contra aid and the national Pledge office called for a nationwide protest on June 12. When that day arrived, Boston-area Pledge activists returned to the J.F.K. Federal Building to repeat the action of May 7, but federal and city officials effectively preempted the protest by closing the building before the Pledge activists arrived. Hannon, a participant, described what happened next (1991: 321):

> Unable to manufacture a mass arrest, hundreds of Pledge members gathered outside the building and tried to reach consensus on how to respond. After a fairly chaotic discussion, they decided to relocate to a military recruiting station that was thought to house some CIA offices. This building had also been closed. After wandering aimlessly around Government Center for several hours, the group broke up in discouragement and returned to their homes. This failed action was a significant turning point for the Pledge. Much of the momentum established in May was dissipated and many participants felt silly running around trying desperately to get arrested.

By preemptively averting a civil-disobedient confrontation and mass arrest, government officials decisively thwarted one of the Central America peace movement's most powerful tactics, sending the movement—at least temporarily—into disarray and discouragement. This avoidance of arrests occurred in many other cities as well. Phyllis Taylor recalled (1990):

> We had many protests in Philadelphia, with hundreds of people doing sit-ins and vigils. We shut down the Federal Building and the Liberty Bell for a few hours. But, eventually, the city government began to arrange ahead of time not to arrest us, at all costs. It was really very frustrating, because we would have worked out all of these arrest-scenarios in training seminars, but they never arrested us. People would go through such a discernment process before committing civil disobedience, making preparations with their families and work. Then the police would pick them up and drop them in the street. No arrests. That was thwarting, very frustrating.

Thus, when law enforcement authorities believed arresting civil-disobedient protesters would advance the cause of the movement, they often chose *not* to arrest demonstrators. At other times, however, state authorities deliberately chose to arrest Central America peace activists in attempts to discourage further activism. One notable instance was the case of the Sanctuary activists indicted in 1984 and 1985 for transporting undocumented refugees.

When Sanctuary first went public, federal officials publicly downplayed its significance. Initially, high-ranking Justice Department officials instructed regional INS administrators not to go after Sanctuary

workers, because arresting pastors and priests was too politically controversial. INS commissioner Alan Nelson advised his associates,
"Don't let them get our goat. Don't let's make martyrs out of them"
(Crittenden 1988: 78). Local and national INS officials followed that
strategy. Leon Ring, head of the Tucson Border Patrol, for example,
told the *Arizona Daily Star* in December 1982, "The church groups
were baiting us to overreact. Therefore, we have been very low-key.
Certain arrests could have taken place, but we felt the government
would end up looking ridiculous, especially as far as going into church
property." Bill Joyce, Assistant General Counsel to the INS, told the
Christian Science Monitor in August 1982, "If we thought it was a significant problem, then maybe we'd look at it. But there are plenty of
illegal aliens out there" (Davidson 1988: 78). In January 1983, Arizona Border Patrol agent Dean Thatcher even wrote an internal memo
stating that, in his judgment, the Sanctuary movement did not represent a serious threat to INS law enforcement (Crittenden 1988: 140).

At the same time, however, INS officials continually reminded those
in Sanctuary of their liability to prosecution. Word had it that Jim
Corbett's picture was posted in Border Patrol offices all over southern
Arizona and the INS made it clear that they would not hesitate to
prosecute Sanctuary activists caught on the road with undocumented
immigrants. In March 1984, for example, Tucson INS chief William
Johnson told the *Arizona Star* of Sanctuary workers, "If they happen
to get caught, our officers will treat them just like everybody else"
(Tomsho 1987: 157). In 1983, an anonymous INS official acknowledged to the *Washington Post* of Jim Corbett that "there are Border
Patrol officers who would dearly love to catch him" (Davidson 1988:
79). In fact, we now know that the government secretly was keeping
the Sanctuary movement under close surveillance and beginning to
develop strategies to cripple it (Tomsho 1987: 157, 163).

By late 1983 and early 1984, Immigration and Justice Department
officials in Washington began to realize that Sanctuary was not going
to fade away on its own. They also became increasingly convinced
that Sanctuary was shifting from a primarily humanitarian effort to an
anti-administration political movement. Jim Rayburn expressed this
concern when he wrote in an April 1984 request to investigate Sanctuary, "The movement, which may have initially expressed humanitarian motives, has slowly evolved to sanction a more lawless and
political stance" (Crittenden 1988: 141). The relevance of Sanctuary
to White House Central America policy was also becoming more

apparent. In a 1983 PBS "Frontline" special on Sanctuary, INS Commissioner Alan Nelson stated, "Many of them will admit what they are really doing is opposing the President's policy in Central America" (Tomsho 1987: 94). In a June 30, 1983, memo Jim Rayburn wrote, "It is now clear that they plan to force U.S. Immigration to take them to court on either harboring charges or transportation charges. The . . . movement will then use the trial as their stage to challenge both U.S. policy on Central America and INS policy" (Tomsho 1987: 157–58). In early 1984, important Washington officials began to put heavy pressure on regional and local INS officials in the Southwest to investigate and prosecute Sanctuary activists (Tomsho 1987: 166; Crittenden 1988: 116). Operation Sojourner, Arizona INS's response to that pressure, was personally approved by Associate Attorney General Stephen Trott, the third highest ranking official in the Justice Department (Crittenden 1988: 144). According to Sanctuary worker Jane Guise (1990): "The fact that the government went to great lengths to pursue the Sanctuary indictments tells you something, that it was really bothering them."

In February 1984, Texas Sanctuary activists Stacey Lynn Merkt and Sister Diane Muhlenkamp were arrested for transporting undocumented refugees. In March 1984, Tucson Ecumenical Council's director, Phil Conger, and Southside Presbyterian volunteer Katherine Flaherty were arrested on the same charges. The next month, Sanctuary worker Jack Elder was arrested in Texas. In October 1984, Merkt and Elder were indicted again on additional charges. Finally, in January 1985, the Justice Department indicted and arrested sixteen Arizona Sanctuary workers, including John Fife, Jim Corbett, three nuns, two priests, a nurse, a housewife, and a graduate school student. The government had abandoned the strategy of disregarding the movement and replaced it with one of confrontation and punishment.[14] The clear intent of the new strategy was to try to stifle the movement by threatening more widespread arrests of activists if Sanctuary activities continued. After the arrests of Merkt and Elder, Daniel Hedges, U.S. attorney in Texas, stated publicly that he hoped their arrests would "warn those involved in the Sanctuary movement not to expect preferential treatment" (Golden and McConnell 1986: 74). During the Arizona Sanctuary trial, the defense—claiming selective prosecution—questioned Jim Rayburn on the stand as to why the INS arrested Sanctuary activists when his intelligence reports indicated that Sanctuary was transporting relatively few aliens, compared to professional coyotes.

Rayburn replied that, "The deterrence factor was primary, not getting the most number of aliens" (Davidson 1988: 112). And after the convictions and sentencing of the Tucson activists, prosecuting attorney Don Reno concluded: "The convictions were the most startling deterrent they're ever going to receive in a court of law," adding that he expected the convictions would make people think twice in the future before joining the Sanctuary movement (Davidson 1988: 156–57).

Death Squads and Death Threats

Anti-movement repression of the Central America peace movement at times took the form of death-squad operations against U.S. movement activists. As the movement increasingly came to threaten the interests of powerful groups in El Salvador, death squads were formed in the U.S., primarily, it seems, by Salvadoran ex–National Guardsmen living in the U.S. (Garcia 1987: 21; Gelbspan 1987d). These death squads began to terrorize peace activists with death threats, kidnappings, and incidents of torture. Most, though not all, of this activity was based in Los Angeles and was primarily, but not exclusively, directed against Salvadoran- and Guatemalan-born activists, especially women. It appears that the death squads' activities were orchestrated from El Salvador (Garcia 1987). Their operations reveal that they possessed very accurate and reliable information on the activists—their relationships, schedules, and commitments. Sources of that information likely included intelligence materials which Frank Varelli gathered on U.S. activists and fed to the Salvadoran National Guard (Bielski, Forster, and Bernstein 1987: 18; Gelbspan 1989: 20).

In December 1984, for example, a slide show and talk on Nicaragua was canceled and the building where it was to be held evacuated when a member of Omega 7, an anti-Castro terrorist organization, called in a bomb threat. The next day, the minister who was to have made the presentation received another call from Omega 7, saying, "You're a bunch of communists. We're going to blow you up." The minister decided to move his office, because it was located next to a day-care center (Leahy 1987: 240). In April 1985, Sara Murray, a Michigan Central America human rights activist, spoke to a CISPES chapter about Sanctuary in the Southwest. After the meeting, a man from the audience she had never seen before told her death squads were forming in Detroit, that she was a target and should stop her activism. One month later, a hispanic taxi driver waiting outside her office warned her that she might be kidnapped or assassinated and should stop her refugee work (Gelbspan 1991: 29). In July 1987, Father Luis Olivares, a Los Angeles priest, received an anonymous letter on which was written only the initials "E.M.," short for *esquadrón de la muerte,* the brutal Salvadoran right-wing death squads whose initials warned their intended victims that they were marked for torture or assassination (Garcia 1987: 20). That same month, San Francisco Catholic Charities, a regional headquarters of Sanctuary churches, received a phone threat: "You work with the people of El Salvador. Just remember E.M." (Bielski, Forster, and Bernstein 1987: 17). Back in Los Angeles, Marta Alicia Rivera, an Salvadoran activist who had been tortured in El Salvador for her work in the teachers' union, received a list with the names of nineteen refugees targeted for death. An accompanying handwritten note read (Garcia 1987: 20; Gelbspan 1987c):

> For being a traitor to the country, you will die, together with your comrades. You survived in El Salvador. Here, with us, you will not. Do not speak in public. Nothing will save you. Death. Death. Flowers in the desert die.

On July 17, 1987, Guatemalan refugee and activist Ana Maria Lopez was kidnapped at a bus station, pushed into a waiting Toyota, and interrogated at gunpoint for two hours. During the questioning, the masked abductors reeled off names of several dozen Guatemalan and Salvadoran activists from memory. They threatened to kill the activists if they continued their work. "*Tenemos buenos contactos*" ("We have good contacts"), they repeatedly told her. To prove it, they cited to Lopez the names of all of the activists who were attending an organizing meeting that night at a church. "We're going to start with the women," they said, "and you should tell your people that" (Bielski, Forster, and Bernstein 1987: 16). Then in Dallas, on August 5, 1987, a threatening caller warned a Salvadoran refugee group, Proyecto Adelante, "We are observing you. You are communists. What we are doing in Los Angeles, we're going to do here" (Bielski, Forster, and Bernstein 1987: 17–18).

The death squads did not simply threaten Central America peace activists. They sometimes also abducted, interrogated, and tortured them. In one well-known case, for example, in June 1987, Yanira Corea, a twenty-two-year-old Salvadoran CISPES volunteer living in Los Angeles, was driving to the airport with her three-year-old son, Ernesto, when she was forced off the road by a car driven by two hispanic men. One pounded and kicked her car while the other tried to pull Corea out of her door. Before she managed to escape, the men grabbed a book containing a photo of her son. Ernesto was so traumatized that he could not speak for three days afterwards. Two weeks later, Corea received a letter with her son's photo and the traditional Salvadoran death-squad death threat, "Flowers in the desert die." The next week, while on her way to her car outside the CISPES office, three men abducted Corea at knifepoint, taped her mouth shut, and drove her around the city in a van. While they cut the letters E.M. into the palms of her hands, cut her tongue and neck with the knife, burned her face and fingers with cigarettes, and raped her repeatedly with a wooden stick, the three men interrogated her about the activities of CISPES organizers and family members in El Salvador. "We know all the Salvadoran women who are here, and this will keep on," they told her. After six hours of torture and interrogation, they dumped her on a street corner with her eyes taped shut and her underwear tied around her mouth.[15] "They knew exactly what they were doing," Corea later said, "like they had done it a thousand times before." Days later, after moving to a new home with an unlisted telephone, Corea began receiving calls threatening her son. Notes were also left outside her door, with drawings of a decapitated boy's body, asking, "Do you know where and how your son is?" In the next months, Corea's father in El Salvador received intimidating letters from within the country, ordering him to convince his daughter to drop out of political activism (Gelbspan 1987b, 1987d, 1991: 32–34; Bielski, Forster, and Bernstein 1987: 16).

Altogether, between 1984 and 1987, Central America activists reported two hundred incidents of death threats and death-squad activities in scores of cities around the U.S. (Bielski, Forster, and Bernstein 1987: 16). In the month of July 1987 alone, twenty-four different Los Angeles activists received threats from callers with Salvadoran accents saying, "For being a Communist, we will kill you" (Garcia 1987: 20). In Los Angeles, the rash of death threats against activists prompted Mayor Tom Bradley publicly to denounce the death squads and offer a $10,000 reward for information leading to the arrest and conviction of any of their members (Garcia 1987: 21). However, none of the people behind the death threats and abductions were ever apprehended.

State of Emergency Mass Detention

The executive branch of the federal government was apparently prepared to counter and contain the U.S. Central America peace movement no matter how explosive the conflict over Central American policy might have become. Had U.S. involvement in the war in Central America become much more direct and extensive, and the U.S. Central America peace movement able to respond by mobilizing the kind of major social disruption envisioned by the original architects of the Pledge of Resistance, under a reported top-secret government emergency plan, many thousands of peace activists could have been arrested and detained *en masse* without the protection of constitutional rights. While the provisions of government secrecy makes it impossible to verify with certainty or to describe the details, evidence strongly suggests that in 1984, the NSC and the Federal Emergency Management Agency (FEMA) collaborated in designing a top-secret contingency plan, named "Rex 84," to suspend the U.S. Constitution, declare martial law, appoint military commanders to run state and local governments, and detain masses of people considered to be national security threats, in the event the President declared a "State of Domestic National Emergency" (U.P.I. 1987). According to the plan, events expected to precipitate such a declaration included massive domestic opposition to a U.S. military invasion abroad—including a direct invasion in Central America (Reuters 1987; Spiegelman 1987).

According to government sources—such as congressional Iran-Contra investigators, members of Congress, other federal government officials, and leaked FEMA documents—National Security Decision Directive No. 52, signed by President Reagan in April 1984, authorized FEMA to design a secret, national emergency-readiness code. Rex 84 appears to have been written by Lieutenant Colonel Oliver North, NSC White House aide and NSC liaison to FEMA, and John Brinkerhoff, FEMA's deputy director of national preparedness programs. The plan was roughly patterned after a 1970 scheme that FEMA Chief Louis Guiffrida designed while at the Army War College, which proposed the detention of up to twenty-one million "American Negroes" in the event of a national black militant uprising (UPI 1987; Sklar 1988: 358). An internal memo of John Brinkerhoff's, dated June 30, 1982, that was leaked to the press in 1987, outlined the martial law portion of the secret plan (Sklar 1988: 358). Rex 84 arranged, among other things, for the formation of fifty "Defense Forces," composed of local law enforcement and military reserve agencies, to implement the plan at the local level (Gelbspan 1991: 184). Rex 84 also contained preparations for the construction of ten military detention centers within the United States, capable of housing four hundred thousand political prisoners (Nelson-Pallmeyer 1989: 69). Reminiscent of the mass detention of Japanese Americans during World War II, the contingency plan called for the rounding-up and confinement of thousands of U.S. protesters and tens of thousands of illegal aliens in the event of a direct U.S. invasion of Central America (Dubose 1987). In preparation for the potential implementation of Rex 84, an index of FBI dossiers on twelve thousand American citizens considered to be security threats, named ADEX, was actually forwarded—by order of White House counsel Edwin Meese and NSC Adviser to the President Robert McFarlane, and over the objections of FBI Director William Webster—to FEMA headquarters (Dubose 1987).

According to reports, the Rex 84 proposal alarmed Attorney General William French Smith, who wrote an August 1984 letter to Robert McFarlane expressing his objections and urging a delay in accepting the directive. Smith wrote (Reuters 1987): "I believe that the role assigned to the Federal Emergency Management Agency in the revised Executive Order exceeds its proper function as a coordinating agency for emergency preparedness. This department and others have repeatedly raised serious policy and legal objections to the creation of an 'emergency czar' for FEMA."

Smith's objections appear to have gone unheeded. Furthermore, a congressional inquiry into the matter failed to expose fully or terminate the secret emergency plan. On July 13, 1987, during the congressional Iran-Contra hearings, Representative Jack Brooks of Texas attempted to question Oliver North about his involvement in Rex 84. But his question was quickly cut off by committee Co-Chair Sen. Daniel Inouye, who warned, "I believe that question touches upon a highly sensitive and classified area, so may I request that you not touch upon that." When Brooks persisted to cross-examine North about the top-secret plan, Inouye interrupted again, "May I most respectfully request that that matter not be touched upon at this stage. If we wish to get into this, I'm certain arrangements can be made for an executive session." Later that day, the matter was discussed by the Iran-Contra committee in a closed executive session, after which the White House indicated it would allow limited questioning about Rex 84 at the next day's hearing. When questioned the following day, however, Oliver North flatly denied the existence of any such secret plan. This ended any further congressional inquiry into Rex 84 (Spiegelman 1987; Sklar 1988: 357–58).

THE SOCIAL ORGANIZATION OF HARASSMENT
AND REPRESSION

An intriguing question remains: Were these oppositional actions of government agencies and private groups against the Central America peace movement more highly coordinated than the above accounts suggest? If so, was that coordination what we might call an "instrumental" coordination—the work of identifiable, self-conscious, goals-oriented individuals—or a "structural" coordination: the work of some systemic imperative? Certainly, the break-ins, IRS audits, death threats, and group infiltrations do not appear to have been random, accidental, disconnected, or spontaneous. Most of them seem to have been politically calculated and purposeful, possibly having involved a degree of broader coordination or direction. Was there, then, some kind of a higher "center" of anti-movement organization that initiated, mobilized, authorized, financed, or executed these harassing and repressive activities in a coordinated fashion? Without jumping to a grand conspiracy theory involving a unified master plan executed by a single agency, might we be able to identify an organizing entity that may have been "behind" many of these different anti-movement actions in some way?

Unfortunately, the exact organizational arrangement of Central America anti-movement activities remains shrouded in the secrecy that veils state and private domestic covert operations. Identifying precisely who may have authorized and organized the harassment and repression of the peace movement would require gaining access to classified information secured in the files of numerous government agencies and private groups, and eliciting secret knowledge safeguarded by key state officials and heads of private organizations. Such classified files remain inaccessible, and living, potentially enlightening informants remain silent about what they know on the subject. Worse, probably the most illuminating knowledge on the matter was forever buried in the grave of William Casey, CIA director from 1981 to his death in 1987. Hence, we will never completely know about the exact social organization of these anti-movement activities.

Nonetheless, despite this absence of definitive and comprehensive knowledge, we do know more than that described above about a possible organizational catalyst behind much of this anti-movement activity. The available evidence can, admittedly, be interpreted in different ways. But the most plausible interpretation of the evidence suggests—

though does not decisively prove—that a coordinating anti-movement center, reaching out from the NSC and CIA, did, in fact, operate to encourage and order many of the harassing and repressive actions described above. Perhaps the most plausible reading of the available evidence suggests that William Casey—CIA director, White House cabinet member, and campaign director for President Reagan—was responsible for much of this activity and had it implemented through an array of existing and created government agencies and private organizations. These appear to have included some combination of the CIA, the FBI, the INS, the IRS, the Office of Public Diplomacy, the State Department, the Justice Department, the Customs Bureau, and a variety of sympathetic, cooperating private organizations.

What evidence exists to support such an interpretation? Briefly, Casey possessed, as perhaps no one else at the time, the opportunity, the motive, and the means to coordinate anti-movement actions against Central America peace activists. Furthermore, Casey is known to have orchestrated similar politically motivated and sometimes unlawful schemes to protect the President's Central American policy against the Congress, the press, and American public opinion. Finally, other circumstantial evidence strongly implicates the CIA and the White House in the use of federal agencies to oppose the Central America peace movement.

First, Bill Casey clearly enjoyed the *opportunity* to encourage and coordinate the kind of anti-movement activities described above. Casey was the director of the CIA for six years. He was a personal friend of the President's and wielded tremendous influence in the White House. Those in circles of power around the White House perceived Casey as "the real voice of Reagan, the White House, the Administration" (Woodward 1987: 258; Gutman 1988: 271; Ranelagh 1987: 671). No other person in Washington enjoyed the opportunity to orchestrate, had they so wished, opposition to the movement that resisted the President's Central American policy.

Second, Casey possessed a clear *motive* to harass and repress the peace movement. He was a consummate cold-warrior who viewed all political reality as a monumental to-the-death struggle between the U.S. and the Soviet Union. Like others in the White House, he was dedicated to winning back territory from the Soviets, especially to overthrowing the Sandinistas in Nicaragua and defeating the FMLN in El Salvador (Persico 1990: 6–7, 217–18, 320; Judis 1987: 754; Woodward 1987: 112–13; Gutman 1988: 269). In that task, Casey's guiding model for the CIA was the Office of Strategic Services (OSS), the World War II secret intelligence service, for which Casey served as the European theater chief of secret intelligence. In Casey's mind, what made the OSS succeed as it did during its glory days was that it operated by one simple rule: *do whatever is necessary to win the war* (Judis 1987: 753). Applied to the cold-war reality, this meant the goal of rolling back the Soviet empire trumped every other competing social value or domestic restraint. If defeating the Soviets required violating the civil liberties of some U.S. citizens and evading congressional and media oversight through misrepresentations and lies, then so be it. For that conviction, Casey was not apologetic (Judis 1987: 753–54; Watson and Sandza 1987: 25; Persico 1990: 298, 337, 392, 400–401, 538; Ranelagh 1987: 675). Furthermore, in his work, Casey sought to erase the traditional line between intelligence gathering and policy formation and implementation (Watson and Sandza 1987: 28). For Casey, the CIA and other government agencies were to function as proactive tools executing anti-Soviet foreign policy, not apolitical sources of data merely providing reliable information to foreign-policy makers (Persico 1990: 444; Gutman 1988: 29–30). Thus, Casey was convinced of the need to establish an autonomous, self-financing, policy-implementing entity that would operate in complete secrecy, independent of congressional oversight, though sometimes in cooperation with other friendly intelligence services (Woodward 1987: 467). All of this was nourished by Casey's personal penchant for secrecy, love of covert operations, and willingness to operate outside the law if need be (CQ Researcher 1992). Since, in Bob Woodward's words (1987: 264; also see Gutman 1988: 305), "Casey was determined to do everything possible to protect the Nicaragua operation," since the FBI considered certain U.S. Central America peace organizations to be engaged in terrorism and the promotion of communism (Kurkjian 1987), and since the Central America peace movement actually threatened to obstruct the success of White House Central American policy, it would have been supremely unnatural for Casey *not* to have taken steps to encourage actions to counter the peace movement.

Not only did Bill Casey enjoy the ample opportunity and have a compelling motive, he also possessed the *necessary means* to encourage and coordinate the harassment and repression of Central America peace activists. Casey had at his disposal the vast organizational, financial, and technological power of the CIA and other friendly federal intelligence and law enforcement agencies, including the Defense Investigative Service (DIS), a branch of the CIA dedicated to domestic covert operations. To facilitate implementing policy without obstruction, Casey also created a covert action wing of the CIA and the NSC as an independent instrument of foreign policy, not accountable to the State or Defense Departments, the American public, and perhaps even the President (Judis 1987: 752; Persico 1990: 503; Gutman 1988: 147, 203, 319). Casey then staffed this "off-shore" operation with the likes of the loyal and entrepreneurial Lieutenant Colonel Oliver North, for whom Casey was an inspiration, a protector, and a "soulmate" (Woodward 1987: 466; Perry 1992: 48; Persico 1990: 405, 452; Gutman 1988: 313). Casey also appointed Kenneth de Graffenreid—who believed that the Soviets were operating a vast electronic disinformation project in the U.S. and advocated forming a special agency for covert actions that would merge the CIA and FBI into a super domestic surveillance agency—as the CIA's liaison to the NSC (Judis 1987: 754). Furthermore, to establish as much legal cover as possible, from its first days of office, Casey encouraged the Reagan administration to loosen existing restrictions on domestic activities of the CIA, to create a legal authorization for the CIA to infiltrate and influence domestic groups (*Time* 1981; Woodward 1987: 76, 92–93, 118–19; also see Prados 1986: 371). By December 1981, the President had signed Executive Order 12333, which authorized the CIA, FBI, and State Department to "collect, produce, and disseminate foreign intelligence and counterintelligence" through covert domestic operations (Donner 1985: 13). This order *legalized* CIA and FBI break-ins, when conducted under the rubric of foreign intelligence or counterintelligence (Crittenden 1988: 352; Kohn 1986: 75). Consequently, at congressional hearings, Assistant FBI Director Oliver Revell could state categorically that the FBI "is not now engaged in any burglaries or *illegal* activities as an institution." But when Representative Robert Kastenmeier asked Revell, "Do you do it under the cover of law?," Revell responded, "I can't comment on that or on activities that involve foreign counterintelligence" (Crittenden 1988: 352). In addition, guidelines issued by Attorney General William French Smith on March 7, 1983, further strengthened the legal ability of the CIA and FBI to engage in covert, intrusive investigations of administration opponents (Donner 1985: 13; Webster 1984: 11–12). Thus, with these vast organizational, financial, technological resources at his disposal and the newly established legal cover for domestic covert operations, Bill Casey enjoyed more than abundant means to counter effectively the U.S. Central America peace movement.

Besides indications that all of the necessary conditions existed for Bill Casey both to have wanted to and to have been able to organize the harassment and obstruction of the peace movement, additional evidence appears to further implicate the CIA, NSC, and FBI in many intrusive and sometimes illegal actions against the movement. We know that Bill Casey involved the CIA in an illegal covert domestic propaganda effort to "sell" the Contras to the American public and Congress, and that he coordinated Oliver North's network in a campaign, headed by Carl "Spitz" Channell, to discredit Contra opponents (Parry 1992; Persico 1990: 493; Jacoby and Parry 1987; Gutman 1988: 257–58). We know that, according to a report of the Senate Committee on Intelligence, the CIA appears to have collaborated with the Salvadoran National Guard to fabricate a document—purportedly captured from Shafik Handal, head of a Salvadoran communist party—to implicate CISPES in a network of international terrorism, in order to initiate an FBI counterterrorist investigation of CISPES (Committee on Intelligence 1989). Furthermore, we know that Bill Casey sought to coordinate CIA intelligence and counterintelligence programs with the FBI (Woodward 1987: 305). We know from FBI Director William Webster that many of the FBI's counterintelligence investigations were conducted pursuant to "taskings" (assignments) from the CIA and the NSC (Donner 1985: 13). We also know that the extent of FBI domestic electronic surveillance programs expanded rapidly under Reagan administration, as indicated by the almost doubling of applications for secret warrants for electronic surveillance between 1980 and 1984 (Greider 1985: 52; also see Demac 1984: 27), and that the impetus and authorization for the Sanctuary investigation, Operation Sojourner, came from high-level INS and Justice Department officials in Washington, who appear to have been keenly interested in seeing the Sanctuary movement stopped (Tomsho 1987: 166). We know that FBI agents questioning Central America peace activists said they were working in conjunction with the CIA, that a Georgetown University–based refugee organization was being covertly investigated by agents of the State Department for its human rights activities, and that an activist lawyer's organization was under surveillance by the FBI at the same time that he received a death threat

(MSN 1989: 51, 74, 78). Finally, we know from a March 1989 State Department domestic-intelligence report on CISPES and other anti-administration groups that—contrary to FBI denials and consistent with Frank Varelli's claims—information on those groups was to be shared with agencies of the Salvadoran government (Gelbspan 1989).

Furthermore, we know from numerous former federal agents and operatives that at least some federal agents were involved in political burglaries. Philip Mabry, for example—a Fort Worth–based private investigator and former CIA contract agent—claims that Oliver North gave him a list of individuals and organizations opposed to U.S. policy in Central America, saying, "A good way to get these assholes is to let the FBI check them out. This list includes pro-Marxists, communists, traitors." North then instructed Mabry on how to organize a letter-writing campaign that would give the FBI a legal mandate to investigate the groups (Gelbspan 1991: 185–86). Furthermore, Mabry claims that he was asked by a member of North's secret network if he would be willing to conduct a break-in at the Christic Institute, a legal-aid organization helping to defend the indicted Arizona Sanctuary workers (Gelbspan 1991: 188). One member of Oliver North's private Contra supply network, who asked to remain anonymous, suggested that a book based on FBI intelligence and published by the Office of Public Diplomacy, called *The Latin America Establishment: A Survey of Involvement,* was actually used by covert operatives as a handbook for break-ins at Central America organizations (Gelbspan 1991: 176–78). Plus, Frank Varelli testified that he personally saw physical evidence that his two supervisory agents had broken into the offices and apartments of CISPES members on at least three different occasions (Subcommittee on Civil and Constitutional Rights 1987: 441; Berman 1987: 6). Varelli also maintains that he was instructed to make an "armed reconnaissance" of offices of three different Central America peace organizations (Berman 1987: 9). And according to Varelli, three different FBI agents told him that these investigations into Salvadoran activists were ordered by the White House, through the NSC. Supervisory Special Agent Ron Davenport reportedly said, "This operation has the backing of the White House. It has been fully authorized by the National Security Council" (Gordon 1987: 289; Gelbspan 1991: 151). Such allegations, though not absolutely verifiable, are consistent with the historical record of the FBI, which, for example, during the COINTELPRO era of the 1960s and early 1970s, conducted a massive campaign of illegal harassment, defamation, and break-ins against a variety of social-movement activists (U.S. Senate 1976; Glick 1989: 7–18).[16]

Hence, it appears not only quite possible, but also likely that William Casey—while always allowing an escape of "plausible denia-bility"—took the initiative to encourage and coordinate many of the anti–peace movement actions described above. Using his political influence and authority as CIA director and confidant of the President, Casey set up organizational networks within the NSC which not only financially sustained the Nicaraguan Contras, through the Iran-Con-tra intrigue, but also appear to have worked to discredit, harass, and repress domestic groups opposed to administration policy in Central America. Indeed, the initiative and intelligence support for many of the political break-ins of Central America peace organizations that were carried out by hired operatives and members of private anti-communist organizations likely came from this Casey-sponsored NSC-based Cen-tral America network. And the Rex 84 plan, which prepared to detain masses of protesters in the event of a major U.S. invasion of Central America, also derived from the Oliver North NSC operation.

It also appears likely that Casey initiated most of the covert inves-tigations of Central America organizations conducted by the FBI. It is probable that Casey used informal, word-of-mouth channels of com-munication to apprise middle-level FBI supervisors—such as Daniel Flanagan and James Evans, who supervised Frank Varelli—that, as far as the White House and CIA was concerned, political break-ins and exchanges of intelligence information with the Salvadoran National Guard were acceptable, indeed, desirable. According to one senior congressional staff member who was deeply involved in investigations of FBI abuses, who wished to remain anonymous (Anonymous 1993), "The way things work in Washington, all it would take is one sentence from Casey, and he could get done whatever he wished." It is also probable that Casey used the same kind of informal communication channels to prompt middle-level IRS employees to begin auditing indi-viduals and organizations involved in the Central America peace movement, middle-level Customs officials to begin detaining, interro-gating, and searching Central America travelers at U.S. airports, and, possibly, selected postal workers to tamper with activists' mail. In this way, Casey bypassed the objections of more principled federal agency directors, such as William Webster, and was still able to accomplish these harassing and repressive activities, while yet allowing high-level agency spokespeople to declare to Congress and the press truthfully—at least as far as they knew—that their agency was not involved in these illegal activities.

Finally, while most of the reported death threats against and abductions of Central America peace activists appear to have been executed by private Salvadoran death squads, not by federal government agents, it is nonetheless probable that those death squads received intelligence support—either directly from federal operatives or indirectly through Salvadoran channels—from the FBI, INS, or CIA. They also likely received the message that such activities, if kept within "reasonable" limits, would be condoned by federal law enforcement agencies. Thus, death-squad members were confident that the FBI was more interested in investigating the activists they targeted than in investigating the activities of the death squads themselves. Again, the available evidence does not *prove* this interpretation, but only strongly suggests it as most plausible, given the best reading of the data at hand.

Theoretically, this interpretation posits a weak "structural" coordination of anti-movement activities, grounded in the U.S. as a hegemonic power's overall political interest in dominating Central America and in the missions of the preexistent federal intelligence and law enforcement agencies. More immediately, this interpretation assumes a strong "instrumental" coordination of anti-movement actions, embodied in the person of William Casey and other officials and agents—such as Oliver North, Carl Channell, Oliver Revell, and Otto Reich—who promoted and discharged Casey's political program. The harassment and repression of Central America peace activists, in other words, appears to have been generated not simply by some kind of impersonal systemic imperative, but by an identifiable set of intentionally acting individuals who were responsible for defending the interests of groups that the Central America peace movement threatened.

THE CONSEQUENCES: BACKING-OFF OR BACKFIRING?

One final question deserves brief consideration: What effect did these anti-movement activities actually have on the Central America peace movement? The simple answer is that they had mixed effects. In some cases, as intended, the harassing and repressive actions discouraged potential activists from ever becoming seriously involved in the movement and already mobilized activists from deepening or continuing their political work. In many other instances, however, anti-movement actions proved either largely ineffective, or they positively backfired by generating more insurgent consciousness among Central America peace activists and deepening their commitment to and investment in the movement.

The specific outcome in any given instance appears to have depended, in part, on the intensity of repression and on the emotional dynamics provoked by the harassment and repression. Most anti-movement actions—FBI visits, tax audits, mail tamperings, attacks on movement credibility, disrupted demonstrations, group infiltrations, break-ins, death threats—generated in activists emotional combinations of fear and anger. They evoked fear of financial, emotional, reputational, or physical injury. But they also tended to provoke anger and resentment that someone or some group would stoop to such devious tactics to prevail in the battle over Central American policy. When Central America peace activists believed that the U.S. government had participated in the harassing and repressive actions, they were especially likely to feel angry and defiant, because that violated ideals of democracy and civil liberty that define U.S. popular political culture. Fear worked in favor of the anti-movement activists, while anger and resentment worked against the movement's opponents. When the fear overrode anger, the anti-movement actions tended to successfully discourage activism. But when the anger outstripped the fear, those actions tended to backfire, increasing activists' political commitment and investment in activism.

Variations in these emotional dynamics seem to correlate with the repression intensity of the particular anti-movement tactics employed. Viewing the experience of the peace movement's confrontation with anti-movement actions overall, the general relationship between intensity of repression and the effective discouraging of activism appears to have been curvilinear. That is, until a point where the repression became quite severe, increases in the intensity of anti-movement repression seemed to produce corresponding increases in anger over the repression and increases in dedication to activism. However, when the severity of repression became *very* intense, a turning point was often reached where increases in repression produced increasing withdrawal from activism (see Jenkins and Schock 1992: 173).

Thus, activists who had their mail tampered with became rankled, but hardly fearful. Yet, because the import of mail-tampering was so relatively minor, such tactics appears to have only marginally increased the activists' commitment to activism, if at all. When activists had their apartments broken into and ransacked by politically motivated intruders, however, they appear to have experienced a significant amount of fear, but even more anger. This increased their commitment to and involvement in activism. When the Reverend Timothy Limburg's Washington, D.C., church was broken into twice in one month, for example, Limburg responded (Gelbspan 1987e), "At this point, I am far more angry than intimidated. I think it's outrageous that this can happen in this country. It cannot be allowed to go on."

Similarly, when activists were covertly investigated and arrested for their political work, the consequent anger and resentment overrode the fear, producing deeper commitments to activism. Thus, the arrests and convictions of the Arizona Sanctuary activists unified and strengthened the Sanctuary movement, encouraging many church leaders who had previously been silent to speak out in support of Sanctuary (Davidson 1988: 89). According to Golden and McConnell (1986: 77–78):

> All around the country church responses to the indictments and arrests were quick and strong. Local congregations and national church bodies reaffirmed their commitment to sanctuary as a valid ministry of the church and vowed they would not be intimidated by the government. Top religious leaders from the National Council of Churches, the Leadership Conference of Religious Women, the United Church of Christ, the Catholic Mission Society, the American Baptist Church, and others issued a statement saying, "We proclaim our belief in the moral rightness of 'sanctuary.' It will flourish as long as hope, love, and a belief in the ultimate authority of God live in the hearts of the people."

Even the legal convictions of the Sanctuary activists did not put an end to their activism. Quite the contrary, as a report in *The Economist* (1986) described:

> Those acquitted are not resting in peace, and those convicted are not meekly awaiting what the penal system has in store for them. Instead, they were to be found this week fanning out across the country, showing themselves undaunted, rallying their supporters, and doing their best to ensure that the setback in the Tucson courtroom does not deprive the Sanctuary movement of momentum. They do not admit defeat and have no intention of modifying their attitudes.

At the far extreme of repression intensity, however, activists who received death threats from Salvadoran death squads were usually terrified, and their anger about it provided little comfort or security.

Hence, the death-squad activities appear to have been most effective in discouraging activism, especially among Central American refugee activists. According to Garcia (1987), Los Angeles Mayor Tom Bradley's 1987 public denunciation of death-squad activities "did not reassure many refugees, who fear they may become the next target for the death squads. Said a 28-year-old Salvadoran: 'If they want you, they will find you, even here.'" Danny Lewis, head of the New Orleans chapter of CISPES, also observed that visits from federal agents had an intimidating effect on activists, especially on refugees: "When the FBI agents knock on your door, it doesn't do you any good with your neighbors. It doesn't do you any good with your employer." He noted that his CISPES chapter had been virtually "emptied" of Central American refugees, who were frightened away by visits from FBI agents (Gelbspan 1985a). According to one report, most Salvadoran activists who were threatened by death squads ended up abandoning their political work and fleeing to Canada (Bielski, Forster, and Bernstein 1987: 19).

Besides shaping the balance of fear and anger, anti-movement actions affected movement activism in other important ways as well. In addition to generating productive anger, for example, repression also often backfired on movement opponents by generating in activists hope and exhilaration. Many organizers were inspired when harassment and repression convinced them that their political work actually represented a genuine threat to their opponents and that, therefore, their actions might stand a chance of succeeding. Often, to be ignored means one is irrelevant. But to be repressed means one is threatening to somebody. Ironically, then, government repression was often encouraging to activists. This realization of their own political significance often energized them to press even harder against administration policy. According to Witness for Peace organizer Sam Hope (1992), "Some of the younger people working here would get excited when we had a break-in. They always seemed sort of stimulated, actually, thinking that it was *definitely* a CIA break-in."

On the other hand, besides generating activism-discouraging fear, the experience of anti-movement actions often hindered the Central America peace movement by inhibiting the free flow of communication within and between Central America organizations. Sojourners activist Jim Rice (1992), for example, said:

> Even though we knew what we were doing was right, when we became aware that we were under surveillance, especially electronic and telephone surveillance, we began to tell ourselves, "We need to be careful

here." We had to be very cautious about the things we said. You just couldn't make jokes on the telephone anymore that could get you in trouble, even though they were really harmless. People might be listening. So you always had to think about what you said.

Gail Phares (1992) similarly recalled: "Surveillance is a nuisance, mostly. But I just don't say anything that I wouldn't want to have heard by whoever might be listening." Sometimes the threat of state opposition also worked against the Central America peace movement by restricting the range of activities in which individual activists could engage. Pledge of Resistance organizer Anne Shumway (1990) recalled, "I was somewhat involved in Sanctuary. But I had to watch it, to be careful, because of my position in the Pledge. It could have put things in danger to have mixed the two kinds of activism, to mix up illegally transporting refugees with organizing Pledge protests. So I pretty much stuck to Pledge work."

Finally, how did movement organizers try to react to the harassment and repression? To counter fear, movement activists repeated again and again the need to work in the open, to maintain composure, and to keep moving forward. According to Mike Clark (1992), "We just moved along and were open about what we were doing, which was always our approach from the start, that we weren't going to have any secrets, that anyone could know what was happening with us." Gail Phares (1992) observed:

> With surveillance, they're just trying to get you to stop doing what you're doing. So, I'm above board, do what I do publicly, and do it with other people who are credible, so it would be counter-productive for them to come after me. But I never let them stop me. We just keep going. I think the fact that we've kept very above-board with everything gives us credibility. Sometimes it seems like they're just trying to pull us down, which is an annoyance. When they have tried to question me, I've just ignored them and kept doing what I do. I'm not frightened by them. I just press on.

Similarly, Jim Rice (1992) explained what he believes was the best response to surveillance and investigations:

> Their obvious purpose is to intimidate you. So when the knock comes on the door at nighttime, saying, "This is the FBI. We're doing an investigation," well, you just say, "Come back in the morning." You just can't let it intimidate you, especially when you realize that's exactly what they want to do. So, it was important for us to keep our ground-

ing when we knew that stuff was going on, like break-ins and surveillance over the phone lines. We had to say, "Yeah, it's happening, but
we'll just keep doing what we're doing and not let it get to us."

To summarize, opponents of the Central America peace movement
successfully suppressed the movement in cases where—either because
the targeted activists had low fear-thresholds or the anti-movement
tactics were intensely repressive—their harassment and repression
generated more activism-inhibiting fear than anger. In most cases,
however, the intensity of repression was sufficiently moderate and the
nature of the anti-movement actions so infuriating that they actually
provoked Central America activists to greater levels of dedication and
involvement in opposing administration Central American policy.

Eleven

PROBLEMS FOR PROTESTERS
CLOSER TO HOME

We are accustomed to look upon the shackled form of a conquered monster, but there—there you could look at a thing monstrous and free. It was unearthly, and the men were—No, they were not inhuman. Well, you know, that was the worst of it—this suspicion of their not being inhuman. It would come slowly to one. They howled and leaped, and spun, and made horrid faces; but what thrilled you was just the thought of their humanity—like yours—the thought of your remote kinship with this wild and passionate uproar. Ugly. Yes, it was ugly enough; but if you were man enough you would admit to yourself that there was in you just the faintest trace of a response to the terrible frankness of that noise, a dim suspicion of there being a meaning in it which you . . . could comprehend.

Joseph Conrad, *Heart of Darkness*

Social movements are often harassed and repressed by countermovement and anti-movement opponents who purposefully work to neutralize and undermine them. But adversarial forces are not always to be found on the outside. Typically, social movements contain within themselves the seeds of their own potential disintegration and failure. Social-movement organizers, therefore, need not only to counter the attacks of their antagonists, but also to confront inimical forces that emerge from within.

Studies of social movements often analyze the dynamics of repression from external opponents, but less frequently the variety of *internal* problems and dysfunctions that also threaten to undermine movement strength and effectiveness. To help redress this neglect, this chapter offers a brief descriptive exploration of some of the problems closer to home that beset the Central America peace movement. By examining the dark underside of its life we expect to acquire a richer understanding of the kind of forces that helped to shape its durability and disintegration, its achievements and failures.

AUTONOMY AND "ANTI-AUTHORITY-ISM"

Most Central America peace activists believed strongly in the idea of "prefigurative politics," the need for the movement itself to model the kind of world it aspired to help create. The notion of prefigurative politics was rooted, in part, in the movement's abhorrence of the willingness of many twentieth-century leftist political movements to employ authoritarian and violent tactics on the grounds that "the ends justify the means," as well as in a belief in the New Left creed that "the personal is political" (Breines 1982; McAdam 1988: 126–27; Epstein 1991). Hence the popular peace-activism slogan, "There is no way to peace—Peace is the way."

Whatever merits the commitment to prefigurative politics may have had, it also served as the basis—particularly in the Pledge of Resistance—for the development of detrimental themes within the movement's organizational culture. The desire to model in microcosm an egalitarian world that respects diversity and operates by consensus often degenerated into undisciplined, factional assertions of autonomy and the indiscriminate spurning of any exercise of leadership (Hannon 1991: 335–50). Consensus mutated into dissension. Respect for diversity translated into group fragmentation. And anti-authoritarianism evolved into "anti-authority-ism," a generalized suspicion of, and sometimes hostility toward, *any* position or function of leadership or authority. The all too frequent organizational consequences were pernicious: disunity in action and inhibited local leadership. Witness for Peace organizer Bob Van Denend (1992) explored this problem:

> When you throw the bone of independence out to people, they feel like they're unique, like they're doing something special. And as long as they feel that way, they're motivated. Regional and local organizations endured, I think, because of that. You get people excited about doing things if they feel like they have some control, which is what empowerment is all about. But sooner or later you run into problems, because everyone wants to do things their own way.

Tendencies toward fragmenting autonomy and "anti-authority-ism" plagued many regional organizations. According to Boston-area Pledge organizer Anne Shumway (1990), for example, "Anyone could attend our coordinating committee meetings. Affinity groups would send representatives and each would have their own separate idea about what we ought to do. It was all by consensus, so those meetings would go on for hours. Chaos and tension were real problems. It was really hard just to make a decision."

The same tendencies also generated difficulties between the local, regional, and national levels. Pledge of Resistance organizer Ken Butigan has said (1991), "There was tension between the national signal group and local groups. Who decided when to protest? Who had how much autonomy? Local group autonomy was a carry-over from the anti-nuclear movement. But religious people wanted more nationally coordinated action."

National Pledge organizer Dennis Marker, who held a distinctively "national" perspective, confirmed (1992):

> There was often a lack of discipline. In my perception, generally, religious activists were willing to be more disciplined. So when we sent a signal for everyone to do civil disobedience— "Protest on January 12 at 3:00 p.m."—religious activists would actually be there January 12 at 3:00 p.m. But many in the secular community were like, "Hey, in your ear. We'd rather do it on January 15." We used to call them "wildcaters," groups that would say, "The signal's for the 12th, so we'll do the 14th." Boston activists were notorious. They would actually jump the gun and protest ahead of time!

In the words of Pledge activist Angela Berryman (1990), "Even if grass-roots activists wanted national coordination, they did not want national direction." Similar local-national struggles operated within the multilevel Witness for Peace organization: "There were creative tensions, sometimes overt fights, between the regional and the national offices. North Carolina led many of those fights, because they wanted autonomy. They and the Maine people wanted to have a lot of say with what the national organization did. But, in my view, they were unwilling to be accountable themselves to the national organization" (Van Denend 1992).

Ken Butigan (1991), however, who served on the national signal group and was a local San Francisco–area Pledge leader, defended the right of local autonomy:

> Locally, we felt that if the national group wasn't going to act, we had to act anyway. Just before our first independent protest, I got a call from Jim Wallis, setting up a signal group conference call. I had the unpleasant job of telling him that we had already called out our group for protest. Jim was very unhappy, because there was a Contra vote coming up in June for which he wanted to save a national response. He called our's a wildcat action and charged us with diluting the June

protest and undermining the national coalition. I reminded him that, originally, we all had agreed that regional groups were at liberty to make their own decisions, which he conceded. The upshot was that the national signal group did not put out a call for action. But some local groups, like our's and Boston's, protested anyway.

While these kinds of independent actions preserved the widely cherished local-autonomy principle, they also created publicity problems, according to Pledge media coordinator Dennis Marker (1992):

> Wildcaters are a problem when you're trying to do a national media strategy. With our first protests, I could tell the press, "Tomorrow, in 300 cities, people are gathering in the streets," and get good news coverage. But as time went on, it became "This week . . ." and then, "Hopefully this week . . ." and "Maybe the next week . . ." Then the press drops you. Even if you get local press coverage in Boston, it's impossible to sell the story to national television and major newspapers. The Beantown activists said, "Who cares?" But the media does care. If I'm advertising that I've got 200 cities doing civil disobedience over the next ten days, they say, "What kind of clowns are these people? Don't they know how to do something on a single day?"

Marker (1992) discovered that "anti-authority-ism" stifled his publicity work in other ways:

> I always used Jim Wallis' name in press releases, writing his quotes. But I also always got flack for quoting "celebrities." Lots of people in the movement said, "We don't want to use celebrity names. Just use Joe Smith's name." Well, Joe Smith won't get covered. Another common one was, "Let's use a different name every time." Bad idea. You consistently use the best name you can get. I consciously tried to create name recognition. We didn't really have a television-worthy spokesperson. The movement needed to create a couple of celebrities that were media-worthy, religious people with credibility and integrity. But people always said, "We'd rather have less coverage than to have one person getting all the attention." I lost that battle. I fought it many times but it just wasn't winnable. Progressive activists are just bad at working with the media. In fact, they hate it. They often actually resent the few prominent spokespeople we do have, like William Sloane Coffin and Jim Wallis. I actually think the right wing does a much better job at this. They understand the system better. You don't see them attacking emerging leaders as media-hogs. But prominent public figures are unacceptable to progressives.

"Anti-authority-ism" also had the deleterious consequence of promoting burnout in many movement leaders. Pledge organizers, for example, who poured themselves into their work often not only found the value of their work ignored, but were sometimes publicly shunned and even attacked by other activists for usurping authority. Furthermore, according to James Hannon (1991: 339–40), for many leaders, the Boston-area Pledge

> demanded enormous amounts of energy while providing little reward. Salaries for their work as central organizers would have made a great difference in their ability to maintain their leadership roles. . . . The Pledge did not lack funds for paid staff. Early contributions and low overhead provided the Pledge with some financial footing. . . . But in Boston there was strong resistance to the possibility of paid staff from those who believed that hiring staff would undermine democracy.

Consequently, many leaders burned out and dropped out. Later, when the Boston-area Pledge confronted the need for a major strategic reassessment, without capable leaders, it became, "a Babel of confusing and conflicting proposals that never coalesced into a coherent strategy" (Hannon 1991: 343).

To summarize, excessive group autonomy and hostility toward positions of leadership and authority certainly helped to avert hierarchical authoritarianism in the Central America peace movement. But these expressions of prefigurative-politics-gone-awry often promoted organizational fragmentation, hampered effective decision making, bred wearisome planning meetings, discouraged intra-organizational accountability, generated disunified protest campaigns, burned out capable and devoted leaders, and spoiled opportunities to promote the movement's cause in the mass media.

CLASHES IN COALITIONS

Generating the political power of unified, targeted protest actions out of a movement comprised of fifteen hundred to two thousand separate local, regional, and national movement organizations required that those organizations work together in coalitions. Coalition building was facilitated by the common purpose of stopping U.S. governmental Central American policy, as Bob Bonthius (1990) observed, "What drove movement people was righteous indignation, outrage, plain anger at the beast, at the empire. No matter what people's faith or philosophy was, all of us could share that. And given our fallenness, we all love to have an enemy. And the U.S. has been perfect in that respect, because it's been about as devious as any nation we know."

While shared outrage at "the beast" was sufficient to draw activists together, it was often not enough to overcome differences in faith, philosophy, and style that distinguished many of the groups. The religious-secular divide was particularly pronounced. Consequently, coalition politics within the Central America peace movement were often fraught with friction and rancor. According to Dennis Marker (1992), "The Central America Working Group coalition meetings in Washington were both entertaining and depressing at the same time." Sojourners' Jim Rice (1992) commented, "We were not that interested in doing too much coalition stuff because it's often such a waste of energy. You can accomplish things so much quicker on your own. Although sometimes even the most difficult or broad coalitions do get things accomplished, I also saw too much bickering and mutual hacking, the worst and most destructive of which came from the hard-line leftist types."

Some of the clashes in coalitions derived from incompatible strategic or philosophical differences. Phyllis Taylor (1990) recalled, "We had a group called Christians Concerned about El Salvador that was meeting early on. Then CISPES came to one of our meetings and offered a whole different platform. Many of us left that meeting turned off by CISPES' apparent support for armed struggle. We, as religious people committed to non-violence, coming from a pacifist position, felt that we couldn't endorse that."

In addition, turf battles ensued over the proper division of labor within large projects. According to Dennis Marker (1992), such problems troubled Witness for Peace:

> Of course, there were the inner-politics of coalition. Many people didn't want Sojourners involved. And early-on there was a real anger that we didn't create an official letterhead. We said, "Send us one, we'll use it." But no one did, so we kept using the Sojourners letterhead. And people got real mad. They also got really upset that Sojourners was doing the media work. There were big, early-on problems between Jim [Wallis] and Bob [Bonthius] that had to do with turf, really. Bob was part of CALC and wanted CALC to do the media work. But CALC wasn't in Washington and didn't even have a person doing media. There were just a lot of control issues between Jim and Bob. All I knew for sure at the time was that, as far as I was concerned, we were not going to write press releases by committee, involving people from Maine and New

York and wherever. No way. So we took the initiative, sent out press releases, and if others hated it, then they could just fire us.

Clashes also arose in coalitions when certain groups felt they were being used or manipulated by others. Tom Quigley (1990), recollected:

> In 1981, the religious community was organizing a first anniversary remembrance of the four religious women killed in El Salvador. CISPES wanted to get in on the protest. So we let them in. But hostilities eventually developed. Sometimes CISPES could be too overbearing and overreaching. I remembers one of the religious organizers, who was a very tough lady, charging, "These bastards are manipulating us. They're just trying to use us." There were just so many different perspectives.[1]

Another problem that sometimes thwarted collaboration was an unwillingness of certain groups, for a variety of reasons, to be formally associated with others.

> We wanted to keep an arm's length from some of the non-religious groups because we didn't want the association. It was so important for us to keep our religious image. If you're always with groups that are what you say you're not, people get suspicious. If Daniel Ortega shows up in your living room, and you're saying, "We didn't have anything to do with the Sandinistas. Oh, well, yes, the Nicaraguan President, he just happened to come by. Yeah, come on in, have some cookies." (Marker 1992)

Another cause of clashes in coalitions, we saw in chapter 8, were disagreements about whether to accept compromise bills in Congress. According to Cindy Buhl (1993):

> We sat through meeting after meeting of coalition people bashing each other over the head about legislative strategy. Oh, yeah. It was beautiful, it was terrible. The first huge blowout was in 1986 over a "humanitarian" Contra aid compromise. There was an incredible amount of rancor about how to respond. I actually missed those meetings, but heard that everyone was upset at everyone else. I don't know if the bad feelings were due solely to different points of view, or also to poorly facilitated discussions. You can let people talk too much. If I was there, I might have just steamrolled over everybody and created a lot of ill will myself. But I spent a lot of time on the phone telling people to try to be kinder to each other. We had another blowout in 1988 over a compromise bill. Our deliberations went on for days. And people were very accusatory, challenging each other's very integrity. It was very shocking that people who had worked together for so long would actually be doubting each other's good faith.

Finally, most of these problems were exacerbated by the frequent turnover of leadership in many organizations. If and when organizations in conflict could negotiate resolutions to their differences, those resolutions vanished just as soon as the people who negotiated them quit. The new leaders would then have to confront their inherent differences all over again. According to Jim Rice (1992):

> Turnover in the peace movement presents a big difficulty in working out problems in coalitions. Many people, especially paid activists earning $10,000 a year, leave after two years or so. So I would represent Sojourners in a coalition for the third year and be the senior person there. The problem is the lack of both cumulative experience and ongoing, stable working relationships. Of course, we always had a national network of life-long activists to call on, who are always there, carrying the vision forward. But in coalitions, you often get these big turnovers. So working out problems is like *déjà vu* all over again.

As a result of these many conflict-generating problems, positive, movement-strengthening coalition building did not occur to the extent that it might have. According to Joe Nangle (1992), "There was never a single major coalition that could pull all the groups together. There were such big egos in the movement and turf problems. So lots of people just ended up plugging away at their own particular thing for the duration."

Many of the coalitions that did form often proved as troublesome as they were effective. Dennis Marker recalled (1992):

> In the national Pledge meetings, people would be bickering and fighting. The individual people there were generally great. Dick Taylor, for example, is one of my favoritest people in the whole world, he's got tons of integrity, he's solid. But he would just sit there and steadfastly argue, "I really think we need to preserve the religious character of the Pledge with religious symbols, crosses, stars of David, etc." And others would reply, "Forget it. We're not going to accept it." There were hours and hours of disputes like that. I mean, it was torture. I can tell you I got more shoulder, back, and neck aches from those meetings than anything else in my entire life.

Consequently, groups looking for longer-term cooperation tended to gravitate toward their own kind. Witness for Peace's Mike Clark (1992) explained, "For one-day demonstrations with a goal that everybody can support, we're pretty flexible. But if we're going to have some ongoing relationship with another group, we look primarily for faith-based organizations that are committed to non-violence and are politically independent. We always hold on to those things as pretty important."

The occasional inability of different Central America peace groups to get along in coalitions both inhibited the formation of what might have been a more united front for the movement and siphoned off a great deal of activists' energy into internal disputes, both of which diminished the movement's capacity to achieve its external policy goals.

INCOMPATIBLE RELIGIOUS AND SECULAR PROTEST STYLES

The problem of incompatible protest styles deserves further examination, as it is such a basic problem for social movements that comprise both secular leftists and religious progressives. Religious and secular activists did manage to work together on many projects. But general willingness to work with different groups and the ability actually to collaborate smoothly on campaigns were often very different matters. At the heart of many conflicts lay the fact that protest itself often meant very different things to secular and religious activists. For secular leftists, protest was largely a matter of exercising political power. But for the religious activists, protest also involved spiritual devotion, self-sacrifice, and moral witness (Epstein 1991). In Jim Rice's words (1992): "Many protests tended to be very religious. But coalition-protests had a different spirit to them. It wasn't just that secular people wanted to chant and we wanted to sing religious songs. There was the deeper issue of the spiritual values that undergirded the actions and the ultimate reason for even being involved." For example, according to Sojourners' Joe Nangle (1992):

> March 20, 1990 was the 10th anniversary of Archbishop Romero's death. We knew it was going to be a very important day and spent seven months in preparation. The question was: how were we going to commemorate it? CISPES wanted a pounding on the gates of the White House, to go out and do massive civil disobedience. We felt that was legitimate. But there was another dimension of Romero's death for us that was deeply spiritual, deeply theological. And we wanted to highlight that also. Well, we had endless debates, I mean, to the point of just not even being able to talk about it anymore.

These different understandings were hard to overcome, for they led to very dissimilar, mutually offending styles of protest. On the one hand, the religious style often bothered or seemed irrelevant to the secular activists. The prayers, religious songs, restrained processions, crosses and other religious symbols, meetings in church buildings, ceremonies of confession, forgiveness, and mission, and elevation of spiritual faithfulness above political effectiveness often alienated nonreligious movement participants (Nangle 1992; Crites 1992; Marker 1992; Rice 1992). On the other hand, the secular styles often repelled the religious activists. Fran Truitt has recalled (1990), "During one sit-in at a Congressman's office, one of the solidarity guys actually urinated in one of the office's plant pots. Then he took a checkbook out of a desk and wrote a check to the U.S. military-industrial complex and signed his name. Now, a person of faith would never do that." And Dennis Marker remembered (1992), "The worst example, in my opinion, was a Pledge group in Chicago. Their idea of non-violent civil disobedience included throwing rocks through windows of buildings! They were hurting people! They're throwing rocks and I'm telling the press, 'We're totally non-violent, you know, life?' I had to do serious damage control."

These kinds of tactics deeply offended many religious activists. According to Truitt (1990), "When these things began to happen, a lot of faith people just dropped out." Sometimes faith-based activists were able to view these differences as a matter of taste. Phyllis Taylor (1990) explained, "The CISPES style is not one that suits me at all. I don't like chanting or the character assassinations. There is another style that I think communicates better, that I'm more comfortable with."

Others, however, such as Bob Van Denend (1992), found the approach of secular groups inherently defective: "I have worked with organizations like CISPES. They did all the same actions we did, but their involvement was devoid of any spirituality. It was just pure politics. In my estimate, they're just a bunch of angry people that are pissed off. They want to be pissed off. And nothing will ever satisfy them."

At times, the tensions between secular and religious activists became a problem on Witness for Peace delegations, as Betsy Crites (1992) has pointed out:

> Sometimes there were struggles and tensions within delegations when people didn't feel comfortable with religious practices. Secular people might say, "I'm not coming to your reflections." Then the rest of the delegation would feel bad, thinking, "Well, darn it, we want to make this open and comfortable for everyone." But then, the religious element can become so watered down and diluted that it doesn't even feel spir-

itual to people at all. That was a difficult balance to strike. The religious aspect was something we tried to make clear up front without being too heavy-handed. We told people they had to accept that we were a faith-based movement. Still, people could get through the application process, through the training, lay their money down, get all the way to Miami, and even then we might discover a real problem. That happened. And it was very painful when it did. But sometimes delegates were sent back.

The greatest tensions between secular and religious activists occurred in the Pledge of Resistance, which began as a religious organization but was quickly transformed into a secular one. Dennis Marker said regretfully (1992):

> When the Pledge started, we made a conscious decision to invite non-religious anti-interventionist groups if they wanted to participate under a religious umbrella. But of course at that time the Pledge was just an idea, there were no signatures. We had it written very clearly that this was going to be a "Christian endeavor but open to others." The secular people joined, saying, "Sure, this is fine to be religious." And it *was* fine with them—until it succeeded! In a few months we had tens of thousands of signers. And once something succeeds like that, everyone wants to own it. So there developed real tensions, a lot of headaches and frustrations. We were fighting to preserve the religious character that had worked so well for Witness for Peace that we thought would work for the Pledge. I can remember executive committee meetings that were just horrible. All of this because it was successful.

Jim Rice concurred (1992): "The Pledge was birthed in a very religious context, but really wanted to reach out to a more secular constituency. So there was a strong, early move to include secular folks. It went to the extent, however, that some of the church people felt, 'Why are we being pushed aside here?'"

According to Fran Truitt (1990): "Some religious people got mad. There was an Episcopal priest, for example, who called me up and told me off because he didn't like that non-Christians were involved."

This uncomfortable shift to a secular constituency and style also transformed the Pledge's leadership, as Phyllis Taylor (1990) has indicated: "There clearly was an identity tension in the Philadelphia Pledge. Originally, the official office of the Pledge was our house. But as more secular groups joined the Pledge, I pulled out of Pledge leadership and other, more secular leaders took it over."

Anne Shumway (1990) recalled: "Boston has a very strong lesbian movement, and a lot of the lesbian women got involved in Pledge early as trainers in non-violence. They were quite secular, which created tensions between the different styles." Finally, many religious activists became upset over the move away from church-based mobilization. Truitt continued (1990):

> We started out with commissioning services, because we began as a faith community. Those of us who were ministers wore our robes, to be as visible as possible. But as things progressed, there began to be real division in decision-making groups all over. The humanists didn't want religious services. But the faith people couldn't do it without the services. There were some compromises made to integrate secular songs in the services. But it remained quite a struggle.

Dennis Marker elaborated (1992):

> As originally envisioned, protesters were going to gather in churches. Before doing civil disobedience, they were first to gather in their church, have a worship service, and then go out and do their protest. Then all of a sudden these hardcore activists showed up saying, "Straight to civil disobedience! Forget this church, man. We're going to meet at the civic center. And forget prayer services. We're going to yell and scream and bang pots and dance." And the church people said, "Well, that's not really what we intended." That was a real problem.

In sum, the frequently incompatible motivations and protest styles of religious and secular activists presented significant obstacles to movement-wide collaboration, sometimes caused participants on both sides to drop out of activism, and consumed large amounts of activists' energy which otherwise could have been spent fighting administration Central American policy.

THE "POLITICALLY EFFECTIVE REFUGEE" CONTROVERSY

Many of the internal problems described above tended to involve the Pledge of Resistance, Witness for Peace, CISPES, and other Central America organizations more than Sanctuary, since it was relatively more organizationally self-contained and strategically focused than these other organizations. Sanctuary, however, was not without its own serious inner problems. Paramount was a rift that developed in 1983 and 1984 between Sanctuary leaders in Tucson and Chicago that nearly rent the movement into pieces.

Underlying this dispute lay a fundamental discrepancy in the minds of the Tucson and Chicago leaders about Sanctuary's primary objective. The Tucson camp, led by Jim Corbett and John Fife, viewed Sanctuary primarily as a humanitarian endeavor to assist the victims of war. That mission necessarily demanded that the movement help all refugees whose lives appeared to be at risk, regardless of their personal or political commitments and abilities. Organizationally, that vision seemed to call for a decentralized, grassroots, horizontally linked network of churches and synagogues devoted to sheltering the refugees. In contrast, the Chicago Sanctuary leaders, led by the CRTF's Renny Golden and Michael McConnell, viewed Sanctuary as a fundamentally political movement aimed at ending U.S. support for the war in Central America by employing refugees' stories to raise the political consciousness of middle-class U.S. citizens. That vision dictated that the entire movement be united nationally under a centralized organization that could set policies, coordinate political actions, and speak for the movement with one voice. It also required that Sanctuary only work with those refugees who were politically informed, communicated well, and had "good"—that is, politically radicalizing—stories.

"Politically effective" refugees were those who were, in the words of Sanctuary activists in Chicago, "articulate," "very political," "appealing to liberal people in the community," "good speakers with good stories," "a different caliber of people, politically oriented," those who "can help stop the war and change U.S. policies," and "understand immediately that sanctuary work isn't just charity but changing American public opinion and government policy" (Lorentzen 1991: 54). According to Boston Sanctuary activist Jane Guise (1990), whose work reflected the Chicago vision of Sanctuary: "Sanctuary refugees in Boston spoke before hundreds, literally hundreds of church congregations and helped paved the way for Central American support. Those who spoke were selected—sometimes one out of fifty possibilities—as appropriate, based on several criteria. They all had strong religious commitments. They were emotionally quite healthy. They were the ones who had stories that were fairly clear-cut, that wouldn't be difficult for Americans to understand."

For the Chicago Sanctuary activists, "good" stories represented the means to generate the kind of political power needed to overturn Reagan's war in Central America. But solidifying and wielding political power was simply not on the agenda of the Tucson Sanctuary leaders. Their vision involved a relinquishing of the struggle for power, as their Chicago counterparts quickly and unhappily discovered.

The conflict between Tucson and Chicago first emerged in late October 1982. At that time, John Fife, immediately before leaving on a trip to Central America, sent two frightened Guatemalan Indian teenagers, whose village had been bombed by the Guatemalan army, to Chicago to be placed in a Sanctuary church in the North. Two weeks later, after returning from his trip to Central America, Fife discovered a letter from Chicago informing him that the two young Indians had been put on a bus back to Arizona because they were ignorant of the political situation in Central America and were, therefore, not useful. The letter made Fife sick. He began to realize that big problems lay ahead. The two youngsters were never heard from again, and Fife presumed that they had been arrested during their return trip and deported to Guatemala (Crittenden 1988: 90–91).

Over the next two years, the disagreements between Tucson and Chicago escalated into an open and divisive battle of words and actions. Chicago began to push to restrict the use of the refugee transportation network to only those refugees willing to participate in *public* sanctuary. Refugees wanting transport into anonymity or low-visibility shelter could look for help elsewhere. Tucson objected forcefully, rejecting the idea of turning away refugees simply because they were too traumatized to tell their stories to North American audiences over and over again. Though unpersuaded, Chicago yielded for the moment.

The underlying problem immediately reemerged, when the more troubling issue of assisting right-wing refugees surfaced. Among the masses of refugees flowing through Arizona were Salvadoran and Guatemalan army deserters and right-wing families fleeing the perils of left-wing guerrilla attacks. Some even had histories as death-squad members. As far as the Tucson leaders were concerned, if deportation threatened these refugees' lives, they deserved protection. To aid only politically "correct" refugees, Corbett argued, would only replicate in reverse image the government's biased treatment of refugees and reduce Sanctuary to just another political pressure group. Tucson sent Chicago their policy statement: "We provide sanctuary to the persecuted, regardless of the political origins of their persecution or of their usefulness in promoting preconceived purposes" (Davidson 1988: 82). The Chicago leaders were astounded. To them, the idea of sheltering former death-squad members was repulsive. In a February 1984 letter to Corbett, they charged Tucson of reducing "the multidimensional process of solidarity to apolitical humanitarian band-aids rather than expanding it to include all that comes from choosing the side of the oppressed. . . . To separate the religious from the political in this fashion is to create a false dichotomy" (Davidson 1988: 83). The Quaker Corbett responded that Sanctuary was a fundamentally spiritual reality that transcended the world of power struggles. In a September 1984 acceptance speech for the Institute for Policy Studies' annual Letelier-Moffitt Memorial Human Rights Award, Corbett stated (quoted in Davidson 1988: 83–84): "Sanctuary is independent of traditional political activism because the covenant people is formed by creative service rather than competitive struggle. As a result, the movement is politically as well as religiously ecumenical. . . . Sanctuary has germinated, taken root, and flourished in Tucson, not because we are converting to more radical political beliefs, but because faith communities are accepting the yoke of the Kingdom."

The Chicago camp countered (quoted in Davidson 1988: 84), "It's simply not true that sanctuary transcends the political. We have a responsibility not to take what could be the most beautiful position— what could be possible in other worlds—but to do what is historically possible." Back and forth the increasingly heated controversy stormed, in meetings, telephone conversations, private letters, and articles published in the movement's newsletter, *Basta!*. Chicago charged Tucson with naive political escapism, while Tucson denounced Chicago's "rhetoric of rage" (Crittenden 1988: 203). Tucson accused Chicago of playing into the government's hands by turning Sanctuary into a left-wing political lobby, the very thing the government denounced Sanctuary as being. Chicago, in turn, accused Tucson of assisting the U.S. government's evil by passively consenting to its deadly war in Central America in the name of Christian love and service. Corbett began sending a series of letters, called "A View from the Border," which championed his position, to Sanctuary churches and Quaker communities around the country. Incensed by what they took to be Corbett's insinuation that only those living on the border truly understood the refugee problem, Chicago rebutted each of Corbett's contentions. Increasingly, the press began to give media coverage to this hostility and division in the movement, which began to damage its generally favorable public image.

The controversy hit a low point in October 1984, when Chicago refused to send Tucson a copy of its Sanctuary mailing list to be used to help publicize their January 1985 national symposium on Sanctuary. The Chicago leaders stated they were afraid Corbett would use the list to send his "diatribes" to a wider audience, generating even more controversy and division within the movement. Flabbergasted, Tucson interpreted this as an opportunistic power play to take, from the very people who had launched it, total control over the entire Sanctuary movement. Corbett reacted with a ten-page, single-spaced letter, published in *Basta!*, announcing that he was determined to avoid a power struggle and so was resigning from the Tucson Sanctuary task force and withdrawing from a public role in Sanctuary (Davidson 1988: 84). It seemed then that the movement was beginning to unravel.

In an ironic stroke of saving luck for the Sanctuary movement, only days later the U.S. Justice Department unwittingly helped to pull the two warring sides back together by issuing its indictments of the Arizona Sanctuary workers. Facing this new external threat, Sanctuary leaders on both sides, poised on the brink of self-destruction, backed away from their battle and agreed to mediate a solution. Responding in unity to the government's challenge took precedence. John Fife proposed that six negotiators from Tucson and six from Chicago meet at the upcoming symposium. In response, most of the Chicago leadership attended the Tucson symposium, and representatives of the opposing factions stayed on for two additional days negotiating a provisional reconciliation (Crittenden 1988: 204–5). Although the crux of their original ideological differences remained (see, for instance, Davidson 1988: 130–34; Crittenden 1988: 234–35), their January 1985 reconciliation did enable the Tucson and Chicago branches to collaborate effectively, if uneasily, in Sanctuary activism for the remainder of the decade. Had the external threat of state prosection not jarred the Sanctuary leaders into a last-minute, commonsense truce, the movement's central leadership and communication structure, as well as its public image, most likely would have been permanently torn apart by these internal ideological controversies.

RE-ENTRY PROBLEMS

Walker Percy, in his penetrating book *Lost in the Cosmos*, explores the "psychic law of gravity" he claims bedevils scientists, artists, and other moderns who, because they "have trouble living in the ordinary world," launch themselves, through their work, into an "orbit of transcendence" (1983: 142):

> What is not generally recognized is that the successful launch of the self into the orbit of transcendence is necessarily attended by problems of

re-entry. What goes up must come down. The best film of the year ends at nine o'clock. What to do at ten? What did Faulkner do after writing the last sentence of Light in August? Get drunk for a week. What did Dostoevsky do after finishing The Idiot? Spent three days and nights at the roulette table. What does the reader do after finishing either book? How long does his exaltation last?

If re-entry problems afflict scientists and writers who elude ordinary existence through their work, they also plagued many Central America activists who left behind their ordinary lives by launching out on risky, challenging, and often life-transforming journeys to Central America. Those activists typically spent two to three weeks immersed in an entirely new social and political reality at the front line of a major, global military confrontation. For those brief weeks, they beheld firsthand one of the twentieth century's most celebrated and vilified sociopolitical revolutions, witnessed the horrors of low-intensity conflict, absorbed the emotional rush of bonding with the victims of their own president's brutal war, and resolved to return home and spend themselves to force an end to that war. Afterwards, when their planes touched down at the airports from which they had departed, these activists returned to families, friends, church members, and colleagues who had not shared their Central America experiences. People whose worlds had changed significantly collided with others for whom nothing had changed. For some activists, this transition was exceedingly difficult. Central America trip leader Dick Junkin described the common ordeal (1991):

> Central America was truly life-changing for many. But then people returned to unchanged life situations, without others with similar experiences with whom they could figure out what it all meant. Most people were just on their own. Often people came back overwhelmed by what had happened to them. Then people at home would ask them about their experience, but twenty seconds later their eyes would glaze over. And the travelers could tell their listeners didn't really care. Oftentimes, people's loneliness increased, their anger grew, and they just didn't have good ways to deal with it.

Witness for Peace organizer, Mike Clark, confirmed this observation (1992), "People would call us after a week at home, saying, 'I tried to tell somebody what it was like, and I totally lost it. What should I do?' This was heavy stuff. These were by-and-large educated, aware people. But when they came back from Nicaragua, they returned to lives that were no longer the ones they had left. For some that was very dis-orienting."

Complicating these re-entry problems was the issue of whether the Central America travelers enjoyed organizational ties to activism at home. Those that did not tended to have greater difficulty following through with their Central America commitments—made during their "transcendent" Central American travels—in the context of their ordinary lives. Witness for Peace did try to prepare delegates before their travels to become engaged in political activism upon returning home, and did organize regional and state coordinators, yearly retreats, workshops, and newsletters to try to sustain the delegates' critical consciousness after the trips. But these alone were not enough. According to Witness for Peace activist Clark Taylor (1990): "The problems is, unless delegates were also regularly involved in a con-sciousness-raising group, when they came home, much of their energy often dissipated. You need groups to raise consciousness and keep it there." Witness for Peace organizer Sam Hope agreed (1992), "For most delegates, the intensity of their trip probably wore off within six months, as do most other 'mountain-top' experiences. It might last six months, maybe a year. But unless someone was in a community that constantly re-enforced this viewpoint, they became acculturated to 'normality' all over again.[2]

Witness for Peace leaders almost unanimously agreed that isolated delegates represented one of the largest weakness in their organiza-tion's overall strategic program:

> We missed a great opportunity by not working harder to form local Witness for Peace chapters. U.S. networking eluded us. We just couldn't get our acts together to pull off a solid network of Witness for Peace activists. We knew that follow-up was essential but we didn't always do the best job. I volunteered to take on the job of organizing follow-up. I already worked with delegations, so it was natural that I would stick with them when they got back to the states. But that was more than I could handle. Then activists in Santa Cruz volunteered to take it on, but it still didn't get done. So, looking back, we made half-hearted attempts, but really without the strong focus we badly needed. (Crites 1992)

To summarize, the intense political energy generated in travelers by trips to Central America was sometimes blocked by devitalizing re-entry problems—difficulties negotiating transitions from transcendent to ordinary worlds—when they returned home. Those who had encountered the often transforming "Central America experience" were frequently frustrated and sometimes debilitated by a loneliness and alienation that set in when people back home proved unwilling or unable to care about or understand this experience that was so important to them. For those who were also socially isolated, who lacked organizational ties to activism, these re-entry problems sometimes ended up completely dissipating their energy for political activism. Consequently, the frequent inability of Central America organizations, such as Witness for Peace, adequately to manage these re-entry problems through better training, debriefing, and networking resulted in a net loss in the overall political strength of the Central America peace movement.

ONEROUS ACTIVISTS

One final problem that emerged from within the peace movement was the recurrently troublesome presence of misguided, unruly, inexperienced, and contentious activists. These kind of problem people came in many forms. Occasionally, some activists created trouble and irritation in the movement with their romantic glorifications of civil disobedience. Pledge of Resistance organizer Anne Shumway observed (1990):

> Civil disobedience attracts weird people who get involved for many reasons, some good, some bad. There are always people who glamorize and over-dramatize civil disobedience. Others can be self-righteous, projecting the attitude that getting arrested is the ultimate sacrifice and that those who don't are inferior. Well, I'm sorry, but some young mothers just can't go to jail. In reality, getting arrested is often a whole lot easier than doing vigils, leafletting, and lobbying week after week, because those can be so tedious. But for some people, the idea of getting arrested with the Pledge was romantic. They actually thought they were making the ultimate sacrifice to go to jail for a day. In fact, some people were annoyed to have to stay even that long. They wanted to get out right away and were angry to have to stay a night in jail. I also knew people who got indignant when the police refused to arrest us, as if it was their high-and-mighty constitutional right to get arrested. It was like a ritualistic game. They would do outrageous things to get arrested. Then they figured, "if I'm not going to get arrested, then why the hell do this?" These kinds of people are problems.

Anne Shumway (1990) recalled the problems created by another type of onerous activist: inexperienced Pledge of Resistance protesters trying to exercise strong leadership:

There was a tension in Boston between two camps: the traditional, old-style, coalition-organizing activists and the new-style, touchy-feely, New-Age, nuts-and-raisins people. These new people were chaotic, not disciplined. Many of them, totally inexperienced, would come to coordinating committee meetings. Affinity groups would send them as representatives. They would have crazy ideas. There were many novices with naive ideas. I remember, for example, having real arguments over whether we should inform the police about our protests. As an experienced activist, I know the police are not our enemies and we have a responsibility to inform them for the sake of everyone involved. But these younger people actually wanted to set up confrontations with the police by not telling them our plans. They don't know how nasty the police can get.

Furthermore, some Central America activists more committed to ideology than truth proved to be quite offensive. Cindy Buhl recalled (1993):

There were a number of hot and heavy moments around the Nicaraguan elections. I was not absolutely convinced that the Sandinistas were going to win the elections. The polling data on the draft and the economy was weak, and I said so. And can you believe, I was actually *yelled* at by some people. One person from one of the solidarity networks called me a fascist! All because I dared to say there was a slight chance the Sandinistas might lose because of their policies. Some people just couldn't accept that might happen. It was like, the Sandinistas had to win to justify our opposition to Reagan's policy. Well, that's a stupid way to look at any election.

Buhl continued:

Or take human rights violations by the Sandinistas. Here you have Americas Watch putting out these reports about rights violations on both sides. But most of the Central America activists would only talk about the Contra violations. A handful of us said we have to read the report as a whole, that maybe we won't emphasize the other part, but we have to read it if only to know what the administration will be talking about. But that was like blasphemy, a heresy. Some people just believed the Sandinistas could do no wrong: they never committed a human rights abuse, the economy would be perfect without the war, the Miskito indians on the Atlantic coast were collaborators. The list was endless. With some, like the Nicaragua Network people, you just couldn't have a discussion when you disagreed. They would end up screaming at you, "Don't you know people are dying?" Well, what are you supposed to say, "By the way, yes I do?" Some of this was pretty nasty.

Trips to Central America also ran into trouble with "problem people" who came along on the delegations. Phyllis Taylor, for example, had this experience (1990): "I've led eighteen delegations and I've had people come—it actually took me a while to figure these things out—who were alcoholics and drug addicts. Or people who had histories of emotional depression who, although they tend to be very sensitive, good, wonderful, feeling people, just can't handle what happens on a delegation. One time we had a short-termer who had a nervous breakdown out in the jungle. Real problems. So we had to get better at discerning people."

Betsy Crites also recounted (1992):

There would be people disgruntled by disappointed expectations. Sometimes, in the early years, delegates expected a profound non-violent action where they would be facing down armed soldiers. The "Shield of Love" article in *Sojourners* gave that impression, which was hard to counter. So if we went out into the countryside and nothing happened, if we didn't see a single Contra or didn't hear gunfire, people would be very disappointed and say, "This is a sham. This isn't a non-violent witness." Or if you do a vigil in the middle of a town, "Well there's no danger in that, what's the risk?" Some people were very disappointed in that, which created a negative atmosphere.[3]

Crites explained (1992) how Witness for Peace's own inexperience sometimes helped produce unfruitful delegations:

One delegation I led fell apart emotionally and psychologically. The living standards were too difficult and we pushed them too hard on the schedule. We held five meetings a day in tropical heat out in the fields, then returned, fatigued, to hammocks and rice and beans. The delegates got exhausted, they got strange. I mean, they lost it. A couple of people just lost all perspective. It took us a long time to learn, and we're still learning, that you don't have to have delegates experience *everything* in order for them to have a profound experience and understanding of what's going on.

Troubles emerged, too, around coming to consensus on legislative strategy when certain leaders sidestepped the truth in favor of their own political agendas. Cindy Buhl remembered (1993):

Some national groups were actually sending misleading information back to the grassroots. The job of any national office is to take the best reading of what is happening in Washington and relay it back to the grassroots so they can make the most accurate, informed decision on how to respond. But some groups were sending very inflammatory interpretations. I remember one group put something on their hot-line which was patently false, that would lead you to start dumping all over a particular member of Congress. When I first heard it, I thought they had just gotten confused. But no. They thought this person *deserved* to be dumped on, and if you had to change the facts, so be it! As far as I was concerned, that was a breach of contract between that national office and its grassroots. The grassroots deserves straight, accurate information, not distortions. We are not supposed to be the Elliott Abrams of the left, for heaven's sake.

Finally, many Central America peace movement organizations were troubled by ordinary interpersonal conflicts among staff members. Bob Van Denend, for example, acknowledged (1992): "Betsy Crites and I had a lot of differences of opinions—not that Betsy wasn't smart or anything, she just had very different ways of looking at things. So we fought a lot." And Betsy Crites herself recalled one difficult staff conflict among the long-term delegates in Nicaragua (1992):

> We desired to be present on the Atlantic Coast, where there was a very complicated political situation. And we wanted our delegates there to be people of color. So we recruited three black men. But we had major, major problems with that team. They were very biased in their treatment of delegations, singling out certain people as their buddies and considering the others to be racists. It was just a mess. Terrible misunderstandings developed between the black volunteers on the coast and the white long-termers in the West. They just couldn't get along. The best intentioned people in the world, but it was just terrible. I got a call, "You have to come down to deal with this Atlantic Coast problem." It was major crisis, plus financial donations were falling, our executive director was quitting, and the long-term team was totally disillusioned with the State-side staff because they thought we were imposing inappropriate policies. That was a very, very difficult time and I just couldn't take it anymore. So I said, "I will carry us through this budget crisis and these other crises, but somebody else can take over from there."

To summarize, various kinds of onerous activists often diffused devitalizing, negative energy within the movement by rankling the more experienced and balanced activists, distorting movement priorities, subverting the educational experience of trips to Central America, and absorbing energy for interminable policy debates and conflict resolution that could have gone into productive organizing and political activism.

CONCLUSION

It would be wrong to exaggerate the discord and difficulties that arose within the Central America peace movement. By most accounts, inter-personal and inter-organizational relations within the movement were characterized by complementarity, mutual respect, and constructive collaboration. At the same time, however, it would also be misleading to overlook those significant internal problems and dysfunctions that threatened to undermine the strength and effectiveness of the move-ment. Among them, "anti-authoritarianism," clashes in coalitions, incompatible protest styles, battles between Tucson's and Chicago's visions for Sanctuary, re-entry problems for Central America travelers, and onerous activists stand out as having been most problematic. In varying cases and in different ways, these problems promoted organi-zational fragmentation, handicapped effective decision making, bred exasperating planning meetings, discouraged intra-organizational accountability, generated disunified protest campaigns, burned out capable and devoted leaders, caused some activists to drop out of activism altogether, depleted other activists' energy for political engage-ment, spoiled opportunities to promote the movement's cause in the mass media, damaged certain leadership and communication struc-tures, and consumed large amounts of energy which otherwise could have been directed into external political struggle. All of these problems closer to home only impaired the peace movement's ability to challenge and defeat the Reagan administration's Central American policy—the very thing which, all the activists agreed, was their real problem.

Twelve

THE MOVEMENT'S DEMISE

All is flux, nothing stays still. . . . Nothing endures but change.

Heraclitus, *Diogenes Laertius*

By mid-1990, the Central America peace movement had largely dissolved. The wave had passed. The energy was spent. The attention of the nation moved on to other contentious political issues. The question is: Why? Exactly what happened that prompted the movement's decline? Why, precisely, after almost a decade of sustained, intense political battle, did the movement lose momentum and disintegrate?

Social movements—according to the political process model employed in our analysis—live and die by fluctuations in three critical factors: the structure of political opportunities they face, which is primary, the organizational capacity they possess, and the intensity of insurgent consciousness they enjoy. The Central America peace movement successfully emerged and sustained its struggle through the 1980s because it enjoyed relatively open political opportunities, strong organizations, and a passionate insurgent consciousness. But near the decade's end, important political events caused a contraction of the movement's political opportunities. This, in turn, weakened the movement's insurgent consciousness and rapidly depleted its organizational strength. Within a few years, the movement of almost two thousand carrier organizations, which had mobilized more than one hundred thousand activists, was reduced to a few hundred hard-core activists and organizations in financial crisis fighting against the shifts of history to maintain enthusiasm and commitment. For most Americans, the movement's struggle had become passé. This chapter seeks to explicate the specific reasons for this decline, focusing especially on the contraction of political opportunities.

THE IRAN-CONTRA SCANDAL

The beginning of the end of the peace movement actually came, ironically, with revelations in October and November of 1986 that the White House was illegally financing the Nicaraguan Contras with funds acquired through covert sales of arms to the state of Iran, sold in exchange for the promised release of U.S. hostages held in Lebanon. This was ironic because the so-called "Iran-Contra scandal" represented a crippling blow to White House Central American policy and a definitive vindication of that policy's critics. President Reagan had flagrantly breached his repeated and solemn pledge never to negotiate with terrorists and brazenly violated the Congress's constitutionally legitimate ban on aid to the Contras. He also had sanctioned a reckless and unaccountable covert government agency within the NSC and allured numerous foreign state officials into participating in these illegal activities (Report 1987; Kornbluh and Byrne 1993; Henderson 1988: 147–70). In time, it would also become known that top White House officials had arranged a cover-up of these criminal activities to protect the President from possible impeachment (Kornbluh and Byrne 1993: xv–xxii).

Few observers at the time would have predicted that the Iran-Contra exposé would undermine the Central America peace movement. Paradoxically—in a classic case of a movement's apparent triumph precipitating its own downfall—it was precisely the widespread recognition of this political damage inflicted on the administration's Central American policy that worked to undermine the very movement that had crusaded for years to defeat that policy. With the Iran-Contra revelations in 1986 and congressional investigations in 1987, many peace activists began to believe that the tide finally had turned in their favor, that a victorious political outcome was inevitable. This had the effect of somewhat relaxing the intensity of the movement's political struggle. Pledge of Resistance organizer Ken Butigan explained (1991):

> The Iran-Contra Scandal had a very interesting and contradictory impact on the movement. On the one hand, it was really vindicating, that these really were a bunch of scoundrels running a secret war that needed to be stopped once and for all. On the other hand, Iran-Contra proved to be a kind of narcotic. People began to assume, foolishly, I think, that Congress would finally deal with Reagan's war, get to the bottom of it, and stop it. So after the revelations, there weren't a huge

number of protests. Instead, there was a quiet moment when people began presuming that the truth would come out and the guilty would finally be dealt with.

Cindy Buhl, who worked on Capitol Hill, recalled (1993):

> I worked for a political action committee that helped an anti-Contra candidate get elected. Right after Iran-Contra was breaking, she came up to me at a party then and actually said, "Well, I guess I won't have to vote on Contra aid after all." I said, "What? You've got to be kidding!" She replied, "But Tom Foley said it was going to be all over, no more votes, now that Iran-Contra is out." I said, "Oh no. You wait and see." It was a real naive article of faith for a while that Iran-Contra was going to be so damaging to the President's policy that it was all over. But, in fact, it was like The Terminator: nothing could end it or kill it.

Rather than using Iran-Contra as an opportunity to escalate public protests to force an immediate cutoff of funds to the Contras and the Salvadoran military, many movement activists initially began to assume that the established mechanisms of institutionalized politics would adequately resolve the matter. In fact, only two weeks after the initial October revelations about the illegal Contra supply network, President Reagan signed into law $100 million of Congress-approved U.S. aid to the Contras. This massive amount of aid notwithstanding, Iran-Contra continued to be a mild sedative on the Central America peace movement, diminishing the intensity of the protests and lobbying campaigns that followed.

Another protest-inhibiting reaction to Iran-Contra that emerged among many Central America peace activists after the initial tranquilizing effect began to wear off was cynicism and, even later, incredulous discouragement. Anne Shumway observed (1990), "Many people in the movement got rather cynical after the Iran-Contra disclosures. And later, during the hearings, it really became kind of depressing how the American people just accepted many of the facts of Iran-Contra." Cynicism often followed successive disclosures about just how far the White House had gone in employing surreptitious, extra-institutional, and illegal means to maintain its Central American policy. To many activists, all of the movement's campaigns to pressure Congress to block the administration's policy seemed to have been pointless, since the White House had gone ahead and done whatever it pleased in Central America anyway, despite what Congress legislated. No amount of organizing and protesting, it appeared, could have ever thwarted the administration's schemes.

Even more unbelievable and disheartening was that, through his assertive, televised testimony in the 1987 congressional Iran-Contra hearings, the NSC's Lieutenant Colonel Oliver North—who Central America peace activists uniformly considered a heinous criminal— instantly became an admired and honorable national hero in the eyes of millions of Americans. The same American public that had consistently opposed U.S. aid to the Contras had now become infatuated with this hyper-patriotic Contra champion. For many Central America peace activists, that kind of political superficiality, fickleness, gullibility, and sensationalism was utterly dismaying. Both the American public and the U.S. government seemed absolutely hopeless.

Many activists thus began to fall into the sardonic and dispirited paralysis of cynicalized radicalism. That devitalizing attitude was simply reinforced when later President Reagan "couldn't recall" facts concerning his involvement in Iran-Contra; when in 1987 the Senate select committee on Iran-Contra deliberately avoided investigating new evidence of Oval Office illegalities because they thought "the country didn't need another Watergate"; when Independent Counsel Lawrence Walsh was forced to drop an entire criminal case because the Justice Department, for whom he ostensibly worked, refused to declassify key documents needed for the trial; and when on Christmas Eve 1992, President George Bush preempted an exposure of the original White House cover-up by unconditionally pardoning all five government officials who had admitted to or been convicted of criminal wrongdoings related to Iran-Contra (Kornbluh and Byrne 1993: xix–xxi). To an increasingly large number of the peace activists, fighting such an all-powerful, deceitful, and self-protective system seemed absolutely futile. Among them was a seventy-seven-year-old Witness for Peace activist, who in 1990 wrote on his questionnaire: "After serious effort to change U.S. policy over the last six years, today I have developed a sense of hopelessness about having achieved anything from so much focused effort. The fact that Robert McFarlane, Oliver North, and others involved in Iran-Contra got off without punishment is very disturbing, as was Robert Gates' becoming CIA director after his involvement in the illegal Contra network."

Iran-Contra, then, because of the initial overconfidence and eventual cynicism and discouragement it aroused in many activists, began to close off political opportunity and triggered a downward-spiraling process of quelling the Central America peace movement's insurgent consciousness.

THE ESQUIPULAS PEACE ACCORD

Renewed peace talks among Central American leaders helped significantly to accelerate the decline of the Central America peace movement. In January 1987, the U.S. proposed that the presidents of Costa Rica, Honduras, El Salvador, and Guatemala meet on February 14–15 in San Jose, Costa Rica, to sign an accord that would force the Sandinistas to negotiate with the Contras and would call for the "restoration of democracy" in Nicaragua, that is, the replacement of the Sandinistas with a more U.S.-friendly regime. Nicaragua would then have fifteen days to agree to the terms. If they did not, the other Central American governments would enact political and diplomatic sanctions against Nicaragua, designed to force the Sandinistas from power. Costa Rican President Oscar Arias, however, resisted this U.S.-designed proposal, claiming that any successful plan would have to disband the Contras as a precondition for peace. The Reagan administration forcefully objected to this major revision and strongly pressured Arias to endorse the original U.S. proposal. But Arias refused (Roberts 1990; Sklar 1988: 374–75).

On August 7, 1987, the Central American presidents, disregarding a last-minute substitute U.S. peace proposal, met in Esquipulas, Guatemala, and signed a peace accord of their own design. Together, they agreed simultaneously to end outside assistance to insurgent forces, to terminate the use of their border territories to facilitate aggression against neighboring nations, and to pursue ceasefires, amnesty programs, political dialogue, and self-determining democratization (Roberts 1990). This Esquipulas peace accord was quickly endorsed by the Contadora Support Group, the Secretary General of the United Nations, and the Organization of the American States. The next month, Arias addressed the United Nations, calling "on any powers intervening in the region to suspend military aid," and declaring that "We want to take the fate of our region into our own hands." Two months later, the Costa Rican president was awarded the Nobel Peace Prize for his breakthrough negotiating efforts (Sklar 1988: 376–81). Over the next months and into 1988, all of the Central American nations, including Nicaragua, began to implement the agreement. In March 1988, the Sandinistas and the Contras signed a temporary ceasefire truce, and on April 16 they signed a permanent ceasefire accord. Genuine peace in Nicaragua, it seemed, was attainable. In time, peace negotiations also commenced in El Salvador, eventually culminating in a final peace agreement in El Salvador, signed on December 31, 1991, that ended the ten-year war between the FMLN rebels and the government (Vickers 1992).

In the U.S., the Esquipulas peace accord distressed the Reagan administration, which wanted greater control over the terms of the agreement and more concessions from the Sandinistas.[1] It also took the wind out of the sails of the peace movement, as activists began to believe that they were witnessing the fulfillment of their ultimate goal, peace in Central America. According to Jim Rice (1992), "Very simply, people originally got involved because there was a crisis. But when the crisis passed, they went off into other things. The winding down of the Contra war was a major change. It really looked like it was over. When people who had been fighting for ten years became convinced that 'Yes, this really looks like it's over,' you might not have achieved justice, but the fight is over."

Betsy Crites concurred (1992), "We really had to struggle with the new reality that we weren't fighting the Contra war anymore, but something different. Other forms of low-intensity conflict? Okay, but how do you make that exciting? It just didn't have the gripping edge that the Contra war had."

This dynamic undercut almost all of the movement's political organizations, with the possible exception of the Sanctuary network: "The Pledge of Resistance really started to fizzle after people began to perceive that the war would be over. 1987 and 1988. I sort of lost track of it. In fact, that's when I myself stopped even caring about what the Pledge was doing" (Crites 1992).

Witness for Peace's Mike Clark observed (1992):

> From the start, we always had the supply of delegates we needed. But by 1987, with the Esquipulas Agreement, we had to become much more intentional about how we recruited, about what would attract people. Originally, people volunteered when they knew there was an immediate crisis. There was an attraction then and people wanted to put their bodies on the line. But when the crisis began to fade, so did the enthusiasm. By 1988, we began hearing excuses we would have never heard before, like, "Well, that's really when my husband's vacation time is for this year." In 1985 we never heard that. People literally dropped whatever

they were doing. So nobody actually began saying, "Nicaragua is less important now." They just said, "I can't miss my cousin's college commencement." But that's effectively saying the same thing.

This perceived end of crisis also altered the sense of dedication and sacrifice within organizations, placing more demands on their financial resources, just when contributions were plummeting. According to Witness for Peace organizer Sam Hope (1992), "As things felt less like a daily life-and-death struggle, we started to hear more conversations about staff benefits and vacation days and salary levels—the kind of things I heard in church years ago which led me to leave the clergy."

Despite, or perhaps because of, the Esquipulas accords, President Reagan continued to pursue a military overthrow of the Sandinistas, instructing his top advisers that he wanted the Sandinistas forced out of power before the end of his presidency. To that end, the White House continued its pro-Contra media efforts in the U.S. press, urged the Contras to step up their military attacks on Nicaragua, pressed Congress for $36 million in Contra aid, and threatened most of the Central American countries with a U.S. aid cutoff if they continued to negotiate with Nicaragua (Felton 1987; Sklar 1988: 383–88). In spite of this continued policy of U.S. military aggression that the peace movement had fought for years, the more the Esquipulas-based Central American peace process advanced, the more political opportunity contracted, and the more the U.S. Central America peace movement lost its political momentum.

PRESIDENT GEORGE BUSH

Ronald Reagan was unable to force the Sandinistas out of power by the end of his presidency. The man who succeeded Reagan in January 1989—former Vice President George Bush—did not share Reagan's passionate commitment to a Contra overthrow of the Sandinistas (Schorr 1989). President Bush—more pragmatically than ideologically driven—prudently avoided the Central America controversy with great care. As one January 1989 *Business Week* headline stated, "For Bush, Central America Won't Be a Crusade" (Baker, Boyd, and Arana 1989). During his presidential bid, Bush's campaign managers declined even to discuss the Central America issue with Reagan administration officials (Millett 1990: 21).

Many factors played into this fundamental shift in orientation. To begin, Bush had witnessed firsthand the political damage that Reagan's preoccupation with Central America had inflicted on the Reagan presidency and did not wish to incur similar damage himself (Felton 1989a). Also, by any realistic assessment, the Iran-Contra scandal had killed any chance of Congress's passing a significant *military* Contra aid package in the near future (Baker, Boyd, and Arana 1989). Furthermore, years of experience had proven that the Salvadoran army remained unable to prevail over the rebel guerrillas. Besides, George Bush and his new Secretary of State, James Baker, were interested in making their mark, not in Central America, but in the more traditionally dominant area of U.S. international relations, Europe and the Soviet Union. Accordingly, with the inauguration of the Bush presidency, Central America quietly dropped from public view and existing "Reagan Doctrine" policies were deliberately dismantled (Schorr 1989). Rather than battling against Congress, within two weeks of his confirmation by the Senate, Secretary of State Baker adroitly negotiated with Congress a bipartisan agreement on modest nonlethal Contra aid (Roberts 1990: 69–70; Congressional Quarterly 1989). And by late 1989, in a radical departure from the previous administration's policy, the Bush administration was pressuring the Salvadoran government to negotiate a peace agreement with the FMLN rebels that would guarantee their safe participation in a democratic political system. Heading up the diplomatic initiative, Assistant Secretary of State for Inter-American Affairs Bernard Aronson declared that for El Salvador, "The only path to peace is at the negotiating table" (Arnson and Forman 1991: 97–100; also see Felton 1990; Bush 1989; Doherty 1991).

For the very reasons that President Reagan's high-profile approach to Central America abetted the peace movement, President Bush's nearly invisible and more conciliatory approach worked to marginalize the movement. Whereas President Reagan's strategy had eliminated the possibility of public indifference to the region, President Bush's approach made the traditional attitude of public indifference to Central America not only possible, but probable. While Reagan had made Central America a lightning-rod issue that united many of his natural political adversaries for opposition, by avoiding controversy over Central America Bush deprived Central America activists of such a unifying issue. And whereas Ronald Reagan's aggressive policy had inflamed deeply rooted cultural fears of "another Vietnam," George Bush's compromising approach more clearly resonated with the U.S. national self-image, also deeply rooted in American political culture, of the U.S. as a benevolent and enduring champion of peace, freedom, and democracy in the hemisphere. Thus, by greatly reducing the political significance of Central America in Washington politics, President Bush effectively undercut the political opportunities for and relevance of the movement that had based its identity entirely on that issue.

THE SANDINISTA DEFEAT

Iran-Contra, the Esquipulas peace accord, and George Bush's presidency seriously damaged political opportunities for and the vitality and relevance of the Central America peace movement. The decisive death-blow to the movement came on February 25, 1990, when the Sandinistas, led by President Daniel Ortega, were unexpectedly defeated in a national election by UNO, an opposition coalition headed by presidential candidate Violetta Chamorro. The Sandinista defeat was a clear upset. Nicaraguan opinion polls prior to the election showed Ortega leading Chamorro by a 51- to 24-percent margin. And the Sandinistas' closing campaign rally—attended by four hundred thousand people—was more than six times larger than UNO's closing rally, which only drew sixty thousand (Robinson 1992: 294). But in the end, Chamorro won 54 percent of the vote over Ortega's 42 percent.

For its part, the Bush administration had taken all possible steps to promote an UNO victory. In 1989 the Bush administration closed down the Contras' offices in Washington and Miami, pushing key Contra leaders to return to Nicaragua to participate in the election. Then, the CIA, without informing Congress, established the Nicaraguan Exile Relocation Program, a covert operation that funneled more than $600,000 to one hundred Contra exiles to support their political work inside Nicaragua during the eight months prior to the election. Eleven Contras who received funding became candidates for the new legislature. And $100,000 of the funds went to Elfredo Cesar, a former member of the Contra Directorate who had been appointed a key political adviser to UNO's candidate Chamorro (Kornbluh 1992: 299). Beyond that, the CIA channeled more than $28 million directly and indirectly into the UNO campaign. CIA advisers also worked with UNO leadership, effectively designing in detail the opposition's overall campaign strategy. And the U.S. Congress authorized $9 million in overt election assistance through the National Endowment for Democracy, $7.7 million of which went to UNO and its affiliated civic, labor, and press groups (Robinson 1992: 111–32).[2] Hence, U.S. Representative George

Miller of California observed: "We funded the Contras, we have destroyed [Nicaragua's] economy, we have taken Mrs. Chamorro and we pay for her newspaper to run, we funded her entire operation, and now we are going to provide her the very best election that America can buy" (Miller 1989: H6642).

Ultimately, the real cause of the Sandinista defeat was neither the millions of dollars of U.S. campaign aid to UNO nor a genuine disaffection among a majority of Nicaraguans for the FMLN political and economic program. Rather, it was an awareness on the part of most Nicaraguans that another Sandinista electoral victory would mean continued U.S. economic and military hostility toward Nicaragua, whereas a victory for the U.S.-sponsored UNO coalition would bring a conclusive end to the bloody Contra war and a repeal of the economically catastrophic U.S. economic embargo (Vanden and Walker 1991: 173; Kornbluh 1992: 300). In William Robinson's words (1992: 3): "The Nicaraguan elections were a contest, not between the Sandinistas and their domestic opposition, but between the Nicaraguan Revolution and the United States." The Bush administration had abandoned—at least provisionally—attempts to secure military aid to the Contras. But in order to maintain political pressure on the Sandinistas, in April 1989, the White House successfully negotiated with Congress $49.75 million in nonlethal aid to keep the Contras intact until the February elections. In May and October of 1989, the Bush administration twice renewed the ongoing U.S. economic embargo against Nicaragua. Then in September 1989 five thousand Contras reinfiltrated Nicaragua from Honduras and began a series of new military attacks against civilians. Under continued Contra attack, in November—three months before the February election—the Sandinistas were forced to suspend their unilateral ceasefire and launched a major army counteroffensive. Only weeks later, President Bush launched a major military invasion of Panama, demonstrating his readiness, if necessary, to employ U.S. military force in Central America. Altogether, these events sent a clear signal to the Nicaraguan people that as long as the Sandinistas remained in power, both the protracted, indecisive Contra war and the U.S. economic embargo would carry on indefinitely. This was an option that the majority of war- and poverty-weary Nicaraguans were no longer willing to endure.

Whatever the cause of the Sandinistas' electoral defeat, its effect on the Central America peace movement was unambiguous. Caught off guard by the election's outcome, a great many activists, who were typically sympathetic to the Sandinistas, became very disoriented and depressed. According to Phyllis Taylor (1990): "There was a lot of depression after the lost election among activists who were politically aligned. And that was on top of the discouraging disintegration of the Nicaraguan economy and spirit." Joe Nangle observed (1992): "There were a lot of people in the movement who were really shocked, disappointed, and depressed when the FSLN lost the elections." Ken Butigan likewise recalled (1991):

> February was the Nicaraguan election. People had organized around making the elections fair. Fffhhheeeeeeww . . . [long exhale, then pause]. The outcome was a very difficult thing for people in this movement, the kind of thing you would expect to kill a movement. We had a protest already scheduled for the next month and had hoped that people would be mad as hell and come down. Well, people who had their heart in El Salvador—which was still a live issue—did come, and we actually had a good turnout. But most people there were very depressed.

Anne Shumway observed (1990), "The Sandinista loss was heart-breaking—that was such a brave little revolution. There was a sense among activists, 'What can we do now?' The whole movement just began to disintegrate. Today, the groups that are trying to hold on are in grave financial trouble. Every peace group I know is now facing major financial difficulties."

In the words of Bob Bonthius (1990): "The movement's 'Red-and-Blacks' [Sandinista partisans] came out in spades during the election. And people's real feelings came out. There was quite a lot of distress over the Sandinista loss. Central America groups are now in deep trouble, closing up shop all over. The movement has fallen with the fall of the Sandinistas, because the old interpretation of Central America just doesn't make as much sense to people anymore."

And, according to Betsy Crites (1992), "There was a long period of recovering from the loss, of trying to understand what the election meant, why it had happened, why we had miscalculated. I heard a long-termer whom I respect very much say, 'We should have known it was going to happen.' It was just a signal to us that we weren't as tuned in to the Nicaraguan people as we thought we were."[3]

The Sandinista defeat disoriented and depressed many Central America peace activists because most viewed the Sandinistas as a symbol of the Central American people's tenacious resistance to U.S. interventionist bullying. Many activists had also held high hopes that the

Sandinista Revolution could create a Latin American society that would genuinely benefit its people more than its oligarchs. The Sandinistas' defeat, for the activists, both marked the end of Nicaragua's "underdog" resistance and killed the dream of a genuine people's revolution. Indeed, no interpretation of the election results was comforting for Central America peace activists. If the loss represented a genuine and uncoerced rejection of the Sandinistas and embrace of the UNO coalition, including its Contra elements, then, apparently, the U.S. Central America peace movement had been fighting valiantly for a cause in which the Central Americans themselves did not even believe. On the other hand, if the Sandinistas' loss was due primarily to U.S. military, economic, and political manipulation and coercion, then the election merely demonstrated that the U.S. had, in fact, successfully reestablished its dominance over the region, despite all resistance. In short, the movement either had been entirely misinterpreting the Central American reality or had simply failed. Either way, movement activists had reason to feel defeated, disoriented, and depressed. Consequently, any of the movement's insurgent consciousness that had managed to survive Iran-Contra, the Esquipulas peace accord, and George Bush's presidency quickly dissipated. The structure of political opportunities closed completely.

NEWLY EMERGING POLITICAL ISSUES

The Central America peace movement, which by 1989 was rapidly expiring and by 1990 was essentially dead, was finally swept out of American politics by a new set of emerging political issues. Important among these were the collapse of communism in Eastern Europe in 1989 and the breakup of the Soviet Union in 1990; the U.S. confrontation with Panamanian President Manuel Noriega that culminated in the December 1989 "Operation Just Cause" invasion of Panama, in which Noriega was captured and brought to stand trial in the U.S.; America's "drug war," which employed U.S. military resources to combat drug-smuggling from Colombia, Peru, and Bolivia (see, for instance, Felton 1989b); the onset of a U.S. economic recession in 1989; and, most importantly, Iraq's invasion of Kuwait in August 1990, which resulted in a tense, five-month political and military standoff between Iraq and the Allied nations and, eventually, the ejection of Iraq from Kuwait in the full-blown Gulf War (Hooglund 1992). Although each of these issues captured significant political attention in the U.S., none of them, not even the Gulf War, became an issue around which peace and justice activists were able seriously to mobilize. Hence, Central America activists were marginalized by historical change and left without a major movement in which to participate. Anne Shumway stated (1990), "The Central America movement is mostly disintegrated. Let's face it, Americans are a fickle people and Central America is no longer the hot issue. At this stage, everyone is worried about war in the Middle East. The Central America issue has gotten diffused. And it's so hard to know how to get a handle back on it."

CONCLUSION

The demise of the movement was induced by the same kinds of factors that sparked its original emergence: macro-political and social changes that altered the movement's structure of political opportunities, which, in turn, affected its organizational strength and modified the intensity of its insurgent consciousness. To be more precise, we might say that the movement's demise is attributable to a combination of success, failure, and irrelevance. Its decline was partly due to a form of success, as negotiated peace agreements put an end to the region's worst military conflicts. Its disintegration was also the result of a sense of failure, when the Sandinistas were removed from power by the Nicaraguan people. Additionally, the movement's dissolution was due to irrelevance, as a new president and newly emerging political issues pushed concerns about Central America to the sidelines of U.S. politics.

Then, as political opportunities closed, activists "allowed" their sheer exhaustion to set in. Many had been organizing opposition to administration Central American policy for the better part of the decade and had somehow managed to keep going. Each new White House bid for Contra aid, every anniversary of the murders of Archbishop Romero and the four North American churchwomen, each new Guatemalan refugee family in need, every annual appropriations bill containing military hardware and training for the Salvadoran army, and each new revelation of CIA or NSC criminal wrongdoing had required another lobbying campaign, another prayer vigil, another spokescouncil meeting, another clandestine drive from Arizona to California, another protest demonstration, another overnight in jail. As long as political opportunities had remained open, the activists were able to take on this seemingly endless series of physically, emotionally, and financially draining activities—along with the attendant FBI visits, tax audits, mail tamperings, infiltrations, political break-ins, state prosecutions, death threats, clashes in coalitions, conflicts over protest styles, re-entry problems, and onerous activists. But when political opportunities began to contract, the activists simply ran out of steam. According to Pledge of Resistance organizer Anne Shumway (1990): "Political activism is really difficult to sustain year after year after year. We really put ourselves into it, but at the end, people got tired." Likewise, Phyllis Taylor observed (1990): "Many political factors caused the movement's decline, and the fact is, many activists just became very tired." And Bob Van Denend recounted (1992), "Eventually I just left Witness for Peace, which was really the right thing for me to do. So many problems had developed and I was just sick of dealing with them. I mean, I had worked for non-profit organizations most of my adult life and, quite frankly, I was just pretty tired of it all." Finally, Witness for Peace organizer Betsy Crites recalled (1992): "I was getting so burned out trying to deal with all of the responsibilities and problems, I had to take a three-month sabbatical during the summer of 1988 just to keep sane. And when I returned, there were a whole new set of problems to deal with. So, I fulfilled my obligations, then backed out of my prominent position pretty much for good."

This chapter completes our analysis of the Central America peace movement's ongoing struggle to maintain, over the decade, a successful political battle against the Reagan administration's Central American policy. In the following and final two chapters, we turn our attention to assessing the movement. What, we will ask, did the Central America peace movement actually accomplish? And what might the movement teach us theoretically about the dynamics of social movements generally?

Part Four
Assessing the Movement

Thirteen

WHAT DID THE MOVEMENT ACHIEVE?

Nothing worth doing is completed in our lifetime; therefore, we must be saved by hope. Nothing true or beautiful or good makes complete sense in any immediate context of history; therefore, we must be saved by faith. Nothing we do, however virtuous, can be accomplished alone; therefore, we are saved by love. No virtuous act is quite as virtuous from the standpoint of our friend or foe as from our standpoint. Therefore, we must be saved by the final form of love which is forgiveness.

Reinhold Niebuhr, *The Irony of American History*

What did the Central America peace movement achieve? In one sense, that is an impossible question. For, without a comparative "control case" of the Reagan Central American policy *unconstrained* by a Central America peace movement, it is impossible to identify with certainty which of history's actual outcomes are attributable to the influence of the movement and which are not. How would events have differed had President Reagan's Central America crusade met little organized opposition? That we can never precisely know.

But lacking ideal comparative conditions does not mean we are totally helpless to venture even a cautious evaluation of the movement's accomplishments. A tentative assessment is better than no assessment at all. Minimally, we can identify what the movement failed to achieve. Beyond that, we can venture a cautious, educated appraisal of the movement's political successes. Finally, we can assess the movement's impact on its participants, and the potential effects of that on future social movements.

FAILURES

The judgment we can make with greatest confidence concerns what the Central America peace movement did *not* achieve: ultimately, the movement was not able to force the Reagan administration to terminate its wars in Central America (see Brett 1994). Despite the movement's fierce opposition, the administration prevailed in sustaining its well-armed counterrevolutionary forces in the field in Honduras and Costa Rica, and so the Contra war in Nicaragua raged on year after year. The Reagan administration also prevailed in maintaining its generous aid package to the embattled regime in El Salvador, sustaining its only lifeline of economic and military viability. Consequently, El Salvador's civil war also ground on for the entire decade. In the end, the Reagan administration essentially had its way. In Nicaragua, the war-weary Nicaraguans cried "uncle," the Sandinistas were ousted from power, the Nicaraguan revolution was terminated, and a U.S.-friendly regime took political control. In El Salvador, an FMLN victory was thwarted, revolutionary social transformations forestalled, and a regime acceptable to the U.S. retained power. Overall, U.S. influence in the region was reasserted and reinforced.

Central America peace activists uniformly recognize their failure in this regard. According to Mike Clark (1992), "We didn't achieve what we wanted to. On the big questions, they won, we lost." Angela Berryman (1990) agreed, "In the end, the Reagan administration got its way. In that sense, our movement was a failure." According to Sam Hope (1992), "Ultimately, Reagan won the battle." Phyllis Taylor (1990) concurred: "That we didn't stop the war was a failure for us." And Dennis Marker (1992) explained, "We could not stop Reagan and Bush from destroying the Nicaraguan revolution. Could not stop tens of thousands from being killed throughout the region. Could not stop the unbelievable amounts of military aid. In those ways, we failed."

A minority of the peace activists also voice another sense of failure: the failure of the movement to fight as entirely effectively as it might have. Cindy Buhl (1993), for example, lamented,

> We really needed to develop more sophisticated, over-arching, long-term, targeted field campaigns for swing-states, to hire crack field staff to go in and organize. We never did. We spent more than one million dollars on Countdown, a short-term campaign. But there was never money for long-term work. And the Central American people paid the price for it. It was the tyranny of the urgent, the fickleness of funders and executive boards who don't understand long-term programs, who'll only fund familiar, short-term campaigns. Once, they did try the right idea, but implemented it badly and declared the whole thing a mistake. This was the so-called "Southern Strategy." There is still a false folklore that we actually tried to organize South Central states, which

is ridiculous. So we are *still* weak in exactly the same states we have always been. And when the next crisis comes up, we'll *still* lose the same goddam votes in exactly those states. That's a failure.

Similarly, some believe the Sanctuary movement failed to capitalize sufficiently on its potential to use the media to challenge the Reagan policy. If so, this may be because, initially, media coverage came easily for Sanctuary, and therefore its leaders were never forced to develop the organizational facility necessary to generate news coverage in later years. According to Jane Guise (1990), "Early on, the media paid lots of attention to the Sanctuary movement, but after the trials, Sanctuary was dropped." Dennis Marker (1992) elaborated:

> Sanctuary was golden. It was total integrity, a major movement. But it got much less media attention than it should have because there wasn't anyone doing the press work, interpreting the movement to the media. You had one big splash and an occasional story, but there was no one following up, making the day-to-day contacts, pressing the case. I would have loved to have done it, but I was already over my head. There may have been some media work done, but it mostly seemed they were making it up as they went along. So, Sanctuary's real importance and bigness was not being interpreted to the country. That was a major lost opportunity.

But these were a minority of voices. On the whole, most activists believed that their failure to stop Reagan's wars in Central America was not due to a lack of effort. Most believed they had fought their hardest and best, and had failed anyway.

ACHIEVEMENTS

That the Central America peace movement ultimately failed to force the Reagan administration to terminate its wars in Central America does not mean that the movement cannot also be credited with some successes. To begin, from the perspective of many movement activists, particularly religious activists, the baseline measure of success is faithfulness. Many activists view their actions and their movement as partially successful because they believe that they faithfully acted upon their convictions and principles (Taylor n.d.: 1–2).

> For a lot of church people, myself included, success is defined a little differently. Because faith is the reason we get into activism, faithfulness is one of the ways we judge it. Not all the focus is on political goals. Crite-

ria for success can be, Were you true to your beliefs? Did you adhere to non-violence? Did you help to transform people in the church? Of course, you also want to win. But that's not all. Faith and faithfulness are also what we're about, and they keep us going, pressing on. (Rice 1992)

Besides the success, from the activists' perspective, of acting faithfully, the peace movement can also claim one major political accomplishment. Even cautiously judged, it is apparent that the movement made the Reagan administration's Central American policy of low-intensity warfare exceedingly difficult to implement, and therefore helped to limit significantly the severity of its destructiveness. Without the movement's opposition, the administration's policy actions would have been much more overt, intense, and unrelenting, and the human misery and loss of life in Central America would have been greater. Primarily as a result of the massive opposition generated and sustained by the Central America peace movement, with the help of the Vietnam syndrome, the Reagan administration was forced to expend a tremendous amount of political capital to achieve what it *did* accomplish, was prevented from employing as much military force in Central America as it would have liked, and, ultimately, was forced to resort to illegal means to prosecute its war against Nicaragua. In the end, those illegalities threatened to bring down the entire Reagan Presidency. In Sam Hope's (1992) words: "We made a big fight out of something that otherwise would have been a non-issue. We helped escalate the matter to the point that it really became a major bone of contention, and that made a real difference for Central Americans."

The Central America peace movement's primary political leverage consisted in pressuring Congress to cut off or reduce U.S. military aid to Central America. In attempting to procure that aid, the White House's task was made difficult by the Boland Amendment, by congressional hearings on human rights abuses by the Salvadoran regime and the Contras, by congressional oversight and restrictions of CIA covert activities, and by the greatly contested, recurrent Contra aid votes, which the administration often lost. Overall, the Reagan administration was awarded notably less Central American military aid than it requested. And the Central America peace movement was probably the most important force consolidating and sustaining congressional opposition to the Reagan policy. According to Central America Working Group Director and congressional strategist and lobbyist Cindy Buhl (1993), who worked more closely with members of Congress than perhaps anyone else in the movement:

Grassroots activism was critical, not marginal. Without it there never would have been a base of congressional opposition. No one took on Ronald Reagan just for the fun of it. Why should any member of Congress challenge the President at the height of his powers, and put their neck on the line for puny little Central America, unless it were for broad constituent pressure? The Peace movement was active and growing. And members of Congress were acutely aware of that.

Buhl (1993) explains that, in Congress, there were a small committed core of opponents and another of supporters of Reagan's Central American policy. These cores, regardless of what their constituencies said, unwaveringly championed their respective positions because of their firmly held principles and real knowledge about Central America. The rest of the members of Congress were "followers," whose votes—whether they thought the White House Central American policy made sense or not—were decided by the immediate forces of political pressure. This was precisely the Central America peace movement's opportunity:

> When you look at Contra aid votes, over time you see about 180 regular opponents and 180 regular supporters of the policy. Then you have that beautiful, vacillating swing list in between. How did the 180 regular opponents become so constant and loyal? Not because they were educated and committed on this issue. Certainly not because they were Sandinista allies. So, aside from weak party loyalties, why were they always voting against Reagan, no matter how irresolute their personal positions on Central America might have been? Simply because of grassroots pressure. We couldn't have sustained those 180 votes for so many years without the grassroots staying so passionately engaged and constantly growing. Almost all of those 180 regular opponents would say that it was pressure from the grassroots that determined their vote. Even some key swing votes against Contra aid, like Dennis DeConcini in the Senate, credited the movement for exposing them to information that they thought was compelling. (Buhl 1993)

According to Gail Phares (1992): "We messed up White House propaganda quite effectively in Congress. We went face-to-face in Washington with our "What We've Seen and Heard" books, with pictures of Contra violence and everything. We continually went to Congress, sat in their offices, and made sure they read our material and saw the reality, so they knew what this vote was about. We did that very effectively."

In addition to pressuring congressional representatives into oppos-

ing the President's policy, the Central America peace movement provided congressional allies with useful, supportive information. Mike
Clark (1992) has said, "When Congress debated Contra aid, often
Witness for Peace was the only source of information. Senators would
stand up and say, 'There have been 37 attacks in 18 different places
over six months.' They knew those facts because *we* were on the front
lines, gathering and publicizing them! *We* were the source of the information that sometimes influenced votes."

Because the peace movement helped create and sustain major congressional resistance to the Reagan Central American policy, and thus
partially constrained the administration's ability to intervene in Central America, the extent and intensity of the region's military conflicts
were notably diminished. Largely because of movement activism, the
Nicaraguan Contras—who, for some years required Oliver North's
extra-constitutional intrigues simply to stay alive and together, "body
and soul"—had far fewer military resources than they otherwise
would have had with which to wage their destructive war. Some evidence also indicates that, because of the physical presence of Witness
for Peace delegates in Nicaraguan war zones engaging in protective
"interposition," some Contra attacks on Nicaraguan targets were prevented and some Nicaraguan lives were saved (Taylor n.d.: 4–5). Also,
largely because of movement activism, the White House was forced to
exert continual pressure, which otherwise it would not have, on the
regime in El Salvador to curb the army and death squads' gross human
rights violations. And it appears that, although Salvadoran army and
death-squad atrocities were already rampant, they would have been
even worse without the U.S. pressure for improvements. Furthermore,
in response to the 1990 murders of the four Salvadoran Jesuits and
their housekeepers, protest from the Central America peace movement helped spur Congress into cutting Salvadoran aid in half, which
contributed to the negotiated settlement of the civil war: "Just look at
how the Salvador policy has gone last year: the Senate voted 75 to 25
to cut military aid in half. That resulted, in part, from our movement's
protests. Had there been a 'China-movement' around Tienamen
Square, the administration could have never followed its policy of
condoning the Chinese government's crackdown. Movements in this
country make that kind of a difference" (Butigan 1991).

Finally, although it is impossible to determine, short of a high-ranking Reagan administration official acknowledging the fact, it is not so
very unlikely that the peace movement prevented what would have

otherwise been a full-scale U.S. invasion of Nicaragua. This possibility is most difficult to judge, and opinions disagree even within the Central America peace movement and among political analysts. It is certainly possible that, even without the movement's widespread grassroots opposition, the Reagan administration would not have launched a U.S. invasion of Nicaragua. But it is also possible that it would have.[1] Other than disruptive domestic protest, it is not clear what might have prevented the President from doing so.

President Reagan unquestionably believed the Sandinistas represented a major threat to U.S. national security interests and plainly stated that he wanted to see the FSLN overthrown. Strategically, he had clearly rejected the diplomatic option of negotiation and compromise. The President approved preludes to and unambiguous acts of war against Nicaragua, including the CIA mining of Nicaraguan harbors. Furthermore, the U.S. armed forces, having repeatedly rehearsed an invasion of Nicaragua in joint military exercises in the region, were fully capable of launching a U.S. invasion to overthrow the FSLN (see Brinkley 1985a, 1985b). Moreover—with factors such as MIG fighter jets allegedly being imported from the Soviet Union, and thousands of U.S. citizens in Nicaragua whose lives could have been claimed, as in Grenada, to have been in danger—the White House was fully capable of creating a "situation" justifying a U.S. invasion. Most importantly, by invading and overthrowing the governments of Grenada and Panama, both Presidents Reagan and Bush demonstrated their complete readiness and willingness to launch full-scale U.S. invasions in the region. Minimally, it would not have been aberrant behavior for President Reagan to have launched a U.S. invasion of Nicaragua. Whether he actually *would* have without a Central America peace movement, however, and whether he actually did not *because* of the Central America peace movement we cannot conclude. The evidence merely suggests this as a real possibility.

Whether or not the peace movement did prevent a full-scale U.S. invasion of Nicaragua, one final political outcome of the movement is certain. The movement helped to force the administration into a position where it had to choose to resort to extraordinary and illegal means to proceed with its policy in Central America. A good part of why the Central America peace movement ultimately failed, especially on Nicaragua, is not because it was unable to use the rules of the political system to accomplish its goals, but because the Reagan administration, when thwarted, chose simply to *disregard* the rules of the political system. Had the White House actually followed the provisions of the U.S. Constitution and other statutes, the movement could have claimed much greater political success, especially with Nicaragua. Instead, the unyielding Reagan administration chose to skirt congressional oversight of covert activities, fabricate human rights improvements in El Salvador, engage in harassment and repression of domestic dissent, unlawfully use tax dollars to fund public diplomacy campaigns, violate established treaties of international law, reject and belittle the rulings of the World Court, and, most astoundingly, secretly divert to the Nicaraguan Contras millions of dollars from the illegal sale of military arms to Iran, a terrorist enemy of the U.S. Having entangled themselves in this snarl of disreputable and illegal activities, with the Iran-Contra affair at its pinnacle, members of the administration then attempted a failed cover-up of criminal wrongdoings. In the end, most high-ranking members of the Reagan administration were found to have lied about these improprieties, and twelve players in the administration's Central America intrigues—Caspar Weinberger, Robert McFarlane, Duane Clarridge, Clair George, Elliott Abrams, Alan Fiers, John Poindexter, Carl Channell, Albert Hakim, Richard Miller, Richard Secord, and Oliver North—were convicted of Contra or Iran-Contra-related criminal wrongdoing (Arnson 1993: 297–301).[2] The reputations and authority of President Reagan and many in his administration were damaged and weakened. In this way, the Central America peace movement not only helped to force the Reagan administration to pay a very high price for the success of its Central America policy, but also inadvertently contributed to the ultimate, partial demise of the Reagan Presidency and administration. In the words of Ken Butigan (1991), "The Central America Peace movement forced the creation of Oliver North. Implementing this policy meant going underground, relying on secrecy, skirting the law. And all of this eventually came crashing in on Reagan and his lot."

THE FORMATION OF ACTIVIST IDENTITIES

Perhaps the Central America peace movement's most profound consequences were not seen in the 1980s, but will only become evident in future years and decades. It may be that the movement's most important impact was not accomplishing certain political goals in the 1980s, as important as they may have been, but expanding the base of grass-roots activists, especially faith-based activists, who will serve as the core mobilizers of larger, even more consequential peace and justice movements in the future.

Social-movement scholarship has made increasingly clear the critical interconnections between seemingly distinct movements and campaigns. McAdam (1988) has shown that the civil rights movement of the early 1960s was directly responsible for helping to generate the student free-speech, women's liberation, and anti-Vietnam movements of the late 1960s and early '70s. Chatfield (1992) has advanced a view of the U.S. peace movement, not as a single mobilization at one period of time, but as a long tradition comprised of advancing and receding waves. Luker (1984) has posed a comparable view of U.S. anti-abortion campaigns. Rupp and Taylor (1987) have demonstrated the importance of the committed remnant of early twentieth-century suffrage activists in maintaining the women's movement during the doldrum years for its eventual resurgence in the 1960s and '70s. Meyer and Whittier (1994) have revealed that the U.S. women's movement had an important impact on the subsequent U.S. peace movement. And Smith (1991) has shown that the emergence of the liberation theology movement in Latin America was facilitated and conditioned by a host of other prior religious and secular movements and campaigns, which themselves had no intention of generating liberation theology.

Recognizing these interconnections and "spillover effects" (Meyer and Whittier 1994) is vital in assessing the impact of the Central America peace movement. For, not only will that movement likely prove to serve as a sustaining organizational and cultural bridge to important movements in coming years, but, at the individual level, that movement has redirected and transformed the lives of tens of thousands of its participants in ways that will likely promote their involvement in subsequent social movements. As Gail Phares says (1992), "Many of our people will remain active for the rest of their lives. Peace and justice is something you don't just drop. It's a lifelong commitment. We recruited and empowered a lot of people. We taught people how to work with the press, with Congress, with their churches. They know they can make an impact, really do things. That's never going to change."[3]

Theoretically, even limited experience in social movements is significant because it can radicalize participants and familiarize them with the "script" used to play the "social activist" role. When movement activists are seen as engaged in a long-term role-transformation process that gradually deepens their commitment to and participation in political activism, each successive social-movement involvement appears to help activists both become more comfortable with their participation in activism and engage in a broader range of more challenging and disruptive activist tactics. In this way, any significant level of participation may help in the long term to form stronger political-activist identities.

Through the Central America peace movement, a host North Americans with little prior movement experience were politicized, socialized into the activist subculture, and taught the language and skills of organized, disruptive protest. And for a multitude of other Americans with substantial prior movement experience, participation in the movement reaffirmed their activist identities, refined their organizing and protest skills, and strengthened their political commitments. One Witness for Peace delegate wrote this characteristic comment on her questionnaire: "Anyone who comes on a delegation and sees what U.S. policies are doing here in Nicaragua can't go back without questioning everything we were ever taught by our country. The experience challenged us not just about Nicaragua, but about everything we are as North Americans." According to Mike Clark (1992), "You *thought* you were going to Central America to offer solidarity and moral support, then you discover that your *life* had been changed. That's what happened. Thousands of people fought Reagan for years because Central America changed their lives. Lots of people experienced struggle and suffering there for the first time."

Central America activist Clark Taylor (1990) disclosed, "I made my first trip to Nicaragua in 1985 and decided to make Central America the issue for the rest of my life. I learned Spanish, have traveled to Central America more than twenty times since, and have become totally immersed in the struggle for Central America."

Phyllis Taylor (1990) recalled, "People's lives were profoundly transformed. When people sleep on a dirt floor in a sleeping bag for the first time; when very wealthy people, surrounded by kids in a refugee camp sit there weeping, just weeping over the realization of what our government's doing, that is change."4

The actual numbers involved are impressive. After only three years of existence, Sanctuary had drawn in more than seventy thousand participants (Golden and McConnell 1986: 3). In two years, the Pledge of Resistance mobilized eighty thousand U.S. citizens (Butigan 1991). Witness for Peace provided life-transforming experiences for more than four thousand North Americans, and, even as late as 1990, enjoyed a constituency of forty thousand supporters and newsletter readers. Witness for Peace and the Pledge of Resistance alone taught thousands of people how to use the mass media for political activism, and trained more than eighty thousand people in the philosophy and tactics of nonviolent civil disobedience (Taylor n.d.: 5–6). Thousands were arrested for civil disobedience, very many for the first time in their lives. And the more than one thousand other local, state, and national Central America organizations provided similar experiences and training for their members (Central America Resource Center 1986). All told, counting overlapping involvements, well more than one hundred thousand U.S. citizens appear to have been mobilized into some form of Central America peace activism that gave them exposure to and education in grassroots political protest. From what we know about social-movement mobilization and recruitment, we should expect these now more experienced activists to serve as the core mobilizing base and early joiners of social movements that may emerge in years to come. Cindy Buhl (1993) observed:

> We educated and mobilized an incredible number of people on what would have normally been an obscure foreign policy issue. This was the largest mobilization of Americans around a foreign-policy issue since Vietnam, without even having "our boys" fighting there. The educational effect was amazing. Many church, labor, and left-wing people learned a lot about dealing with Congress, policy-making, the media, and about fighting for something worth fighting for. Many religious people have developed a strong, ongoing connection with the poor in Central America. And much of the movement's core has remained intact, unlike the post-Vietnam experience. So there is a core out there, one that can quickly respond again to a new crisis. It will take a long time before we have to start from scratch again.[5]

Dennis Marker (1992) agreed:

> Each new movement involves people from the last movement—Vietnam, anti-nuclear, whatever. Then you also pick up new people. With Central America, we picked up a huge number of religious people. Not everyone joins every succeeding movement. Some may choose to sit out the next issue. But they're still there, a base that's not going to go away. The hope is that you just keep building until it reaches the 100th monkey, when you finally get to where you actually have enough people to make a big difference. Instead of being limited to small changes, you get to where you can actually tip the scales. That's what we're working toward.[6]

Finally, the Central America peace movement also appears to have contributed to the effectiveness of potential social movements in the future by generating two innovative tactics of disruptive political protest. First, Witness for Peace created and implemented the novel idea of an accompanying and interpositioning "shield of love," of sending waves of delegations of ordinary U.S. citizens to hazardous battle zones to try to deter enemy offensives, to document atrocities, and to return to the U.S. as "living media" to challenge and terminate a U.S.-sponsored war. Mike Clark (1992) rightly observes, "Witness for Peace was the first time in American history that large numbers of non-combatant U.S. citizens were put in a war zone to see the war from the other side and, hopefully, through sheer physical presence, to prevent enemy attacks." Second, the Pledge of Resistance formulated and executed the novel idea of proactively organizing the capacity to unleash massive, nationally coordinated civil-disobedient protest *before,* rather than after, a U.S. invasion, in order to deter that invasion from ever happening, rather than trying to reverse the invasion after the fact. Tactical innovations such as these afford challengers important new mechanisms of power with which to struggle against and outmaneuver their adversaries, at least until opponents are able to devise countervailing tactical adaptations (McAdam 1983). Admittedly, the applicability of these particular tactical innovations depends on a particular set of favorable conditions. Nevertheless, the U.S. government throughout the 1980s did seem incapable of adapting an effective tactical response to these innovations. Thus, by expanding the tactical repertoire available to the progressive activist community, the Central America peace movement has enhanced the potential political power of peace and justice movements that may emerge in years to come.

CONCLUSION

The Central America peace movement failed to force the Reagan administration to end its low-intensity wars in Central America. This was partly because the movement was unable to pressure Congress into acting more decisively, especially on El Salvador, and partly because the Reagan administration simply disregarded the law when Congress did act decisively, especially on Nicaragua. Nevertheless, the movement did make the Reagan administration's Central American wars exceedingly difficult to conduct, and, as a result, substantially limited the severity of their destructiveness. As devastating as they were, had the peace movement not challenged the White House, those wars would have been even more devastating. It is possible that the movement even prevented a direct U.S. invasion of Nicaragua. Largely as a result of the movement's resistance to the President's policy, the Reagan administration was forced to pay a very high price for its exploits in Central America. Indeed, the movement helped to create a political context within which the administration felt compelled to make reckless choices and, consequently, began to self-destruct. Finally, the movement innovated new tactics of political protest, and educated and trained tens of thousands of U.S. citizens in the philosophy and methods of grassroots activism and disruptive political rebellion. In so doing, it may very well prove to be a critical wave in the long, historical tradition of grassroots peace and justice activism.

Fourteen

LESSONS FOR SOCIAL-
MOVEMENT THEORY

> The actions of individuals can only be understood by reference to the social con-
> text inside which they are placed, or, more exactly, only by reference to the
> structure of the system of interaction in which they participate. . . . One of the
> fundamental ambitions of sociology [is] to analyze the complex relations
> between the structure of systems of interaction defined by social institutions,
> and the expectations, beliefs, and actions of actors.
>
> Raymond Boudon, *The Logic of Social Action*

What might we learn from the specific case of the Central America
peace movement that can help us to build more analytically useful
models of social-movement emergence, struggle, and decline? This
book contains several theoretical arguments and implications, of various degrees of import. The following six points seem most to merit
reemphasis.

POLITICAL OPPORTUNITIES ARE PARAMOUNT

In the search for key factors that govern the generation and outcome
of social movements, political process theorists—such as McAdam
(1982), Tarrow (1983), Meyer (1990), Smith (1991), and Costain
(1992)—who argue that shifts in political opportunity structures are
of paramount importance, have hit the bull's-eye. The case of the Central America peace movement merely adds to the number of diverse
movements and campaigns whose births, lives, and passings appear
best explained by openings and closings in the structure of political
opportunities. Perhaps more than any other factors, President Reagan's obsessive preoccupation with Central America, the political vulnerabilities generated by the Vietnam syndrome, division and elite
defection in the U.S. government, and repeated White House policy
blunders explain why the peace movement irrupted and flourished.

And the political effects of the Iran-Contra scandal, the Esquipulas peace accords, the ascent of President Bush, the electoral defeat of the Sandinistas, and the displacement by new political issues most adequately explain the movement's demise. Without vital openings of political opportunity, the impressive reserves of organizational capacity, human and financial resources, well-formed collective identities, and moral outrage that the nascent movement would yet have possessed would have been insufficient to activate the massive movement that eventually emerged. And with the eventual contraction of political opportunities all of those resources and energies proved inadequate to sustain widespread mobilization and disruption. This recognition of political opportunities as paramount is an insight that social-movement scholars should fully embrace and exploit.

CROSS-NATIONAL INFLUENCES ARE CRUCIAL

As the world has become more economically, politically, and culturally interdependent, social movements have increasingly been shaped by cross-national influences and processes. Organized disruptive politics have increasingly spilled over the borders of individual nation-states. Hence, movements arise in one country whose issues and beneficiaries reside in another. New grievances, strategies, and tactics are diffused cross-nationally. Campaigns are prompted and financed by international and multinational nongovernmental organizations. And activists in individual countries link up with their counterparts in others to form truly internationalized movements.

In the case of the Central America peace movement, cross-national linkages and processes constituted the heart of the movement's identity and purpose, and help explain the movement's very existence. The movement was, of course, a mobilization of North Americans on behalf of Central Americans, occasioned by ominous developments in the larger geopolitical struggle of the Cold War. Furthermore, the movement's emergence was provoked, in part, by the sometimes deliberate and sometimes serendipitous collision of two disparate worlds. To truly understand the origins of the movement, we must recognize the importance of developing papal social doctrines emanating from the Vatican in Rome, the expanding work of North American Protestant and Catholic missionaries in Central America, the radicalizing influence of Latin American liberation theology on many North American Christians, the international organizational structure of the

Roman Catholic Church and Protestant denominations, the flood of migrating refugees from war-torn Central America who ended up politicizing middle-class North Americans, the encouragement offered by European and Canadian protests against President Reagan and his Central American policy, and the geographical proximity of Central America that made short-term travel to the region feasible for thousands of U.S. citizens. Future social-movement studies will reap fruitful benefits by focusing greater attention on the increasingly critical role that international influences and processes play in the generation and outcomes of disruptive political activism.

RELIGIOUS RESOURCES ARE RICH

Social-movement scholars have badly neglected the important role that religion often plays in the life of social movements. Whether because of theoretical limitations, personal proclivity, or something else, social-movement analysts have inadequately accounted for the empirical reality that religion has served as a rich resource for a host of important movements (see Smith 1996).

The case of the Central America peace movement makes clear the decisive impact that religious faith and organizations can make in generating, sustaining, and legitimating disruptive protest. The core motivation and sustaining nurturance of many, if not the majority, of Central America activists was their religious faith.[1] Organizationally, the movement was brought to birth primarily by a network of religious organizations—the AFSC, Sojourners, Clergy and Laity Concerned, New Jewish Agenda, the National Council of Churches, and a multitude of Quaker meetings, along with various religious congregations, denominations, and task forces. Moreover, religious groups facilitated the movement's growth through network chains of communication and bloc-recruitment. In turn, religion served as a primary factor in the negotiation of the movement's collective identity. Religion also provided a variety of expressive symbols, icons, and rituals which served to rally and focus many activists, and to embody their grievances publicly in emotionally powerful ways. Finally, the strong religious character of the movement's constituency gave it a unique political authority and legitimacy that the White House was unable to undermine. Thus, in an April 23, 1985, *Washington Post* article, Assistant Secretary of State Langhorne Motley conceded (quoted in Cohn and Hynds 1987: 119), "Taking on the churches is really tough.

We don't normally think of them as political opponents, so we don't know how to handle them. It has to be a kid-glove kind of thing. They are really formidable."

CIA Director William Casey is reported (in Woodward 1987: 402) to have remarked, "If Tip O'Neill didn't have Maryknoll nuns who wrote letters, we would have a Contra program." Social-movement analysts will often more fully understand their subjects of study by attending more closely to these and other kinds of resources that religion often contributes to many important social movements.

INSURGENT CONSCIOUSNESS IS SOCIALLY STRUCTURED

Resource mobilization theory did social-movement studies a great service by encouraging analysts provisionally to set aside the traditional, primary focus on grievances, and to concentrate instead on organizations, resources, and strategies. But in recent years many scholars have recognized that grievances cannot be entirely ignored or presumed. The objective grounds for grievances *may* be widespread, but people's subjective interpretations of them as injustices that need redressing through collective action are not. Partly because consciousness is a factor not easily measured and analyzed, however, the renewed attempt to understand grievances has not developed as fully as one might have hoped.

The case of the Central America peace movement invites us to view insurgent consciousness as socially located, as heavily conditioned by people's social-structural positioning—especially in cases where movements' constituencies are not their primary beneficiaries. This approach points beyond differences in people's personal attributes, to socially patterned, situational factors that condition people's likelihood of feeling the moral outrage and political commitment we call insurgent consciousness. Employing a micro-structural approach, informed by insights from phenomenological sociology and the sociology of knowledge, we see that in the Central America peace movement, insurgent consciousness irrupted primarily among people who enjoy two structural characteristics that affected the social distribution of knowledge: "cognitive accessibility" (organizational and relational positioning that afforded exposure to norm-violating information) and "subjective engageability" (cultural and social positioning that propelled these violations into high-priority positions in people's personal relevance structures).

Insurgent consciousness first developed among people of faith, partly because they did not have to rely on news media accounts or White House press briefings for information about Central America. They had their own sources of information on the ground in Central America: missionaries, social service workers, pastors, members of religious orders, denominational leaders, and bishops. They were, in other words, cognitively accessible: relationally and organizationally well-positioned to be exposed to information that deeply violated their moral sensibilities. People of faith were also socially located in ways that ranked the Central America crisis as a matter of personal, immediate concern in their individual and collective relevance structures. Their social ethics, relational ties to Central America, keen interest in liberation theology and the Nicaraguan revolution, outrage over the murders of Archbishop Romero and the four churchwomen, and personal confrontations with Central America through refugees' stories and travel to the region, for many Christians and Jews, thrust the potentially abstract issue into the paramount reality of their every-day consciousness. Because they were subjectively engageable, in these ways, a public concern became their personal crusade.

Future studies of disruptive political activism might benefit by more fully utilizing this kind of micro-structural analysis of the development of insurgent consciousness.

ACTIVIST IDENTITIES ARE ACQUIRED

Social-movement scholars, in recent years, have given increased attention to micro-structural determinants of differential recruitment to activism, to the formation of movements' collective identities, and to the macro-cultural, -social, and -political effects that social movements produce. Less attention, however, has been paid to individuals' *prior life experiences* that appear to draw them into activism, to the formation of *individual* activist identities, and to the consequences of activism on *individual* movement participants. The case of the Central America peace movement invites us to investigate more deeply how individuals acquire personal identities over time, in which the role of "political activist" is salient, and how participation in movements may revise these acquired identities in ways affecting participation in subsequent social movements.

Central America peace movement activists tended to have brought to the movement a significant amount of prior activist experience and political radicalism. Participation in the movement appears to have expanded their activist skills and fostered an increased political radicalization. These activists, therefore, can be viewed as engaged in a long-term role-transformation process, which has gradually deepened their commitment to and participation in political activism. With each successive social-movement involvement, these activists appear to have become more comfortable with their participation in activism, and to have engaged in a broader range of more challenging and disruptive activist tactics. In these ways, experience in movements seem to have tended to radicalize participants and increasingly familiarize them with the "script" used to play the "social activist" role. Thus, through the Central America peace movement, many North Americans with little prior activist experience were politicized, socialized into the activist subculture, and taught the language and skills of organized, disruptive protest. And for many other Americans with substantial prior movement experience, participation in the movement reaffirmed their activist identities, strengthened their organizing and protest skills, and reinforced their political commitments.

All of this suggests the value of further studies employing a life-course or quasi-longitudinal "role adoption" approach (see Turner 1990; Demo 1992; Stryker 1980: 55–65), seeking to answer these kinds of questions: Do social-movement activists come from distinctively different kinds of family backgrounds? What social pattern orders the process whereby individuals are introduced to social-movement activism and subsequently over time acquire activist identities? What factors differentiate between novice activists who increasingly adopt the activist role as part of their identity structures and those who don't? How are activist identities maintained or altered during dormant periods between surges of active movement participation? How do experiences such as impermanent biographical nonavailability—such as having young children or beginning demanding new careers—and activism "burnout" affect activist identities? By taking this approach and seeking to answer these kinds of questions, social-movement scholars may contribute significantly to the depth and sophistication of our understanding of social movement participation.

MORALITY MATTERS

Plausible sociological analyses of social movements, I believe, must employ, explicitly or implicitly, three essential analytical components:

1) an account of the distinctive internal normative commitments and interests that guide the actions of the individual and group actors in question, 2) an account of the external, facilitating and constraining socially structured environment within which those actors act, and, 3) an account of the causal mechanisms operating through meaningful, intentional human behavior that link the factors which are claimed to explain a problem (the *explanans*) and the problem that needs explaining (the *explanandum*).[2] If this is so, then it is essential that we operate with a clear understanding of the model of human motivational social psychology that underlies our analysis. Sociology over the decades has advanced many disparate images of the human person. Humans have variously been depicted as organically bonded components of holistic communities, conflictive cravers of wealth and power, compliant enactors of socialized role expectations, instinct-deficient constructors of meaningful cosmic orders, exchange-making maximizers of self-satisfying utility, passive objects of determinative structural forces, and symbolically interacting self-communicators of identity and intention.

The case of the Central America peace movement suggests that, whatever else humans are or are influenced by, human persons should be understood to be, at their core, normative and moral creatures. This movement erupted, in part, because President Reagan's Central American policy deeply violated the moral beliefs and normative standards of tens of thousands of U.S. citizens. For them, the prospect of using U.S. tax dollars to invade Nicaragua, to sponsor the Contra war against Nicaragua, to prop up El Salvador's military machine and political system, to militarize Honduras, and to deport vulnerable Central American refugees to life-threatening situations was so morally reprehensible that they felt compelled to mobilize a political movement to stop that from happening. This view suggests that people draw on the resources of their cultural traditions and, through a process of lived experience, develop within and among themselves standards of what is right and wrong, appropriate and inappropriate, obliged and prohibited, just and unjust. These standards operate as potent guides and measures of thought, feeling, and action. People conduct their lives, in part, to fulfill the imperatives of their normative standards, and people judge themselves and those around them according to how well they have done so. When dearly held standards are egregiously violated, people sometimes take action to try to oppose and prevent further violations. Thus, many social movements emerge when people's sense of what is right and just is so seriously violated that they feel compelled to organize to set things right.

This account of human motives enables us to explain grievances and self-sacrificial commitments on grounds other than those of rational egoism. Insurgent consciousness can erupt not only when people's own well-being is threatened, but also when their moral standards are flagrantly violated. This helps, in part, to account for "altruistic" movements—such as the animal rights movement, the U.S. anti-apartheid movement, and organized efforts in 1940s Europe to rescue Jews from the Nazis—where actors whose well-being is not immediately threatened mobilize on behalf of others whose well-being *is* threatened, and thereby sometimes endanger their own welfare. Furthermore, moral motivations, in some cases, help to overcome the free-rider problem apart from material, selective, or solidary incentives, indeed, in a way that transcends the very logic of incentives. When commitments are motivated not simply by the expectation of achieving particular ends—teleological motives—but also by the belief that certain actions and commitments themselves are moral imperatives, regardless of their consequences—deontological motives— humans can be propelled into taking the kind of self-sacrificial actions that are critical for generating and sustaining social movements. Social-movement analysts might better understand the sources of mobilization by taking seriously not only activists' interests and incentives, but also the vital moral commitments that motivate and guide their actions.

The Distribution and Activities of Central America

Peace Movement Organizations

The obvious difficulties of systematically analyzing the social distribution and activities of fifteen hundred to two thousand social-movement organizations spread throughout the U.S. are mitigated by the existence of a national directory of Central America organizations, compiled in 1986 by the Central America Resource Center of Austin, Texas. This *Directory of Central America Organizations* contains the names and addresses of 1,061 organizations—a very large sample of all existing Central America peace movement groups—along with brief descriptions of their work. Basic information from this directory with corresponding data about the cities and states in which these organizations were located were combined into one database in order to describe significant features of the network of organizations that carried out the political work of the peace movement. That information was supplemented with data drawn from a second national directory of all four hundred declared Sanctuary groups, compiled in 1987 by the Chicago Religious Task Force on Central America.

According to the Central America Resource Center's *Directory,* by 1986 peace movement groups had been formed in every U.S. state but Mississippi and Nevada. Sixty percent of the groups listed identified themselves as being local, 18 percent as regional, and 22 percent as national organizations. This distribution, however, certainly underrepresents the proportion of local organizations that because of their relative isolation and low-profile were much more difficult for the *Directory* publishers to locate. Few of the 423 declared Sanctuary groups listed in the Chicago Religious Task Force directory, for example, were listed in the Central America Resource Center's *Directory.* Had they been, the distribution of types of organizations would have shifted to 72 percent local, 13 percent regional, and 15 percent national. Hence, most of the Central America peace movement carriers were organized as local groups.

Regionally, 32 percent of the *Directory*'s Central America organizations were located in the northeastern U.S. and 32 percent in the four states that border Mexico. Seventeen percent of the listed organizations were located in midwestern states, 12 percent in western states (excluding the Mexico-border states), and 7 percent in southern states. The number of Central America organizations per state varies enormously, from 222 in California to one each in Wyoming and North Dakota (see table A.1). Calculating the ratio of a state's total population to the number of Central America organizations located in that state establishes a comparative measure of how "well organized" for Central America activism each state was. Those levels also vary widely, from Washington, D.C.'s nine thousand residents per organization to Alabama's 2,026,000 residents per organization (see table A.2).

Further analysis reveals significant differences in the geographical regions' levels of organization for activism ($F=2.59^{***}$, $Eta^2=.50$). Western states and Mexican-border states were the most well organized for activism, with regional averages of 129,900 and 143,600 citizens per Central America organization, respectively. States in the northeast and midwest were moderately well organized for activism, with respective regional averages of 175,800 and 354,200 citizens per organization. Southern states were least well organized, with an average of 691,800 citizens per Central America organization. Significant differences in the regional location of various types of Central America organizations were found as well ($\chi^2=125.31^{**}$). Northeastern and Mexican-border states had extra high densities of national-level Central America organizations, while regional-level groups predominated in the south. Western, midwestern, and southern states possessed relatively high proportions of local groups. Furthermore, significant associations exist between types of groups and the relative levels of organization-for-activism of the states in which those types were located ($F=1.88^{***}$). National organizations tended to be located in the most well-organized states, averaging, as a group, 153,100 citizens per Central America organization. Local groups, on the other hand, predominated in the least well-organized states, averaging 260,000 citizens per organization. And regional-level organizations were most likely found in moderately well-organized states, with a group average of 234,700 citizens per Central America organization.

As to the kinds of activism in which the Central America organizations were involved, 64 percent engaged in political action, 95 percent did educational work, 42 percent were involved in raising and ship-

Table A.1. States with Greatest Number of Central America Organizations

State	Number of Central America SMOs	Percent of All Central America SMOs
1. California	222	20.9
2. New York	124	11.7
3. Texas	76	7.2
4. Washington, D.C.	71	6.7
5. Massachusetts	51	4.8
6. Minnesota	39	3.7
7. Pennsylvania	35	3.3
8. Colorado	34	3.2
9. Illinois	31	2.9
10. Oregon	30	2.8
11. Washington	30	2.8
12. Arizona	24	2.3
13. Wisconsin	24	2.3
14. Ohio	19	1.8
15. Montana	17	1.6

Source: Directory of Central America Organizations 1987.

ping direct assistance to Central America, and 38 percent worked with refugees in the U.S. Different types of organizations appear to have specialized in distinct kinds of work. Local groups, for example— compared to both national and regional organizations—tended to specialize in political action (χ^2=43.13***) and direct-assistance work (χ^2=21.77***). Regional organizations, on the other hand, tended to focus more than local or national groups on refugee work (χ^2=24.22***). National organizations—which were least likely to engage in political, refugee, and direct-assistance work—tended to specialize in educational efforts, but not significantly more so than local and regional groups, since almost every organization (95 percent) undertook educational work as part of its mix of actions.

Eighty-six percent of the Central America organizations listed in the *Directory* were located in college and university towns or cities— an extraordinarily high number, compared to the approximately 15 percent of all U.S. cities and towns which contain colleges or universities. This, however, does not suggest a great correlation between activism and dense student populations, since, as we saw in chapter 7, few Central America peace activists appear to have been university students. Rather, it points to an association between social-movement activism and demographic concentrations of members of the so-called

Table A.2: Most and Least Organized States Relative to State Population

Most Organized	Number SMOs	State Residents per SMO (x1,000)	Least Organized	Number SMOs	State Residents per SMO (x1,000)
1. Wash., D.C.	71	9	15. Ohio	19	566
2. Montana	17	48	14. W. Virginia	3	639
3. Vermont	7	77	13. N. Dakota	1	679
4. Oregon	30	90	12. Tennessee	7	686
5. Colorado	34	96	11. Nebraska	2	799
6. Massachusetts	60	97	10. Michigan	11	831
7. Maine	12	98	9. Florida	14	834
8. New Mexico	14	106	8. New Jersey	9	847
9. Alaska	5	107	7. Georgia	7	872
10. Minnesota	3	108	6. S. Carolina	3	1126
11. California	222	122	5. Arkansas	2	1186
12. Arizona	23	142	4. Kentucky	3	1243
13. New York	124	143	3. Alabama	2	2026
14. Washington	30	149	2. Mississippi	0	——
15. Wisconsin	24	199	1. Nevada	0	——

Source: Directory of Central America Organizations 1987; County and City Data Book 1988.

"knowledge class"—in this case, university faculty and administrators. Members of the knowledge class appear more likely than the average American to possess the social attitudes, political information, and organizational skills associated with activist involvement (Bruce-Briggs 1979; McAdam, McCarthy, and Zald 1988: 711–12).

Analysts have suggested that an important social-structural factor promoting social-movement activism is the increased geographic concentration of people through urbanization. This ecological convergence, many argue, increases the density of human interaction, which facilitates movement organization and recruitment (see, for instance, McAdam, McCarthy, and Zald 1988: 703). Our data confirm this theory. The 1,061 Central America organizations listed in the *Directory* tended, as a whole, to be located in large urban centers. Indeed, the average population of the towns and cities where the organizations were located was well over one-half a million residents—549,058 to be exact—a population larger than that of the cities of Seattle, Pittsburgh, and Minneapolis. And this average population is based on the populations of the cities as distinct political units, not the populations of the entire metropolitan areas—what the Bureau of Census calls

Consolidated Metropolitan Statistical Areas or CMSAs—to which most of the cities belonged. Furthermore, a moderately strong association exists in the data between urbanization and organization for activism. The states that contain the nation's thirty largest cities, for example, also tended to be the states that had the largest number of Central America organizations relative to the state's entire population (r=.392**). In addition, overall the greater the percentage of a state's population that resided in urban areas of twenty-five hundred or more, the larger the number of Central America organizations existed in that state relative to the state's entire population (r=.425**). Significant associations also exist between urbanization and type of organization. National organizations tended to be located in the most urbanized states (averaging 87 percent of the population urbanized), local organizations in the least urbanized states (averaging 76 percent urbanized), and regional organizations in moderately urbanized states (averaging 78 percent urbanized) (F=5.70***, Eta^2=.107). Finally, Central America organizations that engaged in political action tended to be found in towns and cities with smaller populations than those which did not engage in political action (F=8.22**).

Sociologists have also suggested that another important social-structural factor promoting social-movement activism is the economic prosperity of both society in general and activists in particular. Such prosperity is said to provide both the broad social conditions that favor the emergence of collective action—namely, advanced communications systems and a sizable knowledge class—and the resources to support many movement carrier groups (McAdam, McCarthy, and Zald 1988: 702). Clearly, the U.S. in the 1980s was, as a whole, a prosperous society. In 1980, for example, the U.S. per capita Gross National Product ranked third in the world at $17,670. U.S. society at that time possessed all of the social infrastructures and systems that are known to facilitate movement emergence. Additionally, the data reveals a significant association between state prosperity and activism: among all states, the relatively richer states tended to be those that were more organized for activism, relative to their population (r=.33***). At the same time, however, the average per capita money income of cities where the 1,061 Central America groups were located was only 104 percent of the national average. Additionally, the average growth in per capita money income, from 1979 to 1985, for the cities where the Central America organizations were located was exactly that of national average: 49 percent. Nevertheless, at the individual level, which is ultimately most telling, we saw in chapter 7 that Central America peace activists tended to earn relatively high incomes.

Variations in prosperity at the state level also appear to correlate with differences in some of the types of activist work in which the Central America organizations were engaged. Specifically, and somewhat counterintuitively, organizations involved in direct-relief work tended to come from cities with lower per capita money incomes relative to average state incomes ($F=6.96^{**}$). Moreover, organizations engaged in direct relief work and refugee work tended to be located in cities with relatively lower rates of income-growth between the years 1979 and 1985 ($F=4.39^*$ and $F=3.94^*$, respectively). This negative association between direct-relief work and prosperity suggests a few possible explanations. Poorer communities that wanted to become involved in Central America activism may have felt that their relatively limited resources would achieve a more definite and tangible positive effect for the region by being spent on the direct shipment of clothes, medicine, and tools to the Central Americans than by being spent on long-run education and political-action efforts. Moreover, reflecting the well-established negative relationship between social class and political participation, activists from poorer areas may have also felt relatively more alienated from the political system and uncomfortable with participation in it.

Notes

INTRODUCTION

1. As typified in this comment by two social-movement analysts: "The 1980 election of Ronald Reagan, with his strident and bellicose rhetoric, and, simultaneously, the heightened tensions in various hot spots around the world (e.g. . . . Central America) . . . provide any number of events and issues around which a peace activist might rally. Yet, with the revival of the peace movement in the 1980s, attention was focused almost singularly on the nuclear threat" (Snow and Benford 1988: 212).

CHAPTER 1

1. See, for example, Brockett 1990; Weeks 1985; Schoultz 1987; Durham 1979; DeWalt and Bidegaray 1991; Huizer 1972; Carmack 1988; Paige 1975; Sheahan 1987; Singelmann 1981; Diskin 1983; Graham 1984; Eckstein 1989; Fagan 1987; Grindle 1986; Hoeffel 1984; Gorostiaga and Marchetti 1988; Bulmer-Thomas 1987; Barry 1987; Anderson 1984; Schulz 1984; Stein and Stein 1970; Bowen 1984.

2. Wiarda notes: "To think that Central America's growth was . . . almost at a 'miracle' rate comes as something of a surprise. But in fact the growth rates in Central America all through that period [the 1950s–1970s] were in the range of 5 to 7 percent per year—considerably greater than in the United States" (Wiarda 1984: 13).

3. Central American economies, measured in GNP, continued to grow until 1978, but that growth was artificially and temporarily maintained by a relatively strong demand for regional exports and easy access to foreign credit (Gorostiaga and Marchetti 1988: 127).

4. These guerrilla groups had been active for years. Nicaragua's FSLN was founded in 1961; the first of El Salvador's armed guerrilla groups—the Popular Liberation Forces—began in 1970; and Guatemala's guerrilla groups had begun insurgency in the early 1960s. However, it was not until the mid to late 1970s that these guerrilla groups became more unified and grew in popular support. In El Salvador, for example, "only in the late 1970s and early 1980s, when human rights violations increased markedly, did major elements of the Salvadoran center give up all hope of reform and begin to drift toward revolutionary movement" (Coleman 1991: 44). Also, "the Guatemala government had been fighting revolutionaries intermittently since 1960. [However,] the out-

break changed dramatically in political complexion during the mid-1970s when significant numbers of Indians joined the revolutionaries" (LaFeber 1991: 7).

CHAPTER 2

1. "A survey conducted in the first days of 1981 found that respondents ranked the conflict in El Salvador as the fourteenth most important news story of the previous year, just above the marriage of Prince Charles to Lady Diana Spencer. . . . A year later . . . three-fifths of the American public, including two-fifths of college graduates, did not know which side the United States was supporting in El Salvador" (Falcoff 1984: 361).

2. Specifically, Mozambique, Zimbabwe, Angola, Grenada, Nicaragua, Iran, Afghanistan, Laos, Cambodia, Guinea-Bissau, Soã Tomé, Cape Verde, and Ethiopia.

3. According to Pastor (1987: 230): "By the 1980 Presidential election, according to two public opinion analysts, North Americans 'felt bullied by OPEC, humiliated by the Ayatollah Khomeini, tricked by Castro, out-traded by Japan, and out-gunned by the Russians. . . . Fearing that America was losing control of its foreign affairs, voters were more than ready to exorcise the ghost of Vietnam and replace it with a new posture of American assertiveness. As Carter had reflected America's need in 1976 to restore honesty and integrity in government, in 1980, Ronald Reagan reflected America's need to take control of its destiny and the world's."

4. According to Vaky (1984: 237): "Literally, a *vital* interest is one upon which the nation's survival depends. To use the term has traditionally been a portentous step; it means that the nation will use military force."

5. According to Rubin (1984: 301): "President Reagan himself and many of the Reaganites came from California and other western and southwestern states. Latin America loomed larger for them than for the 'realpolitik' faction that was more oriented toward Europe. The Reaganites often had close personal contacts with Latin American conservatives. . . . The battle over the Panama Canal treaties was the first foreign policy test of the newly resurgent right, further sensitizing it to Central American security questions."

6. Haig's advocacy of quick and strong action on Central America was also a political maneuver to jockey for a stronger position in the new administration, according to Rubin (1984: 302; also see Destler 1984: 321): "When Alexander Haig became secretary of state in January, 1981, he immediately opted for a high profile on Central America. The secretary of state was determined to place himself quickly in the leading foreign policy role, but he was aware that the Reaganites thought him too moderate on issues like arms control, the pipeline, and NATO. Members of the White House staff closer to him ideologically distrusted his ambition and questioned his loyalty to Reagan's leadership. By giving Central America top priority in the administration's first weeks, Haig could demonstrate to the Reaganites his anti-Soviet toughness, outmaneuver Secretary of Defense Caspar Weinberger (who was challenging him over NATO and arms control policy), and establish his public credentials

as the administration's 'vicar' on foreign policy. El Salvador would be made into a symbol of U.S. willpower in opposing Soviet-Cuban aggression."

7. This interpretation was drawn, in part, from the analysis of the so-called "Santa Fe Committee" in 1980, published in Francis Bouchey et al.'s *A New Inter-American Policy for the Eighties* (Washington, D.C.: Council for Inter-American Security, 1980), which argued: "America's basic freedoms and economic self-interest require that the United States be and act like a power of the first order. The crisis is metaphysical. America's inability or unwillingness either to protect or project its basic values and beliefs had led to the present nadir of indecision and impotence and has placed the very existence of the Republic in peril. . . . It is time to seize the initiative. An integrated global foreign policy is essential."

8. Indeed, force was not only considered necessary, but honorable. As Richard Allen, one of Reagan's National Security Advisers, stated: "U.S. military power has always been the basis for the development of a just and humane foreign policy" (LaFeber 1984: 274).

9. LeoGrande (1986) and Kenworthy (1991) point out, for example, that there were disagreements within the Reagan administration about exactly how to handle Nicaragua. The argument revolved around the dispute as to whether U.S. policy should be simply the *containment,* or actually the *rollback,* of what was understood as communism in Nicaragua. On the one side, more moderate advocates of containment—mostly State Department professionals—argued for a negotiated settlement with Nicaragua. They advocated acceptance of and coexistence with the Sandinista revolution, on the condition that Nicaragua both end support for the Salvadoran rebels and forswear any strategic alliance with the Soviet Union—essentially the position of the Carter administration. On the other side, hard-line advocates of communist rollback—new political appointees drawn from the Republican Party's ideological right, based in the CIA, the Defense Department, and the National Security Council—argued that nothing short of removing the Sandinistas from power was acceptable. Genuine negotiations with, not to mention concessions to, the Sandinistas were, therefore, pointless and out of the question (Vaky 1984: 244). In fact, at every critical juncture, the hard-line advocates of rollback—who reflected the President's predisposition—won the argument in the administration.

10. The White House had to inform the Congressional Intelligence Committees of this covert action. From the start, the Contras stated that their goal was to overthrow the Sandinista regime (Pastor 1987: 241). But since that was an illegal use of U.S. funding, the administration explained that their mission was really to interdict Nicaraguan arms shipments to the Salvadoran rebels. Later, when this explanation became implausible, Reagan claimed that the Contras really fought to pressure the Sandinistas to negotiate. But by 1985, Reagan himself admitted, "You could say we are trying to overthrow them." The goal, he stated, was to make the Sandinistas "say uncle" (Kornbluh 1987: 1).

11. Hence, training of the covert counterrevolutionary army continued.

"By mid-1982 the military aid provided by the United States had transformed the exiles from a ragtag collection of small groups totaling no more than 1,000 persons into a well-equipped and professional training army of some 4,500" (LeoGrande 1987: 203).

12. According to Vaky 1984: 251): "The administration fell into the 'covert action' gambit the way previous administrations have. Unwilling to incur the costs and disadvantages of overt pursuit of a specific goal, and unwilling to abandon the goal, it is tempting to turn to the CIA and covert action as an easy way out. Covert action, after all, seems attractive—it can be mounted without specific legislative approval, bureaucratic consensus, or public explanation."

13. Vaky (1984: 244) noted: "Pentagon spokesmen have made no secret of their disdain for what they called 'the lure of negotiations.' And a National Security Council document leaked to the press in April 1983 describes one of the policy objectives as 'co-opting cut-and-run negotiations'. . . . The same document recommended that the United States 'step up every effort to co-opt the negotiations issue to avoid congressional mandated negotiations, which would work against our interests.'" And, according to LeoGrande (1986: 119): "Because the Administration was unwilling to commit itself to achieving a diplomatic accord with Nicaragua, the Contadora process was primarily a public relations problem. Contadora was hailed in Congress and among U.S. allies worldwide as the best hope for peace in Central America. This posed a dilemma; the Reagan Administration did not want to be seen as an obstacle to peace, but at the same time did not want to give up the option of waging war. . . . The Administration solved its dilemma by constantly paying lip service to Contadora, but never letting it interfere . . . with the policy of hostility toward Nicaragua."

14. Many scholars argue convincingly that proposed concessions from the Sandinistas and the FMLN often actually invited more U.S. aggression. Typically, when either opponent expressed flexibility in negotiations, the Reagan administration did not see good-faith signs of openings for diplomatic solutions, but indications of a growing weakness to be capitalized on through increased pressures (Smith 1984: 484–85). According to Vaky (1984: 250), with the Sandinistas it seemed that "each Nicaraguan concession [was] simply met with another demand rather than a corresponding conciliation. It [was] tempting to argue that if U.S. pressure forced the recent conciliatory gestures, why not just keep it up until the Sandinistas cry 'uncle'?"

15. A 1983 Americas Watch report argued that "the human rights situation in El Salvador remained as it was during the previous three years—disastrous" and that the administration's certifications "were completely without merit" and "reflected a commitment by the Administration to do whatever was necessary to maintain military support for the government of El Salvador" (quoted in Blachman and Sharpe 1988: 4–5). Reports from Amnesty International, the U.N. Human Rights Commission, the American Civil Liberties Union, and the Salvadoran Catholic Church all drew similar conclusions (Schulz 1984: 232).

16. Many observers argue that the human-rights certification process was

a toothless formality resulting in little more than "an elaborate, and rather unseemly, political ritual" (Destler 1984: 325). "After the first certification debates in 1982, when it became apparent that the administration would comply with the letter but not the spirit of the law, certification hearings became lackluster, biannual rituals" (Arnson 1988: 41). The empty and ineffective nature of the certification process reflects, in part, a weak and irresolute Congress, resigned to political posturing instead of genuine alternative policy formation. "The certification revealed the limits of congressional ability to influence foreign policy through procedural solutions. The Reagan administration complied with the letter of the law by issuing certifications based on its own reading of Salvadoran events, despite vigorous challenges by human rights groups, religious leaders, policy analysts, and former U.S. government officials. . . . Yet Congress remained unwilling to terminate military aid to El Salvador for fear that such a step would lead to a victory by the Salvadoran guerrillas. Both the Reagan administration and the Salvadoran army understood the limits of congressional opposition, an insight that gave them the upper hand in dealing with legislatively imposed aid conditions" (Arnson 1988: 40–41). Thus, "the whole process was a fraud. Congress was dumping on the President's lap a responsibility it was too divided or afraid to assume, all the while leaving its members free to cry out when he did what they knew he would do" (Destler 1984: 326).

17. Four hundred million dollars for the entire region was a relatively small amount—only 15 percent of what the Soviet Union was providing to Cuba each year (Smith 1984: 490).

18. "By the end of 1983, the FMLN was in control of roughly one-third of El Salvador's national territory" (Barry et al. 1988: 87).

19. The administration's new congressional strategy, according to Destler (1984: 330), clearly was "go for broke, threaten Congress with blame for the failures, and watch legislators run for cover." Jeanne Kirkpatrick charged (quoted in LeoGrande 1987: 206): "There are some members of Congress who want to see Marxist victories in Central America."

CHAPTER 3

1. Quoted in Anderson 1984.

2. Low-intensity warfare doctrine was also "based on the accumulated experience of the Germans in World War II, the British in Malaya, Kenya, and Ireland, the Philippine government against the Huk, [and] the French in Algeria" (Frederick 1987: 123). Precursory works on low-intensity warfare include: Kitson 1971 and Barnett 1961. Works that comprised the low-intensity warfare school of thought in the 1980s include: Sarkesian and Scully 1981; Hunt and Schultz 1982; Blair 1983; Kupperman and Taylor (eds.) 1983; Robert Kupperman Associates 1983; Shultz 1984; Waghlestein 1985; Morelli and Ferguson 1984; U.S. Army 1986; Weinberger 1986.

3. A 1986 U.S. army manual on low-intensity warfare (quoted in Kornbluh 1987: 4) states that this type of warfare "involves the proactive, thoughtful, energetic, innovative, and synergistic applications of comprehensive political, social, economic, and psychological efforts."

4. "According to the State Department, 'This Fund [U.S. Economic Support Fund (ESF)] has meant the difference between survival and collapse for several countries, notably for those in Central America.' AID [U.S. Agency for International Development] regards the ESF as 'a flexible means to provide assistance to countries of particular security and political importance to the United States'" (Barry and Preusch 1988: 24). In the plainer language of a scholar and a businessperson, both Salvadoran: "This country could not survive one day if AID cut off economic assistance" and "Our economy is like a junkie waiting for the next hit from Uncle Sam" (quoted in Barry and Preusch 1988: 21, 146).

5. Jonathan Sanford (1984: 9), expert on U.S. foreign aid, agrees: "The ESF [Economic Support Fund] in Central America is basically a security/military program undertaken to prop up the existing regimes and the elites who support them." Also, military-dispensed humanitarian aid, channeled through "civic action projects," was politically targeted to generate good will among the people of Central America (Barry and Preusch 1988: 93–106). In Honduras, these employed U.S. military forces to build roads, pull teeth, and immunize children and livestock. During Big Pine II, 53,000 rural Hondurans received medical or dental care, 200,000 immunizations were given, and 37,000 animals were treated (Gold 1987: 44). In El Salvador, civic action also included army-dispensed food and clothing, medical care, literacy training, and community recreation activities, such as clown shows and 16-mm movies (Fish and Sganga 1988: 88; Antonio Hernández 1988: 336).

6. This is a "soft" estimate. Some estimate the costs to be somewhat lower, at $7 billion a year, others much higher at $19 billion a year (Cohen and Rogers 1986: 48).

7. Ironically, it was Nicaragua's private business sector, not the Sandinistas, that suffered most from U.S. trade sanctions (Kornbluh 1987: 103).

8. Once labeled communists, according to Vanden and Walker (1991: 156), "the Sandinistas could be plausibly charged with committing a myriad of sins commonly associated in the popular mind with Communist regimes."

9. According to Schulz (1984: 234), through economic and military pressure, the Reagan administration actually "hoped the Sandinistas could be provoked into further repression of the democratic opposition, thus driving the latter into the arms of the counterrevolution. If that happened, as one U.S. official told *Newsweek,* the Nicaraguan government would 'fall like a house of cards in the wind.'"

10. Critics claim these CIA activities violated international laws, including the Declaration on Principles of International Law Concerning Relations and Cooperation among States in Accordance with the Charter of the United Nations, October 25, 1970; the International Covenant on Civil and Political Rights, December 16, 1966; U.N. General Assembly Resolution 110(II), November 3, 1947; the International Convention Concerning the Use of Broadcasting in the Cause of Peace, September 23, 1936; and the Convention on the International Right of Correction (Frederick 1987: 140–41).

11. El Salvador's Department of Civic-Military and Psychological Opera-

tions was financed with a $22 million U.S. "counterterrorist" aid package (Fish and Sganga 1988: 88).

12. In the same documentary a former Salvadoran National Guardsman, who admitted torturing fifty to sixty people, spoke of being trained to torture by U.S. Special Forces advisers: "I was trained in Panama by the Red Berets of the United States in guerrilla warfare. Part of the time we were instructed about torture and part of the time we were taught self-defense" (Fish and Sganga 1988: 108).

13. By contrast, major human rights groups—Amnesty International, Americas Watch, the Human Rights Commission of the Organization of American States—reported that the Sandinista armed forces were relatively respectful of human rights abuses (Gorman and Walker 1985: 113–14).

14. Others place the total number of Nicaraguan war deaths at 40,000 (Spykman et al. 1988: 156) and 30,865 (Vanden and Walker 1991: 166). Thirty thousand deaths represented .9 percent of the Nicaraguan population, proportionately equal to 2.25 million American deaths, or thirty-eight times the U.S. death toll in the whole Vietnam War (Vanden and Walker 1991: 166).

15. While the government's forces are responsible for the majority of deaths, it would be unfair not to recognize the FMLN's share. In 1985, "the FMLN reverted back to classic guerrilla tactics and increased its use of land mines, which it called 'popular armament.' In mid-1985 the FMLN, in addition to kidnapping or assassinating numerous military and government officials, began kidnapping and assassinating mayors and burning their offices. It also targeted U.S. military personnel for assassination. . . . Guerrilla sabotage and indirect economic losses caused by the war amounted to nearly $2 billion during 1979–88, more than the total amount of United States economic assistance provided the country during the same period" (Hudson 1990: 242, 244; also see Haig 1984: 117, 137).

16. Walter LaFeber (1984: 10) puts the civilian death toll for 1980 and 1981 at thirty thousand.

17. Gabriel Aguilera Peralta (1988: 158) estimates the number of Guatemalans who died or disappeared at fifty to seventy-five thousand, a number lower than Jonas's.

CHAPTER 4

1. See, for example, Bonner 1981; Phelps 1981; de Onis 1981d, 1981e; Fitch 1982; Blair 1982; Tolchin 1982; Towle 1983; Coston 1981; Alvarez 1981; Miller 1981; Malinowski 1983; Berryman 1982; Asner 1982; Neier 1982; Turner 1983; Shipp 1983; LeMoyne 1984; Serrin 1985; Pressman 1985; Toner 1986; Squires 1986; Brinkley 1986; Lehrich 1987; Chavez 1987; Franklin 1987; Schneider 1987; Brozan 1989; Brett 1991; Rosenthal 1987; Weinraub 1983a, 1983b; *New York Times* 1981a, 1981c, 1981f, 1981g, 1981h, 1981l, 1981n, 1982a, 1982b, 1982e, 1982h, 1982o, 1983a, 1983c, 1984b, 1984d, 1985a, 1985d, 1985f, 1985g, 1986a, 1986b, 1986d, 1988e, 1988i, 1989a.

2. CISPES, the Committee in Solidarity with the People of El Salvador,

probably ranks in a close fourth place, in terms of national importance within the movement.

3. The following account is drawn from these sources: Bau 1985; Crittenden 1988; Davidson 1988; Golden and McConnell 1986; Lorentzen 1991; MacEoin 1985; Tomsho 1987; Austin 1983b; Volsky 1983; Goldman 1984; Narvaez 1984; King 1985; Taylor 1985; Mitchell 1985; Martin 1985; *New York Times* 1981l, 1984c, 1984f, 1984g, 1984h, 1984i, 1985b; *The Economist* 1986. For the best full-length descriptions of the Sanctuary movement, see Crittendon (1988) and Davidson (1988).

4. Wary of most institutions, Corbett insisted on leaving their group's name in lower-case letters.

5. According to Jane Guise (1990): "The groups which got involved were quite varied and included some very conservative churches. They may have started out with largely humanitarian motives, but they certainly developed an awareness of why they were doing Sanctuary. The refugees themselves told why they had to flee and there was no question that we, the U.S., were causing the problem ourselves."

6. This account is based on Griffin-Nolan 1991; Hollyday 1983; Taylor n.d.; Wallis 1983; Phares 1992; Crites 1992; Truitt 1990; Bonthius 1990; Hope 1992; Taylor 1991; Clark 1992; Taylor 1990; and Marker 1992; Toner 1986; Kinzer 1987a, 1987c; Courtney 1987b; *New York Times* 1987a, 1988d. For the best full-length descriptions of Witness for Peace, see Griffin-Nolan (1991).

7. Dan Rather, of *CBS News,* was scheduled to participate, but cancelled at the last minute. And Gail Phares, it turned out, learned an important family reunion had been scheduled for July 4, which she felt obliged to attend (Phares 1992). Most of the 153 participants were men, but most of the group's leaders were women (Griffin-Nolan 1991: 34). According to Fran Truitt (1990): "In choosing the original 153 people, they wanted to get representatives from every major denomination and they wanted two people from every state. They had a lot of states represented. They were shooting for important people, people already involved. People were chosen and recruited through the Inter-Religious Task Force and the AFSC."

8. According to Phares (1992): "We would make a very clear, biblically-based covenant with delegates in preparation. You couldn't go on Witness for Peace unless you made it. People committed themselves to spending significant time and money to make this witness happen. They wouldn't just be going on a lark or a vacation. At every training we went through this, people signed that covenant and we had serious discussions about it. It's still taken very seriously today. People can't go unless they do. We weed people out. Not everybody goes."

9. This account is based on Butigan 1989, 1991, n.d.; The Emergency Response Network 1986; Pledge of Resistance 1986a, 1986b, 1986c, 1987a, 1987b, 1988a, 1988b, 1988c, 1989a, 1989b, 1989c, 1990, n.d.; Hannon 1991; The Editors 1983; Wallis 1984; Shumway 1990; P. Taylor 1990; Epstein 1991; Brinkley 1986a; Bishop 1987; New York Times 1984a, 1985d, 1985e, 1986d, 1987b, 1987c, 1987d, 1987e, 1988e, 1988i.

10. These included the Presbyterian Church, the Mennonite Church, the Episcopal Peace Fellowship, Maryknoll, Inter-Religious Task Force on Central America, the Southern Christian Leadership Conference, Fellowship of Reconciliation, Pax Christi, New Call to Peacemaking, World Peacemakers, Clergy and Laity Concerned, AFSC, SANE, the Nuclear Weapons Freeze Campaign, the Committee in Solidarity with the People of El Salvador, the National Network in Solidarity with Nicaragua, the Chicago Religious Task Force, Mobilization for Survival, Witness for Peace, Sojourners, the Emergency Response Network, and the Central America Peace Campaign.

11. Original members of that group were Richard Barnett, the Institute for Policy Studies; Yvonne Dilling, Witness for Peace; David MacMichael, former CIA analyst; Steve Goose, Center for Defense Information; Valerie Miller, Central America Peace Campaign; Joanne Heisel, National Network in Solidarity with the People of Guatemala; Mike Davis, CISPES; Debbie Ruben, National Network in Solidarity with Nicaragua; Reggie Norton, Washington Office on Latin America; Buddy Summers, Witness for Peace; William LeoGrande, American University; and Jim Wallis, Sojourners.

12. Original members of that group included Suzanna Cepeda, SANE; Timothy McDonald, SCLC; Ken Butigan, Emergency Response Network; Jim Wallis, Sojourners; a Washington Office on Latin America representative; and representatives from the three solidarity networks.

13. In fact, more demonstrators were now committing civil disobedience, but the police in many cities already were beginning the policy of deliberately refusing to arrest protesters. More on this in chapter 10.

CHAPTER 5

1. Seeing that this account of political opportunities, which focuses on increased state and public attention to the issue area and more extreme public policies, differs from McAdam's (1982) account, which concentrates on increased opportunities for blacks to participate in politics and social life, reminds us that, with different cases the exact factors that represent openings in political opportunities will vary.

2. We would expect book publications to lag behind other indicators.

3. On Vietnam, also see: Smith 1982; Lewis 1982; Sharpe 1988: 20; Sklar 1988: 313–14; Whittle 1981; Felton 1983a, 1983b, 1985; Rothman 1984; *New York Times* 1981d; Roberts 1982a; Crossette 1982; Taubman 1982.

4. According to Moberg (1987: 2): "Pollster Stanley Greenberg says the resilient majorities against contra aid that have persisted despite Reagan's pleadings over nearly seven years reflect 'strong antipathies to involvement that go well beyond the contra aid issue.' Although many on the left take the numbers as cheering signs of a latent progressive majority, Greenberg's latest probes of focus groups of political independents in conservative districts show that for many 'there's a strong aversion to the region that goes from misinformation to racism.' Contras and Sandinistas alike are seen as 'unsmiling, dirty, armed Spanish people that [those interviewed] don't want to send their money to.' A deep isolationism and sense that 'even allies kick us in the teeth' lead many to want to avoid involvement despite their hostility to communism.

'You don't come away from this liking us as Americans for our attitudes toward the Third World,' Greenberg said. 'It doesn't reflect the best impulses in people.'"

5. According to one high-ranking Green Beret officer on duty in Central America (quoted in Sklar 1988: 367), a U.S. invasion is "seen as a rebound from Vietnam. The officers who are now in charge of planning *lost* in Vietnam; it's a chance for them to cap off their careers with a victory. I don't think we give a shit about Central Americans."

6. According to Best (1987: 35), "The Joint Chiefs of Staff were reluctant to undertake any military action in the region, placing higher priority on other regions, being concerned that such actions might endanger their burgeoning military budget requests, not wanting to become involved in a difficult and unpopular war."

7. In fact, as early as 1984 and 1985, ample information was available for Congress to suspect violations of the law by the White House (see, for instance, Towell 1984; Cohen 1985). But NSC Director Robert McFarlane (quoted in Sklar 1988: 327) categorically insisted that "at no time did I or any member of the National Security Council staff violate the letter or spirit" of congressional restrictions. Congress believed McFarlane until Hasenfus's capture.

8. Such language automatically raises important questions about the beginnings and ends of movements. Traditionally, analysts have presumed that distinct movements simply emerge, struggle, and die. More recently, however, many have increasingly come to view movements as long traditions that surge and recede in successive waves over decades (for instance, Rupp and Taylor 1987; Chatfield 1992). In fact, both views are correct. It is a matter of looking through different ends of the same telescope. A given surge in movement activism does typically represent one phase of a long movement tradition that in the past has championed and in the future will continue to champion peace, gender rights, racial justice, or whatever cause. At the same time, those long traditions do, in fact, progress or unfold in identifiably distinct "generations." Indeed, tracing the relationships between movement generations is one of the fascinating tasks of social-movement analysis. Recognizing both the continuity and the discontinuity, we freely speak here of the Central America peace movement as having a birth and a death, while simultaneously acknowledging the broader peace movement tradition of which this movement is but one historical wave.

9. Aldon Morris, in an influential chapter of his book *The Origins of the Civil Rights Movement* (1984: 139–73), has labeled such organizations "movement halfway houses," which he claims are characterized by their relative isolation from the larger society and lack of broad support among a mass base. According to Morris, previously isolated halfway houses gain access to large audiences through emerging social movements, which, in turn, capitalize on the newly acquired access to the halfway houses' resources. But Morris's conceptualization of these movement-assisting organizations, whatever they be called, seems problematic, at least in terms of the experience of the Central America peace movement. Curiously, Morris's emphasis on the halfway houses' lack of integration in and isolation from the larger society seems more to reflect clas-

sical theory's preoccupation with anomie and isolation than his own resource mobilization's emphasis on solidarity and integration. Moreover, Morris's depiction of the halfway house as lacking a mass base and a visible platform inadequately captures the full range of organizational possibilities. In fact, in 1956, the Fellowship of Reconciliation, one of Morris's important halfway houses, enjoyed an membership constituency of 11,879, according to FOR records. In the case of the Central America peace movement, the groups that assisted the formation of key movement-carrier organizations were as important as they were *precisely because* they were both socially integrated and possessed mass constituencies. That is exactly what gave them the relational and organizational resources so valuable for the newly forming movement organizations. What made these movement midwives conceptually distinct from "the movement" was not their social isolation nor lack of mass constituencies, but their trans-movement identities and the specialized role they played in facilitating the formation of new movement-carrier organizations without becoming protest organizations themselves.

10. See chapter 4, note 10. Movement midwives were also important in assisting the Pledge's coordination at regional levels. According to Hannon (1991: 263–64), the original organizers of the Pledge in the Boston area "were able to call on the resources of their own organizations and networks in the first stages of Pledge mobilization. These resources included members, mailing lists, office space . . . allocation of staff time . . . and [the] ability to bring to the Pledge . . . grant[s]."

11. According to Fran Truitt (1990): "Different people began to go after money. John Collins got $20,000 from the women of the Methodist church. Jubilee gave $5,000, the Presbyterians gave $5,000. This came through informal contacts and formal proposals. You have to have the contacts and then do the proposals. A lot of people sent in money through Sojourners because of the article. Then delegates began to pledge. One retired man in New England pledged $100 a month and later upped it to $150."

12. Phares continues (1992): "You've got to get people who are established, people who are well-known in their churches, who have lots of credibility. Nurses, teachers, lawyers, doctors, college professors, and pastors of churches. People who others listen to when they speak, who can go to talk to people in power, who get interviewed in the newspaper. You need people who when they call their congressional representatives, their representative answers the phone. People who are listened to by their churches."

13. The actual numbers are certainly higher for Witness for Peace activists, the majority of whom reported having first heard of Witness for Peace through former Witness for Peace delegates and through friends and family, many of whom were probably known by the respondents through common memberships in religious organizations.

14. These include the United States Catholic Conference, the Washington Office on Latin America, Coalition for a New Foreign and Military Policy, Clergy and Laity Concerned, Ecumenical Program for Inter-American Communication and Action, National Council of Churches Human Rights Office, Unitarian Universalist Service Committee, Maryknoll Fathers and Brothers

Justice and Peace Office, Friends Committee on National Legislation, Presbyterian Washington Office, Council for Hemispheric Affairs, Center of Concern, The Quixote Center, Central American Historical Institute, Religious Task Force on Central America, and Impact (Keller 1982; Powell 1986; Winsor 1987; Tyson 1986).

15. According to Schoultz (1981: 86): "Any discussion of interest groups concerned with human rights in Latin America would be incomplete if it failed to mention the central role of an enormous variety of churches and church-related organizations. Of the thirty-six formal members of the Coalition for a New Foreign and Military Policy . . . for example, nearly half were church-related, and a majority of the remainder were at least partially funded by churches."

16. Thus, we agree with Burstein (1991: 1203) that "successful movements generally utilize proper channels as well as outsider tactics and . . . an adequate understanding of movements must therefore consider both," and also with Freeman (1975: 2) that "political change does not involve isolated efforts either within or without the system. . . . Rather it involves a dynamic system of reciprocal influences whose effects are determined by their mutual relationships."

CHAPTER 6

1. I use the term "moral outrage" purposefully. Barrington Moore (1978: xiii–xiv) has suggested that the expression "'moral outrage' suggests too strongly the agonies of intellectuals trying to interpret, judge, and change the world. It smacks too much of the preacher. People of little education and refinement are certainly capable of feeling anger, but the word 'moral' carries overtones of condescension and introspection that miss both the tone and concreteness of much popular anger." It is exactly because I believe Moore is correct that I employ the term "moral outrage" here. For most of the protagonists of the Central America peace movement were not people of little education, but, in fact, intellectuals in agony. Indeed, we will see, an extraordinary number precisely were preachers trying to interpret, judge, and change the world.

2. The number of Protestant missions agencies grew from 58 in 1960 to 71 in 1964 and to 93 in 1972 (Dayton 1973; Directory 1964).

3. According to Quigley (1990): "Early on, many went to Latin America to 'save' Latin America: there were programs of financial assistance and so on. But by the end of the 1970s, a great deal of naiveté had sloughed off and we were more trying to dialogue, maintain solidarity and support. So, we got to hear how U.S. policy was impinging on their lives."

4. In addition to missionaries serving in Central America, a far greater number of North American missionaries had been living and working in South America: 8,282 Protestant and 3,653 Catholic missionaries in 1968, 8,383 Protestant and 2,701 Catholic in 1972, 9,987 Protestant and 2,107 Catholic in 1979, and 9,753 Protestant and 1,941 Catholic missionaries in 1985 (U.S. Catholic Mission Association 1993; Dayton 1973; Directory 1968; Wilson and Siewert 1986). Despite not actually having worked in Central America, when Central America became an important political issue the

Latin American commonalities fostered a similar attention and bonding dynamic for many of the South American missionaries and their North American sponsors. Of course, it should be recognized that not all North American missionaries opposed Reagan's policy in Central America. There were a number of conservative fundamentalist and evangelical missionaries, sometimes associated with North American televangelists, that vehemently opposed the FMLN and supported the Contras and the regime in Guatemala.

5. The transnational structure of the Catholic Church hierarchy also contributed to this flow of information between North and Central Americans. According to Quigley (1990): "There was consultation between North and Central American bishops on a regular and informal basis for a long time. It's a general principle of the USCC that before we take a policy position, we check it out with the bishops of the region effected. We visit and consult together. I spent a lot of time in Central America, talking with bishops and coming back and writing reports. There was a flow of information. There is also a structure for international meetings of bishops, who exchange experiences and what's on their minds. Then there is regular visiting that goes on, when Latin American bishops come up here."

6. For a detailed account of the history of liberation theology, see Smith (1991).

7. According to Central America congressional lobbyist Cindy Buhl (1993): "Everyone and their puppy went to Nicaragua. It was like a revolving door down there in Nicaragua. There were good things to see in Nicaragua as well as bad things. At any given time, you could go down, walk into the main hotels, and meet half the world, including well-known news people, former heads of state, foreign ministers, and a three-church delegation from DeKalb, Illinois. Everybody was there."

8. The term "relevance-structure" is Berger and Luckmann's (1966: 45).

CHAPTER 7

1. Pledge of Resistance mailing lists proved impossible to obtain for reasons of membership confidentiality.

2. These interviews yielded 576 pages of typed transcripts.

3. Unlike McAdam's (1986, 1988) data on Freedom Summer activists, the Witness for Peace and Sanctuary data did not provide for a logit-regression comparison between activists and "no-shows"—people who took initial steps toward activism then backed away. Neither Witness for Peace nor Sanctuary had analogous cases of no-shows on record. Consequently, this study uses tests for differences between means and differences between proportions, comparing relevant traits of Witness for Peace and Sanctuary activists with those of the population from whom those activists were drawn. Since both were national organizations that consciously tried to mobilize people from all walks of life, to strengthen their political credibility, that population is regarded as all adult Americans.

4. The standard deviation is 4.7 for Witness for Peace activists and 5.2 for Sanctuary activists.

5. Fifty-three percent of Sanctuary and 49 percent of Witness for Peace

activists, the majority of whom were already leftists in 1979, experienced no ideological shift.

6. Among Witness for Peace activists, participation in protests, marches, demonstrations, sit-ins, and vigils increased by 14 percent; participation in nonviolent civil disobedience or tax resistance increased by 8 percent; and arrests for protesting or committing civil disobedience increased 8 percent. Among Sanctuary activists, participation in protests, marches, demonstrations, sit-ins, and vigils increased by 22 percent; participation in nonviolent civil disobedience or tax resistance—besides the civil disobedient nature of Sanctuary activism itself—increased by 3 percent; and arrests for protesting or committing civil disobedience increased 14 percent.

7. Comparatively, McAdam's subjects were considered to be biographically available because they were young enough to be free from family and employment responsibilities (1988: 53). His subjects had not hit the biographically unavailable years of the late twenties and the thirties, whereas Central America peace activists tended to have already moved beyond those years.

8. According to survey data, only 5 percent were students. Butigan (1991) concurs on the Pledge of Resistance: "Agewise, the Solidarity movement people are younger, whereas the Pledge had a much broader sample. We had a large number of older people with us. Our organizers tended to be middle aged, with a few exceptions both ways. We did not have so many younger people, in their 20s. Younger people tended to gravitate more to solidarity groups. CISPES organized very well on campuses and brought large contingencies of students to protests. The Pledge was more like 30 and up." The mean age of Lorentzen's sample of Sanctuary activists was identical to this study's, forty-four years old (Lorentzen 1991: 205).

9. This high average is even more impressive when one realizes that it includes the incomes of very many priests and nuns who voluntarily lived at the poverty level.

10. The particular nature of refugee work appears to have been more compatible with marriage than, for example, Witness for Peace activism. Interestingly, the percent of married Sanctuary workers in Lorentzen's sample, 65 percent, is again (see note 8) identical to that of this study (1991: 205).

11. Viewed in the reverse, the price of activism for parents of young children are evident in this "cautionary tale" told by Jim Rice (1992): "I was signed up and ready to do a Pledge action. But the House postponed their vote, as usual, and I stopped paying attention for a while. Then suddenly the House voted again and I said, 'Oh, yeah, I'm doing this one.' I went down to the State Department and got arrested. But by this time I had a three-month-old daughter. I wasn't ready for jail at all. It was tough. I got before the judge and was thinking, 'I going to get 30 days here. I'm just not ready for this.' I was pretty distraught by the whole thing."

12. The percentages are even larger if you count "religious publications" and "Witness for Peace mailings" as evidence of organizational ties. This would be justified in many cases, since many religious publications, such as newsletters, are merely the communication arms of organizations to which

people belong, and since receiving a promotional mailing often indicates that one belongs to an organization whose mailing list the promoter, that is, Witness for Peace, purchased.

13. One might suggest that the survey question was misleading, that the activists really did make cost-benefit calculations, but only in rather casual and unconscious ways. But that suggestion is problematic. Besides the fact that it begins to dismantle the essential utility of the concept "calculation," the activists' making casual and unconscious calculations seems rather unlikely, given the objective costs and risks involved in Sanctuary and Witness for Peace activism.

14. These were: writing protest letters to Congress or the President; working to politically educate others in church, synagogue, school, neighborhood, and workplace; writing letters to the editor of local newspapers; helping to organize local citizen activism; donating money or volunteering time to a political organization; participating in political protests, demonstrations, marches, sit-ins, or vigils; committing nonviolent civil disobedience or tax resistance; and being arrested for political protesting or civil disobedience.

15. The following argument draws heavily on Amitai Etzioni's theory of bi-utility (1986, 1988) and Charles Taylor's penetrating work on the essential link between human identity and inescapable moral frameworks (1989). Also see: Oliner and Oliner 1988; Coles 1993; Zey 1992; Mansbridge 1990, 1992; Wilson 1993.

16. Pleasure-motivated actions are here defined in the classical utilitarian sense of self-oriented, hedonistic actions performed because they are expected, directly or indirectly, to reduce pain and/or to increase what one likes, enjoys, finds gratifying, pleasurable, or satisfying according to one's scale of preferences (see Etzioni 1988: 24–25).

17. According to Etzioni (1988: 12), "Actions are morally right when they conform to a relevant principle or duty." More precisely, Etzioni writes (1988: 42–43): "It suffices to consider moral acts as those that meet four criteria: moral acts reflect an imperative, a generalization, and a symmetry when applied to others, and are motivated intrinsically. . . . The *imperative* quality of moral acts is reflected in that persons who act morally sense that they 'must' behave in a prescribed way, that they are in fact obligated, duty bound. . . . Individuals who act morally are *able to generalize* their behavior—they are able to justify an act to others and to themselves by pointing to general rules. . . . *Symmetry* is required in that there must be a willingness to accord other comparable people, under comparable circumstances, the same standing or right. . . . Finally, moral acts *affirm or express a commitment,* rather than involve the consumption of a good or service. Therefore, they are intrinsically motivated and not subject to means-end analysis."

18. Of course, sometimes the pleasure and morality motives complement and reinforce each other.

19. In Etzioni's words (1988: 46), "Moral internalization turns constraints into preferences." Examples of such experiences include parents who in the middle of the night, despite their own exhaustion, *feel gratified* staying awake to comfort a troubled or sick child, and people who voluntarily and *happily*

forfeit sunny Saturday afternoons at the beach in order to work in smelly soup kitchens for the poor and homeless. For a cogent critique of the attempt to include other people's pleasure in the rational calculator's own utility scheme, see Etzioni (1988: 25–31).

20. One resulting asset of the prior experience in Central America, not to be underestimated, was that about one-half of Witness for Peace's original organizers spoke Spanish fluently.

21. Jim Wallis and Joyce Hollyday later married.

22. According to Truitt (1990): "My activism in civil rights and the peace movement in the 1960s led to a divorce, because my husband was liberal but not a churchgoing Christian and our values changed. He thought I was involved in the latest fad and began wanting me to be at home. That led to a divorce. I chose to leave. I went to seminary, I was being called. He couldn't understand that." And according to Anne Shumway (1990): "I was married so young. My husband was a scientist and developed an interest in the Pennsylvania long rifle. Today he is *the* expert on the Pennsylvania long rifle. There developed a contradiction. He and his friends would dress up in eighteenth-century garb and shoot clay pigeons and I would go around with my anti-war petitions collecting signatures. We gradually drifted further apart. He, in fact, did not want me to become involved with the anti-war movement at all, primarily because of the threats people were making on my life, but I said I was sorry, that I had to do it. We each did what we had to do. We were divorced in 1979."

Chapter 8

1. According to Dennis Marker (1992): "We started the Pledge as a totally Christian thing, but it soon became much broader. We talked more vaguely about 'religious' in later years, but back in 1983 and 1984 it was definitely 'Christian,' though open to Christians, Jews, and anyone else who wanted to come."

2. From another point of view, Bob Van Denend (1992) argues: "I think Witness for Peace actually got carried away trying to be all things to all people—gays, lesbians, blacks, non-Christians, Jews, nonbelievers, and on and on. The preoccupation came at the expense of its mission. This naïve, white organization wanted to be so inclusive that the organization's sense of purpose got sidetracked. We got into issues that weren't at all related to our primary mission. Hours and hours of conference calls we would have, thirty people on a conference call arguing endlessly about how to be more inclusive. We allowed ourselves to get bogged down with issues that weren't really ours. It's so hard to be inclusive and open, yet maintain your original purpose and values. Inclusivity and consensus-building really can be counterproductive when they make you lose your core organizational vision and purpose."

3. CAWG was formally named as such in 1987. Before then, the same legislative coalition was coordinated by Cindy Buhl as head of the human rights program of the Coalition for a New Foreign and Military Policy (Buhl 1993).

4. According to Tom Quigley (1990), on El Salvador: "There were divergent voices. Many in the Peace and Justice movement were saying, 'Not

Another Dime!' for El Salvador, that the whole thing was wrong and must be ended. But others, including the Catholic bishops—both U.S. and Central American—didn't want a unilateral, destablizing aid cut-off. They wanted more realistic cuts and incremental changes toward an end to external military aid from *all* sources. Also, Congress at the time was not in any mood to cut off all Salvadoran aid. So, do you settle for making *some* changes? Or do you stick to all-or-nothing demands? That was the question. The bishops chose the former strategy. Many in the movement, the later."

CHAPTER 9

1. According to Dennis Marker (1992): "If I ever said one thing to the press that wasn't true, they'd never talk to me again. Ollie North got caught lying 50 times. What does that get him? An hour on Ted Koppel's *Nightline*." And Cindy Buhl remarks (1993): "You have to recognize working with the media, that the White House is more quotable than you are. That's just a given. It doesn't matter if the President is lying or doesn't have the faintest idea of what he's talking about. What the President says is news. It doesn't matter that Elliott Abrams is just the sleaziest thing that ever walked on earth. He's the Secretary of State for Inter-America affairs, so he gets on all the talk shows."

2. Spence's (1987) content analyses of television and newspaper coverage of Central America, for example, shows that out of the 181 *New York Times* stories published on Nicaragua from January to June 1986—a time of heated debate on Contra aid in the U.S.—the stories focused primarily on politics and not the substance of U.S. Nicaragua policy, very rarely offered views contrary to the administration's, habitually mentioned press censorship and election fraud in Nicaragua, but not in U.S.-supported El Salvador where both are far more rampant, and contained a total of one sentence alluding to land distribution and redistribution in Nicaragua, a crucial issue in Nicaraguan politics. Spence concludes (1987: 198–99): "Coverage of Nicaragua's Sandinistas amplified the President's condemnation. It did so literally by repeating the President's repetitions. [The lack of] evidence supporting the President's charges was not relevant; stories never said 'the charge could not be independently confirmed. . . .' The two case studies demonstrate that the press substantially replicated Washington biases, covering over or distorting Nicaraguan political dynamics in the process. Views outside acceptable Washington limits were eliminated."

3. According to Angela Berryman (1990): "The media has the attitude that if they printed an article on Central America last week, they don't want to repeat with one this week. 'We covered that issue,' they say. Or they don't want to print 'one point of view' too much. Even when newspapers do come out with good articles, they often don't consistently follow the issue. But, of course, when the President says something, no matter what, it's important news." And according to Jane Guise (1990): "We in Sanctuary worked with a reporter from the *Philadelphia Inquirer,* who had been happily developing a 'Sanctuary beat.' Then her bosses removed her from it. They said she wasn't neutral enough."

4. For an alternative view, see Falcoff 1984: 372–76.

5. In addition, the majority of Americans' opposition to administration Central American policy was also fueled by large measures of political and geographical ignorance and anti-Latino racism, factors Central American peace activists were generally reluctant to exploit (see Clymer 1983; Shipler 1986; Judis 1987; Kenworthy 1991: 121).

6. According to *NBC Nightly News'* Tom Brokaw, President Reagan received "a more positive press than he deserves. . . . Ronald Reagan reminds me of a lot of CEOs I know who run big companies and spend most of their time on their favorite charitable events or lunch with their pals and kind of have a broad-based philosophy of how they want their companies run. Reagan's got that kind of broad-based philosophy about how he wants the government run, and he's got all these killers who are willing and able to do that for him" (quoted in Hertsgaard 1989: 5).

7. According to David Gergen: "It was great television. I think every White House would rather see its President in what amounts to a heroic situation . . . and it sure is a hell of a lot better picture than a guy like [Jimmy] Carter, stumbling up in Camp David when he's jogging around up there, falling down. One picture builds support for the President. The other, I think, destroys him" (Hertsgaard 1989: 25).

8. According to *NBC News* Executive Vice President David Burke (quoted in Hertsgaard 1989: 4–5): "You just can't get the stomach to go after the guy. It's not a popular thing. . . . I think it's a perception that the press has in general of Reagan, that he is a decent man. He is not driven by insecurities, by venality, by conspiracies and back-room tactics." Concerning Reagan's repeated gaffes, former Reagan presidential campaign manager John Sears (quoted in Hertsgaard 1989: 47) explains, "If Jimmy Carter were making these mistakes, he would be treated much worse. The press didn't like Carter on the level of a personal human being. But they like Reagan, and this affects their intensity factor." Elsewhere (in Griffith 1984), Sears stated, "[Reagan] walks away from more political car crashes than anyone."

9. According to *CBS Evening News* executive producer Sanford Socolow (quoted in Hertsgaard 1989: 114–15), "We got interested in El Salvador basically because General Haig not only got interested but began to trumpet the dangers of El Salvador and going to the source. . . . We were led to El Salvador by General Haig, and the administration."

10. Amanda Spake, citing weariness from the constant requests of right-wing groups for information and interviews, declined to be interviewed.

11. According to Marker's records (1992): "Our launching was covered by CBS, NBC, and ABC television, both the evening and morning news. We also had NBC radio and a special half-hour story on ABC television. We ran an AP wire service the day before the press conference and UPI wire service the same day. We were also covered by CNN, National Public Radio, Canadian Broadcasting, British Broadcasting, in the *Philadelphia Inquirer,* and many other major local papers, all on the day of the press conference. Then *Newsweek* and *Time* came out a week later, along with articles in the *New Yorker Magazine, The Nation, Mother Jones,* and *Off Our Backs.* The *Wall Street Journal* and *New York Times* also ran articles one week later."

12. Marker concurred (1992): "I would call one reporter to give them an exclusive, same as the White House does. That reporter gets the exclusive, looks good, gets kudos. You always try to provide them with something good. Then they like you and want to work with you."

13. Indeed, advocates for reestablishing U.S. hegemony in Central America understood the need to control media coverage even before President Reagan was elected. The right-wing Committee of Santa Fe's influential 1980 report, "A New Inter-American Policy for the Eighties," for example, recommended that (quoted in Golden and McConnell 1986: 86): "U.S. policy formulation must insulate itself from propaganda appearing in the general and specialized media which is inspired by forces explicitly hostile to the U.S. . . . Coverage of Latin America's political reality by the U.S. media is both inadequate and displays a substantial bias favoring proponents of radical socioeconomic transformation of the less developed countries along collectivist lines."

14. To protect CIA operations in Nicaragua against attacks from Congress and the media, Casey also appointed the CIA's director of covert operations, Clair George, as head of the agency's congressional relations, and George Lauder, a thirty-two-year veteran of CIA covert operations, as director of the CIA's public affairs, to stop damaging stories in the news media (Woodward 1987: 264–65).

15. Despite an August 29, 1983, memo of Raymond's recognizing the legal need "to get [Casey] out of the loop," because "the work done within the Administration has to, by definition, be at arms length," DCI Casey remained personally involved in many of the public diplomacy operations. Within weeks of Raymond's memo, for example, Casey convened five commercial advertising consultants in the Old Executive Office Building, next to the White House, to brainstorm strategies "to sell [to the America people] a 'new product'—Central America" (Jacoby and Parry 1987). In February 1986, Casey also spearheaded a lobbying campaign to solidify Republican support for an upcoming Contra aid vote. And as late as mid-1986, Casey was making recommendations for new public diplomacy personnel and receiving status reports on NSC public diplomacy operations. Seeking to explain Casey's illegal involvement to the congressional Iran-Contra committees, Raymond later suggested that Casey had participated in these public relations operations, "not so much in his CIA hat, but in his advisor-to-the-President hat" (Parry and Kornbluh 1988: 10–11; Parry 1992: 16). For a detailed, "insider's" account of extensive CIA involvement in influencing domestic Central America politics, see Chamorro 1987.

16. More specifically, for example, Oliver North maintained a secure telephone line to Otto Reich and met with Walter Raymond in at least seventy public-diplomacy planning sessions (Kornbluh and Byrne 1993: 5).

17. The legal department of the U.S. Government Accounting Office in 1987 judged these Office of Public Diplomacy techniques as "prohibited, covert propaganda activities designed to influence the media and the public to support the Administration's Latin America policies" (Jacoby and Parry 1987; Kornbluh and Byrne 1993: 6).

18. In the spring of 1987, Channell and Miller both pled guilty to charges of conspiring to defraud the United States by using tax-exempt money to purchase weapons to resupply the Contras. Both were sentenced to two years' probation (Parry and Kornbluh 1988: 21; Kornbluh and Byrne 1993: xxiv, xxvii).

19. Chamorro's evaluation of the CIA-Contra program (1987: 4, 57–59) is damning: "The Contra policy . . . depended on disinformation for its very survival. . . . The language used in the campaign to promote the Contras . . . was reminiscent of Orwell's doublespeak. . . . It had no relation to objective reality. . . . We specialized in creatively confusing the general public, Congress, and the press . . . [so that] no one could be sure whose proposals were whose, and which organizations were artificial and which were real. . . . The whole campaign was morally and ethically wrong, based on false premises and carried out unscrupulously. First, there was a blurring of the distinction between means and ends. . . . Second, there was a denial of reality, a replacement by fiction. . . . Third, lies were used to manipulate people and events to such an extent that behind the lies there was nothing but more self-illusion and self-deception. . . . Fourth, there was a negation of the moral distinction between good and evil. The need to be simplistic and to maintain a polarized, black-and-white situation, an antithesis between good and bad, led to a legitimation of concepts such as a good war, a good crime, a good rape, a good lie. This is how murder and torture were justified. . . . Finally, there was a total confusion of reason and faith. What could not be supported by reason and argument became a matter of faith. . . . The constant playing with lies and half-truths became a way of life that [I realized] could destroy my sanity and all capacity to analyze reality. . . . The people involved had no high purposes; they were greedy, ambitious, corrupt adventurers, misfits, and murderers, totally uncaring of others and irresponsible."

20. Later, the U.S. Drug Enforcement Agency conceded that it lacked evidence of any other involvement of Sandinista officials in drug smuggling (Parry and Kornbluh 1988: 12).

21. Noriega reportedly terminated the plan when the U.S. press began publishing stories of his own drug running (Parry and Kornbluh 1988: 12).

22. Of which $2.7 million was siphoned through IBC into a Swiss bank account and spend by Oliver North on weapons for the Contras (Kornbluh and Byrne 1993: 7–8).

23. North also wrote fund-raising appeal letters to wealthy donors, such as the January 1986 letter to Nelson Hunt, Robert Mosbacher, and Ellen Garwood, in which North stated, "Because you cared, the spark of liberty still glows in the darkness of Nicaragua. Once again your support will be essential" (quoted in Kornbluh and Byrne 1993: 7).

24. Carl Channell's NEPL, for example, campaigned during the 1986 Senate primary race to defeat Maryland Democratic Representative Michael Barnes, Chairman of the House Foreign Affairs Subcommittee on Western Hemisphere Affairs, who had opened an investigation of Oliver North's clandestine Contra-supply operation. Undated internal NEPL notes eventually uncovered by the investigation read, "Destroy Barnes, use him as object lesson

to others. . . . Barnes—wants indict Ollie. Watergate babies—want to get at the Pres. through Ollie. Want another Watergate. Put Barnes out of politics. If we get rid of Barnes we get rid of the ring leader and rid of the problem." Kris Littledale, an NEPL official disclosed to Iran-Contra investigators in September 1987, "We all, of course, wanted to nail Barnes' ass." Thus, in 1986, Channell placed a set of newspaper and television ads portraying Barnes as a Sandinista sympathizer. And the evening that Barnes lost the race, Channell sent North a telegram heralding "an end to much of the disinformation and unwise effort directed at crippling your foreign policy goals" (Parry and Kornbluh 1988: 22).

CHAPTER 10

1. Even some Republicans objected to that and similar argumentation. Senator Nancy Kassebaum, for example, rebuked the White House for this "highly offensive" rhetoric (Nyhan 1986).

2. In defending the ill-fated CISPES investigation to Congress, FBI Executive Assistant Director Oliver Revell emphasized (quoted in Mills 1988a), "Although our two-year counterterrorism investigation failed to lead to indictments of CISPES members, we did find indications that some CISPES members were at least discussing and planning violence." Apparently, one activist, in planning a protest campaign, had researched the response times of the city's emergency services, and another had concocted a scheme to shut down a utility company.

3. The list also included Samuel Bowles of the University of Massachusetts, Amherst, Richard Fagan of Stanford University, Salvador Luria of MIT, John Weeks of the American University, John Womack and George Wald of Harvard University, and Howard Zinn of Boston University (Marshall 1985).

4. With the exception of one detailed question about who had initiated a conversation Varelli had with a Texas mercenary about a contract to assassinate Salvadoran President Jose Duarte—Varelli or the mercenary?—to which Varelli answered, "I can't recall." Otherwise, the test showed that Varelli told no lies. At its conclusion, the polygraph examiner declared, "Congratulations. You've passed with flying colors." Weeks later, an FBI examiner reported that, with the exception of the one question, Varelli had spoken truthfully (FBI Document 1A143 in Frank Varelli file, June 7, 1984): "It is the opinion of the examiner that the recorded responses to Series I and Series II [dealing with Varelli's FBI activities] reflect no apparent deception. The responses to Series III [dealing with the Duarte assassination] indicate deception."

5. Originally, in addition to the June 7 report named in note 4, a second report confirming the veracity of Varelli's polygraph answers (FBI Memorandum Document 148, in Frank Varelli file, July 19, 1984) stated: "A technical review of the polygraph examination . . . of Frank Varelli on 6/7/84 has been completed. This review discloses that the examination is satisfactory in all aspects and review personnel concur with the results of the examination" (Gelbspan 1991: 179–81, 209–10). However, an April 24, 1987, FBI Headquarters Memorandum in Frank Varelli's file, released in 1988, stated: "A technical review of the polygraph examination documents pertaining to the

examination of Frank Varelli on 6/7/84 in response to an inquiry regarding this matter has been completed by [blanked out] FBIHQ. This review discloses that the responses indicate that the examinee was deceptive. It was noted during this review that the report erroneously concluded the examinee truthful to the first two series of questions. This was an error in the report and should be disregarded." In handwriting on the same memorandum, an official in the Dallas FBI Field Office wrote: "Pls prepare AT [airtel] to HQ suggesting they consider review of [Varelli's] file pursuant to [blank] FCIM and corrective action be taken by HQ if appropriate inasmuch as they have had the file for years."

6. A tape recording of Varelli's 1984 interview with Secret Service agent Jerry Kluber confirms that Varelli believed a potential attack on the President would be carried out by terrorists who would infiltrate CISPES, not by CISPES members themselves (Gelbspan 1991: 245). For further analysis of Varelli's credibility, see Gelbspan 1991: 1–11, 210–216; Berman 1987: 6.

7. At times, the efforts of government agencies to control potentially damaging information involved the exercise of force and unreasonable seizure. In 1981, for example, INS officials seized a news photographer, Octavio Gomez, for taking pictures of other INS agents breaking up a demonstration against the Service's treatment of Salvadoran refugees. They confiscated his camera and demanded to see his immigration papers. One week later, INS agents again seized Gomez and confiscated his camera as he tried to photograph them conducting a neighborhood sweep for illegal aliens. Subsequently, a Federal Court found the INS guilty of intentionally violating Gomez's First Amendment rights, awarding Gomez and his newspaper $295,000 in punitive damages (NYT 1985k).

8. In fact, everyone later learned, what they actually heard was ladders being quickly dragged across the boat's corrugated tin roof, which, over the crackly radio—all who heard it agreed—sounded exactly like machine-gun fire (Griffin-Nolan 1991: 145).

9. Another means of disrupting demonstrations was preventing protest organizers from ever reaching the demonstration site. According to Ken Butigan (1991): "There were scattered cases of key people really being screwed around with, like batteries taken out of their cars or electrical cables broken on the days of big protest events."

10. Little is known about "Sanchez," her undercover name, because within days, she bungled her cover and was taken off the case (Crittenden 1988: 166).

11. In the late 1970s, Cruz, a resident alien from Mexico, had worked as a coyote transporting illegal immigrants to Florida farmers who used them as inexpensive field workers. When in 1980 that operation was discovered and Cruz's employers arrested for running a slave camp, Cruz turned state's evidence rather than stand trial with his bosses. Later, it was discovered that Cruz perjured himself to secure the government's case in that trial. From there, Cruz became a regular paid INS informant for Jim Rayburn, where he completed eight cases before being assigned to infiltrate Sanctuary. Cruz was paid $18,000 for his work against Sanctuary (Davidson 1988: 115–17).

12. At the Pico Rivera Methodist Church near Los Angeles, to evade alarms, intruders actually cut a hole in the wall rather than go through a window or door (Davidson 1988: 113).

13. The FBI also consistently denied charges that they were involved in the break-ins. In March 1987, for example, Assistant FBI Director Floyd Clarke stated (quoted in Davidson 1988: 113; also see Subcommittee on Civil and Constitutional Rights 1987: 356–57; Crittenden 1988: 302–4), "I can tell you with certainty that there were no break-ins that were authorized, suggested, approved or considered by FBI management or supervisors." FBI Director William Webster took the same position in a personal interview with the author (Webster 1993).

14. The judge assigned by random drawing to preside over the Arizona Sanctuary trial, Earl Hamblin Carroll, proved to be heavily biased against the Sanctuary activists. He excluded, in pretrial rulings, all possible defense strategies as irrelevant to the case (Davidson 1988: 102), publicly expressed his disapproval of Sanctuary arguments with scowls and grimaces (Davidson 1988: 128), publicly belittled the Latin American refugees who were called to testify ("I think that people from Latin America perhaps have a difficulty in just answering the question 'yes' and 'no' by nature of their personal attitudes," Crittenden 1988: 278), and ridiculed the Sanctuary movement ("I thought Sanctuary was something for birds," Davidson 1988: 106). The defense lawyers, who complained that they had never in twenty years of legal practice seen a judge display such bias from the bench, repeatedly requested, unsuccessfully, that Judge Carroll remove himself from the trial (Crittenden 1988: 279).

15. The Los Angeles police officer assigned to Corea's case, detective Ron Elena, doubted that political motives were behind her abduction. "How political can a twenty-two year old be?," he asked (quoted in Bielski, Forster, and Bernstein 1987: 18). "I don't know what difference it makes. I'm just looking for some asshole to put in jail."

16. One former FBI agent, M. Wesley Swearingen, has admitted to performing five hundred burglaries himself, before leaving the Bureau in 1977 (Gelbspan 1987e). In another instance of covert domestic spying, the FBI has also kept confidential dossiers on members of U.S. Supreme Court since 1932 (*The Progressive* 1988).

CHAPTER 11

1. Conflict between religiously based groups and CISPES was a recurrent theme in interviews. One organizer, who asked to remain anonymous on this subject, confided: "Off the record, my dealings with CISPES were more like, 'We got a campaign to do and CISPES is going to be there. So how do we deal with them?' They weren't provocateurs or anything, just pains in the ass. And their commitment to non-violence was something less than absolute. We mostly had to do damage-control with them. We had the church involved in activism and wanted the media to get that message through our symbols, songs, etc. Then CISPES comes along, doing their chants, and conveys a totally different impression."

2. Gail Phares, another Witness for Peace organizer, concurred (1992): "Delegates return home, and for six months or so, they'll be quite active. But if they don't belong to a peace group of some kind, they will stop activism after six months. When we send our newsletter, they'll put it in their 'To Be Read' file and never read it."

3. Sometimes clashing expectations also proved to be a problem in the Sanctuary movement. According to a Sanctuary volunteer from Ithaca, New York, who asked to remain anonymous (1992): "Our group had one good refugee, but the second one was bad. He expected to be taken care of, not to have to work or anything. We raised thousands of dollars for him, but he took it and promptly moved to Canada. Some of us felt burned and taken advantage of. Another thing: in 1985, we tried putting refugees on our decision-making board. But they didn't know how meetings were run and decisions were made, so they were rather disruptive. They actually brought to us big plans for revolutionizing the U.S. from above. Really, nobody in our group had a clue about what the end goal of Sanctuary was, and our work ended up dying of neglect."

CHAPTER 12

1. On September 21, 1987, President Reagan declared to the General Assembly of the United Nations: "To the Sandinista delegation here today I say: your people know the true nature of your regime. . . . Understand this: we will not, and the world community will not, accept phony 'democratization' designed to mask the perpetuation of dictatorship." And on October 7 Reagan told the Organization of American States: "I make a solemn vow: as long as there is breath in this body, I will speak and work, strive and struggle for the cause of the Nicaraguan freedom fighters." One nonplussed U.S. official remarked, "Our cover story has become a reality. We talked about wanting peace. Well, here it is" (all quoted in Sklar 1988: 379).

2. By comparison, the Sandinistas received $3,017,085 in contributions of material aid (T-shirts, posters, and baseball caps) and $400,000 in cash contributions from overseas (Robinson 1992: 132).

3. One Witness for Peace long-termer, Kevin Kresse, quite likely the one to whom Betsy Crites referred, explained in a 1992 interview the difficulties he experienced in assessing the Nicaraguan situation at the end of the decade: "I found myself really reassessing the solidarity movement, the way the Contra war was framed, the kind of space we had to resist the war, and the kinds of truth-vs.-propaganda issues that were raised in my experiences by the Nicaraguan reality. I came back as committed as ever to opposing U.S. policy. But I also came back not really sure what to say. In the early years, what long-termers had to say fit with the official story. Later it became a more complicated reality. I found myself speaking to hard-core movement activists and wanting them to hear a certain story. But I had lived the Nicaraguan reality and come up against an analysis from some of the Nicaraguan people that didn't jive with what we had been saying for many years. At issue was whether the Contras had a significant social base in Nicaragua and whether the Sandinistas, in ways beyond excusable errors, had some very fundamentally

flawed institutional practices. The point is, it's gotten very difficult for solidarity people to talk about Nicaragua with much authority anymore. And I think that's part of the reason why people have moved on: Nicaragua is no longer sexy, no longer an easy country to explain."

CHAPTER 13

1. According to Brett (1991: 24), for example: "Robert White, the former U.S. ambassador to El Salvador, [stated] that he believed the work of the religious groups, more than any other factor, kept the U.S. from invading Nicaragua in the 1980s."

2. Weinberger, McFarlane, Clarridge, George, Abrams, and Fiers were pardoned by President Bush shortly before his term ended, on Christmas Eve 1993, partly, according to many, to divert attention from his own involvement in the Iran-Contra affair (see, for instance, Levin 1993; Doherty 1993; Bruning 1993; Idelson 1993). North's and Poindexter's convictions were overturned on grounds that their trials were tainted by their immunized testimony before Congress. Channell, Hakim, Miller, and Secord were each sentenced to two years' probation and combinations of modest fines and community service (Arnson 1993: 297–301).

3. Dick Junkin (1991) recounted: "The other day I ran into a guy doing peace work in his church around the Gulf War crisis. He said, 'You realize I would not be here if it weren't for the trip you led in Central America.' Here's a guy who was a career military man, working with missiles, and is now deep into peace work in the church. Some of the most moving experiences that happened to people on these trips were with career military people. Central America face-to-face dredged up all kinds of memories. It was a major challenge for them. And I was delighted, because I knew they would be the most credible witnesses back home."

4. Taylor (1990) continued: "One Catholic woman, who was the Assistant Attorney General for the state of Missouri, was so moved by her trip that she went to language school and has worked in Central America ever since, using her legal expertise to document human rights abuses. Another woman, who used to work for the government, and whose son was killed in Vietnam, went as a short-termer and was transformed. Here is this dumpy woman in her mid-50s, who had lost a son to war, in Nicaragua, encountering Nicaraguans who have also lost sons to war. There was a real bonding. She now works at Harvest House. Sam Goldman, a Jew who only knew Christianity as the Inquisition and the Crusades, was overcome by the suffering in Central America and met some real Christians in Nicaragua, came back transformed, and began to work with Catholic Peace Fellowship in Long Island. I know people who had been alienated and withdrawn from activism since the Vietnam movement who got back involved because of Central America."

5. At the same time, it must be acknowledged that one frequently disempowering result of political consciousness-raising was cynicism. Buhl (1993) admitted: "Many people who worked on Central America in the 1980s are very cynical now, extremely disaffected people. It's very hard to like your government when you know up-close and personal it has been habitually lying to

you and killing people. Those two things really upset activists, and I'm not sure how long it will take for them to recover. They are very cynical about our democracy. Some don't even vote anymore. Paradoxically, Central America organizing was very empowering. But, when it came to feelings about our government, it was also *very* alienating."

6. According to Angela Berryman (1990): "Our main goal is to build an educated, active constituency that can analyze U.S. foreign and domestic policy and can speak out and put their bodies on the line for those issues. Because of Central America, many people are much more aware of foreign policy issues and their ability to organize and challenge their own government. In that way, we have been a success."

CHAPTER 14

1. David Meyer, more appreciative than most of the importance of religion, speaking with regard to the Nuclear Freeze movement, observed (1990: 106): "Religious faith . . . provides a more easily sustainable motivation for activism than do more instrumental or pragmatic incentives. Religiously motivated people were among the first to address passionately the dilemmas of the nuclear age partly because they were not necessarily searching for battles that could easily be won. Religious faith can make political activity personally rewarding, even when it does not seem to be immediately or even potentially efficacious. It can justify and even encourage actions against both the state and the odds, which gain meaning for activists in the context of religious commitment rather than realpolitik."

2. Thus, every plausible structuralist explanation actually assumes, at least implicitly, that the outcome being explained is a result of norm- and/or interest-directed human agents actively responding to the social structures they encounter. Likewise, every plausible methodological-individualist explanation—including rational-choice explanation—assumes, at least implicitly, not only that purposive individuals act within social-structural constraints, but also that individual preferences and goals themselves are not stable and uniform, but are variably inculcated and shaped by the socializing environment of culture. Structure cannot escape agency, and agency cannot escape structure. Wherever they start, plausible analyses eventually come around to and employ the other.

Bibliography

AFSC. n.d. "Introduction to the American Friends Service Committee." Organizational pamphlet. Philadelphia: American Friends Service Committee.

Aguilera Peralta, Gabriel. 1988. "The Hidden War: Guatemala's Counterinsurgency Campaign." In Nora Hamilton et al. (eds.), *Crisis in Central America: Regional Dynamics and U.S. Policy in the 1980s*. Boulder, Colo.: Westview Press.

Agus, Jacob. 1981. "The Covenant Concept: Jewish Ethics and the Doctrine of Creation." *Conservative Judaism* 28.

———. 1983. "A Jewish View of World Community." In *The Jewish Quest: Essays on BasicConcepts of Jewish Theology*. New York: Ktav Publishing House.

Alter, Jonathan, Thomas DeFrank, and Margaret Warner. 1984. "Reagan: The Cocoon Strategy." *Newsweek* 104 (September 17).

Alexandre, Laurien. 1987. "In the Service of the State." *Media, Culture, and Society* 9.

Alvarez, Carmelo. 1981. "A Close-Up View of the Struggle in El Salvador." *New York Times* (March 16): 22.

America. 1986. "'When I Use a Word,' Humpty Dumpty Said . . ." *America* 159 (November 29).

Americas Watch. 1984. *Failure: The Reagan Administration's Human Rights Policy in 1983*. New York: Americas Watch.

Anderson, Jack. 1984. "CIA Joins with Extremists in Nicaraguan War." *Washington Post* (September 30).

Anderson, Thomas. 1971. *Matanza: El Salvador's Communist Revolt of 1932*. Lincoln: University of Nebraska Press.

———. 1984. "The Roots of Revolution in Central America." In Howard Wiarda (ed.), *Rift and Revolution*. Washington: American Enterprise Institute for Public Policy Research.

Anonymous. 1992. Anonymous Interview, June 18. San Diego, California.

Anonymous. 1993. Anonymous Interview, November 29. Washington, D.C.

Antonio Hernández, Colonel Leopoldo. 1988. "A Most Successful Operation—Civil Affairs." In Max Manwaring and Court Prisk (eds.), *El Salvador at War: An Oral History*. Washington, D.C.: National Defense University.

Apple, R. W. 1982. "Salvador Stirring Concern in Europe: U.S. Policy in Latin

Nation Is Adding to Tension between Washington and Allies." *New York Times* (March 11): 19.

Applebome, Peter. 1988a. "Talks over Convoy Reach Dead End." *New York Times* (June 15): 6.

———. 1988b. "Aid Convey Is Turned Back at Border." *New York Times* (June 16): 8.

Arnson, Cynthia. 1988. "The Reagan Administration, Congress, and Central America: The Search for Consensus." In Nora Hamilton et al. (eds.), *Crisis in Central America: Regional Dynamics and U.S. Policy in the 1980s.* Boulder, Colo.: Westview Press.

———. 1993. *Crossroads: Congress, the President, and Central America, 1976–1993.* University Park: Pennsylvania State University Press.

Arnson, Cynthia, and Johanna Mendelson Forman. 1991. "United States Policy in Central America." *Current History* 90 (544) (March).

Asner, Edward. 1982. "We're on the Wrong Side in El Salvador." *New York Times* (February 20): 23.

Austin, Charles. 1983a. "L.I. Bishop Asks the End of Salvador Aid." *New York Times* (July 19): 2.

———. 1983b. "More Churches Join in Offering Sanctuary for Latin Refugees." *New York Times* (September 21): 18.

Baker, Stephen, Larry Boyd, and Ana Arana. 1989. "For Bush, Central America Won't Be a Crusade." *Business Week,* no. 3087 (January 16).

Barnes, Samuel, Max Kaase, et al. 1979. *Political Action: Mass Participation in Five Western Democracies.* Beverly Hills, Calif.: Sage Publications.

Barnett, Frank. 1961. "A Proposal for Political Warfare." *Military Review* (March).

Barry, Deborah, Raúl Vergara, and José Rodolfo Castro. 1988. "'Low Intensity Warfare': The Counterinsurgency Strategy for Central America." In Nora Hamilton et al. (eds.), *Crisis in Central America: Regional Dynamics and U.S. Policy in the 1980s.* Boulder, Colo.: Westview Press.

Barry, Tom. 1987. *Roots of Rebellion: Land and Hunger in Central America.* Boston: South End Press.

Barry, Tom, and Deb Preusch. 1988. *The Soft War: The Uses and Abuses of U.S. Economic Aid in Central America.* New York: Grove Press.

Bau, Ignatius. 1985. *This Ground Is Holy: Church Sanctuary and Central American Refugees.* Mahwah, N.J.: Paulist Press.

Beach, Harlan, and Charles Fahs (eds.). 1925. *World Missionary Atlas.* New York: Institute for Social and Religious Research.

Benford, Robert. 1992. "Social Movements." In Edgar Borgatta (ed.), *Encyclopedia of Sociology.* New York: Macmillan Publishers.

Berger, Peter. 1967. *The Sacred Canopy: Elements of a Sociological Theory of Religion.* New York: Anchor Books.

Berger, Peter, and Thomas Luckmann, 1966. *The Social Construction of Reality.* Garden City, N.Y.: Anchor Books.

Berman, E. Bruce. 1987. "Project Terror: the FBI's El Salvador Obsession." *The Boston Pheonix* (March 3): 1, 6–9, 20.

Bermann, Karl. 1986. *Under the Big Stick: Nicaragua and the United States since 1848.* Boston: South End Press.

Berryman, Angela. 1990. Interview, November 26. Philadelphia, Penn.

Berryman, Phillip. 1982. "Mr. Reagan, Press El Salvador to Negotiate." *New York Times* (February 14): IV, 19.

———. 1984. *The Religious Roots of Rebellion: Christians in Central American Revolutions.* Maryknoll, N.Y.: Orbis Books.

Best, Edward. 1987. *U.S. Policy and Regional Security in Central America.* New York: St. Martins Press.

Bielski, Vince, Cindy Forster, and Dennis Bernstein. 1987. "The Death Squads Hit Home: Which Side Is the FBI On?." *The Progressive* (October 16): 15–19.

Billingsley, K. L. 1990. *From Mainline to Sideline: The Social Witness of the National Council of Churches.* Washington, D.C.: Ethics and Public Policy Center.

Bishop, Katherine. 1987. "Protesters, Angered by Injury, Return to Arms Site." *New York Times* (September 3): 22.

Blair, Aurthur. 1983. "Unconventional Warfare: A Legitimate Tool for Foreign Policy." *Conflict* 4(1).

Blachman, Morris, and Kenneth Sharpe. 1988. "Central American Traps: Challenging the Reagan Agenda." *World Policy Journal* 5(1) (Winter).

Blair, William G. 1982. "Ivy Editors Unite on Salvador." *New York Times* (March 24): 14.

Blanchard, Tzi. 1975. "Our Social Concerns Have a Jewish Ground." *Sh'ma* 5.

Blasier, Cole. 1983. *The Giant's Rival: The USSR and Latin America.* Pittsburgh: University of Pittsburgh Press.

Blumenthal, Sidney. 1983. "Reagan the Unassailable: How Come the Gaffes Never Seem to Hurt Him?" *The New Republic* 189 (September 12).

Bock, Paul. 1974. *In Search of a Responsible World Society: The Social Teachings of the World Council of Churches.* Philadelphia: Westminster Press.

Bonner, Raymond. 1981. "Protests on Salvador Are Staged across U.S." *New York Times* (March 25): 3.

Bonthius, Bob. 1990. Interview, October 16. Ellsworth, Maine.

Booth, John. 1985. *The End and the Beginning: The Nicaraguan Revolution.* Boulder, Colo.: Westview Press.

Bouchey, Francis, Roger Fontaine, David Jordon, and Gordon Sumner. 1980. *A New Inter-American Policy for the Eighties.* Washington, D.C.: Council for Inter-American Security.

Bowen, Gordon. 1984. "Guatemala: The Origins and Development of State Terrorism." In Donald Schulz and Douglas Graham (eds.), *Revolution and Counterrevolution in Central America and the Caribbean.* Boulder, Colo.: Westview Press.

———. 1989. "Presidential Action and Public Opinion about U.S. Nicaraguan Policy: Limits to the 'Rally 'Round the Flag' Syndrome." *PS: Political Science and Politics* (December).

Brand, Karl-Werner. 1990. "Cyclical Aspects of New Social Movements: Waves of Cultural Criticism and Mobilization Cycles of New Middle-Class Radicalism." In Russell Dalton and Manfred Kuechler (eds.), *Challenging the Political Order.* Oxford: Oxford University Press.

Braude, Samuel. 1970. "Civil Disobedience and the Jewish Tradition." In Daniel Silver (ed.), *Judaism and Ethics.* New York: Ktav Publishing House.

Breines, Wini. 1982. *Community and Organization in the New Left, 1962–1968: The Great Refusal.* New York: Praeger.

Breslauer, S. Daniel. 1983. *A New Jewish Ethic.* New York: The Edwin Mellon Press.

———. 1986. *Modern Jewish Morality.* New York: Greenwood Press.

Brett, Donna Whitson, and Edward Brett. 1988. *Murdered in Central America: The Stories of Eleven U.S. Missionaries.* Maryknoll, N.Y.: Orbis Books.

Brett, Edward. 1991. "The Attempts of Grassroots Religious Groups to Change U.S. Policy toward Central America: Their Methods, Successes, and Failures." *Journal of Church and State* 36(4) (August): 773–94.

Bricker, Victoria Reifler. 1981. *The Indian Christ, the Indian King.* Austin: University of Texas Press.

Briggs, Kenneth. 1981. "Catholic Bishops Criticize Aid to El Salvador." *New York Times* (November 20): I, 17.

———. 1982. "U.S. Catholic Bishops Opposing Administration's Salvador Policy." *New York Times* (February 21): 1.

Brinkley, Joel. 1985a. "Nicaragua and the U.S. Options: An Invasion Is Openly Discussed." *New York Times* (June 5): 1.

———. 1985b. "U.S. Said to Have Weighed Raid on Training Camp in Nicaragua." *New York Times* (July 24): 1.

———. 1986a. "Four Veterans Ending Fast on Policy in Nicaragua." *New York Times* (October 17): 16.

———. 1986b. "U.S. Aides Fear Crisis Will End Contras' Effort." *New York Times* (December 8): 1.

Brint, Steven. 1984. "'New Class' and Cumulative Trend Explanations of the Liberal Political Attitudes of Professionals." *American Journal of Sociology* 90: 30–71

Brinton, Crane. 1965. *The Anatomy of a Revolution.* New York: Vintage Books.

Broadcasting. 1982. "Photo Opportunity Standoff: Networks vs. White House." *Broadcasting* 102 (April 19).

———. 1984. "Michael Deaver: The President's New Communicator." *Broadcasting* 106 (January 30).

Brockett, Charles. 1990. *Land, Power, and Poverty: Agrarian Transformation and Political Conflict in Central America.* Boulder, Colo.: Westview Press.

Brockman, James. 1982. *The Word Remains: A Life of Oscar Romero.* Maryknoll, N.Y.: Orbis Books.

Brody, Reed. 1985. *Contra Terror in Nicaragua: Report of a Fact-finding Mission: September 1984–January 1985.* Boston: South End Press.

Broude, S. G. 1970. "Civil Disobedience in the Jewish Tradition." in D. J. Silver (ed.), *Judaism and Ethics*. New York: New York: Ktav Publishers.

Browning, David. 1971. *El Salvador: Landscape and Society*. Oxford: Clarendon Press.

Brozan, Nadine. 1989. "160 Demonstrators Are Arrested in U.S. for Salvador Sit-Ins." *New York Times* (March 21): 8.

Bruce-Briggs, B. (ed.). 1979. *The New Class*. New York: McGraw-Hill Publishers.

Bruning, Fred. 1993. "The Time Bomb That Ticks for George Bush." *Maclean's* 106(3) (January 18).

Buchanan, Patrick. 1986. "The Contras Need Our Help." *The Washington Post* (March 5): A19.

Buhl, Cindy. 1993. Interview, November 28. Washington, D.C.

Bulmer-Thomas, Victor. 1987. *The Political Economy of Central America since 1920*. Cambridge: Cambridge University Press.

Burnham, David. 1985. "Foes of Reagan Latin Policies Fear They're under Surveillance." *New York Times* (April 19): II, 20.

Burnham, Walter. 1982. *The Current Crisis in American Politics*. New York: Oxford University Press.

Burns, E. Bradford. 1987. *At War in Nicaragua: The Reagan Doctrine and the Politics of Nostalgia*. New York: Harper and Row.

Burstein, Paul. 1991. "Legal Mobilization as a Social Movement Tactic." *American Journal of Sociology* 96:5 (March).

Bush, George. 1989. "Bush Seeks 'New Partnership' on Central America Policy." *Congressional Quarterly Weekly Report* 47(18) (May 6).

Butigan, Ken. 1991. Interview, January 8. Berkeley, Calif.

———. 1989. *The Pledge of Resistance: A Special Pledge Report*. Washington, D.C.: The Pledge. n.d. "Pledge of Resistance Chronology." photocopied leaflet.

C-5 Spokesperson. 1988. "In the Beginning They Took No Prisoners." In Max Manwaring and Court Prisk (eds.), *El Salvador at War: An Oral History*. Washington, D.C.: National Defense University.

Carmack, Robert (ed.). 1988. *Harvest of Violence: The Maya Indians and the Guatemala Crisis*. Norman, Okla.: University of Oklahoma Press.

Cayetano Carpio, Salvador. 1988. "Murder, Assassination, and Death Squads." In Max Manwaring and Court Prisk (eds.), *El Salvador at War: An Oral History*. Washington, D.C.: National Defense University.

Central America Resource Center. 1986. *Directory of Central America Organizations* (third ed., 1987). Austin, Tex.: Central America Resource Center.

Chamorro, Edgar. 1987. *Packaging the Contras: A Case of CIA Disinformation*. New York: Institute for Media Analysis.

Chatfield, Charles. 1992. *The American Peace Movement: Ideals and Activism*. New York: Twayne Publishers.

Chavez, Lydia. 1987. "Nicaragua Is Aided by Sister City Projects." *New York Times* (February 1): IV, 6.

Clark, Jeanne. 1988. *Prophetic Rhetoric and the Sanctuary Movement*. Ph.D.

dissertation. Department of Speech Communication, University of Arizona.

Clark, Mike. 1992. Interview, July 28. Washington, D.C.

Clendinen, Dudley. 1986. "Friends and Foes of Contras Rally at Florida Base." *New York Times* (December 14): 20.

Clymer, Adam. 1983. "Poll Finds Americans Don't Know U.S. Positions on Central America." *New York Times* (July 1): 1.

———. 1985. "Most Americans in Survey Oppose Aid for Overthrow of Sandinistas." *New York Times* (June 5): 1.

Cockburn, Alexander. 1987. "Whistle and They'll Come to You." *The Nation* 244 (May 16).

———. 1989. "The Files of Counterrevolution." *The Nation* 249 (August 7).

———. 1990. "From the Jaws of Defeat." *The Nation* 251 (November 19).

Coffin, William Sloane. 1985. "The Tasks Ahead." In Gary MacEoin (ed.), *Sanctuary.* New York: Harper and Row.

Cohen, Jean. 1985. "Strategy or Identity: New Theoretical Paradigms and Contemporary Social Movements." *Social Research* 52(4) (Winter).

Cohen, Joshu, and Joel Rogers. 1986a. *Inequity and Intervention: The Federal Budget and Central America.* Boston: South End Press.

———. 1986b. *Rules of the Game: American Politics and the Central America Movement.* Boston: South End Press.

Cohen, Martin. 1979. "The Mission of Israel after Auschwitz." In Helga Croner and Leon Klenicki (eds.), *Issues in the Jewish-Christian Dialogue: Jewish Perspectives on Covenant, Mission, and Witness.* New York: Paulist Press.

Cohen, Richard. 1986. "The Propagandist at His Best." *The Washington Post* (March 21): A23.

Cohen, Samuel. 1973. "The Universal and the Particular in Judaism." In Robert Gordis and Ruth Waxman (eds.), *Faith and Reason.* New York: Ktav Publishing.

Cohen, Shari. 1985. "Hill Probes into 'Contra' Funds Stalled over Lack of Evidence." *Congressional Quarterly Weekly Report* 43(46) (November 16).

Cohn, Betsy, and Patricia Hynds. 1987. "The Manipulation of the Religious Issue." In Thomas Walker (ed.), *Reagan Versus the Sandinistas: The Undeclared War on Nicaragua.* Boulder, Colo.: Westview Press.

Coleman, Kenneth. 1991. "The Consequences of Excluding Reformists from Power: The View from the 1990s." In Kenneth Coleman and George Herring (eds.), *The Central American Crisis: Sources of Conflict and the Failure of U.S. Policy.* Wilmington, Del.: Scholarly Resources.

Coleman, Kenneth, and George Herring (eds.). 1985. *The Central American Crisis: Sources of Conflict and the Failure of U.S. Policy.* Wilmington, Del.: Scholarly Resources.

Coles, Robert. 1993. *The Call to Service: A Witness to Idealism.* Boston: Houghton Mifflin Co.

Collins, Joseph. 1986. *Nicaragua: What Difference Could a Revolution Make?* New York: Grove Press.

Collins, Sheila. 1990. "On the Death of Archbishop Oscar Romero and the

First Anniversary of Three Mile Island." In Mar Peter-Raoul, Linda Forcey, and Robert Hunter (eds.), *Yearning to Breath Free: Liberation Theologies in the U.S.* Maryknoll, N.Y.: Orbis Books.

Collum, Danny. 1986. "Trespassing in the Basin: A History of U.S. Intervention." In Emergency Response Network (ed.), *Basta! No Mandate for War.* Philadelphia, Penn.: New Society Publishers.

Committee on Intelligence. 1989. *The FBI and CISPES.* Report of the Select Committee on Intelligence, United States Senate (July 14).

Congressional Quarterly. 1989. "Bipartisan Agreement Reached on Central America Policy." *Congressional Quarterly Weekly Review* 47(12) (March 25).

Connors, Joseph. 1973. "Roman Catholic Missions." In Edward Dayton (ed.), *Missions Handbook.* Monrovia, Calif.: Missions Advanced Research and Communications.

Conroy, Michael. 1987. "Economic Aggression as an Instrument of Low-Intensity Warfare." In Thomas Walker (ed.), *Reagan Versus the Sandinistas: The Undeclared War on Nicaragua.* Boulder, Colo.: Westview Press.

Conroy, Michael, and Manuel Pastor. 1988. "The Nicaraguan Experiment: Characteristics of a New Economic Model." In Nora Hamilton, Jeffry Frieden, Linda Fuller, and Manuel Pastor Jr. (eds.), *Crisis in Central America: Regional Dynamics and U.S. Policy in the 1980s.* Boulder, Colo.: Westview Press.

Conway, M. Margaret. 1985. *Political Participation in the United States.* Washington, D.C.: Congressional Quarterly Press.

Cooper, Marc, and Lawrence Soley. 1990. "How to Get on TV, Win Newscaster Friends and Influence People: An Interview with Sam Donaldson." *Mother Jones* (February/March).

CQ Researcher. 1992. "Attempts at Reform." *CQ Researcher* 2(46) (December 11): 1084–86.

Corn, David, and Jefferson Morley. 1988a. "CISPES Is Not Alone." *The Nation* 246(8) (February 27): 27.

———. 1988b. "Shocked (Shocked?) to Find F.B.I. Spying." *The Nation* 246 (March 12).

Costain, Anne. 1992. *Inviting Women's Rebellion.* Baltimore: Johns Hopkins University Press.

Coston, Carol. 1981. "No U.S. Arms for El Salvador." *New York Times* (March 1): 18.

Courtney, Marian. 1987a. "New Jersey Group Seeks Answers in Nicaragua." *New York Times* (September 6): XI, 1.

———. 1987b. "3 People Who Chose to Work in Nicaragua." *New York Times* (September 6): XI, 10.

Coutin, Susan. 1990. *The Culture of Protest: Religious Activism and the U.S. Sanctuary Movement.* Ph.D. dissertation. Department of Anthropology, Stanford University.

Craig, Robert. 1992. *Religion and Radical Politics: An Alternative Christian Tradition in the United States.* Philadelphia: Temple University Press.

Crites, Betsy. 1992. Interview, August 1. Durham, North Carolina.

Crittenden, Ann. 1988. *Sanctuary: A Story of American Conscience and Law in Collision.* New York: Weidenfeld and Nicolson.

Crossette, Barbara. 1982. "4 Democrats Urge U.S. to Seek a Truce in Salvador." *New York Times* (February 11): I, 8.

Crucible. 1984. "Keeping the Backyard Safe." In *Crucible of Hope.* Washington, D.C.: *Sojourners* magazine.

Cutler, Lloyd. 1984. "Foreign Policy on Deadline." *Foreign Policy* (Fall).

Dalton, Russell, and Manfred Kuechler (eds.). 1990. *Challenging the Political Order.* Oxford: Oxford University Press.

Damboriena, Prudencio. 1962. *El Protestantismo en América Latina.* Bogotá, Colombia: FERES.

Davidson, Miriam. 1988. *Convictions of the Heart: Jim Corbett and the Sanctuary Movement.* Tucson: University of Arizona Press.

Davis, Shelton. 1983. "State Violence and Agrarian Crisis in Guatemala: The Roots of the Indian-Peasant Rebellion." In Martin Diskin (ed.), *Trouble in Our Backyard: Central America and the United States in the Eighties.* New York: Pantheon Books.

———. 1988. "Introduction: Sowing the Seeds of Violence," in Robert Carmack (ed.), *Harvest of Violence.* Norman: University of Oklahoma Press.

Dayton, Edward (ed.). 1973. *Missions Handbook.* Monrovia, Calif.: Missions Advanced Research and Communications.

de Onis, Juan. 1980a. "Catholic Bishops Ask End of Arms Aid to El Salvador." *New York Times* (November 9): 15.

———. 1980b. "Carter Reported Undecided on Salvador Military Aid." *New York Times* (December 24): 8.

———. 1981a. "Reagan Aides Meet Sharp Attack In House on New Salvadoran Aid." *New York Times* (March 6): 6.

———. 1981b. "President Terms Aid for Salvador a Help to Rights." *New York Times* (March 7): 1.

———. 1981c. "Killings in Salvador Deplored by U.S." *New York Times* (April 10): 3.

———. 1981d. "Foes and Supporters of Reagan Policies Plan Rallies." *New York Times* (May 3): 23.

———. 1981e. "Capital Rally Assails Arms to Salvador." *New York Times* (May 4): 3.

Demac, Donna. 1984. *Keeping America Uninformed: Government Secrecy in the 1980s.* New York: Pilgrim Press.

Demo, David. 1992. "The Self-Concept over Time." *Annual Review of Sociology.* 18: 303–26.

Destler, I. M. 1981. "Dateline Washington: Congress as Boss?" Foreign Policy, no. 42 (Spring).

———. 1984. "The Elusive Consensus: Congress and Central America." In Robert S. Leiken (ed.), *Central America: Anatomy of a Conflict.* New York: Pergammon Press.

DeWalt, Billie, and Pedro Bidegaray. 1991. "The Agrarian Bases of Conflict in Central America." In Kenneth Coleman and George Herring (eds.), *The*

Central American Crisis: Sources of Conflict and the Failure of U.S. Policy. Wilmington, Del.: Scholarly Resources.

Diamond, Edwin. 1985. "Seeing Things the White House Way." *New York* 18 (May 27): 20–22.

Dickey, Christopher. 1983. "Central America: From Quagmire to Cauldron." *Foreign Affairs* 62 (Annual: America and the World).

Directory of North American Protestant Foreign Missionary Agencies (4th ed.). 1960. New York: Missionary Research Library.

Directory of North American Protestant Foreign Mission Agencies (6th ed.). 1964. New York: Missionary Research Library.

Directory of North American Protestant Missionaries Overseas. 1968. Waco, Tex.: Word Books.

Diskin, Martin. 1983. *Trouble in Our Backyard: Central America and the United States in the Eighties.* New York: Pantheon Books.

———. 1987. "The Manipulation of Indigenous Struggles." In Thomas Walker (ed.), *Reagan Versus the Sandinistas: The Undeclared War on Nicaragua.* Boulder, Colo.: Westview Press.

Dodson, Michael, and Laura Nuzzi O'Shaughnessy. 1985. "Religion and Politics." In Thomas Walker (ed.), *Nicaragua: The First Five Years.* New York: Praeger Publishers.

Doherty, Carroll. 1991. "Bush Holds Off on Military Aid That Congress Had Resisted." *Congressional Quarterly Weekly Report* 49(11) (March 16).

———. 1993. "Walsh Says Pardon Thwarted New Evidence on Arms Deals." *Congressional Quarterly Weekly Report* 51(7) (February 13).

Donner, Frank. 1985. "The F.B.I. Is Watching: Travelers' Warning For Nicaragua." *The Nation* (July 6–13): 13–17.

Dorr, Donal. 1983. *Option for the Poor: A Hundred Years of Vatican Social Teaching.* Maryknoll, N.Y.: Orbis Books.

Draper, Theodore. 1987. "The Iran-Contra Affair: An Autopsy." *The New York Review of Books* 34(20) (December 17): 67–77.

Dubose, Louis. 1987. "The Next Round-Up." *The Texas Observer* (May 15).

Duff, Edward. 1956. *The Social Thought of the World Council of Churches.* New York: Association Press.

Durham, William. 1979. *Scarcity and Survival in Central America.* Stanford, Calif.: Stanford University Press.

Dyck, Cornelius. 1980a. *Responding to Worldwide Needs.* Mennonite Central Committee Story Series II. Scottdale, Penn.: Herald Press.

———. 1980b. *Witness and Service in North America.* Mennonite Central Committee Story Series III. Scottdale, Penn.: Herald Press.

Eckstein, Susan. 1989. "Power and Popular Protest in Latin America." In Susan Eckstein (ed.), *Power and Popular Protest: Latin American Social Movements.* Berkeley: University of California Press.

Economist, The. 1986. "Refugees: No Hiding Place." Vol. 299 (May 10): 26.

Editors, The. 1983. "A Promise of Resistance." *Sojourners* (December).

Emergency Response Network. 1986. *Basta! No Mandate for War: A Pledge of Resistance Handbook.* Philadelphia, Penn.: New Society Publishers.

English, Raymond. 1989. "A Counterintelligence and Counterterrorism Case: CISPES and the FBI." *Harvard Journal of Law and Public Policy* 12.

Epstein, Barbara. 1991. *Political Protest and Cultural Revolution: Non-Violent Direct Action in the 1970s and 1980s.* Berkeley: University of California Press.

Etzioni, Amitai. 1986. "The Case for a Multi-Utility Conception," *Economics and Philosophy* 2(2) (October): 159–83.

———. 1988. *The Moral Dimension: Toward a New Economics.* New York: The Free Press.

Evans, G. Russell. 1973. *Apathy, Apostacy and Apostles: A Study of the History and Activities of The National Council of Churches of Christ in the U.S.A. with Sidelights on Its Ally: The World Council of Churches.* New York: Vantage Press.

Fackenheim, Emil. 1968. "Religious Responsibility for the Social Order." In *Quest for Past and Future: Essays in Jewish Theology.* Bloomington, Ind.: University of Indiana Press.

Fagan, Patricia Weiss. 1988. "Central American Refugees and U.S. Policy." In Nora Hamilton et al. (eds.), *Crisis in Central America: Regional Dynamics and U.S. Policy in the 1980s.* Boulder, Colo.: Westview Press.

Fagan, Richard. 1987. *Forging Peace: The Challenge of Central America.* New York: Basil Blackwell.

Falcoff, Mark. 1984. "The Apple of Discord: Central America in U.S. Domestic Politics." In Howard J. Wiarda (ed.), *Rift and Revolution: The Central American Imbroglio.* Washington D.C.: American Enterprise Institute.

———. 1986. "Revolutionary Tourism." *Public Opinion* 9 (Summer): 6–8.

Farer, Tom. 1988. "Looking at Looking at Nicaragua: The Problematique of Impartiality in Human Rights Inquiries." *Human Rights Quarterly* 10.

Felton, John. 1983a. "Compromise Appears Likely on El Salvador Military Aid." *Congressional Quarterly Weekly Report* 41(11) (March 19): 549.

———. 1983b. "Three Committees Wrestle with El Salvador Aid Request." *Congressional Quarterly Weekly Report* 41(12) (March 26): 606.

———. 1984a. "Reagan Tactic on Central America Funds Fails." *Congressional Quarterly Weekly Report* 42(10) (March 10): 542.

———. 1984b. "Administration Defends Mining of Harbors." *Congressional Quarterly Weekly Report* 42(15) (April 14): 835.

———. 1984c. "Administration Moves to Placate, Pressure Hill." *Congressional Quarterly Weekly Report* 42(17) (April 28): 957.

———. 1985. "Reagan Misled Hill on El Salvador, Report Says." *Congressional Quarterly Weekly Report* 43(7) (February 16): 315.

———. 1987. "Arias' Plan Has Yet To Bring Real Peace." *Congressional Quarterly Weekly Report* 45(33) (August 15): 1892–93.

———. 1989a. "New Accord Alters Equation for Contras, Hill Allies." *Congressional Quarterly Weekly Report* 47(32) (August 12).

———. 1989b. "Bush Turns to Military Aid to Stanch Narcotics Flow." *Congressional Quarterly Weekly Report* 47(36) (September 9).

———. 1990. "Carrots-and-Sticks Policy Yields Possible Truce on the Hill." *Congressional Quarterly Weekly Report* 48(18) (May 5).

Fields, A. Belden. 1986. "U.S. Anti-Imerialist Movements in Two Contexts: The War in Indochina and the Intervention in Central America." *Scandinavian Journal of Development Alternatives* 5(2,3) (June–September).

Fields, Howard. 1984. "The White House versus the News Media: Are the Networks Correspondents Being 'Used'?." *Television-Radio Age* 32 (November 26).

Fish, Joe, and Cristina Sganga. 1988. *El Salvador: Testament of Terror.* New York: Olive Branch Press.

Fishburn, Janet. 1993. "Mainline Protestants and the Social Gospel Impulse." In Dieter Hellel (ed.), *The Church's Public Role.* Grand Rapids, Mich.: Wm. B. Eerdmans.

Fitch, Stona. 1982. "El Salvador Dispels Apathy at Princeton." *New York Times* (March 16): XI, 16.

Fowler, Robert. 1982. *A New Engagement: Evangelical Political Thought, 1966–1976.* Grand Rapids, Mich.: Wm. B. Eerdmans.

Franklin, Ben. 1987. "Contra Aid Protesters Found Guilty." *New York Times* (February 16): 9.

Frederick, Howard. 1987. "Electronic Penetration." In Thomas Walker (ed.), *Reagan Versus the Sandinistas: The Undeclared War on Nicaragua.* Boulder, Colo.: Westview Press.

Freeman, Jo. 1975. *The Politics of Women's Liberation.* New York: David McKay.

Freidman, Maurice. 1974. "The Community of Otherness and the Covenant of Peace." In *The Hidden Image: A Heartening Answer to the Dehumanizing Threats of Our Age.* New York: Dell Publishing.

Friedrich, Otto. 1983. "'Anybody Want to Go to Grenada?' Angry Reporters Finally Get to a Story after It Is All But Over." *Time* 122 (November 14).

Frontline. 1986. "Revolution in El Salvador." Public Broadcasting Service.

Gailey, Phil. 1985. "Poll Shows Most Americans See Reagan Tax Plan as Fair." *New York Times* (June 5): 8.

Gamson, William. 1975. *The Strategy of Social Protest.* Belmont, Calif.: Wadsworth.

———. 1989. "News as Framing." *American Behavioral Scientist* 33(2) (November–December): 157–61.

Gamson, William, and Andre Modigliani. 1989. "Media Discourse and Public Opinion on Nuclear Power: A Constructionist Approach." *American Journal of Sociology.* 95(1) (July): 1–37.

Gamson, William, David Croteau, William Hoynes, and Theodore Sasson. 1992. "Media Images and the Social Construction of Reality." *Annual Review of Sociology* 18: 373–93.

Gans, Herbert. 1979. *Deciding What's News.* New York: Vintage Books.

Garcia, Cristina. 1987. "Death Squads Invade California." *Time* (August 3): 20–21.

Garst, Rachel, and Tom Barry. 1990. *Feeding the Crisis: U.S. Food Aid and Farm Policy in Central America.* Lincoln, Nebr.: University of Nebraska Press.

Gelbspan, Ross. 1984. "Break-ins, Threats Hit Political Activists." *Boston Globe* (December 30): 21, 25.

———. 1985a. "Opponents of U.S. Latin Policy Charge FBI Harassment." *Boston Globe* (March 26): 11.

———. 1985b. "Sanctuary Groups See Trend of Harassment." *Boston Globe* (December 9): 1.

———. 1986a. "Civil Liberties Lawyers Seek Sanctuary Link to Break-ins." *Boston Globe* (April 25): 25.

———. 1986b. "Central America Activists Call for Probe of Break-ins." *Boston Globe* (December 7): 28.

———. 1987a. "Boston Church Scene of Break-in." *Boston Globe* (January 6): 13.

———. 1987b. "Foe of Latin Policy Reports Rape in LA." *Boston Globe* (July 12): 18.

———. 1987c. "LA Activists Report Receiving Death Threats." *Boston Globe* (July 14): 7.

———. 1987d. "Tentacles of Salvador Death Squads Feared Stretching to United States." *Boston Globe* (November 7): 38.

———. 1987e. "A Political Threat Entwines Break-ins." *Boston Globe* (December 7): A23.

———. 1988a. "Groups Give FBI Data on Foes of U.S. Latin Policies." *Boston Globe* (March 15): 1.

———. 1988b. "Documents: Moon Group Aided FBI." *Boston Globe* (April 20): 1.

———. 1988c. "More Probes Found on Latin Policy Foes." *Boston Globe* (June 18): 1.

———. 1989. "Covert U.S.-Salvador Action against Activists Feared." *Boston Globe* (December 15): 1.

———. 1991. *Break-Ins, Death Threats, and the FBI: The Covert War against the Central America Movement.* Boston: South End Press.

Gendler, Everett. 1978. "War in the Jewish Tradition." In Menahem Kellner (ed.), *Contemporary Jewish Ethics.* New York: Sanhedrin Press.

Giniger, Henry. 1981. "Reagan Arrives in Canada to Heckling and Applause." *New York Times* (March 11): 10.

Ginsberg, Benjamin, and Martin Shefter. 1990. *Politics by Other Means: The Declining Importance of Elections in America.* New York: Basic Books.

Gitlin, Todd. 1980. *The Whole World Is Watching: Mass Media and the Making and Unmaking of the New Left.* Berkeley: University of California Press.

Glick, Brian. 1989. *War at Home: Covert Action against U.S. Activists and What We Can Do About It.* Boston: South End Press.

Gold, Eva. 1987. "Military Encirclement." In Thomas Walker (ed.), *Reagan Versus the Sandinistas: The Undeclared War on Nicaragua.* Boulder, Colo.: Westview Press.

Golden, Renny, and Michael McConnell. 1986. *Sanctuary: The New Underground Railroad.* Maryknoll, N.Y.: Orbis Books.

Goldman, Ari L. 1984. "Sheltering of Salvadorans Is Debated." *New York Times* (June 4): II, 3.

Goodfellow, William. 1987. "The Diplomatic Front." In Thomas Walker (ed.), *Reagan Versus the Sandinistas: The Undeclared War on Nicaragua.* Boulder, Colo.: Westview Press.

Gordon, Diana. 1987. "Varelli: In from the Cold." *The Nation* 244 (March 7).

———. 1989. "Can Sessions Tame the Bureau?" *The Nation* 249 (October 30).

Gorman, Stephen, and Thomas Walker. 1985. "The Armed Forces." In Thomas Walker (ed.), *Nicaragua: The First Five Years.* New York: Praeger Publishers.

Gorostiaga, Xabier, and Peter Marchetti. 1988. "The Central American Economy: Conflict and Crisis." In Nora Hamilton et al. (eds.), *Crisis in Central America: Regional Dynamics and U.S. Policy in the 1980s.* Boulder, Colo.: Westview Press.

Gouldner, Alvin. 1978. "The New Class Project I." *Theory and Society* 6: 153–204.

Graham, Douglas. 1984. "The Economic Dimensions of Instability and Decline in Central America and the Caribbean." In Donald Schulz and Douglas Graham (eds.), *Revolution and Counterrevolution in Central America and the Caribbean.* Boulder, Colo.: Westview Press.

Granovetter, Mark. 1973. "The Strength of Weak Ties." *American Journal of Sociology* 78.

Greenberg, Moshe. 1970. "Rabbinic Reflections on Defying Illegal Orders: Amasa, Abner, and Joab." *Judaism* 19.

Greenberg, Simon. 1977. *The Ethical in the Jewish and American Heritage.* New York: The Jewish Theological Seminary of America.

Greider, William. 1985. "Reagan's Moles." *Rolling Stone* (May 23): 51–52.

Gremillion, Joseph. 1976. *The Gospel of Peace and Justice: Catholic Social Teaching Since Pope John.* Maryknoll, N.Y.: Orbis Books.

Griffin-Nolan, Ed. 1991. *Witness for Peace: A Story of Resistance.* Louisville, Ky.: Westminster/John Knox Press.

Griffith, Thomas. 1983. "Going Too Easy on Reagan?" *Time* 122 (July 11).

———. 1984a. "Coming to Grips with Reagan." *Time* 123 (March 26).

———. 1984b. "Proving Lincoln Was Right: Reagan 'News Management.'" *Time* 123 (October 22).

———. 1986. "Being Too Easy on Reagan." *Time* 128 (November 17).

Grindle, Merilee. 1986. *State and Countryside: Development Policy and Agrarian Politics in Latin America.* Baltimore: John Hopkins University Press.

Grunwald, Henry. 1983. "Trying to Censor Reality." *Time* 122 (November 7).

Gruson, Lindsey. 1983. "Poll Reveals Fear of El Salvador as a New Vietnam." *New York Times* (July 24): 15.

Guise, Jane. 1990. Interview, August 9. Cambridge, Massachusetts.

Gutman, Roy. 1988. *Banana Diplomacy: The Making of American Policy in Nicaragua, 1981–1987*. New York: Simon and Schuster.

Gwertzman, Bernard. 1984. "Haig Cites Advice to Press Havana: In Memoirs, Says He Sought Early Salvador Solution to Avoid a 'Vietnam.'" *New York Times* (March 25): 11.

———. 1985. "Shultz in Warning on Combat Troops for Latin Region: Fears 'Agonizing Choice', He Says Failure to Aid Rebels in Nicaragua Adds to Risk of U.S. Military Role." *New York Times* (May 24): 1.

Haig, Alexander. 1984. *Caveat: Realism, Reagan, and Foreign Policy*. New York: MacMillan Publishing Company.

Hallin, Daniel. 1987. "Hegemony: The American News Media from Vietnam to El Salvador, a Study of Ideological Chang and Its Limits." in David Paletz (ed.), *Political Communication Research*. Norwood, N.J.: Ablex Publishing.

Halloran, James, Philip Elliot, and Graham Murdock. 1970. *Demonstrations and Communication: A Case Study*. Baltimore: Penguin Books.

Hamburger, Tom. 1982. "How the White House Cons the Press." *Washington Monthly* 13 (January).

Hamilton, Nora, Jeffry Frieden, Linda Fuller, and Manuel Pastor Jr. (eds.). 1988. *Crisis in Central America: Regional Dynamics and U.S. Policy in the 1980s*. Boulder, Colo.: Westview Press.

Hannon, James. 1991. *Identity and Participation in a Social Movement Organization: The Boston-Area Pledge of Resistance*. Ph.D. dissertation. University of Wisconsin, Madison.

Hatfield, Mark, Jim Leach, and George Miller. 1987. *Bankrolling Failure: United States Policy in El Salvador and the Urgent Need for Reforms*. Washington, D.C.: U.S. Congress, Arms Control and Foreign Policy Caucus.

Henderson, Phillip. 1988. *Managing the Presidency: The Eisenhower Legacy—From Kennedy to Reagan*. Boulder, Colo.: Westview Press.

Henriot, Peter, Edward DeBerri, and Michael Schultheis. 1988. *Catholic Social Teaching: Our Best Kept Secret*. Maryknoll, N.Y.: Orbis Books.

Herring, George. 1991. "Vietnam, Central America, and the Uses of History." In Kenneth Coleman and George Herring (eds.), *The Central American Crisis: Sources of Conflict and the Failure of U.S. Policy*. Wilmington, Del.: Scholarly Resources.

Hertsgaard, Mark. 1989. *On Bended Knee: The Press and the Reagan Presidency*. New York: Schocken Books.

Hertzke, Allen. 1988. *Representing God in Washington*. Knoxville: University of Tennessee Press.

Hildreth, Anne Marie. 1989. *Collective Action, Individual Incentives, and Political Identity: The Sanctuary Movement*. Ph.D. dissertation. Political Science, University of Iowa.

Hirsch, Richard. 1970. "Social Values in Judaism and Their Realization in the Reform Movement." *Journal of the Central Conference of American Rabbis* 18.

———. 1971. "Toward a Theology for Social Action." In Daniel Silver (ed.), *Judaism and Ethics*. New York: Ktav Publishing House.

Hirshson, Paul. 1988. "Central America Relief Agency Ransacked." *Boston Globe* (May 4): 30.

Hitchens, Christopher. 1988. "Minority Report." *The Nation* (March 5).

Hoeffel, Paul Heath. 1984. "Autumn of the Oligarchs." In Donald Schulz and Douglas Graham (eds.), *Revolution and Counterrevolution in Central America and the Caribbean*. Boulder, Colo.: Westview Press.

Hollyday, Joyce. 1983. "The Witness for Peace in Nicaragua." *Sojourners* 12(10) (November).

Hollyday, Joyce (ed.). 1984. *Crucible of Hope: A Study Guide for the Churches of Central America*. Washington, D.C.: Sojourners.

Honey, Martha, and Tony Avirgan. 1987. "Peace Efforts Cost Costa Rica Dearly." *San Francisco Bay Guardian* (August 26).

Hooglund, Eric. 1992. "The Persian Gulf." In Peter Schraeder (ed.), *Intervention into the 1990s: U.S. Foreign Policy in the Third World*. Boulder, Colo.: Lynne Rienner Publishers.

Hope, Sam. 1992. Interview, July 28. Washington, D.C.

Howell, Leon. 1982. *Acting in Faith: The World Council of Churches since 1975*. Geneva, Switzerland: World Council of Churches.

Hudson, Rex. 1990. "National Security." In Richard Haggerty (ed.), *El Salvador: A Country Study*. Washington, D.C.: U.S. Government Printing Office.

Huizer, Gerrit. 1972. *The Revolutionary Potential of Peasants in Latin America*. Lexington, Mass.: Lexington Books.

Hunt, Richard, and Richard Schultz. 1982. *Lessons from Unconventional War: Reassessing U.S. Strategies for Future Conflicts*. New York: Pergamon Press.

Idelson, Holly. 1993. "Bush Leaves Partisan Mark with Surprising Pardons." *Congressional Quarterly Weekly Report* 51(1) (January 2).

Ignatius, David. 1986. "The Contrapreneurs Skirting Congress and the Law for Years." *Washington Post* (December 7).

Iklé, Fred. 1983. "Toward Victory." In Robert Leiken and Barry Rubin (eds.), *The Central America Crisis Reader*. New York: Summit Books.

Inglehart, Ronald. 1990. *Cultural Shift in Advanced Industrial Society*. Princeton, N.J.: Princeton University Press.

International Finance. 1982. *International Finance 1982: Annual Report of the Chairman of the National Advisory Council on International Monetary and Financial Policies to the President and to the Congress for Fiscal Year 1982*. Washington, D.C.: U.S. Department of Treasury.

Iosso, Christian. 1993. "Changes in Ecumenical Public Witness, 1967–1990." In Dieter Hellel (ed.), *The Church's Public Role*. Grand Rapids, Mich.: Wm. B. Eerdmans.

Isaacson, Walter. 1982. "Calling Plays for the Gipper." *Time* 120 (August 23).

Israel, Richard. 1970. "Jewish Tradition and Political Action." In Alfred Jospe (ed.), *Tradition and Contemporary Experience: Essays on Jewish Thought and Life*. New York: Schocken Books.

Jacoby, Tamar, and Robert Parry. 1987. "Casey's Domestic Covert Op: a Propaganda Operation Right Here at Home." *Newsweek* (October 12): 36.

Jenkins, C. Craig, and Kurt Schock. 1992. "Global Structures and Political Processes in the Study of Domestic Political Conflict." *American Sociological Review* 18 (Annual).

Jonas, Susanne. 1991. *The Battle for Guatemala: Rebels, Death Squads, and U.S. Power.* Boulder, Colo.: Westview Press.

Joppke, Christian. 1991. "Social Movements during Cycles of Issue Attention." *British Journal of Sociology* 42:1 (March).

Judis, John. 1987a. "The CIA and the Legacy of William Casey." *Commonweal* (December 18): 752–56.

———. 1987b. "We Love Contras, We Love Them Not." *In These Times* (September 30–October 6): 2.

Junkin, Dixon. 1991. Interview, January 7. Pasadena, Calif.

Kaiser, Robert. 1982. "El Salvador: A Rerun of Vietnam Movie?" *Louisville Courier-Journal* (March 14).

Kamm, Henry. 1982. "Pope Denounces 'Fratricidal War' in El Salvador." *New York Times* (March 1): 5.

Karl, Terry. 1988. "Exporting Democracy: The Unanticipated Effects of U.S. Electoral Policy in El Salvador." In Nora Hamilton, Jeffry Frieden, Linda Fuller, and Manuel Pastor Jr. (eds.), *Crisis in Central America: Regional Dynamics and U.S. Policy in the 1980s.* Boulder, Colo.: Westview Press.

Karnes, Thomas. 1984. "The United States and the Caribbean Basin in Historical Perspective." In Donald Schulz and Douglas Graham (eds.), *Revolution and Counterrevolution in Central America and the Caribbean.* Boulder, Colo.: Westview Press.

Keller, Bill. 1982. "Interest Groups Focus on El Salvador Policy." *Congressional Quarterly Weekly Report* 40(17) (April 24): 895–900.

Kenworthy, Eldon. 1985. "United States Policy in Latin America: A Choice Denied." *Current History* 84(500) (March).

———. 1987. "United States Policy in Central America." *Current History* 86(524) (December).

———. 1988. "Where Pennsylvania Avenue Meets Madison Avenue: The Selling of Foreign Policy." *World Policy Journal* 5(1) (Winter): 107–27.

———. 1991. "The Permanent Campaign's Impact on the U.S. Central American Policy." In Kenneth Coleman and George Herring (eds.), *The Central American Crisis: Sources of Conflict and the Failure of U.S. Policy.* Wilmington, Del.: Scholarly Resources.

Kimmelman, Reuven. 1968. "Non-Violence in the Talmud." *Judaism* 17.

———. 1970. "Rabbinic Ethics of Protest." *Judaism* 19.

King, Wayne. 1985. "9 Plead Not Guilty in Tucson to Smuggling Illegal Aliens." *New York Times* (January 24): 10.

Kinzer, Stephen. 1985a. "29 U.S. Activists Reportedly Freed in Nicaragua." *New York Times* (August 9): 8.

———. 1985b. "Reporters Say Pastora Rebels Held 29 in Nicaragua." *New York Times* (August 11): 8.

———. 1987a. "Nicaragua Says Contras Killed American Civilian." *New York Times* (April 29): 3.

————. 1987b. "American Died in Rebel Ambush, Nicaragua Says." *New York Times* (April 30): 12.

————. 1987c. "Contras Accused of Killing 84 in Raids." *New York Times* (September 24): 3.

Kirschenbaum, Aaron. 1974. "A Cog in the Wheel: The Defense of Obedience to Superior Orders in Jewish Law." In *Israel Yearbook on Human Rights* 4.

Kitson, Frank. 1971. *Low Intensity Operations: Subversion, Insurgency, Peace-Keeping*. Harrisburg, England: Stackpole Books.

Klandermans, Bert, Hanspeter Kriesi, and Sidney Tarrow (eds.). 1988. *From Structure to Action: International Social Movement Research*. Greenwich, Conn.: JAI Press, Inc.

Klandermans, Bert, and Sidney Tarrow, 1988. "Mobilization into Social Movements: Synthesizing European and American Perspectives." In Klandermans, Bert, Hanspeter Kriesi, and Sidney Tarrow (eds.), *International Social Movement Reasearch*. Greenwich, Conn.: JAI Press, Inc.

Klare, Michael. 1992. "The Development of Low-Intensity-Conflict Doctrine." In Peter Schraeder (ed.), *Intervention into the 1990s: U.S. Foreign Policy in the Third World*. Boulder, Colo.: Lynne Rienner Publishers.

Kohn, Alfie. 1986. "Political Burglaries: The Return of Cointelpro?" *The Nation* (January 25): 74–76.

Konvitz, Milton. 1978. "Conscience and Civil Disobedience in the Jewish Tradition." In Menachem Kellner (ed.), *Contemporary Jewish Ethics*. New York: Sanhedrin Press.

Kornbluh, Peter. 1987a. *Nicaragua: The Price of Intervention*. Washington, D.C.: Institute for Policy Studies.

————. 1987b. "The Covert War." In Thomas Walker (ed.), *Reagan Versus the Sandinistas: The Undeclared War on Nicaragua*. Boulder, Colo.: Westview Press.

————. 1988. "The War at Home." *Southern Exposure* (Winter).

————. 1992. "Nicaragua." In Peter Schraeder (ed.), *Intervention into the 1990s: U.S. Foreign Policy in the Third World*. Boulder, Colo.: Lynne Rienner Publishers.

Kornbluh, Peter, and Malcolm Byrne. 1993. *The Iran Contra Scandal: The Declassified History*. A National Security Archives Document Reader. New York: The New Press.

Kresse, Kevin. 1992. Interview, August 3. Durham, North Carolina.

Kupperman, Robert, and William Taylor (eds.). 1983. *Strategic Requirements for the Army to the Year 2000*. Cambridge, Mass.: Center for Strategic Studies.

Kurkjian, Stephen. 1987. "FBI Agent Says He Lost Job over Latin Views." *Boston Globe* (September 21): 3.

Lacayo, Ricard. 1988. "Bad Habits Die Hard: The FBI Is Accused of Political Snooping and Racial Harassment." *Time* (February 8): 33–34.

LaFeber, Walter. 1984. *Inevitable Revolutions: The United States in Central America*. New York: W. W. Norton.

———. 1991. "Introduction: The Reagan Policy in Historical Perspective." In Kenneth Coleman and George Herring (eds.), *The Central American Crisis: Sources of Conflict and the Failure of U.S. Policy.* Wilmington, Del.: Scholarly Resources.

Lake, Anthony (ed.). 1976. *The Vietnam Legacy.* New York: New York University Press.

Lamperti, John. 1988. *What Are We Afraid Of? An Assessment of the "Communist Threat" in Central America.* Boston: South End Press.

Landman, Leo. 1969. "Civil Disobedience: The Jewish View." *Tradition* 10.

Leahy, Margaret. 1987. "The Harassment of Nicaraguanists and Fellow-Travellers." In Thomas Walker (ed.), *Reagan Versus the Sandinistas: The Undeclared War on Nicaragua.* Boulder, Colo.: Westview Press.

Ledbetter, James. 1985. "I Was a Spy for Accuracy in Academia: Campus Double Agent." *New Republic* (December 30): 14–16.

Lehrich, Tamar. 1987. "Nicaragua Visited to Learn and Help." *New York Times* (January 25): XXIII, 10.

Leiken, Stephen (ed.). 1984a. *Central America: Anatomy of Conflict.* New York: Pergamon Press.

Leiken, Robert. 1984b. "Soviet and Cuban Policy in the Caribbean Basin." In Donald Schulz and Douglas Graham (eds.), *Revolution and Counterrevolution in Central America and the Caribbean.* Boulder, Colo.: Westview Press.

LeMoyne, James. 1984a. "Salvadorans Begin Fast at Church in Manhattan." *New York Times* (January 7): 26.

———. 1984b. "Split Feared in Salvador on Church's Social Role." *New York Times* (September 8): 3.

———. 1987. "Salvadorans Stream into U.S. Fleeing Poverty and Civil War." *New York Times* (April 13): 1.

Leogrande, William M. 1986. "Rollback or Containment?: The United States, Nicaragua, and the Search for Peace in Central America." *International Security* 11(2) (Fall): 89–120.

———. 1987. "The Contras and Congress." In Thomas Walker (ed.), *Reagan Versus the Sandinistas: The Undeclared War on Nicaragua.* Boulder, Colo.: Westview Press.

———. 1991. "After the Battle of El Salvador." In Kenneth Coleman and George Herring (eds.), *The Central American Crisis: Sources of Conflict and the Failure of U.S. Policy.* Wilmington, Del.: Scholarly Resources.

Levin, Carl. 1993. "Yes: Above the Law." *ABA Journal* 79 (March).

Lewis, Anthony. 1983. "Why Are We in Vietnam?" *New York Times* (March 6): IV, 19.

———. 1985. "What Country Is It?: A Miami Incident with Soviet Echoes." *New York Times* (February 28): A23.

———. 1986a. "A Fear and Intimidation Campaign." *Patriot Ledger* (February 25): 20.

———. 1986b. "Policing Our Thoughts: When Ideas Get Detained at the Border." *New York Times* (April 28): A28.

————. 1986c. "Harassment at Customs." *San Francisco Chronicle* (September 17): 55.

Lewis, Flora. 1982. "Vietnam and Salvador—A Battle for Hearts and Minds." *New York Times* (February 21): 4.

Lipman, Eugene. 1970. "The Mission of Israel and Social Action." In Daniel Silver (ed.), *Judaism and Ethics*. New York: Ktav Publishing House.

Little, Sara. 1989. "The Place of Education in the Sanctuary Event at the Church of the Covenant." In Nelle G. Slater (ed.), *Tension between Citizenship and Discipleship: A Case Study*. New York: Pilgrim Press.

Livezey, Lowell. 1989. "U.S. Religious Organizations and the International Human Rights Movement." *Human Rights Quarterly* 11(1) (February).

Lowenthal, Abraham. 1985. "The United States and Central America: Reflections on the Kissinger Commission." In Kenneth Coleman and George Herring (eds.), *The Central American Crisis: Sources of Conflict and the Failure of U.S. Policy*. Wilmington, Del.: Scholarly Resources.

Lorentzen, Robin. 1991. *Women in the Sanctuary Movement*. Philadelphia: Temple University Press.

Luker, Kristin. 1984. *Abortion and the Politics of Motherhood*. Berkeley: University of California Press.

MacEoin, Gary (ed.). 1985. *Sanctuary: A Resource Guide for Understanding and Participating in the Central American Refugees' Struggle*. San Francisco: Harper and Row, Publishers.

Malinowski, Jack. 1983. "Prerequisite to Central American Democracy." *New York Times* (May 12): 22.

Manoff, Robert Karl. 1986. "State-Sponsored Journalism." *The Progressive* 50 (June).

Mansbridge, Jane (ed.). 1990. *Beyond Self-Interest*. Chicago: University of Chicago Press.

Manz, Beatriz. 1988. *Refugees of a Hidden War: The Aftermath of Counterinsurgency in Guatemala*. New York: State University of New York Press.

Marker, Dennis. 1992. Interview, November 17, 20. Santa Fe, New Mexico.

Marshall, Eliot. 1985. "New Group Targets Political Bias on Campus." *Science* 229 (August 30): 841–42.

Martin, Douglas. 1985. "Salvadorans Find a Haven in Canada." *New York Times* (July 4): 2.

Marx, Karl. 1978. "The Eighteenth Brumaire of Louis Bonaparte." In Robert Tucker (ed.), *The Marx-Engels Reader* (2nd ed.). New York: W. W. Norton.

Marx, Gary. 1988. "External Efforts to Damage or Facilitate Social Movements." In Mayer Zald and John McCarthy (eds.), *The Dynamics of Social Movements*. Lanham, Md.: University Press of America.

Matthews, Christopher. 1984. "Your Host, Ronald Reagan: From the G.E. Theater to the Desk of the Oval Office." *New Republic* 190 (March 26).

McAdam, Doug. 1982. *Political Process and the Development of Black Insurgency, 1930–1970*. Chicago: The University of Chicago Press.

———. 1983. "Tactical Innovation and the Pace of Insurgency." *American Sociologial Review* 48 (December): 735–54.

———. 1986. "Differential Recruitment to High Risk Activism: The Case of Freedom Summer." *American Journal of Sociology* 92(1) (July): 64–90.

———. 1988. *Freedom Summer.* Oxford: Oxford University Press.

McAdam, Doug and Ronnelle Paulsen. 1993. "Social Ties and Activism: Toward a Specification of the Relationship." *American Sociologial Review.* 99:3 (November).

McAdam, Doug, John McCarthy and Mayer Zald. 1988. "Social Movements." in Neil Smelser (ed.), *Handbook of Sociology.* Newbury Park: Sage.

McCartney, James. 1986. regular collumn, *Lexington Herald-Leader* (March 22).

McCreery, David. 1976. "Coffee and Class: The Structure of Development in Liberal Guatemala." *Hispanic American Historical Review.* 56(3): 438–460.

McDonald, Ronald. 1985. "El Salvador: The Politics of Revolution." in Howard Wiarda and Harvey Kline (eds.), *Latin American Politics and Development.* Boulder, CO: Westview Press.

McManus, Philip and Gerald Schlabach (eds.). 1991. *Relentless Persistence: Nonviolent Action in Latin America.* Philadelphia: New Society Publishers.

Meyer, David. 1990. *A Winter of Discontent: The Nuclear Freeze and American Politics.* New York: Praeger Publishers.

Meyer, David and Nancy Whittier. 1994. "Social Movement Spillover." *Social Problems.* 41:2 (May).

Meyer, Thomas. 1985. "Media Critic Forms New Organization to Monitor Disinformation in Class." *Chronicle of Higher Education* (July 3).

Miles, Sara. 1986. "The Real War: Low Intensity Conflict in Central America." *NACLA Report on the Americas.* 20(2) (April/May).

Millbrath, Lester and M. L. Goel. 1977. *Political Participation: How and Why Do People Get Involved in Politics?.* Chicago: Rand McNally Publishing.

Miller, George. 1989. *Congressional Record* (House) (October 4).

Miller, Judith. 1981. "Congress Mail Heavy On El Salvador Issue: Legislators Receiving Hundreds of Dollars a Week Opposing U.S. Dispatch of Military Help." *New York Times* (March 26): 7.

Millett, Richard. 1990. "Nicaragua: A Glimmer of Hope." *Current History* 89:543 (January).

———. 1988. "The United States and Central America." *Current History* 87(533), (December).

Millman, Joel. 1984a. "Reagan's Reporters: How the Press Distorts the News from Central America." *The Progressive* 48 (October).

———. 1984b. "Harassing the Peace Movement." *Mother Jones* 9(10), (December).

Mills, Mike. 1988a. "FBI Tells Congress CISPES Probe Was Justified." *Congressional Quarterly Weekly Report* 46(9) (Feb 27): 520.

———. 1988b. "FBI Chief Laments 'Mistakes' in CISPES Probe." *Congressional Quarterly Weekly Report* 46(38) (September 17): 2575.

Mitchell, Peter. 1985. "Salvadorans Living in Church Hold to Hope." *New York Times* (March 10): II, 1.

Moberg, David. 1987. "The Grassroots Push to End Contra Aid." *In These Times* (September 2–8): 2.

Molander, Earl, and Roger Molander. 1990. "A Threshold Analysis of the Antinuclear War Movement." In Sam Marullo and John Lofland (eds.), *Peace Action in the Eighties*. New Brunswick, N.J.: Rutgers University Press.

Molotch, Harvey, and Marilyn Lester. 1974. "News as Purposive Behavior." *American Sociological Review* 39 (February): 101–12.

Montgomery, Tommie Sue. 1983. "Liberation and Revolution: Christianity as a Subversive Activity in Central America." In Martin Diskin (ed.), *Trouble in Our Backyard: Central America and the United States in the Eighties*. New York: Pantheon Books.

Moore, Barrington. 1978. *Injustice: The Social Bases of Obedience and Revolt*. White Plains, N.Y.: M.E. Sharpe.

Morelli, Donald, and Michael Ferguson. 1984. "Low-Intensity Conflict: An Operational Perspective?" *Military Review* (November).

Morganthau, Tom, and Eleanor Clift. 1984. "Master of the Media." *Newsweek* 103 (June 18).

Morley, Sylvanus, and George Brainard. 1983. *The Ancient Maya* (4th ed.), Stanford, Calif.: Stanford University Press.

Morris, Aldon. 1984. *The Origins of the Civil Rights Movement*. New York: Free Press.

Morris, Aldon, and Carol Mueller (eds.). 1992. *Frontiers in Social Movement Theory*. New Haven, Conn.: Yale University Press.

MSN. 1989. *Movement Support Network Harassment Update*. New York: Movement Support Network.

Nangle, Joe. 1992. Interview, July 27. Washington, D.C.

Narvaez, Alfonzo. 1984. "Jersey Church Is Salvadoran Haven." *New York Times* (September 20): II, 6.

Nation, The. 1987. "Has the F.B.I. Really Changed?" *The Nation* (October 17): 399–400.

Neier, Aryeh. 1982. "'Empty Arguments' over El Salvador." *New York Times* (August 8): IV, 18.

Nelson-Pallmeyer, Jack. 1989. *War against the Poor: Low-Intensity Conflict and Christian Faith*. Maryknoll, N.Y.: Orbis Books.

New York Times. 1981a. "40 Americans Invade U.S. Embassy in Managua." January 17: 6.

———. 1981b. "Demonstrators protesting . . ." February 1: 4.

———. 1981c. "Let the People of El Salvador Decide!" February 3: 7.

———. 1981d. "Senate Leader Predicts Backing for Increase in Military Aid to El Salvador." March 4: 4.

———. 1981e. "Swedes Protest over Salvador." March 6: 4.

———. 1981f. "In Memoriam: Oscar A. Romero, Archbishop of San Salvador." March 22: IV, 6.

New York Times. 1981g. "The top elected officers . . ." March 27: 5.

―――. 1981h. "Reagan Mail Opposes Involvement." March 29: 17.

―――. 1981i. "Top Salvadorian Prelate Opposes U.S. Arms Aid." April 5: 9.

―――. 1981j. "U.S. Church Leaders Urge Halt to Salvador Arms Aid." April 18: 4.

―――. 1981k. "A group of Episcopalian bishops . . ." April 21: 5.

―――. 1981l. "Tucson Protest Group Links Bible to El Salvador." April 27: 13.

―――. 1981m. "Haig Asserts Soviet Wanes Spiritually, But Rises as Threat: Syracuse Speech Disrupted." May 10: 1.

―――. 1981n. "80 Arrested in Protest at White House." July 4: 7.

―――. 1981o. "5,000 Protest in Ottawa." July 20: 16.

―――. 1981p. "Belgians Seize an Embassy." October 8: I, 17.

―――. 1981q. "About 15,000 people marched . . ." November 29: 4.

―――. 1982a. "Salvadoran Troops Start Infantry Training in U.S." January 12: 4.

―――. 1982b. "Rally at Fort Benning Deplores the Training of Salvadoran Troops." January 25: 4.

―――. 1982c. "Reagan Is Challenged by Maryknoll Leaders." February 4: 11.

―――. 1982d. "More Salvador Aid Opposed." February 18: 4.

―――. 1982e. "Salvador Policy Protest Is Staged in New York." February 21: 21.

―――. 1982f. "Dutch Leftists Protest." March 20: 6.

―――. 1982g. "Dutch Stage a Protest at American Embassy." March 21: 22.

―――. 1982h. "To End the Killing in El Salvador—Give Peace—and Democracy—a Chance." March 21: IV, 22.

―――. 1982i. "Germans Protest U.S. Policy." March 25: 6.

―――. 1982j. "Protests Seen in Amsterdam." March 27: 6.

―――. 1982k. "West Berlin Protest Dispersed." March 28: 18.

―――. 1982l. "West Germans Stone Consulate." March 28: 18.

―――. 1982m. "Swiss Protest over Salvador." April 4: 14.

―――. 1982n. "Pro-American Rally in Amsterdam." May 6: 3.

―――. 1982o. "400 Rebels Reported Killed in El Salvador." July 8: 5.

―――. 1983a. "Dozens Arrested in Protest." January 25: 12.

―――. 1983b. "The Salvadoran Cross." March 3: 26.

―――. 1983c. "Salvador Furor Comes to a Town in Vermont." March 20: 1.

―――. 1983d. "The *New York Times*/CBS News Poll: Attitudes on U.S. Foreign Policy." April 15: 13.

―――. 1983e. "Death of German Prompts Protests: Marchers Say Anti-Sandinists Who Killed a Doctor Were Backed by Washington." May 4: 9.

―――. 1984a. "Pledge by Church Leaders." January 10: 13.

―――. 1984b. "U.S. Volunteers Help Nicaragua with the Harvest." February 16: 4.

―――. 1984c. "Reporter Is Arrested with Five in Texas in Aiding of Aliens." February 19: 39.

―――. 1984d. "Connecticut Journal." March 4: 3.

―――. 1984e. "Salvador Military Is Accused of Bombing Displaced People." April 11: 10.

New York Times. 1984f. "Refugee Center Operator Is Arrested in Texas." April 14: 8.

————. 1984g. "Social Worker Defends Actions on 2 Aliens." May 8: 19.

————. 1984h. "Church Members Back Sanctuary for Refugees." June 11: II, 2.

————. 1984i. "Bishop Assails Arrests of Sanctuary Activists." December 10: II, 13.

————. 1985a. "Shultz's Visitor Rebuffed." January 24: 22.

————. 1985b. "Clerics Denounce Curbs on Aiding Latin Aliens." March 1: I, 10.

————. 1985c. "Spaniards in Protest against Reagan's Visit." March 6: 13.

————. 1985d. "300 Seized in San Francisco in Nicaragua Protest." May 9: 6.

————. 1985e. "7 Protesters Arrested." May 11: 60.

————. 1985f. "40 Held in New York Protest as Duarte Receives Reward." May 21: 12.

————. 1985g. "San Francisco Harbor 'Mined' by Protesters." May 31: 17.

————. 1985h. "Anti-U.S. Protest in Berlin." July 20: 4.

————. 1985i. "Court Rules Agents Violated News Photographer's Rights." July 30: 20.

————. 1985j. "Nicaraguan Rebels Are Said to Abduct 29 U.S. Activists." August 8: 8.

————. 1985k. "Freed U.S. Activists in Nicaragua Town." August 10: 3.

————. 1985l. "Clergymen Assert Abduction in Nicaragua Wasn't Staged." August 15: 3.

————. 1986a. "Religious Figures Protest Contra Aid." March 5: 4.

————. 1986b. "To Catch Reagan's Eye." April 14: 14.

————. 1986c. "U.S. Bars an Oxfam Shipment of Farm Tools to Nicaragua." September 4: 25.

————. 1986d. "War Medals Returned to Protest U.S. Policy." October 10: 22.

————. 1987a. "Corrections." May 5: 3.

————. 1987b. "Arms Protester Injured by a Munitions Train." September 2: 10.

————. 1987c. "R.O.T.C. Building Is Stormed over Maiming of a Protester." September 4: IV, 15.

————. 1987d. "Maimed Protester, 46, Vows He Will Continue." September 12: 7.

————. 1987e. "Injured Protester Returns to Lead Rally." September 30: 18.

————. 1988a. "A.F.L.-C.I.O. Urges Aid Cut." January 8: 3.

————. 1988b. "Rebellion by Mayors." January 21: 7.

————. 1988c. "Meese to Make F.B.I. Inquiry." January 29: 36.

————. 1988d. "American Volunteer Is Seized by the Nicaraguan Guerrillas." March 5: 3.

————. 1988e. "Reagan Action in Honduras Stirs Demonstrations in U.S." March 19: 5.

————. 1988f. "Police Seize Eight in Convoy Carrying Aid to Nicaraguans." July 10: 20.

————. 1988g. "Convoy Member Is Arrested." July 12: 14.

————. 1988h. "Supply Convoy to Nicaragua Crosses Border." July 16: 6.

New York Times. 1988i. "200 Arrested near Pentagon in Protest of Salvador Policy." October 18: 8.

———. 1988j. "Suit Seeks to Force F.B.I. to Seal Data in Terrorism Inquiry." November 30: 21.

———. 1989a. "1,200 Hold Rally in New York against U.S. Role in Salvador." March 19: 3.

Newsweek. 1981. "The White House Image Man." Vol. 97 (June 29).

Nyhan, David. 1986. "Waving the Flag on Nicaragua." *Boston Globe* (March 9): A25.

Oliner, Samuel, and Pearl Oliner. 1988. *The Altruistic Personality: Rescuers of the Jews in Nazi Europe.* New York: The Free Press.

Ovryn Rivera, Rachel. 1987. *A Question of Conscience: The Emergence and Development of the Sanctuary Movement in the United States.* Ph.D. dissertation. City University of New York.

PACCA. 1984. *Changing Course: Blueprint for Peace in Central America and the Caribbean.* Washington, D.C.: Institute for Policy Studies.

Paige, Jeffrey. 1975. *Agrarian Revolution.* New York: Free Press.

Parker, Franklin. 1964. *The Central American Republics.* London: Oxford University Press.

Parry, Robert. 1992. "The Advertising Agency: How the CIA Flouted the Law Using Madison Avenue Techniques to Arm-Twist for the Contras." *The Washington Monthly* 24(11) (November): 15–18.

Parry, Robert, and Peter Kornbluh. 1988. "Iran-Contra's Untold Story." *Foreign Policy* 72 (Fall): 3–30.

Pastor, Robert. 1982. "Our Real Interests in Central America." *The Atlantic Monthly* (July): 27–39.

———. 1987. *Condemned to Repetition: The United States and Nicaragua.* Princeton, N.J.: Princeton Press.

Persico, Joseph. 1990. *Casey: From the OSS to the CIA.* New York: Viking.

Percy, Walker. 1983. *Lost in the Cosmos.* New York: Farrar, Straus, and Giroux.

Perry, Mark. 1992. *Eclipse: The Last Days of the CIA.* New York: William Morrow.

Phares, Gail. 1992. Interview, July 31. Raleigh, North Carolina.

Phelps, Timothy. 1981. "U.S. Role in El Salvador Protested." *New York Times* (April 19): 26.

Piven, Frances Fox, and Richard Cloward. 1979. *Poor People's Movements: Why They Succeed, How They Fail.* New York: Vintage Books.

Pledge of Resistance. 1986a. *Pledge of Resistance Newsletter* (Summer). Washington, D.C.: The Pledge of Resistance.

———. 1986b. *Pledge of Resistance Newsletter* (Fall). Washington, D.C.: The Pledge of Resistance.

———. 1986c. *Stop the Lies* tabloid. Washington, D.C.: The Pledge of Resistance.

———. 1987a. *Pledge of Resistance Newsletter* (Winter). Washington, D.C.: The Pledge of Resistance.

———. 1987b. *Pledge of Resistance Newsletter* (Fall). Washington, D.C.: The Pledge of Resistance.

———. 1988a. *The Pledge of Resistance: The Local Military Connections Campaign* tabloid. Washington, D.C.: The Pledge of Resistance.

———. 1988b. *The Pledge of Resistance: Acting to Stop The New Vietnam—Before It's Too Late* tabloid. Washington, D.C.: The Pledge of Resistance.

———. 1988c. *The Pledge* tabloid newsletter 3(1) (Spring). Washington, D.C.: The Pledge of Resistance.

———. 1989a. *The Pledge* tabloid newsletter 4(1) (Winter). Washington, D.C.: The Pledge of Resistance.

———. 1989b. *The Pledge* tabloid newsletter 4(2) (Fall). Washington, D.C.: The Pledge of Resistance.

———. 1989c. *Five Years of Resistance—Now More Than Ever: The Pledge of Resistance* promotional brochure. Washington, D.C.: The Pledge of Resistance.

———. 1990. *The Pledge* tabloid newsletter 5(2) (Summer). Washington, D.C.: The Pledge of Resistance.

———. n.d. *The Pledge of Resistance for Peace in Central America* brochure. Washington, D.C.: The Pledge of Resistance.

Posner, Michael. 1981. "Playing the Presidency by Cue." *Maclean's* 94 (November 23).

Poulantzas, Nicos. 1973. *Political Power and Social Classes*. London: New Left Books.

Powell, S. Stephen. 1986. *Second Front: Advancing Latin American Revolution in Washington*. Washington, D.C.: Capital Research Center.

Prados, John. 1986. *Presidents' Secret Wars*. New York: William Morrow.

Pressman, Steven. 1985. "Massive Lobbying Campaign Waged over Aid for 'Contras.'" Congressional Quarterly Weekly Report (April 20): 715.

Progressive. 1988. "Licence to Spy." Vol. 52, no. 10 (October): 9–10.

Quebedeaux, Richard. 1974. *The Young Evangelicals: The Story of the Emergence of a New Generation of Evangelicals*. New York: Harper and Row.

Quigley, Thomas. 1990. Interview, November 28. Washington, D.C.

Radolf, Andrew. 1987. "Reagan Aide Defends Lack of Prime-Time Press Conferences." *Editor and Publisher* 120 (October 17).

Ranelagh, John. 1987. *The Agency: The Rise and Decline of the CIA*. New York: Simon and Schuster.

Reagan, Ronald. 1983. "Address to Joint Session of Congress." in Robert Leiken and Barry Rubin (eds.), *The Central America Crisis Reader*. New York: Summit Books.

Report. 1987. *Report of the Congressional Committees Investigating the Iran-Contra Affair*. Washington, D.C.: U.S. Government Printing Office.

Reuters. 1987. "North Drew Up Plans to Suspend U.S. Constitution, Report Says." Reuters North European Service. July 5.

Reuther, Rosemary Radford. 1986. "Foreword." In Renny Golden and Michael McConnell. *Sanctuary: The New Underground Railroad*. Maryknoll, N.Y.: Orbis Books.

Rice, Jim. 1992. Interview, July 27. Washington, D.C.

Riding, Alan. 1982. "Mexicans Pessimistic on Talks between U.S. and Caribbean Leftists." *The New York Times* (May 10).

Roark, Anne. 1986. "Reagan Hits Professor's Nicaragua Story." *Los Angeles Times* (March 12): Part 1, 18.

Robert Kupperman Associates. 1983. *Low Intensity Conflict.* U.S. Army Training and Doctrine Command.

Roberts, Kenneth. 1990. "Bullying and Bargaining: The United States, Nicaragua, and Conflict Resolution in Central America." *International Security* 15(2) (Fall).

Roberts, Steven. 1982a. "Rift on Salvador Grows in Congress." *New York Times* (February 4): 1.

———. 1982b. "A Majority in Poll Want U.S. to Stay out of Salvador War." *New York Times* (March 21): 1.

Robinson, John. 1986. "O'Neill Denounces $100m Aid Plan for Contras." *Boston Globe* (February 21): 3.

Robinson, William. 1992. *A Faustian Bargain: U.S. Intervention in the Nicaraguan Elections and American Foreign Policy in the Post-Cold War Era.* Boulder, Colo.: Westview Press.

Rogers, William, and Jeffrey Meyers. 1982. "The Reagan Administration and Latin America: An Uneasy Beginning." *Caribbean Review* 11 (Spring).

Roper, James. 1985a. "The Great Communicator?" *Editor and Publisher* 118 (March 9).

———. 1985b. "Protecting the President." *Editor and Publisher* 118 (May 18).

Rosenthal, Andrew. 1987. "Campaign Formed Opposing Contras: Political and Religious Groups Seek Funds to Fight Drive by Conservatives." *New York Times* (August 14): 8.

Ross, David. 1985. "The Caribbean Basin Initiative: Threat or Promise?" In Kenneth Coleman and George Herring (eds.), *The Central American Crisis: Sources of Conflict and the Failure of U.S. Policy.* Wilmington, Del.: Scholarly Resources Inc.

Roth, S. 1971. "The Morality of Revolution: A Jewish View." *Judaism* 20.

Rothman, Robert. 1984. "Senate Agrees to Cut El Salvador Funds." *Congressional Quarterly Weekly Report* 42(13) (March 31): 702.

Rubin, Barry. 1984. "Reagan Administration Policymaking and Central America." In Robert Leiken (ed.), *Central America: Anatomy of Conflict.* New York: Pergamon Press.

Rupp, Leila, and Verta Taylor. 1987. *Survival in the Doldrums: The American Women's Rights Movement, 1945 to the 1960s.* Oxford: Oxford University Press.

Ryan, Charlotte. 1991. *Prime Time Activism: Media Strategies for Grassroots Organizing.* Boston: South End Press.

Sanford, Jonathan. 1984. "U.S. Foreign Assistance to Central America." Report No. 84–34F. Washington, D.C.: Congressional Research Service.

Sarkesian, Sam. 1986. *The New Battlefield: America and Low-Intensity Conflicts.* Westport, Conn.: Greenwood Press.

Sarkesian, Sam, and William Scully. 1981. *U.S. Policy and Low-Intensity Conflict.* New Brunswick, N.J.: Transaction Books.

Schlesinger, Stephen, and Stephen Kinzer. 1983. *Bitter Fruit: The Untold Story of the American Coup in Guatemala*. New York: Doubleday.

Schneider, Keith. 1986. "Pattern Seen in Break-Ins at Latin Policy Group." *New York Times* (December 3): A13.

———. 1987. "A Liberal Group Makes Waves with Its Contra Lawsuit." *New York Times* (July 20): 16.

Schorr, Daniel. 1989. "Undoing the Reagan Doctrine." *The New Leader* 72(7) (April 3).

Schoultz, Lars. 1981. *Human Rights and United States Policy toward Latin America*. Princeton, N.J.: Princeton University Press.

———. 1983. "Guatemala: Social Change and Political Conflict." In Martin Diskin, *Trouble in Our Backyard: Central America and the United States in the Eighties*. New York: Pantheon Books.

———. 1987. *National Security and United States Policy toward Latin America*. Princeton, N.J.: Princeton University Press.

Schraeder, Peter. 1992. *Intervention into the 1990s: U.S. Foreign Policy in the Third World*. Boulder, Colo.: Lynne Rienner Publishers.

Schultz, Richard. 1984. "Low Intensity Conflict." In Heritage Foundation, *Mandate for Leadership II: Continuing the Conservative Revolution*. Washington, D.C.: Heritage Foundation.

Schulz, Donald. 1984. "El Salvador: Revolution and Counterrevolution in the Living Museum." In Donald Schulz and Douglas Graham (eds.), *Revolution and Counterrevolution in Central America and the Caribbean*. Boulder, Colo.: Westview Press.

Schulz, Donald, and Douglas Graham (eds.). 1984. *Revolution and Counterrevolution in Central America and the Caribbean*. Boulder, Colo.: Westview Press.

Schutz, Alfred. 1971. *Collected Papers: The Problem of Reality*. Vol. 1. The Hague: Martinus Nijhoff.

Schwartz, Michael. 1976. *Radical Protest and Social Structure*. New York: Academic Press.

Schwarzschild, Steven. 1966. "The Religious Demand for Peace." *Judaism* 15.

Serrin, William. 1985. "Labor Criticizes U.S. Role in Central America." *New York Times* (October 30): II, 6.

Shapiro, David. 1978. "The Doctrine of the Image of God and *Imitatio Dei*." In Menachem Kellner (ed.), *Contemporary Jewish Ethics*. New York: Sanhedrin Press.

Shapiro, Walter. 1984. "Stagecraft? Leave It to Deaver." *Newsweek* 103 (May 28).

Sharpe, Kenneth. 1988. "U.S. Policy toward Central America: The Post-Vietnam Formula under Siege." In Nora Hamilton et al. (eds.), *Crisis in Central America: Regional Dynamics and U.S. Policy in the 1980s*. Boulder, Colo.: Westview Press.

Shatz, David. 1978. "The Jewish Idea of Community." *Tradition* 17.

Shaull, Richard. 1984. "Christian Faith and the Crisis of Empire." *Monthly Review* (April).

Sheahan, John. 1987. *Patterns of Development in Latin America*. Princeton, N.J.: Princeton University Press.

Shenon, Philip. 1988a. "F.B.I. Faces Review over Surveillance of Foes of Policy: President Concerned, He Orders an Internal Inquiry into Watch Put on Critics of the Administration." *New York Times* (January 30): 1.

———. 1988b. "F.B.I. Word Due on Penalty in Surveillance of Policy Foes." *New York Times* (September 13): 22.

———. 1988c. "F.B.I. Chief Disciplines Six for Surveillance Activities." *New York Times* (September 15): 20.

———. 1988d. "F.B.I. Is Willing to Erase Names from Its Records: Chief Restricts Access to Data on Reagan Foes." *New York Times* (September 17): 5.

Sherman, William. 1979. *Forced Native Labor in Sixteenth Century Central America*. Lincoln, Nebr.: University of Nebraska Press.

Shipler, David. 1986. "Poll Shows Confusion on Aid to Contras." *New York Times* (April 15): 6.

Shipp, E. R. 1983. "3 in Hunger Strike over Salvadorans at U.S. Base." *New York Times* (August 16): 9.

Shorter, Edward, and Charles Tilly. 1974. *Strikes in France: 1830–1968*. London: Cambridge University Press.

Shultz, George. 1985. "The Meaning of Vietnam." U.S. State Department *Bulletin* 85 (June).

Shumway, Anne. 1990. Interview, December 17. Cambridge, Massachusetts.

Sider, Ronald (ed.). 1974. *The Chicago Declaration*. Carol Stream, Ill.: Creation House.

Siegman, Henry (ed.). 1966. *Judaism and World Peace: Focus Vietnam*. New York: Synagogue Council of America.

Simonson, S. 1968. "Violence from the Perspective of the Ethics of the Fathers." *Tradition* 10.

Singer, C. Gregg. 1975. *The Unholy Alliance*. New Rochelle, N.Y.: Arlington House Publishers.

Sivard, Ruth Leger. 1991. *World Military and Social Expenditures: 1991*. Washington, D.C.: World Priorities.

Skidmore, Thomas, and Peter Smith. 1984. *Modern Latin America*. Oxford: Oxford University Press.

Skillen, James. 1990. *The Scattered Voice: Christians at Odds in the Public Square*. Grand Rapids, Mich.: Zondervan.

Sklar, Holly. 1988. *Washington's War on Nicaragua*. Boston: South End Press.

Skocpol, Theda. 1979. *States and Social Revolutions*. Cambridge: Cambridge University Press.

Smith, Christian. 1991. *The Emergence of Liberation Theology: Radical Religion and Social Movement Theory*. Chicago: University of Chicago Press.

———. 1996. *Disruptive Religion: The Force of Faith in Social Movement Activism*. New York: Routledge.

Smith, Hedrick. 1982. "Struggle in Salvador Pinches Washington's 'Vietnam' Nerve." *New York Times* (February 7): IV, 1.

Smith, Wayne. 1984. "Reagan's Central America Policy: Disaster in the Making." In Donald Schulz and Douglas Graham (eds.), *Revolution and Coun-*

terrevolution in Central America and the Caribbean. Boulder, Colo.: Westview Press.

Snow, David, and Robert Benford. 1988. "Ideology, Frame Resonance, and Participant Mobilization." In Bert Klandermans, Hanspeter Kriesi, and Sidney Tarrow (eds.), *International Social Movement Reasearch.* Greenwich, Conn.: JAI Press, Inc.

Snow, David, E. Burke Rochford, Steven Worden, and Robert Benford. 1986. "Frame Alignment Processes, Micromobilization, and Movement Participation." *American Sociological Review* 51: 464–81.

Sobel, Richard. 1989. "The Polls—A Report: Public Opinion about United States Intervention in El Salvador and Nicaragua." *Public Opinion Quarterly* 53 (Spring): 114–28.

Spence, Jack. 1987. "The U.S. Media: Covering (over) Nicaragua." In Thomas Walker (ed.), *Reagan Versus the Sandinistas: The Undeclared War on Nicaragua.* Boulder, Colo.: Westview Press.

Spiegelman, Arthur. 1987. "Committee Rules out Testimony on Suspending Constitution," Reuters News Service story (July 13).

Spykman, Gordon, Guillermo Cook, Michael Dodson, Lance Grahn, Sidney Rooy, and John Stam. 1988. *Let My People Live: Faith and Struggle in Central America.* Grand Rapids, Mich.: Wm. B. Eerdmans.

Squires, Patricia. 1986. "Aiding Contras Opposed." *New York Times* (March 16): XI, 4.

Stackhouse, Max. 1987. *Public Theology and Political Economy.* Grand Rapids: Eerdmans.

Steele, Colonel James. 1988. "Psychological Operations and Civic Action." In Max Manwaring and Court Prisk (eds.), *El Salvador at War: An Oral History.* Washington, D.C.: National Defense University Press.

Stein, M. L. 1986. "Controlling the Flow of News." *Editor and Publisher* 119 (June 14).

———. 1987. "More Presidential Press Conferences?" *Editor and Publisher* 120 (May 2).

Stein, Ricardo. 1988. "Civil War, Reform, and Reaction in El Salvador." In Nora Hamilton et al. (eds.), *Crisis in Central America: Regional Dynamics and U.S. Policy in the 1980s.* Boulder, Colo.: Westview Press.

Stein, Stanley, and Barbara Stein. 1970. *The Colonial Heritage of Latin America.* New York: Oxford University Press.

Stout, Angela. 1989. *Sanctuary in the 1980s: The Dialectics of Law and Social Movement Development.* Ph.D. dissertation. Department of Sociology, University of Deleware.

Stryker, Sheldon. 1980. *Symbolic Interactionism: A Social-Structural Version.* Menlo Park: Benjamin/Cummings.

Subcommittee on Civil and Constitutional Rights of the Committee on the Judiciary, House of Representatives: Hearings before. 1987. *Break-Ins at Sanctuary Churches and Organizations Opposed to Administration Policy in Central America.* Washington, D.C.: U.S. Government Printing Office.

————. 1988. *CISPES and FBI Counter-Terrorism Investigations*. Washington, D.C.: U.S. Government Printing Office.

————. 1989. *FBI Investigation of First Amendment Activities*. Washington, D.C.: U.S. Government Printing Office.

Sundquist, James. 1981. *The Decline and Resurgence of Congress*. Washington: Brookings Institute.

Tarrow, Sidney. 1983. *Struggling to Reform*. Ithaca: Center for International Studies, Cornell University.

Taubman, Philip. 1982. "El Salvador as 'Domino'." *New York Times* (February 20): 8.

————. 1983. "21 Nicaraguanists in 6 Consulates Expelled by U.S." *New York Times* (June 8).

Taylor, Charles. 1989. *Sources of the Self: The Making of the Modern Identity*. Cambridge: Harvard University Press.

Taylor, Clark. 1990. Interview, November 15. Boston, Massachusetts.

Taylor, Phyllis. 1990. Interview, December 23. Philadelphia, Penn.

Taylor, Richard. n.d. "Witness for Peace: An Assessment." Unpublished manuscript.

Taylor, Stuart. 1985. "16 Indicted by U.S. in Bid to End Church Smuggling of Latin Aliens." *New York Times* (January 15): 1.

Tilly, Charles. 1978. *From Mobilization to Revolution*. New York: Random House.

Time. 1981. "Spooks on Ice: Unleashing the CIA." Vol. 118 (November 9).

————. 1982. "There He Goes Again." *Time* 119 (February 1).

Tolan, Sandy, and Carol Ann Bassett. 1985. "Informers in the Sanctuary Movement." *The Nation* (July 20).

Tolchin, Martin. 1982. "Thousands in Washington March to Protest U.S. Policy in Salvador." *New York Times* (March 28): 18.

Tomsho, Robert. 1987. *The American Sanctuary Movement*. Austin, Tex.: Texas Monthly Press.

Toner, Robin. 1986. "They Who Beg to Differ on Aid to Nicaragua." *New York Times* (March 14): 4.

Torres Rivas, Edelberto. 1988. "The Central American Crisis and the Common Market." In Nora Hamilton et al. (eds.), *Crisis in Central America: Regional Dynamics and U.S. Policy in the 1980s*. Boulder, Colo.: Westview Press.

Torres, Sergio, and John Eagleson. 1976. *Theology in the Americas*. Maryknoll, N.Y.: Orbis Books.

Towell, Pat. 1984. "House Erupts over Central America Issue." *Congressional Quarterly Weekly Report* 42(21) May 26.

Towle, Reverend Joseph. 1983. "Salvadorans Forced Back Into Hell." *New York Times* (March 3): 26.

Truitt, Fran. 1990. Interview, October 16. Ellsworth, Maine.

Tuchman, Gaye. 1973. "Making News by Doing Work: Routinizing the Unexpected." *American Journal of Sociology* 79(1).

Turner, Ralph. 1990. "Role Change." *Annual Review of Sociology* 16: 87–110.

Turner, Wallace. 1983. "Berkeley Devided by a New Dispute over Freedom of Speech." *New York Times* (March 7): 10.

Tushnet, Mark. 1988. *Central America and the Law: The Constitution, Civil Liberties, and the Courts.* Boston: South End Press.

Twersky, Isadore. 1982. "Some Aspects of the Jewish Attitude toward the Welfare State." *Studies in Jewish Law and Philosophy.* New York: Ktav Publishing House.

Tyson, James. 1986. *Prophets or Useful Idiots?: Church Organizations Attacking U.S. Central America Policy.* Washington, D.C.: Center for Public Diplomacy Studies/Council for the Defense of Freedom.

U.M.C. 1976. *Journal of the 1976 General Conference of the United Methodist Church.* Vol. 2.

UMI. 1973–87. University Microfilms International Dissertation Information Service. Ann Arbor, Mich.

U.P.I. 1987. "Report Says North Authored Plan to Suspend Constitution." United Press International news story (July 6).

U.S. Army, 1986. "Joint Low-Intensity Conflict Project Final Report, Executive Summary." Joint Low-Intensity Conflict Project, United States Army Training and Doctrine Command, Fort Monroe, Virginia, August 1.

U.S. Catholic Mission Association. 1993. *Annual Report on U.S. Catholic Overseas Mission 1992–1993.* Washington, D.C.: U.S. Catholic Mission Association.

U.S. News. 1981. "The White House Image Man." *U.S. New and World Report* 91 (July 20).

U.S. Senate. 1976. *Supplementary Detailed Staff Reports on Intelligence Activities and the Rights of Americans, Book III, Final Report of the Select Committee to Study Government Operations with Respect to Intelligence Activities.* Report no. 94–755, Washington, D.C.: Government Printing Office (April 23).

Vaky, Viron. 1984. "Reagan's Central American Policy: An Isthmus Restored." In Robert Leiken (ed.), *Central America: Anatomy of Conflict.* New York: Pergamon Press.

Valenta, Jiri, and Virgiania Valenta. 1984. "Soviety Strategy and Policies in the Caribbean Basin." In Wiarda, Howard (ed.), *Rift and Revolution: The Central American Imbroglio.* Washington, D.C.: American Enterprise Institute for Public Policy Research.

Vanden, Harry, and Thomas Walker. 1991. "The Reimposition of U.S. Hegemony over Nicaragua." In Kenneth Coleman and George Herring (eds.), *The Central American Crisis: Sources of Conflict and the Failure of U.S. Policy.* Wilmington, Del.: Scholarly Resources Inc.

Van Denend, Bob. 1992. Interview, August 3. Durham, North Carolina.

Van Denend, Pat. 1992. Interview, August 3. Durham, North Carolina.

Vickers, George. 1992. "El Salvador: A Negotiated Revolution." *Report on the Americas* 25:5 (May).

Volsky, George. 1983. "U.S. Churches Offer Sanctuary to Aliens Facing Deportation." *New York Times* (April 8): 1.

Waghlestein, John. 1985. "Post Vietnam Counterinsurgency Doctrine." *Military Review* (January).

Walker, Thomas. 1987. *Reagan Versus the Sandinistas: the Undeclared War on Nicaragua.* Boulder, Colo.: Westview Press.

Walker, Thomas (ed.). 1985. *Nicaragua: The First Five Years.* New York: Praeger Publishers.

Wallis, Jim. 1983. "Witness for Peace: Accion Permanante Cristiana Por La Paz." *Sojourners* 12(10) (November).

———. 1984. "A Pledge of Resistance: A Contingency Plan in the Event of a U.S. Invasion of Nicaragua." *Sojourners* 13(7) (August).

———. 1991. "For Still the Vision Awaits Its Time: Reflection on *Sojourners'* 20 Years." *Sojourners* 20(7) (August–September).

Walsh, Kenneth. 1986. "'Spin Patrol' on the March." *U.S. News and World Report* 101 (December 1).

Watson, Russell, and Richard Sandza. 1987. "Cleaning Up the Mess." *Newsweek* (October 12): 24–28.

Weaver, Jerry. 1984. "Guatemala: The Politics of Frustrated Revolution." In Howard Wiarda and Harvey Kline (eds.), *Latin American Politics and Development.* Boulder, Colo.: Westview Press.

Webster, William. 1993. Interview, November 29. Washington, D.C.

———. 1984. "The FBI vs. Domestic Terrorism." *USA Today Magazine* 112 (March): 11–13.

Weeks, John. 1985. *The Economies of Central America.* New York: Holmes and Meier.

Wein, Berel. 1969. "Jewish Conscientious Objectors and the Vietnamese War." *Jewish Life* 37.

Weinberger, Caspar. 1986. "Low Intensity Warfare." In *Vital Speeches* (February 15).

Weinraub, Bernard. 1983a. "U.S. Catholic Conference Asks Shift on El Salvador." *New York Times* (March 8): 7.

———. 1983b. "U.S. Is Condemned over Salvadorans: Refusal to Grant Them Asylum Stirs Protest in Congress and by Church Groups." *New York Times* (May 21): 5.

White, Ronald, and C. Howard Hopkins. 1976. *The Social Gospel: Religion and Reform in Changing America.* Philadelphia: Temple University Press.

Whittle, Richard. 1981. "Reagan El Salvador Policy Clears First Hurdle." *Congressional Quarterly Weekly Report* 39(13) (March 28): 557.

Wiarda, Howard (ed.). 1984. *Rift and Revolution: The Central America Imbroglio.* Washington, D.C.: American Enterprise Institute for Public Policy Research.

Wiesel, Elie. 1972. *One Generation After.* New York: Random House.

Willey, Gordon, and Demitri Shimkin. 1973. "The Maya Collapse: A Summary View." In T. Patrick Culbert (ed.), *The Maya Collapse.* Albuquerque: University of New Mexico Press.

Williams, Harvey. 1987. "The Social Impact in Nicaragua." In Thomas Walker (ed.), *Reagan Versus the Sandinistas: The Undeclared War on Nicaragua.* Boulder, Colo.: Westview Press.

Wilson, James. 1993. *The Moral Sense.* New York: Free Press.

Wilson, Robert. 1988. *Biases and Blind Spots: Methodism and Foreign Policy since World War II.* Wilmore, Ky.: Bristol Books.

Wilson, Samuel, and John Siewert. 1986. *Mission Handbook: North American Protestant Ministries Overseas* (13th ed.). Monrovia, Calif.: Missions Advanced Research and Communications Center.

Wiltfang, Gregory, and Doug McAdam. 1991. "The Costs and Risks of Social Activism: A Study of Sanctuary Movement Activism." *Social Forces* 69(4) (June): 987–1010

Winsor, Curtin. 1987. *The Washington Battle for Central America: The Unmet Challenge of the 'Red Chorus'.* Washington, D.C.: Washington Institute for Values in Public Policy.

Winston, Diane. 1978. "Vietnam and the Jews." In Jack Porter (ed.), *The Sociology of American Jews.* Washington, D.C.: University Press of America.

Wood, Floris (ed.). 1990. *An American Profile—Opinions and Behavior 1972–1989.* Detroit: Gale Research Inc.

Woodward, Bob. 1987. *Veil: The Secret Wars of the CIA 1981–1987.* New York: Simon and Schuster.

Zimmerman, S. 1971. "Confronting the Halakha on Military Service." *Judaism* 20.

INDEX